D1130413

U•X•L Encyclopedia of

Native American Tribes

THIRD EDITION

U•X•L Encyclopedia of

Native American Tribes

THIRD EDITION

VOLUME 5

GREAT BASIN

PACIFIC NORTHWEST

ARCTIC

Laurie J. Edwards, Editor

U·X·L
A part of Gale, Cengage Learning

GALE
CENGAGE Learning·

Detroit • New York • San Francisco • New Haven, Conn • Waterville, Maine • London

GALE
CENGAGE Learning·

U•X•L Encyclopedia of Native American Tribes, 3rd Edition

Laurie J. Edwards

Project Editors: Shelly Dickey, Terri Schell

Rights Acquisition and Management: Leitha Etheridge-Sims

Composition: Evi Abou-El-Seoud

Manufacturing: Wendy Blurton

Imaging: John Watkins

Product Design: Kristine Julien

For product information and technology assistance, contact us at
Gale Customer Support, 1-800-877-4253.
For permission to use material from this text or product,
submit all requests online at **www.cengage.com/permissions.**
Further permissions questions can be emailed to
permission request@cengage.com

Cover photographs reproduced by permission of Shoshone on Painted Horse, ©Steve Bly/Alamy; Totem for Kwakwaka'wakw, ©Corbis Flirt/Alamy.

While every effort has been made to ensure the reliability of the information presented in this publication, Gale, a part of Cengage Learning, does not guarantee the accuracy of the data contained herein. Gale accepts no payment for listing; and inclusion in the publication of any organization, agency, institution, publication, service, or individual does not imply endorsement of the editors or publisher. Errors brought to the attention of the publisher and verified to the satisfaction of the publisher will be corrected in future editions.

LIBRARY OF CONGRESS CATALOGING-IN-PUBLICATION DATA

U•X•L Encyclopedia of Native American Tribes / Laurie J. Edwards ; Shelly Dickey, Terri Schell, project editors. -- 3rd ed.
  5 v. . cm.
  Includes bibliographical references and index.
  ISBN 978-1-4144-9092-2 (set) -- ISBN 978-1-4144-9093-9 (v. 1) -- ISBN 978-1-4144-9094-6 (v.2) -- ISBN 978-1-4144-9095-3 (v.3) -- ISBN 978-1-4144-9096-0 (v. 4) -- ISBN 978-1-4144-9097-7 (v. 5),
  1. Indians of North America--Encyclopedias, Juvenile. 2. Indians of North America--Encyclopedias. I. Edwards, Laurie J. II. Dickey, Shelly. III. Schell, Terri, 1968-

E76.2.U85 2012
970.004'97003--dc23   2011048142

Gale
27500 Drake Rd.
Farmington Hills, MI, 48331-3535

978-1-4144-9092-2 (set)   1-4144-9092-5 (set)
978-1-4144-9093-9 (v. 1)   1-4144-9093-3 (v. 1)
978-1-4144-9094-6 (v. 2)   1-4144-9094-1 (v. 2)
978-1-4144-9095-3 (v. 3)   1-4144-9095-X (v. 3)
978-1-4144-9096-0 (v. 4)   1-4144-9096-8 (v. 4)
978-1-4144-9097-7 (v. 5)   1-4144-9097-6 (v. 5)

This title is also available as an e-book.
ISBN 13: 978-1-4144-9098-4 ISBN 10: 1-4144-9098-4
Contact your Gale, a part of Cengage Learning, sales representative for ordering information.

Printed in U.S.A.
1 2 3 4 5 6 7 16 15 14 13 12

Contents

Tribes Alphabetically

First numeral signifies volume number. The numeral after the colon signifies page number. For example, 3:871 means Volume 3, page 871.

Reader's Guide

Long before the Vikings, Spaniards, and Portuguese made land-fall on North American shores, the continent already had a rich history of human settlement. The *U•X•L Encyclopedia of Native American Tribes, 3rd Edition* opens up for students the array of tribal ways in the United States and Canada past and present. Included in these volumes, readers will find the stories of:

- the well-known nineteenth century Lakota hunting the buffalo on the Great Plains
- the contemporary Inuit of the Arctic, who in 1999 won their battle for Nunavut, a vast, self-governing territory in Canada
- the Haida of the Pacific Northwest, whose totem poles have become a familiar adornment of the landscape
- the Anasazi in the Southwest, who were building spectacular cities long before Europeans arrived
- the Mohawk men in the Northeast who made such a name for themselves as ironworkers on skyscrapers and bridges that they have long been in demand for such projects as the Golden Gate Bridge
- the Yahi of California, who became extinct when their last member, Ishi, died in 1916.

The *U•X•L Encyclopedia of Native American Tribes, 3rd Edition* presents 106 tribes, confederacies, and Native American groups. Among the tribes included are large and well-known nations, smaller communities with their own fascinating stories, and prehistoric peoples. The tribes are grouped in the ten major geographical/cultural areas of North America in which tribes shared environmental and cultural connections. The ten sections, each beginning with an introductory essay on the geographical area and the shared history and culture within it, are arranged in the volumes as follows:

- Volume 1: Northeast and Subarctic
- Volume 2: Southeast and Great Plains
- Volume 3: Southwest
- Volume 4: California and Plateau
- Volume 5: Great Basin, Pacific Northwest, and Arctic

The *U•X•L Encyclopedia of Native American Tribes, 3rd Edition* provides the history of each of the tribes featured and a fascinating look at their ways of life: how families lived in centuries past and today, what people ate and wore, what their homes were like, how they worshiped, celebrated, governed themselves, and much more. A student can learn in depth about one tribe or compare aspects of many tribes. Each detailed entry is presented in consistent rubrics that allow for easy access and comparison, as follows:

- History
- Religion
- Language
- Government
- Economy
- Daily Life
- Arts
- Customs
- Current Tribal Issues
- Notable People

Each entry begins with vital data on the tribe: name, location, population, language family, origins and group affiliations. A locator map follows, showing the traditional homelands and contemporary communities of the group; regional and migration maps throughout aid in locating the many groups at different times in history. Brief timelines in each entry chronicle important dates of the tribe's history, while an overall timeline at the beginning of all the volumes outlines key events in history pertinent to all Native Americans. Other sidebars present recipes, oral literature or stories, language keys, and background material on the tribe. Color photographs and illustrations, further reading sections, a thorough subject index, and a glossary are special features that make the volumes easy, fun, and informative to use.

A note on terminology

Throughout the *U•X•L Encyclopedia of Native American Tribes, 3rd Edition* various terms are used for Native North Americans, such as *Indian, American Indian, Native,* and *aboriginal.* The Native peoples of the Americas have the unfortunate distinction of having been given the wrong name by the Europeans who first arrived on the continent, mistakenly thinking they had arrived in India. The search for a single name, however, has never been entirely successful. The best way to characterize Native North Americans is by recognizing their specific tribal or community identities. In compiling this book, every effort has been made to keep Native tribal and community identities distinct, but by necessity, inclusive terminology is often used. We do not wish to offend anyone, but rather than favor one term for Native North American people, the editors have used a variety of terminology, trying always to use the most appropriate term in the particular context.

Europeans also had a hand in giving names to tribes, often misunderstanding their languages and the relations between different Native communities. Most tribes have their own names for themselves, and many have succeeded in gaining public acceptance of traditional names. The Inuit, for example, objected to the name Eskimo, which means "eaters of raw meat," and in time their name for themselves was accepted. In the interest of clarity the editors of this book have used the currently accepted terms, while acknowledging the traditional ones or the outmoded ones at the beginning of each entry.

The term *tribe* is not accepted by all Native groups. The people living in North America before the Europeans arrived had many different ways of organizing themselves politically and relating to other groups around them—from complex confederacies and powerful unified nations to isolated villages with little need for political structure. Groups divided, absorbed each other, intermarried, allied, and dissolved. The epidemics and wars that came with non-Native expansion into North America created a demographic catastrophe to many Native groups and greatly affected tribal affiliations. Although in modern times there are actual rules about what comprise a tribe (federal requirements for recognition of tribes are specific, complicated, and often difficult to fulfill), the hundreds of groups living in the Americas in early times did not have any one way of categorizing themselves. Thus, some Native American peoples today find the word *tribe* misleading. In a study of Native peoples, it can also be an elusive defining term. But in facing the challenges of maintaining traditions and heritage in modern times, tribal or community identity is acutely important to many Native Americans. Tremendous efforts have been undertaken to preserve native languages, oral traditions, religions, ceremonies, and traditional arts and economies—the things that, put together, make a tribe a cultural and political unit.

Comments and suggestions

In this third edition of the *U•X•L Encyclopedia of Native American Tribes* we have presented in-depth information on 106 of the hundreds of tribes of North America. While every attempt was made to include a wide representation of groups, many historically important and interesting tribes are not covered in these volumes. We welcome your suggestions for tribes to be featured in future editions, as well as any other comments you may have on this set. Please write: Editors, *U•X•L Encyclopedia of Native American Tribes, 3rd Edition,* U•X•L 27500 Drake Road, Farmington Hills, Michigan 48331-3535; call toll-free 1-800-877-4253; or fax 248-699-8097; or send e-mail via http://www.gale.com.

Words to Know

Aboriginal: Native, or relating to the first or earliest group living in a particular area.

Activism: Taking action for or against a controversial issue; political and social activists may organize or take part in protest demonstrations, rallies, petitioning the government, sit-ins, civil disobedience, and many other forms of activities that draw attention to an issue and/or challenge the authorities to make a change.

Adobe: A brick or other building material made from sun-dried mud, a mixture of clay, sand, and sometimes ashes, rocks, or straw.

Alaska Native Claims Settlement Act (ANCSA): An act of Congress passed in 1971 that gave Alaska Natives 44 million acres of land and $962.5 million. In exchange, Alaska Natives gave up all claim to other lands in Alaska. The ANCSA also resulted in the formation of 12 regional corporations in Alaska in charge of Native communities' economic development and land use.

Allotment: The practice of dividing and distributing land into individual lots. In 1887 the U.S. Congress passed the General Allotment Act (also known as the Dawes Act), which divided Indian reservations into privately owned parcels (pieces) of land. Under allotment, tribes could no longer own their own lands in common (as a group) in the traditional ways. Instead the head of a family received a lot, generally 160 acres. Land not alloted was sold to non-Natives.

American Indian Movement (AIM): An activist movement founded in 1966 to aggressively press for Indian rights. The movement was formed to improve federal, state, and local social services to Native Americans in urban neighborhoods. AIM sought the reorganization of the Bureau of Indian Affairs to make it more responsive to Native American needs and fought for the return of Indian lands illegally taken from them.

Anthropology: The study of human beings in terms of their populations, culture, social relations, ethnic characteristics, customs, and adaptation to their environment.

Archaeology: The study of the remains of past human life, such as fossil relics, artifacts, and monuments, in order to understand earlier human cultures.

Arctic: Relating to the area surrounding the North Pole.

Assimilate: To absorb, or to be absorbed, into the dominant society (those in power, or in the majority). U.S. assimilation policies were directed at causing Native Americans to become like European-Americans in terms of jobs and economics, religion, customs, language, education, family life, and dress.

Band: A small, loosely organized social group composed of several families. In Canada, the word band originally referred to a social unit of nomadic (those who moved from place to place) hunting peoples, but now refers to a community of Indians registered with the government.

Boarding school: A live-in school.

Breechcloth: A garment with front and back flaps that hangs from the waist. Breechcloths were one of the most common articles of clothing worn by many Native American men and sometimes women in pre-European/American settlement times.

Bureau of Indian Affairs (BIA): The U.S. government agency that oversees tribal lands, education, and other aspects of Indian life.

Census: A count of the population.

Ceremony: A special act or set of acts (such as a wedding or a funeral) performed by members of a group on important occasions, usually organized according to the group's traditions and beliefs.

Clan: A group of related house groups and families that trace back to a common ancestor or a common symbol or totem, usually an animal such as the bear or the turtle. The clan forms the basic social and political unit for many Indian societies.

Colonialism: A state or nation's control over a foreign territory.

Colonize: To establish a group of people from a mother country or state in a foreign territory; the colonists set up a community that remains tied to the mother county.

Confederacy: A group of people, states, or nations joined together for mutual support or for a special purpose.

Convert: To cause a person or group to change their beliefs or practices. A convert (noun) is a person who has been converted to a new belief or practice.

Coup: A feat of bravery, especially the touching of an enemy's body during battle without causing or receiving injury. To "count coup" is to count the number of such feats of bravery.

Cradleboard: A board or frame on which an infant was bound or wrapped by some Native American peoples. It was used as a portable carrier or for carrying an infant on the back.

Creation stories: Sacred myths or stories that explain how Earth and its beings were created.

Culture: The set of beliefs, social habits, and ways of surviving in the environment that are held by a particular social group.

Dentalium: Dentalia (plural) are the tooth-like shells that some tribes used as money. The shells were rubbed smooth and strung like beads on strands of animal skin.

Depletion: Decreasing the amount of something; depletion of resources such as animals or minerals through overuse reduces essential elements from the environment.

Dialect: A local variety of a particular language, with unique differences in words, grammar, and pronunciation.

Economy: The way a group obtains, produces, and distributes the goods it needs; the overall system by which it supports itself and accumulates its wealth.

Ecosystem: The overall way that a community and its surrounding environment function together in nature.

Epidemic: The rapid spread of a disease so that many people in an area have it at the same time.

Ethnic group: A group of people who are classed according to certain aspects of their common background, usually by tribal, racial, national, cultural, and language origins.

Extended family: A family group that includes close relatives such as mother, father, and children, plus grandparents, aunts, and uncles, and cousins.

Fast: To go without food.

Federally recognized tribes: Tribes with which the U.S. government maintains official relations as established by treaty, executive order, or act of Congress.

Fetish: An object believed to have magical or spiritual power.

First Nations: One of Canada's terms for its Indian nations.

Five Civilized Tribes: A name given to the Cherokee, Choctaw, Chickasaw, Creek, and Seminole during the mid-1800s. The tribes were given this name by non-Natives because they had democratic constitutional governments, a high literacy rate (many people who could read and write), and ran effective schools.

Formal education: Structured learning that takes place in a school or college under the supervision of trained teachers.

Ghost Dance: A revitalization (renewal or rebirth) movement that arose in the 1870s after many tribes moved to reservations and were being encouraged to give up their traditional beliefs. Many Native Americans hoped that, if they performed it earnestly, the Ghost Dance would bring back traditional Native lifestyles and values, and that the buffalo and Indian ancestors would return to the Earth as in the days before the white settlers.

Great Basin: An elevated region in the western United States in which all water drains toward the center. The Great Basin covers part of Nevada, California, Colorado, Utah, Oregon, and Wyoming.

Guardian spirit: A sacred power, usually embodied in an animal such as a hawk, deer, or turtle, that reveals itself to an individual, offering help throughout the person's lifetime in important matters such as hunting or healing the sick.

Haudenosaunee: The name of the people often called Iroquois or Five Nations. It means "People of the Longhouse."

Head flattening: A practice in which a baby was placed in a cradle, and a padded board was tied to its forehead to mold the head into a desired shape. Sometimes the effect of flattening the back of the head was achieved by binding the infant tightly to a cradleboard.

Immunity: Resistance to disease; the ability to be exposed to a disease with less chance of getting it, and less severe effects if infected.

Indian Territory: An area in present-day Kansas and Oklahoma where the U.S. government once planned to move all Indians, and, eventually, to allow them to run their own province or state. In 1880 nearly one-third of all U.S. Indians lived there, but with the formation of the state of Oklahoma in 1906, the promise of an Indian state dissolved.

Indigenous: Native, or first, in a specific area. Native Americans are often referred to as indigenous peoples of North America.

Intermarriage: Marriage between people of different groups, as between a Native American and a non-Native, or between people from two different tribes.

Kachina: A group of spirits celebrated by the Pueblo Indians; the word also refers to dolls made in the image of kachina spirits.

Kiva: Among the Pueblo, a circular (sometimes rectangular) underground room used for religious ceremonies.

Lacrosse: A game of Native American origin in which players use a long stick with a webbed pouch at the end for catching and throwing a ball.

Language family: A group of languages that are different from one another but are related. These languages share similar words, sounds, or word structures. The languages are alike either because they have borrowed words from each other or because they originally came from the same parent language.

Legend: A story or folktale that tells about people or events in the past.

Life expectancy: The average number of years a person may expect to live.

Linguistics: The study of human speech and language.

Literacy: The state of being able to read and write.

Loincloth: See "Breechcloth".

Longhouse: A large, long building in which several families live together; usually found among Northwest Coast and Iroquois peoples.

Long Walk of the Navajo: The enforced 300-mile walk of the Navajo people in 1864, when they were being removed from their homelands to the Bosque Redondo Reservation in New Mexico.

Manifest Destiny: A belief held by many Americans in the nineteenth century that the destiny of the United States was to expand its territory and extend its political, social, and economic influences throughout North America.

Matrilineal: Tracing family relations through the mother; in a matrilineal society, names and inheritances are passed down through the mother's side of the family.

Medicine bundle: A pouch in which were kept sacred objects believed to have powers that would protect and aid an individual, a clan or family, or a community.

Midewiwin Society: The Medicine Lodge Religion, whose main purpose was to prolong life. The society taught morality, proper conduct, and a knowledge of plants and herbs for healing.

Migration: Movement from one place to another. The migrations of Native peoples were often done by the group, with whole nations moving from one area to another.

Mission: An organized effort by a religious group to spread its beliefs to other parts of the world; mission refers either to the project of spreading a belief system or to the building(s)—such as a church—in which this takes place.

Missionary: Someone sent to a foreign land to convert its people to a particular religion.

Mission school: A school established by missionaries to teach people religious beliefs as well as other subjects.

Moiety: One of the two parts that a tribe or community divided into based on kinship.

Myth: A story passed down through generations, often involving super-natural beings. Myths often express religious beliefs or the values of people. They may attempt to explain how the Earth and its beings were created, or why things are. They are not always meant to be taken as factual.

Natural resources: The sources of supplies provided by the environment for survival and enrichment, such as animals to be hunted, land for farming, minerals, and timber.

Neophyte: Beginner; often used to mean a new convert to a religion.

Nomadic: Traveling and relocating often, usually in search of food and other resources or a better climate.

Nunavut: A new territory in Canada as of April 1, 1999, with the status of a province and a Inuit majority. It is a huge area, covering most of Canada north of the treeline. Nunavut means "Our Land" in Inuki-tut (the Inuit language).

Oral literature: Oral traditions that are written down after enjoying a long life in spoken form among a people.

Oral traditions: History, mythology, folklore, and other foundations of a culture that have been passed by spoken word, often in the form of stories, from generation to generation within a culture group.

Parent language: A language that is the common structure of two or more languages that came into being at a later time.

Parfleche: A case or a pouch made from tanned animal hide.

Patrilineal: Tracing family relations through the father; in a patrilineal society, names and inheritances are passed down through the father's side of the family.

Per capita income: The average personal income per person.

Petroglyph: A carving or engraving on rock; a common form of ancient art.

Peyote: A substance obtained from cactus that some Indian groups used as part of their religious practice. After eating the substance, which stimulates the nervous system, a person may go into a trance state and see visions. The Peyote Religion features the use of this substance.

Pictograph: A simple picture representing a historical event.

Policy: The overall plan or course of action issued by the government, establishing how it will handle certain situations or people and what its goals are.

Post-European contact: Relating to the time and state of Native Americans and their lands after the Europeans arrived. Depending on the part of the country in which they lived, Native groups experienced contact at differing times in the history of white expansion into the West.

Potlatch: A feast or ceremony, commonly held among Northwest Coast groups; also called a "giveaway." During a potlatch goods are given to guests to show the host's generosity and wealth. Potlatches are used to celebrate major life events such as birth, death, or marriage.

Powwow: A celebration at which the main activity is traditional singing and dancing. In modern times, the singers and dancers at powwows came from many different tribes.

Province: A district or division of a country (like a state in the United States).

Raiding: Entering into another tribe or community's territory, usually by stealth or force, and stealing their livestock and supplies.

Ranchería: Spanish term for a small farm.

Ratify: To approve or confirm. In the United States, the U.S. Senate ratified treaties with the Indians.

Red Power: A term used to describe the Native American activism movement of the 1960s, in which people from many tribes came together to protest the injustices of American policies toward Native Americans.

Removal Act: An act passed by the U.S. Congress in 1830 that directed all Indians to be moved to Indian Territory, west of the Mississippi River.

Removal Period: The time, mostly between 1830 and 1860, when most Indians of the eastern United States were forced to leave their homelands and relocate west of the Mississippi River.

Repatriation: To return something to its place of origin. A law passed in the 1990s says that all bones and grave goods (items that are buried with a body) should be returned to the descendants. Many Native American tribes have used that law to claim bones and other objects belonging to their ancestors. Museums and archaeological digs must return these items to the tribes.

Reservation: Land set aside by the U.S. government for the use of a group or groups of Indians.

Reserve: In Canada, lands set aside for specific Indian bands. Reserve means in Canada approximately what reservation means in the United States.

Revitalization: The feeling or movement in which something seems to come back to life after having been quiet or inactive for a period of time.

Ritual: A formal act that is performed in basically the same way each time; rituals are often performed as part of a ceremony.

Rural: Having to do with the country; opposite of urban.

Sachem: The chief of a confederation of tribes.

Shaman: A priest or medicine person in many Native American groups who understands and works with supernatural matters. Shamans traditionally performed in rituals and were expected to cure the sick, see the future, and obtain supernatural help with hunting and other economic activities.

Smallpox: A very contagious disease that spread across North America and killed many thousands of Indians. Survivors had skin that was badly scarred.

Sovereign: Self-governing or independent. A sovereign nation makes its own laws and rules.

Sun Dance: A renewal and purification ceremony performed by many Plains Indians such as the Sioux and Cheyenne. A striking aspect of the ceremony was the personal sacrifice made by some men. They undertook self-torture in order to gain a vision that might provide spiritual insight beneficial to the community.

Sweat lodge: An airtight hut containing hot stones that were sprinkled with water to make them steam. A person remained inside until he or she was perspiring. The person then usually rushed out and plunged into a cold stream. This treatment was used before a ceremony or for the healing of physical or spiritual ailments. Sweat lodge is also the name of a sacred Native American ceremony involving the building of the lodge and the pouring of water on stones, usually by a medicine person, accompanied by praying and singing. The ceremony has many purposes, including spiritual cleansing and healing.

Taboo: A forbidden object or action. Many Indians believe that the sacred order of the world must be maintained if one is to avoid illness or other misfortunes. This is accomplished, in part, by observing a large assortment of taboos.

Termination: The policy of the U.S. government during the 1950s and 1960s to end the relationships set up by treaties with Indian nations.

Toloache: A substance obtained from a plant called jimsonweed. When consumed, the drug causes a person to go into a trance and see visions. It is used in some religious ceremonies.

Totem: An object that serves as an emblem or represents a family or clan, usually in the form of an animal, bird, fish, plant, or other natural object. A totem pole is a pillar built in front of the homes of Natives in the Northwest. It is painted and carved with a series of totems that show the family background and either mythical or historical events.

Trail of Tears: A series of forced marches of Native Americans of the Southeast in the 1830s, causing the deaths of thousands. The marches were the result of the U.S. government's removal policy, which ordered Native Americans to be moved to Indian Territory.

Treaty: An agreement between two parties or two nations, signed by both, usually defining the benefits to both parties that will result from one side giving up title to a territory of land.

Tribe: A group of Natives who share a name, language, culture, and ancestors; in Canada, called a band.

Tribelet: A community within an organization of communities in which one main settlement was surrounded by a few minor outlying settlements.

Trickster: A common culture hero in Indian myth and legend. tricksters generally have supernatural powers that can be used to do good or harm, and stories about them take into account the different forces of the universe, such as good and evil or night and day. The Trickster takes different forms among various groups; for example, Coyote in the Southwest; Ikhtomi Spider in the High Plains, and Jay or Wolverine in Canada.

Trust: A relationship between two parties (or groups) in which one is responsible for acting in the other's best interests. The U.S. government has a trust relationship with tribal nations. Many tribes do not own their lands outright; according to treaty, the government owns the land "in trust" and tribes are given the use of it.

Unemployment rate: The percentage of the population that is looking for work but unable to find any. (People who have quit looking for work are not included in unemployment rates.)

Urban: Having to do with cities and towns; the opposite of rural.

Values: The ideals that a community of people shares.

Vision quest: A sacred ceremony in which a person (often a teenage boy) goes off alone and fasts, living without food or water for a period of days. During that time he hopes to learn about his spiritual side and to have a vision of a guardian spirit who will give him help and strength throughout his life.

Wampum: Small cylinder-shaped beads cut from shells. Long strings of wampum were used for many different purposes. Indians believed that the exchange of wampum and other goods established a friendship, not just a profit-making relationship.

Wampum belt: A broad woven belt of wampum used to record history, treaties among the tribes, or treaties with colonists or governments.

Weir: A barricade used to funnel fish toward people who wait to catch them.

Timeline

25,000–11,000 BCE Groups of hunters cross from Asia to Alaska on the Bering Sea Land Bridge, which was formed when lands now under the waters of the Bering Strait were exposed for periods of time, according to scientists.

1400 BCE Along the lower Mississippi, people of the Poverty Point culture are constructing large burial mounds and living in planned communities.

500 BCE The Adena people build villages with burial mounds in the Midwest.

100 BCE Hopewell societies construct massive earthen mounds for burying their dead and possibly other religious purposes.

100 BCE–400 CE In the Early Basketmaker period, the Anasazi use baskets as containers and cooking pots; they live in caves.

1 CE: Small, permanent villages of the Hohokam tradition emerge in the southwest.

400–700 In the Modified Basketmaker period, Anasazi communities emerge in the Four Corners region of the Southwest. They learn to make pottery in which they can boil beans. They live in underground pits and begin to use bows and arrows. The Anasazi eventually design communities in large multi-roomed apartment buildings, some with more than 1,200 rooms.

700 CE The Mississippian culture begins.

700–1050 The Developmental Pueblo period begins. The Anasazi move into pueblo-type homes above the ground and develop irrigation methods. A great cultural center is established at Chaco Canyon. Anasazi influence spreads to other areas of the Southwest.

800–950 The early Pecos build pit houses.

900 The Mississippian mound-building groups form complex political and social systems, and participate in long-distance trade and an elaborate and widespread religion.

984 The Vikings under Erik the Red first encounter the Inuit of Greenland.

1000–1350 The Iroquois Confederacy is formed among the Mohawk, Oneida, Onondaga, Cayuga, and Seneca nations. The Five Nations of the Haudenosaunee are, from this time, governed by chiefs from the 49 families who were present at the origin of the confederation.

1040 Pueblos (towns) are flourishing in New Mexico's Chaco Canyon. The pueblos are connected by an extensive road system that stretches many miles across the desert.

1050–1300 In the Classic Pueblo period, Pueblo architecture reaches its height with the building of fabulous cliff dwellings; Acoma Pueblo is a well-established city.

1200 The great city of Cahokia in the Mississippi River Valley flourishes.

1250 Zuñi Pueblo is an important trading center for Native peoples from California, Mexico, and the American Southwest.

1300–1700 During the Regressive Pueblo period, the Anasazi influence declines. The people leave their northern homelands, heading south to mix with other cultures.

1350 Moundville, in present-day Alabama, one of the largest ceremonial centers of the Mound Builders, thrives. With twenty great mounds and a village, it is probably the center of a chiefdom that includes several other related communities.

1400s Two tribes unite to start the Wendat Confederacy.

1494 Christopher Columbus begins the enslavement of American Indians, capturing over 500 Taino of San Salvador and sending them to Spain to be sold.

1503 French explorer Jacques Cartier begins trading with Native Americans along the East Coast.

1524 The Abenaki and Narragansett, among other Eastern tribes, encounter the expedition of Giovanni da Verrazano.

1533 Spaniards led by Nuño de Guzmán enter Yaqui territory.

1534 French explorer Jacques Cartier meets the Micmac on the Gaspé Peninsula, beginning a long association between the French and the Micmac.

1539–43 The Spanish treasure hunter Hernando de Soto becomes the first European to make contact with Mississippian cultures; De Soto and Spaniard Francisco Coronado traverse the Southeast and Southwest, bringing with them disease epidemics that kill thousands of Native Americans.

1540 Hernando de Alarcón first encounters the Yuman.

1570 The Spanish attempt to establish a mission in Powhatan territory, but are driven away or killed by the Natives.

1576 British explorer Martin Frobisher first comes into contact with the central Inuit of northern Canada.

1579 Sir Francis Drake encounters the Coast Miwok.

1590 The Micmac force Iroquoian-speaking Natives to leave the Gaspé Peninsula; as a result, the Micmac dominate the fur trade with the French.

1591 Spanish colonization of Pueblo land begins.

1598 Juan de Oñate sets up a Spanish colony and builds San Geronimo Mission at Taos Pueblo. He brings 7000 head of livestock, among them horses.

1602 Spanish explorer Sebastián Vizcaíno encounters the Ohlone.

1607 The British colonists of the Virginia Company arrive in Powhatan territory.

1609 The fur trade begins when British explorer Henry Hudson, sailing for the Netherlands, opens trade in New Netherland (present-day New York) with several Northeast tribes, including the Delaware.

1615 Ottawa meet Samuel de Champlain at Georgian Bay.

1621 Chief Massasoit allies with Pilgrims.

1622 Frenchman Étienne Brûlé encounters the Ojibway at present-day Sault Sainte Marie.

1634–37 An army of Puritans, Pilgrims, Mohican, and Narragansett attacks and sets fire to the Pequot fort, killing as many as 700 Pequot men, women, and children; Massacre at Mystic ends Pequot War and nearly destroys the tribe.

1648–51 The Iroquois, having exhausted the fur supply in their area, attack other tribes in order to get a new supply. The Beaver Wars begin, and many Northeast tribes are forced to move west toward the Great Lakes area.

mid-1600s The Miami encounter Europeans and provide scouts to guide Father Jacques Marquette and Louis Joliet to the Mississippi River.

1651 Colonists establish first Indian reservation near Richmond, Virginia, for what is left of the Powhatans.

1675–76 The Great Swamp Fight during King Philip's War nearly wipes out the tribe and the loss of life and land ends a way of life for New England tribes.

1680 The Hopi, Jemez, Acoma, and other Pueblo groups force the Spanish out of New Mexico in the Pueblo Revolt.

1682 Robert de la Salle's expedition descends the Mississippi River into Natchez territory.

1687 Father Eusebio Francisco Kino begins missionary work among the Tohono O'odham and establishes the first of twenty-eight missions in Yuman territory.

1692 The Spanish begin their reconquest of Pueblo land; Pecos make peace with Spaniards, in spite of protests from some tribe members.

1700 Pierre-Charles le Sueur encounters the Sioux.

1709 John Lawson discovers and writes about the "Hatteras Indians."

1729 French governor Sieur d' Etchéparre demands Natchez land for a plantation; Natchez revolt begins.

1731 The French destroy the Natchez, the last Mississippian culture. Most survivors are sold into slavery in the Caribbean.

1741 Danish-born Russian explorer Vitus Bering sees buildings on Kayak Island that likely belong to the Chugach; he is the first European to reach the Inuit of Alaska.

1760–63 The Delaware Prophet tells Native Americans in the Northeast that they must drive Europeans out of North America and return to the customs of their ancestors. His message influences Ottawa leader Pontiac, who uses it to unite many tribes against the British.

1761 The Potawatomi switch allegiance from the French to the British; they later help the British by attacking American settlers during the American Revolution.

1763 By the Treaty of Paris, France gives Great Britain the Canadian Maritime provinces, including Micmac territory.

1763 England issues the Proclamation of 1763, which assigns all lands west of the Appalachian Mountains to Native Americans, while colonists are allowed to settle all land to the east. The document respects the aboriginal land rights of Native Americans. It is not popular with colonists who want to move onto Indian lands and becomes one of the conflicts between England and the colonies leading to the American Revolution.

1769 The Spanish build their first mission in California. There will be 23 Spanish missions in California, which are used to convert Native Californians to Christianity, but also reduces them to slave labor.

1769–83 Samuel Hearne and Alexander Mackenzie are the first European explorers to penetrate Alaskan Athabascan territory, looking for furs and a route to the Pacific Ocean. Russian fur traders are not far behind.

c. 1770 Horses, brought to the continent by the Spanish in the sixteenth century, spread onto the Great Plains and lead to the development of a new High Plains Culture.

1776 Most Mohawk tribes side with the British during the Revolutionary War under the leadership of Thayendanégea, also known as Joseph Brant.

1778 The Delaware sign the first formal treaty with the United States, guaranteeing their land and allowing them to be the fourteenth state; the treaty is never ratified.

1778 The treaty-making period begins when the first of 370 treaties between Indian nations and the U.S. government is signed.

1786 The first federal Indian reservations are established.

1789 The Spanish establish a post at Nootka Sound on Vancouver Island, the first permanent European establishment in the territory of the Pacific Northwest Coast tribes; Spain and Great Britain vie for control of the area during the Nootka Sound Controversy.

1791 In the greatest Native American defeat of the U.S. Army, the Miami win against General Arthur St. Clair.

1792 Explorer George Vancouver enters Puget Sound; Robert Gray, John Boit and George Vancouver are the first to mention the Chinook.

1805 The Lewis and Clark expedition ecounter the Flathead, Nez Percé, Yakama, Shoshone, Umatilla, Siletz, and are the first to reach Chinook territory by land.

1811 Shawnee settlement of Prophet's Town is destroyed in the Battle of Tippecanoe.

1813 Chief Tecumseh is killed fighting the Americans at Battle of the Thames in the War of 1812.

1816 Violence erupts during a Métis protest over the Pemmican Proclamation of 1814, and twenty-one Hudson's Bay Company employees are killed.

1817 The First Seminole War occurs when soldiers from neighboring states invade Seminole lands in Florida looking for runaway slaves.

1821 Sequoyah's method for writing the Cherokee language is officially approved by tribal leaders.

1827 The Cherokee adopt a written constitution.

1830 The removal period begins when the U.S. Congress passes the Indian Removal Act. Over the course of the next thirty years many tribes from the Northeast and Southeast are removed to Indian Territory in present-day Oklahoma and Kansas, often forcibly and at great expense in human lives.

1831 Some Seneca and Cayuga move to Indian Territory (now Oklahoma) as part of the U.S. government's plan to move Native Americans westward. Other Iroquois groups stand firm until the government's policy is overturned in 1842.

1832 The U.S. government attempts relocation of the Seminole to Indian Territory in Oklahoma, leading to the Second Seminole War.

1838 The Cherokee leave their homeland on a forced journey known as the Trail of Tears.

1846–48 Mexican-American War is fought; San Juan lands become part of U.S. territory.

1847 Another Pueblo rebellion leads to the assassination of the American territorial governor. In retaliation U.S. troops destroy the mission at Taos Pueblo, killing 150 Taos Indians.

1848 Mexico gives northern Arizona and northern New Mexico lands to the United States. Warfare between the Apache people and the U.S. Army begins.

1850 New Mexico is declared a U.S. territory.

1851 Gold Rush begins at Gold Bluff, prompting settlers to take over Native American lands. As emigration of Europeans to the West increases, eleven Plains tribes sign the Treaty of Fort Laramie, which promises annual payments to the tribes for their land.

1851 Early reservations are created in California to protect the Native population from the violence of U.S. citizens. These reservations are inadequate and serve only a small portion of the Native Californians, while others endure continued violence and hardship.

1854 The Treaty of Medicine Creek is signed, and the Nisqually give up much of their land; the treaty also gives Puyallup lands to the U.S. government and the tribe is sent to a reservation.

1858 Prospectors flood into Washoe lands after the Comstock lode is discovered.

1859 American surveyors map out a reservation on the Gila River for the Pima and Maricopa Indians. It includes fields, but no water.

1861 Cochise is arrested on a false charge, and the Apache Wars begin.

1864 At least 130 Southern Arapaho and Cheyenne—many of them women and children—are killed by U.S. Army troops during the Sand Creek Massacre.

1864 The devastating Long Walk, a forced removal from their homelands, leads the Navajo to a harsh exile at Bosque Redondo.

1867 The United States buys Alaska from Russia for $7.2 million.

1870 The First Ghost Dance Movement begins when Wodzibwob, a Paiute, learns in a vision that a great earthquake will swallow the Earth, and that all Indians will be spared or resurrected within three days of the disaster, returning their world to its state before the Europeans arrived.

1870–90 The Peyote Religion spreads throughout the Great Plains. Peyote (obtained from a cactus plant) brings on a dreamlike feeling that followers believe brings them closer to the spirit world. Tribes develop their own ceremonies, songs, and symbolism, and vow to be trustworthy, honorable, and community-oriented and to follow the Peyote Road.

1871 British Columbia becomes part of Canada; reserve land is set aside for the Nuu-chah-nulth.

1874–75 The Comanche make their last stand; Quanah Parker and his followers are the last to surrender and be placed on a reservation.

1875 The U.S. Army forces the Yavapai and Apache to march to the San Carlos Apache Reservation; 115 die along the way.

1876 The Northern Cheyenne join with the Sioux in defeating General George Custer at the Battle of Little Bighorn.

1876 The Indian Act in Canada establishes an Indian reserve system, in which reserves were governed by voluntary elected band councils. The Act does not recognize Canadian Indians' right to self-government. With the passage of the act, Canadian peoples in Canada are divided into three groups: status Indian, treaty Indian, and non-status Indian. The categories affect the benefits and rights Indians are given by the government.

1877 During the Nez Percé War, Chief Joseph and his people try fleeing to Canada, but are captured by U.S. Army troops.

1879 The Ute kill thirteen U.S. soldiers and ten Indian agency officials, including Nathan Meeker, in a conflict that becomes known as the "Meeker Massacre."

1880s The buffalo on the Great Plains are slaughtered until there are almost none left. Without adequate supplies of buffalo for food, the Plains Indians cannot survive. Many move to reservations.

1884 The Canadian government bans potlatches. The elaborate gift-giving ceremonies have long been a vital part of Pacific Northwest Indian culture.

1886 The final surrender of Geronimo's band marks the end of Apache military resistance to American settlement.

1887 The General Allotment Act (also known as the Dawes Act), is passed by Congress. The act calls for the allotment (parceling out) of tribal lands. Tribes are no longer to own their lands in common in the traditional way. Instead the land is to be assigned to individuals. The head of a family receives 160 acres, and other family members get smaller pieces of land. All Indian lands that are not alloted are sold to settlers.

1888 Ranchers and amateur archaeologists Richard Wetherill and Charlie Mason discover ancient cliff dwellings of the Pueblo people.

1889 The Oklahoma Land Runs open Indian Territory to non-Natives. (Indian Territory had been set aside solely for Indian use.) At noon on April 22, an estimated 50,000 people line up at the boundaries of Indian Territory. They claim two million acres of land. By nightfall, tent cities, banks, and stores are doing business there.

1890 The Second Ghost Dance movement is initiated by Wovoka, a Paiute. It includes many Paiute traditions. In some versions the dance is performed in order to help bring back to Earth many dead ancestors and exterminated game. Ghost Dance practitioners hope the rituals in the movement will restore Indians to their formal state, before the arrival of the non-Native settlers.

1896 Discovery of gold brings hordes of miners and settlers to Alaska.

1897 Oil is discovered beneath Osage land.

1907 With the creation of the state of Oklahoma, the government abolishes the Cherokee tribal government and school system, and the dream of a Native American commonwealth dissolves.

1912 The Alaska Native Brotherhood is formed to promote civil rights issues, such as the right to vote, access to public education, and civil rights in public places. The organization also fights court battles to win land rights.

1916 Ishi, the last Yahi, dies of tuberculosis.

1920 The Canadian government amends the Indian Act to allow for compulsory, or forced, enfranchisement, the process by which Indians have to give up their tribal loyalties to become Canadian citizens. Only 250 Indians had voluntarily become enfranchised between 1857 and 1920.

1924 Congress passes legislation conferring U.S. citizenship on all American Indians. This act does not take away rights that Native Americans had by treaty or the Constitution.

1928 Lewis Meriam is hired to investigate the status of Indian economies, health, and education, and the federal administration of Indian affairs. His report describes the terrible conditions under which Indians are forced to live, listing problems with health care, education, poverty, malnutrition, and land ownership.

1934 U.S. Congress passes the Indian Reorganization Act (IRA), which ends allotment policies and restores some land to Native Americans. The IRA encourages tribes to govern themselves and set up tribal economic corporations, but with the government overseeing their decisions. The IRA also provides more funding to the reservations. Many tribes form tribal governments and adopt constitutions.

1940 Newly opened Grand Coulee Dam floods Spokane land and stops the salmon from running.

1941–45 Navajo Code Talkers send and receive secret messages in their Native language, making a major contribution to the U.S. war effort during World War II.

1942 As hostilities leading to World War II grow, the Iroquois exercise their powers as an independent nation to declare war on Germany, Italy, and Japan.

1946 The Indian Lands Commission (ICC) is created to decide land claims filed by Indian nations. Many tribes expect the ICC to return lost lands, but the ICC chooses to award money instead, and at the value of the land at the time it was lost.

1951 A new Indian Act in Canada reduces the power of the Indian Affairs Office, makes it easier for Indians to gain the right to vote, and helps Indian children enter public schools. It also removes the ban on potlatch and Sun Dance ceremonies.

1954–62 The U.S. Congress carries out its termination policy. At the same time laws are passed giving states and local governments control over tribal members, taking away the tribes' authority to govern themselves. Under the policy of termination, Native Americans lose their special privileges and are treated the same as other U.S. citizens. The tribes that are terminated face extreme poverty and the threat of loss of their community and traditions. By 1961 the government begins rethinking this policy because of the damage it is causing.

1955 The Indian Health Service (IHS) assumes responsibility for Native American health care. The IHS operates hospitals, health centers, health stations, clinics, and community service centers.

1958 Alaska becomes a state; 104 million acres of Native land are taken.

1960 The queen of England approves a law giving status Indians the right to vote in Canada.

1964 The Great Alaska Earthquake and tsunami destroys several Alutiiq villages.

1965 Under the new U.S. government policy, the Self-Determination policy, federal aid to reservations is given directly to Indian tribes and not funneled through the Bureau of Indian Affairs.

1968 Three Ojibway—Dennis Banks, George Mitchell, and Clyde Bellecourt—found the American Indian Movement (AIM) in Minneapolis, Minnesota, to raise public awareness about treaties the federal and state governments violated.

1969 Eighty-nine Native Americans land on Alcatraz Island, a former penitentiary in San Francisco Bay in California. The group calling itself "Indians of All Tribes," claims possession of the island under an 1868 treaty that gave Indians the right to unused federal property on Indian land. Indians of All Tribes occupies the island for 19 months while negotiating with federal officials. They do not win their claim to the island but draw public attention to their cause.

1971 Quebec government unveils plans for the James Bay I hydroelectric project. Cree and Inuit protest the action in Quebec courts.

1971 The Alaska Native Claims Settlement Act (ANCSA) is signed into law. With the act, Alaska Natives give up any claim to nine-tenths of Alaska. In return they are given $962 million and clear title to 44 million acres of land.

1972 Five hundred Native Americans arrive in Washington, D.C., on a march called the Trail of Broken Treaties to protest the government's policies toward Native Americans. The protestors occupy the Bureau of Indian Affairs building for a week, causing considerable damage. They present the government with a list of reforms, but the administration rejects their demands.

1973 After a dispute over Oglala Sioux (Lakota) tribal chair Robert Wilson and his strong-arm tactics at Pine Ridge Reservation, AIM leaders are called in. Wilson's supporters and local authorities arm themselves against protestors, who are also armed, and a ten-week siege begins in which hundreds of federal marshals and Federal Bureau of Investigation (FBI) agents surround the Indian protestors. Two Native American men are shot and killed.

1974 After strong protests and "fish-ins" bring attention to the restrictions on Native American fishing rights in the Pacific Northwest, the U.S. Supreme Court restores Native fishing rights in the case *Department of Game of Washington v. Puyallup Tribe et al.*

1978 U.S. Congress passes legislation called the Tribally Controlled Community College Assistance Act, providing support for tribal colleges, schools of higher education designed to help Native American students achieve academic success and eventually transfer to four-year colleges and universities. Tribal colleges also work with tribal elders and cultural leaders to record languages, oral traditions, and arts in an effort to preserve cultural traditions.

1978 The American Indian Religious Freedom Act is signed. Its stated purpose is to "protect and preserve for American Indians their inherent right of freedom to believe, express, and exercise their traditional religions."

1978 The Bureau of Indian Affairs publishes regulations for the new Federal Acknowledgement Program. This program is responsible for producing a set of "procedures for establishing that an American Indian group exists as an Indian tribe." Many tribes will later discover that these requirements are complicated and difficult to establish.

1982 Canada constitutionally recognizes aboriginal peoples in its new Constitution and Charter of Rights and Freedoms. The Constitution officially divides Canada's aboriginal nations into three designations: the Indian, the Inuit, and the Métis peoples. Native groups feel that the new Constitution does not adequately protect their rights, nor does it give them the right to govern themselves.

1988 The Federal Indian Gambling Regulatory Act of 1988 allows any tribe recognized by the U.S. government to engage in gambling activities. With proceeds from gaming casinos, some tribes pay for health care, support of the elderly and sick, housing, and other improvements, while other tribes buy back homelands, establish scholarship funds, and create new jobs.

1990 Two important acts are passed by U.S. Congress. The Native American Languages Act is designed to preserve, protect, and promote the practice and development of Indian languages. The Graves Protection and Repatriation Act provides for the protection of American Indian grave sites and the repatriation (return) of Indian remains and cultural artifacts to tribes.

1992 Canadians vote against a new Constitution (the Charlotte-town Accord) that contains provisions for aboriginal self-government.

1995 The Iroquois request that all sacred masks and remains of their dead be returned to the tribe; the Smithsonian Institution is the first museum to comply with this request.

1999 A new territory called Nunavut enters the federation of Canada. Nunavut is comprised of vast areas taken from the Northwest Territories and is populated by an Inuit majority. The largest Native land claim in Canadian history, Nunavut is one-fifth of the landmass of Canada, or the size of the combined states of Alaska and Texas. Meaning "Our Land" in the Inukitut (Inuit) language, Nunavut will be primarily governed by the Inuit.

2003 The first official Comanche dictionary is published, compiled entirely by the Comanche people.

2004 Southern Cheyenne Peace Chief W. Richard West Jr. becomes director of the newly opened National Museum of the American Indian in Washington, D.C.

2006 The United Nations censures the United States for reclaiming 60 million acres (90%) of Western Shoshone lands. The federal government uses parts of the land for military testing, open-pit gold mining and nuclear waste disposal. The Shoshone, who have used it for cattle grazing since the Treaty of Ruby Valley in 1863, have repeatedly had their livestock confiscated and fines imposed.

2011 The government gives the Fort Sill Apache 30 acres for a reservation in Deming, New Mexico.

2011 Tacoma Power gives the Skokomish 1,000 acres of land and $11 million.

N

Makah
Skokomish Duwamish
Puyallup Lake Spokane Blackfoot
Nisqually Umatilla Colville Salish
Chinook Flathead
Yakama
Siletz Nez Nakota
Percé
Crow Lak
Yurok Northern
Chilula Modoc Cheyenne A
Hupa Pit River Northern Paiute Northern
Shoshone Arapaho
Cahto Maidu Western Eastern Pawn
Pomo Shoshone Shoshone
Washoe
Miwok
Costanoan Kawaiisu
Yahi and Yana
Southern Paiute Ute Southern
Cheyenne
Chumash San Carlos
Anasazi Pueblo
Navajo Jemez Jicarilla Kiowa
Hopi San Juan Taos
Cahuilla Mohave Apache
Luiseño
Yuman White Mountain Zuñi
Yaqui Acoma Pecos
PACIFIC Tohono O'odham Comanche
OCEAN Pima
Chiricahua

California

Great Basin

Great Plains

Northeast

Pacific Northwest

Plateau

Southeast

Southwest

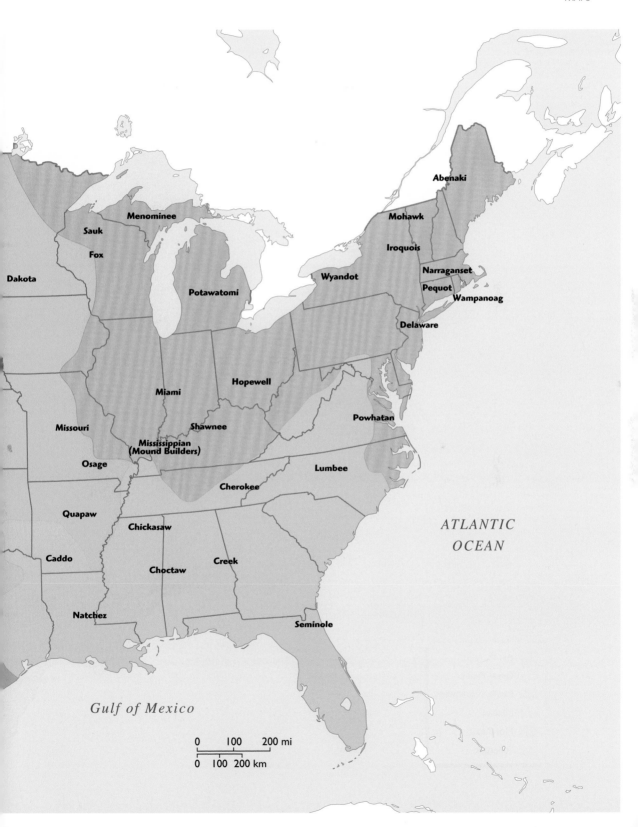

Abenaki

Mohawk

Iroquois

Narraganset

Menominee

Sauk

Fox

Wyandot

Pequot

Wampanoag

Dakota

Potawatomi

Delaware

Hopewell

Miami

Powhatan

Missouri

Shawnee

Mississippian
(Mound Builders)

Osage

Lumbee

Cherokee

Quapaw

Chickasaw

Caddo

Choctaw

Creek

ATLANTIC
OCEAN

Natchez

Seminole

Gulf of Mexico

0   100   200 mi

0   100 200 km

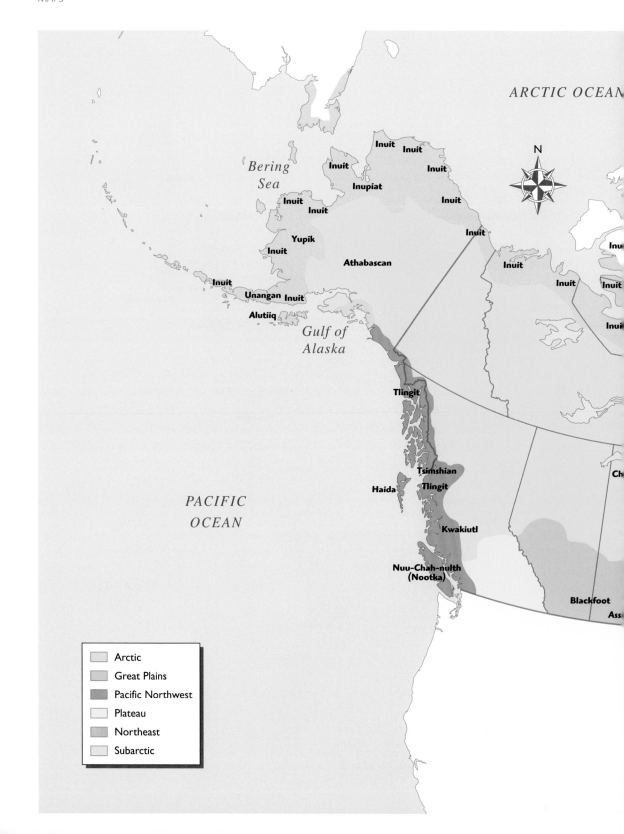

ARCTIC OCEAN

*Bering
Sea*

Inuit **Inuit**

Inuit

Inuit

Inupiat

Inuit

Inuit

Inuit **Inuit**

Inuit

Yupik

Inuit

Athabascan

Inuit

Inuit

Inu

Inuit

Inuit

Inuit **Inuit**

Inuit

Inuit

Unangan **Inuit**

Alutiiq

*Gulf of
Alaska*

Tlingit

*PACIFIC
OCEAN*

Tsimshian

Haida **Tlingit**

Kwakiutl

**Nuu-Chah-nulth
(Nootka)**

Ch

Blackfoot

Ass

	Arctic
	Great Plains
	Pacific Northwest
	Plateau
	Northeast
	Subarctic

Baffin
Bay

Labrador
Sea

Inuit

Inuit

Inuit

Inuit

Inuit

Inuit

Inuit

Inuit

Inuit

Inuit

Inuit

Inuit

Inuit

Inuit

Inuit

Inuit

Inuit

Hudson
Bay

Innu

Cree

Micmac

ATLANTIC
OCEAN

Ojibwa

Algonkin

Ottawa

Huron

Wyandotte

0	250	500 mi
0	250	500 km

Great Basin

The Great Basin

The vast, expansive region of the American West between the Rocky Mountains in the east and the Sierra Nevada Mountains in the west is commonly referred to as the Great Basin. The region is roughly comprised of what are now known as the states of Nevada, western Colorado, eastern Oregon, southern Idaho, and parts of eastern California. With no river outlets to the sea or easily traveled trails, this dry, sparsely populated region was the last area of the continental United States to be explored and settled by Europeans and Euro-Americans; it was finally mapped and crisscrossed in 1844. Although the term "Great Basin" has gained popular usage, the area is in fact not simply one immense basin but a series of mountain ranges and river valleys.

For thousands of years, the Great Basin region has been home to hundreds of Native groups that spoke similar languages but were distinct from each other politically. These groups have undergone profound cultural and political changes in the centuries following European contact and colonization and have skillfully adapted to the many changes brought by the foreigners.

Archaeologists and geologists (scientists who study the history of the earth and its life, especially as recorded in rocks) have determined that great lakes and glaciers covered this region during the Ice Ages and began to evaporate roughly around 11,000 to 8,000 BCE. One of the oldest mummified skeletons in the world has been found in the Lahontan Cave outside Fallon, Nevada, and is estimated to be more than nine thousand years old. Researchers debate over how much meaning can be attributed to the Lahontan Mummy and other archaeological findings from this area, which provide only faint glimpses into the material conditions of these ancient societies. Whatever meanings, beliefs, and rituals these peoples attributed to their practices and lives over countless centuries cannot be adequately assessed. It is, therefore, difficult to make extensive, meaningful determinations about the lives of the Native peoples throughout that time.

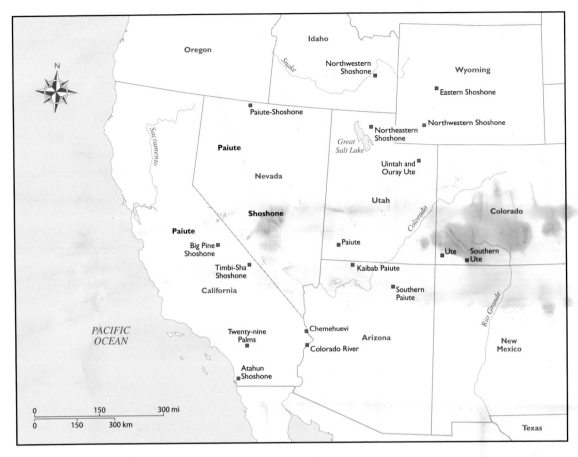

A map showing some contemporary Native American communities in the Great Basin region. MAP BY XNR PRODUCTIONS. CENGAGE LEARNING, GALE. REPRODUCED BY PERMISSION OF GALE, A PART OF CENGAGE LEARNING.

The Spanish bring horses

Beginning in the early 1600s, the European presence greatly changed the lives of the Great Basin peoples living in what are now eastern Utah and Colorado. Located directly north of the Spanish colony of New Mexico, the Ute became the first Great Basin group to experience the pressures introduced by Europeans in the American West. In the seventeenth century, Spanish-introduced trade items, particularly the horse, began to make their way out of New Mexico and into the eastern Great Basin. The Ute at this time were not one unified tribal group but many different political units organized under different leaders and living in different parts of Utah and Colorado. The Eastern Ute quickly adopted the horse and began hunting buffalo and trading in the southern Plains and New Mexico. Many of the Western Ute, however, were slower to adopt the equestrian (horse-riding) culture and economy of their eastern brethren.

With the adoption of the horse, the Ute changed many aspects of their economies and cultures. Previously, like most of the other Numic-speaking (see "Language") peoples of the Great Basin, they had hunted on foot and gathered useful foods from their local environments. The Ute now vigorously competed for precious Spanish resources in and around New Mexico with the many other tribes around them, such as the Comanche to the east, Navajo to the southwest, and Apache to the southeast. To gain firearms, horses, and other goods to meet the demands of the New Mexican market, these tribes often raided each other and other neighboring groups. Their economies and political relations now revolved around the horse, whereas many other Great Basin peoples still lived in societies without horses.

Europeans settle in the Great Basin

In addition to introducing the horse trade, beginning in the mid-1700s the Spanish began solidifying their control on the American Southwest and established settlements in California in 1769. To link the New Mexican and California colonies, Spanish traders and explorers forged the Spanish Trail between Santa Fe and Los Angeles, which led directly through parts of the southern Great Basin, home to Southern Paiute (see entry) groups in southern Nevada, western Utah, and northern Arizona as well as Chemehuevi, Kawaiisu (see entry), Owens Valley Paiute, and Western Shoshone (see entry) groups. These Native peoples now experienced the negative effects of European trading, particularly the newcomers' need for Native American slaves, food resources, and water supplies.

The 1800s brought revolutionary changes to all the Great Basin groups. The Western Shoshone of Nevada and eastern California, the Gosiute Shoshone of eastern Utah, the Northern Paiute of northern Nevada and eastern Oregon, and the Southern Paiute, Chemehuevi, Kawaiisu, and Washoe (see entry) of California all found their previous economies, political organization, and cultural practices fundamentally disrupted by first British and then American traders and settlers. Previously organized in hundreds of small bands that moved seasonally

EMIGRANTS FORDING THE SNAKE RIVER.

A pioneer wagon fords the Snake River on the Oregon Trail in the 1800s. Pioneers traveled this route through the Great Basin in massive numbers, destroying the fragile ecology of the region. © NORTH WIND PICTURE ARCHIVES/ ALAMY.

throughout local environments hunting and gathering needed resources, some smaller groups were forced to band together under powerful leaders, whereas others migrated out of areas infested with European disease into more remote mountain locations.

In the early 1800s, both Great Britain and the United States vied for control of the western half of North America. Quickly displacing the Spanish, British and then American traders moved rapidly into the northern Great Basin along the Snake and Humboldt Rivers and, with the aid of local Bannock, Shoshone, and Paiute guides, trapped any animals they could. With the American conquest of northern Mexico in the Mexican-American War (1846–48; a war in which Mexico lost about one-half of its national territory), the United States acquired control of the Southwest and California in 1848. In the late 1840s and 1850s, the California Gold Rush attracted more than one hundred thousand miners and settlers. Tens of thousands of these pioneers on their way to California and Oregon passed directly through the Great Basin along both the Overland Trail and Oregon Trail, destroying the fragile ecology with their many horses and cattle, as well as sometimes attacking whatever small bands of Northern Paiute and Western Shoshone they encountered.

Greed becomes abuse

Because of their limited technologies, non-equestrian cultures, and sparse material possessions, Europeans often considered most Great Basin peoples to be inferior. Racism was a precondition for American expansion and development throughout California and the Great Basin as U.S. settlers firmly believed in their right to take Native lands and abuse Native peoples. The settlers used both religious and intellectual justification for their violent and criminal acts. Thousands of Native American peoples, especially around the mining settlements in California and Nevada, did not survive these turbulent years of foreign intrusion, and others struggled desperately.

Eastern California and Nevada proved to be extremely abundant in timber, water, and minerals, resources that the growing American economy sought. The American public wanted Native lands, and there was little protection for the Great Basin groups. Although the United States negotiated treaties in the mid-1800s with nearly all the Great Basin groups outside California, the government played only a limited role in supervising the rights these agreements granted to Native peoples. Consequently, reservation lands and annual annuities payments legislated by these treaties were not sufficiently enforced to meet the survival needs of many of these peoples. With the near-destruction of their subsistence economies (systems in which individuals work to provide goods for their own survival but not for trade or money) and their lands occupied by foreigners, the Great Basin peoples experienced extreme hardships. Forced to work on ranches, in mines, as domestic servants, or in any capacity possible, many Native people throughout the region found themselves dealing with wage labor for the first time.

U.S. policies

This period of difficult transitions was made even harder in the late 1800s and early 1900s when the U.S. government began policies that attempted to assimilate Native peoples into the mainstream of American society. Boarding schools were established for Native groups that attempted to stop children from using their traditions and languages and, often painfully, separated them from their parents. New laws, such as the General Allotment Act of 1887 (also known as the Dawes Act), were passed that curbed tribal ownership of lands and gave reservation lands to individual Natives. The results of these policies were disastrous. The Southern Ute

Reservation in western Colorado lost over eight million acres, or 99 percent of the reservation. The Ute Mountain Reservation lost 94 percent.

Throughout the early 1900s, the Native peoples of the Great Basin continued to deal with harsh economic, political, and social impositions by state and federal institutions. Only in the 1930s did the federal government policy move away from these assimilation efforts as Native nations and their tribal governments received some limited autonomy (self-rule). This Indian New Deal (1930s) also led to the recognition of many new Native governments as well as the creation of new reservations, such as several for the Western Shoshone of Nevada. Unfortunately for Native peoples, this era of limited autonomy was quickly followed in the 1950s by another attempt by the government to end the unique legal status of the tribes. This policy of termination directly affected several Southern Paiute reservations, such as the Shivwits Reservation in Southwestern Utah, which lost its status as a tribal government. This status had entitled it to federal resources and exempted it from state laws and taxation. In addition, the U.S. government attempted to integrate Native peoples into the larger U.S. economy through relocation programs that moved Native peoples away from their reservations to work in cities. Only in the 1970s did these assimilation efforts give way to an era of Native nations' self-determination, after which Native peoples and tribal governments helped determine and enforce the laws under which they lived.

Great Basin Native nations have maintained their distinct political and cultural identities despite the tremendous changes brought by European and American contact and colonization. Although American pressures have irrevocably altered the quality of life for the Great Basin Native nations, throughout this vast region, Native peoples continue to live according to their own beliefs and traditions. From Colorado to California, they maintain cultures that are thousands of years old despite the loss of most of their ancestral lands, the economic difficulties of reservation life, and the often overwhelming presence of an intrusive American culture. Struggling to learn the many complexities of living in American society and dealing with a powerful, imposed American government, Native nations throughout Nevada, California, Utah, eastern Oregon, southern Idaho, and western Colorado have become politically and economically active and productive members of their societies. The Native nations of the Great Basin have survived and creatively adapted to their changing world by learning the ways of the larger society and blending their own unique traditions with those of American society.

Religion

The dramatic disruptions accompanying American contact and colonization have irrevocably altered the ways in which Great Basin peoples understand and give meaning to their lives. Through Native oral histories and the work of anthropologists (people who study human societies and cultures), it is relatively clear that many Great Basin peoples at the time of European contact lived in a highly spiritual world where humans were simply one part of a greater universe. Animals, the deceased, mountains, and the land itself all had spiritual significance in Great Basin spirituality.

Although it is difficult to measure the amount of religious change brought by European contact, a great deal of religious blending and mixture has occurred throughout the region. Different religious missionaries and denominations, such as the Mormon religion in Utah, have achieved small to large followings among contemporary Native peoples. Following a new religion, however, does not necessarily mean that these individuals and groups no longer follow ancestral teachings and practices. The adoption of certain religious teachings from American society in many ways parallels the many other adaptations Great Basin peoples have undergone. Gaining spiritual strength from outside religions and using it for everyday guidance are integral aspects of communities and cultures that have changed and continue to change according to their own needs.

Language

Related to linguistic groups found outside of the Great Basin, such as the Hopi of Arizona and the Comanche of the southern Plains (see entries), Numic, the primary Great Basin language, has been divided by linguists into three subgroups: Western, Central, and Southern, depending on the location in the Great Basin. Numic is a branch of a larger language family known as Uto-Aztecan, one of the largest North American language families, which stretches south of the Great Basin all the way into central Mexico. The different Paiute, Shoshone, Ute, Chemehuevi, and Kawaiisu peoples of the Great Basin all speak similar, yet regionally unique, versions of Numic. The Washoe people of western Nevada and eastern California are the only Great Basin groups that do not speak the Numic language. Washoe is a unique language, only distantly related to another North American language family, known as the Hokan. Linguists guess that this uniqueness comes from the long-standing presence of Washoe peoples in their Sierra Nevadan homeland near Lake Tahoe, California.

The Great Basin languages have fallen into disuse in recent years. Children at boarding schools in the region were punished for speaking their language, and discrimination in surrounding English-speaking communities forced many Great Basin peoples to learn English in order to survive. Elders and more traditional Native nations have fought to keep the language alive, and many tribal leaders have instituted language-retention programs in their tribal schools. Only in recent decades have some Great Basin languages been written down and translated. Recording the languages either electronically on tapes or textually on paper is another example of Great Basin nations adapting their cultures to a technologically changing world.

Subsistence

For centuries, the economies of the Great Basin peoples revolved around the gathering of local plants and seeds, and the hunting of deer, antelope, rabbits, and various small game. Fishing was common for many groups, such as the Pyramid Lake Paiute, who had access to fish in this generally water-scarce region. For the Northern and Eastern Shoshone, the Bannock, and the Ute, the adoption of the horse brought a fundamental change to their economy. Mounted and mobile, these equestrian hunters roamed the northern plains in search of buffalo. The groups also hunted larger game, such as bear and elk, in the mountain regions of the Rockies. For most Great Basin groups, however, the gathering of local foods remained the main form of subsistence for centuries. The pine nut, or piñon, is a delicious and nutritious nut found in the mountains throughout the Great Basin. Shoshone, Paiute, and other groups have gathered this food for centuries and use it in many different ways. Ground up, pine nuts form a paste that can be either rolled into dough for bread or boiled with other vegetables to form soup. Roasted, the nuts keep well for many months. Nearly all Great Basin groups harvested piñons in the fall and then saved much of their supply for the cold winter months in underground storage areas. The pine nut plays a significant cultural as well as an economic role as it appears in many Great Basin stories and legends.

European contact fundamentally altered the subsistence economies of all Great Basin tribes. For the Great Basin peoples who hunted on the Northern Plains, the virtual extermination of the buffalo forever changed

A basket of piñon. Nearly all Great Plains tribes relied on piñon as an important part of their diet. © NORTH WIND PICTURE ARCHIVES.

their lives. For the non-equestrian Great Basin nations, the settlements of American miners and ranchers disrupted their extremely fragile ecologies. Since small bands so heavily depended on the seasonal harvest of pine nuts and other grasses as well as the hunting of small game, the loss of access to mountain ranges and water supplies plunged many groups into terrible poverty. The mining industries of Nevada and eastern California, for instance, sometimes used up all local timber and water resources, killing entire stands of piñon trees. Ranching and pioneer travel through the region destroyed fertile marshes and grasslands along the major rivers. Cattle, horses, and sheep ate many of the grasses and seeds that some groups depended on to live. Following these ecological disasters, Great Basin peoples came to depend heavily on local U.S. communities and the federal government for their survival. The government has administered food and other payments to these groups, but poverty and economic problems continue to plague many of these communities.

Customs

All Great Basin groups have maintained social practices and customs that reflect as well as reinforce many of the broader cultural values of their communities. Although it is difficult to make generalizations that apply to all of these different groups, the various artistic, marital, child-rearing, puberty, and burial traditions of these groups offer interesting comparisons and contrasts.

In general, artistic expression and traditions have served both functional and creative purposes. Many of the equestrian Great Basin groups developed artistic styles combining their pre-equestrian traditions with those of their Plains neighbors. The Ute, for instance, embellished their child-carrying cradleboards with many beading and decorative techniques utilized by Plains groups, but they also used a willow cover for the child's head as practiced among other Great Basin groups. (Such woven, willow covers serve to protect the child from the sun as well as to designate the gender of the child.) The equestrian groups likewise adopted some of the Plains buffalo dances and ceremonies not found throughout the Great Basin. They also took up the hide-painting traditions of their Plains neighbors, often depicting important events and ceremonies on the hides of large elk and buffalo.

Most Great Basin nations did not have access to the same animal, leather, and wood resources as the equestrian tribes, yet these groups did develop highly sophisticated forms of functional art, such as baskets. Intricate Washoe, Paiute, Shoshone, and other Great Basin baskets provide clear examples of the creativity and intellectual traditions of these different peoples. Made of woven and coiled branches and other grasses, Great Basin baskets are considered among the highest quality in the world. Washoe baskets became so highly coveted by art collectors in the early 1900s that weavers could not fulfill the demand.

Current tribal issues

In the second decade of the 2000s, the Great Basin tribes were mainly located on reservations and colonies in Idaho, Utah, Nevada, Oregon, and eastern California. The federal government legally recognized some of these lands as home to specific tribes, meaning that the reservations or colonies are subject to the particular laws of the tribes who reside there. Many smaller political groups make up the larger Paiute, Ute, and Shoshone tribes. The Ute live on the largest Great Basin reservation, the

Uintah-Ouray Reservation, in eastern Utah and on two other reservations in southwestern Colorado. There are three main Shoshone groups, the Western, Northern, and Eastern, each with numerous different tribes and reservations. The many Shoshone reservations are quite spread out and stretch from eastern California to Wyoming. The Southern and Northern Paiute, like the Western Shoshone, consist of numerous smaller tribes living on many different reservations throughout southern Nevada and Utah for the Southern Paiute, and in northwestern Nevada and eastern Oregon for the Northern Paiute. The Washoe live close to the Nevada-California border, near their ancestral homes around Lake Tahoe. The Kawaiisu, once scattered around the country, have been making a comeback, and some are concentrated in Kern County, California.

Numerous interrelated concerns and challenges confronted these different tribes and reservation communities. In their efforts to combat the many social problems that stemmed from economic poverty and joblessness, tribes throughout the region attempted various economic development plans. Some nations used the federal court system to sue the government for failed treaty payments and lands. Others, who received federal resources for education and other anti-poverty programs, channeled the money into job training and job placement programs. Many of the Great Basin nations, however, were located in remote locations, far from economic centers. Several tribes adopted ranching on the open ranges as well as various other timber and water resource development projects.

In addition to economic concerns, numerous cultural and political issues are of critical importance. Most of the Great Basin groups are attempting to develop strong education programs for their youth and to introduce their children to some of the older traditions and teachings. Many pan-Indian (including Native peoples from all tribes) cultural and recreational activities, such as powwows and athletic tournaments, became increasingly popular in the 2000s. Politically, tribes throughout the region resisted state and federal incursion onto their lands and jurisdictions (places where they have the authority to make and enforce their own law). Some groups went to court hoping to recover some of the millions of acres of land lost to the U.S. government in the nineteenth century; others accepted settlement money for these lost lands. In addition, the U.S. Bureau of Land Management (BLM) and Department of Defense had illegal ownership of nearly 90 percent of Nevada's land. Meanwhile, the BLM and military used the lands in ways that were offensive to Native American peoples. The military, for instance, were testing nuclear and other weapons in Nevada, and the BLM prohibited Native American cattle ranching and pine nut harvesting on traditional tribal lands. Throughout the Great Basin, contemporary political, economic, and social issues continue to concern these many different neighboring Native nations.

BOOKS

Bergon, Frank. *Shoshone Mike.* New York: Viking Penguin, 1987.

Cassinelli, Dennis. *Preserving Traces of the Great Basin Indians.* Reno, NV: Jack Bacon & Company, 2006.

Doherty, Craig A., and Katherine M. Doherty. *Great Basin Indians.* Minneapolis, MN: Chelsea House, 2010.

Gibson, Karen Bush. *The Great Basin Indians: Daily Life in the 1700s.* Mankato, MN: Capstone Press, 2006.

Fowler, Catherine S., and Don D. Fowler. *The Great Basin: People and Place in Ancient Times.* Santa Fe, NM: School for Advanced Research, 2008.

Hyde, Dayton O. *The Last Free Man: The True Story behind the Massacre of Shoshone Mike and His Band of Indians in 1911.* New York: Dial Press, 1973.

Kuiper, Kathleen. *American Indians of California, the Great Basin, and the Southwest.* New York: Rosen Educational Services, 2012.

McDaniel, Melissa. *Great Basin Indians.* Des Plaines, IL: Heinemann, 2011.

Quinlan, Angus R. *Great Basin Rock Art: Archaeological Perspectives.* Reno: University of Nevada Press, 2007.

Simms, Steven R. *Ancient Peoples of the Great Basin and Colorado Plateau.* Walnut Creek, CA: Left Coast Press, 2008.

Vander, Judith. *Shoshone Ghost Dance Religion: Poetry, Songs, and Great Basin Context.* Urbana: University of Illinois Press, 1997.

WEB SITES

Beckman, Tad. "Indians of the Great Basin." *Harvey Mudd College.* http://www4.hmc.edu:8001/humanities/basin/gb-title.htm (accessed on August 15, 2011).

Great Basin Indian Archives. http://www.gbcnv.edu/gbia/index.htm (accessed on August 15, 2011).

"Great Basin Indian Collection." *University of Nevada, Reno.* http://knowledge center.unr.edu/specoll/gbi.html (accessed on August 15, 2011).

"Great Basin Indians." *University of Washington.* http://courses.washington.edu/anth310/basin.htm (accessed on August 15, 2011).

Great Basin National Park. "Historic Tribes of the Great Basin." *National Park Service: U.S. Department of the Interior.* http://www.nps.gov/grba/historyculture/historic-tribes-of-the-great-basin.htm (accessed on August 15, 2011).

National Library for the Environment. "Native Americans and the Environment: Great Basin." *National Council for Science and the Environment.* http://www.cnie.org/nae/basin.html (accessed on August 15, 2011).

Redish, Laura, and Orrin Lewis. "Indian Tribes and Languages of the Great Basin." *Native Languages of the Americas.* http://www.native-languages.org/basin-culture.htm (accessed on August 15, 2011).

Smith, C. R. "The Native People of North America: Great Basin Culture Area." *Cabrillo College.* http://www.cabrillo.edu/~crsmith/noamer_basin.html (accessed on August 15, 2011).

Kawaiisu

Name

Kawaiisu (pronounced *kah-WHY-soo* or *kah-WHY-i-soo*) comes from the Yokutsan name for the tribe. The people called themselves *Niwi* (also *Nuwu* and *Nuwa*), meaning "person," or *Niwiwi,* the plural form of the word, which meant "people." The Kawaiisu have also been called Kowash, Kahwissah, Kawiasuh, Nuwa, or Nuooah.

Location

Some anthropologists believe the Kawaiisu were living in the Mojave Desert area by the first century BCE. The Kawaiisu homeland in the Sierra Nevada was nestled in the Tehachapi Valley between Walker Pass and the Tehachapi Mountains of southern California (Kern County) near the Nevada border. Gathering food may have taken them as far east as the Panamint Mountains, west to Death Valley, and north to Antelope Valley. Some Kawaiisu still live in Kern County.

Population

The Kawaiisu have always been a small group. Their population was estimated to be 500 around the time of European contact in the 1700s; that number decreased to around 150 people in 1910. The 1936 U.S. Census showed 100 Kawaiisu. By 1984, that figure had dropped to about 35. From that point on, the few people left blended into the mainstream of society or lived on the Tule River Reservation or to the west in Tejon Pass. Since 2002, the Kawaiisu have been reviving their language and culture, and as of 2011, the nation numbered 250.

Language family

Uto-Aztecan.

Origins and group affiliations

The Kawaiisu may have arrived in their traditional homelands from the Mohave Desert more than two thousand years ago. Early writers sometimes considered the Kawaiisu as Caliente, Tehachapi, or Paiute (see entry).

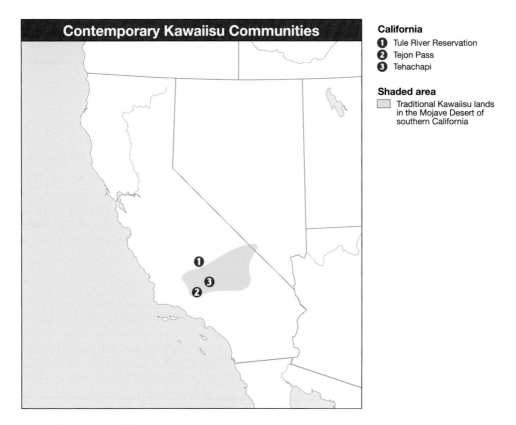

Contemporary Kawaiisu Communities

California
1. Tule River Reservation
2. Tejon Pass
3. Tehachapi

Shaded area
Traditional Kawaiisu lands in the Mojave Desert of southern California

A map of contemporary Kawaiisu communities. MAP BY XNR PRODUCTIONS. CENGAGE LEARNING, GALE. REPRODUCED BY PERMISSION OF GALE, A PART OF CENGAGE LEARNING.

Some sources say they were an offshoot of the Chemehuevi. The Kawaiisu culture or language was similar to that of the Chemehuevi, Ute (see entry), and Southern Paiute. Kawaiisu allies included their neighbors, the Kitanemuk and the Yokuts, with whom they held antelope drives. They also maintained friendly relations with the Yauelmani.

The Kawaiisu, who may be one of the earliest California tribes, have roots going back more than two thousand years. Although the Kawaiisu included the desert as part of their homeland, most of the year they roamed the mountains, particularly the southern Sierra Madre area, which provided safety and natural resources. When the weather grew cold, the Kawaiisu settled on a ridge in the Tehachapi Mountains. Tomo-Kahni, one of their winter homes, still exists as a historic landmark. As a group, the Kawaiisu people almost died out during the twentieth century, but they have made a comeback and are making efforts to restore their language and culture.

HISTORY

Early history

As early as 2000 years ago, the Kawaiisu may have settled near the California-Nevada border. Some archaeologists believe ancestors of the Kawaiisu created the bedrock mortar holes and ancient rock art in the tribe's traditional homelands. Tribe members, however, attributed the artwork to Rock Baby, an evil spirit. The people avoided the pictographs because they believed that contact with the art could cause blindness or even death.

The first Kawaiisu encounter with Europeans may have been in 1776 when Padre Francisco Garcés (1738–1781) passed through their territory. In his diary, he called them the *Cobaji*. He noted that the people were friendly and shared their food, seeds, and baskets.

Important Dates

1776: Padre Francisco Garcés becomes the first European to enter Kawaiisu territory.

1850s: The discovery of gold brings hundreds of prospectors to the Kawaiisu homelands.

1863: Soldiers led by Captain Moses A. McLaughlin massacre thirty-five unarmed Kawaiisu.

2002: The Kawaiisu start to revive their language and culture.

2010: The Kawaiisu Tribe of Tejon begin a lawsuit to stop construction on a site they consider sacred.

Relations with settlers

By the 1800s, settlers and trappers had begun moving into the area and settling on Kawaiisu lands. The numbers of newcomers increased in the1850s when gold was discovered. Soon, Kawaiisu lands were overrun by prospectors.

Difficulties did not arise, however, between the two groups over outsiders settling in Kawaiisu traditional territory. The conflicts occurred because of alleged stealing. The settlers accused the Kawaiisu of taking their horses and cattle, both of which the tribe used for food. At the same time, the tribe resented the newcomers taking their women.

Government decisions affect Kawaiisu

As more miners arrived and conflicts escalated, the state of California passed a law in 1850 that they said was to protect the tribes. In actuality, the Act for the Government and Protection of Indians caused great harm. Settlers could adopt Indian children and benefit from their labor until they became adults. Natives could not testify against any California citizen, but they had to obey all California laws or be subject to penalties.

If bail was set, a settler could pay the bond and take the Indian as a worker. Any Native declared a vagrant or beggar could be hired out to the highest bidder. For many Native peoples, including the Kawaiisu, this proved to be a slave law.

In 1853, the U.S. government decided to move the Kawaiisu to the Sebastian Indian Reservation in the Tejon Canyon. They believed it would make the people into a settled agricultural society and ease the tensions between the settlers and the Kawaiisu. The superintendent of Indian Affairs for California, Edward Beale (1822–1893), who set up the reservation on a Mexican land grant, did so because he claimed the Native nations were a "barrier to rapid settlement of the state."

Over the next decade, disease, insects, and drought caused repeated crop failures. In addition, some settlers moved onto reservation land and allowed their livestock to graze on or trample the crops the Natives had planted. Agents sold the government supplies sent to the reservation and pocketed the money. Meanwhile, the people went hungry. In 1863, all crops, with the exception of thirty tons of hay, were lost.

Massacre of 1863

When settlers heard that the Kawaiisu and several other tribes were meeting near Keysville in 1863, they became concerned that the Indians planned to attack, so they alerted the U.S. Army. Captain Moses A. McLaughlin and his soldiers went to the area, where they massacred thirty-five unarmed Natives. Even many of the settlers believed that McLaughlin's actions were unjust.

Until that time, relations between the two groups had not been hostile. Nanna Ramkin, a daughter of one of the settlers who lived near the Kawaiisu, quoted years later in the *Handbook of the Indians of California,* stated that the "Indians were generally friendly and peaceable. … They had a high standard of integrity and honesty and were honorable men and women." Occasional conflicts had arisen, but for the most part, relations had remained calm. Pioneers and Kawaiisu had even intermarried, and some Kawaiisu descendants still retained the names of the early pioneers.

Decline of the Kawaiisu

Over time, the Kawaiisu gradually assimilated into mainstream American society. They lost their language and traditions as they tried to become more like the settlers around them. A high rate of intermarriage also decreased the full-blooded Kawaiisu population. In 1910, the number of Kawaiisu had dropped to about 150 people. By 1984, only an estimated 35 people still claimed Kawaiisu heritage, and they were scattered throughout California and other nearby states.

Revival of Kawaiisu culture

In the early 2000s, major efforts were made to resurrect the Kawaiisu language and traditions. From a handful of survivors in the late 1980s, the Kawaiisu population has grown to 250 members. Elders have established the Kawaiisu Language and Cultural Center to pass on their knowledge to the younger generation.

In 2002, the center developed a curriculum to teach classes in language and culture. Supported by a variety of grants, the program has expanded to include online materials, tape recordings, and a variety of methods to revitalize the traditional Kawaiisu ways (see "Language"). The Kawaiisu are determined to keep their culture alive as they move into the next decades of the twenty-first century.

RELIGION

Supernatural beings

One of the most important Kawaiisu's supernatural beings was the *inipi,* a cross between a soul and a ghost. The Kawaiisu believed every person and most animals had an inipi. This spirit left the body when a person slept and returned when they awakened. Sometimes this spirit warned people of their impending deaths. After an individual died, the inipi remained behind. Not all inipi were harmless. Some tried to harm the living. Only witches or wicked people could control these evil spirits.

Other supernatural beings that were part of the Kawaiisu culture were the *yah^we'era* and the Rock Baby. The yah^we'era, which looked like a bird with a long tail, lived in an underground cave, and the Rock Baby dwelled in the canyons. Both were feared, but the Rock Baby instilled the most terror. The Kawaiisu attributed the pictographs scattered around their homeland to Rock Baby and said that touching one could cause blindness. Seeing or hearing the Rock Baby brought bad luck and might even result in death.

Omens and dreams

Omens were important in Kawaiisu culture. Unusual events were considered *tuuwatuugidi,* or signals of bad luck about to arrive. A few of the many signs of this impending doom were a ring around the moon, a dead eagle, a falling star that touched the horizon, a drop of blood or a rattlesnake in the house, or a coyote howling nearby several nights in a row.

Dreams played a huge role in the people's everyday lives. They could happen whether the person was asleep or awake. The Kawaiisu induced dreams by drinking jimson weed root, eating tobacco, walking naked through nettles, or swallowing a ball of eagle down filled with live red ants. Dreams could also come from talking to the darkness or the mountains alone at night. Those who saw a singing deer became healers (see "Healing"). Clear water or snow meant an ill person would recover. Rolling rocks indicated that a hunter would find game.

Bad dreams revealed something terrible about to happen. For example, dreaming of falling off a cliff foretold death. Nightmares of a grizzly bear, coyote, or rattlesnake may have been sent by a witch. People who experienced such dreams asked a *huviagadi* (song-possessor), or curing shaman, to identify the witch. The huviagadi might also persuade the witch to stop, or the family might threaten or bribe the witch. If nothing worked, the witch might be killed.

LANGUAGE

The Kawaiisu spoke a Southern Numic division of the Uto-Aztecan language. The Chemehuevi to the east of them also shared a similar language, so they are considered relatives. Most of the other tribes in the area did not speak Numic languages.

During the twentieth century, the Kawaiisu moved into the American culture around them (see "History"). Over time, the people lost their culture and languages. By the turn of the twenty-first century, only five fluent speakers of Kawaiisu were still alive, and all of them were between the ages of sixty and ninety-five. Realizing they had little time left to teach and document the language, the elders formed the Kawaiisu Language and Cultural Center in 2002.

Supported by grants, this nonprofit organization began digitally recording language and cultural information to pass on to future generations. Younger Kawaiisu began actively learning their language.

The center developed a variety of programs to aid in educating the youth. They set up master-apprentice teams, where a fluent speaker is paired with a learner. In time, the apprentice goes on to teach others. A program called Voices in Your Pocket provides digital recordings for people to listen to on digital music players, so they can practice while engaged in other chores. The center has piloted programs for teaching infants, developed curriculum and games for school children, and collected stories and vocabulary for their archives. They hope that by compiling as much material as they can and increasing the number of fluent speakers, they will ensure that Kawaiisu language and culture will once again become a strong influence in the lives of their people.

GOVERNMENT

Chiefs did not inherit their positions but were usually selected based on their wealth and knowledge. Chiefs were responsible for sponsoring all festivities, so they needed to have both money and a generous spirit. Because a chief's possessions were destroyed when he died, his son had no access to them; therefore, sons took over leadership from their fathers only if they had amassed their own property.

The Kawaiisu were peaceful and had little need for a war chief. Most conflicts and disagreements, even intertribal ones, were handled between individuals, so they did not escalate into battles.

ECONOMY

As hunter-gathers, the Kawaiisu migrated from the mountains to the desert to gather food and supplies. They spent the months from spring through fall collecting and preserving food for the winter months. When it became cold, they moved to winter homes in the Sand Canyon area, where women made baskets and men made weapons from chert and obsidian.

The people also traded with nearby tribes, but some of the goods the early Kawaiisu obtained, such as shells, showed that their trading expeditions may have gone as far as the coast. The Kaw's medium of exchange was acorns from the seven different oak species that grew in their territory. Because many tribes used acorns as a staple food, the Kawaiisu could easily get the supplies they needed, such as obsidian for tools.

After the settlers and miners moved into their territory, the Kawaiisu were unable to hunt and gather as they had for centuries. To cope, many became part of the American culture around them and lost their traditional ways. Their livelihoods now came from wage labor, cattle grazing, prospecting, or hunting.

DAILY LIFE

Families

The Kawaiisu lived together in large groups of sixty to one hundred people during the winter months. In the spring, they divided into smaller groups that hunted and gathered together. People usually worked and lived together in small family units. Most of these groups became interrelated through marriage. They visited each other often and exchanged goods. This constant contact resulted in a system of trails that connected the various areas that they frequented.

Buildings

In the winter, the Kawaiisu lived in circular, above-ground homes called *tomo kahni* that were about 15 to 25 feet (4 to 8 meters) in diameter. They built these structures with willow or juniper poles bound together and connected with smaller branches tied to the inside and outside of the poles. To fill the openings between the branches, they stuffed brush into them and then covered the exterior with bark and tule mats. Stones were placed around the base to hold the home in place. Mats served as doors.

Inside, a central fire was ringed with stones, and a hole in the roof allowed the smoke to escape. People slept with their feet facing the fire. The heated rocks in the fire pit kept them warm at night.

Villages included granaries and a *tivi kahni,* or sweathouse, located near water. Granaries, used for storing nuts and acorns, were built at least 2 feet (about half a meter) off the ground so animals and rodents could not burrow into the food. Sweat houses were constructed in a similar manner to the houses, but they were covered with dirt. Most camps were surrounded by a windbreak made of brush. Brush enclosures might also be used for village meetings. Nearby caves served for births, ceremonies, storage, and even for lookouts.

For use in warmer weather, the people had *hava kahni.* These open, flat-roofed houses provided shade. Women worked under the hava kahni when it was sunny.

Clothing and adornment

The Kawaiisu wore little clothing most of the year. Men used breech-cloths (an apronlike piece of fabric attached at the waist), and women had two-piece skirts. The Kawaiisu used bark and tule for clothing, but they added skins and pelts to their wardrobes in winter. Men made rabbit fur into ponchos and blankets that kept their families warm during cold weather. It could take as many as one hundred rabbit skins to make a blanket. The Kawaiisu used deer or rabbit skin to wrap their babies; diapers were made from cattail fluff or from shredded tule or juniper bark. Most children wore little clothing, if any.

Moccasins of tanned deer hide were the usual footwear. The Kawaiisu covered the soles with piñon pitch and ashes to make them durable for long trips. In the winter, they wore snowshoes of heavy cord that they lined with pounded sagebrush bark.

Adults had long hair that they wore in braids down their backs, but they burned their children's hair to keep it short. Women had pierced noses and ears in which they wore plugs or strings of beads. They often painted their bodies, but men generally only used paint for ceremonies. Both men and women might have tattoos on their arms, hands, and faces.

Food

As hunter-gatherers, the Kawaiisu lived mainly on deer and the plants that they gathered in the wild. They were careful about what they harvested and always left enough behind so the plants could reproduce. The people replanted some bulbs and roots, and used fire to clear invasive plants so deer could graze.

Men hunted deer, antelope, brown bear, birds, rodents, and reptiles. At times, they fished using bone hooks or by spreading buckeye meal on the water. This stupefied, or numbed, the fish, making them easier to catch. The Kawaiisu also ate insects. Animals they never ate were skunk, buzzard, rattlesnake, bat, crow, eagle, grasshopper, and grizzly bear. Men collected salt from Koehn Lake, thirty miles away from their winter homes, or in Proctor Lake in Tehachapi Valley if the water was low.

Women collected wild rice, chia, sunflower seeds, pine nuts, buckwheat, juniper, and yucca. The desert yielded mesquite and screwbeans. One of the most important foods was the acorn. Buckeye nuts substituted when acorn harvests were slim. Women ground the shelled acorns or buckeye nuts and soaked them in water. Flour made from acorns

Kawaiisu Sweets

Mesquite

Although the Kawaiisu harvested most of their food in the mountains, they collected mesquite from the desert. Like the California Indians, they ate the young pods raw or cooked them, or they ground the older pods into flour. The seeds could be toasted, and flowers were edible both raw and roasted.

Mesquite could also be used to sweeten things. The pods took the place of sugar. The tree sap could be used to make candy. To obtain the tree sap, the Kawaiisu cut a gash in the trunk and collected the drippings. It was also chewed like gum.

Sugar pine

Seeds from the sugar pine tree were eaten raw or were roasted or boiled. They could also be mashed and mixed with water. Like mesquite, the sugar pine tree could provide a sweet treat. The Kawaiisu collected sugar pine sap. After it dried, it tasted like powdered sugar. This sugar was also an ingredient in many recipes.

could be added to soups and stews, cooked into mush, or baked into breads. Mush was sometimes formed into cakes and then dried until it hardened.

Many of the plants, berries, and seeds the women collected were eaten raw. The women also pounded and ground some of them for winter storage. Some were molded into cakes and dried.

The Kawaiisu ate raw meat, and they also boiled it, roasted it in pits over ashes, or dried it on trays over hot coals. Deer meat was preserved by making jerky (strips of dried meat).

Education

Children learned their adult roles at an early age. Girls participated in gathering and preparing food, and they learned to make baskets. Young boys played games to develop their hunting abilities. By age nine, a boy was expected to hunt for his family. Boys also learned to make cord and create rabbit skin blankets.

Elders used story times to teach values and morals. Important lessons were conveyed through passing along oral history and other tales. In this way, the young learned to respect others and care for the environment and the plants and animals in it (see "Oral literature").

Healing practices

The Kawaiisu had an extensive knowledge of herbs and plants. Records indicate that they used more than one hundred different plants for healing. Some of the most widely used were the sugar pine, flannelbush, and blue oak (see sidebar, "The Vital Blue Oak Tree"). These plants provided not only medicine but many other necessities as well.

Herbalists ground blue oak galls (round growths on leaves or stems that contain insect larvae) and mixed them with salt to heal sores. This mixture wrapped in cloth and wet with water eased the pain of aching eyes. The Kawaiisu boiled the inner bark of the blue oak and drank that liquid to alleviate arthritis. Dried sugar pine sap reduced bloating, gas, and constipation. Mixed with milk, it relieved sore eyes and improved babies' eyesight. The Kawaiisu soaked the inner bark of the flannelbush in water and drank the liquid as a tonic.

Tobacco was used for religious purposes, but it also had a role in healing. The Kawaiisu used it to stop itching, bleeding, and pain. Other plants commonly used for medicine included holly leaf, nettles, buckthorn, and jimson weed. Sometimes people ate live red ants wrapped in eagle-down balls as medicine (see "Puberty").

Illnesses that could not be cured by herbs had to be referred to *huviagadi* (song-possessor) or curing shamans (pronounced *SHAH-munz* or *SHAY-munz*; healers). A huviagadi received his calling through a dream (see "Omens and dreams"). It could take as long as four to six years before a huviagadi had enough strength to heal people. In this same way, some shamans, called *uwapohagadi,* gained the power to cause rain. The huviagadi had songs for different cures. As he sang throughout the night, he chewed and swallowed a mixture of tobacco in water. He might lay his hands on the patient or suck to draw out the sickness, which he then buried outside. Before the huviagadi began his work, he was paid for his services either in money or with the gift of a horse. A healer refused to take on a case if he knew the patient was going to die.

The Vital Blue Oak Tree

The Kawaiisu used more than two hundred plants in their environment to supply their daily needs and help them survive. One of the most important was the blue oak. It provided food in the form of acorns that the women shelled and ground into flour. This flour found its way into a variety of dishes—soups, breads, and mush, which was sometimes dried into cakes.

The blue oak gave more than food, though. Mixed with water, the acorn flour made a glue to fix cracked clay vessels. The logs were used for building and for fires, especially for cooking yucca bulbs. Different parts of the tree were turned into medicines to help both young and old. California Indians used it for dyes and to make eating utensils, and Kawaiisu baskets had blue oak rims.

Even the shells of the acorn were put to use. They made small tops for children to play with. Adults used them to make dice. Every part of the tree throughout its life cycle benefitted the Kawaiisu.

ARTS

Petroglpyhs

Ancient art found in the Kawaiisu homeland includes petroglyphs. These were made by scraping designs into the surface of a rock. Although archaeologists attributed these drawings to the Kawaiisu, the people themselves deny that they created them. They say the petroglyphs are the work of Rock Baby (see "Religion").

Rock drawings, or petroglyphs, found in the canyons of the Mojave Desert are likely the work of ancient Kawaiisu people. © WITOLD SKRYPCZAK/ ALAMY.

Basketmaking

Kawaiisu women made finely woven baskets with complex and colorful designs. The baskets could be either woven or coiled. Coiled baskets were made of deer grass and split willow. Kawaiisu coiled baskets were unusual because rather than anchoring each row to the next the way other tribes did, the weavers wrapped some of the coils around the foundation of the basket. No other tribes in California or the Great Basin used this method, called *wicikadi,* so these baskets are unique to the Kawaiisu.

Basket makers made many types of containers, including burden baskets, winnowing trays, cradleboards, storage containers, and water bottles. Baskets for holding liquid were tightly woven and then painted with pine pitch to make them watertight. Joshua tree roots created red-brown designs, yucca made orange, and devil's claw or bracken fern was used for black. Women wove in quail crests and bird quills for decoration.

Oral literature

Elders in the family told stories. Most contained important lessons children needed to learn. These accounts passed along the history of the Kawaiisu people and explained many of the natural phenomena of the world as they taught children to respect the environment and the creatures in it.

Passing on these tales occurred around the fire in winter. One reason the people only told stories during that time of year was because Rattlesnake slept in cold weather. If he were awake, the Kawaiisu claimed that Raven, the tattletale, would gossip to Rattlesnake. Rattlesnake, who brought snow and rain and had a fearsome bite, would bring bad luck to the people.

Storytelling was accompanied by making figures with string. If the string broke during the performance, the storyteller's hand was burned on both sides with a hot coal.

CUSTOMS

Social organization

The Kawaiisu had no real social structure except for the family group (see "Families"). They operated independently without a central government, but their language, ceremonies, and trade brought them together. Most relatives lived nearby, and extended families came together to gather food or participate in communal activities.

Birth and childhood

Mothers-to-be had many restrictions. They did not eat animal feet so the baby would not be born feet first. Stepping over a mole burrow could cause the baby to be blind. Expectant mothers beat their stomachs with nettles and took daily cold baths to make themselves strong. The last month before birth, women refrained from salt, fat, and meat. Tobacco mixed with lime was rubbed on woman's stomach if labor took too long.

Afterward, the mother lay over heated rocks that were covered with dirt and wild chrysanthemums. Both parents bathed in a liquid containing chrysanthemums and stayed away from salt, fat, and meat.

Childbirth was a much-celebrated event. Families gathered to feast and dance for several days, and children were named after relatives.

Mothers carried their infants in oval-shaped cradleboards that they wove from willow. The Kawaiisu never used sand bar willow to make their cradleboards because one of their tales told of Quail, who lost her babies because she used it and to this day has a black face from all her weeping. Some cradleboards had Y-shaped legs that could be placed in the ground so the baby could be rocked. Babies were entertained by hanging wing charms, which also kept evil spirits away.

Young boys played with miniature bows and arrows. Dolls for girls were made of clay or of grass-stuffed rodent skins.

Puberty

The Kawaiisu used jimson weed (a poisonous plant that can cause hallucinations) in religious rituals. At puberty, it was given to both boys and girls. The teens often saw visions while under the influence, and these affected their future. For example, a girl who had a scary vision of a bear who did not talk to her was forbidden to eat bear meat.

After drinking the jimson weed, girls had their hair washed in a wild chrysanthemum solution as they were told about the old days and beads were scattered. The girl went to bed and was watched as she stayed in a stupor until the next morning. Friends and relatives came together for a celebration feast that included dancing and scattering seeds, berries, and beads. In the morning, the girl was given warm water until she vomited.

Around age fourteen, young people went through another ritual. Live ants were put in eagle-down balls (see "Healing"). Teens swallowed these and lay in the sun all day. Again, they drank warm water until they vomited the ants. This was considered a form of preventative medicine.

Marriage and Divorce

Couples met and married in spring when smaller family units came together to hunt and gather. The main ceremony consisted of a man giving gifts to his bride's parents. Then the couple moved in together. They could live with either family group. The Kawaiisu had only one spouse but could easily divorce. Either partner could initiate the divorce by separation from the other.

Death and mourning

The people buried the corpse on the day of death unless it was after sunset. They wrapped the dead body in a tule mat and put it into a gap in the rocks. The body was then covered with a split burden basket and a pile of rocks. The deceased's house was burned or abandoned, and most of the dead person's possessions were buried or destroyed at the funeral.

Mourners burned off their hair and did not wash their faces. The dead person's name was never spoken, but a spirit name was used instead. A year or so after a person died, a ceremony was held for several nights. Because a close relative paid for the event, this honor was often limited to important or wealthy people.

Intertribal mourning ceremonies were held to remember the deaths of several people. Each tribe had a space around the central fire pit inside a circle of brush. Bark and brush effigies were made and dressed in the dead person's clothes. These figures were carried on a frame made of poles and tossed in the fire as the women cried. Beads and piñon nuts were thrown into the fire or caught by the children. A dance followed, but the mourners only watched rather than joining in. After a feast, the mourning period ended, and widows could remarry.

Games and ceremonies

Children played hide and seek as well as tag. The person who was "it" was called the "bear." Adults also enjoyed games. Women used shell dice; men entertained themselves with throwing games, such as hoop and dart or ring and pin, that included hitting a target.

The Kawaiisu enjoyed dancing and singing to the accompaniment of clappers. People gathered for births and deaths, and they remained together for several days to feast and dance.

CURRENT TRIBAL ISSUES

One of the main issues facing the Kawaiisu is that their culture and language almost died out during the twentieth century. They are working to revive both through a variety of programs geared to passing on traditions and language (see "Language"). Since 2002, the Kawaiisu Language and Cultural Center has received yearly grants that allow the non-profit organization to continue documenting the language and customs of their people. They have created a Web site, DVDs, CDs, and a multitude of educational materials and programs that perpetuate their language and culture.

Another issue has been brought to the forefront by the Kawaiisu Tribe of the Tejon Indian Reservation, who have been fighting development in the area that once had been set aside for their reservation. The group claims that the land in question contains ancestral remains and artifacts that will be destroyed, so they have gone to court to halt construction.

BOOKS

Bibby, Brian. *Precious Cargo: California Indian Cradle Baskets and Childbirth Traditions.* Berkeley, CA: Heyday Books, 2004.

Garfinkel, Alan P., and Harold Williams. *Handbook of the Kawaiisu.* Kern Valley, CA: Wa-hi Sina'avi, 2011.

Kroeber, A. L. *California Kinship Systems.* Reprint. Charleston, SC: Bibliobazzar, 2009.

Kroeber, A. L. *Handbook of the Indians of California.* Vol. 2. Reprint. Whitefish, MT: Kessinger, 2006.

Zigmond, Maurice L. "Kawaiisu." In *Handbook of North American Indians, Great Basin.* Vol. 11. Edited by Warren L. D'Azavedo. Washington, DC: Smithsonian Institution, 1981, pp. 398–411.

Zigmond, Maurice L. *Kawaiisu Mythology: An Oral Tradition of South-Central California.* Banning, CA: Malki-Ballena Press, 1980.

WEB SITES

"An Act for the Government and Protection of Indians, April 22, 1850." *Indian Canyon.* http://www.indiancanyon.org/ACTof1850.html (accessed on August 15, 2011).

"Antelope Valley Indian Peoples: The Late Prehistoric Period: Kawaiisu." *Antelope Valley Indian Museum.* http://www.avim.parks.ca.gov/people/ph_kawaiisu.shtml (accessed on August 15, 2011).

"Kawaiisu." *Four Directions Institute.* http://www.fourdir.com/Kawaiisu.htm (accessed on August 15, 2011).

"The Kawaiisu Culture." *Digital Desert: Mojave Desert.* http://mojavedesert.net/kawaiisu-indians/related-pages.html (accessed on August 15, 2011).

Kawaiisu Language and Cultural Center. http://www.kawaiisu.org/KLCC_home.html (accessed on August 15, 2011).

"Native American People of the Kern River Valley." *Audubon Kern River Preserve.* http://kern.audubon.org/cultural_resources.htm (accessed on August 15, 2011).

Redish, Laura, and Orrin Lewis. "Kawaiisu Culture and History." *Native Languages of the Americas.* http://www.native-languages.org/kawaiisu_culture.htm (accessed on August 15, 2011).

Robinson, David. "The Kawaiisu Tribe of Tejon." *California State University.* http://www.csub.edu/~crobinson/ (accessed on August 15, 2011).

Thompson, John. "Shoshone, Kawaiisu, and Southern Paiute Food Gathering Cycle in Death Valley, California and Amargosa Valley, Nevada." *Beatty Museum and Historical Society.* http://www.beattymuseum.org/native_americans_in_the_oasis_valley_food_gathering.html (accessed on August 15, 2011).

"Tomo-Kahni State Historic Park." *California State Parks.* http://www.parks.ca.gov/?page_id=610 (accessed on August 15, 2011).

Zigmond, Maurice. "The Supernatural World of the Kawaiisu." *Vredenburgh: Historic and Geologic Resources of South Central California.* http://vredenburgh.org/tehachapi/data/kawaiisu-supernatural.pdf (accessed on August 15, 2011).

Paiute

Name

Paiute (pronounced *PIE-yoot*) means "true Ute." The group was related to the Ute tribe. The Spanish called both the Paiute and the Ute "Yutas," which served as the origin for the name of the state of Utah. The Northern Paiute refer to themselves as *Numa* or *Numu,* whereas the Southern Paiute call themselves *Nuwuvi.* Both of these words mean "the people."

Location

The Paiute occupied the Great Basin desert areas of Nevada, California, Oregon, Idaho, Arizona, and Utah. Modern-day members of the tribe live on more than two dozen reservations located throughout Nevada, California, Oregon, Utah, and Arizona. The largest number of Paiute live in California, Nevada, and Utah.

Population

In 1845, there were an estimated 7,500 Paiute. In the 1990 U.S. Census, 11,369 people identified themselves as Paiute. California was home to 4,605 Paiute; Nevada was home to 3,887; and Utah was home to 753. In 2000, the number of Paiute had dropped to 9,893. Of those, 3,099 resided in California, 4,333 in Nevada, and 652 in Utah. In the 2010 census, 9,340 Paiute were counted, as were a total of 13,767 who claimed some Paiute heritage.

Language family

Numic (Uto-Aztecan).

Origins and group affiliations

Native peoples have lived in the land of the Paiute for many hundreds of years. The Paiute are closely related to the Shoshone peoples of the Great Basin. The tribe is divided into three groups: Northern, Southern, and Owens Valley Paiute. The Northern Paiute were relatives of the Bannock. The Owens Valley Paiute were similar to the Northern Paiute but did not

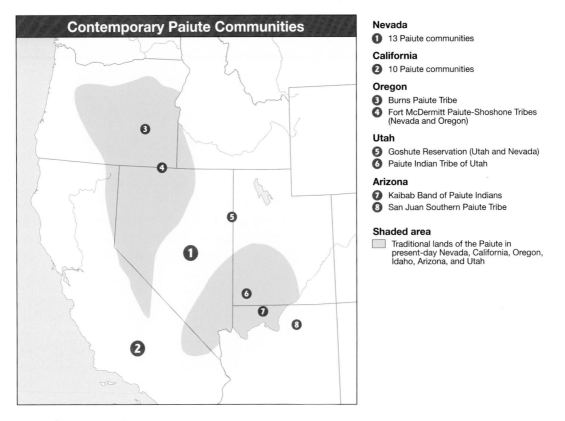

Contemporary Paiute Communities

Nevada
1. 13 Paiute communities

California
2. 10 Paiute communities

Oregon
3. Burns Paiute Tribe
4. Fort McDermitt Paiute-Shoshone Tribes (Nevada and Oregon)

Utah
5. Goshute Reservation (Utah and Nevada)
6. Paiute Indian Tribe of Utah

Arizona
7. Kaibab Band of Paiute Indians
8. San Juan Southern Paiute Tribe

Shaded area
Traditional lands of the Paiute in present-day Nevada, California, Oregon, Idaho, Arizona, and Utah

A map of contemporary Paiute communities. MAP BY XNR PRODUCTIONS. CENGAGE LEARNING, GALE. REPRODUCED BY PERMISSION OF GALE, A PART OF CENGAGE LEARNING.

speak the same language or live in the same area. (They shared their territory with the Washoe tribe.) The Southern Paiute, who moved into the Southwest around the year 1000, lived near the Pueblo people and learned farming from them. A group called the Chemehuevi broke away from the Southern Paiute sometime in the mid-eighteenth century.

Most Paiute were peaceful nomads who roamed through the forested highlands of the Rocky Mountains, the Sierra Nevada, and the desert lowlands between these two mountain ranges. Some Paiute led comfortable, settled lives with abundant resources; others struggled to survive in an extremely harsh environment. Although they tried to resist the hordes of American settlers and gold seekers who swarmed into their territory beginning in the mid-1800s, Paiute lands were taken over, and the people were moved to several small reservations, where many still reside in the twenty-first century.

EARLY HISTORY

Native groups lived in the Great Basin area for ten thousand years or longer. Although no direct connection has been made between these ancient groups and the later tribes who occupied this territory, archaeologists indicate that the Paiute may have lived in the Great Basin for more than one thousand years. Paiute oral history suggests that the people inhabited the land since ancient times.

Before their first contact with non-Natives in the 1820s, the lifestyle of the various bands of Paiute depended largely on the types of foods that were available to them. Groups were often referred to by the names of the foods they ate. For example, some Northern Paiute were called "Fish Eaters," but most bands survived on small game, roots, seeds, and berries. Some of the other groups went by the names of Yellow-Bellied-Marmot Eaters, Cattail Eaters, Groundhog Eaters, Grass-Seed Eaters, Wild-Onion Eaters, Brine-Fly-Larvae Eaters, and Hare Eaters.

Important Dates

1860: The Paiute War between the Southern Paiute and a volunteer army of settlers begins and ends. Removal to reservations increases.

1889: Wovoka, a Southern Paiute, founds the Ghost Dance religion, which soon spreads to other Native peoples throughout the West.

1965: The Southern Paiute in Utah are awarded $8.2 million for land wrongfully taken from them.

1970: The Southern Paiute win $7.25 million for lands taken over by U.S. settlement.

1980: The Paiute Indian Tribe of Utah receives federal recognition.

1990: Congress awards the Fallon Paiute Shoshone Tribe a $43 million settlement.

Northern and Southern Paiute

The Paiute are usually divided into three groups: Northern, Southern, and Owens Valley Paiute. The Northern Paiute lived in parts of what is now Nevada, California, Oregon, and Idaho. The Southern Paiute lived in present-day California, Nevada, Arizona, and Utah. The people had little contact with early European explorers, trappers, and settlers who arrived in the New World in the sixteenth, seventeenth, and eighteenth centuries. Their troubles began in the 1840s with the discovery of gold in the West. American settlers and gold seekers flooded Paiute territory, demanding more and more land and destroying the environment at an alarming rate. The discovery of silver in western Nevada brought another stream of non-Natives in the 1850s and 1860s.

These settlers overran Paiute ancestral land, brought livestock with them, and set up fencing to contain their animals. The livestock destroyed edible plants and spread diseases among local wildlife. The

The Bannock Break Away from the Northern Paiute

Members of the Bannock (pronounced *BANN-uck*) tribe were originally Paiute people who lived in southeastern Oregon. They acquired horses around 1690 and moved east to south-central Idaho, near the Snake River, to gain better access to the region's thriving buffalo-hunting grounds. There they met and intermingled with the Northern Shoshone (see entry) and, like them, were often referred to as Snake Indians. In time, the two groups were practically indistinguishable. The Bannock adapted to the migrating, horse-riding culture of Plains Indians, changing their clothing, lodging, and many customs to fit their new lives as buffalo hunters.

The Bannock began their struggles with American settlers long before many other tribes and quickly gained a reputation for their forceful attacks on pioneers and travelers. In 1814, led by a chief known as "The Horse," they attacked a fur-trading post on the Boise (pronounced *BOY-zee*) River. The Horse continued his campaign against Euro-American fur traders until 1832. In 1863, another chief, Le Grand Coquin ("The Great Rogue"; a rogue is a mischievous person), signed the tribe's first treaty with the U.S. government.

One thousand Shoshone and Bannock reported to the Fort Hall Bannock Reservation in Idaho in 1873. Later, the Bannock lived on reservations situated on or near their homelands of southeastern Idaho and western Wyoming. In the mid-1990s, the population of the Fort Hall Reservation numbered around 5,100 people (including the Shoshone). That figure increased to 5,762 in the 2000 census. By 2010, the census showed a population of 3,201 at the reservation.

fences cut the Paiute off from their hunting and gathering grounds. In addition, settlers cut down the prized piñon trees to use for fuel, displacing local wildlife.

The settlers often looked down on the Paiute because most of them traveled on foot rather than on horseback. When they saw the Paiute digging for edible roots, they expressed their scorn by calling the Natives "Diggers." The Paiute responded by raiding livestock at ranches, farms, mining camps, and wagon trains. Sometimes Paiute who did not own horses carried out these raids on foot. A major clash occurred in 1860 at Pyramid Lake, Nevada, after a group of white men kidnapped two Paiute girls. Warriors responded by attacking and killing five settlers in a rescue attempt. After several minor battles, the pioneers formed an eight-hundred-man volunteer army and defeated the Paiute. This series of conflicts became known as the Paiute War. Thereafter, the move to reservations, which had begun the year before, was increased.

Reservations for Northern Paiute

Several large reservations were established for the Northern Paiute in Nevada and Oregon between 1859 and 1891. By the turn of the twentieth century, the traditional Paiute homelands had been reduced to a mere 5 percent of their original size. Many Paiute bands refused to move to reservations that other bands occupied. Instead, these groups established settlements called colonies on the outskirts of American cities. There they worked as wage laborers. Between 1910 and 1930, the U.S. government established official relations with most of these Native colonies, treating them as reservations.

Southern Paiute and Mormons in Utah

Meanwhile, the Southern Paiute of Utah encountered Mormons (members of the Church of Jesus Christ of Latter-Day Saints), who began settling in the Salt Lake Valley in 1847. Mormons stress the importance of hard work, devotion to family life, and restraint from the use of alcohol and tobacco. They moved to Utah to escape religious persecution from Americans in the East.

The Mormons' firsthand experience with religious intolerance helped them forge a bond with the Paiute, who had already faced discrimination and prejudice from other settlers. Mormons protected the Paiute from bloodthirsty settlers, gold seekers, and Ute (see entry) slave raiders. In return, the Paiute shared their food and their knowledge of the environment with this displaced religious group. Because the Mormons were determined to settle in the area, they gave the Paiute food, clothing, and jobs to foster a relationship of trust and productivity.

Mormon advancement on Paiute land, however, strained relations with the Natives. Too many people crowded onto Native lands, making it impossible for the Paiute to hunt and gather in the old ways. Hostilities grew as starving Natives raided Mormon settlements. U.S. Army troops were called in, and government agents began to handle all Indian matters in the West, including those in Utah. The first Southern Paiute Reservation in Utah was established in the 1880s. Several more were set up there and in Nevada, but most of these lacked sufficient farmland to support the population. Many people had to move away to find work elsewhere.

By the 1950s, the U.S. government had made drastic changes in its Native policies. In 1954, under the terms of a program known as termination, the government declared that the Southern Paiute tribe in Utah no longer existed in the eyes of the government. Several groups filed a lawsuit, and in 1965, the Utah Paiute were awarded $8.2 million to compensate for 30 million acres of land wrongfully taken from them. Fifteen years later, the government granted federal recognition to the Paiute Indian Tribe of Utah. (Federally recognized tribes are those with which the U.S. government maintains official relations. Without federal recognition, the tribe does not exist as far as the government is concerned and therefore is not entitled to financial assistance and other aid.)

Owens Valley Paiute

The Owens Valley Paiute lived near the Owens River in southern California. They were fortunate to have a reliable water supply, which allowed them to settle down, build irrigation canals, and begin farming. By the early 1860s, American settlers in the Los Angeles area were trespassing on the fertile lands of the Owens Valley and casting their eyes on the bountiful waters of Owens River. The Paiute held them off for a time, defeating a volunteer army of settlers in 1862, but they were no match for the increasing number of settlers in the area.

Around the turn of the twentieth century, many Owens Valley Paiute were moved to reservations located on or near the lands where they had once lived. Most of these reservations, however, were far too small to support their former way of life. In 1937, the rapidly growing city of Los Angeles convinced the U.S. Congress to pass laws allowing the city to take over water rights and most of the Owens Valley Paiute land. In exchange, the Owens Valley band was given 1,391 acres in nearby Big Pine, where their largest settlement stood prior to the arrival of American settlers. By the end of the twentieth century, six Owens Valley Paiute reservations were home to about 2,500 people.

On the reservations

In the early 1900s, the Paiute were settled on more than two dozen reservations, most of them small. Federal or state governments controlled the people's land and lives and were often slow in delivering on promises of schools, health care, and adequate housing and sanitation. The Paiute faced ongoing struggles over land and water rights as growing American settlements diverted rivers to fulfill their own needs. U.S. ranchers allowed their cattle to graze on Paiute land, and Native populations declined from diseases and high rates of infant death.

For decades, the Paiute's tribal development was seriously hampered by a lack of funding. This trend did not show signs of reversing itself until the 1960s, when lawsuits over tribal land claims began succeeding in the courts.

RELIGION

The Paiute believed in many supernatural beings that were present in elements of the natural world, such as water, thunder, and animals. For some groups, the most powerful spirit was the sun, called *Thuwipu Uni-pugant,* or "The One Who Made the Earth." Other groups gave credit to Coyote and his wife for populating the earth. The Paiute prayed to the spirits to show their respect or to influence natural events. For example, the people might pray for rain or a successful hunt.

The Mormon influence

Mormon missionaries worked among the Southern Paiute in Utah in the nineteenth century, and some Paiute converted to Mormonism. Other Christian missionaries, who arrived in the late 1800s, influenced additional Paiute. By the late 1990s, most Paiute attended religious services in various Christian denominations. Others participated in religious movements such as the Native American Church (see Makah entry), which combined several Native religious traditions with aspects of Christianity.

Northern Paiute Words

taba	"sun"
muha	"moon"
baabba	"water"
nana	"man"
mogo'ne	"woman"

The Ghost Dance religion

The Paiute played a key role in one of the major Native religious movements of the modern era. In 1889, when most of the tribe had been pushed off their ancestral lands and forced to live on reservations, a Southern Paiute named Wovoka (c. 1856–1932) founded the Ghost Dance religion. Wovoka's underlying message was steeped in Christian sentiment. An advocate of nonviolence, he urged the Native nations to express themselves through song and dance while they awaited the great event—the day when the non-Natives would disappear. A few tribes, such as the Dakota and Lakota (see entries), believed the Ghost Dance could protect them in armed conflicts with American soldiers, but Paiute followers embraced the religion as a source of strength and a form of passive resistance to non-Native culture.

LANGUAGE

Members of the three Paiute groups each spoke a version of the language that could not be understood by the other groups. Paiute groups have maintained their language to varying degrees. The San Juan Paiute, a Southern Paiute band, is the only group that continues to teach Paiute to children as a first language. Other Paiute groups, however, have taken steps to preserve their Native languages.

GOVERNMENT

Paiute groups tended to be small, consisting mostly of an extended family (parents, children, grandparents, and other close relatives) led by a headman. Although the tribe greatly respected the opinion of the head-man, he could not make major decisions without consulting every adult in the community—both male and female. Each morning, he gave a rousing speech, urging his people to live in peace and harmony. The headman held his position only as long as he carried out the wishes of the community.

In early times, the Paiute were peaceful and had no need for war chiefs. So much energy was required to gather food that they had no time for war. After settlers overran their land, however, some groups appointed war chiefs. Modern-day Paiute on reservations are governed by elected tribal councils.

ECONOMY

The early Paiute economy was based on hunting, gathering, and some farming. After the people were relocated to reservations, they were encouraged to farm but were given neither instruction nor modern equipment to do so. Many were forced to leave the reservation to earn their livings by working in nearby towns or on ranches. Some also raised cattle.

In 1970, the Southern Paiute received $7.25 million from the U.S. government in a lawsuit over tribal lands that had been wrongfully taken from them. Many bands used this money to improve living conditions and develop educational and employment opportunities. Some of the more common business ventures included the ownership and management of mini-marts (small convenience stores), smoke shops, and campgrounds.

In the past, the Northern Paiute raised cattle and hay or worked for wages in a variety of professions. In more recent times, they have looked for ways to benefit from tourism. The Las Vegas Paiute, for example, opened a golf course in 1995. The Owens Valley Paiute worked primarily in mining and tourism.

Since the 1960s, when federal funds became available, many Paiute bands have successfully used government development grants to improve conditions on the reservations. They have built houses, roads, community buildings, and sewer and water systems. Because many reservation economies were long hampered by a lack of skilled workers, vocational training among the tribal members became of primary importance. Several Paiute bands opened casinos in the late 1990s or early 2000s; income from gaming helps to fund various tribal initiatives.

DAILY LIFE

Buildings

The migrating Paiute bands built small, temporary huts called wickiups (pronounced *WIK-ee-ups*). These were made of willow poles covered with brush and reeds. The Paiute often constructed wickiups near streams, where they could fish and draw water for irrigation.

Clothing and adornment

Paiute men and women often wore a bark or antelope-skin breechcloths, similar to aprons with both front and back flaps. They wore animal-skin moccasins or woven yucca sandals. (The yucca is an evergreen plant.) In the winter, the Paiute wrapped themselves in blankets made of strips of rabbit fur. Members of some Paiute bands wore hats decorated with bird feathers, and important men wore elaborate feathered crowns. Face and body paints were common for protection from the sun. Ear piercing was associated with long life and was a sign to the god Coyote to allow the souls of the dead to cross to the other world. Some men may have pierced their noses as well.

Food

The Paiute moved around the Great Basin in search of food. They knew and understood their environment—what was ripening when and where. Their diet depended largely on their location; plant foods gathered by the women made up the bulk of the tribes' diets. Many of these wild foods, such as acorns, pine nuts, and agave (pronounced *uh-GAH-vee*; a plant with tough, spiny, sword-shaped leaves that grows in hot, dry regions), were baked or roasted in earth ovens. The Paiute ate other vegetables, fruits, and plants, including cattails, roots, berries, and rice grass. They often used stones to grind seeds and nuts into flour to make bread.

The Paiute also hunted ducks, rabbits, and mountain sheep using bows and arrows or long nets. Some bands in mountainous regions fished, whereas those in arid desert regions dug for lizards, grubs, and insects.

The Southern Paiute learned to grow corn from the Pueblo (see entry). The Owens Valley Paiute developed irrigation techniques and engaged in farming that did not involve planting seeds. Instead their canals brought water to small plots where plants were already growing, thereby allowing the crops to produce better yields.

Writer Sarah Winnemucca and her father, Chief Winnemucca, pose with Natchez and Captain Jim, Paiutes from Nevada, and a European American boy in the 1880s.
© NATIONAL ARCHIVES.

Education

Paiute children learned by observing, imitating, and listening to adults. Sarah Winnemucca (1844–1891) described Paiute teachings passed on to children in her book *Life among the Paiutes: Their Wrongs and Claims*: "My people teach their children never to make fun of anyone, no matter how they look. If you see your brother or sister doing something wrong, look away, or go away from them. If you make fun of bad persons, you make yourself beneath them."

By 1910, all Paiute reservations had at least one government-run school. A number of children from the tribe were sent to boarding schools far from home. Some never returned, either because they died from infectious diseases or because they chose to stay away from the poverty-stricken reservations. The Paiutes have always valued education, and after they received federal recognition, they hired a director of tribal education. In the late 1990s, however, Paiute children attended public schools, but many did not graduate. Small rural communities struggled with the problem of developing bicultural programs in their schools that would meet the needs of their students. By the early 2000s, almost 75 percent of the people between the ages of eighteen and forty had attended college or vocational school.

Healing practices

Many Paiute believed illness was the work of evil spirits, ghosts, or other supernatural causes. Tribal healers were called shamans (pronounced *SHAH-munz* or *SHAY-munz*). Shamans were men or women believed to possess supernatural powers. Shamans formed magical relationships with one or more animal spirits, using the fur or feathers of the animal to call upon the spirits for assistance in their work. A shaman used little else in the way of tools, but often accomplished remarkable feats such as curing poisonous rattlesnake bites, healing wounds, controlling the weather, and assisting in childbirth.

A Paiute woman makes baskets, circa 1902. © THE PROTECTED ART ARCHIVE/ ALAMY.

The Paiute sought the help of shamans well into the 1960s. The two most famous modern Paiute healers were Jimmy George (d. 1969) and Joe Green (d. 1950s). By the 1990s, the people of the Paiute reservations were making many different arrangements for health care. Some bands operated their own health centers to care for minor problems and sent patients with serious health threats to large cities for treatment. Most of the Paiute reservations have access to community health representatives, who provide specific types of health care, including care for diabetic adults. The Paiute, like many Native nations, are at a higher risk of contracting adult-onset diabetes than the rest of the American population.

ARTS

Basketry, rock art, and duck decoys

For centuries, the Paiute were known in international trading circles for their outstanding basketry. Other tribes, and later European traders, often sought out Paiute creations. The tradition continues today on some

Rock drawings, or petroglyphs, made by ancient Paiute people can be found in Owens Valley, California. © ALEXANDER FITCH/ALAMY.

reservations. The National Endowment for the Arts has recognized San Juan Southern Paiute weavers for their excellence.

Much of Owens Valley contains remnants of Paiute rock art, most of which depicts animals such as mountain sheep. These drawings may have served as a decoration, as the mark of a family's territory, or as a symbol that would help bring "hunting magic" to the tribe.

The Northern Paiute were expert makers of duck decoys (artificial ducks used to lure live ducks within gunshot range when hunting). The tribe made decoys from plants gathered from the deserts and marshes and the skin of a recently killed duck.

Oral literature

Aunts, uncles, and grandparents passed on oral history and legends to Paiute children through bedtime stories. The child repeated each line just as the teller told it. One popular creation story described how Coyote carried two boys in a water jug from Canada to the Great Basin, where he released them. One of the boys became the father of the Shoshone tribe, and the other became the father of the Paiute tribe. Because the two tribes were related, they never fought.

CUSTOMS

Festivals and ceremonies

Certain Paiute groups celebrated the desert coming into bloom with a spring Flower Festival. At this festival, Paiute girls, who are often named for flowers, composed songs about their names. Young people from the Paiute bands often engage in the Round Dance. Formerly an all-night social affair, the dance features an ever-widening circle of men and women holding hands, singing, and moving to the beat.

Puberty and childbirth

The Paiute observed two related rituals to celebrate major life events: one for a young woman entering puberty and one for a woman expecting her first child. In the puberty ritual, the young woman was isolated for four days. During this time, she could not touch her face or hair with her hands, eat animal foods, or drink cold liquids. After the four days had passed, she was bathed in cold water, her face was painted, and the ends of her hair were burned or cut. She then ate a special meal of animal foods mixed with bitter herbs and spat into a fire.

The ritual for a woman expecting her first child was very similar, but it traditionally lasted for thirty days instead of four. The pregnant woman also received advice on childbearing from older women.

Courtship and marriage

Potential mates were judged on their performance of gender-based roles. The chief qualification for a good husband was his skill at hunting. A young girl—even one who was not yet physically mature—was considered a good candidate for marriage if she possessed outstanding homemaking skills.

Babies

Fathers buried the umbilical cord of newborn boys in a hole made by a squirrel or in the track of a mountain sheep to ensure their sons' hunting

Why the North Star Stands Still

The Paiute, like many other Native nations, told stories to explain natural phenomena This story explains not only why the North Star is fixed in place, but why the Big and Little Dippers move around it.

Long, long ago, when the world was young, the People of the Sky were so restless and travelled so much that they made trails in the heavens. Now, if we watch the sky all through the night, we can see which way they go.

But one star does not travel. That is the North Star. He cannot travel. He cannot move. When he was on the earth long, long ago, he was known as Na-gah, the mountain sheep, the son of Shinoh. He was brave, daring, sure-footed, and courageous. His father was so proud of him and loved him so much that he put large earrings on the sides of his head and made him look dignified, important, and commanding.

Every day, Na-gah was climbing, climbing, climbing. He hunted for the roughest and the highest mountains, climbed them, lived among them, and was happy. Once in the very long ago, he found a very high peak. Its sides were steep and smooth, and its sharp peak reached up into the clouds. Na-gah looked up and said, "I wonder what is up there. I will climb to the very highest point."

Around and around the mountain he travelled, looking for a trail. But he could find no trail. There was nothing but sheer cliffs all the way around. This was the first mountain Na-gah had ever seen that he could not climb.

He wondered and wondered what he should do. He felt sure that his father would feel ashamed of him if he knew that there was a mountain that his son could not climb. Na-gah determined that he would find a way up to its top. His father would be proud to see him standing on the top of such a peak.

Again and again he walked around the mountain, stopping now and then to peer up the steep cliff, hoping to see a crevice on which he could find footing. Again and again, he went up as far as he could, but always had to turn around and come down. At last he found a big crack in a rock that went down, not up. Down he went into it and soon found a hole that turned upward. His heart was made glad. Up and up he climbed.

Soon it became so dark that he could not see, and the cave was full of loose rocks that slipped under his feet and rolled down. Soon he heard a big, fearsome noise coming up through the shaft at the same time the rolling rocks were dashed to pieces at the bottom. In the darkness he slipped often and skinned his knees. His courage and determination began to fail. He had never before seen a place so dark and dangerous. He was afraid, and he was also very tired.

"I will go back and look again for a better place to climb," he said to himself. "I am not afraid out on the open cliffs, but this dark hole fills me with fear. I'm scared! I want to get out of here!"

But when Na-gah turned to go down, he found that the rolling rocks had closed the cave below him. He could not get down. He saw only one thing now that he could do: He must go on climbing until he came out somewhere.

After a long climb, he saw a little light, and he knew that he was coming out of the hole. "Now I am happy," he said aloud. "I am glad that I really came up through that dark hole."

Looking around him, he became almost breathless, for he found that he was on the top of a very high peak! There was scarcely room for him to turn around, and looking down from this height made him dizzy. He saw great cliffs below him, in every direction, and saw only a small place in which he could move. Nowhere on the outside could he get down, and the cave was closed on the inside....

"Here I must stay until I die," he said. "But I have climbed my mountain! I have climbed my mountain at last!"

He ate a little grass and drank a little water that he found in the holes in the rocks. Then he felt better. He was higher than any mountain he could see and he could look down on the earth, far below him.

About this time, his father was out walking over the sky. He looked everywhere for his son, but could not find him. He called loudly, "Na-gah! Na-gah!" And his son answered him from the top of the highest cliffs. When Shinoh saw him there, he felt sorrowful, to himself, "My brave son can never come down. Always he must stay on the top of the highest mountain. He can travel and climb no more.

"I will not let my brave son die. I will turn him into a star, and he can stand there and shine where everyone can see him. He shall be a guide mark for all the living things on the earth or in the sky."

And so Na-gah became a star that every living thing can see. It is the only star that will always be found at the same place. Always he stands still. Directions are set by him. Travellers, looking up at him, can always find their way. He does not move around as the other stars do, and so he is called "the Fixed Star." And because he is in the true north all the time, our people call him Qui-am-i Wintook Poot-see. These words mean "the North Star."

Besides Na-gah, other mountain sheep are in the sky. They are called "Big Dipper" and "Little Dipper." They too have found the great mountain and have been challenged by it. They have seen Na-gah standing on its top, and they want to go on up to him.

Shinoh, the father of North Star, turned them into stars, and you may see them in the sky at the foot of the big mountain. Always they are travelling. They go around and around the mountain, seeking the trail that leads upward to Na-gah, who stands on the top. He is still the North Star.

SOURCE: Welker, Glenn. "Why the North Star Stands Still." *Indigenous Peoples' Literature.* http://www.indigenouspeople.net/northsta.htm (accessed on August 15, 2011).

ability. A girl's cord was buried in an anthill or small rodent lair to insure that she would be a hard worker.

Death and burial

Author Sarah Winnemucca shed some light on ancient Paiute burial rituals when she described in *Life among the Paiutes* the last hours in the life of her beloved grandfather, who was called Chief Truckee by American settlers. While the chief lay on his deathbed, fires were lit on mountaintops so people would know it was time to pay their last respects. After his death, Chief Truckee's body was wrapped in blankets and buried in the ground. The burial service ended with the killing of six horses. Winnemucca explains, "I do not want you to think that we do this thing because we think the dead use what we put in; or, if we kill horses at any one's death that they will use them in the Spirit-land. No, no; but it is the last respect we pay our dead."

According to Paiute traditions, the dead were either buried or cremated. Paiute mourners abstained from eating meat for four days. Some cut gashes on their arms and legs or cut their hair off. The deceased person's property was destroyed, and his or her name was never spoken again. Often, the tribe moved away from the site where the death had taken place, at least for a time.

A ceremonial funeral rite known as the Cry was introduced to the Paiute in the 1870s. The Cry took place over one or two nights after a person's death, before the funeral. It was repeated a year or two later as a memorial. During the Cry ceremony, which is still held by some groups, two groups of singers perform song cycles known as Salt Songs and Bird Songs. Between the singing, people who had been close to the deceased give emotional speeches, and the person's valuables are distributed among the guests.

CURRENT TRIBAL ISSUES

Conditions on Paiute reservations have improved since the 1960s. The quality of housing has gotten better, and most people of the tribe have access to utilities (electricity, plumbing, heat) and schooling for their children. but the situation for the Paiute is far from ideal. Problems such as substance abuse, low educational attainment, higher than average unemployment, and the loss of Native language and customs still plague the tribe.

Their inability to make a decent living in traditional ways has led the Paiute to seek out new sources of income for tribal members. Economic difficulties prompted two Paiute bands to consider controversial projects in the early 1990s. The Northern Paiute of the Fort McDermitt Reservation in Nevada discussed the possibility of building a storage facility for nuclear waste on their lands, whereas the Southern Paiute of the Kaibab Reservation in Arizona debated about whether to construct a hazardous waste incinerator. The financial rewards of these projects made them appealing, but both tribes ultimately turned down the projects because of environmental concerns.

The Owens Valley Paiute reservations also struggled with environmental concerns. In the early 1900s and again in 1971, the Los Angeles Department of Water and Power (LADWP) built an aqueduct that diverted water from the Owens River, causing the lake to dry up and plants to die. After years of court battles, the LADPW agreed to rewater the lower Owens River by 2003. By 2005, they still had not met the deadlines. After another court case, the LADPW asserted they had met the agreement in 2008.

The San Juan Southern Paiute Tribe, a small tribe with about 265 members, lives in several communities on the Navajo Reservation as well as near the Grand Canyon in Arizona. They received federal recognition in 1990 and, in the early twenty-first century, were engaged in legal proceedings for land of their own.

NOTABLE PEOPLE

Wovoka (c. 1856–1932), known by American settlers as Jack Wilson, was a Southern Paiute who founded the Ghost Dance religion in 1889. He is believed to have been the son of Tavibo (c. 1835–c. 1915), another Paiute who had magnificent visions of unfenced plains full of buffalo, freedom from outsiders, and peaceful communities of Native nations living in harmony with the earth. Sometime in the late 1880s, Wovoka became seriously ill with a high fever. At the height of his illness, he experienced a vision much like that of his father. Wovoka preached that the Native peoples could inherit a virtual paradise by purging themselves of non-Native influences (such as alcohol) and by praying, meditating, and dancing. Wovoka's vision formed the foundation of the Ghost Dance religion, based on the belief that in the future all Native people—the living and the dead—would be reunited on an earth forever free from death, disease, and misery. Word of the new religion spread quickly among Native nations of the Great Basin and Plains regions, even though Wovoka himself never traveled far from his birthplace. The Native peoples revered Wovoka, but local settlers denounced him as an impostor and a lunatic.

Another prominent Paiute was Sarah Winnemucca (Thocmetony, meaning "Shell Flower"; 1844–1891). Her grandfather befriended the settlers and grew to trust them. At his urging, Winnemucca was educated at a Roman Catholic mission school in California. She later served as an interpreter and scout for the U.S. Army. Electrifying audiences with her lectures on indigenous rights, Winnemucca became the first Native woman to publish a book. Titled *Life among the Paiutes: Their Wrongs and Claims,* it describes the history and culture of the Paiute people.

BOOKS

Gray-Kanatiiosh, Barbara A. *Paiute.* Edina, MN: Abdo Publishing, 2007.

Hebner, William Logan. *Southern Paiute: A Portrait.* Logan: Utah State University Press, 2010.

Jackson, Louise A. *The Sierra Nevada before History: Ancient Landscapes, Early Peoples.* Missoula, MT: Mountain Press, 2010.

Lacy, Steve, and Pearl Baker. *Posey: The Last Indian War.* Layton, UT: Gibbs Smith, 2007.

Ray, Deborah Kogan. *Paiute Princess: The Story of Sarah Winnemucca.* New York: Farrar, Straus & Giroux, 2011.

Reeve, W. Paul. *Making Space on the Western Frontier: Mormons, Miners, and Southern Paiutes.* Urbana: University of Illinois Press, 2006.

Shull, Jodie A. *Voice of the Paiutes: A Story About Sarah Winnemucca.* Minneapolis, MN: Millbrook Press, 2007.

Winnemucca, Sarah. *Life among the Paiutes: Their Wrongs and Claims.* Privately printed, 1883. Reprint. Reno: University of Nevada Press, 1994.

WEB SITES

Bishop Paiute Tribe. http://www.bishoppaiutetribe.com/ (accessed on August 15, 2011).

Burns Paiute Tribe. http://www.burnspaiute-nsn.gov/ (accessed on August 15, 2011).

Fallon Paiute-Shoshone Tribe. http://www.fpst.org/ (accessed on August 15, 2011).

Holt, Ronald L. "Paiute Indians." *State of Utah.* http://historytogo.utah.gov/utah_chapters/american_indians/paiuteindians.html (accessed on August 15, 2011).

Kaibab Paiute Tribe. http://www.kaibabpaiute-nsn.gov/ (accessed on August 15, 2011).

Las Vegas Paiute Tribe. http://www.lvpaiute.com/ (accessed on August 15, 2011).

Lewis, David Rich. "People of the Colorado Plateau—The Southern Paiute." *Northern Arizona University.* http://cpluhna.nau.edu/People/southern_paiute.htm (accessed on August 15, 2011).

Lone Pine Paiute-Shoshone Reservation. http://lppsr.org/ (accessed on August 15, 2011).

Paiute Indian Tribe of Utah. http://www.utahpaiutes.org/ (accessed on August 15, 2011).

Pyramid Lake Paiute Tribe. http://plpt.nsn.us/ (accessed on August 15, 2011).

Utah American Indian. "Paiute." *University of Utah.* http://www.utahindians.org/archives/paiute.html (accessed on August 15, 2011).

Utah Indian Curriculum Guide. "The Trade Economy of the Southern Paiutes." *Utah Education Network.* http://www.uen.org/Lessonplan/preview?LPid=27627 (accessed on August 15, 2011).

Walker River Paiute Tribe. http://www.wrpt.us/ (accessed on August 15, 2011).

Shoshone

Name

Shoshone (pronounced *shuh-SHOW-nee*), or Shoshoni, may mean "high growing grass." The Shoshone refer to themselves using several similar words that mean "people." Other tribes and settlers often referred to them as "Snake People" for two reasons: their location near the Snake River, which runs through Wyoming, Idaho, and Oregon, and the tribal warriors' war-time practice of carrying rattles that looked like snakes and using them to frighten enemies' horses.

Location

The Shoshone formerly made their homes in parts of present-day California, Oregon, Nevada, Idaho, Utah, and Wyoming. Most modern-day Shoshone live on or near reservations in their former territory.

Population

In 1845, there were an estimated 4,500 Northern and Western Shoshone. (Earlier estimates are not reliable because they often included members of other tribes.) In the 1990 U.S. Census, 9,506 people identified themselves as Shoshone. The largest number lived in Nevada (2,637), Wyoming (1,752), California (1,595), and Idaho (676). In 2000, the total Shoshone population had dropped to 8,340. Wyoming, with 2,385 Shoshone, still contained the largest number of tribal members. Nevada had 1,713; California had 1,101; Utah had 645; and Idaho had 312. The 2010 census counted 7,852 Shoshone, with a total of 13,002 claiming some Shoshone heritage.

Language family

Uto-Aztecan.

Origins and group affiliations

Early Shoshone most likely moved north from the Southwest between about 1 CE and 1000 CE. Some of the many groups who make up the Shoshone tribe are related to the Paiute, Comanche, and Ute (see entries).

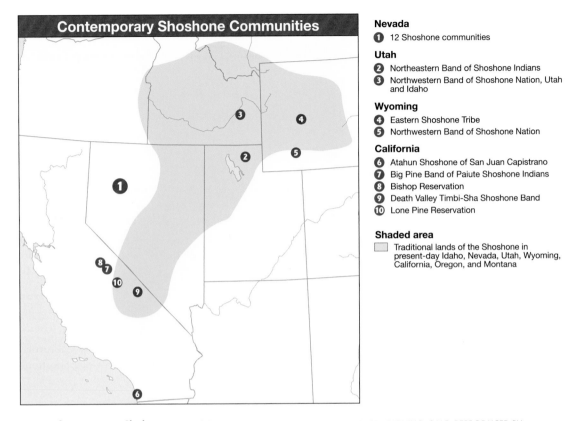

Contemporary Shoshone Communities

Nevada
1 12 Shoshone communities

Utah
2 Northeastern Band of Shoshone Indians
3 Northwestern Band of Shoshone Nation, Utah and Idaho

Wyoming
4 Eastern Shoshone Tribe
5 Northwestern Band of Shoshone Nation

California
6 Atahun Shoshone of San Juan Capistrano
7 Big Pine Band of Paiute Shoshone Indians
8 Bishop Reservation
9 Death Valley Timbi-Sha Shoshone Band
10 Lone Pine Reservation

Shaded area
Traditional lands of the Shoshone in present-day Idaho, Nevada, Utah, Wyoming, California, Oregon, and Montana

A map of contemporary Shoshone communities. MAP BY XNR PRODUCTIONS. CENGAGE LEARNING, GALE. REPRODUCED BY PERMISSION OF GALE, A PART OF CENGAGE LEARNING.

Many different Shoshone groups (called bands) lived throughout the Great Basin—an area located between the Rocky Mountains and the Sierra Nevada. Theirs was a sparsely populated region where life was hard; some groups tried to eke out a living in Death Valley, the lowest point in the Americas, with little rain and very high temperatures. The Shoshone are perhaps best known for being the tribe of Sacajawea (pronounced *sak-uh-juh-WEE-uh;* also spelled "Sacagawea"; c. 1786–1812), who helped guide the historic expedition in which the American explorers Meriwether Lewis (1774–1809) and William Clark (1770–1838) mapped the West for the first time. The Shoshone had friendly relations with American settlers at first, but this changed as they found themselves forced onto reservations. In modern times, they struggle for the rights to their ancestral lands.

HISTORY

Before outsiders arrived

Many bands make up the Shoshone tribe. Members of these bands speak the same language, but they developed different lifestyles based on the areas where they lived and how they supported themselves. Historians call the groups Northern, Western, and Eastern Shoshone, but most Shoshone do not refer to themselves that way.

Around the time of their move from the Southwest into the Great Basin, the Shoshone tribes separated and settled in different areas. They dominated the Great Basin until the arrival of other tribes, such as the Blackfoot and Sioux (see entries) from the East.

The Shoshone adapted well to their new surroundings. The Northern and Eastern groups, for example, adopted a nomadic lifestyle, hunting and gathering where resources were plentiful. They soon began to hunt buffalo, a task made easier after they acquired horses late in the seventeenth century. The tribe eventually expanded its hunting territory and ran into conflict with other buffalo-hunting tribes, such as the Blackfoot and Arapaho (see entry). This constant friction, coupled with a 1782 smallpox epidemic, caused the Eastern Shoshone to move into Wyoming.

Important Dates

c. 1700: The Northern and Eastern Shoshone acquire horses and become buffalo hunters.

1782: The Eastern Shoshone are devastated by smallpox and attacks by the Blackfoot.

1805: The Shoshone meet Lewis and Clark.

January 1863: The Bear River Massacre takes place.

1863: The first Treaty of Fort Bridger is negotiated, setting aside reservation land for Shoshone groups.

1868: The second treaty of Fort Bridger is negotiated, reducing the amount of reservation lands.

1900: Chief Washakie dies.

1930s: Shoshone bands reorganize and form tribal governments.

1990s: Struggles over land rights continue.

2006: The United Nations tells the United States to cease activity on Shoshone land until Shoshone claims are settled.

Shoshone help American explorers and settlers

The first Europeans the Shoshone saw were Spanish settlers, who arrived in the New World in the 1500s. They later encountered other explorers, but contact with foreigners was minimal. Their relations with whites really began with the 1804–06 Lewis and Clark expedition into the American West. The explorers first met a Shoshone Indian when they hired French-Canadian fur trapper Toussaint Charbonneau (1767–1843) to serve as their interpreter. Charbonneau agreed to help the explorers, but it was his Shoshone wife, Sacajawea, who proved to be the important presence

Sacajawea points a way through the mountains to Lewis and Clark.
© BETTMANN/CORBIS.

on the expedition. With her help, Lewis and Clark and their crew made their way from the Missouri River to the Pacific Ocean, encountering many Shoshone bands along the way.

American settlers began arriving soon after Lewis and Clark charted the West. When the explorers returned in 1806 to St. Louis, Missouri, pioneers, trappers, and traders started moving onto Shoshone lands. They were followed by a religious group called the Mormons, who founded Salt Lake City, Utah, in 1847. The lure of gold in California sent more settlers west in 1849, as did the discovery of silver in Nevada in 1857. The American westward movement forever changed the lives of the Shoshone.

Shoshone resistance

Most Shoshone military resistance to American expansion took place in the early 1860s. Native war parties attacked wagon trains, pony express riders (mail carriers on horseback), and telegraph line crews. They were reacting to the disappearance of buffalo herds from overhunting and to the influx of huge numbers of newcomers. To protect American settlers from Native raids, California sent an army to establish Fort Douglas near Salt Lake City. In January 1863, three hundred army troops went on a punishing raid against Chief Bear Hunter (d. 1863) of the Northern Shoshone at Bear Hunter's village, 140 miles (225 kilometers) away from Fort Douglas.

The Shoshone prepared their village for the soldiers' arrival by building barricades. They, however, had never experienced the full force of the U.S. Army. The soldiers flooded the village with gunfire on the morning of January 29. In four hours, they killed 250 Shoshone, ruined 70 homes, and captured 175 horses while suffering only 14 deaths and 49 injuries. The Bear River Massacre (1863), as it came to be called, was the turning point in Shoshone-American relations. According to Virginia Cole Trenholm and Maurine Carley in *The Shoshonis: Sentinels of the Rockies,* Mormons sent to view the battle site reported "the dead eight feet deep in one place.… The relentless slaughter of the Indians, for the first time, served as [a] … lesson. The natives now realized that the [U.S.] army had the power to deal them a crushing defeat."

Northern and Eastern Shoshone make peace

The Northern and Eastern Shoshone were ready to make peace with the whites after the Bear River Massacre. Later in 1863, Shoshone chiefs signed the first of several treaties in which they agreed to sell much of their land to the U.S. government for payments that were usually never made. The federal government began to assign Native Americans to reservations. Many branches of the Shoshone tribe resisted the idea of moving from their homelands, but as time went on, they were left with no choice. Finally, all the Northern Shoshone, together with the Bannock (see Paiute entry), were moved to the Fort Hall Reservation in eastern Idaho.

By the beginning of the twentieth century, most Northern Shoshone were living at Fort Hall, which was located in an area of dry, poor soil. As U.S. timber lords, railroad companies, and miners grabbed Shoshone lands, reservation acreage decreased from 1.8 million acres to 544,000 acres. Hostility toward the Shoshone prevented the Natives from exercising their treaty rights—the rights to hunt, fish, and gather on their own land.

The Wind River Reservation was established for the Eastern Shoshone later in 1863. It consisted of 44 million acres in Wyoming. After about five years, a new treaty reduced the band's land holdings to less than 2.8 million acres, but the Eastern Shoshone did not break their peace with the Americans. In fact, under the leadership of Chief Washakie (c. 1804–1900), they aided the Americans in their wars against the Sioux throughout the 1870s. After all their help, though, the Wind River band felt betrayed when the federal government moved their old enemies, the Arapaho, to the Wyoming reservation in 1878.

After the death of Washakie in 1900, the Eastern Shoshone suffered one tragedy after another. Their population plummeted due to starvation, epidemics of measles and tuberculosis, and other problems. (Tuberculosis, often called TB, is an extremely contagious bacterial disease that usually attacks the lungs.)

Western Shoshone

The Western Shoshone signed the Treaty of Ruby Valley in 1863. In the treaty, they agreed to keep the peace, allow settlers to set up some businesses on their land, abandon "the roaming life," and eventually live on reservations. They did not give up their lands.

For the first three decades of the twentieth century, many of the Western Shoshone avoided or tried to avoid moving to the reservations being established by the federal government. For many of them, the U.S. government agreed to the creation of colonies (small Native settlements near larger white settlements) in Nevada as alternatives to reservation life. By 1927, only about half of the Western Shoshone lived on reservations. This pattern continued into the twenty-first century.

Shoshone in the twentieth century

In the 1930s, new government policies brought reforms to the Shoshone in the form of self-government, and the quality of their lives began to improve. The Shoshone began sharing their culture with non-Natives and worked diligently to retain many of their traditional cultural practices. They taught and used the Shoshone language, built schools and cultural centers, and held powwows (traditional song-and-dance celebrations).

The Shoshone people live on or near more than two dozen reservations and colonies in Utah, Idaho, Nevada, Wyoming, and California. Many of the reservations also serve as homes to Arapaho, Bannock, Paiute, and Goshute peoples.

RELIGION

The many Shoshone peoples have a wide range of religious beliefs and practices. Some believe the sun created the heavens and the earth, whereas others believe that either Coyote or Wolf or a kindly spirit called "Our Father" was the creator. The aid of these and other spirits is often sought, but first the seeker has to undergo purification in a sweat lodge, a building in which steam is produced by pouring water over heated rocks. Many groups do not have priests or other religious leaders. Instead, individuals seek out supernatural powers on their own, through visions and dreams.

A fairly recent addition to Shoshone spiritualism is the Peyote (pronounced *pay-OH-tee*) religion, which originated in Mexico and the southwestern United States and spread throughout North America in the late nineteenth and early twentieth centuries. Many Shoshone welcomed the Peyote religion as a source of comfort and strength in the face of hardship. Peyote is a type of cactus; when parts of it are chewed, the user sees visions. For a people like the Shoshone, who always believed in strong links to the supernatural and the powers of spirits, peyote is a tool to communicate better with spirits and to discover supernatural powers.

The Shoshone also welcomed the messages of the Ghost Dance religions of 1870 and 1889. Ghost Dancers believed that the performance of their special dance would hasten the day when the traditional Native American way of life would be restored and Native peoples would be freed from the burden of non-Native intervention.

Shosone Words	
bungu	"horse"
sadee'	"dog"
weda'	"bear"
buhn'atsi	"skunk"
mumbichi	"owl"
bozheena	"bison"

LANGUAGE

All Shoshone groups speak dialects (varieties) of the same language. Although the dialects differ slightly among the divisions, they are, for the most part, understandable by all Shoshone. In the early twenty-first century, more than one thousand people speak the language, and the tribe is teaching it to its children.

GOVERNMENT

The small, nomadic bands of Western Shoshone sometimes had headmen, leaders who had little real authority. Shoshone groups who hunted buffalo were more likely to have chiefs with a greater degree of authority. This type of organization was necessary for the group to be effective against enemies intruding on their buffalo-hunting territory. These chiefs made decisions

A Shoshone moose skin painting from the early 1900s depicts a buffalo hunt, with tribe members performing the Sun Dance. © WORLD HISTORY ARCHIVE/ALAMY.

after consulting with a council, and they came and went as their popularity rose or fell.

Among the Eastern Shoshone, chiefs played a more important role. Men such as Washakie—older men who had proved their worth in past battles—were chosen to lead. In modern times, the many Shoshone reservations and colonies are governed by elected tribal councils and business councils.

ECONOMY

The Shoshone were hunter-gatherers, but the food they ate differed according to where they lived. For example, those who lived near water could fish. No groups owned land; it was shared by all, as were the fruits of their labors. The Shoshone also engaged in extensive trade. They received metal arrow points from the Crow (see entry) in exchange for horses. Later, they traded furs with American settlers for horses and weapons.

In the late 1800s and early 1900s, many Shoshone who refused to move to reservations became dependent on wages paid by non-Native employers. Those who lived on reservations were encouraged to farm, even where the land was not at all suitable for farming. They suffered hardships when government agents failed to deliver promised supplies, seeds, and instructions on how to farm. At the turn of the twenty-first century, many Shoshone still lived in poverty. Since that time, some groups have opened casinos, which provide jobs and bring economic advantages to the reservations.

The Eastern Shoshone at Wind River were hit the hardest by economic suffering. Their reservation is located in a rugged, remote, mountainous area, with limited opportunities for agricultural activity. Traditionally, income has been generated by leasing land for grazing and by raising horses and cattle. The people also earn some money from tourists, who are drawn by the excellent fishing, tours of Fort Washakie Historic District, and the reservation's location near the Rocky Mountains, the Continental Divide, and Yellowstone and Grand Teton National Parks. A large percentage of tribal members are employed in government programs, such as social services. In the early twenty-first century, casinos brought in additional income for the reservation.

The Northern Shoshone fared better, in part by opening a variety of shops and gambling establishments as well as by farming. Their reservation covers some prime farming land. The tribe grows potatoes, grain, and alfalfa; raises cattle; and leases land to other farmers. The Northern Shoshone have won many contracts and grants from the federal government for various projects, and tribal members are employed on those projects. Nevertheless, the tribe suffered when a phosphate mine on the reservation closed after nearly fifty years in operation.

The Western Shoshone support themselves by cattle ranching, smoke shops, and mining revenues. Although some tribal members support mining on land many believe belongs to the Shoshone nation, others oppose it, claiming that it interferes with their rights and blocks access to sacred sites. Some Western Shoshone continue their struggles with the U.S. government over land rights. (See "Current Tribal Issues.")

DAILY LIFE

Buildings

Some Northern Shoshone lived in tepees made from buffalo hides or interwoven rushes (marsh plants with hollow stems used for weaving) and willows. Others built conical dwellings of brush and grass. All Northern

Shoshone people gather outside of their tepees, which were usually made of buffalo hide or woven plant material. © EVERETT COLLECTION INC./ALAMY.

Heebe-tee-tse of the Shoshone tribe, circa 1899. © EVERETT COLLECTION INC./ALAMY.

groups built and maintained sweat lodges and huts where women retreated during their menstrual period. (Menstrual blood was considered evil or even dangerous.)

The Western Shoshone lived in more permanent camps than other Shoshone communities because they did not chase buffalo. They usually did not use animal hides in their homes and buildings. For the winter months, they constructed cone-shaped huts with bark walls. Rings of stone supported the walls and kept the structure erect. Some built sunshades and circular cottages out of brush and light timber. Many of the mountain-dwelling Western Shoshone lived in wickiups (pronounced *WIK-ee-ups*), frame huts covered with brush or bark matting. Others did not build homes at all but sought shelter in caves when the weather turned bad. All Western Shoshone built sweat lodges, and most built menstrual huts.

The Eastern Shoshone built substantial tepees. Each of these structures required the hides of at least ten buffalo. The chief's tepee might be painted with a yellow band to set it apart from the others.

Clothing and adornment

Most Shoshone wore few clothes, especially during the summer months. Women and girls usually wore only skirts and hats, while young boys went naked. To keep warm in times of extreme cold, women sewed small animal furs and hides into dresses, shirts, and robes. The best hunters and their kin wore larger pieces of clothing made from deer and antelope skins. The clothing of the Eastern Shoshone tended to be more decorative than the Northern and Western divisions.

Groups that hunted large game wore buffalo robes in winter and elk skins in summer. Also common were leggings and breechcloths (garments with front and back flaps that hung from the waist). Many went barefoot; those who did not wore moccasins of buffalo hide.

Both sexes pierced their ears and wore many necklaces. The Western Shoshone also practiced face and body painting and some facial tattooing.

Food

Shoshone bands were often named for the main foods they consumed, so names such as "Salmon Eaters" and "Squirrel Eaters" were typical. Like many of the tribes of the region, some Northern and Eastern Shoshone bands depended on buffalo hunts for their main food. Men also chased down sheep and antelope to add to their wild game menu. In September, the people often combined forces with the Bannock and Flathead (see entry) for a massive buffalo hunt. Some caught fish—primarily salmon, sturgeon, and trout—and gathered other wild foods. They used torches to attract fish at night, then netted or trapped them.

Shoshone women were skilled at making cakes from dried berries, nuts, and seeds of all sorts. They cooked turnips and other tubers in pits beneath hot rocks until the vegetables were soft and brown.

The Western Shoshone used sticks to dig up a variety of nuts and roots; they also picked berries. They migrated more than other Shoshone bands, looking for places where edible plants and wild growth were most plentiful. The Western Shoshone did not hunt buffalo; they confined their hunting to smaller game—antelope, rabbits, and rodents—and to fishing. They also collected grasshoppers in large numbers by sweeping through open fields to send the insects scattering.

Education

Children were taught by the elderly and the handicapped, who sang songs and told stories while parents were busy gathering food. At the beginning of the twentieth century, when the U.S. government was handling Indian affairs on the reservations, Christian missionaries were invited to establish schools. Some Shoshone children were sent to boarding schools located far from home and family. At these schools, children were encouraged to speak English and to give up their Native tongue, but among the Shoshone these efforts to eliminate Native traditions were largely unsuccessful.

In the 1950s, Shoshone children were integrated (merged or blended) into America's public school system. Educational attainment improved, but test results from the 1990s showed that some Shoshone children still lagged behind other students. One reason for low test scores may have been related to language and cultural differences.

Frequently, the public schools were the Shoshone child's first encounter with mainstream American society. Native students were often hampered by the language barrier and the lack of Native history and culture in the curriculum. In recent decades, many school districts have attempted to integrate Native studies into the classroom. Most reservation schools emphasize Shoshone culture and language.

Healing practices

The Shoshone had healers, men or women called shamans (pronounced *SHAH-munz* or *SHAY-munz*), who knew how to use roots, herbs, charms, and chants to cure ailments. More serious cases were cured by spirit power. The shaman obtained spirit powers through visions, usually seen during a fast in a secluded place such as a mountain peak. The shaman applied spirit power while laying hands on the patient or sucking out the disease-causing object.

Old rituals and ways declined after the move to reservations. People starved when the government did not provide adequate food, and tuberculosis was common. Government reforms that began in the 1930s brought better health care. The last half of the twentieth century saw many improvements in health care, and as a result the Shoshone population increased.

ARTS

Painting and crafts

All Shoshone groups have long and unique artistic traditions. The Eastern Shoshone at Wind River Reservation preserve hundreds of ancient pictographs depicting Water Ghost Beings, Rock Ghost Beings, and other fearful creatures.

Once they began using horses to travel greater distances, many Shoshone learned skills from their new Plains neighbors. They recorded tribal history in elk- and buffalo-hide paintings. In addition, like other tribes, they used mineral paints to decorate leather parfleches, pouches or containers for carrying food. Each tribe, however, developed its own distinctive designs.

Western Shoshone crafts are quite different from those of the Northern and Eastern tribes. Lacking water and wood, Western Shoshone societies made extremely complex baskets and tools for carrying water, food, and other objects over greater distances. Not having leather like other groups, the Western Shoshone perfected the weaving of various willows, grasses, and other materials into beautiful, yet functional, art.

The Lemhi Shoshone made bows from the horns of mountain sheep. It could take two months to complete one bow, but the bows were accurate and powerful enough to shoot big game. The Lemhi softened and uncurled the horn by soaking it in hot water. They then whittled it and tied the pieces together with tightly wrapped hide. They decorated finished bows with designs made from porcupine quills. Other tribes traded for these highly prized weapons. The Lemhi also produced watertight bags from salmon skins that they tanned.

The Shoshone are also known for their beadwork. Early designs were more geometric, or boxlike, whereas later ones appear more realistic. Key colors were white, green, blue, and cobalt. During the mid-1900s, the Shoshone Rose became a familiar motif.

Literature

The Shoshone have a long-standing commitment to the written word. Sacajawea's brother is credited with producing the first written Shoshone story. Shoshone authors have written tribal histories, and some reservations produce their own newspapers.

CUSTOMS

Festivals and ceremonies

All three Shoshone divisions practiced a variety of dances and ceremonies. Major dances with religious themes included the Round Dance, the Father Dance, and the Sun Dance. The Round Dance (also done by the Paiute; see entry) was performed when food was plentiful or as part of an annual mourning ceremony. The Father Dance, possibly a form of the Round Dance, paid tribute to the creator and asked him to keep the people healthy.

In the early days, the Sun Dance was performed after a buffalo hunt. The head of the buffalo was prepared so that it seemed to be alive. In modern times, a mounted buffalo head is used. It is then kept at the home of the sponsor of the following year's Sun Dance. Sponsoring a Sun Dance is an expensive proposition, but is a great honor. The Sun Dance has become a focal point for all Shoshone people. It expresses tribal unity and renews the people's connections to their spiritual side.

Coyote Wants to Be Chief

The Shoshone have many tales of Coyote, the trickster and alleged creator of people. Coyote is a prominent figure in many tales from the western tribes of North America.

People from all over the country—all kinds of animals, even Stink Bug—gathered together in a valley for a council. Rumors were going around that a lot of them wanted to make Coyote the head man. Meadowlark told Coyote that Coyote was going to be a great chief. As he was going along, Coyote met Skunk, who told him the same thing, that Coyote was going to be the biggest chief there ever was. Then Coyote met Badger and he said the same thing. Every time Coyote heard this he got so swelled and he wished he would meet some more people who would tell him the same things.

Coyote wanted to find [Wolf] his brother. Wolf had been away for a long time. Coyote ran around that valley so fast, looking for Wolf, that he got all tired out.

The council was to start before the sun came up. Coyote didn't sleep the night before, [so] he was so weary. In the middle of the night Coyote got sleepy. He still had a long way to go to get to the council. Coyote sat down to rest a little while in some timber. He didn't want to go to sleep but he was very weary. His eyes began to close. He picked up some little yellow flowers and propped his eyelids open with them. He fought sleep but he was so tired. Finally he fell asleep and didn't wake up till noon the next day. He got up and ran toward the valley. To his surprise he began meeting people. They were coming back from the council. He started asking, "What did you talk about? Who became a chief?" And they all told him, "Your brother did. He is the biggest man in the country now. He is the chief."

Coyote wanted to find his brother. Then Coyote found his brother and asked him if he were the biggest chief. Wolf said, "Yes." The people all wanted him to be the biggest chief.

SOURCE: Steward, Tom. *Shoshone Tales.* Edited by Anne M. Smith. Salt Lake City: University of Utah Press, 1993.

Modern-day Shoshone host celebrations called fandangos (festivities that include prayers and games) and powwows. The powwow, a traditional song-and-dance celebration, is a recent introduction, having come to the Shoshone in 1957. Shoshone powwows include dancers from many Plains tribes.

War rituals

Some Shoshone warriors took the scalps of their enemies as a symbol of victory. Upon returning to his village, a triumphant warrior would place each scalp atop a pole and dance around it.

Military societies called the Yellow Brows and the Logs existed among the Eastern Shoshone. Yellow Brows were young men who underwent an initiation ritual in which they spoke backwards, so that "yes" meant "no," for example. They painted their hair yellow and took a vow to remain fearless in battle, never giving up even in the face of death. When preparing for an attack, a Yellow Brow and his horse performed a frenzied dance called Big Horse Dance. In battle, Yellow Brows went first; behind them came the older soldiers called Logs, with their faces painted black.

Courtship and marriage

Courting couples looked forward to socializing at Round Dances, although some men kidnapped their brides, not caring if the women were single or already married. Good hunters made especially desirable husbands, so they often had more than one wife. Divorce was common, and frequent remarriage was normal. The choice of residence for the newlyweds, with either the bride's or the groom's family, varied from group to group.

Women's roles

In early times, Shoshone women were considered inferior to men, especially when they were young. This is partly because they menstruated, and menstrual blood was considered evil. (Women were isolated in special huts during their periods.) A woman's status in society was based upon that of her husband. As women grew older, they could attain a higher status by curing, assisting at births, and demonstrating skill at gambling. The coming of Europeans elevated the status of Shoshone women, because many women, as Sacajawea did, acted as go-betweens with trappers and traders.

By the late 1990s, Shoshone women had expanded their roles in many ways, especially in tribal ceremonies. Because of their efforts, many traditional dances and songs (formerly performed only by men) have been kept alive.

Death and burial

When food was extremely scarce, the old and the feeble were sometimes abandoned by their group and soon died. Some Shoshone wrapped their dead in blankets and placed them in rock crevices. They believed the souls of the departed journeyed on to the lands of Coyote or Wolf. Mourners cut their hair and destroyed the deceased's property, horse, and tepee. The Western Shoshone practiced cremation, and they often burned the dead in their dwellings. The ghosts of the dead were feared; even dreaming about someone who had passed on was a bad omen.

CURRENT TRIBAL ISSUES

Land claims

The Western Shoshone had long-standing land claim disagreements with the federal government. They continued to reject government offers of money and instead hoped to regain some of the 22 million acres lost since the nineteenth century, when nearly all their homeland was seized illegally. The treaty they signed in 1863 permitted railroad, mining, and timber activities on their territory, but the Shoshone could not have imagined how many people would come and live on—and mistreat—the land.

The federal government continues to permit various businesses to use Shoshone land. Shoshone outrage at the misuse of their land led to radical action. In 1972, the tribe joined an organization known as the American Indian Movement (AIM) in a demonstration called the Trail of Broken Treaties. Five hundred Natives arrived in Washington, D.C., to protest government policies toward Native peoples; they occupied the U.S. Bureau of Indian Affairs building for nearly a week. The group used other types of civil disobedience to raise public awareness about treaties the federal and state governments violated. (For more information, see Ojibway entry.)

For decades, Shoshone activists continued their legal battles. The tribe blocked plans for nuclear waste disposal on their land. They also postponed the detonation of a bomb that would send vast pollution over the desert. In 2006, the United Nations instructed the U.S. government to cease activities on the land until the Shoshone claim is settled. The United States, however, continued to use Shoshone land for military testing and mining. A lawyer for the tribe estimates that gold worth more than $20 billion has been taken from the area over the years.

In spite of many protests among the Western Shoshone, some tribal leaders made the decision to accept the cash settlement from the U.S. government. In 2011, the first distributions were made to those tribal members who qualified as one-quarter or more Shoshone. Those who opposed the cash distribution believe that it will derail their claim for land to replace their traditional homelands taken by U.S. settlers and businesses. Under the Ruby Valley Treaty the Shoshone signed, they never gave up their ownership of millions of acres in Nevada, Utah, Idaho, and Southern California.

Federal recognition

For decades, the Lemhi-Shoshone people have pursued federal recognition. The government has yet to acknowledge them, but in 1999, it honored their ancestor, Sacajawea, with a coin celebrating the bicentennial of the Lewis and Clark expedition. The government also gave the town of Salmon, the Lemhi's former homeland, a $12 million grant to open a museum in her honor. Sacajawea's descendants, however, will not benefit, nor have they received federal recognition, which would entitle them to government benefits and allow them to live as a sovereign (independent) nation.

NOTABLE PEOPLE

Washakie (c. 1804–1900) was a chief of the Eastern Shoshone and became the most powerful leader of his tribe. His name may be translated as "Gourd Rattle," "Rawhide Rattle," or "Gambler's Gourd." During battle, he rode toward his enemies and shook his rattle to frighten their horses. In the 1820s and 1830s, Washakie and the Shoshone were on good terms with the American pioneers, trappers, and traders. The Shoshone participated in Rocky Mountain get-togethers with fur trappers and joined them in battles against the Sioux, Blackfoot, and Crow, all traditional enemies of the Shoshone. Washakie signed the Treaty of Fort Bridger in 1863, guaranteeing U.S. travelers safe passage through his band's territory. His good relations with the U.S. government made it possible for him to secure the Wind River Reservation in Wyoming for the Eastern Shoshone. Washakie died in 1900 at Flathead Village in Montana's Bitterroot Valley and was buried with full military honors at Fort Washakie, Wyoming.

Sacajawea (c. 1786–c. 1812) played an important role as a guide to American explorers Lewis and Clark during their westward trek (1804–06) across the country. She was born sometime between 1784 and 1790 among the Lemhi-Shoshone. When she was between ten and twelve years old, Sacajawea was kidnapped by the Hidatsa tribe in a raid. In 1804, a French-Canadian trader, Toussaint Charbonneau, purchased her and married her. Charbonneau joined Lewis and Clark as an interpreter shortly before Sacajawea gave birth to their child, Jean Baptiste Charbonneau. The only woman on the expedition, Sacajawea proved invaluable in leading the explorers through the wilderness. She was a symbol to all people they encountered that theirs was a peaceful mission. Sacajawea's date of death is even less certain than her date of birth. One account reported that she died of a disease in 1812, six years after the return of the expedition, aboard a trader ship on the Missouri River. Another account suggested that she returned to her homeland, lived with the Wind River Shoshone led by Washakie, and died at about one hundred years of age. (This would put her death date around the year 1884, rather than 1812.)

Other notable Shoshone include Pocatello (c. 1815–84), who put up the fiercest Shoshone resistance to white settlement; Bear Hunter (d. 1863), killed resisting a U.S. Army raid; and Shoshone-Goshute-Paiute author Laine Thom (1952–), who edited two critically acclaimed books about the Native American experience: *Becoming Brave: The Path to Native American Manhood* and *Dancing Colors: Paths of Native American Women*.

BOOKS

Hendricks, Steve. *The Unquiet Grave: The FBI and the Struggle for the Soul of Indian Country*. New York: Thunder's Mouth Press, 2006.

Himsl, Sharon M. *The Shoshone*. San Diego, CA: Lucent Books, 2005.

Johnson, Thomas H., and Helen S. Johnson. *Also Called Sacajawea: Chief Woman's Stolen Identity*. Long Grove, IL: Waveland Press, 2008.

Johnson, Thomas H., and Helen S. Johnson. *Two Toms: Lessons from a Shoshone Doctor*. Salt Lake City: University of Utah Press, 2010.

Lowe, Robert Harry. *Dances and Societies of the Plains Shoshone*. Whitefish, MT: Kessinger Publishing, 2010.

Mann, John W.W. *Sacajawea's People: The Lemhi Shoshones and the Salmon River Country*. Lincoln, NE: Bison Books, 2011.

Owings, Alison. *Indian Voices: Listening to Native Americans*. New Brunswick, NJ: Rutgers University Press, 2011.

Slater, Eva. *Panamint Shoeshone Basketry: An American Art Form.* Berkeley: Heyday Books, 2004.

Sonneborn, Liz. *The Shoshones.* Minneapolis, MN: Lerner Publications, 2006.

Stamm, Henry E., IV. *People of the Wind River: The Eastern Shoshones, 1825–1900.* Norman: University of Oklahoma Press, 2010.

Stout, Mary. *Shoshone History and Culture.* New York: Gareth Stevens, 2011.

Trenholm, Virginia Cole, and Maurine Carley. *The Shoshonis: Sentinels of the Rockies.* Norman: University of Oklahoma Press, 1967.

Wilson, Elijah Nicholas. *The White Indian Boy: The Story of Uncle Nick among the Shoshones.* Kila, MN: Kessinger Publishing, 2004.

WEB SITES

"Archives: Oral History Collection." *Chief Washakie Foundation.* http://www.windriverhistory.org/archives/oralhistory/oralhistory1.html (accessed on August 15, 2011).

"Ely Shoshone Reservation" *Great Basin National Heritage Route.* http://www.greatbasinheritage.org/great-basin-heritage-Ely-Shoshone.html (accessed on August 15, 2011).

Ely Shoshone Tribe. http://elyshoshonetribe-nsn.gov/departments.html (accessed on August 15, 2011).

Lemhi-Shoshone Tribes. http://www.lemhi-shoshone.com/ (accessed on August 15, 2011).

Redish, Laura, and Orrin Lewis. "Shoshoni (Shoshone) Indian Language." *Native Languages of the Americas.* http://www.native-languages.org/shoshone.htm (accessed on August 15, 2011).

Stamm, Henry E. "A History of Shoshone-Bannock Art: Continuity and Change in the Northern Rockies." *The Wyoming Council For The Humanities: Chief Washakie Foundation.* http://www.windriverhistory.org/exhibits/ShoshoneArt/index.html (accessed on August 15, 2011).

Te-Moak Tribe of Western Shoshone Indians of Nevada. http://www.temoaktribe.com/ (accessed on August 15, 2011).

Timbisha Shoshone Tribe. http://timbisha.org/ (accessed on August 15, 2011).

Utah American Indian. "Shoshone." *University of Utah.* http://www.utahindians.org/archives/shoshone.html (accessed on August 15, 2011).

Wind River Indian Reservation: Eastern Shoshone Tribe. http://www.easternshoshone.net/ (accessed on August 15, 2011).

Ute

Name

The Ute (pronounced *yoot*) call themselves *Noochew*, which means "Ute people." The name of the state of Utah comes from the Spanish description for the Ute (*Yutah*), which means "high land" or "land of the sun."

Location

Ute territory once included most of Colorado and Utah and parts of New Mexico, Arizona, and Wyoming. In the early twenty-first century, the Northern Ute live on the Uintah and Ouray Ute Reservation, the second-largest reservation in the United States, with headquarters in Fort Duchesne, Utah. The Southern Ute live on their own reservation in the southwestern corner of Colorado near Ignacio. The Ute Mountain Ute moved to the western end of the Southern Ute Reservation in 1897; their reservation is located near Towaoc, Colorado, and includes small sections of Utah and New Mexico.

Population

In the 1600s, there were about 4,000 Ute. In the 1990 U.S. Census, 7,658 people identified themselves as Ute (572 Uintah Ute, 5,626 Ute, and 1,460 Ute Mountain Ute). The 2000 census counted 7,309 Ute, and the 2010 counted 7,435 Ute, with a total of 11,491 people claiming some Ute ancestry.

Language family

Uto-Aztecan.

Origins and group affiliations

The seven to twelve bands (groups) who made up the Ute people probably left western Canada and Alaska and moved into their current homeland during the thirteenth century. Some historians believe their presence may have forced the ancient Anasazi to move from the mesa tops to sandstone caves for protection. The Ute themselves, though, say the Anasazi were

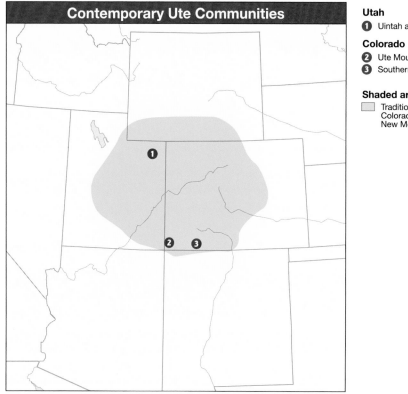

Contemporary Ute Communities

Utah
1 Uintah and Ouray Ute Tribe

Colorado
2 Ute Mountain Ute Reservation
3 Southern Ute Tribe

Shaded area
☐ Traditional lands of the Ute in present-day Colorado and Utah and parts of northern New Mexico and southern Wyoming

A map of contemporary Ute communities. MAP BY XNR PRODUCTIONS. CENGAGE LEARNING, GALE. REPRODUCED BY PERMISSION OF GALE, A PART OF CENGAGE LEARNING.

gone before they arrived. In their search for food, the Ute fought with numerous other tribes, including the Arapaho, Cheyenne, Comanche, Sioux, Kiowa, Pueblo, Apache, Hopi, Navajo, Shoshone, and Paiute (see entries).

In modern times, the Ute bands form three main groups: the Northern Ute (the largest), the Southern Ute, and the Ute Mountain Ute.

The Ute were a fearless people; some historians say they were equal in skill and cunning to the Apaches. They once roamed over 79 million acres of the Great Basin area. Through many centuries, their feet carved out trails in the beautiful mountainous landscape of the West, and the signs they left to guide themselves proved invaluable to the U.S. settlers who took their lands from them. Although the Ute struggle with poverty and other problems today, they retain an unconquerable spirit, a sense of humor, and many of their ancient customs.

HISTORY

Life before European arrival

Before they first met Europeans, the Ute were a varied and widespread tribe. They ranged from the forested slopes of the Rocky Mountains to the barren deserts of Utah. They never really formed a "tribe," in the true sense of the word. Instead, individual members gave their loyalty to their extended family group or to a small, independent band led by a chief. They did this because food was scarce, and small groups needed to cover a great deal of territory to find enough to feed themselves.

At first, the Ute wandered their territory on foot, hunting and gathering food. In the 1600s, they acquired horses from the Spanish, and their lives underwent a tremendous change. Because their land was well suited to grazing livestock, they raised horses, cattle, and sheep. Whereas they had once gathered and hunted small game, they later began to hunt buffalo.

Early relations with Spanish

Riding on horseback increased the Ute's ability to travel long distances and into territory claimed by other tribes. They began raiding neighboring tribes and the Spanish settlements springing up in New Mexico. Ute warriors took hostages, horses, and other goods; their raiding skills earned them a reputation as a warlike people.

The Spanish sent expeditions into Ute country in the 1600s looking for gold, and many written records tell of their meetings with the Ute. One account noted: "They were said to be very skillful with the bow and arrow and were able to kill a buffalo with the first shot." In 1670, the Spanish signed a peace treaty with the Ute, but this did not stop the Ute from raiding for horses. Soon, the Spanish penetrated farther into previously unknown Ute territory to set up an extensive trading network.

Important Dates

1637: First known contact between the Ute and the Spanish. The Ute acquire horses, and their lifestyle changes.

1670: The Ute sign a peace treaty with Spanish.

1861: Uintah Reservation (later the Uintah and Ouray Reservation) is established in Utah.

1868: A reservation is established for the Colorado Ute.

1879: The Ute kill thirteen U.S. soldiers and ten Indian agency officials, including Nathan Meeker, in a conflict that becomes known as the "Meeker Massacre."

1895: The Weminuche band moves to the western end of the Southern Ute Reservation and becomes the Ute Mountain Ute.

1896: Colorado and Utah (Northern) Ute form the Confederated Bands of Ute Indians and file claims for lands illegally taken.

1950: The Confederated Ute Tribes receive $31 million from the U.S. government for lands wrongfully taken in the 1800s.

Loss of land to Mexicans

When Mexico took control of the territory (lands that would later be parts of Colorado, Utah, Arizona, and New Mexico) in 1821, the pattern of trading and exploration of Ute land continued. The Mexicans wanted to own Ute land, because it was beautiful and excellent for grazing livestock. The Mexican government granted its citizens farm and ranch land in Ute territory, which angered the Native peoples. As the years went by, Ute raids on Mexican settlements increased.

When the United States won the Mexican-American War (1846–48; a war in which Mexico lost about one-half of its national territory to the United States) and took over the land of the Ute, the federal government agreed to respect the land grants given to settlers by the Mexican government. The Ute were unhappy about the outcome of the war but believed the Americans would make better trading partners than the Mexicans had been. Up to that point, the Ute had had good relations with American trappers and mountain men who came into their territory. Those men had no interest in settling on Ute land. The Ute shared their knowledge of the vast area of their homelands with these early visitors.

In 1849, the Ute and the United States signed their first treaty. Ute bands acknowledged that the United States was now in charge and agreed to peace and friendship. They promised not to leave their usual territory without permission and to allow U.S. citizens to build military posts and Indian agencies on Ute lands.

Losing land to Americans

Utah was at the time being settled by Mormons, members of the Church of Jesus Christ of Latter-Day Saints, who began moving there in the 1840s. Soon, they were trying to convert the Ute and began calling Ute land their own. The fighting that resulted led President Abraham Lincoln (1809–1865; served 1861–65) to establish the Uintah Valley Reservation for the Ute in Utah in 1861. In 1886, the reservation became the Uintah and Ouray Ute Reservation.

In 1859, gold was discovered in Colorado, and U.S. miners and settlers poured into the area. In 1863, some Ute signed a treaty in which they agreed to give up mineral rights (gold) in exchange for an 18-million-acre reservation (it later became the Southern Ute Reservation). The bands who signed the treaty kept their own hunting grounds and signed over the lands of other Ute who were not present at the treaty meetings.

In 1868, most Colorado Ute signed a treaty reducing their land to 15 million acres. Indian agencies were established at White River and Los Pinos. Five years later, when more gold was discovered, the Ute were forced to give up 3.4 million acres of their Colorado reservation.

Conflict erupts in "massacre"

Tension increased between American settlers and Ute bands in Colorado. Missionaries and Indian agency officials tried to convert the Ute to Christianity and to convince them to adopt an agricultural lifestyle, but the Ute resisted. They did not want to farm or stay on reservations, where the hunting was poor and there was little room to roam. After Colorado became a state in 1876, non-Native inhabitants decided "the Utes must go."

The conflict came to a head in 1879 when Nathan Meeker (1817–1879), an Indian agent at White River, grew frustrated by the Ute's refusal to become farmers. He called in government troops to help him plow the Native's horseracing track, so they would stop amusing themselves and begin farming. The Ute considered Meeker's actions a declaration of war and warned that the army would not be allowed to enter their territory. When a force of 150 U.S. soldiers arrived, the White River Ute ambushed them at Milk Creek. After nearly a week of fighting, the Ute had killed thirteen soldiers and wounded forty-eight others. With the support of two late-arriving backup regiments, the U.S. troops pushed forward to the Indian agency, where they found Meeker and nine of his employees dead. The Ute had also taken several women and children hostage.

Chief Ouray (c. 1833–1880), a respected Ute leader, helped negotiate an end to the hostilities and arranged for the release of the women and children. American settlers, however, used the "Meeker Massacre" as a rallying cry in their battle to remove the Ute from Colorado. The Meeker tragedy was one of the last major Native uprisings in the United States. After Ouray died in 1880, the White River Ute were forced to move to the Uintah Reservation in Utah. Members of other Colorado Ute bands were driven at gunpoint to the Ouray reservation adjacent to Uintah in 1882.

Ute men from southern Colorado, circa 1800s. © NORTH WIND PICTURE ARCHIVES.

The allotment period

The Ute (and many other Native nations) did not settle down to farming fast enough to suit the Americans. Many settlers also protested that too much land had been set aside for Native groups. To respond to their complaints, the U.S. Congress passed the General Allotment Act in 1887.

The Allotment Act was intended to hasten assimilation, a process whereby Native peoples were expected to blend intomainstream American society. Reservation land was divided into parcels (allotments) that would be owned by individual Native heads of households rather than by the tribe as a whole. The leftover land was opened to U.S. settlement.

To the Ute, who did not like farming and did not believe in individual ownership of land, the allotment policy was unwelcome. Some successfully resisted, perhaps because their land was not considered desirable. They occupied the western end of the Southern Ute Reservation, and that area eventually became the Ute Mountain Ute Reservation. Parcels of land at the Southern Ute Reservation and the Uintah and Ouray Reservation were allotted to the Ute who lived there. The remainder of the property was sold, so that both reservations today are checkerboards of Native-owned and non-Native-owned land.

The Ute in modern times

In 1896, the Colorado and Utah (Northern) Ute formed the Confederated Bands of Ute Indians. They pressed the U.S. government to pay them for land they said was wrongfully taken from them, both by treaties and by the allotment policy. Finally, in 1950, the Ute were awarded $31.7 million. Since then the people have engaged in many complex talks with local governments, trying to clarify issues such as hunting and water rights, taxes, and territorial boundaries. They have met with successes (gaining permission to hunt outside the state-ordered hunting season, for example) and frustrating delays (defining their water rights; see "Current Tribal Issues").

RELIGION

The Ute believe in a supreme being and a number of lesser gods, such as the gods of war, peace, thunder and lightning, and floods. The people also have a strong faith in life after death and believe that a good spirit will lead them to the Happy Hunting Ground when they die. They also believe in an evil spirit called the skinwalker. Long ago, skinwalkers were esteemed Navajo warriors who could change themselves into coyotes or foxes and sneak into enemy camps. Once the Indian wars were over, skinwalkers used their powers for evil. The Ute believe that skinwalkers can steal a person's soul.

Some Utah Ute converted to the Mormon religion in the 1800s. In 1898, a Catholic Church was established in Ignacio, Colorado, and found some converts among the Southern Ute. Many Ute today participate in the Native American Church, which formed in Oklahoma in 1918. The church brought together several groups of Native North Americans who had been practicing the Peyote (pronounced *pay-OH-tee*) religion since the 1880s. Peyote is a substance obtained from cactus; when eaten, it causes a person to see visions. The religion involves an all-night service held in a tepee.

LANGUAGE

The language spoken by the Ute people is called Shoshonean; it is a variation of the Uto-Aztecan language that was spoken by the Hopi, Paiute, Shoshone (see entries), and others. According to the 1990 U.S. Census, more than 1,100 people spoke Ute at home; the tribe also used their language during cultural events and public meetings. According to another study done that year, about half of the residents of the Ute Mountain Ute

Reservation and about one third of the residents of the Northern and Southern Ute Reservations knew at least some of their Native language in addition to English. Growing numbers of young people on all three reservations spoke only English, however, causing some concern about how long the Native language could last.

Early in the twenty-first century, approximately 1,500 people spoke the language. Because it has always been an oral language, the Ute are now developing an alphabet. One of the difficulties they face is that some sounds have no equivalent letters in English, so new symbols must be created. Having a written language will help in passing on their heritage. The Ute Mountain Ute have begun language classes in Head Start programs so for preschoolers will become fluent in their native language. Under the direction of some elders, the Ute Language Program was developed to provide workshops classes, language materials, and training. People are encouraged at all times to *Nooh ah pahguh!* ("Speak Ute!"). By 2009, more than 75 percent of the people had become literate in their language.

GOVERNMENT

Ute were organized into extended family groups or small independent bands led by a chief, who was chosen for his wisdom or skills. Families were held together by their respect for their chief. Those who lost their respect for the chief left and moved in with relatives.

After they began to hunt buffalo, the Ute organized into larger groups with more powerful leaders. These leaders were in charge of moving camp and directing hunts, raids, and war parties.

After many years under the supervision of U.S. government agents on the reservations, the three major Ute groups adopted elective forms of government in the 1930s. The Uintah and Ouray Reservation is overseen by a tribal business committee, whereas the Ute Mountain Ute and the Southern Ute are governed by tribal councils.

ECONOMY

Early livelihoods

Early Ute economy was based on hunting and gathering and some trade with neighboring tribes. After they acquired horses, the people traded more extensively, raised cattle, and raided to provide for themselves.

The Ute traded dried buffalo meat and hides for Pueblo (see entry) farm products, cotton blankets, pottery, salt, and turquoise. From the Hopi (see entry), they acquired the red ocher paint (obtained from minerals) they sometimes used to decorate their faces and bodies. The tribes on the Pacific Coast provided the Ute with seashells.

The Ute often took women and children in raids. They either adopted them as tribe members or traded them for products. For example, the Spanish traded horses for children, whom they used as slaves.

After the arrival of U.S. settlers in the 1800s, Ute territory disappeared at an alarming rate. Eventually, the tribes were confined to reservations and attempts were made to force them to become farmers. Most Ute strongly resisted the agricultural lifestyle; instead, they raised livestock and continued to hunt and gather food.

Chief Sevara of the Ute tribe poses with his family in 1899. © DETROIT PHOTOGRAPHIC CO./BUYENLARGE/GETTY IMAGES.

Between the 1890s and the 1930s, the Ute had difficulty supporting themselves. They lived on government handouts (mostly salt and beans) and raised small herds of livestock (cattle and sheep). Many took jobs as day laborers; most still lived in tents. The Ute also received some income from land leases.

Modern economy

In 1950, the Confederated Ute Tribes received $31 million from the U.S. government after winning a lawsuit over territory that had been wrongfully taken in the 1800s. The three major Ute groups divided the money. Around the same time, oil and natural gas deposits were discovered on the reservations, giving the Ute another source of income. This allowed the tribes to make a number of improvements on their reservations, including the construction of modern homes for most of the people. The Ute also used some of the money to start businesses related to tourism, such as motels, restaurants, convention facilities, craft shops, a pottery factory, rodeos, and horseracing tracks. Tourism became the leading industry. By the early 2000s, the Ute had established casinos, which provided additional jobs and income. An additional source of revenue includes trust land with significant oil and gas deposits.

DAILY LIFE

Families

The extended family (parents, children, grandparents, and close relatives) was the basic unit of Ute society. Everyone shared responsibility for caring for children, but the primary caretakers were often young girls, who took over the job when they were about ten years old. The girls carried infant siblings around on wooden boards called cradleboards. Both boys and girls assisted with food gathering as soon as they were old enough.

Education

For centuries, everyone in a camp shared in the education of young children. Once they were confined to reservations, Ute parents were encouraged to send their children to government-run boarding schools, where students were not allowed to speak their own language and were punished for observing their old ways. In spite of this, some Ute held on to their old customs.

In the twentieth century, the Ute demanded nonsegregated public schooling for their children. (Native American children were educated separately from non-Native students.) Since the 1960s, Ute children on the reservations have been attending public schools in nearby communities.

Difficulties arose, though, because the children did not speak English well enough to understand what was going on in the classroom. Children suffered from poverty and poor self-esteem, and schools were often insensitive to the Native culture. Most schools now have introduced curriculums that include the Native experience, and Ute students have the opportunity to learn more about their language and culture through classes and workshops provided by the Ute Language Program.

Buildings

Ute homes varied depending on where the people lived. Most common were domed houses; they were round because the Ute believed the circle was a sacred shape. These houses were about 8 feet (2 meters) high and 15 feet (4.5 meters) around and consisted of a pole frame covered with willow branches or bark. Some groups built cone-shaped houses with pole frames covered with brush, bark, or reeds.

Groups who hunted on the Great Plains used small tepees covered with elk or buffalo skin. They often painted the tepees with brightly colored scenes and symbols. Sweathouses (or sweat lodges, buildings for ritual cleansing in which steam was produced by pouring water over heated rocks) were common then, and they are still used in modern times.

The Ute lived in traditional types of homes until the 1950s, when settlements and housing funds allowed them to build modern homes.

Food

In the centuries before the Ute had horses, the seven bands divided into small family groups for a large part of the year to gather what they could find in the large territory they occupied. Food was scarce, and groups had to cover great distances to locate it.

From the spring until fall, family units hunted for deer, elk, and antelope. They gathered roots, seeds, and wild fruits and berries. They caught insects, lizards, rodents, and other small game. Crickets and grasshoppers were dried and mixed with berries to form a fruitcake. Some groups planted corn, beans, and squash in the meadows and returned to harvest them in the fall.

In the late fall, the small groups rejoined the larger band and left the mountains to find sheltered areas for the winter. After they acquired horses in the 1630s, the Ute could hunt farther afield and capture more animals. Buffalo became a major source of food, clothing, and tools. The Ute were especially fond of jerky (buffalo or deer meat cut into strips and dried). This specialty is still prepared on the reservations; today, the people use deer and elk meat. Jerky is mixed with corn to make stew, ground up and fried in lard, or eaten as a snack. Another modern specialty is frybread, plate-sized disks of bread fried in hot fat (see Flathead entry).

Clothing and adornment

Ute women were described by early observers as being extremely skilled at tanning hides, which were used in trade and for making clothing. They used the hides of buffalo, deer, elk, and mountain sheep. Ute women wore long belted dresses, leggings, and moccasins. Men wore shirts, leggings, and moccasins for everyday activities, and they added elaborate feathered headdresses on special occasions. Many men decorated their bodies and faces with paint, using yellow and black during times of war. Women sometimes painted their faces and the part in their hair. Some Ute pierced their noses and inserted small polished animal bones in the hole; some tattooed their faces using cactus thorns dipped in ashes. Necklaces of animal claws, bones, fish skeletons, and juniper seeds were sometimes worn by both sexes.

Paint, fringes of hair, rows of elk teeth, or porcupine quills dyed in bright colors decorated the clothing worn in early Ute ceremonies. Later, when the Ute acquired beads from European traders, their costumes included intricate beadwork.

Healing practices

Among the Ute, shamans (pronounced *SHAH-munz* or *SHAY-munz*), or medicine men and women, were healers as well as religious leaders. They acquired supernatural powers through their communication with the spirits of animals and dead people. Most shamans knelt down next to a sick person and sang a special curing song, often accompanied by the patient's family. Some shamans also carried small bags containing special materials to aid in healing, including deer tails, small drums and rattles, and herbs. Sometimes medical treatment included placing sick people in a sweathouse and then plunging them into cold water to make their bodies unappealing to evil spirits.

By the early twenty-first century, all the old-time Ute healers were dead. People use modern health-care facilities in urban areas, but those who still wish to consult medicine men can call on Navajo (see entry) medicine men in Arizona.

ARTS

The traditional Ute crafts had nearly died out by the 1930s but have since been revived. Some Ute maintain tribal customs by weaving baskets, creating pottery (the Ute Mountain Ute began their own pottery manufacturing plant), or working with beads or leather. They use these traditional works of art in ceremonies or sell them in gift shops.

Oral literature

Many Ute stories explained features of their natural surroundings. For example, they tell the legend of Sleeping Ute Mountain, which resembles a sleeping Indian with his headdress pointing to the north. This mountain was once a Great Warrior God who was wounded and fell into a deep sleep. Blood from his wound became water, and rain clouds fell from his pockets. The blanket that covers him changes colors with the seasons.

An Ute warrior and his bride on horseback, circa 1874. © CORBIS.

CUSTOMS

Child rearing

Children were loved and treated gently. Grandparents or older siblings in the family usually took care of the younger children. The only form of discipline used was ridicule.

Marriage

Parents or relatives usually arranged the marriages, but couples could also choose their own mates. Often, there was no ceremony. Once the couple slept together at the girl's home, they were considered married. Couples lived with the bride's family.

Men could have more than one wife. Divorce was common, and children usually stayed with the mother.

Hunting rituals

An Ute boy was considered a man when he proved he could provide meat. He was forbidden to eat his first kill. A woman was forbidden to eat deer meat during her menstrual period because to do so would spoil her husband's hunt.

Ute used deerskins as disguises when hunting that animal. They hunted elk on snowshoes, driving the animals into deep snow before killing them.

Dances

The two ceremonies that were most important to the Ute were the Sun Dance and the Bear Dance; both are still performed annually.

Sun Dances The Sun Dance is a personal quest by the dancer for power given by the Great Spirit. Each dancer also represents his family and

A father and daughter from the Ute tribe dance at the National Powwow in Washington, D.C. © TIME SLOAN/STAFF/AFP/GETTY IMAGES.

community, so the ceremony is a way of sharing. The Sun Dance originated from a legend in which a man and a woman left the tribe during a time of terrible famine. While on their journey, the couple met a god who taught them the Sun Dance ceremony. After they returned and performed the ritual with the tribe, a herd of buffalo appeared and the famine ended.

The Sun Dance ceremony includes several days of secret rites followed by a public dance performance around a Sun Dance pole, which is the channel to the creator. The rites involve fasting, praying, smoking, and preparing ceremonial objects.

Newspaper reporter Jim Carrier described a modern Sun Dance on top of Sleeping Ute Mountain: "Night and day, for four days, the dancers charged the pole and retreated, back and forth in a personal gait. There were shuffles, hops, a prancing kick. While they blew whistles made from eagle bones, their bare feet marked a 25-foot (7.5-meter) path in the dirt."

Bear Dances The Bear Dance takes place every spring and honors the grizzly bear, who taught the Ute strength, wisdom, and survival. In the early days, the tribe held the Bear Dance when bears emerged from hibernation. The dance was intended to waken the bear so he could lead the people to places where nuts and berries were plentiful. It was a grand social occasion after a long hard winter.

The Bear Dance involves building a large circular enclosure of sticks to represent a bear's den. Music played inside the enclosure symbolizes the thunder that awakens the sleeping bears. The dance is "lady's choice"; it allows a Ute woman to show her preference for a certain man. The Bear Dance ceremony traditionally lasted for four days and four nights. Dancers wore plumes that they would leave on a cedar tree at the east entrance of the corral. Leaving the feathers behind represented discarding past troubles and starting fresh.

CURRENT TRIBAL ISSUES

Recent struggles

One of the major issues facing the Ute involves water rights. Treaties dating back as far as 1868 guarantee water rights on reservation lands. Nonetheless, the Ute Mountain Ute in Colorado did not have safe drinking water on the reservations until the mid-1990s, when one part of a proposed $73 million water project was completed. For decades, Ute

Thunderheads over the Rocky Mountains are seen in a view from the Ute Mountain Ute Reservation in Colorado.
© NORTH WIND PICTURE ARCHIVES.

Mountain land was parched because non-Native farmers dammed the rivers that used to irrigate it. The Delores Irrigation Project, which brings water to the reservation by canal, has enabled the tribe to farm and ranch. It also pipes in drinking water, the first time the reservation has had access to a safe water supply. However, maintaining water rights is an ongoing process.

The Ute Mountain Ute became involved in another controversy in 1986, when they began a business venture to transport tourists from Ute lands by helicopter to view ancient Anasazi ruins at the adjacent Mesa Verde National Park. The National Park Service argued that vibrations from the frequent helicopter flights damaged the ruins. The Ute had hoped to use the income from this and other tourist enterprises to improve the tribe's education levels and employment opportunities. Now they engage in low-impact tourism (sightseeing that has does not cause as much damage to the environment) and have set up a nonprofit foundation to stabilize the ruins and protect and preserve the environment.

The Ute have been involved in political and legal action to defend their rights and sovereignty. For example, the Uintah-Ouray Reservation began a lawsuit in 2008 against a company that was emitting chemicals from its natural gas compressor stations. Major health concerns, including cancer and birth defects, can result from these toxins being released into the air. At the same time, tribal officials were fighting for recognition as a sovereign, or self-governing, nation. In 2010, the tribe asserted its rights for criminal and civil jurisdiction over tribal lands. The Ute resent outside law enforcement making traffic stops and arrests on reservation land.

Today, the Ute struggle with health issues such as obesity, diabetes, strokes, and alcoholism. On the Ute Mountain Ute Reservation in the late 1990s, life expectancy for men was only 38 years because of the high number of deaths from alcohol-related accidents and violence. By 2006, life expectancy had increased 48 for men and 52 for women, but was still much lower than the national average of 77.5 years.

Past triumphs

Scientists in the early twenty-first century are expanding on a technique that the ancient Ute used to construct ceremonial rattles. Called piezoelectricity, this technology puts crystals under pressure to produce electricity. The early Ute filled leather rattles with quartz crystals. When shamans shook them, they produced flashes of light. In modern times, microphones and igniters on gas grills and other modern devices use this basic design, which the Ute came up with centuries before the rest of world discovered it.

NOTABLE PEOPLE

Chief Ouray (c.1833–1880) became a prominent spokesman and negotiator on behalf of the Ute people because of his ability to speak several languages. He was born in Taos, New Mexico, and spent his youth working as a shepherd on Mexican-owned ranches, where he learned to speak Spanish. He moved to Colorado at the age of eighteen and soon became a leader in the Ute tribe. At first, he was revered as a cunning and dangerous warrior, but his career shifted as he came to realize that U.S. settlement in his tribe's territory could not be halted.

Ouray helped to arrange treaties between the Ute and the U.S. government in 1863 and 1868. In 1867, he assisted Kit Carson (1809–1868) a U.S. Army officer, in suppressing a Ute uprising. In 1868, he accompanied Carson to Washington, D.C., and acted as spokesperson for the seven Ute bands. In the negotiations that followed, the Ute retained 16 million acres of land. More miners trespassed on Ute lands, and in 1872, Ouray and eight other Ute again visited Washington, D.C., in an attempt to stress peace over warfare. In these talks, the government pressured the Ute into giving up four million acres for an annual payment of $25,000. For his services, Ouray received an additional payment of $1,000.

After the Nathan Meeker massacre (see "History"), both the Native nations and the U.S. government chose Ouray to represent them in peace talks. In 1880, Ouray again traveled to Washington, D.C., where he signed the treaty that relocated the White River Ute to the Uintah-Ouray Reservation in Utah. Soon after his return from Washington, Ouray died in 1880 while on a trip to Ignacio, Colorado, where the Southern Ute Agency had been relocated. Lacking a strong voice for their interests, the Ute were removed from Colorado the following year.

Another notable Ute was tribal leader Walkara (1801–1855), one of the most powerful and renowned Native American leaders in the Great Basin area from 1830 until the time of his death.

BOOKS

Becker, Cynthia S. *Chipeta: Ute Peacemaker.* Palmer Lake, CO: Filter Press, 2008.

Carrier, Jim. *West of the Divide: Voices from a Ranch and a Reservation.* Golden, Colorado: Fulcrum, 1992.

Daniels, Helen Sloan, compiler. *The Ute Indians of Southwestern Colorado.* Lake City, CO: Western Reflections, 2008.

Decker, Peter R. *"The Utes Must Go!": American Expansion and the Removal of a People.* Golden, CO: Fulcrum Publishing, 2004.

Farmer, Jared. *On Zion's Mount: Mormons, Indians, and the American Landscape.* Cambridge, MA: Harvard University Press, 2008.

Osburn, Katherine M.B. *Southern Ute Women: Autonomy and Assimilation on the Reservation, 1887–1934.* Lincoln: University of Nebraska Press, 2008.

Ryan, Marla Felkins, and Linda Schmittroth. *Ute.* San Diego: Blackbirch Press, 2003.

Simmons, Virginia McConnell. *The Ute Indians of Utah, Colorado, and New Mexico.* Boulder, CO: University Press of Colorado, 2000.

Silbernagel, Robert. *Troubled Trails: The Meeker Affair and the Expulsion of the Utes from Colorado.* Salt Lake City: University of Utah Press, 2011.

William, Wroth, ed. *Ute Indian Arts and Culture: From Prehistory to the New Millenium.* Colorado Springs: Taylor Museum of the Colorado Springs Fine Arts Center, 2000.

Wyss, Thelma Hatch. *Bear Dancer: The Story of a Ute Girl.* Chicago: Margaret K. McElderry Books, 2010.

PERIODICALS

Van Meter, David. "Energy Efficient." *University of Texas at Arlington,* Fall 2006.

WEB SITES

"History of Northern Ute Indian, Utah." *Online Utah.* http://www.onlineutah.com/utehistorynorthern.shtml (accessed on August 15, 2011).

"People of the Colorado Plateau: The Ute Indian." *Northern Arizona University.* http://cpluhna.nau.edu/People/ute_indians.htm(accessed on August 15, 2011).

Redish, Laura, and Orrin Lewis. "Ute Indian Culture and History." *Native Languages of the Americas.* http://www.native-languages.org/ute_culture.htm (accessed on August 15, 2011).

Southern Ute Indian Tribe. http://www.southern-ute.nsn.us/ (accessed on August 15, 2011).

"The Story of the Ute Tribe: Past, Present, and Future." *Ute Mountain Ute Tribe.* http://www.utemountainute.com/story.htm (accessed on August 15, 2011).

Utah American Indian. "Ute." *University of Utah.* http://www.utahindians.org/archives/ute.html (accessed on August 15, 2011).

The Ute Indian Tribe. http://www.utetribe.com/ (accessed on August 15, 2011).

Ute Language Program. http://uteed.net/utelanguage.htm (accessed on August 15, 2011).

"Ute Nation." *Utah Travel Industry.* http://www.utah.com/tribes/ute_main.htm (accessed on August 15, 2011).

Washoe

Name

Washoe (pronounced *WAH-show*) comes from the word *washiu,* meaning "person." The tribe calls itself *Wa she shu,* or "the people." The name is sometimes spelled Washo. The four main divisions of the tribe include *Pa-wa-lu* ("valley dwellers"), *Tanlelti* ("westerners"), *Welmelti* ("northerners"), and *Hanalelti* ("southerners").

Location

The Washoe territory ran from Walker Lake in Nevada to Honey Lake in northeastern California. In the west, it was bordered by the Sierra Madre, and it stretched as far as the Pine Nut and Virginia Ranges in the east. Most of the people lived in west-central Nevada in the foothills of the Sierra Nevada near present-day Carson City. Modern-day Washoe live on several tracts in Nevada and California, on parts of their original homeland close to Lake Tahoe. Some Washoe live with the Paiute and Shoshone in the urban Reno-Sparks Indian Colony in Reno, Nevada; the colony also has a reservation in Hungry Valley north of Reno. Other Washoe share the Susanville Indian Ranchería in Lassen County, California, with several other Native nations. About one-third of the Washoe live in various locations throughout the United States.

Population

Before the Europeans arrived, the Washoe may have numbered 3,000. During the 1800s, the population decreased to about 1,500. By the mid-1900s, that figure had fallen to 900. The 1990 U.S. Census showed 1,520 Washoe, but in 2000 the population had decreased to 1,317. In 2009, statistics from the tribal council indicated the Washoe Tribe of Nevada and California had 1,550 members.

Language family

Hokan.

Origins and group affiliations

Washoe oral history states that they have lived in their homeland from the beginning of time. Historians, though, say the people may have moved to

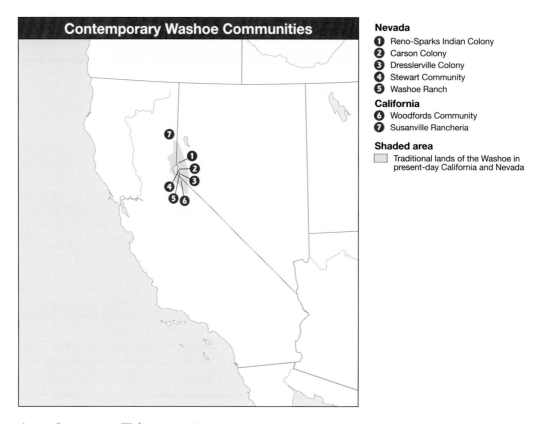

Contemporary Washoe Communities

Nevada
1. Reno-Sparks Indian Colony
2. Carson Colony
3. Dresslerville Colony
4. Stewart Community
5. Washoe Ranch

California
6. Woodfords Community
7. Susanville Rancheria

Shaded area
Traditional lands of the Washoe in present-day California and Nevada

A map of contemporary Washoe communities. MAP BY XNR PRODUCTIONS. CENGAGE LEARNING, GALE. REPRODUCED BY PERMISSION OF GALE, A PART OF CENGAGE LEARNING.

Nevada from California in 4000 BCE. Their location kept the Washoe somewhat isolated from other tribes and U.S. settlers, although some Washoe did intermarry with their neighbors, the Miwok and Paiute (see entries). The Northern Paiute were enemies of the Washoe and may have conquered them in the mid-1800s, although that is subject to dispute. The two groups settled their differences with a 1890 peace council.

For more than 10,000 years, people have dwelled in the area surrounding Lake Tahoe, or *Dao w aga,* as the Washoe called the heart of their homeland. These ancestors of the Washoe lived by hunting, fishing, and gathering in this breathtaking landscape surrounded by natural beauty, much as later generations did. Because their land was divided between present-day Nevada and California, the Washoe melded the lifestyles of two different Native populations. They gathered acorns and built conical houses like the California tribes, and they relied on piñons and game as the Great Basin peoples did. Respect for nature was central to Washoe beliefs, and the people saw the environment as intricately connected with their language and their lives. Caring for the environment has remained a central focus for the Washoe people, who in modern times are working to protect important cultural sites, such as *De ek Wadapush* (Cave Rock) and *Lo'om* (Hobo Hot Springs).

HISTORY

Prehistory

The Washoe claim they have inhabited the territory around Lake Tahoe from the beginning of time. Evidence shows that people have dwelt in this area for more than 10,000 years. The early cultures fished in the lakes and streams, hunted in the woodlands, and gathered the plants that grew wild.

Archaeologists say the Washoe may have moved from Nevada to California around 4000 BCE. The people's lifestyle changed little over the next five millennia. Each year, they migrated from the Sierra Nevada, where they spent summers fishing and gathering plants, to the valleys, where they harvested wild grass seeds. Fall took them to the mountains again to gather pine nuts and hunt small game. When the weather grew cold, they retreated to the conical bark shelters of their winter villages and lived on the food they had dried and stored. Life continued to follow this seasonal pattern until the nineteenth century brought outsiders into their territory.

Encounters with American explorers

The Washoe first met Spaniards at the end of the 1700s, and their first encounter with Americans occurred when Jedediah Strong Smith (1799–1831) arrived in their territory during his 1825–26 travels. For more than a century, most Washoe avoided the Euro-Americans who crossed their lands. They may have feared being sold into slavery because some of

Important Dates

1825–26: The Washoe's first contact with Americans occurs when Jedediah Strong Smith arrives in their territory.

1857: American settlers kill several Washoe for digging up potatoes, sparking a conflict that came to be known as the Potato War.

1858: Prospectors flood into Washoe lands after the Comstock lode is discovered.

1917: The U.S. government sets aside land near Carson, Nevada, for the Washoe.

1924: The Washoe become U.S. citizens.

1936: The Washoe constitution is drafted and the official name, the Washoe Tribe of Nevada and California, is adopted.

1970: The Indian Claims Commission awards the Washoe $5 million for the loss of their lands.

1980: The Washoe win a court case, allowing them to hunt and fish in their traditional areas.

1991: The Tribal Strategic Plan is implemented with a goal of self-governance.

their ancestors had been forced to work in Spanish mines or because they had heard stories of others being thus mistreated. Other than a meeting with government surveyor John Charles Frémont (1813–1890) in 1844, the Washoe had little contact with outsiders until the 1850s.

They did, however, have struggles with the Northern Paiute throughout the 1800s. Although the Washoe deny that the Paiute (see entry) conquered them, some accounts indicate the Northern Paiute kept the Washoe from obtaining guns and horses for decades. Along with this intertribal conflict, the Washoe suffered as an influx of settlers moved to the area in the mid-1800s.

Conflicts with U.S. settlers

Not only did the newcomers' takeover of land cause tensions between the Washoe and their Northern Paiute neighbors, but the Washoe experienced brutality at the hands of the colonists. In 1857, several Washoe took potatoes from a farm that a settler had planted on their land. The Washoe were killed in what was later called the Potato War.

After the Comstock Lode was discovered in 1858 in western Nevada, miners flooded into the area and took over Washoe homelands. Relations between the settlers and Washoe grew ever more strained as commercial fisheries, logging, and cattle herds destroyed the Native's hunting, fishing, and gathering areas. Although some Indian agents requested that reservations be set aside for the Washoe, others felt they were not necessary. The requests were ignored for decades.

Lifestyle changes

Some Washoe moved into town and worked on cattle ranches. Others sold game and fish to restaurants. These Washoe adopted the clothing of the settlers but still gathered for their traditional ceremonies and activities such as the pine nut harvest and rabbit drives (see "Games, rituals, and ceremonies").

After sending several petitions and a delegation to Washington, D.C., to speak with the president, the Washoe were offered land in Paiute territory and $1,000. They did not want to share land with their enemies. In 1892, the Washoe were given tracts, but much of the land was in the now-barren pine nut forest. Settlers had cut most of the trees to build homes. Few of the allotments had water rights. Some Washoe were given land in California, so the people could not all live together.

Washoe expand their landholdings

In 1916, Congress gave the people $10,000 to buy land and water rights. The Washoe bought five pieces of property, amounting to about 236 acres. This land, however, was without good water resources. Many people lived in one room without electricity or plumbing. Later, four-room houses were put up.

By 1940, the Washoe had an additional 95 acres added to their holdings. This property in Carson Valley, called the Washoe Ranch, enabled the people to farm and raise animals.

Compensation for lost lands

Through the Indian Claims Commission, the people filed a claim for the lands that had been taken from them. The process began in 1951 but was not settled until 1970. The Washoe received $5 million, only a small portion of what their original lands were worth.

That year, Congress gave the Washoe people 80 acres in California called the Woodfords Community. The people themselves began purchasing land in their former territory and using some of those properties for conservation. Over the next decades, Washoe landholdings increased. As of 2011, the Washoe had land in trust in Nevada and California that included the Carson Colony, Dresslerville Community, Reno-Sparks Indian Colony, Stewart Community, and Woodfords Community; they also had additional tribal trust parcels located in Alpine, Carson, Douglas, Placer, Sierra, and Washoe Counties.

RELIGION

The Washoe saw all living and nonliving things as sacred. This deep devotion showed in their great respect for the environment. They offered prayers before gathering food or killing animals. They also thanked the Maker, or *Ti-kái,* who lived above.

The Washoe creation story said that Wolf put cattail-down, grass, and seeds in a basket. When humming started, he dumped out the contents, which turned out to be the Miwok, Maidu (see entries), Paviotso, and Washoe. Another part of the story says that the older brother, Wolf, and younger brother, Coyote, argued. This is similar to other California Indian stories. Other Washoe creation accounts are reminiscent of those found in the Plains and Great Basin.

Washoe Words

hunga mi' heshi	"hello"
su'ku	"dog"
tibe	"sun; moon"
timme	"water"
ta'mo'mo'	"woman"
telihu	"man"

During the 1920s, the Northern Paiute and Washoe were introduced to the Peyote religion. (Peyote is a nonaddictive drug that brings on altered mental states and hallucinations in people who chew it or drink it in green tea.) The religion became more widespread in the next decade when Ute (see entry) Peyotist Raymond Lone Bear married into the Washoe tribe. He converted the healer Sam Dick, who in turn taught Ben Lancaster. During the late 1930s, Lancaster, who had some Washoe heritage, spread Peyotism to fourteen Washoe villages. Public disapproval of the religion caused many people to keep their beliefs secret. The religion, later called "New Tipi Way," was part of the Native American Church (see Makah entry). Followers practiced honesty, charity, self-reliance, brotherly love, and avoidance of alcohol. In the later twentieth century, people became more open about their beliefs, and some Washoe continue to follow the teachings of the Native American Church.

LANGUAGE

Because the Washoe speak the Hokan language rather than the Numic or Uto-Aztecan languages of the other nearby tribes, some experts believe the Washoe may have migrated from California to their Nevada homelands. The Washoe language may be related that of the Chumash (see entry) in California; it is also similar to the southeastern languages spoken by the Chickasaw, Creek, and Seminole (see entries).

The three Washoe groups—the *Hung a lel ti* to the south, the *Wel mel ti* to the north, and the *Pau wa lu* to the east—each spoke a different dialect. When students were forced to attend boarding schools in the late 1800s, many children were made to learn English, which led to a decline in the number of Native speakers. In recent years, the Washoe have been working to restore their language by offering classes.

GOVERNMENT

In the early Washoe communities, most leadership was informal. The people looked for guidance from those who were wise, honest, and generous. Men who dreamed of game habitats took the role in organizing a hunt. This person might be called "Antelope Boss" or "Rabbit Boss," depending on what hunt he was leading.

The tribe's traditional approach to government changed after U.S. settlement in Washoe territory. In 1934, Congress passed the Indian Reorganization Act, under which tribes were required to set up central governments. The Washoe wrote a constitution and organized as the Washoe Tribe of Nevada and California. In 1966, the tribe set up a nine-member council, which expanded to twelve members in 1990. The present-day council consists of two representatives from each of the five communities along with two off-reservation members.

ECONOMY

For millennia, the Washoe lived from season to season on the meat, fish, and plants they could gather (see "Food"). They also collected acorns and sometimes shells from the Pacific shores to trade with neighboring tribes. This subsistence lifestyle changed drastically when an influx of settlers arrived and took over Washoe homelands. Loggers cut down the piñon pines, commercial fisheries depleted the fish supply, construction and sport shooting decreased the game and fowl, and cattle trampled or ate the native plants. All of the resources the Washoe had depended on for food soon disappeared.

The Washoe, who had always shared with others in need, could not understand the settlers' possessiveness with their harvests. Whenever Washoe harvested crops on land the settlers considered theirs, the tribe members were accused of stealing. If they asked for assistance, they were said to be begging. Some Washoe went into town to work for wages. Others sold crafts or various goods to the settlers, but many had to eke out their livings on land without sufficient water supplies or resources.

Over time, the Washoe acquired more land, and by the latter part of the twentieth century, several tribal businesses had been established. The Washoe Tribal Ranch raises hay, grass, and alfalfa as well as cattle. The Tribal Development Group oversees and expands tribal businesses, such as the food mart, gas station, and smoke shops.

DAILY LIFE

Families

The family unit was central to the Washoe people; they lived and worked together. Most family groupings consisted of a couple and their children, but they could include other relatives or even friends who shared a *galis dungal,* or winter house. The average size of the group sharing a home was between five and twelve people.

Buildings

Villages consisted of about four to ten families who stayed together all year. In the winter, each family lived in a *galis dungal.* The Washoe often set up their camps near the hot springs in the Sierra Mountains.

The people built their conical winter homes of layers of bark and brush over a strong frame of poles that met at the top. Grass, thatch, or deer hide sometimes covered the exterior. A rock-lined pit in the center of the home held a fire. Doorways faced east to greet the sunrise. Skins hanging from the ceiling separated the interior into rooms.

Cone-shaped summer houses, called *gadu,* were often partially open and built of available materials, such as branches and leaves. These served more as windbreaks than shelters.

Clothing and adornment

Women made most clothing—breechcloths, aprons, leggings, shirts, and capes—from buckskin. Both men and women wore kilts of deer-skin or groundhog fur. Strips of rabbit skins sewed into blankets kept the people warm in winter. The Washoe went barefoot or wore sandals when it was warm but switched to deer hide moccasins when it grew cold.

Women had shoulder-length hair and bangs. Men plucked their faces and wore their hair in braids or knotted at the backs of their heads. Both sexes had pierced ears and wore necklaces. Clamshell beads were used for adornment. Burnt rabbitbrush (a plant similar to sagebrush), acorn juice, and water were mixed as ink for tattoos. Grease and ocher paint protected people's skin.

Food

The seasons of the year determined the Washoe diet. The hardest part of the year was early spring, when winter food stores had been eaten and little had begun to grow. The people ate seeds, pine nuts, and whatever dried meats they had left. Sometimes, they supplemented this with fresh fish or meat, if available. Once the bulb plants and early grasses sprouted, they added those to their diets.

After the fish spawned in the summer, people caught them in baskets and even fished at night under torches. The women cleaned the fish and then dried or smoked them. They wrapped large fish in sunflower leaves before drying and cooked small fish in baskets heated with hot rocks or coals.

The Washoe collected berries, bulbs, and roots from the abundance that grew in the area, but they had to know the exact location and growing times because most plants only lasted about a week. Some of the plants that grew wild were onions, mustard, rhubarb, turnips, celery, potatoes, spinach, oats, and sweet potatoes. The women also gathered berries, plums, grapes, tule root, and various seeds—sunflower, cattail, tiger lily—along with herbs for medicine.

After the snow melted in the mountains, the men fished in the lakes and hunted quail. As fall arrived, they caught spawning whitefish, and everyone harvested acorns and pine nuts. After roasting the pine nuts and drying the shelled acorns, the Washoe stored them in caves or stone- or grass-lined pits. They ground some of the pine nuts, acorns, and seeds into flour that they used to make mush, biscuits, or soup.

The women boiled, roasted, or dried the rabbits caught during the drives (see "Games, rituals, and ceremonies"). Other game hunted in autumn included antelope, mule deer, bighorn sheep, and birds. The Washoe collected honey as well as bee larvae, caterpillars, and grasshoppers, which they roasted.

Education

Elders held a place of honor in the tribe. They passed on traditions to the next generations. Young people spoke respectfully to the elders, and the elders were served first at feasts.

In 1890, the government opened Stewart Indian School, a boarding school run by the U.S. War Department. Children as young as five were forced to attend this boarding school, which was run in military style. Their hair was cut, and they were issued uniforms. Students who tried to run away were caught and punished.

The Shoshone, Paiute, and Washoe students were forced to give up their language and culture to learn Euro-American ways of life. Mornings were spent in the classroom. Students worked at chores the rest of the day. Girls learned cooking, sewing, and nursing. Boys trained to be carpenters, mechanics, plumbers, or electricians. Many children experienced physical or sexual abuse, and deaths from the rapid spread of diseases were common.

Healing practices

Both men and women could become healers, but they had to receive repeated calls to the profession in their dreams. The special powers healers received allowed them to cure both mental and physical illnesses. They used cocoon rattles, eagle feathers, and prayers to aid the sick. The healer, or shaman (pronounced *SHAH-mun* or *SHAY-mun*), sucked out poisoned blood, whereas herb doctors, after dreaming of the location of a specific plant, used that for curing.

Some healers used their powers for evil. If a family suspected a shaman of making a relative ill, they might kill him or her.

ARTS

Crafts

Washoe baskets were intricate, with up to thirty-six stitches per inch. Most were made of willow with accents of black bracken roots. Women created the red designs with redbud and brown patterns by soaking fern roots in mud. Each maker invented her own designs, although some symbols were inherited. In the early 1900s, thanks to several talented

A coiled basket is an example of the intricate work of Washoe artists. © AMBIENT IMAGES INC./ALAMY.

basket weavers (see "Notable People" for important basket makers of that era), the tribe's baskets became so desired by art collectors that the Washoe could not fulfill the demand.

Tightly woven baskets could hold water and be used for cooking. Loosely woven ones served as sifters for nuts and seeds. Conical burden baskets carried acorns and fuel, and cradle baskets, made to hold babies, had sunshades.

Oral literature

The Washoe had many tales of beings who had supernatural powers. A giant who lived near Cave Rock ate lazy people. The *Ong*, a man-eating bird who nested in Lake Tahoe, bent trees with the wind from his huge wings. After he died, his nest sank underwater (see "Monster Bird," in which this creature is called an *óan*).

The *Metsunge,* or Water Babies, lived in the lakes and streams. They traveled through a passageway at *De-ek Wadapush,* or Cave Rock, to reach their homes in the depths of Lake Tahoe. When Washoe traveled past Cave Rock, they left offerings and said a prayer, because Water Babies could cause sickness or death. Only those who had a Water Baby as a guardian spirit, the healers, ventured inside the caves. To them, the Water Babies could bring good luck; healers consulted Water Babies for powers and guidance.

CUSTOMS

Social organization

The three groups that lived to the north, south, and east met for ceremonies or war. When they hunted, each group used their own side of the lake, but they came together for important events,

Monster Bird

The narrator of this tale, Captain Pete, was one of several Washoe who went to Washington, D.C., to ask the government to give his people some land during the late 1800s. He recounted several traditional stories to Edward S. Curtis (1868–1952), a photographer who took pictures of many of the tribes throughout the United States and recorded their history, customs, and stories.

> In the lake [Tahoe] stood a great pine. In the top was a mass of large branches, the nest of óan, an enormous bird that ate human beings. Its winter home was a cave on the lakeshore [near Glenbrook, Nevada]. One day it carried a man into its nest and left him sitting there while it ate. He covered his head with a rabbit-skin blanket and peered out through the holes, and each time the bird took a bite, he could see into its great mouth and down into its gullet. He threw an arrow-point into the bird's mouth, and it swallowed the piece of obsidian along with the meat. Repeatedly he did this, and soon the bird began to tremble, and it died from the poison on the arrow-points. Then the man cut off its wings and tied them together. He climbed down the tree, placed the wings on the water like a boat, and sat on them, and the wind wafted him ashore.

SOURCE: Captain Pete as told to Edward S. Curtis. "Monster Bird." In *The North American Indian*. Vol. 15. Edited by Frederick Webb Hodge. Norwood, MA: The Plimpton Press, 1926: 149–51. Available online from Northwestern University. http://curtis.library.northwestern.edu/curtis/viewPage.cgi?showp=1&size=2&id=nai.15.book.00000235&volume=15#nav (accessed on August 15, 2011).

particularly the major dances and ceremonies related to seasonal food gathering (see "Games, rituals, and ceremonies").

Birth and naming

Female relatives and friends cared for the new mother. The baby's parents gave out presents to the village, and both parents stopped eating meat and salt.

A month later, the baby got a haircut and the mother bathed during a special celebration. After these rituals, infants stayed in cradleboards until they became toddlers. Once children could talk, their parents named them, usually after a word they said.

Mothers rubbed sagebrush bark until it was soft and used it to diaper their babies. Children were treated kindly and gently, and never punished.

Puberty

For a boy to be considered a man, he had to kill a full-grown buck. A girl still celebrates her first menses with a dance. During the four-day ritual, she receives lectures from her mother, sings special songs, and performs the Round Dance, Jumping Dance, and Morning Round Dance. Feasts and throwing gifts into the crowd are part of the ceremony to mark her passage into adulthood.

In the early days. the girl fasted, drank warm water, and walked through the chores she would do in adulthood. She and some of her friends then climbed the mountain, building fires as they went. At dark, they returned to the community for the dance. The next day before sunrise, her mother, uttering wishes for her daughter's health, poured a basketful of cold water over the girl's head; the mother then ritually bathed her daughter. Afterward, the basket was thrown to the crowd. Her father hid an elder stick and returned to make a speech of good wishes for his daughter's health, beauty, and a good marriage. The girl did not eat meat or fish and went through the ritual again a month later. At that point, she was considered marriageable.

Marriage

Parents arranged their children's marriages. Following a gift exchange and a yearlong engagement, the couple either moved in together or participated in a ceremony where they danced beside each other. A rabbit skin blanket draped over their shoulders united them in marriage.

When people married, they usually stayed in the area where they grew up, because they knew the hunting and gathering areas well. The couple moved in with either set of parents. Because property could be inherited from both the father and the mother, the Washoe had no traditions about where a married couple would live.

Death customs

People usually burned the houses of those who died at home and built a new home. Otherwise, bodies were buried under logs or in a remote place, cremated, or placed on a scaffold or in a tree. Possessions were buried or burned with the body.

The mourning period included saying prayers, and women cut their hair. A widow had to wed her husband's brother if he wanted to marry her.

Hunting rituals

Because they believed that all life was sacred, hunters prayed for forgiveness before they killed an animal. People offered a prayer of thanksgiving before meals and always left a gift of food for the Maker. The Washoe held dances and prayers prior to their rabbit drives, salmon spawning, or pine nut harvesting.

To catch deer, hunters wore a deer head with the skin wrapped around them and imitated the call of fawn. They also held deer or antelope drives, similar to the rabbit drives (see "Games, rituals, and ceremonies").

Arrows were tipped with poison, which was made by grinding up the liver of a deer that had been bitten by a rattlesnake. These poisoned tips were used to shoot large game or for war. Quivers were made of coyote, deer, or antelope skin, turned so the fur or hair was inside. The men used obsidian blades for knives.

Games, rituals, and ceremonies

Washoe life was tied to the seasons. The community gathered at *Da ow aga,* or Lake Tahoe, in the spring to play games and compete in archery and races. Summer and autumn meant gathering food to store for winter, but the highlight of the fall season was the *tah gum* (piñon, or pine nut) harvest. The harvest began with *goom sa bye,* a celebration that lasted four or five days. A runner invited all the family groups by bringing a knotted rope, showing how many days would pass until the festival began. After everyone gathered, they prayed, danced, and feasted. They then all worked together to gather the nuts, a process that could take up to six weeks.

The next autumn event was the rabbit drive, which also began with a ceremony of thanks and prayer. Afterward, lines of people flushed the rabbits out and into sagebrush nets, where they were clubbed. The hunters left some rabbits in the nets for the old and sick.

Dances related to the food cycle were the main Washoe celebrations. At times, members of a departing war party might dance with their female relatives, but this was rare, because the Washoe engaged in few battles.

CURRENT TRIBAL ISSUES

The tribe has begun many cultural and social programs to aid their people. Some programs include Culture Camp and language classes, educational scholarships, the Washoe Warrior Society, and the White Bison Society. The Washoe are also encouraging a return to traditional fishing and hunting methods.

In addition, the people are focusing on restoring areas that are valuable to their heritage. In the twenty-first century, they were working on twenty different restoration and conservation projects. They aimed to restore the environment by reintroducing species that had been over-harvested. Other projects include protecting sacred sites important to Washoe culture, such as *De ek Wadapush* and *Lo'on.*

From early times, De ek Wadapush ("rock standing gray"), or Cave Rock, has been a sacred place for the Washoe. Their healers went to this huge rock at the shore to renew their powers. It is also the home of the Water Babies (see "Oral literature").

In 1931 and in the 1950s, holes were blasted through the rock to create and enlarge a highway. The Washoe believed the flooding that followed came from stirring up the Water Babies. New threats to the rock occurred during the 1990s when De ek Wadapush gained a reputation as a popular rock-climbing area.

The Washoe protested, and after several legal battles, they succeeded in preventing rock-climbing. They then removed the climbing pegs by 2009 and worked to restore the site. In 2011, the Washoe tried to have the land transferred into trust. The court denied their request but did authorize the secretary of agriculture to close the land to the general public to protect the history and heritage of the site. A nomination to the National Register of Historic Places will provide an additional safeguard.

Another restoration project is now benefiting the Washoe community, particularly the elderly. For centuries, the Washoe people enjoyed the healing waters of Lo'on, Washoe Hot Springs, also called Hobo Hot Springs. Development in the area beginning in the 1960s disrupted the field that held the pools. In 2001, restoration began, and the Washoe reopened the hot springs the following year with a traditional ceremony. The mineral-filled warm water and mud provides healing relief for those who suffer with arthritis and similar ailments. At the same time, the Washoe, who place a strong value on harmony with the environment, have now healed another valuable part of their landscape.

NOTABLE PEOPLE

Two famous basket weavers were Datsolalee (c. 1835–1925) and Lena Frank Dick (1889–1965). Datsolalee, also known as Louise Keyser, defied the Paiute who, in the 1850s, had prohibited the Washoe from selling goods to the American settlers. In 1895, she contacted the owner of a large clothing store called the Emporium, Abraham Cohn, who bought 120 baskets from her over the next decades. Her work was so prized that one of her baskets reportedly sold for $10,000 in 1930. In more recent times, they have been priced at $1,000,000. Lena Frank Dick, whose work was sometimes mistaken for Datsolalee's, began selling baskets in the 1920s. Dick's work is valued for its fine details and color. She and her sister Lillie Frank James (1885–1948) both became well-known weavers, as were Maggie Mayo James (1870–1952) and Tillie Snooks.

BOOKS

Barrett, S. A. *The Washo Indians.* 1917. Reprint. Charleston, SC: Kessinger Publishing, 2010.

Bibby, Brian. *Precious Cargo: California Indian Cradle Baskets and Childbirth Traditions.* Berkeley, CA: Heyday Books, 2004.

Curtis, Edward S. "The Washoe." In *The North American Indian.* Vol. 15. Edited by Frederick Webb Hodge. Norwood, MA: The Plimpton Press, 1926: 89–98. Available online from Northwestern University. http://curtis.library.northwestern.edu/curtis/viewPage.cgi?showp=1&size=2&id=nai.15.book.00000141&volume=15 (accessed on August 15, 2011).

Dangberg, Grace, translator. *Washo Tales.* Reprint. Carson City: Nevada State Museum, 1968.

D'Azevedo, Warren L., compiler. *Straight with the Medicine: Narratives of Washoe Followers of the Tipi Way.* Berkeley, CA: Heyday Books, 2006.

Kroeber, A. L. *California Kinship Systems.* Reprint. Charleston, SC: BiblioBazaar, 2009.

Life Stories of Our Native People: Shoshone, Paiute, Washo. Reno, NV: Inter-tribal Council of Nevada, 1974.

Makley, Michael J. *Cave Rock: Climbers, Courts, and a Washoe Indian Sacred Place.* Reno: University of Nevada Press, 2010.

Makley, Michael J. *A Short History of Lake Tahoe.* Reno: University of Nevada Press, 2011.

Nevers, Jo Ann. *Wa she shu, A Washo Tribal History.* Reno, NV: Inter-Tribal Council of Nevada, 1988.

Sanchez, Thomas. *Rabbit Boss.* Reprint. New York: Vintage Books, 1989.

Siskin, Edgar E. *Washoe Shamans and Peyotists: Religious Conflict in an American Indian Tribe.* Salt Lake City: University of Utah Press, 1983.

PERIODICALS

ICTMN Staff. "Washoe Tribe's Cave Rock a No-go for Bike Path" *Indian Country Today Media Network,* February 10, 2011. Available online at http://indiancountrytodaymedianetwork.com/2011/02/washoe-tribes-cave-rock-a-no-go-for-bike-path/ (accessed on August 15, 2011).

WEB SITES

"Cave Rock." *National Cultural Preservation Council.* http://www.ncpc.info/projects_caverock.html (accessed on August 15, 2011).

Dodds, Lissa Guimarães. "'The Washoe People': Past and Present." *Washoe Tribe of Nevada and California.* http://www.Washoetribe.us/images/Washoe_tribe_history_v2.pdf (accessed on August 15, 2011).

Redish, Laura, and Orrin Lewis. "Washoe (Washoe) Language." *Native Languages of the Americas.* http://www.native-languages.org/Washoe.htm (accessed on August 15, 2011).

Stern, Robert. Edited and updated by Nate Chappelle. "Cave Rock, NV (Washoe)." *The Pluralism Project: Harvard University.* http://pluralism.org/reports/view/49 (accessed on August 15, 2011).

Van Etten, Carol. "If Stones Could Speak." *Tahoe Country.* http://www.tahoecountry.com/oldtimetahoe/grindingrock.html (accessed on August 15, 2011).

"Washoe." *Four Directions Institute.* http://www.fourdir.com/washoe.htm (accessed on August 15, 2011).

"Washoe Hot Springs." *National Cultural Preservation Council.* http://www.ncpc.info/projects_washoe.html (accessed on August 15, 2011).

"Washoe Indian Tribe History." *Access Genealogy.* http://www.accessgenealogy.com/native/tribes/washo/washohist.htm (accessed on August 15, 2011).

Pacific Northwest

Pacific Northwest

The Pacific Northwest extends from Yakutat Bay, Alaska, in the north to roughly the California-Oregon border in the south. There are more than three dozen identifiable Native groups in the Pacific Northwest, representing a variety of different language groups and cultures. Because they live between the Pacific Ocean and the coastal mountain ranges, the Native people of the Pacific Northwest are traditionally oriented toward coastal and riverine (full of rivers) areas. Their oral traditions and religious expression emphasize the importance of the resources found in these environments.

The Pacific Northwest culture area can be divided into five cultural regions based on similarity of culture or language:

- In the northern area, the defining characteristic is the matrilineal kinship system. This means that family name and inheritance, as well as rights to property and privileges, are passed down through the mother's side of the family. The Tlingit (pronounced *KLINK-it*), Haida (*HIGH-da*), and Tsimshian (which includes the Nisga'a, Gitksan, and coastal and southern Tsimshian; *CHIM-she-an* or *SIM-she-an*) are often called the "northern matrilineal tribes."

- The Wakashan area, found along the south-central coast of British Columbia and the nearby eastern shores of Vancouver Island (both in Canada), is composed of the Kwakwala-speaking peoples, including the Haisla, Heiltsuk (Bella Bella), Oweekeno, and Kwakwaka'wakw, as well as the Nootkan-speaking Nuu-chah-nulth, Ditidaht, and Makah.

- The Salish include the contiguous tribes and bands of southwest British Columbia, Canada, and western Washington State, the outlying Nuxalk of the central British Columbia coast, and the Tillamook of the northern Oregon coast.

- Along the Columbia River, from its mouth to the Cascade Mountains, are the several groups of Chinookan-speakers.

- Along the Oregon Coast are numerous bands of Penutian and Athabaskan speakers.

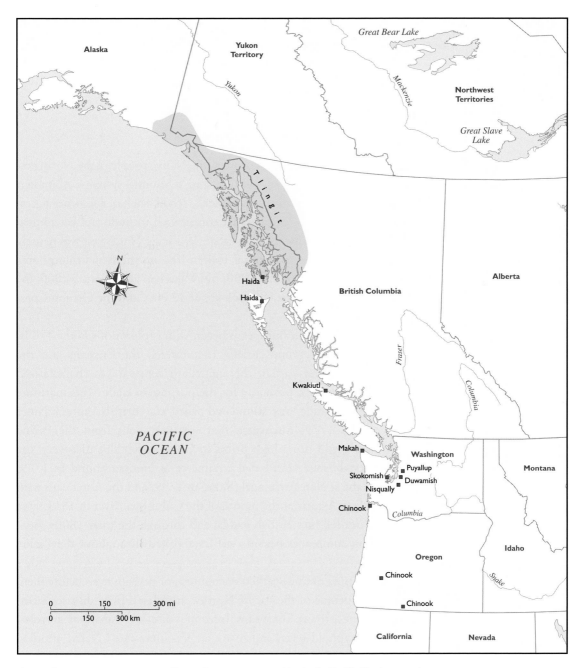

A map showing some contemporary Native American communities in the Pacific Northwest region. MAP BY XNR PRODUCTIONS. CENGAGE LEARNING, GALE. REPRODUCED BY PERMISSION OF GALE, A PART OF CENGAGE LEARNING.

The variety of culture and experience of the Pacific Northwest tribes presents interesting comparisons. Not only is there a great deal of difference in language and culture, but the political boundaries have created historical and contemporary issues that differ significantly as well.

European contact

At the time of first European contact, the Native people of the Northwest Coast had well-developed political and economic systems. Abundant resources met their needs for subsistence (food, shelter, and other necessities) and provided a surplus that contributed to trade and ceremonial life. Population estimates suggest that the Pacific Northwest was densely populated for a nonagricultural region. The northern matrilineal area probably numbered about 42,000, the Wakashan area about 34,000, the Salish about 48,000, the Chinook about 22,000, and the Oregon Coast groups about 30,000.

First contact with Europeans began with explorations in the 1700s; Pacific Northwest groups briefly encountered the Russians and the Spanish. The latter part of the eighteenth century was characterized by more encounters, primarily for the purpose of trade. This maritime (sea-oriented) trade was stimulated when the British captain James Cook (1728–1779) discovered that sea otter pelts from the Pacific Northwest could bring high prices in China. After this discovery, the Spanish established land-based commerce at Nootka Sound in 1789, the Russians at New Archangel (Sitka) in 1799, and the Americans with a post at Fort Astoria at the mouth of the Columbia River in 1811. Fort Astoria later fell into British hands, and through the early 1800s, British trading companies became well established throughout the Pacific Northwest.

At the time of these earliest encounters, or perhaps even before then, the Native people of the Pacific Northwest suffered from diseases introduced by the arriving Europeans. Infectious diseases—smallpox, measles, influenza, typhoid fever, and many others—devastated Native peoples, who had no resistance to them. Thousands died. Estimates suggest that there was a population decline of more than 80 percent by the late 1800s. This had a profound impact on Native culture, and it was at this time, when Native people were most vulnerable, that the European influx began.

New boundaries

In 1846, the boundary between the United States and British North America was established at 49 degrees north latitude, and in 1867, Russian America (Alaska) became a U.S. possession. Since these events, the Native people of the Pacific Northwest have experienced somewhat different political and economic forces that have figured prominently in their lives. The Tlingit and Haida in southeastern Alaska had cool relations with the Russians. Although some Native people adopted the Russian Orthodox Church as their religion and most traded for Russian goods, for the most part, Russian influence was small. When Alaska became part of the United States, interactions between Natives and non-Natives continued at a minimal level until the Yukon gold rush of 1897 brought in a flood of settlers. By 1900, the non-Native population outnumbered the Native population, bringing about a major change in political and economic life. Many Tlingit and Haida participated in wage labor in fish canneries and other economic enterprises. Political and educational systems modeled after those of other states soon became common in communities in southeast Alaska. Nevertheless, the Tlingit and Haida have maintained strong ties with their traditional culture and language.

In 1971, the Alaska Native Claims Settlement Act established Native corporations throughout the state of Alaska. A regional corporation for Alaskan Tlingit and Haida, along with a number of village corporations, was founded in southeast Alaska. The corporations were begun with the intent to use Native-owned land and resources to promote economic development, but success has varied.

The Canadian province of British Columbia maintains different relations with Native groups, or First Nations as they are known in Canada, than Alaska or Washington and Oregon. Throughout the late 1800s, reserves (land set apart for First Nation use, similar to U.S. reservations) were established for the Native groups; in the early twenty-first century, British Columbia had more than two hundred reserves. In Canada, the Indian Act defined Native rights; it was first put into place in 1876 and has been revised or amended many times since. The Indian Act determines who can claim status as a Native, outlines the relationship between Native peoples and the Canadian government, and establishes band (tribe or Native community) government. One of the most controversial actions of the Indian Act was when the potlatch (a very important ceremony in Pacific Northwest cultures; see "Customs") was outlawed in 1884. Although the law was repealed in 1954,

Native Americans tend to their encampment on the shore of Puget Sound. © NORTH WIND/NORTH WIND PICTURE ARCHIVES. ALL RIGHTS RESERVED.

the Native people of British Columbia are still angered over this government action. In the early 2000s, land and resource rights were a major issue, especially as British Columbia, the federal government of Canada, and the First Nations entered into treaty negotiations. Landmark legislation, the Canadian Human Rights Act, took effect in 2011 and gave the aboriginal peoples of Canada rights that had been denied them for centuries. The funding to ensure the needed benefits, however, continues to be an issue.

The experience of Native peoples in Washington and Oregon have more in common with other Native peoples of the contiguous United States. Many of the tribes signed treaties with the United States in the 1850s that established reservations, reserved certain resource rights, and instituted relations with the federal government of the United States.

Political and economic forces have played an important role in the lives of the Native peoples of Washington and Oregon, who have had to adjust to changing and often contradictory federal policy, compete with non-Native interests for land and resource rights, and struggle to maintain ties with traditional language and culture against the forces of the dominant society. Treaty issues have occupied much of the attention of Native groups in recent decades as increasing development in the Northwest decreases the resources upon which Native peoples depend for their economic and spiritual well-being.

Oral literature

Pacific Northwest oral traditions are as varied as the numerous tribes that live in this area. All groups have origin myths, which tell of the first people, migrations, or the origin of kin groups. Each group in the Pacific Northwest differentiates between oral traditions that tell of mythical times and those that tell of historical events. Among northern Pacific Northwest tribes, these traditions may be displayed on totem poles or in other art forms. Raven, as trickster (a cultural hero), is common as a character responsible for much of the natural world. The transformer (one who can change something's outward form) also plays an important role in the oral traditions of many Pacific Northwest tribes as a sometimes benevolent teacher and a sometimes harmful or evil transformer of people into natural objects.

Religion

Pacific Northwest religion is animistic, meaning that the people traditionally believe in the existence of spirits and souls in all living, and in some nonliving, objects. These beliefs are acted out in ceremony and ritual, but they also are part of everyday life. Winter ceremonies are an important series of events that celebrate the religious belief system. These ceremonies may express a personal relationship with a spiritual entity, or they may involve a community expression of supernatural understanding.

A common community event is the First Salmon Ceremony, which all Pacific Northwest groups celebrated. Honoring the first fish taken from the most important run of salmon was a way of paying respect to the resource and ensuring its continuation. The First Salmon Ceremony is still practiced by many Pacific Northwest tribes.

Language

The diversity of languages in the Pacific Northwest has been a puzzle to linguists (people who study languages) for more than a century. The region is comprised of speakers from several not very closely related North American language groupings. In fact, several languages and language groups have no known relation to any other language.

One result of this diversity of languages was the development of Chinook Jargon, a trade language used to communicate across these language barriers. Most of the languages of the Pacific Northwest are still spoken, but many are in danger of becoming extinct. Many tribes in the Pacific Northwest culture area have instituted programs to preserve their language and to teach it to younger tribal members.

Buildings

Multi-family longhouses were the norm throughout the Pacific Northwest. The people built these long, narrow dwellings of planks split from cedar logs. Homes commonly housed from five to ten related families. In general, each family lived in a section of the house with the central area open for cooking and heating fires. When they held celebrations, the homeowners removed the partitions dividing the family units. The Pacific Northwest longhouse was no longer used as a dwelling after about 1900, but the structures continue to be built and used as community buildings and for winter ceremonies or potlatches (see "Customs").

Subsistence

The most important sources of sustenance throughout the Pacific Northwest are the salmon runs, in which the fish swim up the rivers from the ocean. Several different species of salmon are native to the west coast of North America, but not all species are available in various local areas. Fishing in the Pacific Northwest involved a variety of techniques ranging from simple spears and dip-nets to complex weirs (traps) and seines (nets). Salmon provided a staple food and also a surplus for trade and ceremony.

Although salmon was important, it was by no means the only food. Some groups fished for marine (ocean) species, such as halibut, and most groups gathered shellfish. Land-mammal hunting provided food for many groups; sea-mammal hunting was important for others. The Nootkan-speaking peoples were especially known as whale hunters, and many groups utilized whales that had become beached, or stranded, on land. Plant foods included tubers and berries, camas and wapato (common bulbs harvested as starchy foods), and fern roots. The Native groups also used plants for technology and medicinal purposes.

Clothing and adornment

The traditional Pacific Northwest style of garb included cedar-bark skirts and capes and, during cold weather, a blanket worn around the shoulders. Cedar bark was either shredded or woven into material to make clothing. Some groups used leather clothing. Most made rain hats out of cedar bark or spruce root. Blankets were items of wealth as well as clothing and bedding. They were made of cedar bark, plant fibers, mountain goat wool, or dog fur. As cloth blankets became available through trade with Euro-Americans in the late 1700s and early 1800s, they largely replaced the blankets of Native manufacture.

Ceremonial garb was quite different from daily wear. Clothing worn at ceremonies and potlatches might be highly decorated with clan or family symbols or with wealth items, such as precious shells. One of the items of wealth often used in decoration was the dentalium shell. This small shell, harvested by the Nuu-chah-nulth people of the west coast of Vancouver Island, was traded north and south along the Pacific Coast and as far inland as the American Plains. During ceremonies, Pacific Northwest people often painted their faces to express a spirit relationship.

Healing practices

The shaman (pronounced *SHAH-mun* or *SHAY-mun*; a traditional medical practitioner) played an important role in all Pacific Northwest tribes. Shamans could practice both good and evil medicine. Although some practitioners cured with herbs or other medicines, people generally called upon shamans to cure supernatural ailments. This included removing foreign objects from a person's body that had been placed there to make them ill or performing an elaborate ceremony designed to rescue an individual's lost soul. Often in this latter case, the shaman would travel to the Land of the Dead or some other place where the lost soul had strayed and return it to the person's body.

Shamans still practice among many Pacific Northwest societies. Among groups from the Salish southward, the Indian Shaker Church has taken over many of the responsibilities of spiritual healing that were formerly the responsibility of shamans. The Indian Shaker Church originated with the experiences of John Slocum, a Salish man, who in the 1880s had a near-death experience that led him to form this new religion.

Customs

Of all cultural practices, the Pacific Northwest people are best known for the potlatch. A potlatch is a public ceremony that involves giving away accumulated goods. Feasting, ceremonies, rituals, and other activities might also surround the potlatch event. The climax of the potlatch was the display and distribution of goods, which demonstrated the status or inherited privilege of the giver. Potlatching was carried out for a variety of reasons, including naming a child, marriage, funerals, house raising, totem pole raising, or to show affluence.

The Canadian government in 1884 banned potlatching, and the United States actively discouraged the practice. Nevertheless, many Northwest groups continued holding potlatches in secret or in a disguised form until recent years, when they revived the ceremony. Potlatches have since returned as a central activity in many Pacific Northwest communities.

Other customs centered on rites of passage, including birth, naming, puberty, marriage, and death. All of these life stages were recognized by ceremony and ritual, often involving a potlatch.

Current tribal issues

The Native peoples of the Pacific Northwest are politically active on local and national levels. Because political boundaries have separated them into different jurisdictions, their actual experiences vary somewhat. Current interests tend to revolve around land and resource claims, tribal sovereignty (self-rule), and cultural resource control.

The Native peoples of Alaska are subject to provisions of the Alaska Native Claims Settlement Act of 1971, which established regional enterprise and made tribal members shareholders in the corporations. Generally, the Native corporations have maintained some control over certain lands and resources but are expected to use these lands and resources to generate profits in the U.S. economic system. This often conflicts with traditional uses of the land for subsistence-based resource gathering and is often at odds with Native perceptions of how development should proceed. In recent years, the Tlingit and Haida in Alaska have strengthened tribal government by extending jurisdiction (their power to apply law and legislate) over certain legal matters. A tribal court system exists to hear cases and determine punishment. Current efforts include the attempt to increase the power of tribal government and strengthen the control of the clan system. As the influence of the tribes has increased in the educational system, Native language and cultural programs have been instituted in most Tlingit and Haida communities.

In British Columbia, the First Nations entered into treaty negotiations with the province and the federal government of Canada. In 1992, the British Columbia Treaty Commission was established, putting into place a negotiation procedure by which the individual bands could begin the treaty process. This is the culmination of nearly one hundred years of conflict over aboriginal (native) rights in the province. Most bands in British Columbia never entered into treaty negotiations, so this process has been one of the most influential events in their history. Coupled with treaty negotiations is the conflict over natural resources, especially salmon. In 1990, a court ruling clarified that fishing is an aboriginal right protected by the Canadian Constitution. Since that decision, Native peoples of British Columbia have participated in salmon fishery under provisions of the Aboriginal Fisheries Strategy (AFS), a federal action designed to avoid conflict. The AFS is highly controversial and fuels the ongoing debate over what is included in constitutional aboriginal rights in British Columbia.

The Native peoples of Washington and Oregon are embroiled in issues concerning land and resource control, tribal sovereignty, gaming, and cultural resources. As treaty tribes, many of the groups have treaty-assured access to resources, such as salmon; however, the serious decline of many of these resources in recent years has often meant that the right exists, but the resource does not. Tribal groups have attempted to increase the power of tribal government in the decision-making process, but with mixed success. As sovereignty issues emerged, including gaming (running gambling casinos), the tribes found themselves constantly battling to maintain the control they had managed to gain in previous decades. This control often includes land and resources off-reservation as well as on-reservation and tends to center on the religious or subsistence use of public lands, which the bands maintain are protected by treaty or the American Indian Religious Freedom Act, which was signed in 1978 "to protect and preserve for American Indians their inherent right of freedom to believe, express and exercise their traditional religions." These issues promise to command the attention of tribal leaders into the foreseeable future.

BOOKS

Aderkas, Elizabeth, and Christa Hook. *American Indians of the Pacific Northwest.* Oxford: Osprey Publishing, 2005.

Boxberger, Daniel L. *To Fish in Common: The Ethnohistory of Lummi Indian Salmon Fishing.* Lincoln: University of Nebraska Press, 1989.

Boyd, Robert T. *The Coming of the Spirit of Pestilence: Introduced Infectious Diseases and Population Decline among Northwest Coast Indians, 1774–1874.* Seattle: University of Washington Press, 1999.

Braje, Todd J., and Torben C. Rick, eds. *Human Impacts on Seals, Sea Lions, and Sea Otters: Integrating Archaeology and Ecology in the Northeast Pacific.* Berkeley: University of California Press, 2011.

Carlson, Roy L., ed. *Indian Art Traditions of the Pacific Northwest.* Burnaby: Simon Fraser University Press, 1976.

Clark, Ella E. *Indian Legends of the Pacific Northwest.* Berkeley: University of California Press, 2003.

Harmon, Alexandra. *Indians in the Making: Ethnic Relations and Indian Identities around Puget Sound.* Berkeley: University of California Press, 2000.

Glass, Aaron. *Objects of Exchange: Social and Material Transformation on the Late Nineteenth-Century Northwest Coast.* Berkeley: Denver: Bard Center, 2011.

Jonaitis, Aldona, and Aaron Glass. *The Totem Pole: An Intercultural History.* Seattle: University of Washington Press, 2010.

Kuiper, Kathleen. *Indigenous Peoples of the Arctic, Subarctic, and Northwest Coast.* New York: Rosen Educational Services, 2012.

Malin, Edward. *Northwest Coast Indian Painting: House Fronts and Interior Screens.* Portland, OR: Timber Press, 2006.

Mauze, Marie, Michael Harkin, and Sergei Kan, eds. *Coming Ashore: Northwest Coast Ethnology, Past and Present.* Lincoln: University of Nebraska Press, 2004.

Miller, Bruce Granville, ed. *Be of Good Mind: Essays on the Coast Salish.* Vancouver: University of British Columbia Press, 2007.

Moss, Madonna L. *Northwest Coast: Archaeology as Deep History.* Washington, DC: Society for American Archaeology, 2011.

Moss, Madonna L., and Aubrey Cannon, eds. *The Archaeology of North Pacific Fisheries.* Fairbanks: University of Alaska Press, 2011.

Raibmon, Paige. *Authentic Indians: Episodes of Encounter from the Late-Nineteenth-Century Northwest Coast.* Durham, NC: Duke University Press, 2005.

Stewart, Hilary. *Cedar: Tree of Life to the Northwest Coast Indians.* Seattle: University of Washington Press, 1984.

Sonneborn, Liz. *Northwest Coast Indians.* Chicago: Heinemann Library, 2012.

Suttles, Wayne, ed. *Handbook of North American Indians,* Vol. 7: *Northwest Coast.* Washington, DC: Smithsonian Institution, 1990.

Tennant, Paul. *Aboriginal Peoples and Politics: The Indian Land Question in British Columbia, 1849–1989.* Vancouver: University of British Columbia Press, 1990.

Tomalin, Marcus. *And He Knew Our Language: Missionary Linguistics on the Pacific Northwest Coast.* Philadelphia, PA: John Benjamins, 2011.

Youst, Lionel. *She's Tricky Like Coyote: Annie Miner Peterson, an Oregon Coast Indian Woman.* Norman: University of Oklahoma Press, 2005.

PERIODICALS

Adams, John W. "Recent Ethnology of the Northwest Coast." *Annual Review of Anthropology* 10 (1981): 361–92.

WEB SITES

"Aboriginal Fisheries Strategy." *Fisheries and Oceans Canada.* http://www.dfo-mpo.gc.ca/fm-gp/aboriginal-autochtones/afs-srapa-eng.htm (accessed on August 15, 2011).

Alaska Native Collections. "Peoples of Alaska and Northeast Siberia." *Smithsonian Institution.* http://alaska.si.edu/cultures.asp (accessed on August 15, 2011).

Alaska Native Heritage Center. http://www.alaskanative.net/ (accessed on August 15, 2011).

"Alaska Native Language Center." *University of Alaska Fairbanks.* http://www.uaf.edu/anlc/languages/ (accessed on August 15, 2011).

"Alaska's Heritage." *Alaska Humanities Forum.* http://www.akhistorycourse.org/articles/article.php?artID=148 (accessed on August 15, 2011).

"American Indians of the Pacific Northwest Collection." *University of Washington Libraries.* http://content.lib.washington.edu/aipnw/ (accessed on August 15, 2011).

Bill Holm Center. "Pacific Northwest Coast Totem Poles." *Burke Museum of Natural History and Culture.* http://www.burkemuseum.org/static/totempoles/ (accessed on August 15, 2011).

British Columbia Archives. "First Nations Research Guide." *Royal BC Museum Corporation.* http://www.royalbcmuseum.bc.ca/BC_Research_Guide/BC_First_Nations.aspx (accessed on August 15, 2011).

Buerge, David M. "Native Americans of the Pacific Northwest: An Introduction." *University of Washington Libraries.* http://nooksack.lib.washington.edu/aipnw/buerge1.html (accessed on August 15, 2011).

Flora, Stephenie. "Northwest Indians: The First People.'" *Oregon Pioneers.* http://www.oregonpioneers.com/indian.htm (accessed on August 15, 2011).

"Northwest Coastal People." *Canada's First Peoples.* http://firstpeoplesofcanada.com/fp_groups/fp_nwc5.html (accessed on August 15, 2011).

"Pacific Northwest Native Americans." *Social Studies School Service.* http://nativeamericans.mrdonn.org/northwest.html (accessed on August 15, 2011).

Chinook

Name

The name Chinook (pronounced *shi-NOOK*) may have been taken from the Chehalis name *Cinuk* for the people and the village on Baker Bay, Washington. Europeans sometimes called the tribe (and all the people who lived along the lower Columbia River) "Columbians" or "Flatheads" for their practice of flattening the skulls of babies, which they did because they thought it looked more attractive. A sea breeze is sometimes called a "chinook"; the term may have been used by early settlers because winds came from the coast, the direction of the Chinook territory.

Location

The Chinook formerly lived along the shore of the Columbia River in western Washington and Oregon. In modern times, they are divided into three main groups: the Shoalwater Bay Chinook, who live on the Shoalwater Reservation in Pacific County, Washington; the Wahkiakum Chinook, who live on the Quinault Reservation in the southwest corner of Washington's Olympic Peninsula; and the Chinook Indian Tribe, who live in various towns and cities in Oregon and Washington.

Population

In 1825, there were approximately 720 Chinook. By 1840, there were only 280. In the 1990 U.S. Census, 813 people identified themselves as Chinook (32 identified themselves more specifically as Clatsop and 33 as members of other Chinook groups). The 2000 census showed 609 Chinook, and 1,682 people who had some Chinook heritage.

Language family

Penutian.

Origins and group affiliations

The Chinook have lived in their homeland for thousands of years. Historically, they provided a link between the Northwest and Plateau tribes. The Chinook Nation was made up of many groups, including

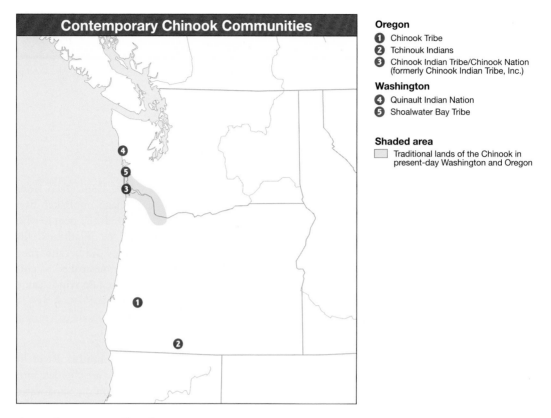

Contemporary Chinook Communities

Oregon
1. Chinook Tribe
2. Tchinouk Indians
3. Chinook Indian Tribe/Chinook Nation
   (formerly Chinook Indian Tribe, Inc.)

Washington
4. Quinault Indian Nation
5. Shoalwater Bay Tribe

Shaded area
☐ Traditional lands of the Chinook in
present-day Washington and Oregon

A map of contemporary Chinook communities. MAP BY XNR PRODUCTIONS. CENGAGE LEARNING, GALE. REPRODUCED BY PERMISSION OF GALE, A PART OF CENGAGE LEARNING.

the Cathlapotle, the Kathlamet, the Clatsop, the Clackamas, the Multnomah, Wasco, Wishram, and the Chinook Tribe proper, also known as the Lower Chinook. In the early twenty-first century, they share reservations with the Chehalis, Quinault, Quileute, Hoh, and Cowlitz tribes.

For thousands of years, the Chinook lived in Washington State along the northern shore of the Columbia River where it flows into the Pacific Ocean. The people carried out extensive trade with other Native tribes and with European explorers who came to the region by sea and later by land. Until around 1900, a special trade language known as the Chinook Jargon was used by over one hundred thousand people throughout the West. For more than one hundred years, the Chinook have been trying to establish a relationship with the U.S. government that would recognize them as a tribe.

HISTORY

Contact with explorers

The first contact the Chinook had with non-Native peoples took place in the 1500s, when European explorers arrived on the Pacific Coast by ship. By the early 1800s, American and European trade ships regularly dropped anchor near Chinook territory to engage in trade. In 1805, American explorers Meriwether Lewis (1774–1809) and William Clark (1770–1838) became the first U.S. explorers to reach Chinook territory by land. By then, the fur trade had become very profitable. In 1811, John Jacob Astor (1763–1848), the wealthy owner of the American Fur Company, constructed on Chinook land a trading post called Fort Astoria. At first, the Chinook resisted this invasion of their territory. Later, they began a productive trade relationship with the "Astorians," as the residents of the fort were called.

Over the next thirty years, many traders and settlers arrived and trespassed on Chinook lands. They brought diseases to which the Natives had little or no resistance. Between 1830 and 1840, nearly two-thirds of the Chinook tribe died of an illness they called the "cold sick," probably a strain of Asian flu. Soon after the tribe struggled with this devastating epidemic, their lands were taken.

In 1851, the Chinook signed the Tansey Point Treaty, which would have assured the tribe of land and water rights in their ancestral territory. The U.S. Senate, however, failed to approve the treaty. The tribe refused another treaty that would have forced them to share a reservation in central Washington with the Quinault Indians, their traditional enemies. With their options dwindling and their land being taken over, most Chinook ended up living with other tribes on the Warm Springs, Yakama, Chehalis, Quinault, and Grand Ronde reservations in Washington and Oregon.

Important Dates

1792: Robert Gray and John Boit—and, later, George Vancouver—are the first to mention the Chinook.

1805: Explorers Meriwether Lewis and William Clark are the first American explorers to reach Chinook territory by land; they establish a trading relationship with the tribe.

1811: Fort Astoria is built in Chinook territory.

1851: The Lower Chinook sign a treaty that is never ratified by the U.S. Senate. The tribe therefore loses its chance for federal recognition and its ability to collect money for lands wrongfully taken.

1897: The Chinook become one of the first tribes to bring a successful land claims lawsuit against the United States. They receive partial compensation for their claims in 1913.

1973: The U.S. government pays the tribes on Quinault Reservation more than $2 million for their loss of land in the 1800s.

1979: The Chinook Heritage Program is launched to help establish legal status of tribe.

2001: The Chinook petition for federal recognition is accepted.

2002: The Chinook's federal recognition status is revoked.

Legal battles

Around 1900, the Chinook undertook the first of what would become a long series of legal battles with state and federal governments seeking payment for their lost lands. The tribe became one of the first to gain the right to bring a land claims lawsuit against the United States. After a lengthy court battle, the Chinook received a token (insignificant) settlement of $20,000 for 213,815 acres of their homeland in 1913.

Later that year, the tribe began fighting to secure allotments on an expanded Quinault Reservation that had been set aside for "fish-eating Indians." Allotments were privately owned parcels (pieces) of land into which the federal government divided the reservations. During their struggle to attain allotments, the Chinook helped found an organization that involved many tribes called the Northwest Federation of American Indians.

Shoalwater Chinook gain recognition

The payments the Chinook received in legal settlements from the federal government during the twentieth century were a very small part of what they had requested to make up for the more than three-quarters of a million acres of land they had lost. The Chinook people were finally granted allotments on the Quinault Reservation in 1932. The remaining Chinook lived with other Native groups or on their own in small towns and cities.

Only one of the three major groups of Chinook has gained recognition by the federal government. Without federal recognition, a tribe does not exist as far as the government is concerned, and it is not entitled to financial or other help. The Chinook who share the Shoalwater Bay Reservation with Chehalis and Quinault people were federally recognized in 1979.

Recognition efforts continue

The Wahkiakum Chinook, who live on the Quinault Reservation, have not won recognition. They did, however, win a case against the U.S. government in 1974 that gave them the right to use their ancestors' fishing areas. It also entitled them to one-half of the fish caught by Natives and non-Natives at those sites.

The third group, which incorporated as the Chinook Indian Tribe, was recognized by the state of Washington in 1955. The federal government still refuses to acknowledge them as a nation. This is largely because of complications regarding their treaties that occurred in the last century.

The Chinook Indian Tribe, Inc., entered the Federal Acknowledgment Program in 1978 in an effort to attain recognition from the U.S. government. Tribal elders launched the Chinook Heritage Project in 1979 to collect historical and cultural data on the tribe to restore some of its traditions and establish its legal status as a tribe. In 2001, the tribe received federal acknowledgment, but this was withdrawn in 2002 when the government disallowed some of the documentation supporting its claim. This lack of recognition prevents the tribe, which has since changed its name to the Chinook Indian Tribe/Chinook Nation, from settling land claims, having fishing and gambling rights, or receiving money from the U.S. government.

RELIGION

The Chinook were a religious people who believed in spiritual forces that guided individuals through life. Some guardian spirits took the form of animals, whereas others came as invisible spirits that entered a human being's soul. At about age ten, a Chinook youngster was sent on a vision quest to meet his or her guardian spirit (see "Vision quest").

The Chinook believed that all objects contained powers. Christian missionaries tried to change the Chinook custom of worshiping sculptures and wooden objects. Both Catholic and Methodist missionaries eventually gave up their efforts to convert the Chinook.

Around 1900, many Chinook adopted the Indian Shaker religion, based on a combination of traditional Native and Christian beliefs. Its followers are called "Shakers" because, when they experience the power of God, they shake, groan, and cry. Many Shaker beliefs fit well with Native traditions, so the religion was readily accepted. The Indian Shaker religion emphasized that people did not need Bibles or written materials; they could communicate directly with the creator. Dancing and physical movement were important religious practices. In modern times, some members of the tribe continue to participate in the Shaker religion.

LANGUAGE

Use of the Chinook language declined around the mid-1800s after many tribe members died of fatal diseases. The remaining members mixed with other tribes on reservations and adopted their languages.

Chinook Jargon

The Chinook language formed the basis for the special trade language known as the Chinook Jargon or the Oregon Trade Language. The language was widely used by traders during the eighteenth and nineteenth centuries. It began as a mixture of Native languages spoken by tribes of the Northwest who gathered to trade with the Chinook near the Columbia River. Later, when the Chinook began large-scale trading with Europeans, the Chinook Jargon incorporated words from many other languages, including Japanese and Russian. Chinook Jargon became known and used throughout the Northwest from Alaska to California. In the early 1900s, English replaced the language. Some Chinook still speak it today, but they call it *Wawa*.

Some examples of Chinook Jargon are *hootch*, meaning "homemade liquor"; *tzum SAM-mon*, meaning "spotted salmon"; *PAHT-lum man*, meaning "drunkard"; *BOS-ton il-LA-hee*, meaning "United States"; and *TUP-so KO-pa la-ta-TAY*, meaning "hair." Some additional words are below:

illahee	"land"
cloish tillicum	"good friend"
chickamin	"money"
canim	"canoe"
chodups	"flea"
łixw	"three"

In the 1890s, Franz Boas (1858–1942), a pioneering anthropologist (someone who studies ancient cultures), discovered two Chinook speakers living on Washington's Wilapa Bay. He recorded their accounts of Chinook legends, customs, and the authentic language. By 1900, the last fluent speakers of the language had died. In the early twenty-first century, Chinook people were working with the information collected by Boas and others to reconstruct their ancestral language.

GOVERNMENT

Chiefs of Chinook villages were members of the tribe's highest social class, and the position of chief passed from father to son. If a village did not think a chief's son was worthy of his position, they did not accept him and instead took their problems to a male relative of his that they trusted. Chiefs took control of the game that hunters and fishermen brought back to the village and distributed it as they liked. Chiefs could also sell orphans into slavery. For the most part, though, a chief's job was mainly advisory; he often helped to settled disputes. For difficult cases, the chief might call together a group of elders to give him advice.

In 1925, the tribe formed a business council to secure land allotments and protect fishing rights, electing William Garretson as the first council president. As of 2011, the Chinook Tribal Office in Chinook, Washington, was the site of the tribal government.

ECONOMY

In the early years, fish were so plentiful and easily caught that gathering food took little time or effort. The tribe had more than enough for their needs and to share, so the Chinook economy revolved around trade. They traded excess fish (especially salmon) to other Native nations, some from as far away as the Rocky Mountains and Alaska. The people also scraped, stretched, and smoked skins of sea otter, beaver, elk, deer, and bear to make handsome hides. They bartered these hides, excess food, basket hats woven from cedar bark and spruce root, and other handmade objects. The Chinook also specialized in blubber and canoes. Both men and women acted as traders.

Items the Chinook obtained from the Europeans, such as iron and copper goods, teapots, swords, tobacco, pots, pans, cloth, blankets, and buckets, were packed into canoes. Chinook traders then sailed as far away as 200 miles (300 kilometers) to exchange these items with other tribes, usually for furs they could trade back to the Europeans. Over time, the number of fur-bearing animals drastically declined because of overhunting. Other items the Chinook traded included a shell called *dentalium* used as money, cedar boards and bark, animal horns, copper, baskets, and slaves.

In modern times, many Chinook make their living by fishing in the Columbia River and on the Pacific Ocean. Some make yearly trips to Alaska to fish or work in canneries there. For many years, the timber industry also supplied jobs on the Quinault Reservation, but because the allotment policy (see "History") divided the land into small plots and sold many of them to non-Natives, it became difficult for the people to maintain their timber reserves. Tribal government employs a large number of people, and tourism and casinos provide jobs and much needed income for the tribe. In spite of these and other available opportunities in fisheries and service businesses, many people cannot obtain employment and must leave the reservation to find work.

A Chinook mother holds a baby contained between boards to flatten its head, circa 1830. © MARY EVANS PICTURE LIBRARY/THE IMAGE WORKS. REPRODUCED BY PERMISSION.

DAILY LIFE

Families

Chinook children received a great deal of attention from their parents and grandparents, and they respected their elders for their wisdom. Once children learned to walk, their mothers no longer carried them about.

National Park Service personnel dig for artifacts after an apparent discovery of a Chinook Indian plank house near the town of Chinook, Washington. © AP IMAGES/THE DAILY NEWS, ROGER WERTH.

Boys spent a lot of time swimming. Men did the fishing and hunting, and women took care of the children, sewed, wove baskets, gathered food, and made blankets. According to the accounts of Lewis and Clark, the women were "treated very badly"—they were bought, traded, or won by gambling; their husbands then put them to work so the men could purchase more wives.

Buildings

The Chinook usually lived in large, rectangular houses with cedar plank walls and steeply sloped roofs thatched with cedar bark. The houses stood about 8 feet (2.4 meters) high and were 20 to 60 feet (6 to 18 meters) long and 14 to 20 feet (4 to 6 meters) wide. Each house might shelter up to ten families. A Chinook village was usually made up of a long row of up to thirty houses.

The inside of each house featured an open living area with a fire in the center, surrounded by small rooms where the different families slept. The entrance and inner walls were decorated with colorful paintings. The floor of hard-packed earth was covered with woven mats, and beds were woven out of cedar bark or rushes.

When they left the village to hunt or trade, the Chinook sometimes built temporary mat shelters to protect themselves from the rain. They also set up these mat shelters near fishing areas in summer villages. The people constructed their temporary homes from two forked poles, which held up the roof pole, then covered this with matting. Sheds with cedar bark roofs stood nearby for drying fish. In very cold weather, some Chinook people built underground rooms to stay warm.

Clothing and adornment

Early Chinook wore little to no clothing. When they did, both men and women used only a small apron. After the Europeans arrived, they began wearing more clothes. Men put on low-hanging collars of porcupine quills on deerskin. Later, these covered their shirts. Women also wore collars; over the years, these eventually became longer until they reached the knees.

Because of the constant dampness, the Chinook did not wear leather, which would soon be ruined. Instead, they used plant material. Men wore mat robes and wide-brimmed hats made of bear grass or cedar bark. Women donned knee-length, fringed dresses made of silk grass or cedar bark.

In the winter, they covered themselves with fur blankets and robes made from the skins of dogs, muskrats, wood rats, sea otters, beavers, raccoons, rabbits, or mountain sheep. Women sometimes twisted strips of fur together with feathers to make winter dresses. Body armor made of layered elk skin, called *clamons,* was a popular clothing item the Chinook received in trade.

Both men and women had tattoos and ear and nose rings made of teeth, beads, or copper. Some put bones through their nose holes. Nose decorations distinguished the wealthy from the slaves. The Chinook also covered their hair and skin with fish oil. A chief adorned his hair with strips of deerskin decorated with dentalium shells and placed two eagle feathers in his hair.

Food

Using dugout canoes up to 50 feet (15 meters) long, the Chinook caught fish and sea mammals near the mouth of the Columbia River. In the early spring, they used long, curved blades to rake thousands of tiny smelt into their boats. Later in the year, they probed the river bottom with sharp poles and caught sturgeon weighing hundreds of pounds. The highlight of the fishing season came in late spring, when the Chinook salmon made its yearly spawning run up the Columbia.

The Chinook viewed salmon as sacred, and the people offered the year's first several salmon to the gods during special ceremonies. They caught many fish using nets and hooks, and they dried the meat for later use or for trade. Men used harpoons to hunt the sea lions and hair seals that sunned themselves near the mouth of the Columbia. The tribe also collected clams and oysters and ate the occasional whale that washed up on shore. They used bows and arrows to hunt deer and elk.

Women gathered edible plants and fruits. Some of the plants that were abundant in the area were salmonberries, cranberries, currants, crab apples, cow parsnips, wild celery, cattails, skunk cabbage, and various roots.

Education

Children in Chinook families were taught the value of hard work. Girls helped their mothers gather food, water, and wood and learned to make baskets and weave mats out of cattails. They also learned how to dry fish on racks or hang them from the rafters to smoke. Boys were taught to hunt, fish, and build houses. They learned the arts of tool making, canoe building, and making nets for fishing.

Healing practices

The two types of Chinook shamans (medicine men; pronounced *SHAH-munz* or *SHAY-munz*) were highly respected, and sometimes feared, by the people. Doctors called *keelalles* provided medical aid. *Etaminuas* helped the souls of dying people travel safely to the land of the spirits. Children learned during their vision quests if they were destined to be healers. The chosen few trained for about five years and then began to practice on their own.

Healers often used "power sticks" smeared with grease and decorated with feathers and paint to rid people of evil spirits that were making them sick. Healers might spend several days chanting and beating the sticks on special diamond-shaped boards or on the frames of houses. Sometimes they discovered an object in a patient's body, such as a piece of wood or a stone that represented the evil spirit. These objects were destroyed in a special ceremony.

ARTS

The Chinook carved bowls and utensils from wood and animal horn. They decorated everyday items with designs of parallel lines made in wavelike or sawtooth patterns. Women created baskets from vegetation such as roots, bark, or rushes. They twined and bent several spruce root ropes into a shape, then wove in more ropes horizontally to create the sides of the basket. Designs might be animal shapes or geometric patterns. Men and women carved and painted crests (family symbols) on everyday objects, such as sticks, dance rattles, and boards.

Oral literature

Children were told to listen carefully when elders related stories about the ancient days of the tribe. Sometimes the children were asked to repeat a story exactly as it was told; no mistakes were permitted. This system ensured that the stories of Chinook life, which did not exist in written form, would be preserved accurately.

CUSTOMS

Social classes

Chinook society was divided into three social classes: the upper class, commoners, and slaves. The small upper class included chiefs and their families, warriors, leading shamans, and traders. Although the majority, the commoners, could become wealthy by working, they rarely rose above the class into which they were born. Sometimes, however, an outstanding person, such as a great healer, was permitted to join the upper class.

Slaves were usually women and children, and they worked at cooking, canoeing, gathering food, and cutting wood. They sometimes helped the men with hunting and fishing. Upper-class Chinook purchased slaves from neighboring tribes, and they seized others in raids on their enemies.

Coyote in the Cedar Tree

Many Chinook stories centered on Coyote, who often played the role of trickster. A trickster is an animal figure that appears in stories to teach lessons by presenting the problems that humans live with. Trickster stories show reality, making it clear that the world is not perfect. They also bring out the conflicting forces at work in the world: day and night, male and female, up and down, sky and earth.

Once Coyote was traveling from the country of the Tillamooks to the country of the Clatsops. Coyote passed the mountains and the headlands of the coast. Then he followed the trail through the deep woods. As he was traveling along Coyote saw an immense cedar. The inside was hollow. He could see it through a big gap which opened and closed as the tree swayed in the wind. Coyote cried, "Open, Cedar Tree!" Then the tree opened. Coyote jumped inside. He said, "Close, Cedar Tree!" Then the tree closed. Coyote was shut inside the tree.

After a while Coyote said, "Open, Cedar Tree!" Nothing happened. Once more Coyote said, "Open, Cedar Tree!" Again nothing happened. Coyote was angry. He called to the tree, he kicked it. Then Coyote remembered that he was Coyote, the wisest and most cunning of all animals. He began to think.

After he had thought, Coyote called the birds to help him. He told them to peck a hole through the Cedar Tree. The first to try was Wren. Wren pecked and pecked at the Cedar Tree until her bill was blunted. But Wren could not even make a dent. [Here, Coyote calls other birds, but they cannot help, either. Finally the big Yellow Woodpecker makes a hole, but it is not big enough for Coyote to escape.]

Coyote began to think hard. After he had thought, Coyote began to take

Slaves could buy their freedom; some were only enslaved for a given number of years. Slaves were usually treated well; they lived in the house with their owners and ate the same food as the rest of the household, but in a separate place. Ordinary households may have had two or three slaves, whereas wealthy ones might have had as many as ten.

Head flattening

The Chinook flattened the heads of their children, but usually only upper-class Chinook did so. Flattened heads were considered beautiful. An infant was placed in a cradle, and a padded board was tied to its himself apart. He took himself all apart and slipped each piece through Yellowhammer's hole. First he slipped a leg through, then a paw, then his tail, then his ears, and his eyes, until he was all through the hole, and outside the Cedar Tree. Then Coyote began to put himself back together. He put his legs and paws together, then his tail, his nose, his ears, and then his body. At last Coyote had himself all together except for his eyes. He could not find his eyes. Raven had seen them on the ground and had stolen them. Coyote was blind.

But Coyote did not want the animals to know he was blind. He smelled a wild rose. He found the bush and picked two leaves. He put the rose leaves in place of his eyes. Then Coyote traveled on, feeling his way along the trail. Soon he met a squaw. The squaw began to jeer, "Oh ho, oh ho, you seem to be very blind!"

"Oh no," said Coyote. "I am measuring the ground. I can see better than you can. I can see tamanawus [spirit] rays."

The squaw was greatly ashamed. Coyote pretended to see wonderful things at a great distance.

The squaw said, "I wish I could see tamanawus rays!"

Coyote said, "Change eyes with me. Then you can see everything."

So Coyote and the squaw traded eyes. Coyote took the squaw's eyes and gave her the rose leaves. Then Coyote could see as well as ever. The squaw could see nothing. Coyote said, "For your foolishness you must always be a snail. You must creep. You must feel your way on the ground."

SOURCE: Ramsey, Jarold. *Coyote Was Going There: Indian Literature in Oregon Country.* Seattle: University of Washington Press, 1977.

---

forehead to mold the head into the desired shape. The Chinook were skilled in this practice, and their children did not suffer any brain damage or health risks as a result.

Vision quest

At about age ten, Chinook boys set out on a "vision quest" to find the guardian spirit who would help them get through life successfully. Taking along a special stick, a Chinook boy traveled alone to a sacred place several miles from the village. He would place the stick in the ground and fast for up to five days until his guardian spirit appeared in a vision. The guardian spirit, often in the form of an animal, told the boy what role he was expected to play as an adult member of the tribe. Sometimes the spirit taught the child a special dance or song that could be used to summon the spirit in the future. If a boy did poorly in his assigned task or career, it indicated that he had not been brave when his spirit first visited him.

War and hunting rituals

Although war was not an important aspect of Chinook life, the people occasionally used violence to respond to insults or injuries from other tribes. One description of a Chinook war dance tells of excited men shouting war threats and firing their rifles in the air. The Chinook men, wearing red, yellow, and black paint, danced in a circle, yelling loudly every two or three minutes. Those with knives swiped at the air. Battles rarely resulted in any widespread loss of life. Fighting sometimes began at an agreed-upon time and continued only until the first person was killed. The conflict was declared over as quickly as it had begun.

Courtship and marriage

Families of a Chinook bride and groom exchanged gifts. Upper-class families traded beads, axes, cloth, knives, and kettles. The exchange was followed by a festive meal. If the family could afford it, they repeated the exchanges and meals as many as five times. Each time, the gifts had to be more expensive than the time before. At the final feast, the couple decided where they would live. If they stayed with the bride's family, the husband provided fuel. If they lived at his house, the bride cleaned and fetched water.

Wealthy men sometimes had more than one wife; some had as many as eight. Some Chinook encouraged their daughters to marry important men, either Native or non-Native, so the family could benefit from the husband's trading businesses.

A woman suspected of adultery was whipped or tied near a fire until she confessed. The man involved was killed, often by a hired assassin; if the man was wealthy, he paid a price to the woman's father-in-law.

Funerals

The night after a death, everyone gathered at the house. Two men sat at the head and feet of the body. These men had special powers for communicating with the dead. The other relatives and friends sang and danced on the opposite side of the room, using the deceased's special medicine songs. Meanwhile, the men near the body listened to find out how the dead person wanted to be dressed. Near the end of the night, they prepared the body and painted the face yellow while the crowd sang the proper songs for that ritual.

Both men and women had objects that were special to them, and these items were buried with them. Many times the wealthy also buried a slave with the deceased. Sometimes they placed a body in a canoe and suspended it from a tree. Cremation and underground burial in wooden boxes became common after disease epidemics killed many Chinook.

CURRENT TRIBAL ISSUES

In the early twenty-first century, members of the Chinook Indian Tribe continue their efforts to gain recognition from the federal government. They have problems with recognition because the treaty signed by their people in 1851 never became legal and because they refused to sign a later treaty proposal. The tribe's petition for federal recognition was placed on active review status in 1993. In 2001, the tribe received federal recognition, but it was withdrawn the following year. In 2008, a bill called the Chinook Nation Restoration Act was presented to Congress. Although it passed the House, it ended up tabled in 2011.

A 2005 excavation for highway improvements in the state of Washington uncovered remains that were later identified as Chinookan. The tribe guarded and protected the site while the bones were unearthed and saw that they were treated in accordance with proper Chinook practices. According to recent laws, all remains must be turned over to the tribes, who are responsible for their burial. The site where the bones were discovered was a Chinook settlement known as Middle Village, a place where the Lewis and Clark expedition camped for ten days before crossing the Columbia River to establish Fort Clatsop.

Other archaeological sites have also been discovered. A site on Bachelor Island contains the remains of a Chinook village more than 2,300 years old. Another, a large settlement called Cathlapotle, once held fourteen plank houses, some of them more than 200 feet (60 meters) long. Homes that large had sleeping space for as many as sixty-five people. Studying these sites will give researchers more information about early Chinook life.

Another part of Chinook history was restored in the twenty-first century. In 1806, the Chinook had assisted the members of the Lewis and Clark expedition. Even though the Chinook kept the party alive all winter, the explorers stole a canoe from the tribe when they continued on their voyage in the spring. This was an insult to the Chinook people, who considered their boats sacred. Descendants of the explorers paid for a replica of the stolen canoe and presented it to the Chinook in a ceremony in 2011. They hoped to make amends for this wrong from two centuries ago.

NOTABLE PEOPLE

Chief Comcomly (c. 1765–c. 1835) was a powerful Chinook leader who dominated trade along the Columbia River during the early nineteenth century. Euro-American traders held him in high regard, and Comcomly received a peace medal and an American flag from explorers Lewis and Clark in 1805. After Comcomly's death during the flu epidemic in 1835, a doctor named Meredith Gairdner robbed his grave. He removed Comcomly's head and sent it to England for scientific study. After more than a century of protests by the Chinook, the head was returned to the Chinook people and reburied in 1972.

BOOKS

Boas, Franz. *Chinook Texts.* Washington, DC: U.S. Bureau of American Ethnology, Bulletin no. 20, 1894. Available online from http://www.sacred-texts.com/nam/nw/chinook/index.htm (accessed on November 2, 2011).

Boas, Franz. *Folk-tales of Salishan and Sahaptin Tribes.* Reprint. Aurora, CO: Biblographical Center for Research, 1988.

Brown, John A., and Robert H. Ruby. *The Chinook Indians: Traders of the Lower Columbia River.* Norman: University of Oklahoma Press, 1988.

Brown, John A., and Robert H. Ruby. *John Slocum and the Indian Shaker Church.* Norman: University of Oklahoma Press, 1996.

Brown, Tricia. *Children of the Midnight Sun: Young Native Voices of Alaska.* Anchorage: Alaska Northwest Books, 2006.

Gibbs, George. *Dictionary of the Chinook Jargon, or Trade Language of Oregon.* New York: Dodo Press, 2007.

Holton, Jim. *Chinook Jargon: The Hidden Language of the Pacific Northwest.* San Leandro, CA: Wawa Press, 2004.

Huntington, Karen. *Jennie Michel: A Woman of the Clatsop Tribe of the Chinook Nation.* Pomeroy, WA: Sweeney Gulch Press, 2003.

Lang, George. *Making Wawa: the Genesis of Chinook Jargon.* Vancouver: UBC Press, 2008.

Ruby, Robert H., John A. Brown, and Cary C. Collins. *A Guide to the Indian Tribes of the Pacific Northwest.* Norman: University of Oklahoma Press, 2010.

Ryan, Marla Felkins, and Linda Schmittroth. *Tribes of Native America: Chinook.* San Diego, CA: Blackbirch Press, 2004.

PERIODICALS

Duara, Nigel. "Descendants Make Amends to Chinook for Lewis and Clark Canoe Theft." *Missourian,* September 23, 2011. Available online from http://www.columbiamissourian.com/stories/2011/09/23/descendants-make-amends-chinook-lewis-clark-canoe-theft/ (accessed on November 2, 2011).

WEB SITES

Chinook Indian Tribe/Chinook Nation. http://www.chinooknation.org/ (accessed on November 2, 2011).

"Chinookan Family History." *Access Genealogy.* http://www.accessgenealogy.com/native/tribes/chinook/chinookanfamilyhist.htm (accessed on November 2, 2011).

"Lewis & Clark: Chinook Indians." *National Geographic.* http://www.nationalgeographic.com/lewisandclark/record_tribes_083_14_3.html (accessed on November 2, 2011).

"Lewis and Clark: Native Americans: Chinook Indians." *PBS.* http://www.pbs.org/lewisandclark/native/chi.html (accessed on November 2, 2011).

"Lower Chinook and Clatsop: Language." *TrailTribes.org.* http://www.trailtribes.org/fortclatsop/language.htm (accessed on November 2, 2011).

Redish, Laura, and Orrin Lewis. "Chinook Indian Fact Sheet." *Native Languages of the Americas.* http://www.bigorrin.org/chinook_kids.htm (accessed on November 2, 2011).

Sanders, Angela. "Chinook Nation." *The University of Portland.* http://www.up.edu/portlandmag/2005_winter/chinook/chinook_01.html (accessed on November 2, 2011).

Duwamish

Name

The name Duwamish (pronounced *dew-AH-mish*) means "inside people," referring to Native peoples living inside "the bay," or the Puget Sound (*PYEW-jit*), an arm of the Pacific Ocean that stretches up through western Washington State. The Duwamish tribe is composed of two groups. The "People of the Inside" (*Dxʷ'Dəw?Abš;* pronounced *doo-AHBSH*) lived around Elliott Bay, and the "People of the Large Lake" (*Xacuabš;* pronounced *hah-choo-AHBSH*) lived around Lake Washington. In modern times, the people call themselves *Dkhʷ'Duw'Absh.*

Location

Formerly, the Duwamish lived in the Puget Sound area of Washington State, on the Black and Cedar Rivers and at the outlet of the Duwamish River at Lake Washington. They had at least seventeen villages in the area now known as Seattle. In modern times, the Duwamish people are scattered throughout the Puget Sound area.

Population

In 1780, about 1,200 Duwamish people were known to exist; by 1856, that number was down to 378. In the 1990 U.S. Census, only 215 people identified themselves as Duwamish. The Duwamish Tribe recorded about 400 enrolled members in 1991 and about 500 in 2004. In 2007, tribal sources indicated approximately 600 enrolled members. Tribal enrollment in 2011 was 572.

Language family
Salishan.

Origins and group affiliations

The Duwamish were one of about three dozen groups called the Coast Salish who lived in western Washington State, in southwest British Columbia, Canada, and on the southeastern side of Vancouver Island, Canada. Their main ally was the Suquamish (or Squamish) tribe.

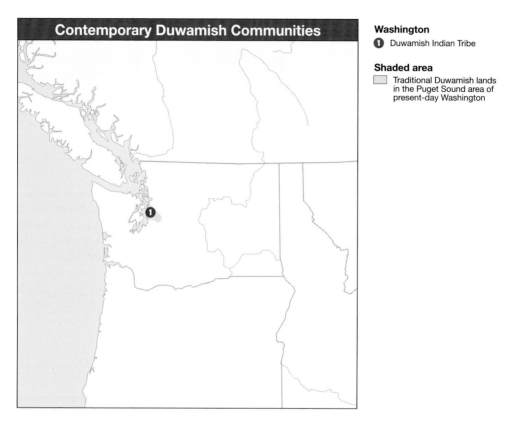

Contemporary Duwamish Communities

Washington
❶ Duwamish Indian Tribe

Shaded area
◻ Traditional Duwamish lands in the Puget Sound area of present-day Washington

A map of contemporary Duwamish communities. MAP BY XNR PRODUCTIONS. CENGAGE LEARNING, GALE. REPRODUCED BY PERMISSION OF GALE, A PART OF CENGAGE LEARNING.

The Duwamish lived in villages on the east side of the Puget Sound near present-day Seattle. The great Chief Seattle, for whom the Washington city is named, was born to a Duwamish mother. The tribe's history after contact with Europeans is a sad one: the people separated, lost all their lands, and dwindled in number, becoming nearly extinct. By the end of the twentieth century, though, the Duwamish people had started to reclaim and preserve their traditional tribal culture and to enhance their economic development.

HISTORY

Prehistory

The traditional Duwamish homelands have been inhabited since around 8,000 BCE. Sites that are at least four thousand years old have been found at what is now Discovery Park, Washington. The remnants of villages found around the area of the Duwamish River that date back to the sixth century indicate that the tribe lived in the area for hundreds of years before Europeans arrived.

Early European contact

The Duwamish and other Native nations of the Puget Sound first met Europeans in 1792 when British explorer George Vancouver (1757–1798) entered the area. Europeans had little contact with the Native people in the area for the next thirty years, because they were primarily interested in trade, and the Puget Sound region had few of the sea otter furs they sought.

At the time of European contact, the Duwamish were involved in ongoing wars with the Suquamish tribe under Chief Schweabe. Schweabe had a son with a Duwamish woman. This child grew up to be the famed Chief Seattle (*si'ábSi'ahl* in Duwamish; c. 1786–1866). Seattle negotiated peace among the Duwamish, the Suquamish, and other Salish-speaking tribes, but he continued warring with other tribes.

Important Dates

1792: Explorer George Vancouver enters Puget Sound.

1855: Chief Seattle signs Point Elliott Treaty exchanging Duwamish lands for reservation parcels.

1855–56: Some Duwamish fight in Indian Wars.

1925: The Duwamish form a government and create a constitution.

1996: Duwamish tribe is denied federal recognition.

2001: U.S. government recognizes Duwamish tribe.

2002: Duwamish tribe loses federal recognition, ruling is reversed by new administration, citing procedural errors.

Giving up lands

By the mid-1800s, Isaac Ingalls Stevens (1818–1862) had become the governor of Washington Territory (it was not yet a state) and superintendent of Indian Affairs in the region. He considered the Native tribes an "impediment to civilization"—an obstacle to the spread of U.S. power throughout the New World. Stevens believed strongly in Manifest Destiny, a popular theory of the 1840s that held that the United States was meant to dominate the entire Western Hemisphere. Beginning in 1854, Stevens attempted to establish treaties with nearly every tribe in the region, hoping to take over as much land as possible for settlers. His goal was to place the tribes on reservations (pieces of land set aside for the Native nations) and convince the Native peoples to assimilate, or adopt the mainstream American way of life.

In 1849, the California gold rush filled the Pacific Northwest with settlers seeking the natural wealth of the area. Seattle was then the principal

Chief Seattle of the united Suquamish and Duwamish nations urged friendship and cooperation with white settlers. LIBRARY OF CONGRESS.

chief of the united Suquamish and Duwamish nations. A religious man who had converted to Catholicism, Seattle encouraged friendship and open trade with U.S. settlers. He agreed to sign the Point Elliott Treaty in 1855. According to the terms of the treaty, the Duwamish gave up their lands in exchange for seven small reservation parcels throughout the area. No reservation lands belonged to the Duwamish alone; other tribes inhabited the lands with them.

Settlers poured in and took over Native American lands. Chief Seattle tried to maintain friendly relations with the newcomers, and when they founded a city on the site of a Duwamish winter village, the grateful settlers named the town Seattle. Other tribes, however, felt the treaty had not been honored, and several of them banded together to attack the new settlement. The loss of their lands and resources also fueled the Indian War of 1855–58. Despite this, Chief Seattle insisted on honoring the treaty and worked for peace between the Native peoples and the new settlers. In accordance with the treaty he had signed, he and his people moved to the Port Madison Reservation across the Puget Sound from the city of Seattle.

A people divided

The Duwamish at Port Madison soon found themselves in conflict with the Suquamish who lived there. Many Duwamish families left and wandered around the area. The federal government pressured some to move to a reservation they had established for the Muckleshoot tribe. By the winter of 1857, most Duwamish had returned to living in two communities on their original homelands along the Duwamish River. After settlers in Seattle burned down their homes, the displaced Duwamish moved to Ballast Island.

Ballast Island had been used as a dumping ground for ships preparing to take on cargo. The oceangoing vessels unloaded heavy boulders and other ballast there before they took on loads of goods for the return trip. By 1885, many displaced Duwamish had set up cattail shelters (later replaced by canvas tents) on the island. They lived among the refuse without a fresh water supply to avoid staying on reservations with their traditional enemies. This location also enabled them to stay close to their former villages and ancestral burial grounds. Soon, though, the island became valuable to the surrounding U.S. community, and the tribe was forced to move once again. By the early 1900s, most Duwamish had moved to the growing town of Seattle.

Modern tribal history

In 1910, the only remaining Duwamish village was at Foster, south of Seattle. By the 1920s, the Duwamish had surrendered all their land. The people scattered throughout western Washington, losing much of their sense of unity as a group. In 1925, some of the surviving Duwamish people reunited. They formed a government and wrote a constitution, hoping the U.S. government would grant them recognition. Federal recognition would make the tribe eligible for government funds and programs. In 1996, their request for recognition was turned down.

Beginning in 1926, the tribe took legal action, seeking money from the U.S. government for lands taken from them. Nearly four decades later, in 1962, it was awarded a payment of $62,000, only $1.35 per acre. In 1974, the Duwamish joined other tribes in seeking 50 percent of the annual salmon harvest in their region. Although other tribes were granted this right, the Duwamish were excluded because they had not received federal recognition. At the start of the twenty-first century, the Duwamish people remained scattered throughout the Puget Sound area. They owned no tribal lands. Some, however, lived as registered members on the reservations of other tribes so they could receive services and health benefits from the U.S. Bureau of Indian Affairs.

Led since 1975 by one of Chief Seattle's descendants, Cecile Hansen, the Duwamish have attempted to gain federal recognition and to regain some of the land they lost. In 1977, they filed the necessary paperwork, but the Bureau of Indian Affairs denied their request in the mid-1980s because the tribe had no land; the decision stated that without land, they could not be considered a tribe.

In 1983, the tribe established a nonprofit group, Duwamish Tribal Services, to preserve its culture and provide for the educational, health, and social needs of the tribe. Without federal recognition, the tribe receives no benefits from the U.S. government, so the non-profit has been striving to meet those needs. The Duwamish continued to fight for their rights, and in 2001, they received federal recognition. The victory was short-lived, however, as that decision was overturned in 2002, when a new presidential administration took over and declared the previous ruling void. The Duwamish have not given up hope and continue to petition the government for federal recognition.

To help its people in the meantime, the tribe created the Duwamish Management Corporation in 2004. This for-profit organization has been working to create businesses whose profits will fund the tribe's many cultural and social programs. One of these programs is put on by *T'ilibshudub*, which means "Singing Feet." This cultural heritage group teaches traditional oratory, dancing, singing, and ceremonial practices to the tribe and also presents programs for the outside community. By teaching their language and traditional practices, the Duwamish are not only supporting tribal artists, musicians, and elders of the tribe, but they are keeping their culture strong and passing it on to the younger generations.

RELIGION

The tribes of the Puget Sound believed that beings with both human and animal qualities existed long ago. One such figure, called the Transformer, came into the world and defeated the dangerous creatures there. These creatures included the soul-stealing earth dwarves, the food-stealing forest giants, and the wife-stealing underwater people. The Transformer, *Duk'wibael,* then taught the people the right way to live and helped them establish their customs. Like other Puget Sound tribes, the Duwamish believed in a land of the dead and in the possibility of the dead being reborn.

Salmon held a place of importance in the lives of the people. Not only were salmon one of the tribe's main sources of nourishment, but they also held religious significance. Most of the Salish people believed that salmon were once people and that they willing gave up their lives to become food for the tribe. To honor this sacrifice, the Duwamish held a ceremony of welcome and thanks when they caught the first fish each year.

In the early 1800s, some Duwamish, including Chief Seattle, converted to the Catholic religion, although many people still retained their Native beliefs. Seattle had been converted by French missionaries and baptized as "Noah." With his new faith, he started morning and evening church services among Native peoples that continued even after his death.

One of the traditional beliefs of the Duwamish was that speaking the name of a dead person would disturb its spirit. For this reason, when Chief Seattle agreed to give his name to the city of Seattle, he asked for a small payment to make up for the trouble his spirit would experience each time his name was mentioned.

In the early 1900s, great numbers of Duwamish converted to the Indian Shaker Church, which combined elements of both Christianity and tribal religions (see Chinook entry).

LANGUAGE

The Duwamish spoke the Southern Lushootseed dialect of the Coast Salish language family. Many other tribes in the area also spoke this dialect, including the Nisqually, Puyallup (see entries), and Suquamish. Although only a few people were fluent in the Duwamish language in recent years, the tribe has been working to revitalize the language. A cultural heritage group is teaching Duwamish culture and language to the community (see "History").

Lushootseed Salish Words

The Duwamish spoke a dialect (variety) of Lushootseed Salish, also called Whulshootseed or Puget Sound Salish. Here are a few Lushootseed words; for others see Nisqually and Puyallup entries.

dəč'u'	"one"
sáli'	"two"
łixw	"three"
búus	"four"
cɔlác	"five"
słádəy'	"woman"
stubš	"man"
alqwu'	"water"
słukwálb	"moon"
łúkwał	"sun"

GOVERNMENT

The Duwamish had no formal village leader, but the wealthiest head of a house was usually accepted as the headman. He took charge of making economic and political decisions. In the late 1990s, some of the remaining Duwamish people lived on the Suquamish and the Muckleshoot reservations and participated in the governmental systems of those tribes.

The Muckleshoot Reservation has a general council and a tribal council. They also have a tribal court system. On the Port Madison Reservation, the Suquamish General Council meets twice a year and is composed of all enrolled tribal members. The seven members of the tribal council are elected to staggered three-year terms. The tribe also has both elder and youth councils to offer advice to the tribal council.

The Duwamish who did not move to the reservations wrote a tribal constitution and bylaws in 1925. In 1975, they organized under the leadership of the great, great grandniece of Chief Seattle, Cecile Hansen, and have a six-member tribal council. Hansen, the elected chair of the tribe, founded Duwamish Tribal Services in 1983 to administer social service programs for the tribe because the tribe was unable to secure federal recognition and gain access to government benefits for her people. For more than thirty-five years, Hansen has remained the chair and still continues the fight for tribal recognition.

ECONOMY

Before contact with Europeans, the Duwamish gathered and fished for their food. In the 1850s, they were forced off their ancestral lands and onto reservations. American officials and religious leaders expected the Native people to give up their traditional ways. Although the U.S. government provided some goods and food to the reservation, supplies were limited, and the Duwamish suffered many hardships. Corrupt officials sometimes kept or sold supplies that were meant for Duwamish people. Left with no other alternatives, many Duwamish began to work in sawmills, in commercial fisheries, and on farms, as some still do today.

On the reservation many people are employed in forestry, fishing, agriculture, and tourism. Casinos also bring in revenue for the tribes. The Duwamish Tribe established Duwamish Management Corporation to create businesses that strengthen the economic well-being of tribal members who live off-reservation.

DAILY LIFE

Families

Family has traditionally been very important to the Duwamish. Villages were composed of extended families (parents, children, and other relatives). These groups of relatives resided together in a large house, where each family had their own section of the house. Homes were one big open area, divided by mats to form areas for the individual families. Family names related to the place where their home was located. Most Duwamish families were made up of a man and one or more wives, their children, and sometimes unmarried relatives and slaves.

Buildings

The Duwamish built plank homes, a popular housing style in the Pacific Northwest. Some of the homes were open in the center, with roofs supported by posts. In the summer, the tribe constructed temporary campsite structures covered with woven mats. A series of forts surrounded by stake-filled ditches protected the Duwamish from invaders.

After moving to the Port Madison Reservation, Chief Seattle lived in the Old Man House, a community building constructed by the Suquamish. It was 500 feet long (150 meters) and 50 to 60 feet (15 to 18 meters) wide. The Duwamish attended ceremonies at the Old Man House and may have built smaller versions of this structure prior to the twentieth century.

Clothing and adornment

In the summer, men went naked or wore breechcloths (pieces of material that went between the legs and fastened at the waist). Women donned aprons and skirts made of cedar bark. In cool weather, both men and women wore blankets woven of mountain goat wool, adding leggings, shirts, and moccasins as it got colder. Women wore necklaces made of shells, teeth, and claws; they also tattooed their legs and chins. Both sexes wore shell earrings. Hair was usually long and braided. Young men plucked out their facial hair; older men let it grow. People decorated their faces and bodies with oil and paint, and wealthy people wore nose ornaments.

Food

The Duwamish diet centered on fish, especially salmon. The people caught and gathered many freshwater and saltwater creatures, including herring, smelt, flounder, halibut, sturgeon, clams, crabs, crayfish, mussels, and oysters. Overall, the Duwamish relied more on wild foods and game than did the tribes closer to the coast or farther north. Their main prey was deer or elk, but they also hunted and trapped black bear, beaver, raccoon, otter, muskrat, and twenty kinds of waterfowl. Berries, ferns, roots, nuts, bulbs, and sprouts added variety to their diet.

Education

Because they lived on the water and fishing was their livelihood, one of the most vital aspects of a child's education was knowledge of the rivers and the ocean. Both boys and girls learned to read the tides, knew where rocks and logjams were located, and understood the currents. Canoe building and repair were also important skills.

In modern times, many students attend public schools, although some children study at the Muckleshoot Tribal School on the reservation.

The tribe also owns and operates the Muckleshoot Tribal College and an Occupational Skills Training Program. Language classes are available both on and off the reservation.

Healing practices

The Duwamish believed that illnesses were caused by the loss of one's soul or by the presence of a disease-causing object within the body. Some ailments could be cured by the use of plants and herbs, but other diseases required a medicine man called a shaman (pronounced *SHAH-mun* or *SHAY-mun*) to either recapture the missing soul and return it to the body or to remove the disease-causing foreign object through chants and rituals.

Most shamans were male, and their training started at the age of seven or eight. Ultimately, the trainee embarked on a vision quest (see "Customs")—a search for revelation and awareness about the shaman's role as healer and as mediator between humans and supernatural powers.

In modern times, many Duwamish rely on traditional herbs for healing. In the Pacific Northwest, they have access to hundreds of herbs and use them, along with knowledge passed down through the generations, to prevent and cure many illnesses.

ARTS

Carving and basketmaking

Like other people of the Pacific Northwest, the Duwamish carved the images of mythical figures onto the wooden posts they placed in front of their houses. They also used their carving skills to build and decorate their houses and to construct their canoes. Women created baskets from plant fibers; these baskets were woven tightly enough to hold liquids and foods for cooking.

CUSTOMS

Class divisions

Duwamish society was made up of free people and slaves. The free population was divided into upper and lower classes. Only the wealthy upper classes were allowed to take part in ceremonial activities. Slaves were usually women and children who had been seized from enemy tribes during raids.

Princess Angeline, also known as Kikisoblu, was the daughter of Chief Seattle.
© TRANSCENDENTAL GRAPHICS/
GETTY IMAGES.

Secret societies

Like many other Native nations, the Duwamish formed secret societies. Members were wealthy adolescent boys and girls called "growling or black *tamanawis*" (pronounced *tah-MAN-ah-wus;* meaning power or guardian spirit). New members went through a ceremony lasting several nights. They danced and sang, were possessed by spirits, and fell into trances. On the final night of the ritual, their hosts presented them with gifts.

Festivals and ceremonies

The most important ceremonies among the Duwamish were the potlatch, the winter dance, and the soul-recovery ceremony (known among the Duwamish as the "spirit canoe ceremony"). Potlatches were gift-exchange ceremonies sometimes used as offerings of peace to other tribes. The festivities included songs, dances, and games.

A person who had been cured of an illness by a shaman sponsored the winter dance. During the course of the evening, the cured individual performed the special song that had aided in his or her healing. The spirit canoe ceremony was especially popular among the Duwamish. Several men of the tribe—often, but not always, shamans—acted out a journey to the land of the dead to rescue living souls that had been stolen. The ceremony lasted for two nights.

Like other Coast Salish tribes, the Duwamish had ceremonies to honor the abundant salmon of the region. They held similar festivities in thanksgiving for other animals, such as elk.

Childhood and puberty

No special ceremonies took place at the time of a child's birth, but within a short time, parents began flattening the heads of their infants with boards. Flattened heads were considered attractive among the Duwamish.

Girls were separated from the rest of tribe at the time of their first menstruation, and during puberty, both boys and girls were expected to embark on their own vision quests. They set out for the forest alone and fasted (went without food or water) until they fell into a trancelike state and received a vision from a guardian spirit. The vision was said to provide the youths with the power to lead successful lives. Spirits usually appeared in the form of animals but could also appear as humans, plants, and events in nature such as thunderstorms.

Courtship and marriage

Upper-class families arranged the marriages of their children, often to members of families from different villages. The families of the bride and groom exchanged goods, and the bride's relatives gave the new couple gifts. Newly married couples usually lived with the wife's parents until they had their first child, and sometimes longer. Divorce was uncommon in Duwamish society. Widows and widowers (people whose spouses had died) were expected to remarry within the same family to preserve the benefits they had gained from being linked by marriage.

Funerals

When a Duwamish person died, a wake (or watch over the body of a dead person prior to burial) was held, and gifts were brought for the deceased. Mourners cut the dead person's hair, prepared the body, placed it in a canoe or a box, and hung it from a tree or buried it in the village cemetery. A feast was held and the deceased's personal property was distributed among friends and family.

CURRENT TRIBAL ISSUES

Federal recognition

In 1996, the Duwamish were denied the recognition they had been seeking from the U.S. federal government since 1925. According to the Bureau of Indian Affairs, the Duwamish did not satisfy all of the requirements for federal recognition: they had not sustained a separate community over the years; they had not exercised authority over their people throughout history; and they had not had a continuous tribal identity. Therefore, the U.S. government maintained that it had no responsibility to provide benefits and other assistance to the Duwamish people.

After gathering proof that they did meet these requirements, the Duwamish reapplied. In 2001, their petition was successful, and the tribe received federal recognition, making it eligible for government aid and benefits. A new presidential administration, however, rescinded the tribe's recognition the following year. In the second decade of the 2000s, the Duwamish were still fighting for their status as a recognized tribe. To provide for the community's needs, they started Duwamish Tribal Services in 1983 and Duwamish Management Corporation in 2004, both of which continue to meet their people's needs in the absence of the government benefits that come with federal recognition.

Everything Is Sacred

In this selection, Chief Seattle describes the Native American view that everything is sacred.

Every part of all this soil is sacred to my people. Every hillside, every valley, every plain and grove has been hallowed by some sad or happy event in the days long vanished. The very dust you now stand on responds more willingly to their footsteps than to yours, because it is rich with the blood of our ancestors and our bare feet are conscious of the sympathetic touch.

Even the little children who lived here and rejoiced here for a brief season love these somber solitudes, and at eventide they greet shadowy returning spirits.

And when the last red man shall have perished, and the memory of my tribe shall have become a myth among the white men, these shores will swarm with the invisible dead of my tribe; and when our children's children think themselves alone in the field, the store, the shop, upon the highway, or in the silence of the pathless woods, they will not be alone.

At night when the streets of your cities and villages are silent and you think them deserted, they will throng with the returning hosts that once filled and still love this beautiful land.

The white man will never be alone.

Let him be just and deal kindly with my people, for the dead are not powerless. Dead, did I say? There is no death, only a change of worlds.

SOURCE: "Chief Seattle—Suqwamish and Duwamish." *First People.* http://www.firstpeople.us/FP-Html-Wisdom/ChiefSeattle.html (accessed on November 2, 2011).

Environmental problems

The Duwamish have also struggled with environment issues. One of the worst problems occurred on a five-mile (eight-kilometer) stretch of the Duwamish River, which was declared a federal Superfund Site, meaning that the toxic waste was extremely dangerous and needed to be cleaned up. Around 2007, the worst of the contaminationwas dredged and capped. Since that time, the area has been closely watched, health and environmental concerns are being monitored, and many groups have been working together to clean up the area and restore the habitats along the river.

Another environmental concern is the water supply at Port Madison Indian Reservation. The growing area, along with the submarine base construction at Bangor, Washington, has strained the water resources in the area. In 2010, studies were begun to assess water needs and plan for the future.

NOTABLE PEOPLE

Chief Seattle (c. 1786–1866), also known as *Si'ahl*, was born to a Duwamish mother and a Suquamish father. He became chief of both those tribes and of other Salish-speaking tribes in the Puget Sound area. Chief Seattle maintained peaceful relations with American settlers. In 1854, during treaty talks with Isaac Ingalls Stevens, governor of Washington Territory, Chief Seattle delivered a powerful speech on his people's future. The speech has become famous and remains the topic of discussion in historical circles: at least four different versions of it exist, and no one has been able to determine with certainty which of the four, if any, is the original. Chief Seattle is regarded as the last great Native leader in the Pacific Northwest. He married twice and had six children before his death on June 7, 1866, at his home on the Port Madison Reservation.

BOOKS

Averill, Lloyd J. *Northwest Coast Native and Native-Style Art: A Guidebook for Western Washington*. Seattle: University of Washington Press, 1995.

Behrman, Carol H. *The Indian Wars*. Minneapolis, MN: Lerner Publications, 2005.

Chehak, Gail, and Jan Halliday. *Native Peoples of the Northwest: A Traveler's Guide to Land, Art, and Culture*. Seattle: Sasquatch Books, 2002.

Cook, R. Michael, Eli Gifford, and Warren Jefferson, eds. *How Can One Sell the Air?: Chief Seattle's Vision*. Summertown, TN: Native Voices, 2005.

Hodge, Frederick Webb. "Dwamish." *Handbook of American Indians North of Mexico*. New York: Pageant Books, 1959.

Johnson, Michael. "Duwamish." *The Native Tribes of North America*. New York: Macmillan, 1992.

Kluger, Richard. *The Bitter Waters of Medicine Creek: A Tragic Clash Between White and Native America*. New York: Knopf, 2011.

Raibmon, Paige. *Authentic Indians: Episodes of Encounter from the Late-Nineteenth-Century Northwest Coast*. Durham: Duke University Press, 2005.

Ruby, Robert H., John A. Brown, and Cary C. Collins. *A Guide to the Indian Tribes of the Pacific Northwest*. Norman: University of Oklahoma Press, 2010.

Schein, Michael. *Bones Beneath Our Feet.* Seattle, WA: Bennett & Hastings Publishing, 2011.

Seattle, Chief. *Chief Seattle's Testimony.* London: Pax Christi International Catholic Peace Movement: Friends of the Earth, 1976.

Vanderwerth, W. C. *Indian Oratory: Famous Speeches by Noted Indian Chieftains.* Norman: University of Oklahoma Press, 1979.

PERIODICALS

Jones, Malcolm Jr., with Ray Sawhill. "Just Too Good to Be True: Another Reason to Beware False Eco-Prophets." *Newsweek.* (May 4, 1992). Available online at http://www.synaptic.bc.ca/ejournal/newsweek.htm (accessed on November 2, 2011).

WEB SITES

"Chief Seattle Speech." *Washington State Library.* http://www.synaptic.bc.ca/ejournal/wslibrry.htm (accessed on November 2, 2011).

"Connecting the World with Seattle's First People."*Duwamish Tribe.* http://www.duwamishtribe.org/ (accessed on November 2, 2011).

Dailey, Tom. *Coast Salish Villages of Puget Sound.* http://coastsalishmap.org/start_page.htm (accessed on November 2, 2011).

"Duwamish Indian Tribe History." *Access Genealogy.* http://www.accessgenealogy.com/native/tribes/salish/duwamishhist.htm (accessed on November 2, 2011).

Duwamish River Cleanup Coalition. http://www.duwamishcleanup.org/ (accessed on November 2, 2011).

"Lushootseed Language."*Lushootseed.* http://www.lushootseed.org/(accessed on November 2, 2011).

Redish, Laura, and Orrin Lewis. "Lushootseed Salish (Whulshootseed, Puget Sound Salish)." *Native Languages of the Americas.* http://www.native-languages.org/lushootseed.htm (accessed on November 2, 2011).

Thrush, Coll-Peter. "The Lushootseed Peoples of Puget Sound Country." *University of Washington Libraries.* http://nooksack.lib.washington.edu/aipnw/thrush.html (accessed on November 2, 2011).

Urban Indian Experience. "The Duwamish: Seattle's Landless Tribe." *KUOW: PRX.* http://www.prx.org/pieces/1145-urban-indian-experience-episode-1-the-duwamish (accessed on November 2, 2011).

Haida

Name

Although Haida (pronounced *HIGH-duh*) has been the most commonly used spelling since the late 1800s, the tribe's name has been spelled many different ways over the years: Haidah, Hai-dai, Hydah, and Hyder. The name Haida can be translated as "us" or "people." In the early 1700s, some Haida migrated to Alaska, where they called themselves *Kaigini*. A few early writers indicated that the Haida called themselves *Hidery*, or "people."

Location

For centuries the Haida lived on the Queen Charlotte Islands, now called *Haida Gwaii* (meaning "homeland" or "islands of the people"), west of the Canadian province of British Columbia. Most present-day Canadian Haida live in two villages there called Old Masset and Skidegate. Old Masset is on the north end of Graham Island, and Skidegate is located on the southeast corner. Alaskan Haida live on Prince of Wales Island in southeast Alaska, just north of the Queen Charlotte Islands, mainly in the village of Hydaburg.

Population

In 1787, 10,000 Haida lived on Queen Charlotte Islands, Canada; in 1896 the number had dwindled to 1,600. By the 1700s, 8,000 Haida lived on Prince of Wales Island; almost two centuries later in 1890, that number was down to 1,200. In the 1990 U.S. Census, 1,936 Americans identified themselves as Haida. According to the 2000 census, 1,357 Haida resided in the United States, and 4,333 people had some Haida ancestors. A total of 4,040 Haida lived in or around the Canadian villages of Old Masset and Skidegate in 2007. In the 2005–2009 American Community Survey, Hydaburg, the main Haida town in the United States, had a population of 408, of which 329 claimed a Native heritage. The 2010 U.S. Census counted 15,256 people as Tlingit-Haida.

Language family

Athabaskan or Haida. Some linguists (people who study languages) classify the Haida language as part of the Athabaskan (Na-Dene) group. Others say it is a distinct language and stands alone.

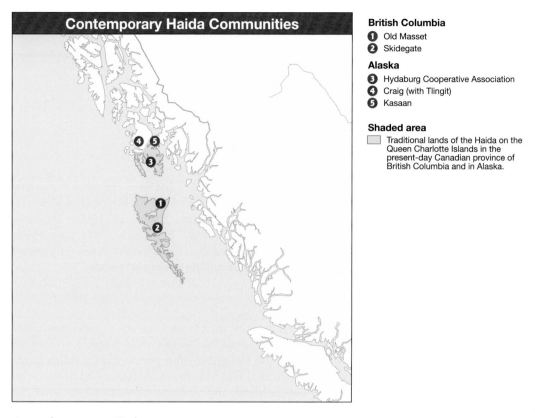

Contemporary Haida Communities

British Columbia
1 Old Masset
2 Skidegate

Alaska
3 Hydaburg Cooperative Association
4 Craig (with Tlingit)
5 Kasaan

Shaded area
Traditional lands of the Haida on the Queen Charlotte Islands in the present-day Canadian province of British Columbia and in Alaska.

A map of contemporary Haida communities. MAP BY XNR PRODUCTIONS. CENGAGE LEARNING, GALE. REPRODUCED BY PERMISSION OF GALE, A PART OF CENGAGE LEARNING.

Origins and group affiliations

The Haida may have come to the American Northwest thousands of years ago from Asia, crossing a land bridge between Alaska and Russia. They reached British Columbia around 800, making their way to the Queen Charlotte Islands a few centuries later. The Haida traded frequently with the Tsimshian, Tlingit (pronounced *KLINK-it*), and Kwakiutl (pronounced *kwak-ee-YEW-tul*) tribes (see Kwakwaka'wakw), but they sometimes warred with them and with the Bella Bella.

For thousands of years, the Haida have lived on islands along the coast of the Canadian province of British Columbia and in the nearby American state of Alaska. Because the area is a relatively warm, rainy region abundant with plant and animal life, the people did not have to spend all their time looking for food, so they were able to pursue artistic and cultural interests. Considered superior among the Northwest Indian groups in terms of arts and warfare, the Haida were known for their ornately carved totem poles and powerful ocean-going canoes. They spoke a language all their own, said to sound like the cries of birds and the crashing of waves on the shore.

HISTORY

Ancient floods

When the Haida people first settled in their lands on the Pacific Coast about ten thousand years ago, melting glaciers flooded the shoreline. People were forced to move farther inland as the waters rose and covered their homes. Haida oral history recalls these events in stories of destruction and rebirth that resemble the biblical story of Noah and the ark.

For centuries, the Charlotte Haida lived a comfortable life in their villages by the sea. Endowed with a bountiful supply of food, they settled in permanent villages and developed a rich culture. From time to time, the Haida set off in huge cedar canoes for the West Coast of British Columbia or south to the areas of present-day Washington and Oregon to raid or trade. Legends also tell of voyages to the southern tip of South America and of encounters with Polynesians and Maori (New Zealand Natives) in the Pacific Ocean. The Haida sometimes captured slaves or acquired them through trade.

Trade with Europeans

The first European ship to reach the Queen Charlotte Islands was most likely the *Santiago,* piloted by Spanish captain Juan Pérez (c. 1725–1774). He passed by the islands in 1774 on his way to investigate the activities of the Russians in Alaska. The French and the British also sailed through the region about the same time. In 1787, a British sea captain arrived on the islands and named them after his ship, the *Queen Charlotte,* which in turn had been named in honor of the wife of King George III. Trading between the Haida and Europeans soon began. The British

Important Dates

1774: First European contact between Spanish captain Juan Pérez and the Haida.

1797: Trading begins between the Haida and the British.

1912: The Hydaburg Indian Reservation is established in Alaska.

1936: Hydaburg, Alaska, adopts a constitution and petition the U.S. government for a 905,000-acre reservation.

1968: The Haida and Tlingit tribes are awarded $7.5 million compensation by the U.S. Court of Claims for their land.

1980: The Council of the Haida Nation unites the Canadian bands under one government.

1985: Seventy-two Haida and their supporters are arrested for preventing logging on Queen Charlotte Islands.

1987: Canadian leaders establish a national park and marine reserve on the Queen Charlotte Islands.

were interested in furs, especially the skins of sea otters, which brought large profits from Chinese buyers.

Move to Alaska

Driven off their Native lands by warfare with neighboring tribes, one group of Haida left the Queen Charlotte Islands in the mid-1700s and established villages in southern Alaska. For the rest of the century, nearly eight thousand Haida resided in five villages at the southern end of Prince of Wales Island, just north of the Queen Charlotte Islands. Before 1867, the Haida of Alaska lived in an area claimed by Russia. Although the Russian Orthodox Church converted some Haida to Christianity, Russian culture had little real impact on the Haida there. Russia sold Alaska to the United States in 1867 for $7.2 million.

With the discovery of gold in Alaskan territory in 1889, settlers swarmed to the area, and the Haida lost much of their land as well as access to many of their hunting and fishing areas. They were then forced to participate in the area's growing economy as fishers and loggers for American companies.

The U.S. Bureau of Education and the Presbyterian Church determined to "educate and civilize" the Haida. In 1911, a mission called Hydaburg was established in Alaska. Without support from the U.S. government, three nearby Haida villages had to be abandoned, and the people from those villages reluctantly moved to Hydaburg. In addition to Hydaburg, some Haida also made their homes in Craig and Kasaan, Alaska, and in Seattle, Washington. By the 1990s, many Haida had left Hydaburg to find employment in large cities.

Masset and Skidegate settlements

The Charlotte Haida, fearing they would lose all their land to the ever-growing number of Canadian settlers, signed a treaty in 1854 giving up most of their land, including their hunting territories, to the Canadian government. In return, they kept their villages and farm areas and retained the right to hunt and fish in all their former territories.

A trading post opened in the town of Masset on the Queen Charlotte Islands in 1869. There, and at forts in the area, the Haida traded meat, dried fish, and potatoes with merchants and sailors in exchange for European products. In 1871, British Columbia became part of Canada, and the government established two Haida reserves (the term

A Haida storage chest is decorated with carvings and painted details.
© TOPHAM/THE IMAGE WORKS. REPRODUCED BY PERMISSION.

Canadians use for reservations, or parcels of land set aside for the Native nations) near the town of Masset and in the town of Skidegate. (See "Government.")

Impact of Europeans

Contact with Europeans had both a positive and negative effect on the Haida who lived on the Queen Charlotte Islands, but it changed the Native way of life. The Haida traded furs with the Europeans for copper and iron tools, kettles, knives, and needles. The tools allowed the Haida to make larger and more elaborate totem poles, canoes, and houses. In the early 1800s, Haida artists started to sell carved wooden boxes, bowls, and utensils to foreign settlers, traders, and sailors. By the mid-nineteenth century, they were trading ceremonial robes, elaborate garments decorated with copper and silver buttons, to the Europeans. In return, the Haida purchased European firearms, cloth, and blankets.

Although the Haida profited from the fur trade, the environmental repercussions were disastrous. By 1830, the sea otter was nearly extinct from overtrapping. In addition, the salmon population was declining. Europeans then traded for other furs, such as deer, mink, and beaver.

Lavina White: Fighting for Tradition

Native activist Lavina White is working to change social conditions and government policies for Native peoples. Her main goal is to reverse the damage done by whites to the Haida tribal homeland. A strong critic of the Canadian government's move to create Gwaii Hanaas National Park, White claims that the benefit of the $38 million park was reaped solely by the non-Native community. She also alleges that: (1) other Haida lands beyond South Moresby are being clearcut (all the trees are being sawed down) by the logging industry, and (2) the Canadian government is to blame for the depletion of fish stocks in Haida waters. White believes that the Haida people—indeed all Native nations—can heal themselves only by reasserting their rights to their traditional lands and resources and reestablishing their Native ways.

When asked how things would be different if the land reverted to Haida control, White said priorities would change. She explained: "We've been here from the beginning of time and we had direction from our creator. We understood our environment completely. Now I see the fish is almost all gone, the trees are almost all gone. [Life] would change, it would be better. As long as money is the driving force the destruction will continue."

Contact with European settlers also brought new diseases to the people. Epidemics (uncontrolled outbreaks of disease; in this case, probably smallpox) in 1862 and 1863 led to the deaths of whole families and entire villages on the Queen Charlotte Islands. By the beginning of the twentieth century, the Haida population there—once numbering about ten thousand—had fallen to nine hundred.

Canadian officials, teachers, and Christian church leaders also pressured the Haida to assimilate (adopt the mainstream American way of life). Soon, large extended families no longer lived together in one big house as they had traditionally. By 1884, the Canadian government had banned potlatches (pronounced *POT-latch-ez;* gift-giving ceremonies; see "Customs") and Haida dances. Christian missionaries tried to convince the people that carving and erecting totem poles was evil.

By the late 1800s, many Haida families had their own gardens and kept farm animals such as horses and cows. As trade in food products and animal furs declined over the next few decades, men and women took jobs in fish-canning factories, mines, and sawmills. Some fished on boats owned by Canadian firms; others had their own boats and sold their catch to Canadian companies.

Modern times

About 15 percent of the land on the Queen Charlotte Islands, an area known as South Moresby, is home to one of the world's only remaining coastal rain forests. In the 1970s, the Charlotte Haida began a lengthy battle with the logging industry over the use of sacred tribal lands on the islands. In one incident in 1985, Haida leaders and supporters were arrested, imprisoned, and charged with breaking the law after they blockaded a logging road. Their thirteen-year-long battle was resolved in 1987 when Canadian and Haida officials signed an agreement establishing a national park and marine reserve at the site. (See "Current Tribal Issues.") Some hailed the decision to create Canada's Gwaii Hanaas National Park as a victory for the Haida. Many tribe members disagree, however, saying all traditional tribal lands should be returned to their control.

RELIGION

According to traditional Haida beliefs, the universe had three separate parts: the earth, made up of their islands and the mainland; the area above the earth, supported by a pillar extending upward from the land below; and the seawater beneath the earth. Animals were said to have souls and to be more intelligent than humans.

The Haida believed in *Ne-kilst-lass,* their supreme being who took the form of a raven. He created the world and brought light and order. He also instructed the Haida in their major ceremonies and taught them to establish good relations within the tribe and with other tribes. Ne-kilst-lass had a dark side as well: he was the troublemaker responsible for all things disruptive and evil.

Haida Words and Phrases

Sánuu dáng gíidang?	"How are you?"
Díi 'láagang.	"I'm fine."
Sánuu dáng kya'áang?	"What is your name?"
Káts hláa.	"Come in."
Gunalchéesh.	"Thank you."
Háakwsdaa	"Let's go."
chíin	"fish"
k'íit	"tree"
sáng	"day"
táa	"eat"
tlaahláa	"make"
xitgáay	"flying"
yáahl	"raven"

LANGUAGE

The Native Americans of the Northwest Coast spoke at least forty-five different languages. Although is it sometimes classified as an Athabaskan (Na-Dene) language, the Haida language is not related to any of the others. Two dialects (varieties) of the Haida language have survived at Skidegate and Old Masset on the Queen Charlotte Islands. The Haida who moved to Alaska in the eighteenth century also spoke the Masset dialect. By the dawn of the twenty-first century, only about fifty Haida speakers remained alive, and all were over sixty years old; most were in their eighties and nineties. Although the language seemed to be dying out, even Haida children who no longer spoke their own language were learning traditional Haida songs.

GOVERNMENT

Haida people who were related through the same female ancestor made up groups called lineages. A chief who had inherited his position led each lineage. Chiefs resolved conflicts among the people, made major decisions about the group's welfare, and had the power to declare war.

In the 1870s, the Canadian government gave its First Nations peoples partial control over their own land. Native-run councils could govern the people in their traditional communities, as long as they followed Canadian law. Two Haida reserves were set up. The Old Masset Village Council Reserve is located about 7 miles (11 kilometers) west of the village of Masset, and the Skidegate Reserve is located 120 air miles (190 kilometers) from Prince Rupert, British Columbia. Even in the early twenty-first century, chiefs held considerable power in Canadian Haida communities.

In 1980, the Haida in Canada formed the Council of the Haida Nation to unite all their people under one government. Since then, the council has become involved in many treaty negotiations. None of the treaties between Canada and the Haida were ever signed, so the council began working "to protect and assert Aboriginal Title and the collective rights of the Haida people." Representatives on the council are elected from the villages of Skidegate and Old Masset as well as from the urban areas of Prince Rupert and Vancouver. In 2010, the council signed an agreement with the province of British Columbia that recognized Haida sovereignty (self-government) and set up joint management of natural resources (see "Current Tribal Issues").

Hydaburg, Alaska, home of most Haida in the United States, was the first village to form a council following the Indian Reorganization Act (IRA) amendment in 1936 that included Alaska natives. The agreement that established Hydaburg as a reservation was declared null and void in 1952 by the U.S. District Court, and Hydaburg became an incorporated city with its own elected government. The city is run by a mayor and a city council, as are Craig and Kasaan.

ECONOMY

For centuries, the Haida enjoyed abundant natural resources and much leisure time. They could gather their entire food supply for the year in only three months, and they needed to do very little farming. They used their leisure time to develop their artistic talents. The Haida held craftspeople in high regard, and the reputation of their canoe makers and carvers soon spread throughout the region.

The Haida exchanged their canoes for mountain goat wool and candlefish, a fish so oily it could be dried, then later set on fire and burned like a candle. With the coming of Europeans, the Haida traded furs, food, and artwork for many European items.

With the passage of the Alaska Native Claims Settlement Act in 1971, the Haida in Alaska faced changes to their traditional ways of life. Although one goal in establishing these nonprofit corporations was to provide the Natives with a more secure economic future, the government did not take into account the difficulties it posed for tribes who did not believe in owning land. It also meant some Haida had to give up traditional subsistence occupations to learn business management. Along with the Tlingit (see entry), the Haida are now part of the Sealaska Corporation.

In the early 2000s, many Alaskan and Charlotte Haida earned their living from logging, a business that has faced opposition for causing damage to Native lands. Others worked in canning or fishing, which has also had its share of trouble. (See "Current Tribal Issues.") The Queen Charlotte Islands have become a center of ecotourism (a type of tourism that features animals and vegetation in their natural habitat), and the Haida provide a variety of services for visitors. With the revival of traditional crafts, Haida carvers and painters create valuable artworks that are praised by art critics and sold throughout the world.

DAILY LIFE

Families

Traditional Haida society consisted of many villages of related families. For centuries, Haida children were considered part of an extended family made up of a mother, her sons and daughters, her daughter's children, her granddaughter's children, and so on.

Haida Canoes

One of the treasures of the American Museum of Natural History in Washington, D.C., is a 63-foot-long (19-meter-long) canoe built by Haida people on the Charlotte Islands in 1878. The canoe exhibit, created in 1910, depicts a group of Native people arriving at an important ceremonial feast. The two men with long poles at the front of the canoe and the three sets of paddlers on both sides of the canoe are captured slaves.

Haida carved canoes from the trunks of large cedar trees. Craftspeople hollowed out the trunk with hand tools, then towed the 40- to 60-foot (10- to 20-meter) log to the village. Next, they softened it with boiling water until they had widened it to more than 8 feet (2.4 meters). To do this, they partially filled the canoe with water and dropped in red-hot rocks to create steam. They then offered prayers for guidance before they pulled the pliable wood sides into shape. If the steam was too hot, the sides would fall open; if it was too cool, the sides could not be moved. After the canoe dried and hardened into its proper shape, an artist carved and painted the bow and stern pieces.

The front of the canoe in the Natural History exhibit is decorated with the carving of a wolf and a painted killer whale. It may have been created for a chief of the nearby Bella Bella tribe. Although the identity of the creator of this particular canoe is unknown, the vessel serves as a fine example of the artistry that made the Haida renowned canoe builders.

(Societies that trace descent through the maternal line, or the mother's side of the family, are called *matrilineal.*)

Haida families—identified as either Eagles or Ravens—owned their own property, were assigned special areas for gathering food, and, depending on their affiliation (either Eagle or Raven), lived at one of two separate ends of the village. The Eagle and Raven groupings were divided even further into a complicated system of subgroups, each with its own land, history, and customs. By the end of the nineteenth century, though, the elaborately structured Haida social system had changed a great deal. Most of the Haida lived in nuclear families—groups made up of a father, a mother, and their children. In modern times, members of the same group (Ravens, for example) could marry one another; such unions had been forbidden earlier in Haida history.

Buildings

The Haida lived in large homes called longhouses that ranged from 30 to 60 feet (10 to 20 meters) or more in length and were 30 to 50 feet (10 to 15 meters) in width. The longhouses were made of cedar logs that had been notched and fitted together so expertly that no pegs were needed to join them. The Haida built roofs of cedar bark slabs and walls of planks split from standing trees. Carved log pillars supported the roof beams. At first, these pillars served merely to make the entryway more elegant; later, the carved pillars, some as tall as 50 feet (15 meters), evolved into one of several kinds of totem poles. (See "Customs.")

The longhouses were permanent dwellings built on seaside sites that offered protection from the weather and enemies. Several families shared the area around a central fireplace within each longhouse, but each group prepared its own meals. Family members retired at night to private sleeping quarters.

On the Queen Charlotte Islands, the longhouses were built on a narrow strip of land facing the ocean. Backed by forests of cedar trees and with large totem poles in front, they made an impressive sight when traders passed by in canoes and ships.

When the salmon returned in spring, the Haida moved to locations along the rivers. They sometimes removed planks from their permanent homes to build temporary shelters, then carried the wood back in the fall. They often tied the planks across two canoes to serve as a platform for carrying belongings.

The Haida built other buildings to house girls who were about to come of age and women about to give birth. Some buildings held the remains of the dead. Celebrations were held in large community buildings.

Clothing and adornment

The early Haida wore little clothing and generally went barefoot. Women wore bark aprons that extended from the waist to the knees. They made clothing from red and yellow cedar bark by peeling long strips from the trees and shredding the softer inner layer. They processed this into soft felt-like fabric strips that they braided or sewed to make cloth.

The Haida were excellent weavers. They made their everyday clothing from spruce tree roots and reeds woven into fabric and then sewed it into hats, capes, and robes. Women sometimes wore skirts and capes of cedar bark, whereas men wore long capes of bark with mountain goat wool decorations. Chief's capes often had trophy head decorations and otter fur collars. Later, people used clan symbols for their cape designs. After the Europeans arrived, the Haida traded for blankets, which they wore wrapped around their bodies in the daytime and covered themselves with at night. Slaves wore blankets their owners no longer wanted.

For ceremonial wear, the Haida sewed garments of dog fur and mountain goat wool with thread made of bark. They also created masks representing different creatures such as the eagle and the salmon and donned headdresses decorated with fur, carvings, and sea lion whiskers.

Food

The Haida enjoyed a bountiful supply of plants, fish, and meat. Women picked berries, clover, roots, seaweed, and crab apples. Men did the fishing and hunting and, along with women, gathered clams, crabs, and scallops inshore and offshore. Seal, sea otter, sea lion, oysters, mussels, halibut, cod, herring, trout, and abalone (a type of shellfish) were taken from the sea.

The 500-pound (230-kilogram) halibut and 20-foot (6-meter) sturgeon the Haida caught were so large they had to be stunned with clubs before they could be pulled on board the canoes. Nearby rivers teemed with salmon so plentiful they could be caught by hand. The Haida did not hunt whales, but they did make use of any stranded whales that washed ashore.

On land, they hunted black bear, caribou, deer, land otter, and bird eggs. Meat, such as deer or seal, was roasted or boiled, cut into strips, and preserved by drying or smoking it. The Charlotte Islands were home to a number of species of plants and animals that are unique, such as the alpine lily, the Steller's jay, and the hairy wood-pecker. Bald eagles and peregrine falcons also thrived there. An equally bountiful supply of plant and animal food was available to the Haida in Alaska.

Education

Haida children played a lot; they also learned songs and dances from older tribal members. By observing their elders, they learned about hunting, fishing, food gathering, and food preparation. Boys sometimes went to live with one of their mother's brothers to learn stories and ceremonies important to the tribe. They fasted and swam in cold waters to "toughen up" and develop survival skills.

In the late 1880s, Methodist missionaries took over the education of Haida children on the Charlotte Islands. The missionaries set up boarding schools that reinforced Christian beliefs. Children who attended them learned to speak English rather than their Native language. These schools contributed to the loss of traditional culture because children no longer received their instruction from tribal elders as they had in the past.

Later, Old Masset and Skidegate opened their own public schools. With the help of elder Natives, these school systems began offering studies in Haida culture, language, and dancing. The New Skills Centre in Old Masset blended traditional values with business management training courses. The public school in Hydaburg, Alaska, introduced a Haida language program as well as classes in traditional drawing and carving.

Healing practices

Because they wore their hair long and tied it on top of their heads, Haida medicine men and women were called *skaggies,* a shortened form of the Haida words for "long-haired ones." Skaggies organized into secret societies and received their power from ocean beings.

Earlier in Haida history, skaggies served as both priests and doctors. They were believed to have the power to heal the sick, foresee the future, and bring success to hunting and fishing expeditions. When called upon for their gift of healing, skaggies usually announced their arrival on the scene by shaking a loud rattle. This same rattle—used in conjunction with a series of sharp, pointed bones they poked into the sick person's body—served as one means of eliminating the cause of illness. The carved bone tubes the healers used were called "soul catchers," because they were intended to return the sick person's soul to his or her body. The return of the soul was believed to promote healing.

Haida men carve a battle-victory memorial.
© NATIONAL GEOGRAPHIC IMAGE COLLECTION/ALAMY.

ARTS

Weaving and woodworking

Most Haida art stood as a lasting symbol of an artist's ancestors, status, and wealth. Traditionally, men made sculptures, carvings, and paintings, and women crafted various types of cedar and spruce baskets and woven items. Many Haida objects have great artistic value. The tribe remains well known for designing and weaving spectacular button blankets, named for the pearl buttons that outline the blankets' designs. The Haida were also very skilled in the construction of large canoes—some up to 75 feet (23 meters) in length and able to carry as many as forty people and two tons of freight.

In artistic terms, the Haida people are probably best known as master wood-carvers who covered virtually any flat surface with engraving or painting. Their carvings were inspired by both realistic figures and mythical creatures, and they adorned totem poles, house posts, grave markers, painted house fronts, interior screens, large dishes, and canoes. Popular smaller carved objects included rattles, cooking and serving implements, and decorative boxes. In the early 1800s, the Haida gained recognition for their intricate carvings in a black stone called argillite (pronounced *AR-juh-lite*). They were the only Native group known to carve from this

A Haida totem pole shows the intricate carving style for which the tribe is known.

particular stone, and they controlled the only source from which it could be obtained.

Totem poles

The Haida were famous for their totem poles, which they decorated with symbols of Eagle or Raven. Red cedar totem poles, covered entirely with carvings, often commemorated important events in the life of the head of a family. Some poles even had little drawers that held the remains of the home's deceased owners. After the Haida acquired iron tools from the Europeans, they were able to produce much larger poles, some as tall as 50 feet (15 kilometers). Only the upper classes could afford totem poles; commoners painted images on their houses. In the late 1800s, Christian missionaries to the Queen Charlotte Islands destroyed many totem poles. Soon after, the pole-carving tradition came to an end. It was not until the 1970s that totem poles were once again being made on the Queen Charlotte Islands, as a result of the efforts of Haida artist Bill Reid (1920–1998).

CUSTOMS

Social classes

The Haida people were divided into two main social classes: commoners and the wealthy upper class. Any Haida commoner who worked hard enough could one day rise to the upper class. Slaves captured in battle made up the lowest class in Haida society. They lived in their owners' houses and were usually treated well.

Tattoos represented a person's rank in society and often included the likeness of a family's crest (a symbol of that family). Young men were tattooed on the chest. A woman's rank was reflected in the types of tattoos found on her arms and legs and in the size of her *labret* (pronounced *LAY-bret*), a wooden ornament that was inserted into a piercing in the lower lip—the larger the labret, the higher a woman's rank.

Festivals

Most Haida ceremonies were held in the winter, which was the rainy season. In fact, the Haida usually held an event of some kind every night from November until March.

Potlatches

Potlatches—elaborate gift-giving ceremonies common among American Indians of the Northwest Coast—were held when a tribal chief wished to celebrate an event of importance, such as the death of the chief who came before him, a marriage, a child's coming of age, or the unveiling of a new totem pole. A major potlatch required years of planning and lasted for several days. The guest list included members of the host's tribe as well as people from neighboring villages. The host was judged by his generosity: possessions such as baskets, cloaks, shell ornaments, blankets, and canoes were given to the guests. Guests were judged by their ability to consume huge bowls of delicacies such as seal and bear meat or berries preserved in fish oil. In fact, eating became a kind of competition at the feast. A host was usually reduced to poverty by the time the potlatch ended, but he could expect to be repaid in double on a future occasion.

The Canadian government banned potlatches in 1884. Only since the 1950s have they again become legal. Despite the longtime ban, the Haida on the Charlotte Islands continued for many years to hold a modified form of potlatch.

How the Haida Got Fire

The Haida believed that the supreme being *Ne-kilst-lass,* in the form of a raven, brought forth the first Haida people from a clamshell. He supplied them with fire to battle the cold and darkness on the earth. This excerpt from a Haida tale describes how Raven brought fire to the people.

> Ne-kilst-lass heard that a great chief who lived on an island in the Pacific had all the fire in the world. So donning his coat of feathers he flew over to this island. Reaching the chief's island, he soon found his house. After a long conversation with him about the merits of his fire, Choo-e-ah seized a brand and with it flew over again to the mainland, letting fall, as he passed along, a few sparks amongst certain sorts of wood and stones. This sort of wood and these stones absorbed all the fire and gave it out again, when struck with a hard substance. The wood also gave it out when two pieces were quickly rubbed together. The Hidery say [that] when Choo-e-ah reached the land, part of his beak was burnt off.

SOURCE: "Of How They First Got Fire." *Tales from the Totems of the Hidery.* Volume 2. Chicago: Archives of the International Folk-Lore Association, 1899.

Puberty and the spirit dance

When a Haida girl began to menstruate, she was taken to a special part of the family house and separated from the rest of the household by a screen. For a month or longer, her father's sisters visited her and taught her about the traditional duties of a woman in the tribe, especially the

A Haida woman wears a labret, or wooden ornament, through her lower lip.
© HULTON ARCHIVE/GETTY IMAGES.

gathering and cooking of food and the raising of children. To toughen herself, she slept on a stone pillow and ate and drank sparingly. At the end of the month, the young woman took a ritual bath, and a celebration was held in her honor.

Boys had no special ceremony, but their uncles (mother's brothers) taught them proper behavior and family history. They swam in the cold ocean to strengthen themselves. To become rapid swimmers, boys ate dragonfly wings. Eating duck tongues increased their ability to hold their breath underwater, and blue jay tongues helped them climb well.

Both boys and girls embarked on vision quests, searching for revelation and awareness. Each youth wandered alone for days through deep forests, hoping for contact with the special spirit who would serve as a guide through life. The greatest spirit power a young man (and occasionally a young woman) could receive was that of Eagle or Raven. Often, the spirit made its presence known by singing a song. The song was then incorporated into the quester's spirit dance, a dramatization of the lesson taught by the spirit visitor. Wearing masks, face paints, and elaborate costumes, spirit dancers reenacted their experiences.

Courtship and marriage

Haida marriages were arranged, and young people accepted their elders' choice of a partner. The bride's family hosted the marriage feast, and the two families exchanged gifts. If a man treated his wife poorly, her family could reclaim her and her children. If he ran away and married another woman, he had to make a financial settlement with his first wife. Failure to do so could result in death. A man who abandoned his wife but did not remarry suffered no negative consequences. Historically, Haida marriages lasted a short time.

Birth

The Haida believed the spirits of the dead came back to life as newborn babies. Girls were especially prized. At birth, children were given undesirable names so they would work hard on their personal growth. Once people acquired property or wealth, a chief rewarded them with a "good and honorable" name. A person could also achieve a good name by hosting a potlatch.

Funerals

Funerals were the most important of the Haida rituals. Women washed and dressed the body of the deceased and painted his or her face. Mourners sobbed loudly and shared their sorrow. They burned the bodies and placed the ashes inside the family totem pole or in boxes inside special buildings set aside for the purpose. After the cremation, a funeral potlatch was held, and the dead person's possessions were distributed among the mourners. Sometimes the Haida placed the dead in carved grave houses overlooking the ocean; only shamans could visit these open coffins.

CURRENT TRIBAL ISSUES

Traditional livelihoods endangered

Commercial fishing, an important part of the economy of Haida villages in British Columbia since the 1800s, took a downturn in the 1990s. Canada's federal fisheries department lowered catch limits (the amount of fish that could legally be kept) that year. Two years later, they banned all Chinook salmon fishing and further restricted other fishing. The Chinook salmon, known in Alaska as the king salmon, had fallen victim to decades of overfishing.

The decline of salmon fishing has greatly affected the Canadian village of Old Masset. Although Old Masset's two fish processing plants once employed ninety full-time workers, by 1996, the number of employees had fallen to twenty-two, more than half of them part-timers. That same year, the catch intended for Old Masset's fish processing plants declined to 50,000 pounds (23,000 kilograms) of fish from about 250,000 pounds (113,000 kilograms) the previous year. Around 2009, Chinook salmon fishing was also banned on the West Coast of the United States, so the Alaskan Haida lost a major food and income source as well.

Cultural restoration

Teams of professional archaeologists (scientists who study the culture and artifacts of ancient peoples) and Haida trainees began studying the area in recent decades. Their discoveries indicate that humans lived in the area for more than nine thousand years.

The Sgan Gwaii archaeological venture represents a turning point in the way Canada handles Native archaeological projects. In the past, objects excavated from abandoned Native villages were removed from the scene and examined in museums. Current policy gives the Haida people control over Native human remains and stipulates that all artifacts be returned to the Queen Charlotte Islands Museum within six months of their release.

In recent times, a totem pole restoration project began in Sgan Gwaii (also known as Anthony Island), a Canadian national park. After missionaries banned totem poles, the Haida did not construct them; the

Haida are now working to revive this important part of their traditional culture. In the twenty-first century, totem pole restoration and creation are once again part of the Haida culture.

Haida-Canadian agreements

The Canadian Haida have always called the Queen Charlotte Islands *Haida Gwaii,* which means "islands of the people." In the 1980s, the name came into common usage, but not until 2009 was a move made to make the term official. In June 2010, this name change received royal assent, and the islands are now known by the First Nations designation of Haida Gwaii in all Canadian government records.

This name change was one of the important agreements made in 2010 between the Haida Nation and Canada. That year, British Columbia and the Council of the Haida Nation signed the Kunst'aa guu–Kunst'aayah Reconciliation Protocol. This document set up a joint decision-making process for land and natural resource management on Haida Gwaii and recognized the Haida government on these islands.

NOTABLE PEOPLE

The greatness of Haida chief Eda'nsa (c. 1810–1994; his name means "Melting Ice from a Glacier"; also called Captain Douglas), who became a Haida Eagle chief in 1841, is the subject of much debate because he was a slave trader. (These slaves had been acquired from other tribes by barter or raid.) He was known for guiding the Europeans through the difficult waters of the Queen Charlotte Islands. Eda'nsa became a Christian in 1884 and sought new trading opportunities in the islands until his death in 1894. His title passed to his nephew Charles Edenshaw (c. 1839–1920), a skilled woodcarver and silversmith who achieved great wealth and fame and was chosen chief of the Haida village of Yatza.

Bill Reid (1920–1998), Edenshaw's nephew, may be the most famous Haida artist of the twentieth century. Credited with ushering in a rebirth of Haida art in the 1950s, he has many sculptures on public display throughout North America. Reid is also an accomplished author.

BOOKS

Augaitis, Daina, Lucille Bell, and Nika Collison. *Raven Travelling: Two Centuries of Haida Art.* Seattle: University of Washington Press, 2008.

Beck, Mary L. *Heroes and Heroines: Tlingit-Haida Legend.* Anchorage: Alaska Northwest Books, 2003.

Bringhurst, Robert. *A Story as Sharp as a Knife: The Classical Haida Mythtellers and Their World.* 2nd ed. Vancouver, BC: Douglas & McIntyre, 2011.

Brown, Tricia. *Silent Storytellers of Totem Bight State Historical Park.* Anchorage: Alaska Geographic Association, 2009.

Collison, Pansy. *Haida Eagle Treasures: Tsath Lanas History and Narratives.* Calgary, Canada: Detselig Enterprises, 2010.

Eastman, Carol M., and Elizabeth A. Edwards. *Gyaehlingaay: Traditions, Tales and Images of the Kaigani Haida.* Seattle: Burke Museum Publications, distributed by University of Washington Press, 1991.

Gill, Ian. *All That We Say Is Ours: Guujaaw and the Reawakening of the Haida Nation.* Vancouver, BC: Douglas & McIntyre, 2010.

Gill, Ian. *Haida Gwaii: Journeys Through the Queen Charlotte Islands.* Vancouver, BC: Raincoast Books, 2004.

Horwood, Dennis, and Tom Parkin. *Haida Gwaii: The Queen Charlotte Islands.* 3rd ed. Custer, WA: Heritage House, 2009.

Jonaitis, Aldona. *Art of the Northwest Coast.* Seattle: University of Washington Press, 2006.

Murdock, George Peter. *Rank and Potlatch among the Haida.* New Haven, CT: Yale University Publications, Human Relations Area Files Press, 1970.

Swanton, John R. *Haida Texts and Myths: Skidegate Dialect.* Reprint. Whitefish, MT: Kessinger Publishing, 2010.

Worl, Rosita. *Celebration: Tlingit, Haida, Tsimshian Dancing on the Land.* Edited by Kathy Dye. Seattle: University of Washington Press, 2008.

PERIODICALS

Farnsworth, Clyde H. "Where Salmon Ruled, End of the Line." *New York Times,* August 11, 1996: 8Y.

Johnston, Moira. "Canada's Queen Charlotte Islands: Homeland of the Haida." *National Geographic,* July 1987: 102–27.

Kowinski, William Severini. "Giving New Life to Haida Art and the Culture It Expresses." *Smithsonian,* January 1995: 38.

WEB SITES

Central Council: Tlingit and Haida Indian Tribes of Alaska. http://www.ccthita.org/ (accessed on November 2, 2011).

Council of the Haida Nation (CHN). http://www.haidanation.ca/ (accessed on November 2, 2011).

Deans, James. "Tales from the Totems of the Hidery." *Early Canadiana Online.* http://www.canadiana.org/ECO/PageView/06053/0003?id=986858ca5f bdc633 (accessed on November 2, 2011).

"Haida." *The Kids' Site of Canadian Settlement, Library and Archives Canada.* http://www.collectionscanada.ca/settlement/kids/021013-2061-e.html (accessed on November 2, 2011).

Haida Gwaii Community Futures. http://www.haidagwaiifutures.ca/about-us/introduction/ (accessed on November 2, 2011).

"Haida Heritage Center at Qay'llnagaay." *Haida Heritage Centre.* http://www.haidaheritagecentre.com/ (accessed on November 2, 2011).

"Haida Language Program." *Sealaska Heritage Institute.* http://www.sealaskaheritage.org/programs/haida_language_program.htm (accessed on November 2, 2011).

"Haida Spirits of the Sea." *Virtual Museum of Canada.* http://www.virtualmuseum.ca/Exhibitions/Haida/nojava/english/home/index.html (accessed on November 2, 2011).

"Haida Totem Pole Raising, Old Massett, Haida Gwaii, Queen Charlotte Islands." YouTube video, 2:42. Posted by "archievideo35," July 1, 2009. http://www.youtube.com/watch?v=BWwlfWkqmWY (accessed on November 2, 2011).

MacDonald, George F. "The Haida: Children of Eagle and Raven." *Canadian Museum of Civilization.* http://www.civilization.ca/cmc/exhibitions/aborig/haida/haindexe.shtml (accessed on November 2, 2011).

Redish, Laura, and Orrin Lewis. "Haida Indian Fact Sheet." *Native Languages of the Americas.* http://www.bigorrin.org/haida_kids.htm (accessed on November 2, 2011).

"Reg Davidson, Haida Artist." *Tennessee Tech University.* http://iweb.tntech.edu/cventura/reg.htm (accessed on November 2, 2011).

"Skidegate Haida Model Houses & Poles." *Burke Museum of Natural History and Culture.* http://www.burkemuseum.org/bhc/haida_models/ (accessed on November 2, 2011).

"Totem Pole Websites." *Cathedral Grove.* http://www.cathedralgrove.eu/text/07-Totem-Websites-3.htm (accessed on November 2, 2011).

Kwakwaka'wakw (Kwakiutl)

Name

The name Kwakiutl (pronounced *kwak-ee-YEW-tul*) has two meanings: "smoke of the world" and "beach at the north side of the river." In the past, the name referred to all the related tribes or groups, those who spoke the Kwakiutl language and the individual band. In the early twenty-first century, the only group to bear the name Kwakiutl is the band located at the village of Fort Rupert, British Columbia. Since the 1980s, members of the Kwakiutl First Nation have called themselves *Kwakwaka'wakw* (pronounced *kwalk-walk-ya-walk* or *kwalk-walk-ya-walk-wuh*), which means "those who speak the language *Kwak'wala*."

Location

For centuries, the Kwakwaka'wakw lived along the Northwest Coast in British Columbia, Canada. Kwakwaka'wakw communities existed at Queen Charlotte Sound on northern Vancouver Island, on various small islands around Vancouver Island, and on mainland British Columbia from Douglas Channel to Bute Inlet. Present-day Kwakwaka'wakw still reside in these areas.

Population

Prior to European contact the population numbered 19,125. In 1750, there were about 5,000 to 6,000 Kwakwaka'wakw; in 1904, that number had dropped to 2,173, and by 1924, it was 1,039. A census of the Canadian population in 1991 reported that there were 4,120 Kwakwaka'wakw living in Canada. The 1996 census indicated 5,517 resided in Canada. In 2005, that figure decreased to 4,896. The Kwakiutl Band Council showed a tribal enrollment of 510 persons in 2011.

Language family

Wakashan.

Origins and group affiliations

Scientists believe that thousands of years ago the ancestors of the Kwakwaka'wakw crossed an ancient land bridge from Asia to North America and eventually settled on the Northwest Coast near the present-day

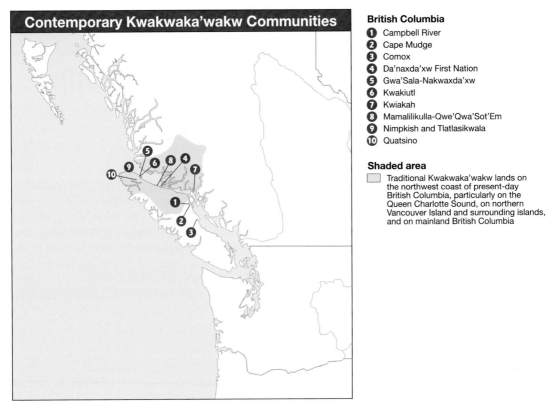

Contemporary Kwakwaka'wakw Communities

British Columbia

1. Campbell River
2. Cape Mudge
3. Comox
4. Da'naxda'xw First Nation
5. Gwa'Sala-Nakwaxda'xw
6. Kwakiutl
7. Kwiakah
8. Mamalilikulla-Qwe'Qwa'Sot'Em
9. Nimpkish and Tlatlasikwala
10. Quatsino

Shaded area

Traditional Kwakwaka'wakw lands on the northwest coast of present-day British Columbia, particularly on the Queen Charlotte Sound, on northern Vancouver Island and surrounding islands, and on mainland British Columbia

A map of contemporary Kwakwaka'wakw communities. MAP BY XNR PRODUCTIONS. CENGAGE LEARNING, GALE. REPRODUCED BY PERMISSION OF GALE, A PART OF CENGAGE LEARNING.

U.S. state of Washington. At one time, about thirty groups were considered part of the Kwakwaka'wakw, and they fell into four main divisions: the Kwakiutl, the Haisla, the Heiltsuk (Bella Bella), and Wuikinuxv (Owekeeno or Rivers Inlet people). The latter three groups were called the Northern Kwakiutl but were later reclassified as separate tribes. In the twenty-first century, the Kwakwaka'wakw consist of thirteen bands.

For centuries, the Kwakwaka'wakw enjoyed the natural bounty of the Pacific Ocean and the surrounding forests. Because their need for food was easily met, the people were able to devote much of their time to artistic pursuits and ceremonies such as potlatches (pronounced *POT-latch-ez;* gift exchanges). The Kwakwaka'wakw were widely known for their totem poles, elaborate wooden houses, and seaworthy log canoes, as well as for dramatizing myths and performing magic tricks.

HISTORY

Before European contact

The many groups that made up the Kwakwaka'wakw tribe stayed apart from one other for much of their history before the Europeans arrived. Those that were close neighbors were often on unfriendly terms. Most historians agree that the Kwakwaka'wakw fought with their neighbors to gain slaves, territory, goods, and even revenge. If a person within the tribe was killed, his or her relatives often retaliated by taking the life of someone of equal social rank or several people of lower rank. Major conflicts among Kwakwaka'wakw groups ceased by about 1865.

Trading with Europeans

The first known contact between the Kwakwaka'wakw and Europeans took place in 1786 when James Strange, a British trader, discovered the Queen Charlotte Strait, which separates northern Vancouver Island from mainland Canada. By 1792, American, Spanish, and British traders flocked to the area in search of sea-otter pelts that could be sold to the Chinese.

Important Dates

1792: Regular trading with Europeans begins.

1849: Fort Rupert, the main Kwakwaka'wakw trading center, is established.

1850: The British destroy the village of Nahwitti.

1857: The Bella Coola destroy the village of Gwayasdums.

1865: The British navy destroys Tsahis, the largest Kwakwaka'wakw village.

1849: The Alert Bay salmon cannery is established.

1877: Missionary A.J. Hall arrives at Fort Rupert.

1881: The Kwawkewlth Agency is established to help the Natives assimilate (adopt mainstream American ways).

1884: The Canadian government bans potlatches.

1897: Franz Boas studies the tribe.

The Kwakwaka'wakw were described as "smart traders" by some of the first British people to make contact with them. The Natives exchanged furs with Europeans in return for iron and copper that they used to make tools, weapons, jewelry, and decorative items. They later bartered for European food items such as rice, tea, flour, and sugar, as well as for tools, mirrors, cloth, and cooking pots. The Kwakwaka'wakw maintained friendly relations with the Europeantraders, but the two groups were known to cheat each other on occasion.

Forts established

Fort Langley was built as a trading center in 1827, and Fort McLoughlin followed in 1833. The Kwakwaka'wakw stationed themselves at the mouth of the Fraser River and bought furs intended for Fort Langley, then sold them to Fort McLoughlin for a higher price. After Fort Victoria was built in 1842, it became the major trading post for all the tribes in the area, including the Kwakwaka'wakw. Seven years later, Fort Rupert was established near Kwakwaka'wakw land. The Kwakwaka'wakw and three other tribes soon moved to a new village they founded nearby, which they called Tsahis. Tsahis became the largest Kwakwaka'wakw community in the region.

Series of tragedies

The discovery of gold on Kwakwaka'wakw land in the mid-nineteenth century brought many settlers and gold miners to the area. Some of them claimed places where Native nations had fished for centuries. By the 1860s, non-Natives greatly outnumbered the Native population, and they pressured the British officials in charge of Canada into adopting legislation to take away Native lands. One 1865 law made it illegal for Native families to own more than 10 acres; on the other hand, non-Natives could own up to 640 acres.

Government agents, who were supposed to protect Native rights, failed to do so. In fact, they were often hostile toward the Native groups. In 1865, the British navy destroyed the Kwakwaka'wakw village at Fort Rupert. It was rebuilt, but by then many Natives had lost faith in the Canadian government.

The arrivals of Europeans in the region had other disastrous effects on the Native peoples. Smallpox epidemics struck in the late 1700s and again in the 1880s, and many died. Still more Kwakwaka'wakw were killed in battles with Canadian authorities, including the battles that destroyed the village of Nahwitti in 1850 and Tsahis in 1865.

Relocation to cities

When the gold rush ended in the 1860s, many prospectors and settlers stayed in British Columbia, which became a province (similar to an American state) of Canada in 1871. A large number of Kwakwaka'wakw settled in the capital city of Victoria and became fishers, hunters, loggers, or crew on whaling ships. Many poor Kwakwaka'wakw ended up in the city's ghetto (an area of a city where poorer members of a minority group live).

The town of Alert Bay, which began as a salmon cannery in 1870, replaced Fort Rupert as the central trading post for the people of the region by 1900. In 1881, the Canadian government established the Kwawkewlth Agency to help the Kwakwaka'wakw and other tribes assimilate (adopt the mainstream American lifestyle) at Fort Rupert, but the agency later moved to Alert Bay. In the last two decades of the 1800s, government agents opened a school, a sawmill, and an industrial school for boys at Alert Bay for the Kwakwaka'wakw and other First Nations.

Scholar studies tribe

In the late 1800s, the pioneering anthropologist (someone who studies the cultures of different peoples) Franz Boas (1858–1942) visited the Kwakwaka'wakw, whom he called the Kwakiutl, many times. He was especially interested in their art, their rituals, and their complex social system. Boas befriended members of the tribe, and they shared tribal secrets with him. He attended their potlatches and even hosted his own.

As Boas was writing about the Kwakwaka'wakw culture, the Canadian government began to take away tribal rights and sell off Native lands. In time, the First Nations peoples no longer had enough land to supply them with food, and many went to work in low-paying jobs. The government also passed laws prohibiting the Kwakwaka'wakw and other First Nations from voting or participating in potlatches.

The 1920s

In the late 1800s, the Kwakwaka'wakw started to earn high incomes by becoming professional fishers. This time of wealth and prosperity declined for the tribe when powerboats were first introduced in the 1920s. Powerboat fishers could take much larger hauls of salmon and other fish. With the number of salmon greatly reduced, salmon fishing declined rapidly, and many Kwakwaka'wakw lost their jobs in the fishing industry.

Fight for rights begins

Most historians agree that the Canadian government overstepped its bounds in its dealings with the Kwakwaka'wakw, intruding on the traditions and the rights of tribal members. For example, when Native groups formed in the 1930s and 1940s to fight against the illegal takeover of their lands, the Canadian government made it a crime for these groups to fund any campaign that might take the government to court. Finally, in 1951, the Canadian government reformed its Indian policy. Native voting rights were restored, and potlatches were made legal.

Hamasaka, a Kwakwaka'wakw chief, holds a ceremonial staff and a shaman's rattle, circa 1914. © BUYENLARGE/CONTRIBU- TOR/ARCHIVE PHOTOS/GETTY IMAGES.

Throughout the twentieth century many Kwakwaka'wakw moved from small villages to cities to find a better life. Those who remained on the reserves (the term Canadians use for reservations, tracts of land set aside specifically for use by First Nations) faced dismal prospects for employment.

Canadian government reforms in the early 1960s provided the people with medical care, educational opportunities, and unemployment insurance. Some people were able to return to their traditional villages and take up the age-old Kwakwaka'wakw enterprise of fishing. A decline in the fishing industry in the 1990s, however, forced many Kwakwaka'wakw to seek other ways of making a living. (See "Economy.")

RELIGION

The religion of the Kwakwaka'wakw was based on a complicated system of privileges that were said to be given to certain families by supernatural powers. The Kwakwaka'wakw believed that such powers were found in all things in nature. They said daily prayers to the spirits, often asking to be granted powers. Other prayers were said in thanks to the sun, to the beaver, to a woodworking tool, to a weapon, to a plant for its curative ability, or to the wind for changing directions.

In the late nineteenth century, Christian missionaries ventured to the land of the Kwakwaka'wakw and succeeded in converting some of the people to the Christian faith. The missionaries pressured the people to give up their traditional practices, including various ceremonies, burial rites, and even the construction of totem poles. Christian converts had to live in single-family homes rather than with larger groups of relatives. Some Kwakwaka'wakw converted to Christianity so they could obtain medical care or gain access to education. Others completely changed their beliefs but continued to take part in rituals such as potlatches (see "Customs").

LANGUAGE

The Wakashan language of the Kwakwaka'wakw is only spoken on the Northwest Coast of the North American continent. In modern times, the language is called *Kwak'wala*. It is a tonal language, and words can be spoken in high, middle, low, rising, or falling tones, so sentences sound musical. The language is written with markings above the vowels to indicate tone. For example, "à" is a low tone, and "ǎ" is a rising tone.

Most modern-day Kwakwaka'wakw speak English as their first language, but since the 1970s, the people have taught their children traditional language, mythology, art, and culture. Language teachers are also working with adults, because they believe that it will reinforce the

Kwak'wala Words

bagwanam	"man"
t'sadak	"woman"
'wat'si	"dog"
t'łisala	"sun"
'makwala	"moon"
'wap	"water"
həmsa	"eat"
duqʷla	"see"
nla	"sing"
bau	"leave"

children's learning. Two tribal museums provide instruction in the Kwak'wala language.

GOVERNMENT

In earlier times, communities were led by the heads of the wealthiest families, who were known as *taises,* or chiefs. Some were warriors, some were medicine men, and others were in charge of trading activities with other tribes or villages.

Since 1974, a district council has governed the bands that make up the Kwakiutl First Nation. The district council oversees tribal affairs and makes its opinions known to the government agency that runs the Campbell River District, formerly the Kwawkewlth Indian Agency. The Kwakwaka'wakw maintain businesses, health-care facilities, educational facilities, and a variety of social services.

The Kwakiutl Band Council has six councilors and a chief councilor. Elections are held in March to vote on three councilors, and in November to select four. The councilors each serve two-year terms. They generally meet biweekly, unless pressing issues arise. Meetings, which are held in the Fort Rupert administration building, are open to all members of the band, except when discussions are confidential in nature.

ECONOMY

Traditionally, the Kwakwaka'wakw were fishers and gatherers. Fishing season began in spring with Chinook salmon and extended until the chum fishing season ended in the fall. In the winter, the people stayed in their winter villages and did very little food gathering. During that time, they produced such items as boxes, spoons, dishes, and canoes.

The twentieth century brought ups and downs to the Kwakwaka'wakw economy. The fishing industry boomed after 1945. Overfishing and overcutting of trees led to a decline in the fishing and logging industries by the 1990s, and many tribal members have had to find other employment. Some began their own small businesses in the hotel, restaurant, and laundry industries. Others took jobs as janitors, clerical workers, teacher's aides, and homemaker assistants. Some Kwakwaka'wakw obtained college degrees and went into in professional fields. Nonetheless, a high unemployment rate exists among the Kwakwaka'wakw people, many of whom must rely on government assistance, because they cannot find jobs.

DAILY LIFE

Families

Extended families (parents, children, grandparents, and other relatives) lived together. The families shared rights to certain fishing and food gathering areas, their large houses, and the totem poles that depicted the family crest or symbol. Each family had a sacred name and its own songs and dances that told the story of its creation.

A Kwakwaka'wakw chief's house on Vancouver Island, British Columbia, is painted with an eagle and a whale. COURTESY OF THE PENN MUSEUM, IMAGE # S4-142218.

Buildings

Traditionally, the Kwakwaka'wakw lived in large houses—sometimes up to 100 feet (30 meters) long, 40 feet (12meters) wide, and 20 feet (6 meters) high—designed to hold several families. Villages were made up of rows of such houses, sometimes built on stilts, with a large boardwalk running the entire length of the village.

The area where the chief and his family lived was often separated from the rest of the house by an elaborately carved screen. Other families lived along the walls in areas separated by mats. Sleeping areas were assigned according to social rank: the higher a family's rank, the better their sleeping area. Slaves slept inside on blankets near the entrance of the house. Everyone used the cooking fire in the center of the house.

By the late nineteenth century, Kwakwaka'wakw houses were being built of cedar beams and milled lumber and were decorated with elaborately painted fronts and complex carvings of family crest figures. Some houses had doorways surrounded by large carved figures; an opening for the entryway was cut out between the figure's legs.

Clothing and adornment

During warm weather, Kwakwaka'wakw men went naked or wore a breechcloth (flaps of material at the front and rear suspended from the waist), whereas women wore aprons made of bark strands. As it grew colder, the Kwakwaka'wakw wrapped themselves in blankets made of bark or animal skins, which they fastened with a belt. Most Kwakwaka'wakw went barefoot. On rainy days, they donned rain hats and coats made of bark mats. Men left their long hair loose and sported long beards. Women braided their hair and wore necklaces, bracelets, and anklets made of teeth. They also wore a tight anklet designed to keep the feet from growing. Wealthy people wore nose and ear decorations of abalone shells. Everyone painted their faces and bodies to protect against sunburn, but they did not have tattoos.

Food

Kwakwaka'wakw bands collected and ate whatever foods were available in their area. For example, those near Fort Rupert ate clams, whereas other groups ate mostly salmon. The people gathered berries, roots, sea grass, and common marine food such as smelt, cod, halibut, and sea urchins. They also ate seal and sea lion. Some hunted elk, deer, wolf, bear, mink, marten, otter, whale, or mountain goat.

Families had their own territories for hunting, fishing, and food gathering. Some of the groups arranged to share sites, but other areas were considered the common property of all. The Kwakwaka'wakw dried and smoked the fish they caught in the warm months for use during the long winters.

Education

Kwakwaka'wakw children of the late twentieth century learned traditional Native customs from their elders, as their ancestors had. Organized efforts to educate children in the ways of the mainstream Canadiansociety began in 1881, when Anglican missionary A. J. Hall opened a school at Alert Bay, and his wife began teaching homemaking skills to several young Native girls in the Hall home. In 1894, the Department of Indian Affairs established an industrial school for boys in the town; by that time, Mrs. Hall's program had become a live-in school for girls. The Department of Indian Affairs school closed in 1974.

In the 1960s, many Kwakwaka'wakw moved from smaller communities to larger villages that had Indian schools. Some people who believed their children were not well served by the public schools began their own schools with programs in fishing, forestry, and carpentry in addition to standardized classes in reading, mathematics, history, and the sciences. Since the 1970s, children are also being taught their language, ceremonial dancing, mythology, and the traditional arts.

Healing practices

Kwakwaka'wakw healers were either witches or shamans (pronounced *SHAH-munz* or *SHAY-munz*; traditional religious healers). Witches harmed people by casting spells using the hair or bodily wastes of their

How to Cure a Fish, Kwakwaka'wakw Style

The Kwakwaka'wakw were masters at preserving fish so that it could be consumed all year long. Here is a description of one method they used:

To ready a fish for curing (preserving), the fish is opened at one side of the backbone, which is then detached from the head and placed aside. The roe (eggs) are put on another pile, the innards and gills are disposed of, and the fish is rubbed inside and out with a handful of green leaves. The strip running along each side of the back is cut off and sliced into a very thin sheet. The fish, now of uniform thickness at the belly, is held open by skewers and hung up to dry. It is first placed in the sun and later put in the smoke of the house's cook fire. The thin sheets are hung on poles and partially dried in the sun, with skewers inserted so they won't curl up as they dry. Five tiers of racks are hung above the fire, and each group of salmon meat spends a day on each of the first four tiers, beginning with the lowest. After lying on the topmost shelf for five more days, the cured flesh is placed in large baskets or cedar chests. The containers are kept in dry places until it is time to eat the fish.

A spirit bird mask is an example of the elaborately carved and decorated masks made by Kwakwaka'wakw artists for ceremonies and dances.
© CHRIS CHEADLE/ALAMY.

victims. If victims also knew how to cast spells, they could cancel the effects of the spells cast on them.

The people used herbs to cure diseases and injuries, but they turned to shamans when traditional methods failed. Shamans drew their power from relationships with animal spirits, who taught special dances, songs, and magic tricks that were useful in curing the sick or in healing injuries. Some shamans also had the power to cause diseases. They used these abilities to protect the chief and kill his enemies.

ARTS

Woodworking

The Kwakwaka'wakw were gifted woodworkers. They used simple tools to make remarkable canoes, large food bowls, and everyday utensils. They were also known for their superb baskets and chests made from split cedar roots, spruce roots, and grasses. Both baskets and chests were so finely made that they were watertight.

The people also carved elaborate masks, often adding feathers and hair, and used them in ceremonies and dances. One unusual feature of many masks was that they could transform from one character to another. For example, a mask of a human face had a cord on each side. If the wearer pulled the cord, wings popped out on each side of the face, and a heron's head on top stretched out its neck and opened its beak. The human face then looked as if it were part of the heron's body. Pulling on the other cord made the heron wings disappear. In addition to a variety of transformation masks, carvers also created masks with moveable parts: jaws snapped, tails spread and folded, spines fanned out, and wings flapped.

Kwakwaka'wakw artworks, with their realistic and geometric patterns, had their golden age between 1890 and 1921. Art critics call the works exceptional. Artwork could be found everywhere: on house fronts, on furnishings, on tools, and on totem poles. The American Museum of Natural History in New York sponsored a traveling exhibit of Kwakwaka'wakw art and culture called "Chiefly Feasts" that toured the country from 1992 to 1994.

A Kwakwaka'wakw longhouse and totem pole stand at Thunderbird Park on Vancouver Island, British Columbia. © GUNTER MARX/ ALAMY.

Totem poles

Master Kwakwaka'wakw craftspeople were in charge of carving totem poles (large wooden poles depicting the animals and family symbols believed to link a family to the spirit world). Other figures on the pole represented important incidents in the family's history. Another type of totem pole, the memorial pole, stood from 20 to 30 feet (6 to 9 meters) high and honored a chief who had died. Smaller totem poles, carved from large timbers, supported the roofs of houses. The Kwakwaka'wakw sometimes placed food in front of the poles as an offering to the spirits.

Oral literature

Kwakwaka'wakw families told creation stories about larger-than-life supernatural ancestors who came to the people from the sky, the sea, or the earth. One such figure was Thunderbird, who took on a human form and created his relatives, who then became the Thunderbird family.

CUSTOMS

Social classes

Each Kwakwaka'wakw family was made up of three or more groups. Each group, in turn, held property in its village—usually at least one house and various hunting, fishing, and food gathering areas. Families marked their property with special decorations, especially posts and poles that featured family crests. The family unit organized and controlled village life and directed economic activities (hunting, fishing, and so on), social relations, and ceremonial events on a daily basis.

Traditionally, a person's social rank was determined by the family into which he or she was born. People from high ranks did not perform physical labor. Instead, people called *michimis,* who cut down cedar trees, built houses, hunted game, and repaired fish traps, did such work. People with artistic skills, such as carvers, were sometimes permitted to join the upper class, but this was rare. This type of social organization began to disappear around 1875 when diseases reduced the Kwakwaka'wakw population and people moved away from their historic villages to live and work elsewhere.

Secret societies

The identity of a person's guardian spirit was revealed through prayer and fasting. Some guardian spirits were animals, such as Grizzly Bear, whereas others were figures such as Cannibal or Warrior. Those who shared the same guardian spirit formed secret societies, including the Hamatsa or Shaman Society and the Bear Society.

To gain membership in the Hamatsa Society, certain chosen children took part in the Hamatsa Dance. As part of the ritual, adults of the tribe abducted the children and took them to a spot in the forest. There, covered only by a few hemlock boughs and in a frenzy of hunger, the youths appeared to be trying to "eat" bystanders. (Europeans who observed these ceremonies thought the participants were cannibals. In fact, the children pretended to consume pieces of flesh donated by volunteers. Later the flesh was returned to the "victim," along with an apology and a small gift.) The elder members of the tribe would then seize the youngsters and force them to control themselves. Once the children became peaceful, they took part in public and private ceremonies involving magic and became members of the Hamatsa Society.

Potlatches

The Kwakwaka'wakw held potlatches, or gift-giving ceremonies, to mark births, marriages, deaths, and acceptance into secret societies. Potlatches were usually held in winter and could be simple or elaborate.

The greatest of all potlatches was called *max'wa,* meaning "doing a great thing." Visitors were invited to hear speeches, eat, dance, and marvel at their host's display of wealth. Guests received gifts of blankets, animal furs, carved boxes, shell necklaces, fish oil, weapons, and those of greatest value—engraved metal slabs called "coppers." The more lavish the potlatch, the more honor it reflected on its host. Sometimes a chief hosting a potlatch gave away all his possessions, burned down his house, and killed his slaves. These actions were considered honorable and right.

The Winter Ceremony

One of the most significant religious events in Kwakwaka'wakw society was the annual Winter Ceremony. This event involved the entire tribe and often many visiting tribes and lasted for up to twenty days. The Kwakwaka'wakw believed that powerful spirits came and visited them during this time and granted special powers to young people. While under the spell of the spirit, the young people acted insane, and the purpose of the ceremony was to "tame" them. A potlatch followed.

Head flattening

The Kwakwaka'wakw used special boards that forced the heads of their infants to take on particular shapes as they grew; these head shapes showed the person's rank in society. For example, the rather cone-shaped heads of the women of Vancouver Island showed their high social rank. People from a lower class were identified by their flatter and broader heads.

Potlatches Reach the Extreme

A person who ended up poverty-stricken after hosting a potlatch knew the condition would not last long. It was customary for a person who had received a gift of four dugout canoes at a potlatch to repay the giver eight dugout canoes at the next potlatch. By the early twentieth century, when the Kwakwaka'wakw were enjoying a fair amount of wealth, potlatches became very elaborate. Family members sometimes worked year-round at several jobs to pay for the ceremony, even pooling their life savings just to hold a single potlatch. Modern products such as sewing machines, musical instruments, boat motors, furniture, and pool tables were freely given. Families would compete to show their superiority by setting fire to large mounds of valuable goods.

An enormous potlatch took place near Alert Bay in 1921. Eighty of the three hundred guests were arrested. Without regard for the traditional significance of the ceremony, the Canadian government concluded that large-scale potlatches were bringing economic ruin to the people and decided to ban them. The authorities took many ceremonial items, such as masks and costumes, from Alert Bay and did not return them until the 1960s.

War and hunting rituals

The Kwakwaka'wakw believed that each living thing, whether plant or animal, had its own spirit. Animals did not mind being caught and eaten, because they could return to the spirit world and take on a new body. Hunters showed great respect for the animal spirits. For example, when they caught salmon, they thanked it and put its bones back into the water, believing that the bones would float back to the house of the Salmon People in the world of the spirits.

Marriage

Marriage was an opportunity to gain property and other rights and privileges, so the arrangement of a child's marriage was taken very seriously. Kwakwaka'wakw marriages might occur between two children of the same father but of different mothers, or between a man and his younger brother's daughter.

Most modern-day marriages are performed in Christian churches. They are followed by a potlatch celebration that features traditional practices such as a mock competition for the bride, a gift exchange between the families of the bride and groom, and the couple's departure to start their new life together in the groom's village (unless job demands necessitate other arrangements).

Funerals

Kwakwaka'wakw groups had different burial customs. Those of the north cremated their dead, while those to the south buried their dead in trees or caves. Important chiefs were sometimes buried in their canoes.

CURRENT TRIBAL ISSUES

In April 1997, the government of Canada and the Kwakiutl First Nation, also known as the Fort Rupert Band, reached a final settlement in a land claim filed back in 1992. The Kwakwaka'wakw claimed that Deer Island and Eagle Island should have been made Kwakwaka'wakw reserves. In exchange for the land, Canada agreed to pay the Kwakiutl First Nation $500,000 for final settlement of the claim.

Since the late 1990s, the members of the Kwakiutl Band have been pursuing treaty negotiations with the Canadian government. In 2003, they began to work on issues concerning the Kwakiutl Douglas Treaty from the late 1800s. As the first step in the treaty process, the Kwakiutl prepared a map of their territories, identified issues to be discussed, and completed background research. Although the process tends to be lengthy, the band hoped to receive a fair and equitable settlement for agreements made long ago.

By 2011, after the Canadian government continued to ignore their requests, the Kwakwaka'wakw began civil protests. The people, in war canoes or on the ground, peacefully blocked the passage of a British Columbia ferry in August of that year. The Kwakwaka'wakw protestors then went to the Forestry Office with a letter indicating they wanted to meet with government officials to discuss stopping the commercial forestry in their territory. They also wanted their rights affirmed to their traditional territory. Along with other First Nations, the Kwakwaka'wakw threatened to continue protests and civil disobedience until the British Columbia (BC) provincial government negotiated with the tribe and recognized their rights To halt the protests, the BC government agreed to a meeting to discuss forestry revenue sharing.

NOTABLE PEOPLE

Mungo Martin (Naka'penkim; c. 1881–1962) was a chief, a sculptor, a master carver, and a leader in the campaign to preserve and restore Kwakwaka'wakw totem poles. He also carved his own totem poles, including the world's largest, which stands more than 127 feet (39 meters) high. Martin drowned in 1962 while fishing.

James Sewid (1913–1988) was the chief of the Kwakwaka'wakw at Alert Bay when the ancient system of inheriting leadership positions was replaced by an election process. He began work for the fishing industry at age ten, married at thirteen, and wrote of his life in a remote village in his autobiography entitled *Guests Never Leave Hungry.* Sewid spent his later years helping to revive Kwakwaka'wakw customs. In 1955, he was selected by the National Film Board of Canada to portray his achievements in a movie called *No Longer Vanishing.* In 1971, he was made an Officer of the Order of Canada.

BOOKS

Alfred, Agnes. *Paddling to Where I Stand: Agnes Alfred, Kwakwaka'wakw Noblewoman.* Seattle: University of Washington Press, 2005.

Boas, Franz, and George Hunt. *Kwakiutl Texts.* Whitefish, MT: Kessinger Publishing, 2006.

Codere, Helen. *Fighting with Property: A Study of Kwakiutl Potlatching and Warfare.* New York: AMS Press, 2005.

Jacknis, Ira. *The Storage Box of Tradition: Kwakiutl Art, Anthropologists, and Museums, 1881–1981.* Washington, DC: Smithsonian Institution Press, 2002.

Nowell, Charles James. *Smoke from their Fires: The Life of a Kwakiutl Chief.* Hamdon, CT: Archon Books, 1968.

Schwartz, Virginia Frances. *Initiation.* Markham, Ontario: Fitzhenry and Whiteside, 2003.

Spalding, Andrea. *Secret of the Dance.* Orca, WA: Orca Book Publishers, 2006.

Spradley, James P., ed. *Guests Never Leave Hungry: The Autobiography of James Sewid, a Kwakiutl Indian.* Kingston: McGill-Queen's University Press, 1972.

Thira, Darien Troy. *And I Live It: From Suicidal Crisis to Activism among Members of the Kwakwaka'wakw and Coast Salish Nations.* New York: ProQuest, 2011.

Wolcott, Harry F. *A Kwakiutl Village and School.* Walnut Creek, CA: AltaMira Press, 2003.

WEB SITES

Anonby, Stan J. "Reversing Language Shift: Can Kwak'wala Be Revived?" *Revitalizing Indigenous Languages: Northern Arizona University.* http://jan.ucc.nau.edu/˜jar/RIL_4.html (accessed on November 2, 2011).

"Gifting and Feasting in the Northwest Coast Potlatch." *Peabody Museum of Archaeology and Ethnology.* http://www.peabody.harvard.edu/potlatch/ (accessed on November 2, 2011).

"Kwakiutl." *Four Directions Institute.* http://www.fourdir.com/kwakiutl.htm (accessed on November 2, 2011).

Kwakiutl Indian Band. http://www.kwakiutl.bc.ca/ (accessed on November 2, 2011).

Redish, Laura, and Orrin Lewis. "Kwakiutl Language (Kwak'wala, Kwakwaka'wakw)." *Native Languages of the Americas.* http://www.native-languages.org/kwakiutl.htm (accessed on November 2, 2011).

"Kwakwaka'wakw." *First Nations Land Rights and Environmentalism in British Columbia.* http://www.firstnations.de/fisheries/kwakwakawakw.htm (accessed on November 2, 2011).

Talking Feather. "Kwakiutl." *ESL and American Indians.* http://talking-feather.com/lesson-plans/kwakiutl/ (accessed on November 2, 2011).

"Thunderbird Park—Place of Cultural Sharing." *Royal BC Museum.* http://www.royalbcmuseum.bc.ca/exhibits/tbird-park/main.htm?lang=eng (accessed on November 2, 2011).

U'mista Cultural Society. http://www.umista.org/ (accessed on November 2, 2011).

Makah

Name

The Makah (pronounced *muh-KAW* or *mah-KAH*) called themselves *Qwiqwid-icciat* or *Kwih-dich-chuh-ahtx* (pronounced *kwee-DITCH-cha-uck*), meaning "people who live by the rocks and seagulls," referring to their lands along the rocky coastline. The name Makah was mistakenly applied to the tribe during treaty negotiations with the U.S. government. Officials misunderstood the Salish names other tribes called them—ones that meant "cape dwellers" (they lived on Cape Flattery) or "people generous with food." In the eighteenth century, they were known as the people of *Tatootche,* or *Tutusi* ("Thundering"), one of three thunderbird brothers and a powerful chief. Makah has been spelled many ways, including Ma-caw, Macau, Mak-kah, Mi-caw, and Maccaw.

Location

The Makah lived on the most northwestern point of Cape Flattery on the Olympic Peninsula in the northwestern state of Washington. In the late 1990s, the Makah Indian Reservation covered 44 acres in Clallam County, Washington, and included the village of Neah Bay.

Population

In the late 1700s, there were an estimated 2,000 Makah. In 1834, they numbered about 550. In the 1990 U.S. Census, 1,661 people identified themselves as Makah. According to the 2000 census, 1,704 Makah lived in the United States, and 2,147 people claimed some Makah heritage. According to tribal statistics in 2011, 2,234 Makah were enrolled; of those, 1,260 were living at Neah Bay.

Language family

Wakashan.

Origins and group affiliations

The Makah have lived on the northwestern Pacific Coast for centuries. Long before the coming of Europeans, they lived near and traded with the Nootka (see entry) and Nitinaht tribes, to whom they were sometimes friendly and sometimes hostile. They also traded with the Clallam, but they had conflicts with them as well as with the Quileute.

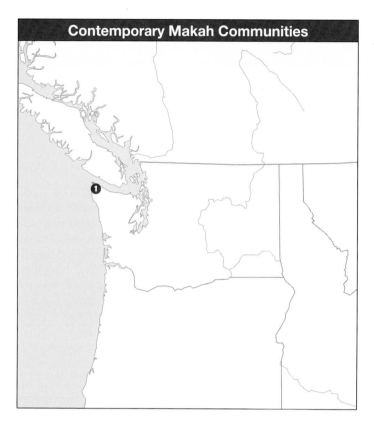

Contemporary Makah Communities

Washington
❶ Makah Indian Reservation, Neah Bay

A map of contemporary Makah communities. MAP BY XNR PRODUCTIONS. CENGAGE LEARNING, GALE. REPRODUCED BY PERMISSION OF GALE, A PART OF CENGAGE LEARNING.

According to tribal legend, the Makah people were conceived when the stars mated with animals. Their lush forest home along the Pacific Northwest coastline is an area battered by storms, soaked with rains, and dwarfed by rugged mountains to the east. The Makah depended on the sea for their livelihood and were expert hunters of whales and seals. They survived the invasion of their homeland by U.S. settlers; at the end of the twentieth century, they were the only Native people with the legal right to hunt whales. The treaty guaranteeing this right has been the subject of controversy in recent years.

HISTORY

European arrival

Before the Makah had contact with Europeans, the people lived in five villages: Bahaada (Baada, Biheda), Deah (Dia; present-day Neah Bay), Waatch (Wyacht, Wayatch), Sooes (Tsuess, Tsoo-yess), and Ozette (an excavation site). The villages were linked by similar cultures and languages as well as through marriages.

The first recorded European contact with the Makah was made by John Meares (c. 1756–1809), a British sea captain who anchored off the coast of the Makah-occupied Tatoosh Island in the spring of 1788 on a fur-trading journey. Two years later, Spaniards sailed into Neah Bay. They established a fort there in 1792, but for unknown reasons, they abandoned the venture after only four months.

Gifted traders

The Makah were already experienced dealmakers when they began trading with Europeans in the early 1800s. Their frequent trading with Europeans sharpened their skills and introduced them to non-Native goods.

Europeans bought sea otter and beaver pelts from the Makah to make hats and coats for the fashion-conscious people of northern Europe. Other tribes, who also became wealthy from this trade, purchased whale oil from the Makah. As the number of U.S. settlers grew in the first half of the nineteenth century, the Makah concentrated on producing oil from whale, seal, candlefish, and dogfish to be used as machine oil in European and American factories. They took their trade items to Fort Nisqually in Washington and Fort Langley in British Columbia, Canada, trading centers built by the U.S. government. In 1852 alone, the Makah sold 20,000 gallons (76,000 liters) of fish and whale oil for use at sawmills in Olympia, Washington; they were, in fact, the chief suppliers of machine oil for the entire Northwest Coast.

Treaty of Neah Bay

Isaac Ingalls Stevens (1818–1862) was the governor of Washington Territory and superintendent of Indian Affairs in the mid-1800s. He considered the Native tribes of the Northwest an "impediment to

Important Dates

1788: In the first recorded contact between the Makah and Europeans, John Meares moors his ship off the coast of Tatoosh Island.

1792: The Spanish establish a fort at Neah Bay but abandon it after only four months.

1855: The Makah are forced to sign the Treaty of Neah Bay, turning all their land over to the U.S. government.

1936: The Makah Tribe writes its constitution.

1970: Tidal erosion uncovers an ancient whaling village at Ozette. The find promotes a renewed interest among the Makah in traditional language and culture.

1997: The Makah regain their right to kill up to five gray whales a year for food and ceremonial use.

1979: Makah Cultural and Research Center opens to house Neah Bay artifacts.

1999: The tribe successfully hunts a gray whale.

2004: The Makah Utility Authority is formed to oversee a wind-generated power plant with its partner, Cielo Wind Power.

civilization," meaning they stood in the way of American settlement in the West. Stevens believed strongly in Manifest Destiny. According to this nineteenth-century philosophy (way of thinking), Euro-American nations—especially the United States—were meant to dominate the entire Western Hemisphere. Beginning in 1854, Stevens attempted to establish treaties with nearly every tribe in his territory (what would become the state of Washington and some surrounding areas). To take over as much land as possible for U.S. settlers, Stevens set out to abolish Native land titles, place tribes on reservations, and persuade the Native nations to adopt the mainstream American way of life.

In the mid-1800s, the Makah experienced a series of epidemics (serious outbreaks of diseases) that killed significant numbers of the tribe. The weakened Makah were convinced to sign the Treaty of Neah Bay in 1855, giving up their land to the U.S. government. In return, Governor Stevens guaranteed them access to health care. He also promised that the U.S. government would send oil kettles and gear to make their fishing more efficient. The treaty granted them "the right of taking fish and of whaling or sealing at usual and accustomed grounds and stations," referring to family-owned sections of ocean in their old territories.

Refusal to farm

U.S. government agents and Christian missionaries tried to turn the Makah, who were expert whalers and fishers, into farmers—on land that was completely unsuitable for agriculture. For the most part, the Makah ignored these efforts and continued to fish. They controlled supplies of fish oil and halibut fish in the region. Late in the nineteenth century, the Makah used their fleet of large whaling vessels to supply oil for logging camps established by American companies in the Northwest.

Makah involvement in the large-scale hunting of fur seals began in 1860. It continued for thirty years, until the ever-increasing number of seal hunters and the growing use of firearms to kill seals led to the end of the seal trade. Even so, the Makah made sure that a 1911 treaty with the U.S. government gave them and some other tribes the right to continue catching seals by the age-old method of harpooning them from canoes. The tribe continued this form of hunting for several more decades. During the twentieth century, tourism and logging activities grew, replacing fishing as the major source of income for the Makah.

Discovery of ancient village

In 1970, archaeologists (scientists who study the life and culture of ancient peoples by examining the things they left behind) made an exciting discovery. They unearthed a prehistoric Makah whaling village at Ozette in present-day Washington State. Parts of the village had been covered by a mudslide more than five centuries before, and the mud had preserved skeletons of the victims, as well as their houses and belongings, in nearly perfect condition. Ozette has been called one of the most significant archaeological discoveries ever made in North America. Many items were found there, including sculptures, harpoons, baskets, and various household utensils. This event led to the founding of the Makah Cultural and Research Center on the Makah Reservation at Neah Bay, Washington. The center highlights the history of the tribe and helps preserve its language and culture.

Culture revived

In 1995, the Makah decided to revive the age-old custom of whale hunting. Since the 1920s, the gray whale population had been endangered. By the 1990s, however, it had made a comeback. After it had been taken off the endangered list, the Makah wanted to exercise their rights. As part of the Treaty of Neah Bay, they had retained the right to catch fish, whales, and seals in traditional tribal territory. Many groups objected, but eventually the Makah received permission to take five gray whales a year.

The first whale hunt in decades ended successfully on May 17, 1999. The discovery of the ancient Ozette village and the return of whaling have paralleled the recovery of many Makah traditions, including arts, ceremonies, and language. The people are eager to revive aspects of their culture that were lost or neglected for centuries.

RELIGION

The Makah people believed in guardian spirits who helped individuals become successful in reaching their life goals. Shamans (pronounced *SHAH-munz* or *SHAY-munz*), healers who could be either male or female, helped people contact their guardian spirits.

At the beginning of the twentieth century, some Makah people joined the Native American church, a religion that combined elements of Christianity with traditional Native beliefs and practices.

Native American Church

The Native American Church formed in Oklahoma in 1918. It brought together several groups of Native North Americans who since the 1880s had been practicing the Peyote religion (pronounced *pay-OH-tay*; named for a stimulant derived from mescal buttons, which are the dried tops of a small cactus). The new religion was first spread by John Wilson (c. 1840–1901), a man of mixed Delaware, Caddo (see entries), and French parentage. He claimed that under the influence of peyote, he had several visions telling him the right way for Native people to worship Jesus Christ. (Peyote, a nonaddictive drug, brings on altered mental states and hallucinations in people who chew or consume it in the form of green tea.) Wilson preached that those who followed the "Peyote Road" would be set free from their sins. This was a welcome message to people who found themselves at the mercy of the U.S. government and settlers—confined to reservations, stripped of the right to worship their Native religions, and seeking a way to combine their traditional beliefs with Christianity.

James Mooney (1861–1921), an employee of the Smithsonian Institution (a center for the study of American culture) in Washington, D.C., became fascinated by the Peyote religion. While traveling among many Native tribes in the 1890s, Mooney came to believe that the Native nations in the United States needed to be brought together through their own religion, so he drew up the legal papers forming the Native American Church.

Attracting a diverse membership from numerous tribes, the church is most active in the American Northwest and Southwest. It combines Christian and Native beliefs and features an all-night ceremony of chanting, prayer, and meditation.

Peyote is considered sacred among church members, but since 1900, attempts have been made to outlaw its use in church ceremonies. In 1990, the U.S. Supreme Court ruled that the possession and use of peyote by Native American church members is not protected by the First Amendment. (The First Amendment to the U.S. Constitution guarantees Americans freedom of religion, among other freedoms.) The Supreme Court's ruling means that each state can decide whether to allow the religious use of peyote.

Although the consumption of peyote has generated considerable controversy and publicity, the church's main goal is quite simple: to promote unity among its members. The Native American Church stresses brotherly love, family ties, self-reliance, and the avoidance of alcohol. From the beginning, it has fought to protect the First Amendment rights of its members.

Because the Native American Church is so loosely organized, it is difficult to estimate its membership with accuracy. In 1922, the church claimed to have about 22,000 members; by 2004, it had more than 250,000 members.

LANGUAGE

The Makah language is similar to the languages spoken by their northern neighbors, the Nootka, Kwakiutl (see entries), and Bella Bella. With the discovery of the ancient city of Ozette, there has been a renewed interest in learning the Makah language. The Makah Cultural and Research

Center is home to a program that works to preserve and teach the Makah language. As a result of such efforts, the number of Makah children who spoke their native language jumped from 33 percent in 1980 to 78 percent by 1985. The last of the fluent Makah speakers died in 2002, so the Makah nation is making sure their language is passed on to the next generations.

Like most Native languages, Makah was not originally written down. It has many unique sounds that are not found in English or other languages, so a special alphabet had to be used. This alphabet, a variation of the international phonetic alphabet, was adopted in 1978. Words are written with special symbols to show how they are pronounced.

GOVERNMENT

The Makah had no chiefs. The men who had the most influence in a Makah village, usually the fur seal hunters or the harpoon throwers who captured whales, were called headmen. They often displayed their wealth and power through gift-giving ceremonies called potlatches.

The Makah adopted a constitution in 1936. A tribal council governs the tribe. It consists of five persons who are elected to staggered, three-year terms; a new council head is chosen each year.

ECONOMY

Early lifestyle

For centuries, the Makah economy was based on trade and fishing. The Makah were among the top whalers in North America until about 1860. Having gained a reputation as clever traders, they managed to control most of the money supply in the Northwest. The Makah used a shell called *dentalium* (pronounced *den-TAY-lee-um*; from the Latin word for "tooth") as money. The shells were polished and strung like beads.

Makah Words

The Makah language belongs to the Southern Nootkan branch of the Wakashan language. It is a very distinct language and the only one in its classification in the United States. Other related languages are spoken in British Columbia, Canada. *Qwiqwidicciat* (the Makah name for their language) became a separate language from its closest relative, Nitinaht, about one thousand years ago.

'cakwà'ak	"one"
atł	"two"
wⁱ	"three"
bù	"four"
Šu'č	"five"
łàXuk	"man"
xad'ak	"woman"
dakà	"sun"
ča'ak	"water"
'tłiXuk	"red"
tupkuk	"black"
'tłisuk	"white"
xusboxuk	"yellow"

Traditionally, the Makah hunted fur seals and whales. Each family had its own section of the ocean for fishing, and the area passed from father to son. During the nineteenth century, however, seals changed their migration patterns and almost disappeared from the tribe's homeland. When fur seals reappeared around 1866, seal hunting resumed because sealskin was in great demand. By the 1880s, U.S. companies were hiring Makah men to serve as seal hunters aboard commercial fishing boats. (Commercial boats work for profit, not for food or an owner's personal use.) The jobs were so profitable that the Makah temporarily gave up whaling, but they continued seal hunting. The seal trade lasted until 1890 when seal hunting was prohibited because the supply had been so severely depleted. Many Makah then returned to whale hunting.

Modern economy

Commercial logging (cutting down trees for money) on Makah land began in 1926. In the 1930s, the first road linked the mainland of Washington to the peninsula where the reservation is located. (Previously the peninsula could only be reached by boat.) The Makah tourist industry developed as more and more people discovered the beauty of the area and set out to learn about Native life. Since then, the building of a breakwater (to shelter the harbor from crashing waves) has attracted individual sailing boats and tourist boats.

Commercial fishing became important to the Makah economy later in the twentieth century, but overfishing and overcutting brought a decline in the fishing and logging industries in the 1990s. As a result, tourism became increasingly important. The opening of the Neah Bay Marina, which harbors more than two hundred sailing and fishing vessels, boosted tribal income. Large and small businesses have opened at the marina and in the village to cater to tourists.

From the later 1990s into the early 2000s, Makah Tribal Bingo provided a considerable amount of money and jobs, but the community rejected the idea of a full-service casino. The Makah did not want to develop a heavy economic reliance on gambling. Instead they concentrated on tourism and building small businesses. Their Cape Flattery Resort and Conference Facility features a lodge, campgrounds, a sweathouse (a steam-heated lodge used for Native American cleansing, purification, and ritual), sports facilities, and a café. Increasing numbers of tourists visit the reservation and surrounding areas to view wildlife, marine mammals, and birds.

In 2004, the tribe completed a feasibility study (a study to determine if something is a good idea) on the use of wind-generated power. They partnered with Celio Wind Power to develop a commercial power plant and sell electricity. Grazing cattle, operating fisheries, and mining of sand, gravel, and rock round out the tribe's economic base. Unemployment is still high on the reservation in the 2000s, however, because many of the jobs are seasonal.

DAILY LIFE

Families

The Makah family consisted of a father, mother, children, and close relatives who lived together in a large house. The bonds between grandparents and grandchildren were especially strong. Aunts and uncles were like second parents, and in-laws were also close. Members of Makah families were ranked in society according to their relationship to the headman of the village; the closer the relationship, the more important the person. Traditionally, each Makah family owned a certain section of beach along Makah territory; the family also had rights to any items that floated ashore on their property.

Buildings

Makah villages consisted of three to twenty flat-roofed longhouses along the beaches. Each longhouse sheltered up to twenty families. The buildings had dirt floors and frames made of planks held in place by pegs. The Makah constructed roofs with flat wooden planks that could be shifted to let in air or removed and transported if the villagers moved to follow a spring salmon run. Removable woven mats served as partitions to separate each family's living area. During the winter months, the Makah took down the partitions to provide a common place for dancing, feasting, and gambling. Although there was a central cooking fire, each family had its own smaller fire.

Clothing and adornment

Because of the mild climate, Makah men (and sometimes women) went naked or wore very little clothing year-round. The clothing they did wear consisted of woven capes, skirts made of cedar bark (soaked and pounded until soft), cattail fluff, and woven downy feathers. Rain gear included cone-shaped hats and bearskin robes. The Makah rarely wore shoes, but in cool weather they sometimes donned moccasins.

Food

Sea mammals, especially whales, were the centerpiece of the Makah diet. Both men and women participated in the butchering of whales, and they used every part for some purpose. For instance, they braided and dried tendons for use as rope and extracted oil from whale blubber. They ate the meat and skin immediately and gave the choicest piece of blubber to the chief harpooner.

Men also fished for salmon and halibut and hunted land mammals and birds. Various fish, shrimp, small octopuses, worms, snails, seagull eggs, and crabs added variety to the diet. The activities of women centered on gathering shellfish, plants, roots, and berries. They also processed the fish and animals the men brought from the hunt. The Makah saved smoked and dried meats for winter or used them for trade. A favorite food among the Makah was a root called camas, which could only be obtained by trading with tribes from the north who were able to grow or harvest it.

Education

From their early years, Makah boys learned fishing techniques and routes to their family's fishing territory. Girls learned about food gathering and preservation from adult women of the village.

After the move to the reservation, representatives of the federal government, called Indian agents, oversaw schools in Neah Bay. The agents showed little respect for Makah language and culture and did their best to make the children assimilate, or take on the mainstream American way of life. To do this, teachers forbid students to speak their own language or practice their customs. Often, the government-run schools were boarding schools, and students were separated from their families for much of the year. Many students missed their relatives and their traditional lifestyles; some tried to run away, but they discovered punishments could be severe.

In 1932, the state of Washington built a public elementary school and high school on the reservation. In the early twenty-first century, most students attend Neah Bay Public Schools. To encourage students to speak their language, the tribe's education department runs the Makah Language Program at the cultural center. Tribal elders assist by recording oral histories, preparing dictionary entries, and developing materials for the public schools to use.

When the Makah Cultural and Research Center opened on the Makah Reservation (see "History"), many young Makah found work there with teams who were studying the Ozette excavation site. They learned about their culture through formal training in anthropology (the study of human societies and cultures).

Healing practices

The Makah depended on shamans (pronounced *SHAH-munz* or *SHAY-munz*) to deal with illnesses. Shamans held curing ceremonies to teach the people how to use plants for healing. By the later 1900s, Makah health care was provided at a clinic run by the tribe and Indian Health Services. The Makah Nation also started substance abuse clinics, mental health programs, and many health-related classes.

ARTS

The Makah Cultural and Research Center

The Makah Cultural and Research Center, which was founded in 1979, depicts the life of the Makah people prior to European contact. It features three-hundred- to five-hundred-year-old articles that were uncovered from the Makah village of Ozette. (See "History.") On display are full-scale replicas of cedar-log longhouses, as well as exhibits on whaling, sealing, and constructing canoes. The museum displays only about 1 percent of the 5,500 articles recovered from the Ozette site. Makah artists and craftspeople have helped revive Makah traditions and are teaching other members to make longhouses, canoes, totems, masks, baskets, clothing, and jewelry.

Oral literature

As is true with many other tribes, storytellers passed on the wisdom of the Makah tribe from one generation to the next. One popular Makah tale describes how the Great Thunderbird, helped by the Wolf Serpent,

Boarding School Runaways

In addition to teaching students trades, the main goal of boarding schools was to assimilate Native Americans (make them more like whites). Students were forbidden to use their Native language or to practice their religion. Some students rebelled by running away. When they were caught, runaways received harsh punishments to discourage other students from following their example. Helma Ward (1918–2002), a former Makah student, recalls an incident from her years at one of these boarding schools.

> Two of our girls ran away … but they got caught. They tied their legs up, tied their hands behind their backs, put them in the middle of the hallway so that if they fell, fell asleep or something, the matron would hear them and she'd get out there and whip them and make them stand up again.

SOURCE: Marr, Carolyn J. "Assimilation through Education: Indian Boarding Schools in the Pacific Northwest" *University of Washington Libraries Digital Collection.* http://content.lib.washington.edu/aipnw/marr.html#schedule (accessed on November 2, 2011).

A Makah woman sits next to several cedar baskets that she made. NATIONAL ARCHIVES.

brought the Makah people their first whale. The Wolf Serpent, who had the head of a wolf and the body of a serpent, braced himself around the legs of the Great Thunderbird. When the bird swooped down on the whale, the Wolf Serpent wrapped itself around the whale's head and tail and helped the Great Thunderbird lift it out of the sea. They then took the whale and presented it to the Makah people, who made use of the sea mammal for food and supplies.

CUSTOMS

Social classes

Makah society had a class system. People in the middle class could gain power by marrying into the upper classes.

Puberty

Adolescent boys went to remote places in the forest on vision quests to find their spiritual protectors. They fasted and entered a trancelike state in which their spirits were revealed to them. Girls acquired their guardian spirits by going alone to a special place when they menstruated and performing certain rites while wearing distinctive shell ornaments on their braids.

When the Animals and Birds Were Created

In this Makah tale, the world is created by two brothers. The first part of the story (recorded here) tells why birds have certain characteristics.

The Indians who live on the farthest point of the northwest corner of Washington State used to tell stories, not about one Changer, but about the Two-Men-Who-Changed-Things. So did their close relatives, who lived on Vancouver Island, across the Strait of Juan de Fuca.

When the world was very young, there were no people on the earth. There were no birds or animals, either. There was nothing but grass and sand and creatures that were neither animals nor people but had some of the traits of people and some of the traits of animals.

Then the two brothers of the Sun and the Moon came to the earth. Their names were Ho-ho-e-ap-bess, which means "The Two-Men-Who-Changed-Things." They came to make the earth ready for a new race of people, the Indians. The Two-Men-Who-Changed-Things called all the creatures to them. Some they changed to animals and birds. Some they changed to trees and smaller plants.

Among them was a bad thief. He was always stealing food from creatures who were fishermen and hunters. The Two-Men-Who-Changed-Things transformed him into Seal. They shortened his arms and tied his legs so that only his feet could move. Then they threw Seal into the Ocean and said to him, "Now you will have to catch your own fish if you are to have anything to eat."

One of the creatures was a great fisherman. He was always on the rocks or was wading with his long fishing spear. He kept it ready to thrust into some fish. He always wore a little cape, round and white over his shoulders. The Two-Men-Who-Changed-Things transformed him into Great Blue Heron. The cape became the white feathers around the neck of Great Blue Heron. The long fishing spear became his sharp pointed bill.

SOURCE: Glenn, Welker. "When the Animals and Birds Were Created." *Indigenous Peoples' Literature.* http://www.indigenouspeople.net/created.htm (accessed on November 2, 2011).

War and hunting practices

Slaves were important to the Makah; their war parties captured them from enemies such as the Quileute and Klallam. The wealthy owned the greatest number of slaves. Children were warned not to wander far away from camp for fear they might be taken as slaves by other tribes.

The Makah ranked among the foremost whalers in North America. Whale hunting was extremely dangerous, and preparations for a hunt went on throughout the year. To condition themselves, whale hunters bathed in cold streams or lakes when the moon was full. To toughen their skin, they rubbed their bodies with hemlock twigs until they bled. At certain times, they fasted and stayed away from women. They practiced diving underwater, holding their breath to increase their lung capacity, and they mimicked the whales' graceful swimming style. When a whale appeared in a dream to the head of the whaling group, it was time for the hunt.

Whale hunters used cedar log canoes manned by crews of eight, who sometimes took the canoes as far as 20 miles (30 kilometers) offshore to hunt for whales. Excellent canoeing skills were needed, because whales could swim under a dugout canoe and flip or smash it with their enormous tails.

The chief whalers were known for having great spiritual powers. One stood in the front of the canoe and sang special songs to lure a whale, promising it many gifts if it let itself be killed, such as in this Makah plea, as quoted in Robert Sullivan's *Whale Hunt: How a Native American Village Did What No One Thought It Could*: "Whale, I have given you what you wish to get—my good harpoon. Please hold it with your strong hands.… Whale, tow me to the beach of my village, for when you come ashore there, young men will cover your great body with blue-bill duck feathers and the down of the great eagle." Whaling songs were very valuable and were passed down through families. It was considered a crime for a whaler to "steal" another's song.

Whale hunters used harpoons tipped with sharp seashells. Seal bladders, which served as excellent flotation devices, were attached to the harpoons with whale sinew rope. After the harpoon entered the whale's flesh, these floats prevented the whale from diving while it was alive or sinking after it had died. Hunters then guided the whale toward the shore to complete the kill.

Festivals and ceremonies

The Makah practiced the Wolf Ritual, a four-day winter healing ceremony. Its purpose was to welcome members into the secret Klukwalle society. Participants in the Wolf Ritual wore masks or headdresses made of thin boards.

The Doctoring Ritual was another four-day winter ceremony. It was believed to cure participants of illnesses. The ceremony was performed by a shaman, who wore yellow cedar bark robes with neck and head rings of shredded cedar bark.

In modern times, Makah Days are held on the reservation each August to honor the Makah heritage. They include canoe races and traditional dancing and singing by children and adults.

CURRENT TRIBAL ISSUES

A controversy erupted in 1995 when the Makah, who had not hunted whales since 1926, informed federal officials that they wanted to kill up to five gray whales a year for food and ceremonial use. The proposal met with disapproval from animal rights activists, who claimed that a sanctioned whale hunt would hamper their efforts to ban whale hunting worldwide and would push the whales closer to extinction. Into the second decade of the 2000s, studies are assessing the current whale population and migration patterns, which have changed over time.

Tribal members themselves were not in agreement on this issue. Still, plans went forward, and the first whaling expedition occurred in spring 1999. Billy Frank Jr. (1931–), chairperson of the Northwest Fisheries Commission, tried to encourage the community at large to support the tribe's return to their traditions:

> Whoever you are, you should join the Makah Tribe in celebrating its harvest of a gray whale. You should celebrate this return of a sacred practice to some of the most culturally connected people in the world. You should celebrate the return of justice and vitality to a tribe that has been repressed over this past century, and celebrate the recovery of gray whale populations to the historic levels needed to sustain harvest. You should understand that life begets life, and that the spirit of the whale lives on in the Makah people. It lives in the rejoicing of the elders, the strength of the warriors and the rekindled excitement of the children. It lives on because that is the way the Creator intended it to be.

NOTABLE PEOPLE

Sandra Osawa (1942–) is a successful television producer and writer, focusing primarily on Native culture and issues. In 1980, she received an Emmy nomination for *I Know Who I Am,* a short film produced for Seattle's KSTW-TV on the traditions and cultural values of the tribes of the Pacific Northwest. She also was the producer of *The Native American Series,* which was the first television series ever to be produced, written, and acted exclusively by Native Americans.

BOOKS

Coté, Charlotte. *Spirits of Our Whaling Ancestors: Revitalizing Makah, and Nuu-chah-nulth Traditions.* Seattle: University of Washington Press, 2010.

Erikson, Patricia Pierce. *Voices of a Thousand People: The Makah Cultural and Research Center.* Lincoln: University of Nebraska Press, 2005.

Goodman, Linda J. *Singing the Songs of My Ancestors: The Life and Music of Helma Swan, Makah Elder.* Norman: University of Oklahoma Press, 2003.

Haig-Brown, Roderick. *The Whale People.* Madeira Park, BC: Harbour Publishing, 2003.

McMillan, Alan D. *Since the Time of the Transformers: The Ancient Heritage of the Nuu-Chah-Nulth, Ditidaht, and Makah.* Vancouver: University of British Columbia Press, 2000.

Nelson, Sharlene, and Ted W. Nelson. *The Makah.* New York: Franklin Watts, 2003.

Norris, Karen and Ralph. *Contemporary Art on the Northwest Coast: Salish, Nuu-chuh-nulth, and Makah.* Atglen, PA: Schiffer, 2011.

Sullivan, Robert. *A Whale Hunt: How a Native American Village Did What No One Thought It Could.* New York: Scribner, 2002.

Tweedie, Ann M. *Drawing Back Culture: The Makah Struggle for Repatriation.* Seattle: University of Washington Press, 2002.

Waterman, T.T. *The Whaling Equipment of the Makah Indians.* Reprint. Charleston, SC: Nabu Press, 2010.

WEB SITES

Frank, Billy Jr. "Everyone Should Celebrate the Makah Whale Hunt." *Hartford Web Publishing.* http://www.hartford-hwp.com/archives/40/191.html (accessed on November 2, 2011).

Makah Cultural and Research Center. http://www.makah.com/mcrchome.html (accessed on November 2, 2011).

"The Makah Indian Tribe and Whaling: A Fact Sheet Issued by the Makah Whaling Commission." *Native Americans and the Environment.* http://ncseonline.org/nae/docs/makahfaq.html (accessed on November 2, 2011).

The Makah Nation on Washington's Olympic Peninsula. http://www.northolympic.com/makah/ (accessed on November 2, 2011).

Moss, Madonna L. "Makah Whaling Misunderstood." *University of Oregon.* http://pages.uoregon.edu/mmoss/makah.htm (accessed on November 2, 2011).

"Native American Church Movement." *Oklevueha Native American Church.* http://www.nativeamericanchurch.net/Native_American_Church/Native_American_Church_Movement.html (accessed on November 2, 2011).

Northwest Indian Fisheries Commission (NWIFC). http://www.nwifc.org (accessed on November 2, 2011).

"Our History." *Makah Cultural and Research Center.* http://www.makah.com/history.html (accessed on November 2, 2011).

Redish, Laura, and Orrin Lewis. "Makah Indian Language (Qwiqwidicciat)." *Native Languages of the Americas.* http://www.native-languages.org/makah.htm (accessed on November 2, 2011).

Renker, Ann M. "The Makah Tribe: People of the Sea and Forest." *University of Washington Libraries.* http://content.lib.washington.edu/aipnw/renker.html (accessed on November 2, 2011).

Nisqually

Name

Nisqually (pronounced *nis-KWALL-ee*) comes from the word *squalli,* meaning "prairie grass." The Nisqually call themselves *s'q"ali? abš* or *Squalli-absch,* which means "people of the grass country" in the Salish language.

Location

The Nisqually's traditional lands were the entire Nisqually River basin in western Washington State. They inhabited the coastal regions and woodlands from Puget Sound (Whulge) to Mount Rainer (Tacobet). Today, they live on the Nisqually Reservation, located by the Nisqually River in Thurston County. It lies on a strip about one mile wide (about one and a half kilometers) surrounded on both sides by Fort Lewis, the second largest U.S. military base. By the early 2000s, the Nisqually Land Trust had acquired more than 3,400 additional acres along rivers and creeks on or near the reservation.

Population

In 1780, there were about 3,600 Nisqually. By the beginning of the twentieth century, the population had fallen to 110. In the 1990 U.S. Census, 436 people identified themselves as Nisqually. The 2000 census indicated there were 460 Nisqually, and 697 people claimed a Nisqually heritage.

Language family

Salishan.

Origins and group affiliations

For thousands of years, Nisqually groups lived in their homelands in what is now the state of Washington. They shared good relations with the nearby Puyallup (see entry) and with the Kittitas and Yakama (see entry), who lived within the same water drainage system. They also traded with the Nuu-chah-nulth (see entry).

The Nisqually thrived for thousands of years on the natural resources their vast tribal lands provided, sharing berry and hunting grounds with

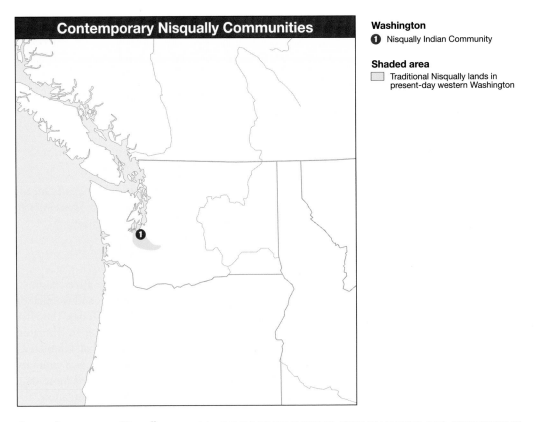

Contemporary Nisqually Communities

Washington

① Nisqually Indian Community

Shaded area

☐ Traditional Nisqually lands in present-day western Washington

A map of contemporary Nisqually communities. MAP BY XNR PRODUCTIONS. CENGAGE LEARNING, GALE. REPRODUCED BY PERMISSION OF GALE, A PART OF CENGAGE LEARNING.

nearby tribes. They roamed the woodlands and coastal waters from Mt. Rainier to the Puget Sound. Their lives were ordered by finding food, feasting, and special rituals. Before the 1970s, a lack of electricity and other modern resources on the reservation caused most Nisqually to move from their tribal lands. Since then, electricity has been introduced, and new buildings have gone up. Hundreds of Nisqually have come back to the area to rebuild their culture and community.

HISTORY

Early history

Nisqually oral history indicates that the *Squalli-absch,* the ancestors of the modern Nisqually, traveled north from the Great Basin. After they traversed the Cascade Mountain Range, they constructed their first village in the basin area of present-day Skate Creek. This settlement was just below the southern end of the Nisqually River watershed, the later home of the tribe. The Nisqually also built a large village near the Mashel River.

First contact

The first contact between Europeans and the Nisqually took place when British captain George Vancouver (1757–1798) explored the Puget Sound area in 1792. The Hudson's Bay Company, a trading business, first wrote about the tribe in 1820 when it entered the region.

Before 1846, the United States and Great Britain jointly occupied the Nisqually lands. In 1846, the two countries agreed that the U.S. government would decide the tribe's fate. In 1848, U.S. officials promised the Native nations that their lands would not be taken from them without their consent, but they later broke that promise.

Treaty of Medicine Creek

In 1854, Isaac Ingalls Stevens (1818–1862) was appointed governor of Washington Territory and was placed in charge of relations with the Native nations. By then, U.S. settlers wanted more acreage. Stevens decided the best way to get land was to take it away from the Native nations and place the tribes on reservations. In December 1854, he offered a treaty to a group of tribes, including the Nisqually. Under the Treaty of Medicine Creek, the Nisqually had to give up their tribal lands and move to a reservation within one year. It was plain to Nisqually Chief George Leschi (1808–1858) that the treaty took away the rivers where his people had always fished and the pastures where they kept their horses. The Nisqually also had to face the threat of being moved farther north. Although Leschi refused to sign the treaty, someone placed an "X" before his name on the treaty, falsely indicating his approval.

Important Dates

1792: George Vancouver explores Puget Sound.

1833: Fort Nisqually is established.

1854: The Treaty of Medicine Creek is signed, and the Nisqually give up much of their land.

1855–56: The Nisqually engage in the Puget Sound War.

1858: Chief George Leschi is convicted and executed.

1884: Nisqually land is divided into thirty family allotments.

1917–18: Tribal land is taken by the U.S. government for building Fort Lewis.

1946: The Nisqually adopt a tribal constitution.

1974: The Boldt Decision affirms Nisqually off-reservation fishing rights.

1978: The Nisqually Tribal Headquarters is built.

1994: Tribal constitution is amended.

2004: Chief Leschi is acquitted, almost 150 years after his death.

Chief Leschi leads uprising

In time, the Nisqually were forced by the U.S. government to relocate to a reservation, and their life changed greatly. The people were upset to leave the grasslands they loved and move to a rocky and barren land away from their accustomed fishing sites. They became afraid when diseases brought by the American settlers broke out among the people. They were dismayed with U.S. government delays in putting certain plans for the tribe into action.

Finally, the Nisqually enlisted the help of men from other tribes and, under the command of Chief Leschi, engaged in an uprising. However, Leschi was unsuccessful in drawing all the tribes of Western Washington into a wider war against the Euro-Americans. The Puget Sound Indian War (1855–56) was short, and the Natives lost. Leschi was captured and executed.

Life on the reservation

The Nisqually settled down to a quiet, but impoverished, life on the reservation. The war had one benefit, however. The federal government removed Governor Stevens from his position and increased the size of the Nisqually reservation. Although the original treaty had given them 1,280 acres, an executive order in 1856 enlarged it to 4,717. Still, the land proved too poor for successful farming.

By the beginning of the twentieth century, some Nisqually were forced to leave the reservation to seek jobs in the lumber and agricultural industries. In time, the population of the reservation declined even further due to disease, poor diet, and alcoholism. By the early 1900s, the Nisqually population had fallen by more the 90 percent.

Loss of rights

During the winter of 1917, without any warning, the U.S. Army ordered the Nisqually to leave their homes. Later, the U.S. War Department seized nearly two-thirds of the Nisqually Reservation land to create Fort Lewis, a military training camp for soldiers going to fight in World War I (1914–18; a war in which Great Britain, France, the United States, and their allies defeated Germany, Austria-Hungary, and their allies). As the years passed, the War Department took over more parcels of Nisqually land.

Around this time, the government also attempted to assimilate Native peoples, or make them more like mainstream Americans. Rather than letting the Nisqually teach their own children, government officials ordered that the children be sent to boarding schools at which teachers forbid them to speak their own language or follow tribal customs. This practice continued until the 1940s.

Protests held on fishing issues

During the 1950s, a growing number of American fishers wanted more fishing areas for themselves. They succeeded in pressuring Washington State officials to limit Nisqually fishing rights to their reservation only, instead of the much wider area the tribe had been used to. The Nisqually defied the order and continued to fish beyond reservation lands.

In 1963, the Washington State Supreme Court upheld the state's right to impose fishing restrictions on the Native nations. As a result, conflicts took place between the Nisqually and state police officials on the banks of the Nisqually and Puyallup rivers. In 1966 a well-known African American comedian named Dick Gregory (1932–) was arrested for supporting the tribe during a "fish-in." The fish-in was held to protest state laws that now required hook-and-line fishing instead of the tribe's traditional methods—nets anchored with rocks that made for a larger catch. A celebrated fishing rights case resulted. The Nisqually claimed that, according to treaties with the federal government, they had the right to engage in net fishing. A complicated series of court battles took place between the Natives and the state government.

The Boldt Decision of 1974 affirmed that the 1854 Treaty of Medicine Creek permitted the tribes of western Washington to fish in their "usual and accustomed" fishing areas away from the reservation. Since this celebrated case, the input of Native peoples has been sought on fishing questions. Since the late 1990s, the Northwest Indian Fisheries Commission has directed off-reservation fishing for the tribes, including the Nisqually.

Meanwhile, by 1973, the Nisqually Reservation had been reduced to a fraction of its former size, and only a small group of Nisqually resided there. In 1974, the Nisqually people, with planning and funding from the federal office of Housing and Urban Development, began preparations to build a tribal headquarters on the reservation. In 1976, they purchased 53 acres of land, and they completed the headquarters in 1978. Nearby, they built facilities for educational services, medical and dental care, programs for seniors and children, a police force, a library, recreational programs, and a natural resources center. In the 1990s, more than one hundred homes were built on the reservation. The Nisqually nation also formed a land trust to acquire and restore shoreline habitats (see "Current Tribal Issues").

RELIGION

Religion played a major role in every aspect of Nisqually life. Spirits gave people certain abilities, attitudes, personality traits, and preferences. Failure to cooperate with the spirits resulted in illness and death. The spirits bestowed powers that might include physical strength, artistic talent, hunting skills, long life, and wealth, among others. The powers usually were given to a person during adolescence, but they could come to those of any age who were physically clean and pure.

The Nisqually believe that their land is a living thing that has been created by the Great Spirit and should not be divided. Mother Earth is sacred and has to be treated with great care (see "Current Tribal Issues"). The people did not accept the typical American concept of private property and refused to break up their land.

In 1839 and 1840, two priests, Francis Norbet Blanchet (1795–1883) and Modeste Demers (1809–1871), traveled around the area to introduce the tribes to Catholicism. Using Chinook Jargon, a language used for trade, they communicated with the various peoples in the Puget Sound area. (For more information on Chinook Jargon, see Chinook entry.) Several Native peoples converted and began holding worship services for their tribes. Later, a Methodist missionary settled at Fort Nisqually, but he was not successful in gaining converts.

The early 1880s saw the rise of interest in the Indian Shaker Church. The founder, John Slocum, reportedly died and was resurrected as a result of his wife's shaking. This religion, with its combination of Christian and Native beliefs, appealed to many of the tribes along the coast, including the Nisqually.

Today, most Nisqually people are members of the Catholic Church, the Indian Shaker Church, or a Nisqually division of the Assembly of God denomination.

LANGUAGE

The Nisqually people spoke Southern Lushootseed, a variety of the Salish language commonly used in the Puget Sound area. In modern times, most Nisqually speak English during their everyday activities. Only a few dozen elders were still fluent in the language at the turn of the century, but the tribe is working to keep its heritage alive by offering classes to the young.

GOVERNMENT

The Nisqually had no chiefs in traditional times, but the advice of the head of the richest household was often sought. His main job was to sponsor feasts and potlatches (gift-giving ceremonies). When he died, his younger brother or son usually took over these duties.

Today, a general council made up of all enrolled tribal members over the age of eighteen governs the Nisqually Reservation. This council elects a seven-member tribal council, which rules according to the Nisqually constitution that was adopted in 1946 and amended in 1994. The Nisqually tribal council has a tribal chair, vice chair, secretary, treasurer, and three other positions for fifth, sixth, and seventh council members. Each member serves a two-year term.

ECONOMY

Before the move to the reservation, the Nisqually economy was based on fishing, hunting, gathering, and trade. Shells obtained in trade from the Nuu-chah-nulth (see entry) of Vancouver Island were polished, strung like beads, and used as money. People's wealth was also measured by the number of blankets, fur robes, pelts, bone war clubs, canoes, and slaves they owned.

In the early 2000s, unemployment on the reservation was high; many people who wanted to work could not find jobs. The tribe currently provides jobs for tribal members and receives income from their casino, aquatic technologies, reservation mart, shellfish business, and various grants. They earn additional funds from their community garden and solar greenhouse, timberlands, and two fish hatcheries. The Nisqually Five-Year Overall Economic Development Program was implemented to encourage economic growth on the reservation, to provide training and employment for tribe members, and to develop tribal resources.

Lushootseed Words

The Nisqually, along with several other Northwest Coast tribes, speak a form of the Lushootseed Salish language. (For more Salish words, see Duwamish and Puyallup entries.) The words listed here are all foods that the Nisqually enjoyed eating.

Sčuhdádx	"salmon"
sbít'	"soup"
quhlítx	"salmonberry"
kʷuhlhú'l	"camas"
s'áxʷu'	"clams"
plíla'ac	"cherry"
xʷsuhbuhd	"honey"
qá'xʷac	"crab apple"
xúhdxuhd	"goose"
Sqígʷuhc	"deer"
Sxʷítl'uhy'	"mountain goat"
sčúhtxʷuhd	"black bear"

DAILY LIFE

Families

In traditional times, four to eight Nisqually families shared a large house. The families usually consisted of a man, one or more of his wives, and all of his children, sometimes unmarried relatives, and (in wealthy families only) one or more slaves.

Buildings

The Nisqually built solid houses out of cedar posts and planks; cedar is a strong wood that can be cut with simple tools. Houses were rectangular and longer than they were wide; they usually sat in rows parallel to a body of water. The insides of the houses were lined with platforms that served as beds; the platforms were about 3 feet (1 meter) wide and had storage spaces built above them. In the summer, these houses often sat empty,

A Nisqually woman in traditional dress places a headdress on a young girl. © NATALIE FOBES/CORBIS.

as most activities took place either outdoors or in square or cone-shaped summerhouses, covered with mats.

Clothing and adornment

During warm weather, Nisqually men often went naked or wore only hide or cedar bark breechcloths (garments with front and back flaps that hung from the waist). In rainy weather, they wore capes made of cedar bark strips. Women wore narrow skirts of cedar bark or full-length dresses. In the winter, both men and women wore animal hides, rubbed with deer brains to soften them. They also wore hide moccasins and blankets woven of mountain goat hair or dog hair.

Nisqually women parted their hair down the middle and wore two braids, sometimes painting the part red. Men let their hair grow to neck-length, parted it down the middle and combed it behind their ears or braided it. They often wore headbands made of skin and tied hawk or eagle feathers into their braids. Younger men plucked out their beards, but older men sometimes let theirs grow. Men often wore rectangular fur hats, whereas older women wore soft hats made of mountain grass. Young girls rarely wore hats.

The Nisqually did not wear body paint, but both men and women used red face paint combined with deer tallow to keep their faces from becoming weather beaten. At ceremonial events they painted designs on their faces, such as lines on the cheeks and on the chin. Both men and young girls wore headbands with tassels. They wore necklaces, bracelets, earrings, and nose rings made of shells polished to look like beads.

Food

The Nisqually mainly fished, but they also hunted and gathered. In spring and fall, men caught salmon; everyone in the tribe helped to smoke and dry them. The men also caught blue fish, flounder, halibut, skate, sole, and devilfish. Fish eggs and shellfish added variety to their diets. Hunters took seals by surprise and clubbed them or drove them into sharpened stakes or nets.

The meat of deer, elk, black bear, beaver, coyote, mountain goat, and rabbit was dried and smoked over fires. Small animals, including squirrel, pheasant, and grouse were caught in nets strung between trees and then roasted. Different kinds of berries, such as blackberries, were crushed, formed into blocks, and dried in the sun or over a fire or were boiled and made into a thick paste for later consumption. The Nisqually also ate licorice roots, wild carrots, ferns, dandelions, sunflowers, camas, tiger lilies, and various other bulbs, leaves, and seeds.

Women used sharpened ironwood sticks to dig cooking pits. Camas bulbs were steamed in a pit for two to three days. Then they were dried and stored in baskets for winter use. The Nisqually ate some plants raw, and they boiled others in baskets filled with water into which they dropped hot stones. Salmonberries and thimbleberries might be eaten fresh, crushed and mixed with water to make juice, or dried on racks over a low fire. Women spread hazelnuts in the sun to dry and roasted acorns to get rid of the acid taste. Acorns could be ground into flour or buried in mud near a stream for later use.

Food was prepared only once a day, in the late afternoon, and eating took place throughout the day. A typical evening meal might be a boiled liquid followed by steamed meat or fish. The tribe ate dried or freshly picked foods at other meals. All winter homes had rows of dried salmon hanging from the ceiling. Women would cut down one fish each day for their families' meals.

Education

Although little is known about how the Nisqually were taught, children likely learned many of the skills needed for survival by observing their elders. In the late 1800s and early 1900s, the U.S. government established schools on the reservation. Children from ages six to sixteen received a basic education in reading, writing, and arithmetic for half a day, and then they worked during the afternoon on farms run by the schools. Boys did repairs, and girls learned to sew clothes and keep house.

By the mid-1900s, more emphasis was placed on teaching children their own culture. In 1974, activist Maiselle Bridges started the Wa He Lut Indian School to integrate Nisqually culture into all subject areas. In 1996, a flood destroyed the school, but with the help of government funding, it reopened in 1998. In the 2000s, the school continued to pass on Nisqually tribal history, language, and beliefs.

Other children at the Nisqually Reservation attend public school. Northwest Indian College established a branch campus on the reservation in 1994 that serves as a training site for tribal employees in addition to offering degree programs.

Healing practices

When people became ill, they consulted medicine men called shamans (pronounced *SHAH-munz* or *SHAY-munz*), but these healers could only cure certain diseases. After a shaman determined the cause of an illness (often an object within the afflicted person's body), he seized the object by using sweeping gestures and passing his hands over the body of the patient, occasionally dipping his hands in water. He then clasped the object in his palms. At times, he bit into the patient, sucked the object out, and then transferred it to his hands. The patient's relatives decided whether to send the object back to its source or let the shaman destroy it. This final part of the process often took many hours and sometimes required the aid of a second shaman. Singing, dancing, and drumming accompanied the healing act.

Many Nisqually people had a knowledge of herbs. They collected or bought them and cured themselves. Today, the staff at a medical clinic on the reservation meet many of the people's health care needs.

CUSTOMS

Social classes

Nisqually society was divided into the upper class, the lower class, and slaves, who were usually war captives and their descendants. Villages were linked by the marriages of leading families and by participation in shared ceremonies.

Birth and babies

When a Nisqually woman was about to deliver, she went to a shelter where a specially trained woman assisted her with the birth. The afterbirth (the substance expelled from a woman's womb after childbirth) was wrapped and then carried by a small boy to the top of a tree—the higher

Folklore of the Tsiatko

The Nisqually tell stories about a group of tall people, called "stick" Indians, who were said to wander through the forests. In the Nisqually language they were called *tsiatko*.

The tsiatko lived like animals in hollowed-out sleeping places in the woods. They wandered on land only, never on the rivers, and usually by night. They communicated by whistling, and their sounds could be heard throughout the darkness.

They played pranks on the villagers, such as stealing fish from their nets. They sometimes played pranks on individual men, whistling to put the men into a trance and then removing their clothing and tying their legs apart.

People who interfered with the tsiatko were hunted down and killed by bow and arrow. The tsiatko sometimes stole children and forced them to become wives or slaves. Women were afraid of them, and they used threats of the tsiatko to keep their children in line.

One man told a story about his relatives capturing a tsiatko boy in 1850 and raising him. The boy slept all day and wandered about at night. In the morning, his captors could see where he had piled up wood or caught some fish. They eventually permitted him to go home to his people. He later returned with some of his people for a visit, then went away for good.

the better for the good luck of the baby. Parents used special boards to mold their infants' heads to form a straight line from the nose to the forehead, as this was considered an attractive feature. Babies stayed in cradleboards until they could walk.

Puberty

Adolescent boys took part in vision quests, looking for the spirits who would guide them throughout their lives. Sweat baths and fasting were elements of these five- to ten-day journeys. What happened on the journeys always remained a secret.

Girls also went on vision quests both before and after puberty. When she had her first menses, a girl went to an isolated hut. She was encouraged to do tasks to make her a good worker later in life. After their daughter's first menstruation, the family of an upper class girl often held a feast, which let the village know she was ready for marriage.

Young Nisqually people reenact a wedding ceremony. © NATALIE FOBES/CORBIS.

Courtship and marriage

Parents arranged marriages for their children, and both boys and girls married at young ages. In *People of the Totem,* author Norman Bancroft-Hunt points out that Salish Indians like the Nisqually made use of "love charms and potions which were designed to make a girl fall in love with the young man who idolized her.... Secret formulas for 'putting names' on a girl's ears, eyes, hands, and head were used … to make it impossible for her to hear, see, touch, or think without being reminded of her suitor."

Marriages usually took place between individuals from unrelated families in different villages. The boy's family approached the girl's with a formal request. A ceremony followed in which the bride was taken to the groom's village. The bride's family gave the couple a dowry, and both families exchanged gifts. The couple stayed in the husband's village and lived with his family.

People who came from wealthy families rarely divorced. If a spouse died, the widow or widower married one of the deceased's relatives to keep the children and money within the same family. Poorer people did not have the same restrictions.

Festivals and ceremonies

First feasts The Nisqually held First Salmon ceremonies, which took place when they caught the first fish of the season. They honored the salmon as if it were a visiting chief. The people presented it with offerings such as eagle down. Then they cooked and ate the fish with reverence. Celebrations honored other fish and creatures, such as seals and elk.

Winter Dance People who had been cured by a shaman (see "Healing practices") held a Winter Dance. A song leader led the ceremony, and the shaman and others worked on the sponsor to draw out his songs. Then the sponsor got up and danced while he sang his song. Other singers followed as their spirits led. Afterward, everyone feasted, and the sponsor distributed gifts.

The dancers who participated in the ceremony each had a different kind of power. For example, one painted his face red, carried deer-hoof rattles, and danced with a knife piercing his body. Another caused a striker (the long pole the people used to keep time by striking the rafters) to move by itself. A third made two boards or hoops pull young men around the room.

Soul-Recovery, or Spirit-Canoe, Ceremony The people believed that the spirits of the dead stole souls, so men with special powers traveled to the land of the dead to bring them back. Each performer had a plank carved and painted with a guardian spirit and a post made to resemble an earth dwarf. The men set them up in a rectangle to form a canoe shape. As they sang their songs, they paddled with staffs, and acted out their journey. The dance lasted two nights with a final battle where the men outwitted the dead and returned with the souls.

Potlatch Those who received wealth power in their vision quest hosted a village potlatch, or giveaway. Messengers went to other villages to announce the ceremony and handed out small sticks to the leading men. Everyone who received an invitation brought other guests with him; the visitors usually took food and gifts to share.

The event could be held either in the host's home or in a potlatch house. Dancers performed on a stage made by putting planks across two canoes. For several days, people played games, participated in contests, danced, and sang. Guests could give out gifts, but the host handled the main give-away. He distributed presents to each of his invited guests. To end the ceremony, the host sang his wealth power song, and then other participants could share their spirit songs.

War and hunting rituals

The Nisqually engaged in occasional raids, but little actual warfare. They had an interesting custom associated with a potlatch. As visitors approached a village where a potlatch was being held, they pretended to be a war party and engaged in a mock battle with their hosts.

Funerals

The family of the deceased held a wake, and relatives brought gifts for the dead. Professional undertakers prepared the body and then removed planks from the side wall of the house so they could exit with the body. They buried the body in rocky ground, or they wrapped it in robes, placed it in a fishing canoe covered by a mat, and suspended the boat 10 to 14 feet (3 to 4 meters) in the air between two trees. They sometimes put bodies in a box that stood on the ground. Cedar plank sheds marked the graves.

After the burial, the family held a feast and gave away the dead person's property. Women cut their hair for the mourning period.

CURRENT TRIBAL ISSUES

Changing history

When Nisqually Chief Leschi was tried for the murder of U.S. militia-man A. B. Moses, many people believed territorial governor Isaac Ingalls Stevens wanted to punish Leschi for refusing to sign the Medicine Creek Treaty. The trial ended in a hung jury, meaning that the jurors could not agree on a verdict. At a second trial, jurors did not know that Chief Leschi had killed Moses during combat. They convicted him, and Leschi was executed in 1858.

In December 2004, almost 150 years later, the Washington State Supreme Court handed down a new verdict. The court unanimously declared Leschi not guilty. They said that when Leschi shot and killed Moses on October 31, 1855, it was an act of war, so Leschi should not have been executed for the crime.

Following the 2004 trial, Billy Frank Jr. (1931–), chairman of the Northwest Indian Fisheries Commission, explained that his father had often talked to him about Leschi:

> He always talked about the war (Washington's Indian War of 1855–56) and the day he [Leschi] was hung. We went up to the place where he was hung. It was a big, natural bowl. He said they came for miles in wagons and watched the hanging. We teach that to all our children about how our leader was hung by this society. We teach our young people about this hanging and it's not a very good story. We want to be able to tell the truth to our children.

The story in the history books will now have a different ending—one the tribe has always insisted is the truth. Nisqually tribal council chairman at the time, Dorian Sanchez, summed it up: "[Now] all will know the name Leschi as we have: warrior, leader, hero and innocent."

Environmental action

In 1974, the tribe established the Nisqually National Wildlife Refuge for the protection of birds and wildlife. By the early twenty-first century, more than 275 bird species arrived yearly to winter and breed in the Nisqually Refuge. The area also provides a habitat for steelhead trout, various salmon species, and many threatened and endangered species. The Nisqually Delta has been named a National Natural Landmark because it is one of the best examples of a coastal salt marsh remaining in the North Pacific.

Their concern for the environment and desire to acquire more of their former homeland has led the Nisqually nation to purchase lands along the shorelines and restore them. Along with other watershed partners, the Nisqually now own 75 percent of the land along the Nisqually River, and they received grants to assist in the restoration. The nation also added to their Yelm shoreline holdings. Other initiatives include land purchases and restoration at Mount Rainier Gateway, Wilcox Flats, Mashel River, and three creeks—Ohop, Powell, and Red Salmon.

NOTABLE PEOPLE

Chief George Leschi (1808–1858) united Native warriors in the western part of Washington during a conflict with the U.S. government in 1855 and 1856. Leading about one thousand troops representing various tribes, Leschi attacked the settlement of Seattle as part of an unsuccessful resistance against Governor Isaac Ingalls Stevens. Leschi and his troops were turned back by U.S. Navy troops. Although Leschi escaped and went to live among the Yakama (see entry), he was taken prisoner by the U.S. Army and executed in 1858 (see "Current Tribal Issues").

Billy Frank Jr. (1931–), is a Nisqually political activist working to change policies that affect the lives of Native peoples. In 1991, Johns Hopkins University officials honored him for the decades he has spent fighting for the land and fishing rights of Native nations in the Pacific Northwest.

BOOKS

Bancroft-Hunt, Norman. *People of the Totem: The Indians of the Pacific Northwest.* New York: Putnam, 1979.

Carlson, Keith Thor, ed. *A Sto:lo-Coast Salish Historical Atlas.* Vancouver, BC: Douglas & McIntyre, 2006.

Carpenter, Cecelia Svinth, Maria Victoria Pascualy, and Trisha Hunter. *Nisqually Indian Tribe.* Charleston, SC: Arcadia, 2008.

Hansen, Carl. *Nisqually.* Denmark: Nationale Forfatteres Forlag, 1912.

Kluger, Richard. *The Bitter Waters of Medicine Creek: A Tragic Clash between White and Native America.* New York: Alfred A. Knopf, 2011.

Middleton, Beth Rose. *Trust in the Land: New Directions in Tribal Conservation.* Tucson: University of Arizona Press, 2011.

Uncommon Controversy: Fishing Rights of the Muckleshoot, Puyallup, and Nisqually Indians. Report prepared for the American Friends Service Committee. Seattle: University of Washington Press, 1970.

Wilkinson, Charles F. *Messages from Franks Landing: A Story of Salmon, Treaties, and the Indian Way.* Seattle: University of Washington Press, 2006.

PERIODICALS

Shapley, Thomas. "Historical Revision Rights a Wrong." *Seattle Post-Intelligencer.* (December 18, 2004). Available online from http://www.seattlepi.com/local/opinion/article/Historical-revision-rights-a-wrong-1162234.php#ixzz1WBFxoNiw (accessed on August 15, 2011).

Wickersham, James. "Nusqually Mythology, Studies of the Washington Indians." *Overland Monthly* 32. (July–December 1898): 345–51. Available online from http://themossback.tripod.com/tribes/nisqually.htm (accessed on August 15, 2011).

WEB SITES

"Before the White Man Came to Nisqually Country." *Washington History Online.* January 12, 2006. http://washingtonhistoryonline.org/treatytrail/teaching/before-white-man.pdf (accessed on August 15, 2011).

Crooks, Drew W. "Leschi and Quiemuth: Honored Leaders of the Nisqually Indians." *Dupont Museum.* http://www.dupontmuseum.com/Documents/Articles/Corrected_Leschi_and_Quiemuth_Essay.pdf (accessed on August 15, 2011).

Curtis, Edward S. "Puget Sound Indians." *The North American Indian.* Northwestern University Digital Library Collections. http://curtis.library.northwestern.edu/curtis/viewPage.cgi?showp=1&size=2&id=nai.09.book.00000034&volume=9 (accessed on August 15, 2011).

"Leschi: Last Chief of the Nisquallies." *Washington History Online.* http://washingtonhistoryonline.org/leschi/leschi.htm (accessed on August 15, 2011).

Lushootseed Research. http://www.lushootseed.org/ (accessed on August 15, 2011).

Nisqually Delta Restoration. http://nisquallydeltarestoration.org/ (accessed on August 15, 2011).

"Nisqually Indian Tribe, Washington." *United States History.* http://www.u-s-history.com/pages/h1561.html (accessed on August 15, 2011).

Nisqually Land Trust. http://www.nisquallylandtrust.org (accessed on August 15, 2011).

Redish, Laura, and Orrin Lewis. "Lushootseed (Whulshootseed, Puget Sound Salish)." *Native Languages of the Americas.* http://www.native-languages.org/lushootseed.htm (accessed on August 15, 2011).

Southern Poverty Law Center. "Against the Current." *Teaching Tolerance.* http://www.tolerance.org/activity/against-current (accessed on August 15, 2011).

Thrush, Coll-Peter. "The Lushootseed Peoples of Puget Sound Country." *University of Washington.* http://content.lib.washington.edu/aipnw/thrush.html (accessed on August 15, 2011).

"Welcome to Nisqually." *Nisqually Indian Tribe, Squally-Absch.* http://www.nisqually-nsn.gov/ (accessed on August 15, 2011).

Nuu-chah-nulth (Nootka)

Name

The Nuu-chah-nulth (pronounced *New-chaa-nulth*), or Nuu-chah-nulth-aht, are a Canadian First Nation composed of fourteen bands. In 1979, the Nuu-chah-nulth Tribal Council adopted this name, meaning "all along the mountains and sea," as their official designation. Prior to that, they were called the West Coast District Society of Indian Chiefs (1973–79) and the West Coast Allied Tribes (1958–73). For centuries after the arrival of the Europeans, however, the people were called *Nootka,* a name the Captain James Cook expedition gave them in 1778. At that time, the people referred to themselves as *Mooachaht.* Although some Nuu-chah-nulth still use the term Nootka, others consider it offensive.

Location

When the first Europeans arrived in the area, the Nuu-chah-nulth homeland stretched along the west coast of Vancouver Island from Port San Juan to Cape Cook in present-day Canada. The people also inhabited the area around Cape Flattery, which was Makah territory. Their land extended from Flattery Rocks to Hoko Creek in what later became the state of Washington. In the twenty-first century, the Nuu-chah-nulth First Nations still live on Vancouver Island's Pacific coast, and their communities are found from Brooks Peninsula in the north to Point-no-Point in the south.

Population

Estimates suggest that the population may have been as large as 30,000 prior to European contact, but that figure might have included other groups, such as the Makah. In the early 1800s, the twenty-two Nuu-chah-nulth villages may have only totaled 6,000 people. An 1835 statistic showed 7,500 people. Disease and alcohol greatly reduced the population, which stood at little more than 5,000 in 1860, slightly more than 3,000 in 1888, and about 2,000 in 1908. The number rose to 4,325 in 1991 and 6,792 in 1996. As of 2011, the Nuu-chah-nulth Tribal Council had 8,147 members, and an additional 2,000 people lived in various off-reserve communities. (A reserve is the Canadian name for reservation.)

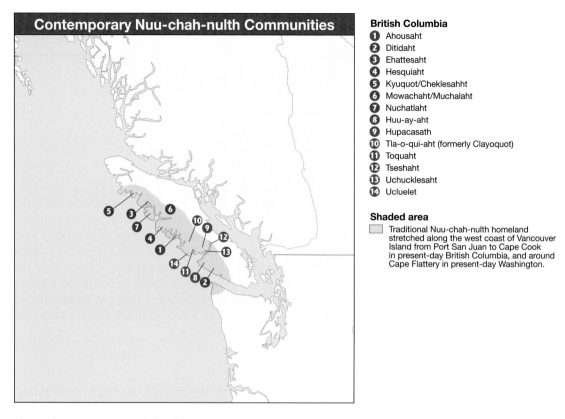

Contemporary Nuu-chah-nulth Communities

British Columbia

1. Ahousaht
2. Ditidaht
3. Ehattesaht
4. Hesquiaht
5. Kyuquot/Cheklesahht
6. Mowachaht/Muchalaht
7. Nuchatlaht
8. Huu-ay-aht
9. Hupacasath
10. Tla-o-qui-aht (formerly Clayoquot)
11. Toquaht
12. Tseshaht
13. Uchucklesaht
14. Ucluelet

Shaded area

Traditional Nuu-chah-nulth homeland stretched along the west coast of Vancouver Island from Port San Juan to Cape Cook in present-day British Columbia, and around Cape Flattery in present-day Washington.

A map of contemporary Nuu-chah-nulth communities. MAP BY XNR PRODUCTIONS. CENGAGE LEARNING, GALE. REPRODUCED BY PERMISSION OF GALE, A PART OF CENGAGE LEARNING.

Language family

Wakashan.

Origins and group affiliations

Sources vary on when the first peoples inhabited the area. Some may have arrived about ten thousand years ago, but they first formed societies several thousand years later. Excavations show that coastal sites were occupied possibly as far back as seven to nine thousand years ago. Various Nuu-chah-nulth tribes lived on Vancouver Island, but the most well-known ones were the Clayoquot, Kyuquot, and Nitinaht. Their neighbors included the Salish, Kwakwaka'wakw (see entry), and Nimkish. The Nuu-chah-nulth are related to the Kwakwaka'wakw, Makah (see entry), Haisla, and the Nitinaht.

In 1958, the fourteen separate Nuu-chah-nulth nations united. These groups occupy three different regions. The Ditidaht, Huu-ay-aht, Hupacasath, Tse-shaht, and Uchucklesaht are from the Southern Region of

Vancouver Island. The Central Region consists of the Ahousaht, Hesquiaht, Tla-o-qui-aht, Toquaht, and Ucluelet. The Ehattesaht, Kyuquot/Cheklesaht, Mowachat/Muchalaht, and Nuchatlahtlive in the Northern Region.

Thousands of years ago, a culture began on the West Coast that centered on whaling. Some of these early peoples were ancestors of the Nuu-chah-nulth, who continue to depend on the sea for sustenance. Like many of the Northwest tribes, the Nuu-chah-nulth developed a class system of the wealthy, commoners, and slaves. They participated in potlatches (elaborate gift-giving events) and adapted to their maritime environment by using sea mammals and fish for food, clothing, and tools. In the late 1700s, the Nuu-chah-nulth began a trade relationship with the Europeans, but they soon gained a reputation as warlike after they retaliated against outsiders' brutality. In recent years, the people have been working to counteract that image and to restore their culture, which had eroded over time. Victoria Wells, the granddaughter of the Ehattesaht Band chief explained in David Neel's *The Great Canoes* about this revival of their heritage: "Our culture is alive. It hasn't died, it's been in the winter phase."

Important Dates

1774: The first Spaniard, Juan Peréz, arrives in Nuu-chah-nulth territory.

1778: Captain James Cook spends a month with the people and names them and their homeland *Nootka*.

1789–94: Spain and Great Britain vie for control of the area during the Nootka Sound Controversy.

1803: The Nuu-chah-nulth kill all but two crewmembers of the European ship named the *Boston*.

1864: The British navy destroys Ahousaht villages.

1871: British Columbia joins Canada; reserve land is set aside for the Nuu-chah-nulth.

1958: The various bands unite as the West Coast Allied Tribes.

1978: The people rename themselves the Nuu-chah-nulth.

HISTORY

Prehistory

Archaeologists have unearthed artifacts at Yuquot, a large prehistoric village located at the entrance to Nootka Sound. The ancestors of the Nuu'chah'nulth lived there beginning about 2350 BCE. Other settlements excavated in this area as well as to the south in Hesquiat Harbour and to the west around Barkley Sound show that the people used bone and antler tools for fishing. They also made awls, needles, harpoon points, and bark shredders. Seal and bear teeth adorned necklaces. Mussel shells served as knives and beaver teeth as woodworking tools. The people created other implements from stone and sometimes from shells or teeth.

A sketch of a Nuu-chah-nulth man and woman was made by a member of Captain James Cook's expedition in the late 1770s. © THE PRINT COLLECTOR/ALAMY.

Different tools found in the Barkley Sound area indicate that that the Nuu-chah-nulth conquered the area in a later historical period.

Ancient villages were constructed on steep bluffs or on small islands to make them easy to defend. The people buried their dead in caves or in rock shelters, usually in boxes or trunks. Grave goods included glass beads, cedar boxes, baskets, mats, and robes made of cedar bark. These early peoples depended on sea mammals and fish for their survival, though at times they ate deer or birds. Thus, their lifestyles closely resembled that of their descendants.

European contact

Because of their location, the Nuu-chah-nulth traded with other groups in the area, but not until 1774 did the first European expedition make its way into their territory. Juan Peréz (c. 1725–1774) sailed from Mexico and landed at present-day Friendly Cove. Two more Spanish ships passed through the area the next year. Those were followed in 1778 by British explorer Captain James Cook (1728–1779), who stayed with the Nuu-chah-nulth for a month and gave the people and the land the name Nootka. After one more visit by Spanish explorers in 1779, the Nuu-chah-nulth did not see another European until the British fur trader James Hanna arrived in 1785.

Hanna's discovery of the rich possibilities for the fur trade spurred other English and American fur traders to head to the area. Mexico, however, had sent Estevan Martínez to claim the land. When the British crews sailed into the area, the Spaniards seized their ships. Although

An illustration from around 1800 shows the native inhabitants of Nootka Sound, British Columbia, greeting European visitors.
© HULTON ARCHIVE/GETTY IMAGES.

Mexico later returned the vessels, the two countries struggled for control of the land in a conflict called the Nootka Sound Controversy (1789–94). Eventually, in 1795, Great Britain took over.

Relations with Europeans

The Nuu-chah-nulth were friendly to the traders, but after the European crew of two ships beat the men of the Nuu-chah-nulth village and raped the women, the chief ordered his warriors to prepare for battle. The two trading ships sailed before the Nuu-chah-nulth could attack, but when another European ship anchored near their shores, the tribe planned an assault. After preparing for battle (see "War and hunting rituals"), the Nuu-chah-nulth concealed weapons under their blankets. They convinced some of the crew to go salmon fishing and, after they had the Europeans in the water, they killed them. The Nuu-chah-nulth then returned to the ship and killed the rest of the European sailors, except for two that they held hostage.

One of these two men, John Jewitt (1783–1821), wrote about his life among the Nuu-chah-nulth people. Jewitt, who lived as a slave of the powerful chief Maquinna (died c. 1795; see "Economy" and "Notable People"), kept a diary using berries as ink. In the diary, he notes that Maquinna spared his life because he wanted to utilize Jewitt's ironmaking skills. The nineteen-year-old Englishman was not rescued for more than two years because traders avoided the area after the attack.

Changes in the economy

During the next fifty years, relations remained hostile as Europeans took over more Nuu-chah-nulth hunting and fishing areas. Some tribes attacked trading vessels, but others continued to look for new goods to barter. The sea otter population had been depleted, so the Nuu-chah-nulth turned to other pelts. Seal, marten, mink, deer, and elk became the new trade goods along with dogfish oil, which the loggers used to grease skids.

By the late 1800s, many Nuu-chah-nulth were working in the commercial seal and salmon processing industries. Some had turned to crafts to make a living. Baskets and totem poles were the major moneymaking items. But fishing, canning, and logging became the mainstays of the economy. In 1871, British Columbia became a part of Canada, and the government set aside reserves for the Nuu-chah-nulth. Only a few reserves were on traditional tribal lands.

The Nuu-chah-nulth suffered during the Great Depression in the 1930s, when industries shut down, leaving them without jobs. Many returned to their traditional subsistence lifestyles and made money by selling furs or crafts. After World War II, fishing and logging once again increased, and some Nuu-chah-nulth continue to make a living in these trades. Others, however, had to leave the reserves to find jobs.

The Pan-Nootkan movement

As more people moved into mainstream Canadian society, they wanted to erase the long-held ideas about their culture stemming from their past encounters with Euro-Canadians. The people also wanted to establish their autonomy by taking control of their own affairs.

One of the ways they did that was to join the Native Brotherhood of British Columbia. The people also banded together as the West Coast Allied Tribes in 1958. That group changed its name to Nuu-chah-nulth Tribal Council in 1978. In 1980, the council made a formal land claim for the territory and resources that had once been theirs. They requested the land and seas from Port Renfrew to the Brooks Peninsula. In January 1995, the council signed an agreement with the federal and provincial governments to begin the treaty process. Along with restoring their land, the Nuu-chah-nulth have also been working to revive their culture.

RELIGION

Ka'uc, the supreme being, dwelt in the "land of the sky" or "sky country." Other important beings were the Four Chiefs Above, the sun, the moon, and Thunderbird, who sent lightning and thunder. Some Nuu-chah-nulth groups, such as the Clayoquot, had other deities, including the Sea Chief, Mountain Chief, and South Chief in addition to the Day (sun) and Night (moon) Luminary. Many groups included the Above Chief *Hahlupihawihl* as an important spirit. The Nuu-chah-nulth prayed to these beings for luck in hunting and good weather. The elder of the household burned feathers and whale oil as he recited the prayers.

The people also believed that objects had spirits and that spirits controlled all aspects of life. Spirit people lived in the ocean, and certain sea mammals—Herring, Whale, Salmon, and Harbor Seal—had houses under the sea. Evil beings also lived underwater and in the mountains and forests. To gain power, the Nuu-chah-nulth went on vision quests so they could take a piece of these powerful beings, who then became their guardian spirits.

LANGUAGE

The Nuu-chah-nulth, along with the Kwakwaka'wakw, speak a Wakashan language. Although the two languages have enough similarities for linguists to classify them as part of the same group, the dialects (varieties of a language) are quite different. Both of these languages consisted mainly of nouns and verbs. The Nootka dialects include Northern Nootka, Central Nootka, Nitinat, Makah, and Ozette. The latter three groups can understand the two Nootka dialects, but the Nootka speakers cannot understand them.

Nuu-chah-nulth Words

huupisi	"cockle"
sac'up	"Chinooksalmon"
haw'a	"eat"
nuu	"sing"
wah	"leave"
kiwitaana	"horse"

The language, which has more consonant sounds than English, is complex. Only a few hundred people speak it fluently; most of them are over age fifty. The people are working to revive their language through Internet lessons and classes.

GOVERNMENT

In the early days, the people were governed by *ha'wiih,* or hereditary chiefs. They also looked to the creator, *n'aas,* and to the elders of the community for guidance. The various bands were composed of several families or local groups, each with its own territory and chief.

The people respected the chief, who was usually the wealthiest member of the band. A chief was responsible for dividing food and giving gifts. He was also expected to be decisive, and it was his responsibility to select the lead singer and dancer as well as to care for the environment. During the ceremonies, the chiefs would "bring out their wolves," according to elder Nelson Keitlah. "These wolves were the law and order of governance and they [the chiefs] lived almost like a secret society."

In 1958, the tribes united as the West Coast Allied Tribes, and later as the West Coast District Society of Indian Chiefs. By 1979, they had become the Nuu-chah-nulth Tribal Council. The council supports the bands in establishing self-government.

ECONOMY

The Nuu-chah-nulth were a nomadic people who depended on fishing and gathering to supply their food needs. The people spent spring and summer in the village, then traveled in autumn for salmon fishing and in midwinter for sprat and herring. Each move meant packing up the plank houses (see "Buildings") and moving them in canoes. Much of the tribe's time was taken up with traveling to food sources and then getting and preparing food, but the Nuu-chah-nulth also had time to partake in the arts, particularly wood carving and basketry (see "Arts").

After the Europeans arrived, the people engaged in trade. They collected sea otter skins from other tribes and traded with both the British and Spanish. One chief in particular, Maquinna, became wealthy from acting as an intermediary in the trading process. He used potlatches to redistribute the goods among his people. Maquinna's skill as a wholesaler increased his power among his own tribe and with neighboring tribes.

Over time, the Nuu-chah-nulth moved from a subsistence economy to dependence on wage labor in the Euro-American-owned fishing, canning, and lumber industries. During the Great Depression of the 1930s, an economic downturn caused many businesses to shut down. Some Nuu-chah-nulth returned to trapping and producing crafts to make a living. Others began picking hops (plants used to make beer). Many people, however, struggled to find employment. They had to move away from the reserves to obtain jobs. Even in the twenty-first century, unemployment continues to be a problem for many.

DAILY LIFE

Families

Several generations usually lived together. Grandparents were vital to the family. They oversaw the care and education of the children (see "Education"). Their role was so important that if a woman did not have elderly relatives to play this role, she was given a medicine to prevent pregnancy.

The highest honor and respect in families went to the eldest person who had the closest connection to the kin's ancestors. Families passed down rights to hunting and fishing areas, clam beds, and camas root sites. Children also inherited songs and dances.

Buildings

Homes were built in rows facing the shore. Five posts in the front and back supported a sloping roof held up by lintel posts and crosswise rafter poles. The Nuu-chah-nulth used flat, moveable boards for roofs and tied the wall planks together with flexible pine-bark branches. They could take planks off the roof to let in sunshine and let out smoke. In rainy weather, they pushed the boards close together. The Nuu-chah-nulth entered their houses through gaps in the boards or by moving overlapping planks.

Houses were usually about 8 to 10 feet (3 meters) high in the front and about 15 feet (4 or 5 meters) high in the back, but some had 20-foot (6-meter) ceilings. The plank homes averaged 60 feet (18 meters) long and 30 feet (9 meters) wide. They had window holes that could be closed off with matting when it stormed. Inside, the Nuu-chah-nulth built long wooden benches for sleeping and eating, which they covered with mats.

Boards separated one family's quarters from another, and although every house had a central fire, individual family groups used their own fires for cooking. The occupants stored their clothing, masks, and other valuables in carved chests that they painted black and decorated with animal teeth. They hung fishing gear, drying fish, whale blubber, and sealskins filled with oil from the rafters. Because they also gutted their fish indoors and threw their bones on the floor, the houses smelled of fish and were often smoky inside.

One of the important features of the homes were the *klumma* or *tlámma,* house posts carved from huge tree trunks. These painted posts had human faces, arms, and hands, and stood about 4 or 5 feet (1 to 2 meters) tall. Larger posts like these formed the outer doorway; visitors passed between the figure's legs to enter the building.

Clothing and adornment

One of the early European arrivals recorded information about Nuu-chah-nulth clothing and admired the men's beautiful ankle-length dresses made of sea otter skin. In honor of the visit, the men had painted their faces with a red-and-black shark's jaw design and had coated their hair with white down taken from birds' soft underfeathers. The chief wore a pointed cap with feathers on top. His hat, like those of the rest of the upper class, was made from spruce roots. Common people used red-cedar bark for their headwear.

For everyday wear, the men used cedar bark or fur robes that they fastened on the right side. Women used cedar bark to make aprons and also wore robes. They fastened tight bands of deerskin around their ankles to make them slimmer. When it rained, they donned bark capes.

The men usually plucked out their facial hair, but they sometimes grew thin beards just on the tips their chins. The older men often had beards and long mustaches that drooped down on the sides. They wore their hair loose or tied into a knot at the tops of their heads. Women had two braids that hung down in back.

The wealthy wore abalone-shell nose rings and dentalium (pronounced *den-TAY-lee-um*; polished shells) earrings. In addition to their earrings, chiefs inserted eagle, hawk, or owl feathers into piercings in their ears for celebrations. Everyday earrings for men were made of wooden circles that had yellow cedar bark streamers attached to them. Women tied dentalia to their braids and made woven bracelets from bracken roots.

Food

The Nuu-chah-nulth considered seal and whale blubber a treat; they also added the oil to many dishes, including berries. Women dried clams, salmon, and other fish to eat when supplies ran low. In addition to these staples, the people also ate roe (fish eggs), cod, porpoise, halibut, dogfish, sprats, herring, sea otter, cockles, and mussels. Some fish were eaten raw, but others were cooked by dropping hot stones into water until it boiled. The women then added the fish to the wooden pot and kept the water hot by adding more stones taken from the fire.

Along with catching seafood, the men sometimes hunted ducks, geese, deer, or bear. After eating bear meat, the Nuu-chah-nulth did not eat fresh fish for two months. Onions, turnips, nettles, roots, and berries such as brambleberries and strawberries were also part of their diet.

The Nuu-chah-nulth carved wooden dishes for eating and serving food. Mussel shells served as utensils, and tree bark was used as napkins. The people used mealtimes for teaching children. They believed that as food nourished the body, words nourished the mind, so both food and edifying conversation were included at every meal.

Education

Because parents were busy gathering food, grandparents taught the children the skills they needed to know. The elders spoke gently and provided encouragement; children were expected to sit, listen, and learn. Girls learned to care for the household; boys learned to hunt and fish. In addition to chores, children learned moral values, such as truthfulness, reciprocity, and cooperation.

Fathers passed down special prayers and songs to their sons. Once a boy had memorized the words, he could accompany the men on short fishing or whaling trips. His father then taught him about bathing rituals. Boys went to the most dangerous parts of the rivers and lakes to learn to be brave.

After the Canadian government passed the Indian Act in 1874, children were forced to attend government or religious schools. Some schools lasted only a decade; others existed for almost a century. Thousands of Native children across Canada died in these boarding schools, and many were physically and sexually abused. Because teachers did not allow students to practice their traditions or speak their languages, much of the Nuu-chah-nulth culture was lost.

A Nuu-chah-nulth totem pole stands at Yuquot Village, Nootka Sound, British Columbia. © DANITA DELIMONT/ALAMY.

Healing practices

The Nuu-chah-nulth valued those who caught fish and whales; as a result, although shamans (pronounced *SHAH-munz* or *SHAY-munz*), or healers, were important and respected, that role went to those who had time to practice it. Women could become shamans, but most were men.

People treated minor illnesses with herbs. Songs often played a part in the healing process. Shamans were called in to treat more difficult diseases. They used rattles and other instruments along with paint and ornaments to affect cures. Sometimes they removed objects from the body. At times, the rituals caused the shaman to go unconscious.

Illness could be caused by different factors. An angry whale or salmon might steal a person's soul, which the Nuu-chah-nulth believed was located in the brain. The person remained alive because the *titicu,* or life force, still breathed in his or her chest. Both the soul and the *titicu* had to depart for a person to die.

ARTS

Music, theater, dance, visual art, and storytelling all held a place of prominence in Nuu-chah-nulth culture. Songs and dances, which were obtained from spirits, were passed along as a family inheritance.

CRAFTS

The Nuu-chah-nulth arts were highly praised. In spite of crude iron tools, the people achieved great skill at woodcarving. Carvings ranged from huge totem poles to ceremonial masks and small decorative items. Homes had carved roof beams; boxes and drums were also carved and painted.

Basketry and weaving were two other arts in which the Nuu-chah-nulth excelled. Women softened cedar bark fibers with bark shredders and beaters and used the fibers for weaving. Designs such as birds and whales were woven into the hats and baskets.

Oral literature

The Nuu-chah-nulth told two different kinds of stories, both of which were believed to be true. The first were the oldest tales that went back to a time when animals were humans and people had not settled into their traditional homelands. Anyone could tell these stories and pass them along.

The second group of stories were accounts of what happened to specific humans in a certain time or place. These recountings could only be told by descendants of the story's hero. The hero of each tale had received special powers that were passed down to each successive generation, just as names, dances, and songs were. These legends became part of a family's inheritance.

CUSTOMS

Social organization

The Nuu-chah-nulth had several levels of society. Those with the most power and wealth formed the upper class, which consisted of chiefs. Commoners made up the middle class. The lower class was composed of slaves, often captives from other tribes.

People owned their property, which was passed down to both sons and daughters. Value was also placed on names, stories, and songs, all of which were considered an important part of an inheritance, along with rights to fishing and hunting grounds.

Birth and naming

The people washed newborns in warm water and put dogfish oil on them. Infants sucked on dried whale blubber until their mothers had enough milk to feed them. After their daily baths, babies were wrapped in shredded cedar bark and put in carriers that held their heads in place. A pad of bark over the forehead flattened their heads into a pointy shape.

Babies had a circle punched out of their ear by a professional ear piercer. He flattened the earlobe onto a block of wood and then struck a sharpened circle of eagle bone onto the ear to cut out the hole. Young children had only one piercing in each ear, but others were added in later years.

One group of Nuu-chah-nulth, the Clayoquot, tattooed a circle around girls' ankles using fishing line that they sewed through the skin. They then blackened nettle fiber with elderberry wood charcoal and pulled that through the holes to leave the permanent color behind.

When a baby began to crawl, relatives and friends gathered for a feast. At the celebration, the father or grandfather named the child, using an inherited name. A girl received an unused name from her mother's or grandmother's side of the family. A boy's name came from the father's or grandfather's side. A feast that included gift-giving was held whenever names were changed later in life.

Parents of twins or deformed children had to live away from the village. For four days, they were confined to a hut hung with black mats. They were expected to drum and sing to the herring and salmon for special power. For the next year, they could not eat either of those fish, and they had to bathe in a pit rather than the river. Twins often died of neglect.

Puberty

At age twelve, boys learned the bathing rituals, songs, and prayers used during whale hunting (see "Education"). They went at night for baths, during which they scrubbed themselves with hemlock to get rid of their human smell so that whales would accept them. After they bathed alone and learned all the proper songs and prayers, young men could take their fathers' places on whaling expeditions.

At puberty, a daughter of the chief sat for five days inside wooden walls in the back of the house, with her chin on her knees, while women sang to her. Wrapped in a cedar-bark robe, the girl kept her hair neat with a wooden comb tied around her neck. Rather than touching herself with her hands, she used a scratching stick. She ate very little—only two pieces of dried fish and a clamshell of water per day.

After her hair was freshly braided and decorated with dentalia (shell ornaments) on the fifth day, the girl went with her mother or an elder woman to bathe in a secret place. The girl prayed and scrubbed herself with four different bunches of hemlock until the branches were shredded. She then donned a robe and a headdress with an eagle feather on either side of her head. Her father, carrying a red wooden bowl, and three men accompanied her through the village. When the chief threw the bowl, the person who caught it received a dentalium shell and an otter skin. Gift-giving also occurred at the house. Every four days after that for the next ten months, the girl washed and scrubbed with four hemlock branches and kept the ornaments in her hair.

Marriage and Divorce

Spouses for chiefs' daughters were usually chosen for political purposes, to unite villages. When a man wanted to marry, he placed a stick with feathers on it outside the woman's home. Everyone in the village watched, sometimes for days, to see the response. If the woman agreed, she took the stick inside. If she was not interested, she broke the stick and threw it on the beach. After a woman accepted his proposal, a man had to pass both physical and intellectual challenges. Gift-giving sealed the arrangement, and presents were exchanged during the marriage ceremony as well. Weddings involved feasts and potlatches.

Women who married outside their villages took a name with them. They also brought their songs, dances, and material possessions, but they did not own the songs and dances. They shared them with their new communities.

Men, particularly wealthy chiefs, had more than one wife. John Jewitt (1783–1821), who lived for two years as a Nuu-chah-nulth captive (see "History"), told of a chief's brother who had his teeth filed into points and bit off his wife's nose as punishment for her refusal to sleep with him.

A man could divorce his wife by sending her back to her family. A woman could also choose to go home to her parents. The wedding gifts did not have to be returned if a couple divorced.

Death and mourning

Whenever someone was about to die, that person was dressed in his or her best clothing, and the family stood around, crying. After death, the body was propped, using robes or blankets, into a sitting position inside a box. Once the lid was tied shut, the Nuu-chah-nulth made a hole in the house roof or the wall for the coffin. It was considered bad luck to take a dead body through the door, because the souls of other people in the household might follow the deceased's spirit. Corpses were usually put coffins in trees or caves. Hunters' graves were marked with carved images of the animals they had hunted. The carving was done on a pole, or the figures were placed in a canoe.

When a chief died, his possessions were buried with him, and a slave might be executed to accompany him. If a chief's son died, the village

A Nuu-chah-nulth man takes a ceremonial bath before a whale hunt, circa 1910. © WORLD HISTORY ARCHIVE/ALAMY.

viewed the body, which was laid out on a mat. After a speech by another chief, ten men carried the coffin to the cemetery, accompanied by crying relatives. Everyone then gathered in the house, where the father sang a mourning song and gave away most of what the deceased had owned. A chief sometimes sent a war party out so that other tribes would experience the same sorrow.

Spouses of the deceased cut their hair, donned old clothes, and leaned on a staff when they walked. The most important of the deceased's possessions were thrown near the grave or destroyed. The eldest son of the dead person took what he wanted and then decided how the rest would be divided. If a man died childless, his widow kept his possessions, but others in the village hauled away the boards of his house. If the wife had no children, her husband got only the bedding; everything else went to her sister or next closest relative.

The Nuu-chah-nulth believed that when people died, the spirits of some of their departed relatives met them and helped them cross a river in a canoe. The spirits occupied a world under the earth similar to the village the dead person had left. The spirits lived to old age there and had spirit children with the spouse they loved most.

War and hunting rituals

Whaling traditions The Nuu-chah-nulth hunted whales from May through June. Whale hunting required a long preparation period to ensure success. Whalers took ritual baths twice a day in the morning and evening beginning in October and continuing until the end of whaling season. In addition to abstaining from sex, the men prayed and sang special songs that they had learned in childhood from their fathers.

Whalers depended on amulets (charms to improve their luck). One of these was a foot-long black worm with two heads that they speared and preserved. Another was the chest and right leg of a crab's shell.

Crews of eight went out in canoes but had only one harpooner per canoe. The others paddled or steered. The harpooner was the man with the greatest spiritual power. He used a 14- to 18-foot (4- to 6-meter) spear that had a sharp mussel-shell point at the end, to which floats made of sealskin were attached. Once a harpooner sank his spear into a whale, other canoes surrounded the whale and shot additional harpoons into the wounded animal. After the whale tired, a diver cut a hole in its lip and attached a towline so the canoes could pull it to shore.

The person who speared the whale chose how it was divided among the other hunters. He received the back part of the whale near the fin, but he never kept it for himself. Giving it away ensured that he would be able to spear more whales in the future.

War rituals Raids were common because the Nuu-chah-nulth wanted to acquire slaves. Wars were also undertaken to avenge insults. Before Nuu-chah-nulth warriors engaged in battle, they took a ceremonial bath called *ósŭmĭch.* The *haíitlik,* a dance or pageant led by the chief, came next. The men, wearing masks, then followed the chief's canoe as it snaked through the water to their destination.

Festivals and ceremonies

One of the major celebrations, often held several times during the winter, was the Wolf Ritual. This ten-day ceremony welcomed young men into the tribe. It included elaborate feasts, potlatches (extravagant gift-giving), and performances. Masked dancers acted out comical and magical rituals. The Doctoring Ritual for healing the sick was another common practice among the Southern and Central Nuu-chah-nulth.

The shamans' dance was an important Nuu-chah-nulth ceremony. The performance portrayed the story of an ancestor who was kidnapped by supernatural beings. These spirits later released him, after bestowing supernatural gifts on him. A potlatch followed the reenactment, which reinforced the Nuu-chah-nulth social values and class system.

CURRENT TRIBAL ISSUES

Laws outlawing potlatches were enacted more than a century ago. Many Northwest tribes held their ceremonies in secret during that time. Not until the 1970s did the Nuu-chah-nulth again publicly hold these gift-giving events. Since that time the people have been working to restore the culture and language they lost due to the bans on their traditions and enforced residential schooling. The bands began programs to record elder wisdom and pass on the Nuu-chah-nulth heritage and language to instill cultural pride in the younger generations.

Because the Nuu-chah-nulth never signed treaties with the Canadian federal or provincial governments, they still consider themselves to be the owners of their original territories. In the 1990s, they have been negotiating with British Columbia to establish their rights. Although a framework agreement was signed in 1996 and an amended statement of intent was submitted in 2004, the final treaty agreement remained unsigned as of 2011. Only five of the original Nuu-chah-nulth nations stayed involved in the treaty-planning process; the other nations settled separate agreements from 2000 to 2011. The remaining nations continue to meet to address common concerns and strategic planning.

Although the fishing and logging industries expanded in the mid-1900s, the Nuu-chah-nulth often found themselves shut out of such growth. Many people left the reserves to find jobs, go to college, or obtain better housing. Clear-cut logging that damaged the environment became a problem in some areas; and the Nuu-chah-nulth protested the destruction of natural resources. In addition to environmental issues, unemployment continues to remain a problem in the twenty-first century. Other concerns include social and health problems, land-use planning, resource allocation, and education.

NOTABLE PEOPLE

Maquinna (pronounced *Ma-queen-a*; died c. 1795), one of the richest and most powerful chiefs on the West Coast during the early 1800s, was known for his involvement in trading with the Europeans. He was influential in settling the British-Spanish dispute called the Nootka Sound Controversy (see "History"). Maquinna later gained revenge on the British who mistreated his people by killing the crew of another English ship and taking two men prisoners.

Nuu-chah-nulth artists were known for their carvings and basketry, but over the centuries, the number of people practicing these crafts decreased dramatically. Born on the Nitinaht Indian Reserve on Vancouver Island, Art Thompson (1948–2003) tried to revive these art styles. Originally a carver, silversmith, and silkscreen artist, Thompson moved into working more with wood, using traditional designs, and his work received critical acclaim. Two other artists, carver and printmaker Joe David (1946–) and Ron (Ki-Ke-In) Hamilton (1948–), also rediscovered these long-lost styles. Ki-Ke-In, who studied with renowned Kwakwaka'wakw carver Henry Hunt (1923–1985), is known for his painting, carving, and jewelry design.

BOOKS

Bodega y Quadra, Juan Francisco de la. *Voyage to the Northwest Coast of America, 1792: Bodega y Quadra and the Nootka Sound Controversy.* Norman: University of Oklahoma Press, 2012.

Coté, Charlotte. *Spirits of Our Whaling Ancestors: Revitalizing Makah and Nuu-chah-nulth Traditions.* Seattle: University of Washington Press, 2010.

George, Earl Maquinna. *Living on the Edge: Nuu-chah-nulth History from an Ahousaht Chief's Perspective.* Winlaw, British Columbia: Sono Nis Press, 2003.

Hoover, Alan L. *Nuu-chah-nulth Voices, Histories, Objects, and Journeys.* Victoria: Royal British Columbia Museum, 2000.

Jacobsen, Rowan. *The Living Shore: Rediscovering a Lost World.* New York: Bloomsbury, 2009.

Jewitt, John R. *The Captive of Nootka, or the Adventures of John R. Jewitt.* Philadelphia, PA, 1815.

Jewitt, John R. *A Journal Kept at Nootka Sound.* Boston, 1807. Available online from http://www.canadiana.org/view/90038/0003

Jonaitis, Aldona, and Aaron Glass. *The Totem Pole: An Intercultural History.* Seattle: University of Washington Press, 2010.

Miller, Frederic P., Agnes F. Vandome, and John McBrewster, eds. *Nuu-chah-nulth People.* Beau Bassin, Mauritius: Alphascript Publishing, 2011.

Neel, David *The Great Canoes: Reviving a Northwest Coast Tradition.* Vancouver: Douglas & McIntyre, 1995.

Norris, Karen and Ralph. *Contemporary Art on the Northwest Coast: Salish, Nuu-chuh-nulth, and Makah.* Atglen, PA: Schiffer, 2011.

Sapir, Edward. *The Origin of the Wolf Ritual: The Whaling Indians West Coast Legends and Stories.* Gatineau, Quebec: Canadian Museum of Civilization, 2007.

Umeek (E. Richard Atleo). *Tsawalk: A Nuu-chah-nulth Worldview.* Vancouver: University of British Columbia Press, 2004.

WEB SITES

Gregg, Andrew, Gail Gallant, et al. "When the World Began: John Jewitt's Diary: Maquinna." *Le Canada: A People's History.* http://www.cbc.ca/history/EPCONTENTSE1EP1CH7LE.html (accessed on August 15, 2011).

"Ha-Shilth-Sa." *Nuu-chah-nulth Tribal Council.* http://www.hashilthsa.com/ (accessed on August 15, 2011).

"Man of Nootka Sound." *Oregon Historical Society.* http://ohs.org/education/oregonhistory/historical_records/dspDocument.cfm?doc_ID=2CA04DAF-C490-7D6A-3A631D57C9CB2493 (accessed on August 15, 2011).

"Nootka Indian Music of the Pacific North West Coast." *Smithsonian Folkways.* http://www.folkways.si.edu/albumdetails.aspx?itemid=912 (accessed on August 15, 2011).

"Nuu-chah-nulth." *Royal British Columbia Museum.* http://www.royalbcmuseum.bc.ca/Content_Files/Files/SchoolsAndKids/nuu2.pdf (accessed on August 15, 2011).

"Nuu-chah-nulth (Barkley) Community Portal." *FirstVoices.* http://www.firstvoices.ca/en/Nuu-chah-nulth (accessed on August 15, 2011).

Nuu-chah-nulth Tribal Council. http://www.nuuchahnulth.org/tribal-council/welcome.html (accessed on August 15, 2011).

"Pacheedaht History." *Vancouver Island Networking Services.* http://www.portrenfrew.com/pacheedaht1.htm (accessed on August 15, 2011).

Redish, Laura, and Orrin Lewis. "Nuu-chah-nulth (Nootka) Indian Language." *Native Languages of the Americas.* http://www.native-languages.org/nootka.htm (accessed on August 15, 2011).

"Traditional Nuu-chah-nulth Food Harvesting." *School District 70.* http://www.sd70.bc.ca/_Programs/Ab_Ed/AbEdCurrNTC/Foods-Curr.pdf (accessed on August 15, 2011).

Puyallup

Name

The name Puyallup (pronounced *pyu-ALL-up*) may mean either "the mouth of the river" or "generous and welcoming behavior to all people." Some sources say it means "shadow," in reference to the dense shade forests near the mouth of the stream. The tribe's name for itself is *spuyáluhpabš, spwiya'laphabsh,* or *S'Puyalupubsh,* which means "generous and welcoming behavior to all people (friends and strangers) who enter our lands."

Location

The Puyallup formerly lived along the Puyallup River in present-day Washington, west of the Cascade Mountains between central Oregon and southern British Columbia, Canada. In modern times, many live near the Puyallup Reservation, which covers almost 100 acres near Tacoma, Washington, and is one of the only urban reservations in the United States.

Population

The Puyallup and the Nisqually were longtime allies and were so similar that population figures often included both tribes. In 1780, the estimated total of both tribes was about 3,600 people. Following several major outbreaks of deadly diseases, an 1853 estimate listed 150 Puyallup, and a count in 1854 revealed only 50 people. In the 1990 U.S. Census, 1,013 people identified themselves as Puyallup. The 2000 U.S. Census showed 1,545 Puyallup, and 2,069 people claimed some Puyallup heritage.

Language family

Coast Salish.

Origins and group affiliations

The Puyallup were part of a group called the Southern Coast Salish peoples. Tribes in this group included the Duwamish, Skokomish, Nisqually, Suquamish, Twana, Squaxin, and about forty others. The Puyallup

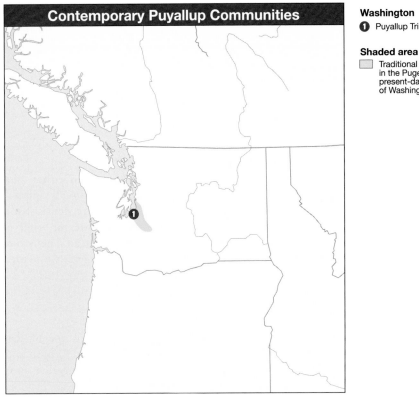

Contemporary Puyallup Communities

Washington
1 Puyallup Tribal Council

Shaded area
Traditional lands of the Puyallup in the Puget Sound area in the present-day Seattle and Tacoma area of Washington state

A map of contemporary Puyallup communities. MAP BY XNR PRODUCTIONS. CENGAGE LEARNING, GALE. REPRODUCED BY PERMISSION OF GALE, A PART OF CENGAGE LEARNING.

were closely associated with the Nisqually and generally maintained good relations with the Kittitas and Yakama. The Lekwiltok Kwakiutl, who raided the area, and the Cowichan were enemies of most Southern Coast Salish tribes.

The Puyallup have long been an active group, looking out for and working in their own best interests. Rather than waiting for the government to provide for them, for example, they often start projects themselves. During the 1960s and 1970s, they became leaders in the fight to restore Native fishing rights. The case went to court, and in 1974, the Boldt Decision upheld Native American rights to fish in their original territories, which they had been promised in treaties they signed in the late 1800s. Since then, the Puyallup have gained fame for what has been called the largest Native American land claim settlement in history.

HISTORY

Early European contact

European fishermen and explorers infected the Puyallup tribe with smallpox before the people ever saw their first outsider. The first European to arrive in Puyallup territory was probably the British explorer George Vancouver (1757–1798), who entered the Puget Sound and Hood Canal area in 1792. By then, disease had seriously reduced the tribal populations in the region.

In 1827, the Hudson's Bay Company, a British trading company, established the Fort Langley trading post in the region where the Puyallup lived. The company founded Fort Nisqually nearby six years later. Soon, many of the Southern Coast Salish tribes were trading at these sites. From these exchanges, the Puyallup received firearms and frontier-style clothing as well as potatoes. In 1839 and 1840, Catholic missionaries entered the Northwest, and they were successful in converting some of the Natives.

Settlers and miners

Isaac Ingalls Stevens (1818–1862) served as the governor of Washington Territory as well as the superintendent of Indian Affairs in the mid-1800s. He considered the Native tribes an "impediment to civilization." He believed strongly in Manifest Destiny, a policy that held that the United States was meant to dominate the entire Western Hemisphere. Beginning in 1854, Stevens attempted to establish treaties with nearly every tribe in the Northwest, hoping to take over as much land as possible for U.S. settlers. His goal was to place the tribes on reservations and convince the people to assimilate (adopt the mainstream American way of life).

In 1854, Governor Stevens convinced the Puyallup to sign the Treaty of Medicine Creek. Under this treaty, the Puyallup gave up a portion of their lands to the U.S. government. Although some Native nations moved to reservations, others refused. Stevens then announced that the lands formerly held by the Natives of the Washington area were available

Important Dates

1792: British explorer George Vancouver makes first contact with the Puyallup.

1854: The Medicine Creek Treaty gives Puyallup lands to the U.S. government; Puyallup are sent to a reservation.

1855–56: A Native revolt against gold miners in their territory results in Yakima War.

1856: The Puyallup reservation is enlarged to 18,062 acres.

1900: Reservation lands are lost to railroad companies.

1936: The Puyallup form a tribal government.

1974: The Boldt Decision affirms Native fishing rights.

1984: The Puyallap receive a settlement of $77.25 million for land taken by the Port of Tacoma in 1950.

1996: The Chief Leschi School for Native American students opens.

for settling, and American pioneers trickled in. When gold was discovered in the area, prospectors and more settlers poured in, trespassing on tribal lands and farms.

Conflicts among the groups erupted in the Yakama War of 1855–56. Some Puyallup joined the Yakama (see entry) and other groups in opposing non-Native settlements and refusing to move onto reservations. The war lasted three years and accomplished very little for either side.

Loss of land

Soon after the war, the U.S. government increased the original 1,280 acres the Treaty of Medicine Creek had granted to the tribe, and the people moved back along the Puyallup River onto 17,463 acres that became known as the Puyallup Reservation. The Puyallup soon adopted a typical American lifestyle. They farmed, attended Christian churches, and sent their children to government-run schools. One observer claimed that the Puyallup were "the most creditable [praiseworthy] specimens of civilized Native Americans to be found in the West."

Thirty years later, the U.S. government divided the reservation land and gave individual tribe members 178 allotments (plots for farming). Only one small area, called the Indian Addition, stayed under tribal ownership. The rest of the land was sold to settlers. In 1893, the federal government authorized the sale of Puyallup lands to commercial ishing companies. In addition, railroad companies had acquired Puyallup lands in 1873, and they did so again in 1899. The Puyallup claimed that they had been forced to give up their lands, but the sale papers bore the signatures of tribal people. By 1900, the Puyallup owned no land. The few remaining Puyallup lived in poor housing on scattered tracts of land along the banks of the Puyallup River.

State of Washington officials, who regulated hunting and fishing, arrested Puyallup fishermen for fishing in the river. The government argued that the Puyallup people were only permitted to fish on their reservation, but they no longer had a reservation. Tribal leaders brought a lawsuit against the United States in 1899 for loss of their lands, but they lost the case.

The struggle for rights

After 1900, the Native population of western Washington greatly diminished, and Puyallup culture began to deteriorate. Marriage with settlers became common, and problems with alcohol increased. Religious rituals such as the potlatch (a gift-exchanging ceremony) disappeared due to the disapproval of religious and other authorities outside the tribe. Children were sent to English-speaking boarding schools, and older members of the tribe spoke English to find work more easily. As a result, the Puyallup language went into decline.

Treaties with the U.S. government dating back to the nineteenth century guaranteed the Puyallup certain rights, including the "right of taking fish at all usual and accustomed grounds and stations … in common with all citizens of the [Washington] territory." For more than one hundred years, the meaning of the phrase remained in question as non-Native settlers and then the state of Washington fought to control access to the region's fisheries. In the 1960s, one Native leader claimed that angry whites shot him while he was fishing; the local police doubted his story.

In 1970, Tacoma police used clubs and tear gas to arrest fifty-nine protestors camped on the Puyallup River. Finally, during that same year, the century-old controversy was settled when the Natives won a federal lawsuit against the state of Washington. In 1974, federal judge George Boldt rendered the Boldt Decision, which allowed Native fishermen half of all harvestable salmon and steelhead on their former fishing grounds.

Planning for the future

That year, the Puyallup joined several other tribes to form the Northwest Fisheries Commission. This group carried out the provisions of the Boldt Decision, but it also actively fought for treaty rights. The following year, in 1975, the Puyallup drafted a Long-Range Management Plan to increase tribal control of fisheries, reduce non-Native fishing in their waters, and plan for seasons when fish harvests were low.

Several land claims that had been filed in the 1950s were settled in the 1970s. Cushman Indian Hospital and the Northeast Tacoma Clubhouse were both returned to the Puyallup. The clubhouse serves as a day care center, senior center, and meeting facility. The tribe also opened its own credit union. In 1990, the Puyallup received compensation for land claims that included money in trust, individual payments, and promises to enhance social services, such as health care and education, over the next fifty years. In addition, they received some of their land—four parcels around the City of Tacoma.

Some money was set aside for economic development and land purchases. The Puyallup also developed their law enforcement and tribal court system. In 1996, they expanded the Chief Leschi School. This educational facility, started in 1975, serves as a model for Native American schools around the country, especially in its use of educational technology (see "Education"). In the early 2000s, the tribe opened the Emerald Queen Casino in two cities. The income from gaming combined with the settlement for land claims has helped the tribe expand its economic base and fund many improvement projects (see "Current Tribal Issues").

RELIGION

The Puyallup believed in a creator called the Transformer, who came into the world and taught the people many things. They thought spirits went to the land of the dead and could later be reborn. Puyallup looked to guardian spirits for guidance and success throughout life but understood their own responsibility in remaining physically clean and pure.

Special powers were received from the spirit world during a ceremony called the vision quest (see "Puberty"), and they were kept secret from other people. It was rude to ask about someone else's spirit power and dangerous to talk about one's own. Disrespect of spirit powers could cause bad luck, illness, or even death.

Some powers could be obtained only in certain geographic locations, and some only came to certain people, such as a shaman (pronounced *SHAH-mun* or *SHAY-mun*; spiritual healer). These powers were most important during ceremonies held in December and January, when spirits visited the people and assisted in rituals. Individuals often expressed their spirit powers through movements and songs during the Winter Dance (see "Festivals").

Catholic missionaries converted many Puyallup to Christianity in the early 1800s, but others retained their traditional beliefs. Presbyterians came in the 1870s, and some tribal members adopted their faith. The Indian Shaker Church, a Christian religion blended with Indian traditions, was popular among the Native nations in the Northwest in the early 1900s and found adherents among the Puyallup.

LANGUAGE

All the Coast Salish tribes spoke different dialects (varieties) of the Coast Salish language, and the names of their villages came from the names of the dialects spoken by the residents. The Puyallup spoke the Southern

Lushootseed dialect, although some scholars have named the tribe's dialect Nisqually (see entry).

In the late 1990s, there were only about thirty speakers of the Southern Lushootseed language, but since then, efforts have been made to keep the language alive. For example, programs at the Chief Leschi School (see "Education") and other programs conducted around the Puget Sound teach the Puyallup language to children and adults.

GOVERNMENT

The village was the Puyallup's principal political unit. Although the people had no formal leader, the wealthiest head of a house was generally accepted as the village headman. People in different villages were linked through marriage.

The U.S. Congress passed the Indian Reorganization Act in 1934. According to that act, reservations wishing to receive certain government benefits had to form their own tribal governments and adopt a new constitution. In 1936, the U.S. Department of the Interior approved the Puyallup constitution and its tribal government. A seven-member elected tribal council now governs the tribe. The Puyallup have health and law enforcement programs as well as a tribal court. A committee oversees funds for housing, senior citizens' programs, education, cultural preservation, social services, and cemetery maintenance.

The Tribal Law Enforcement department has two components—one for people, the other for fish and wildlife. Police officers receive special training in New Mexico as well as in Washington State. The game law enforcement staff oversees fishing and hunting regulations and violations.

ECONOMY

The Puyallup and other Coast Salish tribes kept in contact with their neighbors by canoeing from one seacoast village to another. Because of this constant interaction, they had similar lifestyles. Women and children gathered shellfish near the ocean and collected wild plants, such as camas

Lushootseed Words

The Puyallup, like many other Southern Coast Salish tribes, spoke a dialect (variety) of the Lushootseed language. (For additional words in this language, see Duwamish and Nisqually entries.)

hígwuhl'iduhgwuhs	"brave man"
stiqtiqíw	"horses"
túbšuhduh'	"warrior"
gwigwia'ltxw	"longhouse"
'ácilhtalbixw	"villages"
xwsalikw	"potlatches"
luhluhlwá'suhd	"sleeping platform"
si'áb	"leader, chief"
xwuyubal'txw	"trading post"
sxwúhqwuhb	"Thunderbird"

bulbs (wild lilies), roots, and ferns. Men hunted and fished. Wealthy people sometimes employed their poor relatives to do domestic chores. They also kept war captives as slaves for their own use or traded them with other Native nations for goods.

After signing the Treaty of Medicine Creek in 1854 (see "History"), the Puyallup supported themselves by selling fresh salmon to the new settlements around the Puget Sound. Efforts at farming and raising cattle on the reservation also proved to be quite successful.

In the late 1980s, the Puyallup tribe voted to drop the claims to some very valuable ancestral lands near the city of Tacoma, Washington, in return for a payment of $162 million in cash, as well as other tracts of land and jobs for their people. This historic land claim settlement provided the Puyallup with a strong base on which to further their goals for economic growth.

In modern times, human service programs that benefit the tribe employ nearly 1,500 people. Some of the programs also serve other Native peoples who have relocated to the Puyallup area. Tribal bingo and casino operations provide jobs and are a major source of income for the tribe. A marina, fisheries, service and retail businesses, a shipping company, and tourism also supply money and employment for many people. Puyallup International oversees the economic development of the tribe and is one of the largest employers of its members.

DAILY LIFE

Families

Basic tribal groupings were the village, the household, and the family. A village might have one or more large plank homes and a few smaller ones. Each home held a household, usually consisting of a husband, his wife (or wives), their children, sometimes unmarried relatives, and for those who could afford it, a few slaves. Inside, the house each family had its own living quarters and fireplace. Extended families had land in the village, where they owned exclusive rights to hunt, fish, and gather plants.

Buildings

Like other tribes in the region, the Puyallup built cedar plank houses, sometimes called shed-roof houses. Larger homes could reach 500 feet (150 meters) in length to accommodate the many families that lived within. The people had a spiritual connection to their houses and talked about them as if they were alive. They compared the frame to a body on its hands and knees; the front of the house was its face. The word for "human skin" was similar to the word for "wall." The roof ridge was the house's spine, and the elaborately carved and painted posts that held up the roof were referred to as limbs or pillars supporting the sky.

The houses also revealed status and relationships. The owner of the house lived in the back of the house, where he was safer and away from drafts. Common people slept along the sides, while slaves slept near the doorway. Where people slept, worked, and sat in the home indicated their societal position.

In the summer, people constructed temporary campsites using a pole frame covered by woven mats. They used sweathouses for purifying themselves all year round.

Clothing and adornment

In the summer, Puyallup men wore nothing or only breechcloths (flaps of material that covered the front and back and were suspended from the waist). Women wore cedar bark aprons and skirts. In cool weather, both sexes used woven blankets made of mountain goat wool, and they added leggings, shirts, and moccasins when it got colder.

Women tattooed their chins and legs and donned earrings and necklaces made of shell, teeth, and claws. Men also wore earrings, and wealthy people had nose ornaments. Young men plucked out their facial hair, though older men let it grow. The Puyallup decorated their faces and bodies with oil and paint. They generally wore their hair long and braided.

Food

Families moved from their permanent winter villages to temporary camps in spring and summer to collect their supplies of food. Fish, especially salmon, was the primary staple in their diets. The men fished in both saltwater and fresh water, where they caught five kinds of salmon, steelhead trout, herring, smelt, flounder, flatfish, lingcod, rockfish, halibut, and sturgeon. The Puyallup also gathered shellfish, such as clams, crabs, sea urchins, and oysters. They hunted or trapped deer, elk, black bear, beaver, raccoon, marmot, wild game, and twenty kinds of waterfowl. The women gathered

Student dancers and drummers perform at the Puyallup tribe's Chief Leschi School, which is considered a model for Native education. © AP PHOTOS.

berries, roots, nuts, bulbs, and sprouts. The most important plants were bracken and camas. In the fall, women gathered acorns to roast.

Education

During the second half of the 1800s, the federal government opened special schools for the Puyallup. Henry Sicade (1866–1938), who attended the Puyallup Day School from age seven to fourteen, described it as follows:

> The one-room shack, built of rough lumber about 16 feet [5 meters] square, with one window and a door, contained a few rough benches, and to this primitive school five volunteer students, young men, came to attend each day. There was but one book for this pioneer class, no doubt some sort of a primer, and when the ambitious student had recited, he stepped out to the trail and returned to his primitive home. Each took his turn likewise.

Later, boarding schools were started, and children lived away from home during the school year. One goal of education during this period was to assimilate students (make them more like whites). Students were not allowed to speak their Native languages. They also learned trades: girls studied domestic duties, while boys did manual labor. Many boys objected to this because, in their tribes, many of the jobs they did were "women's work." Life at the schools was harsh, as Henry Sicade pointed out: "Half a day school and half a day work was the system and sometimes all work and no school.... Provisions were always short and we often went home to stock up and those who could not stock up visited the stores and cooked in the woods. When caught in the treacherous act of cooking trout salmon, we were punished or put into jail."

The Puyallup boarding school closed soon after some girls disclosed that they were abused. Eventually, federal funds for education were cut off, and tribal elementary schools closed in the early twentieth century. After that, most students attended public school.

In the late twentieth century, the Puyallup tribe renewed its focus on education. It opened the Chief Leschi Tribal School in 1975 to serve the educational needs of Native children in the region and to keep its heritage alive. The school serves close to one thousand students from thirty different tribes in kindergarten through grade twelve.

Elementary school students learn both English and the Southern Salish languages. Each day begins with a prayer and "circle," where students participate in Native dancing, singing, and drumming. Other programs offered by the school center on teen parenting, family and child education, and cooperative school-to-work vocational training programs. In 2004, Tacoma Public Schools and the Chief Leschi School received a three-year grant of $349,592 per year to improve Native American education and increase opportunities for Native students. In the second decade of the 2000s, the school received funding and assistance from the Puyallup tribe, the Bureau of Indian Affairs, and the Puyallup Tribe Air Quality Program (see "Current Tribal Issues"). College-bound students can apply for tuition assistance through special tribal programs.

Healing practices

The Puyallup believed that serious illnesses were caused by foreign objects in the body or by the loss of one's soul. Although minor ailments could be cured by the use of herbs, more serious illnesses required a shaman's care. Shamans (pronounced *SHAH-munz* or *SHAY-munz*) had to remove the object that was causing the disease, or they had to recapture the missing soul and return it to the sick person's body.

The Transformer

The Puyallup believed in a creator they sometimes called *Dabábet'hw* or the Transformer. He created food and language and made the world less dangerous. He also taught people how to make clothes, fire, fish traps, and medicine. This tale is one of the few published Puyallup stories.

> Over the land Dabábet'hw traveled, everywhere banishing evil, helping the needy, and teaching the ignorant. All the arts and industries the people then learned, and their games. Men were taught how to cure the sick and to baffle evil, and all were shown the mode of acquiring magic power from the spirits.
>
> After a while the great teacher and transformer became hungry, and seeing a salmon leaping in the water he called it ashore, [put it on a spit], and placed it beside a fire. While it was broiling, he fell asleep. Then came a wanderer, who, finding a salmon cooked and its possessor asleep, ate all the fish; and before departing he rubbed a little grease on the sleeper's fingers and lips, placing also some bits of fish in his teeth. When Dabábet'hw awoke he detected instantly the trick that had been played upon him, and following rapidly he soon overtook the thief. As [the wanderer] sat gazing at his reflection in a stream, Dabábet'hw changed him to a coyote.
>
> The news of the transformations wrought by Dabábet'hw preceded him, and caused some to fear him and wish that he might be slain. Such was a man whose occupation was the making of bone points for arrows, and who threatened that if the magic man came within his sight he would shoot him. But when Dabábet'hw actually appeared, the arrow-maker did not know him, and thought him to be an ordinary stranger. The traveler stopped to talk, and learning that he was preparing to slay the man of magic, Dabábet'hw disarmed him by thrusting the bone points into his wrists, at the same time sending him bounding away on all fours. The man, in fact, had been turned into a deer, the same as those which now roam the woods, and the pointed bones are now found in the legs of deer above the dew-claws.
>
> Dabábet'hw now proceeded to the home of his grandmother, Toad, from whose care he had been stolen in his infancy. The earth and all its creatures had been perfected, but it occurred to him that there should be more light. He therefore ascended to the sky and traveled across it by day in the form of the Sun. But he made the days, already warm, so hot that the people could not endure it. Therefore he bade his brother, who had been made from the cradle-board, become the Sun, and Dabábet'hw himself became the night Sun. Before he finally left the Earth he announced that he would take as his wife the girl who could lift and carry his great bundle of handiwork. Only the daughter of Frog was successful and she accompanied him to the sky; and to this day Dabábet'hw, Frog, and the bag may be seen in the Moon.

SOURCE: Curtis, Edward S. *The North American Indian*, Volume 9, 1911. Reprint. New York: Johnson Reprint Corporation, 1970.

Both men and women could become shamans, but most shamans were men. Training for the position began at age seven or eight. Spirits communicated to the aspiring shaman what he or she should do to invoke the spiritual powers of healing. Most villages had shamans to protect them from evil outsiders.

In 1993, the Takopid Health Center opened, offering health care to over 250 tribes throughout the United States. More than ten thousand peoples of various tribal backgrounds living on or near the reservation, along with the Puyallup, enrolled at the health center in 1990. The center provides dental, medical, and community health services as well as a pharmacy, vision care, and physical therapy. The tribe also has a substance abuse clinic, a mental health center, and a "spirit house." All of the medical facilities offer both modern and traditional healing methods.

ARTS

Puyallup woman, like others of the Salish Coast, produced outstanding textiles that had social and spiritual significance. They often carved whorls, the small wooden flywheels that control the speed of a spinning wheel. The whorls had human, animal, and geometric designs incised into them. As the women did their spinning, they often stared at the whorls, which put them into a trance-like state. The Puyallup believed that this gave the spinner the ability to create textiles containing special powers. The ancient Puyallup art of weaving blankets was revived in the 1960s.

CUSTOMS

Infancy

Children were often named during the Winter Dance ceremonies. A child received an ancient family name as a link between the past and the future. The Puyallup, like most Coast Salish tribes, flattened the heads of infants. This was accomplished by strapping boards to the babies' foreheads to mold their skulls. A flattened forehead was considered an attractive feature.

Puberty

A Puyallup girl was separated from the village at the time of her first menstrual period. During that time, she was also expected to work, because that would make her industrious once she married. Afterward, a feast was held for the girl and her family.

Adolescent boys and girls embarked on vision quests, sacred ceremonies in which they went off alone and fasted, living without food or water for a period of days. During that time, they hoped to learn about spiritual matters and have a vision of a guardian spirit who would provide help and strength throughout their lives. These quests took place in the winter, sometimes outside tribal territory, and usually under the guidance of a trainer.

Courtship and marriage

Arranged marriages were common among the upper class, generally to a person of a different village. The families of the bride and groom exchanged gifts with one other, and the bride's family gave gifts to the young couple. Divorce was uncommon. After the death of a spouse, the surviving husband or wife remarried within the same family to preserve alliances.

A man could have multiple wives, and men often had wives of different ages. The older wives had the most power. A man would sometimes marry all the sisters in a family. He had to undergo the entire marriage ceremony with each one of them. Men sometimes gave their wives to shamans or warriors to pay them for their services, and important men often received gifts of wives. Young girls were simply presented to them without any ceremony or exchange of goods.

War and hunting

To catch ducks and other waterfowl, the Puyallup hunted at night. They spread big nets across a series of tall poles that stood along the riverside. When a signal was given, the men came out of the darkness carrying lighted torches and making loud cries. The frightened birds flew off, hit the nets, and fell to the ground. The men quickly gathered up the stunned birds.

Funerals

The Puyallup held wakes to which loved ones brought gifts for the deceased. Some mourners displayed their grief by biting their own hair. The people usually buried the body in a box in the village cemetery, but sometimes they placed corpses in a canoe atop a cedar plank shed (in later years sheds were made of canvas). A feast was held, and the deceased's personal property was distributed among family and friends.

Festivals

The Puyallup held several important winter dances, spirit dances, potlatches, and first salmon ceremonies to celebrate the first catch of the year. Potlatches were ceremonies of gift giving, especially as offers of peace to other visiting tribes. The festivities included songs, dances, and games.

Winter dances were sponsored by an individual who had been diagnosed with an illness brought on by his guardian spirit—the spirit he had received earlier in life on a vision quest (see "Puberty"). This spirit was lodged in his chest in the form of a song. During the evening, his friends used drumbeats and phrases to draw out the song. They painted the sponsor's face. Eventually, possessed by his power, he got up and danced and sang his song. Others joined in the performance, which was followed by a feast.

The first salmon ceremony honored the fish that made up almost 90 percent of the Puyallup diet. The tribe held the celebration at the start of the

Traditional dancers perform at a powwow hosted by the Puyallup tribe. © LISA REESE/DEMOTIX/CORBIS.

salmon-spawning season. The people barbecued the first salmon caught in the year over an open fire and gave small portions of the meat to everyone present. All the bones were saved intact. Everyone then went to the river for dancing, chanting, and singing. The people placed the salmon skeleton in the water with its head pointing upstream in the direction a spawning salmon would go. This was to encourage the salmon to return in great numbers.

In modern times, the Puyallup hold their Annual Powwow and Salmon Bake in Tacoma every Labor Day weekend. Monthly powwows at the Chief Leschi School, like all powwows, feature dancing and singing with drums.

CURRENT TRIBAL ISSUES

The Puyallup people are trying to increase their land base, develop human service programs for tribal and community members, and protect their fishing, environmental, trade, and tribal rights.

Urban problems

One of the major problems facing the tribe is their urban environment. Because of their location in the Puget Sound air shed, stagnation and pollution occur when air gets trapped between the surrounding mountains. The Puyallup Tribal Air Quality Program regulates and suggests alternatives to pollution releases into the air. The program also offers education to increase awareness of the problem.

Another major issue is gang violence and losing children to the streets. To protect their youth, the Puyallup have organized a group of professionals to offer positive alternatives for the young people. This Tribal Strategies team includes members from law enforcement, housing, domestic violence programs, the tribal council, and the community. Safe Futures provides counseling, education, teen parenting classes, and cultural awareness. The tribe hopes that by instilling pride among its youth, it will reduce future difficulties.

Fishing rights

On several occasions, the Puyallup have had to defend their fishing rights. They have used tactics ranging from "fish-in" protest rallies to lawsuits to draw media and government attention to the issue. In 1994, they went to court to preserve their rights to harvest shellfish. Judge Edward Rafeedie's ruling agreed with the Boldt Decision of 1974 (see "History"), asserting the tribe's right to half the shellfish taken each year.

Although the Natives won, many landowners did not know about the tribes' treaty rights when they purchased their land. Realizing that harvesting shellfish could be disruptive to these landowners, the Northwest Indian Fisheries Committee (an organization that represents many Northwest tribes) negotiated a settlement with growers and the government. The agreement has three key provisions: 1) the tribes would forgo their rights to harvest about $2 million worth of shellfish from commercial growers' beds; 2) growers would add $500,000 worth of shellfish to public tidelands for ten years; and 3) $33 million would be put in trust for the seventeen tribes to buy and enhance tidelands for their own use.

NOTABLE PEOPLE

Ramona Bennett (1938–) has been active in tribal government for many years, including roles as principal administrator, controlling the budget, and chair of the Puyallup Tribal Council. She is a well-known spokesperson for Native American rights at the national level, particularly in the areas of fishing rights, Native American child welfare, and Native health and education. In 2003, the Native Action Network awarded her its Enduring Spirit Award.

BOOKS

Adamson, Thelma, ed. *Folk-tales of the Coast Salish.* Lincoln: Bison Books, 2009.

Carlson, Keith Thor, ed. *A Sto:lo-Coast Salish Historical Atlas.* Vancouver, BC: Douglas and Mcintyre, 2006.

Chalcraft, Edwin L. *Assimilation's Agent: My Life as a Superintendent in the Indian Boarding School System.* Lincoln: University of Nebraska Press, 2007.

Chehak, Gail, and Jan Halliday. *Native Peoples of the Northwest: A Traveler's Guide to Land, Art, and Culture.* Seattle: Sasquatch Books, 2002.

Rogerson, George. *Stillness of the Dawn.* Bangor, ME: Booklocker, 2007.

Ruby, Robert H., John A. Brown, and Cary C. Collins. *A Guide to the Indian Tribes of the Pacific Northwest.* 3rd ed. Norman: University of Oklahoma Press, 2010.

Uncommon Controversy: Fishing Rights of the Muckleshoot, Puyallup, and Nisqually Indians. Seattle: University of Washington Press, 1970.

PERIODICALS

Collins, Cary C., ed. "Henry Sicade's History of Puyallup Indian School, 1860 to 1920." *Columbia* 14, no. 4 (Winter 2001–02).

WEB SITES

Chief Leschi School. http://www.leschischools.org/ (accessed on November 2, 2011).

"History of the South Puget Sound: The Indian War of 1855." *Daffodil Valley Times.* http://www.daffodilvalleytimes.com/history/indian_war.html (accessed on November 2, 2011).

Marr, Carolyn J. "Assimilation through Education: Indian Boarding Schools in the Pacific Northwest." *University of Washington Libraries Digital Collections.* http://content.lib.washington.edu/aipnw/marr.html (accessed on November 2, 2011).

Northwest Indian Fisheries Commission. http://nwifc.org/ (accessed on November 2, 2011).

"Puyallup Indian Agency (Washington)." *Family Search.* https://www.familysearch.org/learn/wiki/en/Puyallup_Indian_Agency_%28Washington%29 (accessed on November 2, 2011).

Puyallup Tribal News. http://www.puyalluptribalnews.com/ (accessed on November 2, 2011).

Puyallup Tribe of Indians. http://www.puyallup-tribe.com/ (accessed on November 2, 2011).

Redish, Laura, and Orrin Lewis. "Puyallup Culture and History." *Native Languages of the Americas.* http://www.native-languages.org/puyallup.htm (accessed on November 2, 2011).

Sicade, Henry. "Education." *Puyallup Tribe of Indians.* http://www.puyallup-tribe.com/history/education/ (accessed on November 2, 2011).

Thrush, Coll-Peter. "The Lushootseed Peoples of Puget Sound Country." *University of Washington Libraries Digital Collections.* http://content.lib.washington.edu/aipnw/thrush.html#intro (accessed on November 2, 2011).

Tulalip Lushootseed. http://www.tulaliplushootseed.com/ (accessed on November 2, 2011).

Siletz

Name

The name Siletz (pronounced *SIGH-lets*) comes from the name of the river on which the Siletz tribe lived. The origin of the name is unknown. The Siletz people called themselves *Se-la-gees,* meaning "crooked river." They were also called *Tsä Shnádshamím.*

Location

The Siletz lived along the Pacific Coast in northern Oregon, in parts of what are now Tillamook, Lincoln, and Lane Counties. They were part of a larger group of Native Americans called the Tillamook, whose lands stretched from Tillamook Head in Clatsop County to the Siletz River in Lincoln County, Oregon. They built villages along the mouths of principal rivers that flow west from the Pacific Coast Range. In the early twenty-first century, the Siletz reservation is located in western Oregon, mainly in Lincoln County, but the tribe owns other acreage in Marion County. The tribe also serves an eleven-county area of western Oregon.

Population

Estimates indicate that there may have been around 100 Siletz people in the 1700s to 1800s. In 1855, after epidemics (uncontrolled outbreaks of disease) and starvation, only 21 Siletz remained alive. The Confederated Tribes of Siletz Indians of Oregon formed when twenty-seven bands of Native peoples were forced onto the Siletz Reservation in 1856. After the tribes were relocated, they were no longer counted separately, so a 1934 census did not identify any Siletz at all. However, in the 2000 census, 1,830 people identified themselves as Siletz, and 2,746 people claimed to have some Siletz heritage. Most, if not all, of those who called themselves Siletz may have been members of the bands who adopted the tribal name in the mid-1800s. In 2004, the U.S. Bureau of Indian Affairs showed tribal enrollment on the Siletz reservation as 4,077. In 2011, tribal rolls counted 4,804 members.

Language family

Salishan.

Contemporary Siletz Communities

Oregon
① Confederated Tribes of Siletz Indians

Shaded area
Traditional land of the Siletz in present-day Oregon

A map of contemporary Siletz communities. MAP BY XNR PRODUCTIONS. CENGAGE LEARNING, GALE. REPRODUCED BY PERMISSION OF GALE, A PART OF CENGAGE LEARNING.

Origins and group affiliations

Some historians believe that Salishan speakers were part of a wave of people who migrated via a land bridge across the Bering Strait from Russia to the New World about ten thousand years ago. The Siletz were part of the Tillamook tribe. Meriwether Lewis (1774–1809) and William Clark (1770–1838), during their exploration of the area in the early nineteenth century, mentioned that all the tribes of that area traded with each other regularly. The Tillamook took prisoners from tribes to the south of them and sold them to northern tribes such as the Clatsop and Chehalis. In 1856, the Siletz were moved the reservation that bears their name along with twenty-six other tribes. Some of the main tribes sharing the reservation were the Tillamook, Alsea, Siuslaw, Coos, Coquille, Takelma or Upper Rogue River, Six, Joshua, Tututini, Mackanotni, Shastacosta, Cheteo. The Athapascan and Takelman tribes were called Rogue River Indians.

The Siletz were a proud river people. For thousands of years, they roamed undisturbed through the western portion of present-day Oregon. By the time the U.S. government established a reservation in the heart of their territory in 1855, only 21 Siletz people were known to be alive. The forcible relocation of the Siletz and more than two dozen other Coastal tribes proved disastrous. In the end, most of the original Siletz tribe may have perished, but the reservation bearing their name still thrives.

HISTORY

First contact with outsiders

Of the Pacific Northwest groups who spoke the Salishan languages, the Siletz were members of the southernmost branch. They were living along the coast, next to the Siletz River in present-day Oregon, when the first U.S. explorers crossed into their territory in 1805. The men were part of the Lewis and Clark expedition (1804–06), the first navigators to make a large-scale exploration of what would become the western United States. This and other early contacts between the Siletz and other outsiders were brief, but the consequences for the tribe were dire.

Fur trappers soon followed the expedition, bringing deadly diseases to which the Siletz had no immunity. In 1828 and 1833, measles and smallpox epidemics swept through the region, killing many. A series of destructive fires compounded problems for the tribe in the late 1840s. The Siletz had set the fires deliberately, according to their annual practice of slashing and burning some of their land to promote better growth of food resources. However, these fires burned out of control and did tremendous damage. By 1850, the Siletz tribe, weakened by diseases

Important Dates

1805: Lewis and Clark expedition explores Siletz territory.

1846: United States takes over land from Great Britain, and the Oregon Territory is established.

1850: Gold is discovered in Oregon, prompting settlers to take over Native American lands.

1855: Rogue River Wars begin between settlers and Natives; Siletz Reservation is established on the Siletz homeland.

1856: The Siletz and more than two dozen other tribes are forcibly relocated to the Siletz Reservation.

1892: Reservation land is allotted (divided up); the remainder of the land is given to settlers.

1956: U.S. government terminates Siletz Confederation of Tribes and closes the reservation.

1977: The Confederated Tribes of Siletz Indians of Oregon gains federal recognition and drafts a constitution.

2002: Tribe forms Siletz Tribal Business Corporation (STBC) to oversee economic development.

Rogue River Wars

When gold was discovered in Oregon's Rogue River Valley in the early 1850s, gold miners and settlers put pressure on the U.S. government to remove the Native peoples from their homelands. Hostilities erupted into war in October 1855, when a mob of miners killed more than two dozen Natives camping near the Table Rock Reservation. Many historians believe bored and idle miners, who were unable to pan for gold because of a drought, deliberately started the war. Land was not an underlying reason for the fighting, because by the time the war started, the Native people had already given up most of their land.

After enduring several bloody battles, the Native nations who lived and fought in the mountains moved down the Rogue River to the Pacific Coast, probably to buy time because winter had set in and food was becoming scarce. They nearly succeeded in driving the settlers away from the coast, but by the following spring, the U.S. Army joined the conflict to support the settlers. Volunteers and troops from California attacked the Native nations. Although the Natives almost won the final battle, in the end, the army emerged victorious.

The defeated tribes were forcibly removed to a new reservation constructed under federal government authority in 1855. Some Natives were taken there by steamboat; others had to walk. Although the tribal groups were promised sufficient land to support themselves, their acreage was eventually reduced by three-quarters; no compensation was given to them until many years later.

and starvation, had suffered a severe loss of population.

Settlers and miners arrive

U.S. settlers arrived in the Oregon territory in the 1850s, drawn by the abundant furs, suitable farmland, and impressive forests of old growth timber. Gold miners soon followed. Relations between these groups and the Native inhabitants were hostile. The rapid growth of the non-Native population caused serious problems for the Native nations. Prospectors muddied the river with debris from their mining operations, game became scarce as animals were trapped for their furs, and important food sources disappeared when settlers fenced off Native lands for cattle farms.

Tribes such as the Rogue River Indians (who lived south of the Siletz) were the most severely affected by the arrival of settlers in Oregon. The competition for resources, combined with robbing and looting by both sides, set off the Rogue River Wars in 1855.

Siletz Reservation founded

The U.S. government decided the best way to stop the violence between settlers and Native peoples was to establish a reservation and relocate all of the Coastal Indians there. The government chose a 150-mile stretch of the Oregon coast for the reservation, including the entire Siletz homeland, and in 1855, the Siletz Reservation was founded.

Although they had nothing to do with the Rogue River Wars, the entire Siletz tribe (population now reduced to 21) was relocated onto the Siletz Reservation, along with 2,500 Native Americans from twenty-six other tribes. Many people were forced to make a long overland march—in some cases walking more than 125 miles (200 kilometers).

The people faced new problems adjusting to life on the reservation. Free and autonomous (independent and self-governing) tribes were suddenly obliged to live among other Native nations. Conflicts inevitably broke out. Within fifty years of the founding of the reservation, only 483 of the original group of 2,500 people remained. Some had died of sickness and exhaustion caused by the forced march; others were killed by the devastating effects of overcrowding and introduced diseases; still others were victims of hopelessness and despair; and another segment of the population simply left the reservation.

Allotment

The people who reside on the Siletz Reservation today are descendants of the many tribes who were moved there in the mid-1850s. During the late 1800s, reservation land was allotted (divided up into smaller farming parcels), and each head of a household received one lot. The government sold the rest of the land to settlers, reducing tribally owned land from the original 1,440,000 acres to about 30,000 acres. During the early 1900s, government policies and taxes caused many of the people on the Siletz reservation to lose their allotments. By the 1950s, tribal members owned only 3,200 acres.

In 1954, the U.S. government ended its trust relationship with the Siletz Confederation of Tribes. Under this relationship, the federal government held reservation land in trust and oversaw it for the tribe. When this agreement ended, all tribal assets were dissolved, which left the people with no reservation. It also ended the tribe's official dealings with the government, meaning it could not receive federal money or benefits. In 1973, the Siletz formed a nonprofit organization to provide social services to tribal members. In 1977, the U.S. government once again federally recognized the people as the Confederated Tribes of Siletz. (Federal recognition means that the tribes have a special, legal relationship with the U.S. government that entitles them to federal assistance if necessary.)

Siletz Reservation in the twenty-first century

The Siletz Reservation is situated on noncontiguous (not next to each other) land in the lush, damp coastal mountains of western Oregon. These tribal lands predominantly lie within Lincoln County, Oregon. Some acreage is located in Marion County, Oregon. The Confederated Tribes of Siletz, however, serve a tribal population throughout an eleven-county area in western Oregon. The town of Siletz, located along the north-south running State Highway 229, serves as the tribal headquarters.

The Siletz Tribal Business Corporation (STBC) was chartered in 2002 to oversee economic development and to manage tribal economic enterprises. STBC operates the Siletz Tribal Smokehouse in Depoe Bay that sells fresh seafood and traditionally smoked salmon and tuna. The Siletz economy is primarily supported by profits generated by the Chinook Winds Casino Resort and Hotel. The tribe, with its many branches, programs, and businesses, became the largest employer in Lincoln County.

The Siletz Reservation Forest Resource Management Plan called for harvest of 1.74 million board feet (MMBF) of conifer timber each year from 1999 to 2005 and 1.86 MMBF each year from 2006 to 2010. The timber harvested was generally 130 to 140 years old and consists of Douglas fir, western red cedar, western hemlock, Sitka Spruce, red alder, and big leaf maple. The Siletz continue to update their plan to manage their 8,067 acres of timberlands.

RELIGION

The Siletz called their supreme being *Tk'a,* which means "Transformer." They believed he was their ancestor, the creator of the world and its people, and the being who gave them the gift of salmon. According to Siletz legend, Tk'a's soul left the land of the living, and his body assumed the form of the Medicine Rocks, a site in Siletz territory that resembles three human heads.

The Siletz believed that after death good people went to the land in the sky and bad people went to the land below the earth. The good souls lived in a world where land, fish, and game were plentiful. The bad souls became slaves and were mistreated in the afterlife.

The Ghost Dance religion was introduced to the Siletz Reservation in the 1870s. Believers performed the Ghost Dance to bring good fortune to their people. They were convinced that a time would come when the earth would swallow up all non-Natives, but their own people would be spared.

In 1923, the Indian Shaker Church opened on the reservation. A large number of Siletz became involved with this religion that combined elements of Christianity with Native beliefs. Bellringing, candles, dancing, and shaking all had a part in the services. Traditional Christian churches with their rigid, staid practices did not appeal to the Native peoples who were used to lively, active worship, so the Indian Shaker

Church soon had many converts. Quite a few people claimed to be cured by practicing the religion, which had started after John Slocum was healed by his wife's prayers and shaking.

LANGUAGE

Siletz was part of the family of Tillamook (*Hutyéyu*) languages, one of the first Native language families to die out. The last Tillamook speakers on the Siletz reservation died during the 1970s. Although some of the Tillamook language was recorded in the 1930s, the Siletz dialect (variety) of Salishan was never written down during the speakers' lifetimes, so not much is known about this extinct language. Franz Boas (1858–1942), a famous American anthropologist (someone who studies the cultures of different peoples), interviewed one of the last living members of the tribe and recorded some words. For example, the word for the carved stick or wand used by a healer is *qelqaloxten.*

GOVERNMENT

Each Siletz community had a headman from the upper class who coordinated major activities. He first had to prove his bravery, his speaking ability, and his capacity for settling differences among the people. The headman's leadership position was said to come from supernatural spirits. His main responsibilities were to plan and organize work parties and to serve as mediator. Often, a headman paid fines for poor villagers who had offended someone. Because fines were the usual penalty for any infractions (including murder), his payments helped to maintain peace and friendly relations both within and outside the tribe.

On the Siletz Reservation in the early twenty-first century, the tribal government has

A Siletz Creation Story

Anthropologist Franz Boas conducted interviews at the Siletz Reservation in 1890. He spoke to a Siletz elder, one of the very few survivors of the tribe who remembered the ancient language. The man told him the following story about how the Siletz were created.

> The transformer Tk'a traveled all over the world. He was also called the master of salmon. He created everything and commanded the people to be good. When he came to the mouth of a river he tried to make a cascade [waterfall] at that place. When he was traveling about, he carried a bunch of arrows. When he came to a nice place he would take out some arrows, break them to pieces, and throw them down. Then he began to shout as though he were going to dance, and the arrows would be transformed into human beings and begin to dance. When day came he would take his quiver [carrying case] and the arrows would go back into it. This was his way of amusing himself; he did this every night whenever it pleased him. When he came to Siletz he called the people his relatives. When he left he transformed his body into the rock Tk'a, while his soul went to the country of the salmon from which the fish come every year.

SOURCE: Boas, Franz. "Notes on the Tillamook." *University of California Publications: American Archaeology and Ethnology.* Vol. 20. Edited by A. L. Kroeber. Berkeley: University of California Press, 1923.

A Siletz chief wears a traditional headdress. © EDMUND LOWE/ALAMY.

a nine-member tribal council, a general council, and a tribal court. Members of the tribal council serve for three years, but elections occur every year.

ECONOMY

The Siletz economy was based on fishing and food gathering. Economic life revolved around the seasons. From April to June, the people gathered salmonberry sprouts. They harvested camas (pronounced *KAH-muss*) roots (the edible part of certain lily plants) and lamprey (an eel-like fish) in June and July, and they gathered various berries in July and August. The men caught Chinook salmon in August and September, and Coho salmon in October. During November, the Siletz went elk hunting and fished for chum salmon. Women spent December collecting lily roots and various berries, and from December to April, fishers caught steelhead trout.

Modern economy on the Siletz Reservation is overseen by the Siletz Tribal Business Corporation (STBC). The main sources of tribal income include a smokehouse that sells fresh and smoked fish, a casino and resort hotel, and RV parks, along with forestry, fisheries, tourism, and recreation. The tribe has some service, retail, and manufacturing businesses.

DAILY LIFE

Families

Three or four families often lived together in one large house. Families were made up of a man, his wife, their children, and sometimes a few other close relatives. Wealthy men often had more than one wife. The status of women was dependent on that of their parents, husbands, or other close relatives. Women enjoyed their greatest respect after their childbearing days were over.

Buildings

The tribe's permanent dwellings were rectangular winter houses made of cedar planks. Homes had a central hearth below ground level, and families slept in separate areas of the home, partitioned off by matting. Outside the house was a separate grass-covered structure used in the summer to store food. In warm weather, the Siletz erected temporary huts of reed matting near their food-gathering sites.

Clothing and adornment

The Siletz wove much of their clothing, including rain capes and apron-like dresses, from plant fibers. Siletz women wore unusual woven hats that resembled baskets. Samples of these hats are on display at the Tillamook County Pioneer Museum. Both men and women pierced their ears and wore ankle and wrist bracelets.

Food

Fish and seafood—mainly salmon, mussels, and clams—were the most important part of the Siletz diet. The people caught freshwater fish in nets or traps called weirs and preserved them by drying them over a fire. Beaver, muskrat, bear, and other mammals were eaten fresh. The people extracted salt from dried seaweed and used it to preserve elk meat for winter storage. Crickets, grasshoppers, and caterpillars were ground with berries and animal fat to make a nutritious winter food that would not spoil. Women prepared most foods by steaming them in an earth oven or boiling them in baskets or bowls using hot stones.

Education

After the tribe moved to the reservation, the government adopted a policy of assimilation, trying to make them more like mainstream American society. Children were sent to boarding or day schools, where they were not allowed to speak their native language or practice their tribal customs. In 1908, the Siletz Boarding School was closed and the land sold to settlers. The day school stayed open for about ten more years.

For much of the following century, Siletz students attended public schools. The school on the reservation was poorly equipped with cast-off furniture and used books from other district schools. When that was scheduled to close in 2003, the tribe reopened it as a charter school. Since then, the Siletz tribe has been active in promoting education. In addition to sponsoring a youth conference in 2004 that drew over 230 participants from all over the state of Oregon to learn about career and educational opportunities, they also initiated an Eagle Feather Ceremony to honor high school graduates. By rewarding students for staying in school, they have been encouraging more students to graduate and pursue higher education. The tribe also offers financial assistance to students attending college.

The Siletz place importance on passing along their culture to younger generations. They have language programs, cultural resources programs, and culture camps. All of these give families opportunities to learn more about their heritage and traditions.

Healing practices

Shaman Healers called shamans (pronounced *SHAH-munz* or *SHAY-munz*) learned their craft from guardian spirits who appeared to them in dreams. A black bear, for example, was said to teach a female shaman how to cure serious ailments with water and song. Special sweathouses—secluded huts or caverns heated by steam—were used to cure sickness. These healing sweathouses were made of hemlock bark and covered with dirt.

The people believed some illnesses were caused by objects lodged within the patient's body. Shamans cured patients by waving a carved wand, piercing the skin, and sucking out the object that caused the illness (often something brought along by the shaman). Healers also brewed potions to ensure long life, fertility, and luck in hunting. Being a shaman could be dangerous. Those who were unsuccessful in their healing attempts were often murdered.

Indian Shaker Church After the Indian Shaker Church arrived on the reservation in the 1920s, some people turned to that for healing (see "Religion"). Because the founder, John Slocum, claimed he had died and come back to life, many Native people saw the religion as a powerful force similar to that of the shaman. Following several accounts of miraculous healings, interest grew in the religion.

In one account from 1926, Jimmy Jack, a Klamath man who had moved to the Siletz Reservation, attended a service. A young man there shook his hands over Jack's chest and told him he had seen blood clots there. This stranger did not know that for seventeen years Jack had suffered from a lung disorder that caused him to spit up blood. After that day, Jack claimed he never had any trouble with his chest. He and others who had been healed converted to the Indian Shaker religion.

CUSTOMS

Social divisions

Like other Tillamook tribes, the Siletz people were divided into classes: freeborn individuals and a small group of slaves. When work needed to be done, the people were divided into groups based on their talents. Task leaders led these groups. The task leaders might include shamans (healers), headmen, and warriors. The highest class of people included those with great wealth, professionals such as doctors, and accomplished hunters.

Childbirth

Specially trained women attended the birthing process. In early times, the woman in labor sat on a board equipped with a horizontal gripping bar. Following the birth of her baby, the bar, the mother's clothing, and the floor matting were thrown into the woods. The afterbirth (material expelled from the womb after the baby was born) was placed at the foot of a small spruce tree so that the child would grow tall and strong. When the newborn's umbilical cord fell off, it was placed in a decorated cloth bag that the child wore from toddlerhood until about age six. The loss of this special bag was a bad omen, signaling that the child would become disobedient or foolish.

Puberty

When a girl had her first menstrual period, she went to a secluded place for four or five days. During this time, she lay on planks of wood while her mother explained to her about becoming a woman. The girl usually cooked for herself and danced during the evenings. Later, she went on an overnight trip to the nearby mountains. She was washed with decayed wood and painted with a red dye upon her return. She was then considered a woman.

An adolescent boy was sent into the mountains to find a guardian spirit to guide him through life. The spirit revealed to him whether he would be a hunter, warrior, or shaman. The first animal caught by a young man and the first food gathered by a young woman after the puberty ritual were given as gifts of respect to the elderly of the tribe.

Courtship and marriage

The Siletz held two types of marriage ceremonies: special and common. Special marriages required at least one of the parents to be an important person in the tribe; furthermore, the bride must not have any children, and the groom must not have been married previously. Many people attended these special marriages, which were held outdoors and featured elaborate gift-giving rituals. Common marriages were performed by "good talkers," men with outstanding public-speaking skills. A common marriage bride was brought to the home of the groom's family, gifts were exchanged, and a feast was held.

Promises of gifts for the newlyweds' children were made—the wealthier the family, the more lavish the promises. Grooms were expected to be kind and sensitive to their new wives, and marital relations often did not occur for several nights after the marriage.

Funerals

People usually had a shaman in attendance at their deathbeds. The shaman reassured the dying person that his or her belongings would be distributed properly and that the burial canoe would be prepared according to custom. After death, the body was washed and dressed, the eyes were bandaged, and the face was painted red. The body was then wrapped in a blanket, covered with cedar bark, and laid on a plank. At the two- or three-day wake that followed, people sang and attendants kept each other awake so the dead person would not take their souls. The body was later placed in a canoe, which was removed through a hole in the house and placed on supports at the burial ground. Another canoe was upended and placed over the one containing the body, and goods were placed near the grave. One year later, the canoe might be reopened, the bones cleaned, and new grave goods added.

Festivals and ceremonies

Most Siletz festivals were held in winter, when the cold weather reduced fishing activities. The Siletz celebrated the naming of children with a special ceremony in which the new young members were welcomed into the tribe. Children were often named after dead relatives. All babies had their ears pierced, and boys also had their noses pierced, usually by a shaman using a bone needle. Feasting and dancing followed. The Siletz also held ceremonies to celebrate the onset of puberty, the beginning of salmon season, and lunar and solar eclipses.

After the tribes moved to the reservation, many of their individual traditional festivals and practices were lost, but people still gathered to celebrate. They held an annual Siletz Indian Fair. At hop-picking time, they enjoyed fiddle dances and sometimes feather dances. In the twenty-first century, the Siletz Tribe holds annual powwows (celebrations where people participate in Native singing and dancing). The NesikaIl-lahee Pow-wow in August features competitive dancing as well as arts and crafts. The Restoration Pow-wow is held to commemorate tribal restoration.

CURRENT TRIBAL ISSUES

In 1956, the U.S. government terminated the Siletz Tribe's federal recognition and sold the remaining Siletz lands. Thirty-nine acres, called Government Hill, went to the city of Siletz. The next twenty years were difficult for the people. They lost much of their culture and identity, but they continued to work for recognition. In 1977, they regained their federal recognition, making them eligible for federal benefits and funds again.

Next, they needed to work on restoring the lands they had lost. In 1980, the Siletz Reservation Plan was approved, and in 1981, Government Hill was returned to the tribe. With that 39-acre plot and 3,630 acres of timberland in Lincoln County, as well as several parcels purchased by tribe members, the Siletz began to reestablish their land base. By the early 2000s, they had acquired additional acreage and were working to revive their culture and language.

The Siletz have also achieved greater financial security. The casino and other businesses the tribe now operates have helped the Siletz increase their wealth. Surplus funds are used for charitable contributions. The Siletz have contributed more than $8 million to various charities. They provide charitable assistance within their eleven-county service area (Lincoln, Tillamook, Linn, Lane, Benton, Polk, Yamhill, Marion, Multnomah, Washington, and Clackamas Counties) and donate to Native entities throughout the United States.

BOOKS

Boas, Franz. "Notes on the Tillamook." In *University of California Publications in American Archaeology and Ethnology.* Vol. 20. Edited by A. L. Kroeber. Berkeley: University of California Publications, 1923.

Chehak, Gail, and Jan Halliday. *Native Peoples of the Northwest: A Traveler's Guide to Land, Art, and Culture.* Seattle, WA: Sasquatch Books, 2002.

Du Bois, Cora. *The 1870 Ghost Dance.* Lincoln: University of Nebraska Press, 2007.

Michigan Historical Reprint Series. *Annual Report of the Commissioner of Indian Affairs to the Secretary of the Interior.* Ann Arbor: Scholarly Publishing Office, University of Michigan Library, 2005.

Ruby, Robert H., John A. Brown, and Cary C. Collins. *A Guide to the Indian Tribes of the Pacific Northwest.* 3rd ed. Norman: University of Oklahoma Press, 2010.

Ulrich, Roberta. *American Indian Nations from Termination to Restoration, 1953–2006.* Lincoln: University of Nebraska Press, 2010.

Wilkinson, Charles. *The People Are Dancing Again: The History of the Siletz Tribe of Western Oregon.* Seattle: University of Washington, 2010.

WEB SITES

Confederated Tribes of Siletz. http://ctsi.nsn.us/ (accessed on November 2, 2011).

"Confederated Tribes of Siletz Indians: From the Brink of Oblivion to Front Runners in Achievement." November 25, 2002. *U.S. Department of Housing and Urban Development.* http://www.hud.gov/news/focus.cfm?content=2002-11-25.cfm (accessed on November 2, 2011).

"Confederated Tribes of the Siletz Indians and Coastal Coho." *Oregon State.* http://www.oregon.gov/OPSW/cohoproject/MeetingInfo/11_14_05_ctsi. pdf?ga=t (accessed on November 2, 2011).

Edward S. Curtis's The North American Indian. Vol. 13. Northwestern University Digital Library Collections. http://curtis.library.northwestern. edu/curtis/toc.cgi?sec=nai.09.book,&psec=#nai.09.book (accessed on November 2, 2011).

"History of the Confederated Tribes of the Siletz Indians." *HeeHeeIllahee RV Resort.* http://www.heeheeillahee.com/html/about_tribe_history.htm (accessed on November 2, 2011).

"Lewis & Clark: Tribes: Siletz Indians." *National Geographic.* http://www. nationalgeographic.com/lewisandclark/record_tribes_090_14_8.html (accessed on November 2, 2011).

Native American Document Project. "A Brief Interpretive History of the Rogue River War and the Coast, Alsea, and Siletz Reservations to 1894." *California State Univesity, San Marcos.* http://public.csusm.edu/nadp/subject.htm (accessed on November 2, 2011).

Siletz Tribal Business Corporation. http://www.stbcorp.net/ (accessed on November 2, 2011).

"Tillamook." *Department of Linguistics, University of Oregon.* http://logos. uoregon.edu/explore/oregon/tillamook.html (accessed on November 2, 2011).

"Tolowa." *Four Directions Institute.* http://www.fourdir.com/tolowa.htm (accessed on November 2, 2011).

Skokomish

Name

The name Skokomish (pronounced *sko-KO-mish*) comes from two words—*skookum* and *mish*—that together mean "big river people." The suffix *mish* is found on many Northwest tribal names, and it means "people." These words are most likely a combination of Chinook Jargon (a trade language; see Chinook entry) and Lutshootseed, a language family spoken by most of the Coast Salish tribes. The word came from one of their village names, *sqoqc'bes* ("people of the river"). The tribe began using this name after they moved to the reservation. Prior to that the people called themselves *tuwáduxq* or *Twana*. Some tribe members have returned to using this name.

Location

The Skokomish traditionally lived in the Hood Canal drainage basin west of Puget Sound, Washington. Today they live on the Skokomish Reservation, which covers 5,000 acres on the Skokomish River Delta, where the river empties into the Great Bend of the Hood Canal.

Population

In 1792, there were about 800 Skokomish. The Skokomish Reservation had a population of 1,029. In the 1990 U.S. Census, 737 people identified themselves as Skokomish. The 2000 census showed 698 Skokomish, and 814 people who claimed some Skokomish heritage.

Language family

Salishan.

Origins and group affiliations

Skokomish was the largest of nine Twana Indian communities that lived near one another and shared many customs. What is now known as the Skokomish tribe is mostly made up of Twana Indians and the descendants of the other tribes who share the Skokomish Reservation. The closest neighbors of the Twana were the Klallam (Clallam), the Squaxon, the Suquamish, and the Satsop. The Twana also traded with the Makah and Chehalis. Enemies

Contemporary Skokomish Communities

Washington
❶ Skokomish Indian Reservation

Shaded area
Traditional lands of the Skokomish in present-day Washington

A map of contemporary Skokomish communities. MAP BY XNR PRODUCTIONS. CENGAGE LEARNING, GALE. REPRODUCED BY PERMISSION OF GALE, A PART OF CENGAGE LEARNING.

included the Lekwiltok Kwakiutl, who raided their villages for slaves and possessions, the Chimakum, the Snohomish, and the Cowichan.

For thousands of years, the Skokomish people have had a cultural, spiritual, and economic dependence on the Skokomish River where they make their home. Fishing has always been the mainstay of their economy. In the 1990s, the river was named one of the most endangered in the United States. The Skokomish have been encouraging the state and federal government to restore the river's natural abundance of animal and plant life.

HISTORY

Early contact with Europeans

The Skokomish probably had their first actual contact with Europeans in 1792, when British explorers led by Captain George Vancouver

(1757–1798) explored Puget Sound and Hood Canal. The Skokomish already had experienced an epidemic of smallpox, brought to their region by Europeans, and they already owned European metal goods, probably obtained in trade from other tribes. For three decades after Vancouver's visit, however, the Skokomish had little contact with outsiders.

After the British established trading posts at Fort Langley in 1827 and Fort Nisqually in 1833, the Skokomish had wider contact with Europeans. They were exposed not only to new trade goods but also to the people who worked for British, such as Iroquois (see entry) and Native Hawaiians. The Skokomish traded salmon for European goods, especially firearms and clothing.

Until 1846, the United States and Great Britain jointly occupied the Skokomish lands, and it was around this time Americans first began arriving in the Puget Sound region. In that year, England agreed to place all tribes in the area under the control of the U.S. government. The Skokomish then signed several treaties giving their land to the United States. In a short time, new settlers flooded into the former Twana lands.

Treaties strip Skokomish of land

In 1854, Isaac Ingalls Stevens (1818–1862), governor of Washington Territory, attempted to establish treaties with nearly every tribe in the region. He wanted to take over as much land as possible for the settlers by doing away with Native land titles, placing tribes on reservations, and getting the Native nations to adopt the Euro-American way of life. In 1859, as a result of the 1855 Treaty of Point No Point, the Skokomish were restricted, along with other tribes who spoke a similar language, to a reservation located on a small portion of their former lands.

Originally, the people were moved to a 3,840-acre reservation following the signing of the treaty. Other tribes united under Nisqually

Important Dates

1792: Probable first contact between the Skokomish and Europeans occurs.

1827: Fort Langley is founded, and the Skokomish lifestyle changes as the people begin trading with the British.

1846–55: A series of treaties gives most of the Skokomish homeland to the United States.

1855: The Treaty of Point No Point is signed.

1857: The Skokomish settle on reservation land.

1874: The U.S. government increases the Skokomish Reservation size to 4,987 acres.

1938: The Skokomish tribal constitution is adopted.

1965: The Skokomish tribe receives an award of about $374,000 for claims against the government.

1974: The Boldt Decision reaffirms Native fishing rights.

1976: The Skokomish and several other tribes form the South Puget Intertribal Planning Agency (SPIPA).

2011: Tacoma Power gives the Skokomish 1,000 acres of land and $11 million.

A Skokomish couple at their fishing camp, circa 1912. LIBRARY OF CONGRESS, PRINTS AND PHOTOGRAPHS DIVISION.

(see entry) Chief Leschi (1808–1858) to resist the forced relocation to the reservations. Following the Puget Sound Indian War (1855–56), Stevens was removed from his position, and the government enlarged the size of most reservations. An executive order on February 25, 1874, increased the Skokomish Reservation to 4,986.97 acres. At that time, the tribe took the name Skokomish, one of their nine original village names. Many people, however, did not move to the reservation, deciding instead to take jobs as loggers, mill workers, or canoers.

Fight for tribal rights

In the twentieth century, the Skokomish struggled through many hardships. Around 1900, the tribe lost the sweetgrass it used to make baskets because a farmer built dikes on land at the mouth of the Skokomish River, preventing the grass from growing. Around that time, the government laid claim to the tidelands, severely restricting tribe's shellfish-gathering activities. Then, in the late 1920s, the city of Tacoma built two dams on the North Fork of the Skokomish River. This resulted in the destruction of major tribal sites and limited the people's ability to get to saltwater fishing sites. Finally, Potlatch State Park, which opened in 1960, took over one of the best pieces of Skokomish coastline. The Skokomish were successful in legal cases they brought before the federal and state courts on all four of these issues.

In 1965, the tribe received an award of about $374,000, which they used to improve tribal housing and purchase a fish processing plant. In 1974, the Boldt Decision reaffirmed Native fishing rights obtained under treaties signed in the 1850s. Once again, the Skokomish people could fish in waters outside the reservation. Responsibility for enforcing Skokomish fishing rights now lies with tribal courts and the tribal fish patrol rather than with the state. The Skokomish people have also received training in fish management and biology and have benefited financially from taxes they impose on non-Native fishermen. A court decision led in 2011 to 1,000 acres being restored to the Skokomish along with $11 million and proceeds from the Cushman Hydroelectric Project.

Cultural Renewal

As tribe members regained their traditional livelihoods, the late 1970s and early 1980s ushered in an interest in customs of the past. Ceremonies that had not been practiced for seventy years or more were reestablished. There was also a renewed interest in basketry, carving, and dance. The Skokomish Tribe Historic Preservation Office collected artifacts, and elders taught members of the younger generation these dying arts.

In the 2000s, the Skokomish began offering special classes to high school students. Attendees receive credit for learning about their heritage. Teachers present oral history and traditional literature, and students learn to weave baskets with sweetgrass and cedar as their ancestors did. Language classes also ground the youth in their culture.

RELIGION

Skokomish oral tradition tells of first beings, creatures with both animal and human qualities. A figure called the Transformer changed these first beings into objects such as stones or into guardian spirits or human

Twana Words

Although the last fluent speaker of Twana died in 1980, some of the tribe's elders remember the language, and people are working to bring it back. One man who played an important role in reviving both the Twana language and culture is Bruce Miller (1944–2005). A few basic Twana words are below:

dakas	"one"
usali	"two"
cha'as	"three"
busas	"four"
sts'hwas	"five"
stibat	"man"
sladai	"woman"
sluqatl	"sun"
slutlub	"moon"
ka	"water"

beings. Then, after teaching humans the proper way to live, he sent them to Earth.

The Skokomish worshiped the sun, moon, and earth. They thought the sun rewarded good behavior, and the moon punished bad behavior. The people believed in other spiritual beings, such as earth dwarfs who could steal souls, forest giants who stole food, and underwater creatures who took on the form of humans.

The Skokomish thought that every person possessed two souls: a life soul that caused lingering sickness when it left the body and a heart soul that died with the body. After death, the life soul went on a long journey through the land of the dead and then started life over again in a new form. Souls of dead infants did not go on this journey but became guardian spirits who guided humans on their path through life.

People attained their guardian spirits through vision quests (see "Vision quest"). Guardian spirits granted people different types of power: power for success in war, power in gambling, power in hunting on land or sea, or power in attaining wealth. They sometimes even provided protection from minor things such as fleabites.

In 1839 and 1840, two Catholic priests taught the Skokomish about Christianity. Although the people seemed to be enthusiastic students, priests and missionaries who came later had little luck in finding converts. In modern times, people on the reservation prefer the Indian Shaker Church (see Hupa and Chilula entry) and the Assemblies of God religion.

LANGUAGE

The Skokomish and other Twana people spoke a dialect (variety) of the Salishan language family. Each tribe spoke a slightly different dialect. Between 1975 and 1980, the Twana Language and Culture Project was developed to keep the language alive. Volunteers used recordings from older members of the tribe to create a Twana language dictionary and textbooks, which are used in public schools as well as in the tribe's preschool.

GOVERNMENT

Skokomish villages had no formal government. The head of the wealthiest house in the village usually took on a leadership role in matters such as settling disputes.

The Indian Reorganization Act of 1934 encouraged the tribes to form their own elected governments supervised by the U.S. government. The Skokomish chose that option and established a tribal government in 1938. The tribal council members are elected to staggered four-year terms. The council selects a chairperson, vice chairperson, and secretary/treasurer, and a tribal manager to handle administrative affairs and enforce tribal policies. The people also have a general council led by a president.

ECONOMY

The Skokomish economy was based mainly on fishing and gathering foods. The tribe had three distinct types of hunters: sea hunters, land hunters, and fowl catchers. The sea hunters used harpoons from a two-person canoe. To catch seals, the men surprised them and clubbed them or drove them onto sharpened stakes or into nets. They traded sealskins for European products. Although fishermen made use of beached whales, they did not hunt them.

Skokomish men carved objects out of wood, and women made cords and ropes, mats, and baskets out of cedar bark and blankets of mountain goat wool and dog fur. The people sometimes traded these objects with other tribes or with Europeans.

In the early twenty-first century, many Skokomish people worked in logging and fishing companies, but these industries have been declining because of overharvesting. Since the 1970s, the tribe has been working to support its people through a variety of ventures. With new land purchased for economic development, the tribe created a planning department that assists in the development of retail and service businesses, commercial sites, and community facilities. Tourism and recreation, along with a casino and gas station/convenience store, also create income.

The Skokomish own a fish hatchery and a fish processing plant. The people harvest timber and lease forestland to lumber companies. Although their land is not suitable for most agriculture, the tribe harvests huckleberries, salal, and juvenile cedar in addition to a variety of mushrooms and medicinal herbs. The largest employers, however, are the tribal government and the casino.

DAILY LIFE

Families

Families were made up of a man, his wife or wives, and their children as well as one or two unmarried relatives. Wealthy people sometimes had slaves. Several families lived together in one large house, and each family had its own section of the home.

Buildings

The people built winter and summer homes. The entire community helped members of the upper class build their houses, and they joined in the feasting to celebrate the home's completion.

Winter homes were large rectangular structures made of cedar planks. The roof was sloped and supported by two main posts, painted with symbols of the families' guardian spirits. The dirt floors and walls were covered with mats, and walls were plugged with moss for insulation. Along the walls were bed platforms. Each family had a fireplace next to the bed space, and the area underneath the bed was used for storage.

Lightweight summer shelters that could easily be moved were set up at hunting, gathering, or fishing sites. They were usually square and held a single family. The walls were made of cattail matting and covered with bark. A cooking fire was placed outside the entrance to each home.

A special building was set up for important tribal celebrations such as potlatches (gift-giving ceremonies).

Clothing and adornment

In warm weather, men went naked or wore cedar bark vests and breech-cloths (garments with front and back flaps that hung from the waist). Women wore only a short apron of shredded cedar bark, although upper-class women sometimes added a goatskin skirt that was short in front and long in back. During rainy weather, women covered themselves with square capes of shredded bark tied in the front.

During cooler weather, men added a knee-length buckskin shirt, buckskin trousers or bearskin leggings with the fur left on. Bearskin or coonskin caps and deerskin moccasins and mittens provided warmth in extreme cold. People also wrapped themselves in blankets or fur robes, and the type of fur showed the wealth and importance of the wearer. The wealthiest people had sea otter blankets. Robes made of mountain goat wool were also quite valuable. Deer and raccoon skins, though, were more common.

Both men and women wore ear ornaments made of pieces of shell connected to cattail fiber loops. After contact with Europeans, silver ear pendants and earrings became popular. Wealthy people often wore shell ornaments hanging from their noses. Women had necklaces and bracelets made of shell, bone, and animal claws. Both sexes wore ankle bracelets. Although women usually had their ankles, chins, and lower legs tattooed in stripes, men were rarely tattooed. Face and body painting was done only for ceremonies, such as spirit dances or joining secret societies. On those occasions, the painted design depicted a person's guardian spirit or the special power a person possessed.

Men usually kept their hair shoulder length or longer, gathered in back with a thong or knot. Women left their hair loose or gathered it into a single braid. Slaves and women in mourning had short hair.

Food

Four different kinds of salmon made up the primary food of the Skokomish. Men caught salmon with dip nets and harpoons. The tribe also ate other sea creatures, such as sea lions, seals, mollusks, and beached whales. They hunted deer, black bear, mountain goat, beaver, muskrat, and waterfowl. Each year, an elk hunt took place in the Olympic Mountains.

Women gathered various plants throughout the spring, summer, and fall, so in the winter, the tribe could focus on social and ceremonial occasions. Plant foods that grew in the area included wild carrots, camas, salmonberries, salal, huckleberries, thimbleberries, ferns, and many other sprouts, roots, and bulbs. Many varieties of mushrooms grew well in the marshy soil. Women also harvested nuts and acorns, which they roasted to rid them of their acidic taste.

Healing practices

Tribal healers called shamans (pronounced *SHAH-munz* or *SHAY-munz*) received their curing powers from a guardian spirit. Two kinds of spirits appeared to shamans: a two-headed serpent-like being and an alligator-like being. Healing was a public event, and relatives and neighbors of the patient watched and participated in the ceremony. First, the shaman sang a special power song to find out what ailed the patient. He then treated the person by removing the sick-making object or by returning the life soul or guardian spirit that had been stolen. Shamans could also cause harm and even death. They were often regarded with suspicion and sometimes even killed, if they were suspected of harming someone.

Herbs were an important part of healing. Whereas shamans cured spirit-caused sicknesses, plants aided in recovery from many physical illnesses. The tribe still harvests medicinal herbs such as rhubarb, wild ginger, maidenhair fern, plantain, devil's club, and Labrador plant. Herbs not used for tribal purposes are sold to alternative medicine companies and to the cosmetic industry.

ARTS

Most art was of a religious nature. People used hard, sharp implements to peck at stone to make abstract designs. They made images of supernatural beings on articles used for ceremonial purposes or images reflecting the owner's power on house posts.

Shamans were known for carving unusual wood figures out of red cedar. These sculptures were often legless torsos with oval heads that were flattened in the front and painted in red and black on a white foreground. Instead of legs, they had pointed stakes that were set in the ground during ceremonies. Other common ceremonial objects were staffs topped with deer-hoof rattles used in healing ceremonies.

A Skokomish basket maker holds one of her works, circa 1912. LIBRARY OF CONGRESS, PRINTS AND PHOTOGRAPHS DIVISION.

Women created watertight baskets and waterproof clothing from cedar bark, and women wove blankets of cedar bark, mountain goat wool, dog hair, bird down, and fireweed fluff. They spun their yarn on their thighs without a spindle. To get the materials they needed, the people traded with the upriver tribes for mountain goat wool and with the salt-water tribes, who kept a breed of wool-bearing dogs, for fur. One early explorer reported seeing "about forty dogs in a drove, shorn [shaved] close to the skin like sheep." The people also traded for hemp. With this and other materials they gathered, women created baskets adorned with geometric and stylized animals.

CUSTOMS

Social organization

Tribal members were divided into one of three classes based on wealth and their ancestry: the upper class; the lower class, or freemen; and slaves, who were usually war captives.

Head flattening

Members of the upper class practiced head flattening, a common custom in the Pacific Northwest. Shortly after birth, a baby was placed in a cradle with a padded board tied to its forehead to mold the head into a desired shape. Children were kept in these special cradles until they could walk.

Vision quests

At around the age of eight, both boys and girls engaged in vision quests to find the guardian spirits that would guide them through life. These quests were held both before and after puberty. They started with fasting (not eating or drinking) and bathing. Older boys shaved their beards and body hair. After going without food and drink for several days, the youngsters fell into a trance, made contact with a spirit (who might appear in animal or human form), and received their personal power and a special song. Sometimes, they inherited guardian spirits from other family members.

Puberty

Menstrual blood was considered extremely powerful, even harmful. Upon a girl's first menstruation, she went to an isolated hut. There she sat on a mat and was instructed on how to perform a woman's work, such as food gathering and cooking. When a girl of high social rank came out of this isolation, her parents gave a feast announcing that she was eligible for marriage.

Boys were kept away from girls in an effort to keep them focused on finding their guardian spirit. This forced separation led many boys to decide to marry when they were young.

Marriage and divorce

Most people chose marriage partners from outside their village. Especially in the case of upper-class families, parents usually arranged marriages. The process began with a formal request by the groom's parents to the bride's parents, after which the two families exchanged gifts. Poor couples could easily obtain divorces, but it was more difficult for the rich and therefore was rare. Widows or widowers were expected to marry a close relative of their deceased mate to keep the couple's children in the groom's village.

Festivals

Upper-class families, who were the only ones who could afford it, often held feasts, called potlatches, to show off their wealth. Lavish gifts were given to other members of the tribe.

In August 2007, the Lummi tribe invited Northwest tribes to an Intertribal Potlatch, the first to be held since 1937. Tribal leaders described it as a "healing journey" as well as an expression of native pride. It also was intended to increase the usage of the Native American's traditional waterways and promote closer relationships among the tribes. Each year, a different tribe hosts the canoe journey; in 2011, the Swinomish Indian Tribal Community hosted the event. The Skokomish participate in this movement to reintroduce Native customs to younger tribal members.

In modern times, Skokomish people gather each year with other Native nations for various celebrations, including the Treaty Day celebration in January (which is open to the public), the First Plant Ceremony in April, the First Salmon Ceremony in August, and the First Elk Ceremony in October. The tribe also sponsors an elder's picnic in August.

Funerals

When a Skokomish person died, a series of rituals was held, beginning with a wake given by the family of the deceased. Professional undertakers prepared the body for viewing, and relatives and friends brought gifts to

Legend of the Dog Salmon People

Many Native stories tell of the first beings who had both human and animal characteristics. Some of these beings were later changed into humans. The Skokomish tell this tale of their origin. It also explains why the tribe holds the First Salmon Ceremony when they catch the initial dog salmon (also called chum salmon, Pacific salmon, or Keta salmon) of the season.

> This is the story of how the Dog Salmon people of the North Fork Skokomish River began.
>
> In the time when the first human beings lived in the land and were learning how to survive, they learned from the animals at the beginning of what we would call history.
>
> The chief of the Dog Salmon now knew it was time for his daughter-in-law and his grandchildren to return to the land of their mother's birth.
>
> The killer whales are the guardians of the great salt waters.
>
> They escorted our ancestors, the Dog Salmon People, from the great salt water that we call the land of foods, all the way back to where Hood Canal and the Skokomish River meet.
>
> It was here they danced the dance of the Salmon People.
>
> Hands on their hips, back and forth they danced, out of the water on their tails.
>
> When they reached the home of their mother, they danced from the water on to the land.
>
> Now they were humans.
>
> And it was they who became the ancestors of our Skokomish People.
>
> And it was at this time that our ancestors vowed to honor the Dog Salmon People with the first salmon ritual, till the end of time.

SOURCE: Sobiyax (Bruce Miller). "Skokomish Tribe: Legend of the Dog Salmon People." *United Cherokee Ani-Yun-Wiya Nation.* http://www.ucan-online.org/legend. asp?legend=4960&category=8 (accessed on November 2, 2011).

honor the dead person. The body was removed from the home through a hole in the wall and taken to a cemetery, where it was placed either in a box in the ground or in a canoe on a frame. A funeral feast followed the burial. There the personal property of the deceased was given away, and the widow cut her hair to show her sorrow.

CURRENT TRIBAL ISSUES

Restoring the Skokomish River and tribal land

The Skokomish River has always been the social and economic focus of the tribe. For decades, the river suffered damage because of clear-cut logging (the total removal of a stand of trees) on the river's South Fork and unregulated hydroelectric development on the North Fork. Run-off from the clear-cut slopes clogged the river with sediment, greatly reduced the number of salmon, and contributed to increased flooding in the Skokomish Valley. In the North Fork, the City of Tacoma's Cushman Hydroelectric Project completely blocked fish passage and piped the waters from the North Fork out of its watershed (the area drained by the river system) to a power plant. This starved 17 miles (27 kilometers) of the river of its flows and damaged the conditions of fish and wildlife.

In 1996, the Skokomish Tribe met with conservation groups and nearby residents to form an action plan for restoring healthy conditions for the natural plant and animal life of the Skokomish River. The tribe tried to influence the Federal Energy Regulatory Commission to require the City of Tacoma to restore the river to its watershed and to reduce the damage that has been done to the tribe's lands and that of others who live nearby.

In September 2011, the culmination of the tribe's longstanding legal battle to restore this land and to regain property that is culturally significant to them resulted in Tacoma Power transferring ownership of 1,000 acres of land to the Skokomish as part of the Cushman Hydroelectric Project settlement. The electric company also paid $11 million to the tribe, and it will make annual payments based on the amount of electricity it produces. The tidal estuary at the mouth of the Skokomish River that the Skokomish had been restoring was included in the property deeded to them. In return, the power company received a license to operate their power plant until 2048.

The Skokomish have also joined other tribes to form the South Puget Intertribal Planning Agency (SPIPA). SPIPA's mission is to deliver social, human and health services and provide training and technical assistance, resource development, and planning to members. The agency writes grant requests for funding and helps tribal leadership as well as individual tribe members.

Safety and law enforcement

Violent crime levels are high; many incidents are domestic abuse. In 2010 the Skokomish requested government funds to increase their law enforcement staff from six to eighteen. The tribe had an insufficient number of officers to patrol the 2.2 million acres that make up their treaty-protected hunting and fishing territory. New judges and probation officers were also needed to handle the backlog in the courts.

NOTABLE PEOPLE

Bruce Miller (1944–2005), an artist, teacher, and historian, was also a storyteller and community leader. He retold tales passed down to him by older relatives. Miller also played a key role in reviving the Twana language and culture. A skilled basket weaver and carver, he spoke and taught the Twana language and was responsible for reintroducing the winter longhouse ceremonies and the first elk ceremony. In 1982, he organized the building of the first traditional longhouse on the Skokomish Reservation in more than 110 years. In 1992, he received the Governor's Heritage Award.

BOOKS

Angell, Tony, and John M. Marzluff. *In the Company of Crows and Ravens.* New Haven, CT: Yale University Press, 2007.

Chaney, Ed. *The City of Tacoma's Illegal Condemnation of Land within the Skokomish Indian Reservation for the Cushman Hydroelectric Project Transmission Line.* Tacoma, WA: Chinook Northwest, 1999.

Chehak, Gail, and Jan Halliday. *Native Peoples of the Northwest: A Traveler's Guide to Land, Art, and Culture.* Seattle, WA: Sasquatch Books, 2002.

Clark, Ella E. *Indian Legends of the Pacific Northwest.* Berkeley: University of California Press, 2003.

Eells, Myron. *The Twana Indians of the Skokomish Reservation in Washington Territory.* Washington, DC: Department of the Interior, 1887. Available online from http://www.archive.org/stream/cihm_01084#page/n0/mode/2up (accessed on November 2, 2011).

Montgomery, David R. *King of Fish: The Thousand-Year Run of Salmon.* Boulder, CO: Westview Press, 2005.

Platt, Ward. *The Frontier.* Kila, MN: Kessinger Publishing, 2006.

Raibmon, Paige. *Authentic Indians: Episodes of Encounter from the Late-Nineteenth-Century Northwest Coast.* Durham, NC: Duke University Press, 2005.

Ruby, Robert H., John A. Brown, and Cary C. Collins. *A Guide to the Indian Tribes of the Pacific Northwest.* 3rd ed. Norman: University of Oklahoma Press, 2010.

Suttles, Wayne, and Barbara Lane. "Southern Coast Salish." *Handbook of North American Indians.* Vol. 7: *Northwest Coast.* Edited by Wayne Suttles. Washington, DC: Smithsonian Institution, 1990.

PERIODICALS

Trumbauer, Sophie. "Northwest Tribes Canoe to Lummi Island." *The Daily,* August 1, 2007. Available online at http://thedaily.washington.edu/article/2007/8/1/northwestTribesCanoeToLumm (accessed on November 2, 2011).

WEB SITES

"American Indians of the Pacific Northwest Collection." *University of Washington Libraries Digital Collections.* http://content.lib.washington.edu/aipnw/index.html (accessed on November 2, 2011).

Brian Thom's Coast Salish Home Page. http://home.istar.ca/~bthom/ (accessed on November 2, 2011).

"Culture and History of the Skokomish Tribe." *Skokomish Tribal Nation.* http://www.skokomish.org/historyculture.htm (accessed on November 2, 2011).

Curtis, Edward S. *The North American Indian.* Vol. 9. Northwestern University Digital Library Collections. http://curtis.library.northwestern.edu/curtis/viewPage.cgi?showp=1&size=2&id=nai.09.book.00000030&volume=9 (accessed on November 2, 2011).

Northwest Indian Fisheries Commission. http://nwifc.org/ (accessed on November 2, 2011).

The Skokomish Tribal Nation. http://www.skokomish.org/ (accessed on November 2, 2011).

Tlingit

Name

The name Tlingit (pronounced *KLING-kit*; sometimes *TLING-kit* or *TLING-git*) means "human beings." Over the course of history the tribe's name has been written many different ways: *Clingats, Klinket, Thlinket,* and *Tlinkit.* The Russians called them *Koloshi* or *Kaliuzhi,* which came from the Aleut word *kalu kax,* meaning "wooden dish." This nickname came from the women's practice of putting a *labret,* or wooden ornament, in a piercing in their lower lip.

Location

The Tlingit traditionally lived along the Pacific Coast in what is now southeastern Alaska and northern British Columbia and the southwestern Yukon in Canada. In the twenty-first century, Tlingit communities are scattered throughout those areas.

Population

The Tlingit population numbered about 15,000 prior to European contact. This figure may have included the Haida people, because some early European writers believed the Haida and Tlingit were the same peoples. Following the outbreaks of disease in the 1800s and early 1900s, the Tlingit population figures dropped to 3,895 in 1920. In the 1990 U.S. Census, 14,417 people identified themselves as Tlingit. According to the 2000 census, 9,340 Tlingit lived in the United States, and 17,219 people claimed some Tlingit heritage. In 2007, the three Tlingit reserves (Canadian name for reservation) in British Columbia had a combined population of 1,533. The 2010 U.S. Census counted 15,256 people as Tlingit-Haida.

Language family

Athabaskan (Na-Dene).

Origins and group affiliations

The Tlingit most likely lived along the southeastern coast of Alaska for thousands of years, since the time when the land was covered with glaciers. Major Tlingit tribes include the Sitka, Auk, Chilkat, Huna, Stikine, Yakutat,

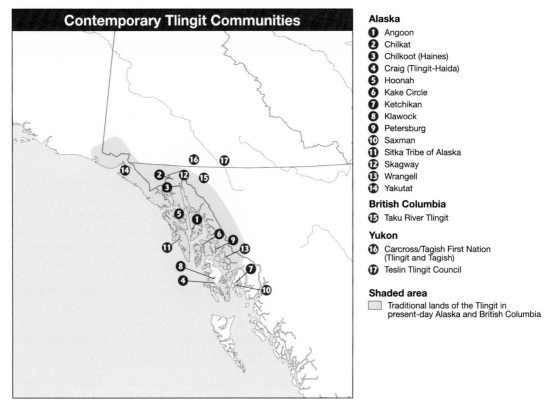

Contemporary Tlingit Communities

Alaska
1. Angoon
2. Chilkat
3. Chilkoot (Haines)
4. Craig (Tlingit-Haida)
5. Hoonah
6. Kake Circle
7. Ketchikan
8. Klawock
9. Petersburg
10. Saxman
11. Sitka Tribe of Alaska
12. Skagway
13. Wrangell
14. Yakutat

British Columbia
15. Taku River Tlingit

Yukon
16. Carcross/Tagish First Nation (Tlingit and Tagish)
17. Teslin Tlingit Council

Shaded area
- Traditional lands of the Tlingit in present-day Alaska and British Columbia

A map of contemporary Tlingit communities. MAP BY XNR PRODUCTIONS. CENGAGE LEARNING, GALE. REPRODUCED BY PERMISSION OF GALE, A PART OF CENGAGE LEARNING.

and Tongass. According to Tlingit oral history, when the Athabaskans faced hunger, they sent out a group to explore the south. Historians believe these are today's Apache and Navajo tribes. An older couple volunteered to explore the dangerous meltwater below a glacier and found a beautiful land; these explorers were the ancestors of the Tlingit. Present-day Tlingit have close ties with the neighboring Haida; both have interests in the Sealaska Corporation.

Over thousands of years, the Tlingit developed a way of life that helped them survive in the rain-drenched area of Alaska known as the Panhandle. Tlingit men burned, steamed, and carved cedar wood to make canoes for fishing because they obtained most of their food from the sea. Before the arrival of European explorers and settlers, groups of Tlingit people traveled by canoe through treacherous waters for hundreds of miles to engage in war, attend ceremonies, trade, or marry. In recent times, the Tlingit have led the fight for Native rights and have become involved in politics.

HISTORY

Relations with the Russians

The first Europeans in the Northwest were the Spanish, British, and Russians who came seeking furs in the mid-1700s. In 1741, the Russian explorer Aleksey Chirikov (1703–1748) sent two boatloads of men on a search for drinking water in Tlingit territory near the site of present-day Sitka, Alaska. Neither boat returned, and there were few attempts to explore Tlingit land again until the 1800s.

During the nineteenth century, the Tlingit people, who controlled trade in their area of southern Alaska, began bartering with the Russians. Relations were friendly until the newcomers tried to settle in the area and control trade routes. The Tlingit objected, and in 1802, Chief Katlian led a successful war party against the Russians in Sitka. The warriors killed many Russians and Aleuts and took thousands of furs; they believed these pelts belonged to them because the animals had been hunted on tribal land. The Russians, however, soon recaptured the site, and a few years later, they built a new fort that became the headquarters of the Russian-American Company, a fur trading center as well as a government center, until the United States purchased Alaska in 1867.

United States takes control

In time, European diseases and other hardships weakened the Tlingit. Between 1835 and 1840, nearly one-half of the population living at or near Sitka died due to epidemics (uncontrolled outbreaks of disease). About this time Americans, who came into Tlingit territory looking for gold, began to occupy and control Tlingit lands. The U.S. purchase of

Important Dates

1741: The Russians lose two boats in Tlingit territory.

1852: Chilkat Tlingit warriors burn Fort Selkirk.

1867: The United States purchases Alaska from Russia.

1882: The Angoon Tlingit seize boats, weapons, and hostages to force the U.S. Navy to compensate them for the deaths of two of their people.

1912: The Tlingit organize the Alaska Native Brotherhood to establish equality.

1959: Alaska becomes a state.

1968: The Central Council of Tlingit and Haida receives a $7.5 million land claim settlement.

1971: The Alaska Native Claims Settlement Act (ANCSA) is passed.

1973: The U.S. government offers $90,000 settlement for Angoon casualties.

1991: The ANCSA is amended.

Alaska from Russia in 1867 brought even more settlers. The newcomers established fish canneries, mines, and logging camps—businesses that were in direct conflict with Native traditions of taking only the resources necessary for survival. The Tlingit protested, but they were no match for American military strength and technology. The tribe was further weakened by the destruction of two of their villages in the late 1800s by the American military, caused by a disagreement over the deaths of two Native people.

Tlingit face threats

Over time, the American government subjected the Alaskan Natives to the same regulations and policies as American Indians in the United States. (Alaska was not yet a state, but its citizens enjoyed many U.S. citizenship rights.) Natives were deprived of land, and they lost their right to deal with criminal matters according to traditional customs. By the beginning of the twentieth century, their way of life had begun eroding.

In response, the Tlingit people joined other tribes in 1912 to found the Alaska Native Brotherhood (ANB). Among its goals was to gain for their members the same citizenship and educational rights enjoyed by non-Natives in Alaska. Their wish for citizenship was granted in 1915, on the condition that they become "civilized" and give up certain tribal customs. Few Alaska Natives were willing to accept these conditions, so they did not become citizens. In the early 1900s, smallpox, influenza (flu), and tuberculosis epidemics struck some Tlingit villages, and the population dropped to less than 4,000.

Tlingit regain some land

At the urging of the ANB, Congress passed a law in 1935 allowing the Tlingit to sue the United States for the loss of their lands. By this time large sections of Tlingit homelands had been claimed for the Tongass National Forest and Glacier Bay National Monument. Farther south in Tlingit territory, the government had set aside Annette Island as a reserve for Natives. Some lands were returned to the Tlingit, but not enough to meet the needs of a hunting and fishing people.

The Tlingit people also actively pursued the right to vote. Unlike many Alaska Native people at the time who wished to continue living as they had lived for many generations, Tlingit leaders sought increased political influence.

Twentieth-century issues

In the first half of the 1900s, disputes developed around such issues as Native citizenship, the right to vote, fishing methods, and discrimination. In the 1930s, 1940s, and 1950s, signs reading "No Indians Allowed" were a common sight on the doors of Alaska businesses. The ANB did much to fight prejudice and raise the social status of the Tlingit people as American citizens.

In the 1940s, the Tlingit people, along with a neighboring tribe, actively pursued land claims. The Central Council of Tlingit and Haida fought for an $80 million settlement, claiming that the money the United States paid the Russians to buy Alaska rightfully belonged to them. After an almost thirty-year court battle, they received $7.5 million in 1968.

In 1959, Alaska became a state. Soon afterward, oil was discovered there, and companies wanted to build a pipeline across Native lands to carry oil south. In 1971, the Alaska Native Claims Settlement Act (ANCSA) allowed Alaska Natives to retain 44 million acres of their land and gave them $962.5 million. In exchange, they gave up all claim to other lands in Alaska—in all, nine-tenths of Alaska. The ANSCA also resulted in the formation of twelve regional corporations to take charge of Native Alaskan economic development and land use.

Ongoing struggles for rights

In the early twenty-first century, although Tlingit people enjoy much more acceptance, their fight for survival continues. Their ability to live off the land and sea is constantly endangered by logging, overharvesting of the waters by commercial fisheries, government regulations, and the area's increasing population.

RELIGION

The Tlingit were closely tied to nature. They believed that everything had a soul, so they respected all of nature. Ignoring or neglecting other inhabitants of the world could bring disaster, so they were careful to always treat animals and inanimate (nonliving) objects well.

Other beliefs centered on a creator and spirit helpers who influenced the weather, hunting, and healing. Raven, who was not only a bird but also a human and a spirit, assisted in creation. Another being called *Shagoon* was the supreme god but also represented many other things—ancestors, history, creation, and future destiny. Shagoon, however, remained distant

The Tlingit Language

Unlike the English alphabet of twenty-six letters, the Tlingit language has at least thirty-two consonants and eight vowels. The alphabet was created not only with the familiar lettering of English but also with periods, underlined letters, and apostrophes to distinguish particular sounds. For example, the word *yéil* means "raven," and *yéil'* (with the apostrophe) means "elderberry."

Tlingit people do not use such greetings as "hello," "good bye," "good afternoon," or "good evening." Some common expressions are:

Yoo xat duwasaakw	"My name is"
Gunalchéesh	"Thank you"
Yak'éi ixwsiteení	"It's good to see you"
Wáa sá iyatee	"How are you feeling?"
Wa.éku.aa?	"Where are you going?"
Haa kaa gaa kuwatee	"It's good weather for us."

and took little interest in human affairs. Traditionally, the Tlingit believed that all members of the tribe were reborn from a common ancestor.

Changes occurred in Tlingit religion during the early 1900s as hundreds of Tlingit died in tuberculosis epidemics and were buried in mass graves. Many Tlingit lost faith in the healing powers of their traditional healers, called shamans (pronounced *SHAH-munz* or *SHAY-munz*), and the Native ceremonies that had brought the people together nearly died out. Tlingit people turned to Christian churches for comfort. When they converted to Christianity, many Tlingit were given new names to replace their Tlingit names, which had been an important basis of identity and status in their society.

The Russian Orthodox and Presbyterian faiths have had a great impact on Tlingit life and are well established in their communities. Smaller numbers of the people belong to other Christian churches. Most who continue to practice the traditional tribal religion usually do so privately.

LANGUAGE

The Tlingit language is not closely related to any other language. Because many Tlingit sounds are made in the back of the mouth, the language sounds similar to German. It has twenty-four sounds not found in English, and the difference in meaning between words often depends entirely on the tone of the speaker's voice.

In the nineteenth century, a Russian Orthodox priest created the first Tlingit alphabet and developed a program to teach the Tlingit to read and write. He based his alphabet on Cyrillic, or Russian, letters. Soon after that, in their desire to have the Tlingit adopt new ways, Americans tried to suppress the use of the Tlingit language. A Native movement to teach the language to the young began in the 1960s, when language experts created the Tlingit alphabet that is commonly used today. This alphabet contains letters used in the English language as well as other symbols such as periods and apostrophes to indicate sounds not found in English.

GOVERNMENT

Tlingit leaders, who headed the various clans, were the chiefs and their close relatives (see "Social system"). In the early twentieth century, Tlingit leaders sought power in state politics. A Tlingit named William Paul was elected to the Alaska Territorial House of Representatives in 1924, marking the beginning of a trend toward Native political power in the state.

In addition to the tribal governments, each clan also chose a leader based on character, abilities, and social standing as well as a commitment to clan welfare. The clan leader was called *Kaa Shaa du Heni* ("headman standing up").

In the twenty-first century, corporations created as a result of the Alaska Native Claims Settlement Act of 1971 (see "History") have a great deal of political power. Their power comes from their ownership of valuable lands and the fact that they represent more than sixteen thousand Tlingit and other Natives. They use their power to influence state lawmakers to pass laws favorable to the Natives.

In the United States, a city council headed by a mayor governs most Tlingit villages. A few villages, though, have tribal councils organized under the Indian Reorganization Act.

In Canada, the Taku River Tlinglit are led by a spokesperson and four clan directors, two each from the Wolf and Crow clans. Carcross/Tagish First Nation, who base their government on the five traditional clans, have four councils: executive, general, elders, and youth. The Teslin Tlingit Council has a twenty-five member general council with five representatives from each of the five clans, elected to four-year terms. They also have an administration to carry out council decisions. Administration and council decisions are guided by advice from the Elders Council, composed of all members age fifty-eight and older.

A fur-trimmed Chilkat robe is an example of the type that was a valuable trading item for the Tlingit people.
© TOPHAM/THE IMAGE WORKS. REPRODUCED BY PERMISSION.

ECONOMY

For centuries, the Tlingit economy centered around trade. The people bartered food, furs, canoes, shells, fish oil, and their beautiful woven Chilkat robes (see "Weaving") with other tribes. The price of a Chilkat robe in the mid-1800s was about $30—a very large sum at that time. Only caribou hides, copper, and later, guns, came close to the value of the Chilkat robe. An elderly woman who was a good bargainer often accompanied a trading party; she also kept track of exchange values.

By 1900, many Tlingit worked in seafood canneries, and their economy came to be based on work for wages and commercial fishing (fishing for profit, not food). A number of people moved from small villages to larger towns where this work was more readily available.

Although the American way of life has greatly altered the Tlingit lifestyle, the people have learned to adapt. Many Tlingit work in logging and forestry, fishing, tourism, and other business enterprises. Because the tribe emphasizes the importance of education, a number of Tlingit work in professional positions as lawyers, health-care specialists, and educators. Corporations created after the passage of the Alaska Native Claims Settlement Act benefit the tribal economy.

DAILY LIFE

Buildings

Before their first contact with Europeans, Tlingit families belonging to the same clan lived together in large homes made of spruce or cedar planks. They painted crests (family symbols) on the front of the house and decorated the interior with intricate carvings and pictures of birds and animals. The only openings were a small oval doorway and a hole in the center of the roof that allowed smoke to escape.

Inside their houses, the Tlingit dug out the center of the floor for the fire and placed platforms around it to make benches for eating. The highest bench was reserved for the head of the household; it also served for funerals (see "Death"). Another layer of higher platforms formed sleeping compartments; wooden partitions divided these. The people built floors of smooth wooden planks and hung large woven mats from the ceiling to separate living areas. Outside walls could be removed to turn the house into an amphitheater for large celebrations.

A house could hold six families plus their slaves; in all, a total of forty to fifty people. The rear of the house was reserved for nobility, the people

The exterior of a Tlinglit clan house is decorated with paintings and carvings. © TOM BEAN/CORBIS.

who owned the house. A carved and painted wooden screen usually hid this area from view. Commoners (poorer kin or laborers) had beds along the sides of the house. Slaves (usually war captives) slept by the front door. Each family had its own small fire, but the central fire was used to cook meals for the nobles or for guests at celebrations.

The four posts that held up the roof were carved and painted with totem or ancestor figures. Dark areas under the benches served as prisons for witches, who were tied up and left to starve until they confessed. Girls were also confined there during their puberty rituals. A trapdoor near the fire led to a small cellar for steam baths. Outside on the beach, families kept canoes, fish drying racks, and fish smoking sheds. Palisades (high fences made of sharpened logs) surrounded some villages. In the summer, the people moved to fishing camps where they lived in temporary shelters.

Europeans influenced the Natives to build their houses on raised wooden posts, but the Tlingit kept their custom of carving wood figures on the posts. They added windows, multiple doors, inside walls, stoves instead of fireplaces, and porches. In modern times, many Tlingit live in cities. Those who remain in villages live in single-family homes of various styles.

Clothing

Tlingit men and women traditionally wore loincloths (two pieces of cloth hanging from the waist in front and back) and skirts made of cedar bark. Because of the frequent rainy weather, they made raincoats from natural substances such as spruce root or cedar bark. The Tlingit wore hair ornaments and bracelets and practiced ear and nose piercing, face painting, and tattooing. The wealth of a Tlingit woman could be determined by the size of her labret, a wooden disc inserted in a slit cut into the lower lip. As a woman grew older and richer, larger and larger discs were inserted, until finally her lip might flap loosely on her chin.

People wore various types of highly decorated robes (see "Weaving") for ceremonies. In modern times, many people wear a button blanket, or dancing robe, made from red, blue, or black felt. Women appliquéd intricate designs of clan emblems outlined with mother of pearl (shell) buttons. These robes are worn to display one's lineage and family crest at gatherings, in much the same way as the people once used the Chilkat robe (see "Weaving").

Headdresses ranged from simple headbands to colorful carved cedar hats inlaid with pretty shells and finished with ermine fur. The wealthy often wore carved hats stacked high with wooden rings; each ring represented a time the headpiece had been given at a potlatch. Today, most Tlingit people dress in modern clothes, but they often display their clan or family crest on clothing or jewelry.

Food

The traditional Tlingit diet centered on foods from the rivers and sea, including seal, seaweed, clams, herring, salmon eggs, and fish (primarily salmon, halibut, cod, and herring). Fish was smoked, baked, roasted, boiled, or dried for later use. Berries, seaweed, and deer meat were also important. Bear provided food and fur for robes. The men also hunted mountain sheep and goats, birds, gulls, and ducks. Ocean catches included seal, sea lion, sea otter, and sometimes small whales. Only poor families ate porpoise, because it gave people a bad body odor.

Before leaving on a hunt, a man purified himself by bathing and fasting (going without food or drink). His wife and children had to stay quiet at home while he was gone to avoid disturbing his luck. After killing an animal, hunters prayed to it to ask forgiveness. The Tlingit never killed land otter because that was the shape a shaman's spirit usually took.

Women gathered roots, ferns, sweet potatoes, cow parsnips, and the sweet inner bark of the hemlock (a special treat). They cooked in watertight boxes or baskets by filling the baskets with water and then dropping in hot rocks to make the water boil. Other cooking implements were spits over fires and earth ovens lined with leaves. To start a fire, the Tlingit used a wooden hand drill or iron pyrite and quartz to make a spark. To help the fire catch quickly, they put wax from their ears on the tinder.

In modern times, the Tlingit use cooking methods learned from the Norwegians, Russians, Chinese, and Filipinos who have immigrated to Alaska, and rice has become one of their most common foods. Frybread is used for everyday meals and for special occasions, and certain fish oils are still considered a luxury.

Education

Traditionally, uncles and aunts taught Tlingit children how to survive and how to participate in society. Anyone within the clan could reprimand or guide a child. Today, most Tlingit children are raised in typical American one-family homes, and the role of the aunts and uncles is not as great. In the smaller Tlingit communities, however, some children are still raised according to the old ways.

Beginning in 1905, two separate systems of education were set up in the Alaska Territory—one for Natives run by the federal government and one for non-Natives run by the territorial government. Not until 1949 did schools in Alaska become integrated.

Many Tlingit go on to receive degrees in higher education. In addition to regular schooling, children sometimes attend dance groups, traditional survival camps, art camps, and Native education projects.

Healing practices

The Tlingit believed that sickness was the sign of possession by an evil spirit, and shamans (pronounced *SHAH-munz* or *SHAY-munz*), or traditional healers, had to drive out the evil spirits. Shaman's spiritual helpers were called *yeks*. Each yek had its own special name and could assume

Tlinglit men wear clan hats during a ceremony in Sitka, Alaska. © AP IMAGES/DAILY SITKA SENTINEL, JAMES POULSO.

both animal and human forms. A shaman's success at healing depended on the number of yeks he controlled and the quality of his relationship with them. Shamans were paid in advance for their services. If they failed to cure someone, they often claimed that bad spirits interfered with them and requested further payment to continue their services.

Although many shamans were men, some powerful women also became healers. Shamans never cut or combed their hair. They wore aprons of animal hides and decorated their shoulder robes and crowns with animal claws and carved bones. When engaged in healing dances, they often wore masks that looked like one of their yeks. Shamans shook rattles and charms; they chanted, groaned, and hissed themselves into a trance-like state.

When a shaman died, he or she passed healing powers on to a younger clan member. These junior healers knew they had been chosen because they would become dizzy or ill following the funeral; they might also faint or have seizures. An assistant then took this novice into the woods to encounter an animal spirit. A land otter was the spirit the healers most often encountered. The shamans would gain the animal's power by killing it and cutting off a slice of its tongue. Every time shamans went into the woods after that, they would obtain other spirit helpers.

In the twenty-first century, Tlingit people have access to modern medical treatment, but healing through diet and traditional local medicines still takes place.

ARTS

Dance

Dances were performed at potlatches (special gift-giving ceremonies) or around the evening fire. People told stories, made fun of others, or extended apologies through dance movements accompanied by the music of drums and carved rattles. One Tlingit dance told the story of a funeral. The "corpse" was dressed in fancy clothing with his back against the wall, and another man danced the part of his widow. The mourner cried sorrowfully as he threw himself on the "corpse" and tickled it. As the dance ended, the "corpse" sat up and grinned.

Dancers wore masks carved and painted with animals and mythical figures. They also wore headdresses made of sea lion whiskers and bird feathers that they showered down on guests to show good wishes. Dancers sometimes put on beautiful Chilkat robes (see "Weaving") with fringe that made a wonderful visual effect as they moved.

Weaving

Two types of traditional ceremonial dress, Chilkat and Raven's Tail robes, are still worn today. The intricately designed Chilkat robe is made from mountain goat wool and cedar bark strips. It can take a weaver up to five years to complete one robe. The Raven's Tail robe is woven of black and white fibers in geometric patterns. Both types of robes were signs of wealth. These art forms nearly died out, but during the twentieth century, the skill revived when elderly weavers were encouraged to pass down their knowledge to younger ones. Chilkat and Raven's Tail weaving techniques are also used in leggings, medicine bags, dance purses and aprons, tunics, and shirts.

Totem poles

The Tlingit carved totem poles in the shape of animals and humans. Totems could be as high as 90 feet (25 meters) tall and told family stories and legends. They honored chiefs or loved ones and commemorated events such as a birth or a successful hunt. Memorial totems held the ashes of deceased loved ones. Occasionally, totems were created to make fun of someone who had wronged the clan or village.

Leaders often hired a carver and selected crest designs from their elite ancestors. They placed the finished pole in a doorway or used it as a pillar honoring a dead relative or as a memorial on the beach. After the totem pole was completed, the owner gave a potlatch. His guests helped him erect the pole, then everyone feasted, gifts were dispensed, and the owner told the tales of each figure on the totem.

Tlingit rock art often has the same clan crests found on totem poles. Other rock art designs include sailing ships, mythological figures, ancestors, and symbols of wealth or victory.

CUSTOMS

Tlingit social system

The Tlingit social system was very complex. From birth, each person belonged to the same group as the mother, either Eagle or Raven, and was only permitted to marry a person from the other group.

The Raven and Eagle groups were divided into clans. Each clan had its own crest (an animal symbol). A person could be an Eagle and belong to the Killer Whale or Brown Bear Clan, or to several other existing clans; Ravens could belong to the Frog Clan, Sea Tern Clan, Coho (Salmon) Clan, and so on.

Clans were further divided into houses or extended families. Before the Tlingit had contact with Europeans, "houses" were real houses or lodges in which members of that clan or family lived. Today, "houses" are one of the ways in which Tlingit people identify themselves and their relationship to others. Some examples of houses include the Snail House, Brown Bear Den House, Owl House, Crescent Moon House, Coho House, and Thunderbird House.

Beyond family and clan groupings, the Tlingit were divided into units called *kwan,* which were communities of people who lived in a mutual area, shared residence, intermarried, and lived in peace.

Festivals

Potlatches have always been an important part of Tlingit life. A potlatch is a great feast where people show respect, pay debts, and display their wealth. The host of the potlatch gives gifts to everyone present. In modern times, potlatches are held for a variety of occasions such as funerals, adoptions, the naming of a baby, raising a totem pole, or building a lodge. They may take years of planning; in the past they lasted four weeks or more, but they seldom last that long today.

War and hunting rituals

The Tlingit were a warlike people who raided neighboring tribes and other clans to seek revenge for insults or injury. Tlingit warriors wore shirts of untanned moose hide covered with armor made of wooden slats that encased the body from the neck to the knees. They sometimes took women and children as slaves, but men were considered too dangerous and were instead slain and their heads or scalps taken.

Courtship and weddings

Marriage was viewed by the Tlingit as a way to strengthen the family's social and financial position, and parents chose spouses for their children. The boy's family gave the girl's family valuable gifts. If her family found the gifts acceptable, they gave generous gifts in return. Gift exchanges continued throughout the couple's married life.

Death

The Tlingit believed that people who died naturally went through a thorny forest and crossed a river to reach the Town of the Dead (the cemetery). They stayed warm from the heat of the cremation fire and ate the food and drink their relatives put in the fire. They were also fed by food people ate in their memory at potlatches. Anyone who died by violence went to heaven, whereas evil people went to Raven's Home or Dog Heaven.

Relatives mourned a man's death for eight days. The clan met to sing songs and give money toward the funeral. Men from the opposite moiety (tribal subdivision) painted the clan symbol on the deceased's face, dressed him in ceremonial clothing, and propped him up on the highest bench in the house with his treasures. His body stayed there for the four days until cremation. Sometimes, important chiefs remained on this bench of honor until they decomposed.

The Ghost Land

Lacking a written language, the Tlingit used storytelling and plays that included music and dancing to pass down their history. In the following story, a young man whose wife has died does not participate in her funeral potlatch ceremony. Instead, he follows the Death Trail, and his unusual action leads to strange results.

> The young wife of a chief's son died and the young man was so sorrowful he could not sleep. Early one morning he put on his fine clothes and started off. He walked all day and all night. He went through the woods a long distance, and then to a valley. The trees were very thick, but he could hear voices far away. At last he saw light through the trees and then came to a wide, flat stone on the edge of a lake.
>
> Now all the time this young man had been walking in the Death Trail. He saw houses and people on the other side of the lake. He could see them moving around. So he shouted, "Come over and get me." But they did not seem to hear him. Upon the lake a little canoe was being paddled about by one man, and all the shore was grassy. The chief's son shouted a long while but no one answered him. At last he whispered to himself, "Why don't they hear me?"
>
> At once a person across the lake said, "Some one is shouting." When he whispered, they heard him.
>
> The voice said also, "Some one has come up from Dreamland. Go and bring him over."
>
> When the chief's son reached the other side of the lake, he saw his wife. He was very happy to see her again. People

Mourners, wearing old clothes and rope around their waists, sang clan songs every morning and evening. Widows cut off their hair and burned it in the cremation fire. They also fasted (did not eat or drink) for eight days, except for a little food in the evening every other day. They always put some of each meal into the fire to feed their dead husbands. People from the opposite moiety cheered up the deceased's family with songs and games. It was considered dangerous to cry too much because grief might cause another relative to die.

On the day of cremation, men removed a plank from the wall and took the body out to be burned. They threw the deceased's most valuable possessions, and sometimes a slave, onto the funeral pyre. Afterward, they collected the ashes in a blanket and put them in a grave box or mortuary totem pole, then everyone feasted at a potlatch.

asked him to sit down. They gave him something to eat, but his wife said, "Don't eat that. If you eat that you will never get back." So he did not eat it.

Then his wife said, "You had better not stay here long. Let us go right away." So they were taken back in the same canoe. It is called Ghost's Canoe and it is the only one on that lake. They landed at the broad, flat rock where the chief's son had stood calling. It is called Ghost's Rock, and is at the very end of the Death Trail. Then they started down the trail, through the valley and through the thick woods. The second night they reached the chief's house.

The chief's son told his wife to stay outside. He went in and said to his father, "I have brought my wife back."

The chief said, "Why don't you bring her in?"

The chief laid down a nice mat with fur robes on it for the young wife. The young man went out to get his wife, but when he came in with her, they could see only him. When he came very close, they saw a deep shadow following him. When his wife sat down and they put a marten skin robe [a marten is a weasel-likemammal] around her, it hung about the shadow just as if a person were sitting there. When she ate, they saw only the spoon moving up and down, but not the shadow of her hands. It looked very strange to them.

Afterward the chief's son died and the ghosts of both of them went back to Ghost Land.

SOURCE: Judsen, Katharine Berry, ed. "The Ghost Land." *Myths and Legends of Alaska*. Chicago: A. C. McClurg, 1911.

For the Tlingit, three potlatches (feasts and giveaways) were required to properly send a deceased person off to the spirit world. During the first, they prepared the body for cremation or burial (more common today), cooked food for the feast, and disposed of the body. Later, they held a potlatch in honor of the deceased person's clan. The third potlatch took place a year later; it ended with a celebration of life and happy stories and songs.

CURRENT TRIBAL ISSUES

Cultural changes

An important issue the Tlingit were dealing with in the early 2000s was having their own tribal courts and judges, because American courts do not understand traditional Tlingit values. Most sentences do not reflect Tlingit ideas of justice. In deciding cases in tribal court, Tlingit judges choose consequences that help the accused learn a lesson and modify future behavior.

Tlingit culture has undergone a rebirth that began in the 1970s. The people have revived their dances, songs, potlatches, language, artwork, and stories. Discussions are taking place about discrimination: how it can actually make people feel sick and what can be done to help the victims.

Environmental concerns

For decades, the Tlinigit in both Alaska and Canada have expressed concerns about the environment. Pollution and overfishing have caused great damage to the fish populations that have sustained the people for centuries. Industrial expansion, takeover of traditional lands, and commercial seafood harvesting have all played a role in the declining fish populations. The Tlingit are determined to restore the ecological balance in their homelands.

The First Nation Regeneration Fund provided financial support so that the Taku River Tlingit could build a run-of-river hydropower plant on Pine Creek. This allowed the Tlingit to stop using a diesel-powered electricity generator that was putting thousands of tons of greenhouses gases into the air. The hydroelectric plant, which opened in 2009, significantly reduced the band's carbon footprint.

At one time, Tlingit elders recall that the shores of Teslin Lake were red with salmon. In recent years, however, overfishing has drastically reduced the Chinook salmon population in the Yukon River. In 2010, the Teslin Tlingit Council initiated a plan to halt the decline of salmon. It voluntarily agreed to lower the tribe's catches, and it encouraged the people to substitute other fish instead. Other efforts include maintaining and enhancing salmon habitats, and making conscious land use decisions that benefit the environment and the fish population.

In 2011, the Taku River Tlingit signed a historic agreement with British Columbia that includes joint decision-making on environmental issues. The agreement helps to safeguard the Tlingit's traditional salmon runs and caribou habitat, but it will allow for industrial growth that plans for responsible and sustainable environmental development of the area.

NOTABLE PEOPLE

Elaine Abraham (1929–), the first Tlingit to enter the nursing profession, went on to a career in education. Her accomplishments include cofounding the Alaska Native Language Center in Fairbanks, teaching the Tlingit language at Anchorage Community College, and working as director of Alaska Native Studies for the University of Alaska in Anchorage. Abraham was inducted into the Alaska Women's Hall of Fame.

Tlingit activist Elizabeth Peratrovich (1911–1958) made a moving plea for justice and equality for Alaska Natives in 1945 that led to the passage of an antidiscrimination bill. The State of Alaska officially recognized her efforts as a civil rights leader in 1988 with the annual Elizabeth Peratrovich Day.

BOOKS

Beasley, Richard A. *How to Carve a Tlingit Mask.* Juneau: Sealaska Heritage Institute, 2009.

Beck, Mary G. *Heroes and Heroines: Tlingit-Haida Legend.* Anchorage: Alaska Northwest Books, 2003.

Bial, Raymond. *The Tlingit.* New York: Benchmark Books, 2003.

Brown, Tricia. *Silent Storytellers of Totem Bight State Historical Park.* Anchorage: Alaska Geographic Association, 2009.

Brown, Tricia, and Roy Corral. *Children of the Midnight Sun: Young Native Voices of Alaska.* Anchorage: Alaska Northwest Books, 2006.

De Laguna, Fredericæ. "Tlingit." In *Handbook of North American Indians: Northwest Coast.* Vol. 7, edited by Wayne Suttles. Washington, DC: Smithsonian Institution, 1990, pp. 203–28.

Grinnell, George Bird. *The Harriman Expedition to Alaska: Encountering the Tlingit and Eskimo in 1899.* Fairbanks: University of Alaska Press, 2007.

Grinev, Andrei Val'terovich. *The Tlingit Indians in Russian America, 1741–1867.* Translated by Richard Bland and Katerina G. Solovjova. Lincoln: University of Nebraska Press, 2005.

Hancock, David A. *Tlingit: Their Art and Culture.* Blaine, WA: Hancock House Publishers, 2003.

Liptak, Karen. *North American Indian Ceremonies.* New York: Franklin Watts, 1992.

Nichols, Richard. *A Story to Tell: Traditions of a Tlingit Community.* Minneapolis: Lerner Publications Company, 1998.

Steward, Hilary. *Looking at Totem Poles.* Seattle: University of Washington Press, 1993.

Swanton, John R. *Social Condition, Beliefs, and Linguistic Relationship of the Tlingit Indians.* Whitefish, MT: Kessinger Publishing, 2006.

Thornton, Thomas F. *Being and Place among the Tlingit.* Seattle: University of Washington Press, 2008.

Victor-Howe, Anne-Marie. *Feeding the Ancestors: Tlingit Carved Horn Spoons.* Cambridge, MA: Peabody Museum Press and Harvard University, 2007.

Worl, Rosita. *Celebration: Tlingit, Haida, Tsimshian Dancing on the Land.* Edited by Kathy Dye. Seattle: University of Washington Press, 2008.

WEB SITES

Carcross Tagish First Nation. http://www.ctfn.ca/ (accessed on November 2, 2011).

Central Council: Tlingit and Haida Tribes of Alaska. http://www.ccthita.org (accessed on November 2, 2011).

"Language Resources." *Sealaska Heritage Institute.* http://www.sealaskaheritage.org/programs/language_resources.htm (accessed on November 2, 2011).

Nicholas Galanin. http://www.nicholasgalanin.com/ (accessed on November 2, 2011).

"Raven Spirit: A Native American Canoe's Journey." *Smithsonian Institute.* http://ocean.si.edu/ocean-stories/raven-spirit-native-american-canoes-journey (accessed on November 2, 2011).

Redish, Laura, and Orrin Lewis. "Tlingit Indian Language." *Native Languages of the Americas.* http://www.native-languages.org/tlingit.htm (accessed on November 2, 2011).

Sealaska: A Native Corporation. http://www.sealaska.com (accessed on November 2, 2011).

Taku River Tlingit First Nation. http://www.trtfn.com/ (accessed on November 2, 2011).

Teslin Tlingit Council. http://www.ttc-teslin.com/ (accessed on November 2, 2007).

The Tlingit Language. http://www.tlingitlanguage.org/ (accessed on November 2, 2011).

"Tlingit Tribes, Clans, and Clan Houses: Traditional Tlingit Country." *Alaska Native Knowledge Network.* http://www.ankn.uaf.edu/ANCR/Southeast/TlingitMap/ (accessed on November 2, 2011).

Tsimshian

Name

Tsimshian (pronounced *CHIM-she-an*, *SIM-she-an*, or TSIM-she-yan), sometimes spelled Chimmesyan, is often used to refer to all the groups in northern British Columbia, Canada, that speak the same language. These include the Nishga (Nisga'a), Gitksan, and Coast Tsimshian. The name means "people of the Skeena." The Skeena is a river that borders their traditional homelands. Tsimshian clans had names that described their location, often in relation to the animals abundant there. For example, the *Kitseesh* were called the "people of the land of the hair seal traps," and the *Kitnakangeaks* were the "people who live where there are many mosquitoes."

Location

The traditional Tsimshian homeland stretched from the Nass to the Skeena Rivers on the northwest coast of present-day British Columbia in Canada. By the time the Europeans arrived, the Tsimshian had villages in southeastern Alaska at Halibut Bay and Hyder. In modern times, many Tsimshian make their homes on the Annette Island Reserve in Metlakatla, Alaska, in addition to settlements in British Columbia. The five Tsimshian First Nations are located along the north coast from Prince Rupert in the north to Klemtu in the south, and their territory stretches east to Terrace.

Population

The Tsimshian population numbered about 8,500 in 1835. From 1862 to the late 1890s, smallpox and other epidemics killed from one-quarter to one-third of the people. In 1857, a report indicated that about 2,300 Tsimshian lived in 140 villages. The Tsimshian population increased, however, during the twentieth century. In 1990, of the 6,982 Tsimshian people, 4,550 lived in Canada and 2,432 in the United States. The 2000 U.S. Census showed 3,489 Tsimshian, and the 2010 census counted 2,307, with 3,755 people claiming some Tsimshian heritage. According to 2011 statistics from Indian and Northern Affairs Canada, the Canadian Tsimshian population was 3,264.

Language family

Tsimshian.

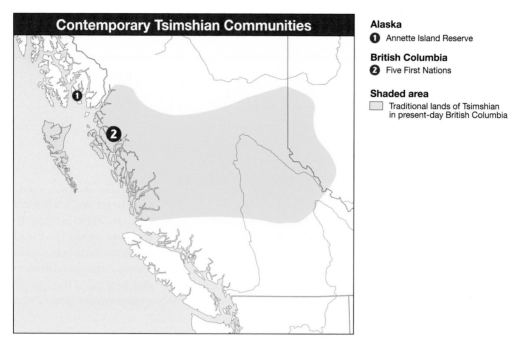

Contemporary Tsimshian Communities

Alaska
1 Annette Island Reserve

British Columbia
2 Five First Nations

Shaded area
▢ Traditional lands of Tsimshian in present-day British Columbia

A map of contemporary Tsimshian communities. MAP BY XNR PRODUCTIONS. CENGAGE LEARNING, GALE. REPRODUCED BY PERMISSION OF GALE, A PART OF CENGAGE LEARNING.

Origins and group affiliations

According to Tsimshian oral history, their people once inhabited a warm land but fled during a great flood. The Raven clan escaped the floodwaters by fleeing to a nearby mountain. After the waters receded, they met the Eagle clan beside a river. Following their custom of intermarriage, the two groups settled together and founded the village that is now called Kitwanga. Archaeologists have found evidence of Tsimshian settlements from five thousand years ago, and people have lived in the coastal area of British Columbia since 9000 BCE. As did other Northwest nations, the Tsimshian engaged in trade with neighboring tribes, particularly the Tlingit (see entry) to their north. Disagreements among trading partners, such as with the Haida (see entry), sometimes erupted into warfare. The Dunne-Za, Kwakwaka'wakw (see entry), and Athapaskan sometimes attacked the Tsimshian.

The Tsimshian are unique because theirs is the longest continuous occupation by any Native nation in North America. They have lived in the Prince Rupert Harbour area for at least five thousand years. Bounded by the Nass and Skeena Rivers and somewhat isolated by the ocean and mountains, the Tsimshian's location allowed their culture to flourish. Trade and their traditional lifestyles gave the people leisure time to develop their arts and ceremonies. The Tsimshian became expert navigators and developed an elaborate class system, which was reflected in their homes, possessions, and burials. In spite of the many changes introduced by the Euro-Canadians beginning in the nineteenth century, the Tsimshian managed to retain much of their original culture and still rely on the sea and forests for sustenance as they had for millennia.

HISTORY

Prehistory

Archaeological evidence dating back more than ten thousand years shows that the Tsimshian homeland was occupied by early cultures. Although these ancient peoples may have been Tsimshian ancestors, direct ties to the present-day Tsimshian extend back only five thousand years. Remains of plank houses and villages unearthed from that period show that the ancient Tsimshian migrated from winter coastal villages to temporary camps each year. These camps, occupied by small family groups, were moved as needed so the people stayed near important food resources.

About 1500 BCE the Tsimshian began constructing larger villages, reflecting their population growth. Homes faced the beach, with the chief's house in the center being the largest. Those of lesser chiefs were placed near the chief's house in order of importance. The differences in housing sizes indicate that these ancient peoples had a similar social class structure to later Tsimshian.

By 500 CE, the culture had developed to the level it was when the Europeans arrived. The wealthy enjoyed privilege and status. In addition to owning large homes, they were given elaborate burials with many grave goods. Men were buried with weapons, whereas women's graves contained jewelry. Commoners had simple graves, but slaves received no coffins and sometimes were mutilated. Around this time, the rights to hunting, fishing, and gathering grounds were established.

Important Dates

1787: The Tsimshian have their first contact with European traders.

1862: Anglican missionary William Duncan sets up a colony at Metlakatla.

1871: British Columbia becomes part of Canada.

1884: The Canadian government bans potlatches.

1891: Annette Island Reserve, Alaska's only reservation, is created.

1931: Native Brotherhood is founded.

1951: Ban on potlatches ends.

1988: Tsimshian Tribal Council is formed.

European contact

In 1787, the first European to arrive in Tsimshian territory was James Colnett (1753–1806), the captain of a fur-trading ship. Jacinto Caamaño (1759–c. 1825), who reached the area in 1792, wrote in his journal about his meetings with the Tsimshian. Over the next few decades, the Tsimshian had occasional contact with traders, but not until 1831 did the Hudson's Bay Company establish trading posts in the area. The British wanted to take advantage of the bounty of pelts and the Tsimshian's hunting abilities. They built their first post at Fort Simpson, and soon the Tsimshian left their villages to relocate near the fort.

The Tsimshian took over as middlemen in the trade. When other First Nations brought goods to the trading posts, they had to sell to the Tsimshian, who then resold the goods to the British. Over the next century, the Tsimshian became a major force in Northwest trade.

Legex (Ligeex or Legiac)

The Tsimshian dominance in trade resulted from the influence of their head chief, Legex (or Stonecliff; d. 1894; see "Government"). Several strong chiefs had come to power among the Haida and Tlingit (see entries). The most powerful chief of all, though, was Legex of the Tsimshian, who subdued many of his rivals through war during the early years of the nineteenth century. He gained additional power by marrying the daughter of a Hudson's Bay Company manager. Legex solidified his position by providing the land where the company built its Port Simpson trading post.

Throughout the rest of the century, his descendants, all also called Legex, maintained control of trade along the Skeena River. They charged the trading company for the use of their canoes, increasing their rates from $30 a ton in 1865 to $90 by 1890. This monopoly ended in 1892, when the Hudson's Bay Company introduced steamboat service.

Influence of William Duncan

In 1857, an Anglican missionary named William Duncan (1832–1918) arrived at Fort Simpson. Until then, potlatches had been the Tsimshian's main economic system (see "Economy" and "Games and ceremonies"). Duncan, along with other Europeans, discouraged this practice. In 1862, accompanied by about fifty converts, Duncan reestablished the old village of Metlakatla, located near Ketchikan, Alaska, where he and his followers set up a Christian community that grew rapidly.

After a dispute with the bishop, in 1887, Duncan and more than eight hundred community members moved to Alaska. At Duncan's request, a reservation, Annette Island Reserve, was established for his followers in 1891. Annette Island became Alaska's only reservation, and the community came to be known for its ideal lifestyle.

Relations with Canada

After British Columbia became a Canadian province in 1871, the Tsimshian lands there came under government rule. Consequently, the people lost their rights to their homelands without a treaty giving them any rights or compensation. A law forbidding potlatches (gift-giving ceremonies) went into effect in 1884, and other Native traditions were banned. This Tsimshian practice, so crucial to their economy, had to go underground (see "Festivals and ceremonies" and "Economy").

In 1931, the Tsimshian were instrumental in starting the indigenous organization called the Native Brotherhood. This group aimed to restore tribal rights and end government interference. After decades of fighting for Native rights, the organization succeeded in getting the potlatch ban lifted in 1951.

In 1988, the provincial government passed the British Columbia Society Act. Under the act, the Tsimshian organized their seven bands under a tribal council, which takes charge of their affairs and deals with legal matters. The Tsimshian Tribal Council in 1994 initiated treaty negotiations with British Columbia over land claims. Several Tsimshian nations dropped out of the joint negotiation process to settle with the government on an individual basis during the 2000s (see "Current Tribal Issues").

Annette Island Reserve

In 1887, Anglican lay missionary William Duncan argued with his bishop over what Duncan had been teaching to the Tsimshian. The Anglican Church seized the land where he and the Tsimshian lived, which belonged to the Tsimshian. The First Nations people wanted to fight to reclaim it, but Father Duncan convinced them to move elsewhere.

Duncan received U.S. government approval for the group to move to Alaska. Scouts were sent ahead, and in 1887, they chose Annette Island because of its sheltered bay. The date they discovered the island, August 7, is still celebrated as Founder's Day.

Sailing in canoes, Father Duncan and 823 Christian converts moved to New Metlakatla ("calm channel"), as they called it. (The village later dropped the "New.") Buildings went up rapidly, and in 1889, the Tsimshian constructed a day school and church. Two years later, Congress set aside the land as the Annette Island Reserve. In 1916, the government enlarged the reserve to include three thousand feet of water surrounding the island.

Duncan remained in charge until his death in 1918. An elected twelve-member council now governs the reserve. Metlakatla has a unique relationship with the government. The residents chose not to accept the Alaskan Native Claims Settlement Act of 1971, which set up for-profit corporations to handle the claims money the government paid for land wrongly taken from the various tribes. Instead, the community opted to remain autonomous; they are the only reservation in the state of Alaska. Metlakatla has gained a reputation as a creative, independent, and progressive community.

RELIGION

Traditional beliefs

The Tsimshian had many deities, including Thunderbird, who sent the lightning and thunder, and creek-women, who controlled the water and fish supply. Light, Raven, and Salmon were important to the culture. People placed a bit of their meals in the fire as an offering for the supreme being, *Shimauget Lahaga* ("Chief of Above"). The people honored the spirits and their personal and family crests by following certain rituals.

To the Tsimshian, the bodies of animals, plants, and humans were only the houses, canoes, or shells that contained the souls. Animals and people were so closely connected that animals were included in the gift-giving traditions too. Animal and plant spirits were asked for permission before they were taken and eaten. The Tsimshian believed that people could transform into animals and vice versa. Animals had villages of their own where their "Real People" gathered and lived the same way humans did.

Guardian spirits played an important role in Tsimshian culture. Ten-year-old children went into the forest on vision quests, but the guardian spirits did not reappear until later in life. These guardian spirits protected those who followed certain rituals that included fasting, bathing, purging, refraining from sexual activity, and solitude. To prevent themselves from being taken over by evil spirits or influences, especially during "crisis" points in life—birth, puberty, and death—people observed certain rituals. Men were also careful to observe these rules before going hunting.

Other religious influences

In the early 1800s, Athapaskan prophets called Bini ("mind") encouraged the people to combine their traditional beliefs with those of the Europeans. The rituals involved "singing and dancing without laughing" along with some Catholic customs.

This religion was supplanted when the Anglican missionary William Duncan arrived in 1857 (see "History"). Duncan had great success among the Coast Tsimshian because he learned their language, and some say he gained greater influence than Legex. His ability to win converts may also have been because, many people lost faith in traditional religious healers following a smallpox epidemic that killed about three thousand people. Duncan convinced his followers to give up their traditional religious practices, including the potlatches (see "Festivals and ceremonies" and "Economy").

In 1862, Duncan and his converts settled in the village of Metlakatla. In 1887, Duncan had a heated disagreement with the bishop, so he and his supporters sought religious freedom in Alaska. The group moved to the Annette Island Reserve, where they created a model cooperative Christian community that still existed in the twenty-first century.

Tsimshian Words

aks	"water"
hana'a	"woman"
yuuta	"man"
gimgmdziws	"sun"
lak	"fire"
suunt	"summer"
gwisgwaas	"bluejay"

LANGUAGE

The Tsimshian people speak Sm'algyax, which means "real or true language." It has four main dialects: Nisga'a, Gitksan, Coastal Tsimshian, and Southern Tsimshian. Some scholars say it is part of the Penutian language, but many think it is a separate language all its own and is unrelated to any other North American languages. Other experts have noted that Sm'algyax is similar to Na-Dene, which is spoken by the Athapaskan to the north.

Because the Tsimshian placed importance on wealth, they have five different way to say each number. The word for each numeral changes according to what the people are counting. Many Sm'algyax words can be as long as twelve syllables.

GOVERNMENT

Clans had four or five chiefs, but one of them held a higher position than the others. Wealth and possessions determined clan status, but the superior chief had *skovalis,* or royal blood, on his mother's side. After trade began with the Europeans, rivalry sprang up among the various chiefs. They held potlatches to gain status. The leader who emerged, Legex, became the grand chief and dominated the fur trade (see "Economy") in the early 1800s.

The status of chiefs changed after British Columbia became a province of Canada. In 1884, the government banned potlatches. Because of their importance in establishing village leadership, these gift-giving ceremonies were still held in secret. In 1931, the Tsimshian joined the Native Brotherhood to gain their right to hold potlatches and end government interference. The restriction on potlatches was lifted in 1951.

Under the 1988 British Columbia Society Act, the seven Tsimshian bands formed the Tsimshian Tribal Council. The council oversees the affairs of all the bands. In 1994, the council began treaty negotiations with the province over land claims, some of which were settled in the second decade of the 2000s (see "Current Tribal Issues").

ECONOMY

Early Tsimshian migrated around the area between the Nass and Skeena Rivers, according to the seasons and animal movements. The men fished in the rivers and in the Pacific Ocean; they hunted game in the forests and mountains. The women collected berries and plants to add to their diets. For thousands of years, the Tsimshian engaged in this hunting and gathering lifestyle.

They also traveled upriver to barter with other nations and soon came to control the candlefish oil trade. They also dealt in furs and arts and crafts, long before the Europeans arrived. The Tsimshian women had a reputation as shrewd bargainers.

After British trading posts were established, many Coast Tsimshian built homes nearby. Over time, the head chief, Legex (see "Government"), dominated the fur trade, and several trade goods became valuable, including the Hudson's Bay Company blankets, metal, guns, and *Din-ne,* a copper worth five or six slaves. Throughout the 1800s, the Tsimshian remained a major influence in trade while continuing their own economic system of potlatches, which redistributed wealth in the communities. In the Tsimshian culture, all goods and wealth went to the chiefs, who decided how it should be distributed. The goods were given to outside communities, who in turn gave to their donors.

When the government outlawed potlatches in the late 1800s, it affected the Tsimshian distribution of wealth. The gift-giving continued to occur in secret, but could not be practiced on the scale it had once been. Over the centuries, the Tsimshian economy changed, but the people continued to depend on the ocean and forest for their major resources, as they still do today.

Tsimshian Clans

The four phratries, or clans, came from supernatural beings that the Tsimshian considered to be their ancestors. Each of these clans had crests, wonders, and privileges. Names were handed down to heirs. If no male heir existed, the name went to a female. Any woman who had a man's name was treated like a male at feasts.

Crests tied the clan to the spirit world. They gave the members a heraldic design and special names. The right to use an animal design on the clan's crest occurred because an animal had killed an ancestor; that person's descendants could place that animal on their crest. The crest came with the right to specific hunting, fishing, and gathering areas.

People sought their *Narnox,* or supernatural power, by going out into to nature and communing with spirits. After doing so, a *yaawk,* or feast, was held, where the event was dramatized using elaborate masks.

To appear in the physical world, Narnox needed a physical symbol, such as the crest, which was visible in the masks used in dramas. Other items might include drums, shakers, horns, or frontlets (a headpiece worn over the forehead and inlaid with abalone shell), which helped the wearer move to other worlds.

Having a "real-time" relationship with the spirit world was called *Halaayt.* Privileges, which came with Halaayt, were for the upper class. Only royal and noble children were initiated into one of the four orders of the Secret Society, and they alone were permitted to practice Halaayt.

Halaayt and Narnox brought the supernatural and natural worlds together. The Tsimshian used drama and storytelling (*adawx*) during their ceremonies to remember their ancestors and let them walk in the physical world again.

DAILY LIFE

Families

The Tsimshian have four *phratries,* or clan groups—Eagle, Raven, Wolf, and Orca (or Killer Whale). One of the groups, the Gitksan, had Fireweed, Wolf, Raven, and Eagle phratries. People selected their mates from another phratry. Each group had special stories, crests, property, and privileges that its heirs inherited.

Inheritance was passed down through the mother's side. A boy received his names, his rank and crest, and the family traditions from his uncle. Kinship also determined ownership of salmon streams, berry patches, and other vital resources.

Women not only determined inheritance lines, but they were allowed to participate in secret societies. They could compose songs for feasts, learn ancestral dances, and become Spirit Doctors (see "Healing"). Women were considered bad luck when they were menstruating, so they were secluded in separate huts during this time and while giving birth.

Buildings

Homes Early Tsimshian villages were located near the water and included a smokehouse, a sweat lodge, and a hut for births and menstruating women. Most villages housed three hundred to five hundred people. In addition to this main winter village, the people built seasonal camps near the areas where they gathered food.

The Tsimshian built rectangular red cedar homes with either excavated or flat earthen floors. Stones held down the bark roof, and a plank covered the smoke hole in the roof when the central fire was not burning. Dishes and wooden boxes for storage and cooking were arranged near the fire.

The windowless homes, which often housed more than thirty people from the same family or clan, had one main room with platforms along the wall for sleeping and storage. The head of the house slept in the central space farthest from the door, with close male relatives on either side. Slaves slept by the doorway. Menstruating women stayed in a separate hut or a cave.

Outside the home families erected a totem that showed their history. Each family had descended from a certain animal spirit, so that was part of the design. The whole village celebrated the raising of a totem pole. Those who could afford it had the exteriors of their homes painted with totem symbols. Chiefs often rebuilt their homes to make them more elaborate. At times, slaves were sacrificed, and a body was buried under each corner post.

Forts During the era of European trade, many Tsimshian built homes near the forts for easy access to trade. The people also built forts of their own to control the trade in their areas. Although some paths were open to all and freely traveled, the routes to scarce items belonged to specific owners, who protected them with forts. These forts, the plans of which came to their owners in dreams, had ingenious hidden compartments, decoys, and booby traps such as rolling logs, deadfall doorways or ceilings, and trapdoors.

Clothing and adornment

During the warmer months, men either wore no clothes or used a breechclout. Women wore cedar bark robes draped over one shoulder and tied at the waist. A poncho kept off the rain, as did waterproof hats woven from spruce roots and cedar bark. Cedar bark was the main material for clothing, but fur, tanned skins, and mountain goat wool were also used.

In the winter, men wore shirts and leggings decorated with fringe, paint, and porcupine quills. Closer to the mountains, women wore animal skin dresses and leggings to the knees. Wealthier Tsimshian wrapped themselves in fur coats made from raccoon, marmot, or sea otter skin. Other people used moose or deer hide pelts. Fur hats kept them warm. People rarely wore shoes, although rich people might wear seal or bear skin moccasins. When it was cold, commoners tied cedar bark mats around their feet.

The Tsimshian never cut their hair. Women braided their long hair, but men left theirs loose. Ear piercings showed social status, with wealthier people having more earrings. The usual materials for earrings were copper, bone, and shell. Women had a slit cut in their lower lip to insert a labret, or disc. Chiefs painted their faces.

Post-contact fabrics changed to cottons, and Tsimshian clothing became more like that of the Europeans, but the people still used traditional designs for ceremonial regalia. One legacy of their earlier years is the button blanket, which is wrapped around the shoulders. Early blankets made from cedar bark and mountain goat hair were called Chilkat blankets. Later, blankets were made from blue or black cloth with a wide red edging, decorated with white buttons. The designs symbolized the clan and crest and denoted social status. Before European traders introduced buttons, women created the designs from shells and copper plates that clinked as people danced.

Tsimshian dancers in traditional dress gather at the ceremony in Anchorage, Alaska. © BLAINE HARRINGTON III/ ALAMY.

Witchcraft

In 1894, a Tsimshian man named Moody explained to anthropologist Franz Boas how sorcerers killed people. Sorcerers were sometimes paid by people who wanted to harm someone else. When sorcerers were discovered, other Spirit Doctors used exorcism to get rid of the evil. If that did not work, the sorcerer was banished. Most who were exiled went mad and soon died.

> When a sorcerer wants to kill a fellow man, he takes some of the man's perspiration, or an old shirt, and takes it to the place where he keeps his witch-box. Then he opens his box, takes a string, and fastens a piece of the old shirt to it. He ties it across the box. When he wants the man to die quickly, he takes a piece of the old shirt, and cuts the string in the box so that the piece of shirt falls on the corpse that is in the box. As soon as this is done, and the string breaks, he pretends to cry for his victim; then the man from whom he has taken the piece of shirt must die. When he knows that the person is dead, he [the sorcerer] goes around the house in which the bewitched dead person is lying. After he has finished going around the house, he stops for a while; and when the dead one is buried, he goes to his grave and walks around it. Then he sits down in the grave and rubs his body, pretending to cry all the time. Then he returns, and his work is finished.

SOURCE: Boas, Franz. "Witchcraft." *Tsimshian Texts.* Washington, DC: Government Printing Office, 1902. Available online at http://www.alaskool.org/native_ed/literature/Tsimshian/Witchcraft.htm (accessed on August 15, 2011).

Food

Salmon was the most important food. The Tsimshian treated it with respect. They offered a prayer to the first catch of the season, and they never sliced salmon with metal. Instead, they used a sharp shell so as not to insult the fish and prevent it from returning to its usual waters. Women then cooked the salmon in wooden kettles.

The men caught other fish, such as halibut, cod, ooligan, and herring. Seals, sea lions, and otters were also part of the Tsimshian diet along with shellfish, herring eggs, barnacles, chitons, and seaweed. Women gathered berries, shoots, bark, and roots. They also collected sea plants, such as goose tongue, which was used to salt food, and beach asparagus. In the autumn, hunters killed birds and game (mountain goat, moose, deer, and bear). Each clan had certain hunting, fishing, and gathering property allotted to them.

The people extracted oil from the ooligan (a type of smelt) into baskets. They used it themselves and also traded it. The ooligan, or candlefish could be set on fire to serve as lighting inside the houses.

To preserve food, families buried it in pits. They dug holes in the ground that they lined with birchbark. They placed bark over the food cache and weighted it down with rocks. To camouflage the pit, the Tsimshian covered it with shells and dirt. When the caches were empty, they filled in the hole with dirt and shells.

Education

The extended family helped to teach the children. Grandparents often taught children the skills they needed, and the matriarch (eldest female) told them their clan history and instructed them in the laws and values of their people. After puberty, aunts and uncles took a major role in the young people's education and in preparing them for marriage.

Later, the missionaries and the government took over the schooling. Youngsters did not learn their language or traditions, which resulted in a loss of much of the Tsimshian culture. Not until later in the twentieth century did the people begin to revive some of these lost traditions. Language revitalization programs helped to reintroduce the various dialects to the younger generations.

Healing practices

Older women in the community who had an extensive knowledge of herbal remedies usually cured the sick. Sweat baths were also common remedies for ailments. Illness that could not be cured by these methods had to be treated by the *shoo-wansh,* or "blower." This healer, who could be male or female, got rid of the evil spirits causing the sickness.

According to the Tsimshian, their Spirit Doctors could move back and forth from the spirit world to the physical world. Some, called sorcerers, used this power for evil (see sidebar "Witchcraft"), but those who used it rightly served as intermediaries between the lower and upper worlds. Spirit Doctors held many roles—mystic, poet, visionary, prophet—but their primary function was to heal. Losing a guardian spirit was thought to cause diseases. The Spirit Doctor searched for and found the spirit, or they brought back another one to replace it.

Tsimshian totem poles stand at a reserve in Gitanyow, British Columbia. © GUNTER MARX/ALAMY.

Men or women could be Spirit Doctors. Before reaching this position, they spent much time soul searching and then began a long initiation process. Older Spirit Doctors taught their skills to the initiates. The main tools these healers used were medicine bundles, drums, rattles to waken the ancestors, walking sticks (decorated with power symbols such as fur, feathers, bells, teeth, ribbon, or hair) for directing energy, and soul catchers.

ARTS

Men created objects from wood, bone, metal, and stone. Wood was used for many household items and crafts. Artists carved and painted totem

K'elku

Anthropologist Franz Boas collected Tsimshian stories and wrote about their customs. In 1984, he wrote this story as it was told to him by a man named Moses.

A number of children played camping every day. Many played this game in one large hollow long. They went into it and played that it was their house. They made a fire in it and ate there. They took a large quantity of provisions into the log. They ate salmon. They did so every day. One day when they were playing camping, the tide rose high and the large tree floated out to sea. The children did not know it. They were playing inside. Now the log had drifted far out to sea. Then one child went out, and he saw that the log had drifted away. Then all the children went out, and they cried. The log was drifting about in the ocean.

One of the children was wise. He saw gulls flying about, and then he returned into the hollow log and said, "Gulls are always sitting on top of us. What can we do to catch them?" Then one boy said, "Let us hit our noses, and we will rub the blood all over the log, then the feet of the gulls will stick to the log." They did so. They hit their noses until they bled. Then they rubbed the blood on the log. Then they entered the log again. Now many gulls came and sat down on the log. About noon their feet dried to the log. Then one of the boys went out. The gulls tried to fly away, but they could not do so because their feet were glued to the log. Then the boy took hold of them and twisted off their necks. He killed many gulls and took them into the log. Then the boys were glad. They ate the meat of the gulls and forgot that they were drifting about on the ocean.

The land was far away. They were on the edge of the ocean. One day they heard a great noise. The boys went out and, behold, they were drifting round in a whirlpool. Then they began to cry. The tree almost stood on its end, because the whirlpool was swallowing it.

While it was drifting there on end a man ran out to it. He had only one leg. He harpooned the great log and pulled

poles, storage chests, bentwood boxes, cooking pots, drums, rattles, and even columns in their homes. Tsimshian masks were carved with large eyes to show the importance of seeing beyond the material world; taking time to look and listen mindfully were attributes the Tsimshian stressed.

Women wove cedar bark into mats, aprons, and hats. They also pounded the inner bark until it was soft and velvety enough for clothing, blankets, and padding for baby cradles.

it ashore. He hauled it ashore. The boys were not dead. He had saved them. Then the boys went up to the house of the man. There were many boys. One-leg gave them to eat.... They ate, and they grew up to be young men.

After a while the children remembered those who they had left behind, and they began to cry. Then One-leg asked the children why they cried, and they told him. Then he said, "The town of your fathers is not far. It is over there. To-morrow morning you shall start. You may use my canoe, which is at the end of the village." Early the next morning One-leg sent the boys, saying, "Take the cover off from my canoe. It is near by yonder." The children went, and grew tired walking about. They could not find the canoe. Finally they returned. Then One-leg asked, "Did you find it?" The boys said, "No." He sent them again, and they went; but again they grew tired walking about, and·they did not find it. Again they returned. Then One-leg himself went. He went to a rotten tree that was there. It was covered with small branches. He took off the branches and they beheld a large canoe. It was made in the shape of a man, with a mouth at one end. It was the same at the other end. Its name was "Wâ'sE-at-each-end." It did not allow anything to cross its bow or its stern. When a man crossed it, it ate him. Then One-leg said, "Don't pass in front of the canoe." And they obeyed because they were afraid. Then they put it into the water. It was a fine, large canoe. They put many seals aboard, which were to serve as food for the canoe. They the boys went aboard. They fed the canoe. Its bow and its stern ate five seals each. Then the canoe went. After it had finished eating the seals, it went very fast. Then they gave five seals more to the bow and five to the stern, and it went on again.

Finally the children landed at the town of their fathers. They went ashore. Their fathers and mothers and all their relatives were crying. Then the boys came back. That is the end.

SOURCE: Boas, Franz. "K'elku." *Tsimshian Texts*. Washington, DC: Government Printing Office, 1902. Available online at http://www. alaskool.org/native_ed/literature/Tsimshian/ Kelku.htm (accessed on August 15, 2011).

The Tsimshian were once considered the finest painters in the Northwest. They were even commissioned to paint homes of the Tlingit chiefs. Tsimshian designs were often abstract and based on oral history, but most designs also contained many human faces. Artists used heavy paints made from ground pigment and salmon eggs to decorate items with rhythmic, flowing forms. The glossy paint colors were mainly yellow, red, black, and blue-green.

In addition to their skills in the visual arts, the Tsimshian had a flair for music, dance, and drama. Dramas consisted of music and symbolic dancing. Performers donned costumes and masks. Transformation masks (for example, raven to human) had one mask inside the other, with ropes to open and close them. Backdrops might include mechanical devices, such as spouting whales and dancing heads, along with painted screens.

CUSTOMS

Social organization

Tsimshian society was divided into distinct classes. At the top were the head chiefs, with their *skovalis,* or royal blood (see "Government"). The upper class, or nobility, were called *ligakets.* People could move into this level if they gained enough wealth. The ten or twelve ligakets served as members of the tribal council.

Below them were the *waheim,* or commoners, who did most of the labor. Servants, poor people cared for by the chief, were also part of this class. The lowest class consisted of *kligungits,* or slaves, often captives of other tribes. Slaves had no family ties or clans, and their children automatically became slaves. Although they were worth money (in the 1800s they sold for as much as a thousand dollars), they were considered worthless when they became too old to work. At that point, they were sometimes put in the woods to die.

Birth and naming

Women who conceived were secluded, and they gave birth in special hut. If she had a boy, a mother sent him at an early age to live with her brother.

Puberty

Boys began their initiation into one of the four phratries (see "Social organization"). Girls went into seclusion for six months. They stayed in a hut in a forest or behind a screen at the back part of the house. Only their mothers could visit them during this time. The girl's lower lip was cut so a labret, or plug, could be inserted. At the end of the seclusion period, the girl's family held a feast and formally presented her.

Teen girls were expected to stay chaste, especially chiefs' daughters. They climbed ladders to get to their sleeping platforms, and a slave woman slept on the floor at the foot of the ladder. The girls also could not leave the house unaccompanied.

Marriage

The groom's mother usually arranged his marriage to someone of a different clan. Weddings were elaborate affairs that involved much gift-giving and ceremony. Both families met, and the young man's father offered symbols of the gifts they planned to give the bride's family. A stone represented a slave; a stick stood for a canoe. If the gifts were acceptable, the parents set a wedding date.

At the ceremony, the bride sat on a mat beside the groom. The groom's uncle on his mother's side held a feast for all the guests. After the wedding, the couple went to live with that uncle.

Funerals and mourning

Death rituals After the family of dead person paid for the funeral, the house chief prepared the body for cremation. The ceremony was held on a clear day so the smoke could easily rise to the unseen world. Chiefs had their hearts buried before cremation, or their bodies were placed in boxes in trees while their internal organs were burned. The ashes were placed in a box and put inside the family totem pole.

A wake, or Black Feast, was then held, where black paint showed mourning. The deceased's relatives cut their hair and wore old clothes. A year later, red paint was worn to a Red Feast to show that mourning had ended. During this commemoration for the dead, a successor was named for the deceased.

A man's property went to his widow and to his oldest sister's eldest son. The nephew was supposed to marry the widow. If he chose not to wed her, he paid money, and she could marry someone else.

Afterlife Souls went west after crossing rivers. Spirit Doctors' souls went to an island. Because their bodies retained certain powers, Spirit Doctors' corpses often were not cremated. Instead, their bodies were placed in grave houses or in secluded caves along with their medical tools (see "Healing"). The bodies might also be wedged into a tree, sitting up. It was a crime to use a Spirit Doctor's possessions.

Reincarnation was part of Tsimshian beliefs. Young Tsimshian saw themselves as reincarnations of their ancestors. Most people returned to their original families when they came back to Earth. If a pregnant woman dreamed about a visit from a deceased relative, she realized her baby was a reincarnation of that person.

To get a soul to return to them, people sometimes placed a piece of corpse in their belt and walked around the funeral pyre eight times. At times, the Tsimshian chose a dog to house the chief's soul. They believed that after the soul wandered the heavens, it would return to the dog's body. After the dog died, the villagers gave it a human burial.

Warfare and raiding

The Tsimshian engaged in skirmishes but had little full-scale warfare. Most raids on other tribes were to avenge insults or injury, or to gain slaves. One warrior, Nekt, surrounded his home with spiked posts. If attacked, he rolled the logs down the hill and crushed his enemies.

Before the Europeans arrived, warriors wore dried animal hides covered with pitch as armor. After they obtained metal through trade, they added face pieces. Special war canoes could hold as many as fifty men.

Festivals and ceremonies

Part of the tradition of winter festivities included placing red cedar bark rings on the doors to sanctify houses. At this time of year, the four dancing societies—Cannibals, Dog-eaters, Destroyers, and Firethrowers—initiated new members. Because shamans could enter death and return, they had a part in these events. The Cannibal Society members, for example, left the world to receive power from the cannibal spirit. From this contact with the supernatural world, members of the society learned that the desire to kill should never overcome reason. The shamans then brought the society members back to the human world and to their human form again.

One of the mainstays of Tsimshian celebrations was the *yaawk,* or potlatch, an elaborate gift-giving ceremony. The wealthy hosted most of these events, but if a commoner could afford to hold one, he could raise his children's status, but not his own.

Potlatches occurred for many different occasions—naming children or clan regalia, honoring the dead, paying off a debt, marking a divorce, erecting a totem pole, building a new house, or celebrating a wedding, birth, or adoption. Sometimes, the host wanted to make amends or get rid of shame. For any of these events, the host sponsored a lengthy gathering marked by feasts and dancing, which ended with the distribution of gifts. After the Canadian government forbid potlatches in 1884, the practice went underground until it again became legal in 1951.

CURRENT TRIBAL ISSUES

When Canada passed the Indian Act in the 1880s, the government's goal was to make all the indigenous peoples fit the Euro-Canadian ideas of correct social behavior. For more than a century, First Nations struggled to maintain their culture. Potlatches, or gift-giving events, which formed the basis of the Tsimshian economy, were outlawed (see "Festivals and ceremonies" and "Economy"). The Tsimshian inherited their rights to food-gathering areas through their mother's line, but the Indian Act forbid women from owning land in their communities. These regulations had a severe impact on the Tsimshian, denying their cultural rights and traditions, and undermining their traditional practices. After decades of practicing their ceremonies in secret and trying to retain their culture in spite of Canadian laws, the Tsimshian, along with many other First Nations, are now insisting on their right to practice their traditions and have begun to pass on their culture to the next generations. They are lobbying for their language to be taught in schools and trying to regain territorial and fishing/hunting rights.

In 1994, the Tsimshian Tribal Council began negotiations with the provincial government to settle land claims from previous centuries. The Tsimshian want a treaty recognizing that their rights to their original homelands were violated. By 2004, they had reached the fourth stage of the six-step process, but after two bands withdrew, the paperwork had to be revised. In 2010, several groups—the Gitga'at, Kitasoo/Xai'xais, and Metlakatla First Nations—signed an agreement with British Columbia, giving the tribes a new ferry terminal, a percentage of resource revenue, and a say in the decision-making. These nations agreed to work with the provincial government to create an Alternative Energy Action Plan.

In 2011, five bands signed a Forest Consultation and Revenue Sharing Agreement (FCRSA). This allows them to make joint decisions on forest management and allots them a portion of the tree-harvesting income. The Tsimshian want to protect and preserve their temperate rainforest. Their concerns extend to protecting the environment in other areas, such as fish and sea mammals. After years of government ownership of the natural resources, the Tsimshian are trying to restore unbalanced ecosystems and assert their claims for ownership and authority over land and coastal resources in what were their traditional homelands.

NOTABLE PEOPLE

Victoria Young (Su-dalth) was the wife of the famous Tsimshian chief Legex. Around 1876, she aided missionary Thomas Crosby after becoming one of the first converts. She was an influential speaker, and she often addressed the people along with other important elders.

Among the many distinguished Tsimshian are William Beynon (1888–1958) and his grandfather, Arthur Wellington Clah (1831–1916), both of whom served as informants for anthropologists. The materials Clah and Beynon supplied helped preserve many stories, oral histories, songs, and other important cultural material. Clah taught the Anglican missionary William Duncan (see "History" and "Religion") to speak the Tsimshian language; in return, Duncan taught him English. Clah kept a diary for about fifty years, and in it he captured many details about Tsimshian life in the 1800s.

Social activist Peter Simpson (1871–1947) served as chairman of the Alaskan Native Brotherhood to lobby for Native rights and for a decrease of government intervention in tribal life. He is sometimes called the "father of land claims" because his work resulted in the treaty claims process with British Columbia.

Important twenty-first century Tsimshian artists include David Boxley, Leanne Helin, Bill Helin, Roy Henry Vickers, and Edward Bryant.

BOOKS

Arctander, John W. *The Apostle of Alaska: The Story of William Duncan of Metlakahtla.* New York: Fleming H. Revell, 1909.

Boas, Franz Reed. *Tsimshian Texts: New Series (1912).* Reprint. Charleston, SC: Forgotten Books, 2008.

Ellis, Donald, Steven Clay Brown, and Bill Holm. *Tsimshian Treasures: The Remarkable Journey of the Dundas Collection.* Charleston, SC: Forgotten Books, 2008.

Johnson, Gertrude Mather. *HaaKusteeyí, Our Culture: Tlingit Life Stories.* Edited by Nora Marks Dauenhauer and Richard Dauenhauer. Seattle: University of Washington Press, 1994.

MacDonald, George F., and John J. Cove. *Tsimshian Narratives 2: Trade and Warfare.* Ottawa: Canadian Museum of Civilization, 1997.

Neylan, Susan. *The Heavens Are Changing: Nineteenth-Century Protestant Missions and Tsimshian Christianity.* Montreal, Quebec: McGill-Queen's Press, 2003.

Pierce, William Henry. *From Potlatch to Pulpit, Being the Autobiography of the Rev. William Henry Pierce.* Edited by J. P. Hicks. Vancouver, BC: Vancouver Bindery, 1933.

Roth, Christopher Fritz. *Becoming Tsimshian: The Social Life of Names.* Seattle: University of Washington Press, 2008.

Swanton, John R., and Franz Boas. *Haida Songs; Tsimshian Texts (1912).* Vol. 3. Whitefish, MT: Kessinger Publishing, 2010.

Worl, Rosita. *Celebration: Tlingit, Haida, Tsimshian Dancing on the Land.* Edited by Kathy Dye. Seattle: University of Washington Press, 2008.

PERIODICALS

Brock, Peggy. "Building Bridges: Politics and Religion in a First Nation Community." *Canadian Historical Review* 81, no. 1 (2000): 67–96.

Brock, Peggy. "Two Indigenous Evangelists: Moses Tjalkabota and Arthur Wellington Clah." *Journal of Religious History* 27, no. 3 (2003): 348–56.

Galois, R. M. "Colonial Encounters: The Worlds of Arthur Wellington Clah, 1855–1881." *B.C. Studies.* No. 115/116 (1997–98): 105–47.

WEB SITES

Council Annette Islands Reserve. "Metlakatla Indian Community." *Hobbs, Straus, Dean & Walker.* http://www.hsdwlaw.com/sites/default/files/classII/Exhibit%207.PDF (accessed on August 15, 2011).

"Eyak, Tlingit, Haida, and Tsimshian." *Alaska Native Heritage Center Museum.* http://www.alaskanative.net/en/main_nav/education/culture_alaska/eyak/ (accessed on August 15, 2011).

ICTMN Staff. "Carving a Red Cedar Mask" (video). *Indian Country Today Media Network.* http://indiancountrytodaymedianetwork.com/2011/06/carving-tsimshian-red-cedar-masks/ (accessed on August 15, 2011).

Miller, Jay. "Alaskan Tlingit and Tsimshian." *University of Washington Libraries.* http://content.lib.washington.edu/aipnw/miller1.html#tsimshian (accessed on August 15, 2011).

Redish, Laura, and Orrin Lewis. "Tsimshian Language (Smalgyax)." *Native Languages of the Americas.* http://www.native-languages.org/tsimshian.htm (accessed on August 15, 2011).

Thunderbird, Shannon. "A Comprehensive Look at the Pacific Northwest Coast: Tsimshian." *TeyaPeya.* http://www.shannonthunderbird.com/Pacific%20Northwest%20Coast.htm (accessed on August 15, 2011).

"'Tsmshian Songs We Love to Sing!" *Dum Baaldum.* http://www.dumbaaldum.org/html/songs.htm (accessed on August 15, 2011).

Arctic

Arctic

It is difficult to define the indigenous (native) peoples of Arctic North America by the recognized boundaries of the modern political world because the geographical context in which they live goes beyond the borders of several countries. The United States (Alaska) and Canada make up the Arctic region of North America, but Alaska's Siberian Yup'ik (pronounced *YOO-pik*) peoples, for example, are also found on the Russian side of the Bering Strait, and the Inupiat (*in-NOO-pee-aht*) people of Alaska's Arctic slope also reside on the Canadian side of the border. In Alaska's northern interior, the Gwich'in (*GWITCH-in*) Athabascan Indians live in both Alaska and in Canada's Yukon Territory. All the indigenous people of Arctic North America therefore belong to a larger community of peoples who live in the Circumpolar North, the area surrounding the North Pole.

The people of the North American Arctic region belong to one of three major cultural and linguistic divisions: Aleut (Unangan), Eskimo, and Athabascan. Whereas the Aleut have traditionally occupied Alaska's Aleutian Islands, the Eskimo, who are further divided into the Yup'ik, Inupiat/Inuit, and Sugpiat language groups, live from Alaska to Greenland. The Athabascan are also further divided into several groups with the Gwich'in being the most northerly. Despite the vast territory separating Arctic peoples, which also includes many different groups in Arctic Siberia and the Sami people of northern Scandinavia, they remain united both culturally and politically. As Caleb Pungowiyi (1941–2011), a Siberian Yup'ik who at the time was president of the Inuit Circumpolar Conference, proclaimed in 1995, "While we are divided by four political boundaries, our common languages, traditions, and ancestry give us common bond and strength to work together."

History

Most archaeologists believe that the Arctic region of North America has been populated only within the last 11,000 to 14,000 years. These scientists base their estimates on the theory that a bridge they call the Bering

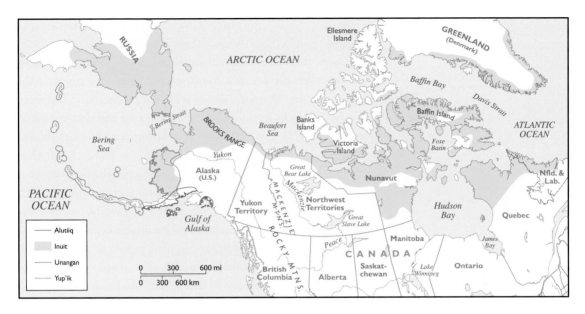

A map showing some contemporary Native American communities in the Arctic Region. MAP BY XNR PRODUCTIONS. CENGAGE LEARNING, GALE. REPRODUCED BY PERMISSION OF GALE, A PART OF CENGAGE LEARNING.

Land Bridge, or Beringia, once spanned the distance from Asia to Alaska with lands that are now under the waters of the Bering Strait. While this land bridge existed, they say, hunters from Asia gradually migrated into Alaska and from there, they and their descendants spread throughout North and South America. Scientists believe that this bridge became submerged by about 12,000 BCE. The Beringia argument is hotly contested by some Native nations, however.

The more recent history of the Arctic is well documented. European contact with the Inuit of Arctic Quebec began in the late sixteenth century as the British, French, and Danish all sent ships in search of a Northwest Passage to China (a water route along the northern coast of North America extending between the Atlantic and Pacific Oceans). The British Hudson's Bay Company was founded in 1667, beginning a long period of trade among Arctic indigenous peoples. By the nineteenth century, the Hudson's Bay Company had expanded westward and was trading with Athabaskan Indians in what is now interior Alaska. A colonization process began in present-day Canada on the margins of Inuit territory in the mid-eighteenth century, as Europeans, particularly the English and French, formed settlements. This process included the establishment of trading posts, missions, and whaling stations.

The Russians rule Alaska The first European contact in Alaska came from the opposite direction, Russia, when Vitus Bering (1681–1741), a Dane serving in the Russian navy, landed in Prince William Sound in 1741. Over the following decades, the Russians made attempts at establishing outposts in the Aleutian Islands and on Kodiak Island but were rebuffed by the Unangan (pronounced *oo-NUNG-an* and also known as Aleut, pronounced *AHL-lee-ay-LOOT*) and the Sugpiat (Alutiiq; *ahl-loo-TEEK*). The Aleut destroyed four Russian sea vessels in 1763, but they paid dearly in the savage retaliation by the Russians. The Sugpiat were able to hold off the Russians for more than twenty years, beginning with the first Russian landing attempt in 1761. In 1784, however, Russian vessels headed by Grigorii Shelikhov made a brutal assault on Kodiak Island that ended with the massacre of many Sugpiaq people at a refuge rock near the present day village of Old Harbor.

The early years of Russian rule in this part of Alaska were marked by the enslavement of Native men, who were forced to hunt sea otters for the Russians. The absence of these men from their communities caused great hardships, as they were not there to provide food and shelter when needed. The Russian Orthodox Church halted many of the atrocities as the clergy complained to the tsar (ruler of Russia) of the mistreatment of the Native nations at the hands of the Russian American Company personnel. The Natives then became employees of the Russians and began adapting to Russian culture. Even today, Russian influence is evident in Aleut and Alutiiq villages, as many people have Russian surnames, prepare many Russian-inspired foods, and maintain the Russian Orthodox Church as the center of village social life.

Americans move into Alaska By the mid-nineteenth century, hundreds of American whaling ships were operating off the Arctic coasts, severely depleting the population of walruses and bowhead whales, which affected the Native residents considerably. In addition to supplying food, the bowhead is crucial to Inupiat culture and identity. The Yankee whalers also brought new diseases and alcohol. In 1867, the Treaty of Cession transferred control of Alaska from Russia to the United States. Before the end of the century, American Christian missionaries had established themselves in all corners of Alaska, including the Arctic—a region that, for the most part, had been left alone by the Russians. While most Alaska Natives are now members of Christian churches, mixed feelings remain for many. "Christianity saved our souls

Inuit whalers haul in their catch, a bowhead whale. The bowhead plays an important role in Inuit culture. © RICHARD OLSENIUS/ CONTRIBUTOR/NATIONAL GEOGRAPHIC/GETTY IMAGES.

but indeed left deep psychological scars in our hearts," Yup'ik Caleb Pungowiyi lamented.

With the firm establishment of the U.S. government in Alaska came the American education system. Under this system, children were often required to leave their villages to attend boarding schools, where they were punished if they spoke in their Native language. One result has been the severe eroding of indigenous languages. The state of language preservation varies greatly throughout Alaska; some villages still speak their language on a daily basis, whereas in others only a few Native-speaking elders remain. A cultural revitalization movement has been taking place in Alaska for the past several decades in which the restoration and protection of languages is a high priority.

The American government unwittingly caused new and severe problems in the North. While attempting to provide services to Alaska

Natives in every aspect of their lives, they created a "culture of dependency." This system replaced proud Native identities with an epidemic of self-destructive behavior. "For many Natives, the sense of personal, familial and cultural identity that is a prerequisite to healthy and productive life is being lost in a haze of alcohol-induced despair that not infrequently results in violence perpetrated upon self and family," the Alaska Federation of Natives stated in its 1989 report called *The AFN Report on the Status of Alaska Natives: A Call for Action*. This report revealed such grim statistics as the fact that Alaska Native males between the ages of twenty and twenty-four were committing suicide at fourteen times the national average and that the homicide rate among Alaska Natives was four times the national average. Conditions worsened even as the federal and state governments spent millions of dollars on Native services. "Rather than feeling comfort in government-built homes and contentment in government-funded food supplies, Alaska Natives felt instead, emptiness and an overwhelming sense of loss," concluded the final report of the Alaska Natives Commission, published in 1994, adding that "the spiritually and psychologically debilitating intervention of government services … has created a culture of dependency." Considerable effort and funding has gone into improving the conditions described in the AFN report. Despite an intensive effort these conditions have persisted into the twenty-first century. According to a 2004 report by the First Alaskans Institute, some progress had been made, but the statistics remained grim.

Beginning in the 1990s, one other major cause of depression and substance abuse came to light. During the era when students were forced to attend government- and church-run schools, a large proportion of Native children and teens in the Arctic were subjected to physical and sexual abuse by their teachers and priests. The church often sent known sexual predators among the clergy to the Far North to keep them away from mainstream society. Thus, the Arctic Native population experienced greater victimization than most other areas of the continent. Many lawsuits against religious groups, particularly the Jesuits and the Catholic Church, were settled during first decade of the 2000s; some were still ongoing. Winning these court cases brought justice and monetary compensation to the victims, but healing will be a long-term process.

Canadian government and the Inuit In Canada, the situation of indigenous peoples became similar to the one in Alaska. Jack Hicks, the director of research for the Nunavut Implementation Commission, found that

"European and Canadian explorers, traders, missionaries, police, soldiers, and administrators brought many things with them to Nunavut—some good and some not so good. Suffice it to say that, as late as the early 1970s, the Inuit of Canada were a thoroughly colonized and economically dependent people."

Culture

If one is to use Alaska as a starting point from which to trace the geographical areas of the various cultures in the North, a logical place to begin would be Prince William Sound, the westernmost home of the Alutiit (plural for Alutiiq) people. The Alutiit also live on the lower Kenai Peninsula, the Kodiak Island archipelago, and the lower Alaska Peninsula. The traditional name for Alutiiq is *Sugpiaq,* meaning "a real human being." The plural is *Sugpiat,* meaning "the real people." The Alutiit are classified as Pacific Eskimo by anthropologists, but most strenuously object to that label. They are, however, closely related linguistically (by the language they speak) to all the Inuit peoples of the Arctic.

Beginning at the tip of the Alaska Peninsula and stretching out the Aleutian Island Chain and into Russia are the Aleut, or as they call themselves, Unangan. The name Aleut was applied to them by the Russian explorers and fur traders of the eighteenth century. The name was also used by the Russians to identify the Sugpiat, thus the name Alutiiq, which is simply the word Aleut in the language of the Sugpiat.

The area populated by the Central Yup'ik, or Yupiaq, people begins at the northern edge of the Alaska peninsula and continues through Bristol Bay and the Yukon-Kuskokwim River Delta and north to the village of Unalakleet. The words *Yup'ik* and *Yupiaq* translate to "a real person." The plural is *Yupiit,* meaning "the real people." The Central Yup'ik language is very close to Alutiiq, such that speakers of the two languages can usually carry on a conversation. Both differ substantially from the Aleut language, however. Another Yup'ik language is Siberian Yup'ik, spoken on St. Lawrence Island and the Chukchi Peninsula of Siberia. The relationship of what are usually referred to as Eskimo languages is quite apparent when one compares a single word, such as the one for "person." The Alutiit say *suk,* and the Yupiit say *yuk,* or in some areas, *cuk.* The Inupiat of Arctic Alaska, the Inuvialuk of Northwest Canada, and the Iglulik of Eastern Canada all use the term *inuk* for "person." Another major indigenous group of the Arctic is the Athabascan Indians. The Athabascans, who call themselves Den'a (Dene), live in vast areas of the interior of Alaska and Northern Canada. They are made up of numerous subgroups who speak eleven different languages.

Subsistence

"Subsistence is a word that means … my way of life," Moses Toyukuk of Manokotak, Alaska, told the Alaska Native Review Commission in 1985. "Our subsistence way of life is especially important to us. Among other needs it is our greatest. We are desperate to keep it," Paul John of Tununak, Alaska, told the same commission. In the Alaska Native Claims Settlement Act of 1971 (ANCSA), all aboriginal hunting and fishing rights were abolished, which created a dilemma for remote Alaska Native villages dependent on such resources for their livelihood. Efforts made to restore these rights met with moderate success. The Marine Mammal Protection Act of 1972 enables coastal Alaska Natives to take marine mammals for food and for use in arts and crafts. In 1980, the Alaska National Interest Lands Conservation Act (ANILCA) provided a subsistence preference for rural residents. As the majority of rural residents in Alaska are Natives, this essentially restored Alaska Natives' right to hunt and fish for subsistence. After the state's implementation of the ANILCA subsistence provision was thrown out by the Alaska Supreme Court in 1985, the Alaska state legislature, in 1986, passed its own law, which is consistent with federal law. In 1989, however, the Alaska Supreme Court ruled that the state law confirming a preference for rural residents to hunt and fish for subsistence is unconstitutional because it discriminates against urban residents. This action resulted in the U.S. government takeover of the regulation of fish and game on federal lands in Alaska in 1990 to guarantee subsistence rights to rural residents. Dr. Angayuqaq Oscar Kawagley, a Yupiaq educator, has summed up the meaning of subsistence for most Alaska Native people: "Alaska Native peoples have traditionally tried to live in harmony with the world around them. This has required the construction of an intricate subsistence-based worldview, a complex way of life with specific cultural mandates regarding the ways in which the human being is to relate to other human relatives and the natural and spiritual worlds."

Current tribal issues

In 1971, the U.S. Congress passed the Alaska Native Claims Settlement Act (ANCSA), starting a controversy that continues today. ANCSA resulted from a drive for settlement from a variety of interests: business and government interests in the oil source, the state of Alaska's desire to develop land, the conservationists' desire to preserve wilderness areas, and the Alaska Natives' wish for their land. Twelve regional profit-making corporations were established that were responsible for distributing money to village corporations and individuals, controlling the subsurface resources, promoting economic development in the region, and supporting the village corporations within the region. Whereas past agreements had been made only between the federal government and individual tribes, ANCSA was an agreement made with these newly created Alaska Native regional associations, which were charged with the responsibility of establishing for-profit business corporations to receive a cash settlement and perhaps more importantly, legal title to the land. Under ANCSA, the corporations received title to 44 million acres of land and a cash settlement of $962.5 million for land lost. This amounted to about three dollars an acre. As discontent mounted in many areas of Alaska with ANCSA, a number of studies were carried out to assess its effectiveness and its legality.

A 1984–85 study conducted by the Alaska Native Review Commission, under the auspices of the Inuit Circumpolar Conference (ICC)—an international organization founded in 1977 to represent the Inuit or Eskimo peoples of the United States, Canada, Greenland, and Russia—recommended that the title to land owned by Alaska Native corporations be transferred to village tribal governments. "A corporation cannot take from the rich and give to the poor without facing a shareholders' suit," claimed Thomas Berger (1933–), a former justice of the Supreme Court of Canada who headed the study. "A tribal government can implement measures designed to achieve social justice." Berger also recommended that "tribal governments established in all of Alaska's Native villages should assert their Native sovereignty (self-government)."

Many scholars believed that under the American legal system, land owned and controlled by Alaska Native village tribal governments would take on the legal status of "Indian Country." According to federal law and the terms of more than four hundred treaties, Native nations have sovereign power—the power to act as independent nations. Although most Native governments are based on reservations, sovereignty can extend beyond reservation boundaries by the terms of the definition of "Indian Country," which includes reservations, scattered Native home sites, and sometimes areas near reservations that are used for subsistence activities and cultural practices. By law, tribal governments in Indian Country have the authority to make and enforce their own laws and to enter into agreements with the United States, just as foreign governments do. The legal debate over whether village-owned land in Alaska was indeed Indian Country, as it would be if located in the forty-eight contiguous states, raged for well over a decade. Then in 1996, the U.S. Ninth Circuit Court of Appeals ruled that there is Indian Country in Alaska, a ruling strongly opposed by the state of Alaska, which appealed to the U.S. Supreme Court. In 1998, the Supreme Court overturned the Court of Appeals in what is known as the "Venetie Decision," ruling that the Alaska Native Claims Settlement Act abolished Indian Country status.

Another political issue that has become very emotional, both within Alaska Native communities and within the general Alaska population, has to do with the potential opening of the Arctic National Wildlife Refuge to oil development. U.S. law currently prohibits oil development within a federal wildlife refuge unless Congress votes to open it and the president concurs by signing the legislation. The Arctic National Wildlife Refuge, or ANWR, as it is usually referred to in Alaska, covers about 19 million acres of remote northeast Alaska. Geologists believe that ANWR contains vast deposits of oil, and the state of Alaska has unsuccessfully pursued opening the area to oil development for several decades. ANWR is also the spring calving grounds for the Porcupine caribou herd that resides in the Canadian Arctic during the winter months. The Gwich'in Athabascan Indians of both Alaska and Canada depend heavily on the Porcupine caribou herd for subsistence and cultural identity, so they strongly oppose ANWR oil development. At the same time, many Inupiat of the North Slope are in favor of opening ANWR for oil development.

The indigenous people of the Canadian Arctic have followed a path similar to that of Alaska Natives in terms of pursuing their aboriginal land claims. In 1975, the Inuit and Cree Indians of northern Quebec and the Canadian government reached a negotiated agreement after the James Bay Hydroelectric Project nearly flooded a large area of traditional hunting lands. The agreement, called the James Bay and Northern Quebec Agreement, conveyed the title to 5,250 acres of hunting grounds, confirmed exclusive hunting and fishing rights on another 60,000 square miles (96,560 kilometers), provided for local administrative control, established autonomy in education decisions for villages, verified control of local justice systems, and supplied a $90 million monetary settlement. In return, the indigenous peoples were required to give up any further aboriginal rights. The settlement was not embraced by all aboriginal people involved, some of whom voiced considerable dissent. In 1984, however, the Inuvialuit of the north-westernmost portion of the Northwest Territories entered into a similar agreement.

The Inuit Tapirisat, an indigenous Canadian political organization formed in the 1960s, actively pursued a land settlement with the Canadian government. The Nunavut, or "Our Land" movement, began in 1974 and ended in 1992 with the signing of Nunavut Land Claim Agreement. The Nunavut agreement involved 18,000 Inuit living in the northeastern portion of the Northwest Territories. Under the agreement, the Inuit gained legal title to the surface of 353,610 square kilometers (136,530 square miles) of land, or about 18 percent of the settlement area, in addition to priority hunting and fishing rights throughout the Nunavut settlement area. They also received subsurface rights to oil, gas, and minerals on 36,257 square kilometers (13,999 square miles), or about 10 percent of the settlement area, as well as a cash settlement of $1.148 billion (Canadian) to be paid by the Canadian government to the Inuit over a period of fourteen years. In addition, the Canadian government must pay the Inuit 50 percent of the first $2 million of royalties from oil, gas, or mineral development. The Inuit were required to give up all rights and claims to land and waters elsewhere in Canada, but they will keep all other constitutional rights, including continued recognition as aboriginal people by the Canadian government. An especially important part of the agreement called for the government of Canada to establish a Nunavut Territory by the year 2000. This thirteenth Canadian province was established in 1999, granting the Inuit, who make up about 85 percent of the population, self-government in their homelands.

Of considerable concern to the indigenous peoples of the Arctic is the issue of climate change or "global warming." Indigenous people throughout the Arctic have noted the melting of glaciers, the shrinking of the Arctic ice cap, and the changes in animal behavior. Many are alarmed at the possibility of losing their food sources because of climate changes. Jose A. Kusugak, president of the Inuit Tapiritt Kanatami in Canada, sums up the climate change: "What it all comes down to was respect for the earth and doing your part in keeping the world as in its original state. Inuit see themselves as part of the ecosystem and want to be included: not as victims, but as a people who can help."

Perhaps the largest issue facing the indigenous people of the Arctic is one of self-determination. They want to control their own affairs and chart their own destinies. They want meaningful input into decisions being made by the governments of the United States and Canada on issues that will have an impact their ways of life. In recent decades, they have become more vocal in pursuing these rights. The United Nations Draft Declaration on the Rights of Indigenous Peoples clearly summarizes their pursuits: "Indigenous peoples have the right of self-determination. By virtue of that right they freely determine their political status and freely pursue their economic, social and cultural development."

BOOKS

Alaska Native Policy Center. *Our Choices, Our Future: Analysis of the Status of Alaska Natives Report 2004.* Anchorage: Alaska Native Policy Center, First Alaskans Institute, 2004.

Berger, Thomas R. *Village Journey: The Report of the Alaska Native Review Commission.* New York: Wang and Hill, 1985.

Bruemmer, Fred. *Arctic Visions: Pictures from a Vanished World.* Toronto, Ontario: Key Porter Books, 2008.

Chaussonnet, Valerie, ed. *Crossroads Alaska: Native Cultures of Alaska and Siberia.* Washington, DC: Arctic Studies Center, National Museum of Natural History, Smithsonian Institution, 1995.

Cone, Marla. *Silent Snow: The Slow Poisoning of the Arctic.* New York: Grove Press, 2005.

Damas, David, ed. *Handbook of North American Indians.* Vol. 5, *Arctic.* Washington, DC: Smithsonian Institution, 1984.

Doak, Robin S. *Arctic Peoples.* Chicago: Heinemann Library, 2012.

Doherty, Craig A., and Katherine M. Doherty. *Arctic Peoples.* New York: Chelsea House, 2008.

Aron Crowell, ed. *Living Our Cultures, Sharing Our Heritage: The First Peoples of Alaska.* Washington, DC: Smithsonian Institution, 2010.

Guigon, Catherine, Francis Latreille, and Fredric Malenfer. *The Arctic.* New York: Abrams Books for Young Readers, 2007.

Heinämäki, Leena. *The Right to Be a Part of Nature: Indigenous Peoples and the Environment.* Rovaniemi, Finland: Lapland University Press, 2010.

Kawagley, A. Oscar. *A Yupiaq Worldview: A Pathway to Ecology and Spirit.* Prospect Heights, IL: Waveland Press, 1995.

Krupnik, Igor, and Dyanna Jolly, eds. *The Earth Is Faster Now: Indigenous Observations of Arctic Environmental Change.* Fairbanks, Alaska: Arctic Research Consortium of the United States, 2002.

Kuiper, Kathleen, ed. *Indigenous Peoples of the Arctic, Subarctic, and Northwest Coast.* New York: Rosen Educational Services, 2012.

McGhee, Robert. *The Last Imaginary Place: A Human History of the Arctic World.* Chicago: University of Chicago Press, 2007.

Marshall, Bonnie. *Far North Tales: Stories from the Peoples of the Arctic Circle.* Edited by Kira Van Deusen. Santa Barbara, CA: Libraries Unlimited, 2011.

Miller, Debbie S., and Jon Van Dyle. *Arctic Lights, Arctic Nights.* New York: Walker Books for Young Readers, 2007.

Wallace, Mary. *The Inuksuk Book.* Toronto, Ontario: Maple Tree Press, 2004.

Wohlforth, Charles. *The Whale and the Supercomputer: On the Northern Front of Climate Change.* New York: North Point Press, 2004.

WEB SITES

"The Arctic." *Russian News & Information Agency: RIA Novosti.* http://www.arctic.ru/ (accessed on August 15, 2011).

"Arctic Circle." *University of Connecticut.* http://arcticcircle.uconn.edu/VirtualClassroom/ (accessed on August 15, 2011).

"The Arctic Is…." *Stefansson Arctic Institute.* http://www.thearctic.is/ (accessed on August 15, 2011).

"The Inuvialuit of the Western Arctic." *Canadian Museum of Civilization.* http://www.civilization.ca/cmc/exhibitions/aborig/inuvial/indexe.shtml (accessed on August 15, 2011).

"Land Claims." *Department of Labrador and Aboriginal Affairs.* http://www.laa.gov.nl.ca/laa/land_claims/index.html (accessed on August 15, 2011).

"Native Quarterly." *First Alaskans Institute.* http://www.firstalaskans.org/index.cfm?section=Alaska-Native-Policy-Center&page=Current-Projects&viewpost=2&ContentId=842 (accessed on August 15, 2011).

"NOAA Arctic Theme Page." *National Oceanic and Atmospheric Administration.* http://www.arctic.noaa.gov/ (accessed on August 15, 2011).

Pastore, Ralph T. "Aboriginal Peoples: Newfoundland and Labrador Heritage." *Memorial University of Newfoundland.* http://www.heritage.nf.ca/aboriginal/ (accessed on August 15, 2011).

Alutiiq (Sugpiaq)

Name

The traditional name for the Alutiiq (pronounced *ahl-loo-TEEK*) is *Sugpiaq,* meaning "a real human being." The plural is *Sugpiat,* or "the real people." Russian explorers and fur traders of the eighteenth century often grouped the Alutiiq with the Aleut. In the 1980s, the name Alutiiq (the plural form is Alutiit) came into common usage for both the people and their language.

Location

The Koniag, one of the three main Alutiiq groups, once occupied Kodiak Island. The Chugach, another group, lived between Prince William Sound and present-day Cordova, Alaska. The third group had land that stretched from Cook Inlet to Kupreanof Point. Today, Prince William Sound is the westernmost home of the Alutiiq people. The Alutiiq also live on the lower Kenai Peninsula, the Kodiak archipelago, and the lower Alaska Peninsula.

Population

When the Vitus Bering expedition arrived in 1741, the Alutiiq population was estimated to be 20,000. That number had dropped to about 9,000 by 1784. The first true census of the region occurred in 1880; it listed 2,458 Koniag, 278 Chugach, and 205 Kenai. In both 1980 and 1990, the figures remained steady at 5,000. The 2000 U.S. Census showed only 193 Alutiiq and 362 Alutiiq Aleut.

Language family

Eskimo.

Origins and group affiliations

For more than 7,500 years, ancestors of the Alutiiq lived in their Arctic homelands. Early cultures were influenced by migrations of various groups into and out of the area. Each influx of newcomers brought changes to the culture and introduced new materials. One of the major influences came

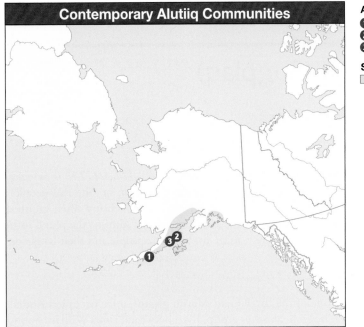

Contemporary Alutiiq Communities

Alaska
1. Perryville
2. Douglas
3. Katmai

Shaded area
Traditional lands of the Alutiiq on Kodiak Island, Prince William Sound, and the Alaska Peninsula

A map of contemporary Alutiiq communities. MAP BY XNR PRODUCTIONS. CENGAGE LEARNING, GALE. REPRODUCED BY PERMISSION OF GALE, A PART OF CENGAGE LEARNING.

from the Bering Sea Eskimo culture. Anthropologists have classified the Alutiiq as Pacific Eskimo, but most Sugpiaq object to that label. They are, however, closely related linguistically (by the language they speak) to all the Inuit (see entry) peoples of the Arctic. The Central Yup'ik (see entry) language is similar to Alutiiq, such that speakers of the two languages can usually carry on a conversation.

For thousands of years, the coast-dwelling Alutiiq developed a strong maritime culture. They thrived on the bounty from the seas surrounding their homelands and used all parts of the sea mammals and fish they caught—for food, fuel, clothing, utensils, and tools. From the 1700s on, the Alutiiq survived domination by the Russians, forced assimilation by the Americans, and environmental disasters, including a volcanic eruption, an earthquake, a tsunami, and an oil spill. Throughout the centuries, the Alutiiq adapted to change and rebuilt their lives. As they moved into the twenty-first century, communities began working together to plan for their future, while reviving the traditions and culture of their past.

HISTORY

Prehistory

Ancient sites show that ancestors of the Alutiiq may have lived in the Kodiak region as far back as 7,500 years ago. These early peoples lived by the bounty of the sea and established trading connections with other cultures. The groups also engaged in warfare with each other. The early cultures produced tools from slate; later groups used bone, ivory, shell, stone, and jet for artwork and carving. Rock art, carved stone tablets, and mummies attest to the sophistication of these ancient peoples.

Archaeologists have labeled several cultures that existed in the present-day Alutiiq homelands. Sources differ on the dates, but the first, Ocean Bay, flourished from approximately 4500 to 1400 BCE. The Kachemak culture followed and lasted until about 1200 CE. Some experts suggest this group may have been destroyed in battle or replaced by the migration of the Koniag. Others believe that the Koniag evolved from the Kachemak. In any event, the final cultural stage, the Koniag, continued until 1784, at which time the Russians settled the area.

Important Dates

1741: Danish explorer Vitus Bering sees buildings on Kayak Island that likely belong to the Chugach.

1784: Russians establish their first permanent settlement in Alaska.

1867: The United States buys Alaska from Russia for $7.2 million.

1941: President Franklin D. Roosevelt creates Kodiak National Wildlife Refuge.

1964: The Great Alaska Earthquake and tsunami destroys several Alutiiq villages.

1971: The Alaska Native Claims Settlement Act gives the Kodiak National Wildlife Refuge to the people, but prohibits development.

1989: The Exxon *Valdez* tanker spills almost 11 million gallons of oil in Prince William Sound.

Arrival of the Russians

After Vitus Bering (1681–1741), a Danish explorer for Russia, sighted the Aleutian Islands, Russian fur traders called *promyshlenniki* set up colonies in present-day Alaska to take advantage of the abundant sea mammal population. The Russians soon exploited the Native groups on the western islands, forcing them to collect sea otter pelts. As natural resources dwindled in the Aleutian Islands, the Russians moved eastward to the Kodiak archipelago.

The Kodiak islanders resisted the newcomers, but the Russians soon subdued them with cannons and guns. The Russians also took hostages, particularly the chief's children, to force the Natives to cooperate. Many Alutiiq died during the early conflicts, including several thousand during an attack near Sitkalidak Island. Once the Russians had gained the upper hand, they established their first settlement in the Kodiak area at Three Saints Bay, near present-day Old Harbor. The Russian government also made the Alutiiq Russian citizens and charged the Russian-American Company, a fur-trading business, with governing the colonies.

Life under the Russians

The Russian-American Company forced many Alutiiq men into service, taking them far from home. The men faced grave danger as they hunted for sea mammals in the treacherous waters to the north, and quite a few died. This left their families without food supplies, so their wives and children starved. The surviving villagers, including the elderly and children, labored to sew waterproof parkas (*kanagllut* or *kamleikas*; see "Clothing") and to gather and prepare the food the hunters needed.

For centuries, the Alutiiq had kept war captives as slaves (*kalgi*). The Russian-American Company took these slaves and any Alutiit who had been accused of treason to Russian posts, where the women processed skins and fish, made nets, sewed clothes, or gathered food. The men made bricks, cut timber and hay, built buildings, and hunted for the company. These *kaiury*, as they were called, had to serve for life unless they were bought back or another family member took their place.

During the Russian occupation, the Kodiak population decreased from about 8,000 to around 2,000 due to starvation, accidents, cruelty, and disease. Epidemics of illnesses brought by the Russians killed many Natives because they had no immunity, or resistance. The Chugach, with their small population and limited natural resources, were not as affected by the Russian settlement.

In 1794, Russian Orthodox priests arrived to convert the Alutiiq people to Christianity. The priests set up a school and an orphanage; they also spoke out against the Russian-American Company's treatment of the people. One of the first monks to arrive, Father Herman, was later canonized. He was credited with miracles such as healing illnesses and stopping a tsunami. Many Alutiiq became Christians and incorporated the feast days and holidays into their traditional celebrations.

American purchase of Alaska

In 1867, Russia sold Alaska to the United States for $7.2 million. Soon, American businesses tried various enterprises, including cattle ranching, whaling, trapping, and gold mining. They hired Native people to do the work. Salmon became one of the greatest revenue producers.

Throughout the late 1800s, canneries opened and closed (sometimes due to sabotage), but the growing industry led to overfishing. Most of the canneries hired Chinese workers rather than the Natives, who had to spend time hunting and fishing to feed their families.

Beginning in the 1890s, the U.S. government and churches established schools for Alutiiq children. One of the goals of these schools was to assimilate the students, or make them more like mainstream Americans. The teachers forbid pupils to speak their language or practice their customs. Over time, this eroded the Alutiiq culture.

Natural disasters

In 1921, Mt. Katmai on the Alaska Peninsula erupted. The volcano covered nearby areas in ash, killing plant life and clogging streams, which decimated the fish population. No commercial fishing could be done that year. Two villages—Douglas and Katmai—were destroyed. The survivors resettled in New Savonoski and Perryville. Later, the ash served as rich fertilizer, so people could grow better crops.

A few decades later, after Alaska had become a state in 1959, an earthquake struck. This 1964 Great Alaskan Earthquake caused tidal waves that engulfed four villages. Three villages were destroyed, and more

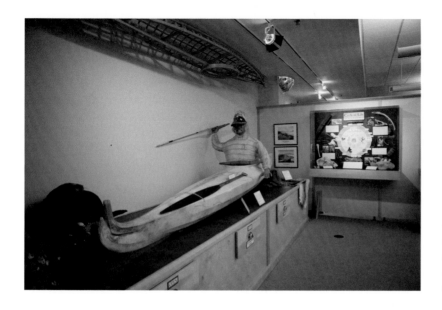

A replica of an Alutiiq kayak and other artifacts are displayed at the Alutiiq Museum in Kodiak, Alaska.
© DANITA DELIMONT/ALAMY.

than thirty people died. The tsunami also damaged the fishing fleet in Kodiak. Many fishers, however, were able to replace their boats with disaster loans and resume their occupations.

Twenty-five years later, an oil tanker, the *Exxon Valdez,* struck Bligh Reef in Prince William Sound. More than 11 million gallons of oil spilled into the sound, causing a major environmental disaster. The slow response times for the cleanup resulted in the death of a large number of sea mammals and birds. Recovery efforts continued over the next decades, but the oil became embedded in the soil of the beaches, and many plants and animals were unable to return to their previous population sizes.

Restoring Native pride

One positive outcome of the spill was that it united the Alutiiq people as they worked together to save the animals and their homeland. This led to increased efforts to restore their culture and language. Schools instituted classes, cultural heritage programs began, and the Alutiiq Museum & Archaeological Repository opened in Kodiak. The younger generations had an opportunity to learn about their traditions. These efforts have paid off in a renewed pride and sense of community.

RELIGION

According to Alutiiq accounts of creation, Kassarpak, who lived in the third of five sky worlds, made all the animals and birds from a little man. This allowed animals to shapeshift into human form. Animals also received a *sua* or *suk* (a human "owner" or consciousness) that appeared as a shining human form. *Lam Sua* (person of the universe) was the most powerful sua. *Imam Sua* (person of the sea) and *Nunam Sua* (person of the land) cared for the animals. If animals were treated properly, their suas were recreated as other animals.

The Alutiiq have long believed in many different magical beings. They left food for dwarves, who were said to bring good luck. Some of the other beings that they believe interact with people include huge man-worms, sea monsters, giants, and people who lived on the smell of meat.

Oral history tells of the *iiyaq* (devil), the soul of an evil person. Unlike good souls that went into the sky at death, the iiyaq remained on Earth, where they lived in caves or the woods and ate human flesh. People could recognize an iiyaq by its pointed head. Only the shamans

Kas'aq Story

An Alutiiq man told this story in 1805 to Uri Lisianski, a Russian trader. This account of creation describes how plants, animals, bodies of water, and Kodiak Island were formed.

> A raven, he said, brought the light from heaven, while a bladder descended at the same time, in which a man and a woman were enclosed. At first, this pair of human beings enlarged their dungeon by blowing and afterward by stretching their hands and feet; and it was thus mountains were constructed, The man, by scattering the hair of his head on the mountains created trees and forests, in which wild beasts sprung up and increased; while the woman, by making water, produced seas and by spitting into ditches and holes formed rivers and lakes. The woman, pulling out one of her teeth, gave it to the man, who made a knife of it; and, cutting trees with the knife, threw the chips into the river, which were changed into fish of different kinds. At last this human pair had children and while their first-born, a son, was playing with a stone, the stone all of a sudden was converted into an island. On this island, which was the island of Cadiak (Kodiak), a man and a she-dog were then placed; and it was set afloat on the ocean, and arrived at its present situation. The man and the she-dog multiplied, and the present generation is their descendants.

SOURCE: Mañosa, Cecilia. "The Alutiiq." *Indigenous Geography: National Museum of the American Indian.* http://www.indigenousgeography.si.edu/uploads/pdfs/Akhiok_4-8_ENG.pdf (accessed on August 15, 2011).

(pronounced *SHAH-munz* or *SHAY-munz*), or religious healers, could kill these evil spirits. In addition to healing, shamans (*kala'alet*) had the power to travel to the spirit world, predict the future, and control the weather. Some could fly or change into animals. Boys who had been raised as girls (*ahnaucit*) often became shamans. They often wore their clothes backward or inside out.

In 1795, the Russian Orthodox Church opened a missionary school on Kodiak Island. Many Alutiiq adopted the Catholic faith of the priests who worked among them, and most still follow the Russian Orthodox religion. The people celebrate feast days and Christian holidays. At the end of the 1800s, the Baptist church gained some influence on the island. Later, Mormons and other Protestant faiths opened churches in the area.

Alutiiq Words

The relationship of what are usually referred to as Eskimo languages is quite apparent when one compares a single word, such as the one for "person." The Alutiit say *suk,* and the Yupiit say *yuk,* or in some areas, *cuk.*

taquka'aq	"bear"
tunturpak	"moose"
keneryaq	"bat"
kauskaanaq	"rabbit"
palauqtaq	"beaver"
qanganaq	"squirrel"

LANGUAGE

The people refer to their language as Alutiiq, Sugt'stun ("like a real person"), or Alutiits-tun ("like an Alutiiq/Aleut"). It is also called Sugpiak, Sugpiaq, Pacific Gulf Yupik, Chugach, Koniag-Chugach, Suk, and Sugcestun. The Alutiiq language is related to Central Alaskan Yup'ik, but is considered a separate language. The two major dialects are Koniag and Chugach.

After the Russians arrived, the Alutiiq people learned Russian but continued to speak their own language. The priests who taught in the Russian Orthodox schools encouraged the Alutiiq to read and write in their own language, which they recorded using the Cyrillic alphabet. Most of the early reading material consisted of translations of Bible passages or prayers.

After the United States bought Alaska in 1867, schools had an English-only policy, and teachers punished students who spoke Alutiiq, a policy that lasted until the 1960s. Children in those generations became trilingual, because they spoke Alutiiq at home, heard Russian at church, and were forced to speak English at school. Most people of that generation could understand Alutiiq but could not speak it. Because the students had been severely punished for using Alutiiq, when they became parents, they did not teach their children the language. As a result, much of the traditional Alutiiq culture and language disappeared.

By 1982, no villages were teaching Alutiiq to their children, and fewer than 900 speakers existed. By 1994, that number had fallen to 450. A 2003 report showed only 50 Koniag speakers left, all over the age of fifty-five. Experts worried that within the next few decades the language would be lost completely, so several linguists began collecting documents and recording Native speakers. They created dictionaries, lesson plans, culture camps, and programs to teach Alutiiq. The Alutiiq Dancers, a group dedicated to spreading Native culture, performed songs in Alutiiq. With this revived interest in learning Alutiiq, the people began passing on their heritage to the coming generations.

GOVERNMENT

Before the Russians arrived, the Alutiiq lived in small and large villages, each of which had a hereditary chief. These leaders were the richest men in the village, but they had to show that they were worthy of the responsibility. They kept their positions by giving advice and gifts. The chief chose his successor from among his relatives. Although the people respected the chief and his guidance, each man made decisions for himself. During the 1800s, villages began selecting a second chief, who was chosen by a council of elders.

Major changes to Alutiiq government occurred after the U.S. Bureau of Indian Affairs required the people to use democratic elections in the 1900s. Some villages conformed to the Indian Reorganization Act (IRA) in 1934 and changed their system of government again. Those who did were able to take advantage of the services the government provides, such as education, health, and welfare.

ECONOMY

Modern economy

For millennia, the Alutiiq lived by fishing for salmon and sea mammals. These provided not only food but oil, clothing, tools, and even frames for houses. They depended on salmon runs in warm weather, picking berries and roots in autumn, and gathering shellfish during colder times of year.

After the Russians arrived, and later the Americans, the economy changed from a subsistence lifestyle to a more industrialized one. Rather than working to feed themselves and their villages, many Alutiiq now worked for wages. They went out on commercial fishing boats or took jobs in canneries. As a result, a people who had once fulfilled their needs by fishing, gathering, and bartering became more dependent on a cash economy.

In 1971, the government settled ongoing land claims by passing the Alaska Native Claims Settlement Act. This law gave land grants and cash settlements to regional corporations. The goal of these Native corporations is to benefit the people who had been forced to give up their land. This new form of organization meant the Natives had to change to a different form of government. Several corporations serve the Alutiiq people: Bristol Bay Native Corporation; Koniag, Inc.; and Chugach, Inc. Also in the 1970s, Alaska passed laws that restricted commercial fishing and offered greater freedom for those who fished for subsistence. This led to decades of court battles over who qualified for these rights.

Today, many Alutiiq still work in the commercial fishing industry, but others have sought work in different professions. Business, education, and politics are some of the many fields where the Alutiiq now find jobs.

DAILY LIFE

Families

Alutiiq villages contain extended families, so children grow up with many relatives nearby. Family ties are strong, and the people can trace their ancestors back for generations. The Alutiiq, who see time as circular and fluid rather than linear (progressing in a straight line), consider these ancestors as close family members. They honor the knowledge and skills that they have inherited from former generations. Living relatives, particularly the mother's brother, held an important place in childrearing. Wealthy families adopted orphans, who then worked for the household in exchange for their food and clothes.

Buildings

The Alutiiq lived in temporary fish camps during the summer months but moved to permanent villages in the winter. In these villages, semi-subterranean sod houses called *ciqlluaq* kept people warm when the weather grew cold. The Russians called these homes *barabaras*. The houses had plank walls over driftwood frames and a sod roof, and could house up to twenty people. Most villages had about one or two hundred residents.

Inside, homes had a main room with a hearth. This was used for gatherings, such as ceremonies and dances. People also worked together in the main room when the weather prevented them from going outdoors. Women sewed and made baskets, while men crafted tools and boat frames. Doorways in the sides of this central room led to several private rooms for sleeping, storage, and sweat bathing. Even the dogs slept in side chambers. People entered these rooms through low doorways.

Homes always had a *maqiq* (or *banya* as the Russians called it). This area for steam bathing had a covered doorway and a low ceiling. Bathers poured water over hot rocks piled in the corner of the room to produce steam. They used bundles of roots to scrub their skin.

Families built a small building near their home for childbirth. They tore these buildings down after the baby was born. Other structures housed menstruating women, mothers mourning a child's death, or dead bodies awaiting burial. Wealthy men sometimes built *kashims,* or men's halls, which they rented out for private events, such as weddings, but these buildings were mainly used for winter ceremonies.

Clothing and adornment

Men and women wore hoodless fur or bird-skin parkas as well as *kamleikas* or *kanagllut,* waterproof hooded parkas made of seal or bear intestines (see sidebar, "Using Gut Skin to Stay Dry"). The parkas had slits in the side rather than sleeves. Women adorned the garments with natural dyes, skins, fur, feathers, puffin beaks, carved ivory figures, and even hair. Clothing decoration showed the person's home village, age, and gender.

In some places, women made mittens from bear paws. People used mitten liners of grass or stuffed their gloves with moss to keep their hands warm. The Alutiiq used boots in cold weather but went barefoot when it was warm.

Women wove cone-shaped hats from beach grass and spruce roots. They painted them and added beaded designs. Men wore hats made from bent wood or spruce root. For special occasions, women donned close-fitting beaded caps strung on sinew. They decorated their caps with feathers dyed in blueberry or cranberry juice and added strings of beads that dangling down their backs. Chiefs' daughters had strands of beads and dentalia (shells) that reached their feet. Men wore hoods of ermine skin embellished with strips of leather and gutskin, feathers, animal hair, and embroidery.

The Alutiiq wore multiple labrets, or small plugs, through their lips. Men also inserted a stick with a bead at each end through their noses. Women had their chins tattooed at puberty in a design some early writers thought resembled a beard. Face paint was common; black paint was made from oil or blood mixed with charcoal.

An Alutiiq woman wears a traditional beaded headdress. © DAVID SANGER PHOTOGRAPHY/ALAMY.

Using Gut Skin to Stay Dry

Because the Alutiiq dwelled in a damp marine climate, they needed waterproof clothing to protect them. Long before modern vinyl and plastic were invented, the Alutiiq came up with an ingenious way to stay dry. They used the gut skin or intestines of seals, sea lions, and bears to make various items. Water cannot penetrate the intestines, which are also flexible, lightweight, and strong.

To make caps, bags, or *kanagllut* (the plural form for *kananluk,* or jacket, in Allutiq), women soaked the guts in urine to remove all the fat. Then they turned the intestines inside out to clean them thoroughly. Before hanging them up to dry, they inflated them to allow air to circulate.

The women cut open the dried intestines to make sections of material that they stitched together. To prevent water from seeping into the needle holes, they sewed folded beach grass into the seams. This caught any drops of water that got through the tiny stitches and kept the parkas water resistant.

Food

Life in Alutiiq villages revolved around an annual cycle that depended on the sea. In the late winter, hunters took fur seals before moving to the islands to hunt sea otter. During the spring and summer, the people ate whale, sea lion, porpoise, salmon, and halibut. From fall to winter, the groups with access to game hunted for duck, ptarmigan, mountain goat, bear, caribou, marmot, fox, and river otter. Most people, though, lived on shellfish—clams, sea urchins, chitons, mussels, periwinkles—during the lean winter months. Hunters and gatherers shared their food with their relatives, the elderly, and the needy.

Women picked roots, bulbs, grasses, greens, and berries, especially cranberries. They mixed these with seal or whale oil. They dried some plants to eat during cold weather, but greens were not a major food source. Women also dried fish and gathered bird eggs for winter use.

Archaeologists have uncovered clay pits for holding water near the remains of hearths. Some pits had stone or wooden lids; others had clay caps. Cooks dropped heated rocks into broth to boil soups and stews. Tightly woven baskets or wooden dishes were also used for cooking. Meats might also be baked in pits with hot coals, cooked on top of heated rocks, roasted over flames, or fermented in pits lined with leaves or beach loveage (a type of plant). Meat and fish were often eaten raw. The Alutiiq dug pits into the floors of their homes and lined them with clay to store food.

One traditional treat, *akutaq*, is still enjoyed today. Nowadays, the recipe can sometimes vary from the traditional ingredients vegetable shortening, seal oil, potatoes, dried fish, sugar, and salmon eggs. These were beaten with berries until fluffy, and then the mixture was frozen. Other favorite foods are fish pie, seal soup, smoked or baked fish, and herring eggs on eel grass.

Education

By the age of six, girls began learning to weave mats. Boys played with small tools. Later, they helped the men at the fish camps. When boys turned twelve, their uncles taught them the skills they needed to become successful hunters. At age sixteen, boys fished alongside the men in their own kayaks.

The Russian Orthodox missionaries started schools soon after their arrival in 1794. A century later, the U.S. government opened schools for Alutiiq children. The goal of these schools was to assimilate Natives by teaching them how to fit into mainstream American society. Teachers forbid students to speak their language or practice their customs. This led to a decline in traditional culture.

In the latter part of the twentieth century, the Alutiiq began to reclaim their heritage. The people began programs to teach the youth crafts and skills that had been important to their culture. They held classes to reintroduce the language (see "Language"). These efforts continued into the twenty-first century.

Boiled Fish Stomach

This recipe is often made with king salmon. The Alutiiq consider this a delicacy. The heart can also be fried and eaten in gravy. The rest of the salmon can be dried or made into a fish pie.

> Stomach
>
> Salt
>
> Water
>
> Gravy (Brown or White)

Take the stomach (NOT intestine) out of the fish, most likely the stomach of a King salmon, turn it inside out and wash it several times throughout the day, and boil it in salted water. Cook till done. Take out and chop it up and then make your brown (or white) gravy and put your chopped stomach in it.

SOURCE: McMullen, Elenore, as told to Jeff McMullen. "Fish Delicacies." *Kenai Peninsula Borough School District.* Available from http://ankn.uaf.edu/ANCR/Alutiiq/Fireweed/Issue1/Fish%20Delicacies/Fish%20Delicacies.htm (accessed on August 15, 2011).

Healing practices

The Alutiiq had a good knowledge of herbal and plant medicines. Doctors for physical ailments were usually women with specialized skills, such as bloodletting (making a small cut to let out blood) and sucking out illnesses. When the doctors could not heal the sickness, the family called in a shaman (pronounced *SHAH-mun* or *SHAY-mun*), or spiritual healer. Both men and women could become shamans.

Common remedies included yarrow for toothaches, charcoal mixed with milk for eye infections, and tree sap for colds. Berries from the high cranberry bush could be made into juice or jelly that took the place of cough syrup. Shavings from the stems of the cranberry bush were heated in water and applied to cuts to drain out infections. Alder berry tea was used to stop diarrhea, and the powdery substance from rotting trees treated earaches, as did warm seal oil.

ARTS

Art has been a part of Alutiiq life for thousands of years. Ancient stone carvings of faces, animals, and geometric patterns preserve the past. Carved masks also date back to earlier centuries. Artists decorated the masks with paint, feathers, fur, and carvings. Performers held their masks with their hands or teeth, or tied them on. The people used some masks in ritual plays, called "six-act mysteries," as well as in religious ceremonies. Afterward, the masks were broken to destroy their power.

Wood was also used for containers for storage and cooking. Like other Northwest and Arctic groups, the Alutiiq bent thin wood into various shapes using steam. The craftspeople built their houses and boats from wood, and carvers made statues and amulets.

Alutiiq baskets are prized for their tight stitching. Women wove them in geometric patterns using as many as 2,500 stitches a square inch. Birchbark, grasses, and spruce roots provided basket materials and dyes. Fibers for baskets came from plants, animal tissue, cords, and fishing line.

CUSTOMS

Social organization

Alutiiq society was divided into classes. The upper class consisted of the chiefs and other wealthy families. The majority of villagers were commoners. Slaves made up the lower class; they were often war captives. Villages also included specialists, such as shaman, healers, midwives, whalers, and weather forecasters. One of the important positions belonged to the *kassat,* or wise men, who created the songs and dances.

Birth and naming

Women had their babies in special houses near the main house (see "Buildings"). They stayed there for five or ten days after birth. Both mother and baby then went for a sweat bath. At this time, lips and noses were pierced (see "Clothing"). Some early sources indicated that the Alutiiq might have practiced head flattening (applying pressure to a baby's forehead so the top of the head became more pointy), but this may have been caused by the cradles babies were put in. To teach their offspring to endure hardships, parents plunged infants into freezing water.

Children played with toys, but in addition to being for fun, each toy had a spiritual meaning or lesson. Toys were also seasonal; children could only play with each toy at a certain time of year. The patterns of play were based on animal and bird migration.

Parents were permissive, but children were expected to be stoic and learn to endure great hardships without complaining. Sometimes, girls were given boys names and reared as men, but more often boys were dressed as girls and raised to be women. The Alutiiq valued these transvestites, and many went on to become shamans.

Puberty

When girls began to menstruate, they were secluded for thirty days. They were not allowed to look up at the sky or eat wild game. Older women taught them the skills they needed for adulthood. A girl's clothing was washed separately, and her urine was dumped where no one would walk or disturb it. During their periods, women were considered bad luck, so they could not go near the beach because they might prevent hunters from catching seals.

Marriage and divorce

Parents of the bride and groom usually arranged the marriage, but individuals could also chose their own partners. The families usually exchanged gifts, and then the man went to live with his wife in her parents' house for a year or until they started their own family The husband hunted for his in-laws while they lived in the bride's home.

Women could have two husbands, but one was more like a servant. Most wealthy men had more than one wife. Couples could separate and remarry, and they often did.

Death and mourning

People kept their dead nearby. After dressing the body in good clothing and jewelry, the Alutiiq wrapped it in sea mammal skins. Some corpses were put in a side chamber of the house. Others were laid in plank-lined graves. Wealthy people mummified their relatives' bodies and placed them in a secluded place. Slaves might accompany their masters into death. The deceased's possessions and tools were often placed on the grave along with a decorated pole marker.

The Alutiiq believed the dead were reincarnated five times before they ascended to the sky, where they could look down on Earth. On their way to the afterlife, though, the deceased had to close their eyes and could not watch the spirits at work. Once they reached the heavens, however, they had excellent vision. The stars are said to be the eyes of the ancestors.

Mourning lasted for at least forty days. Each day at twilight people took food and water to the grave, and sang dirges (sad songs). During this time, the relatives cut or singed their hair and blackened their faces. Some went into seclusion. These rituals sometimes lasted until a special ceremony honoring the dead was held. These feasts for the dead included humorous music and dancing along with gift-giving (see "Games, festivals, and ceremonies"). Attendees burned some of the goods to send them skyward to their dead relatives.

A museum curator holds a collection of 3000-year-old stone bayonet points discovered at an ancient Alutiiq hunting camp.
© AP PHOTO.

War and hunting rituals

Hunters had two animal spirits, which were often birds. One helped with hunting on land, the other at sea. Alutiiq masks and hunting hats reflect the importance of these spirits. Because those two items represent the wearer's spiritual connection, people often decorated them with bird images, beaks, or feathers. The ivory carvings on the hats were of bird wings, heads, eyes, and beaks. Seal hunters wore wooden helmets carved to resemble seal heads; these were painted black, white, and red.

Games, festivals, and ceremonies

Competitions Communities often invited their neighbors, the Tlingit (see entry) and Eyak, to participate in challenges of strength and endurance. Both men and women raced, swam, boated, and played team sports. Wrestling, target throwing, and high jumping were other popular activities. Although some competitions were for enjoyment, people bet on the winners of others. Valuable items—clothing and tools—might be wagered on the outcome.

Some games were thought to influence the sun's movements. Children played *Úmayuwitstaq*, or the Sunrise Game, to help spring come sooner. They jerked a string tied to a nail on the wall to make a bead run as high as they could. The Alutiiq also believed spinning tops brought the sun back earlier. They engaged in guessing games to help summer last longer; teams sang and tried to guess how many sticks their opponents were holding. Many of these traditional games are still played in Alutiiq communities.

Celebrations When winter set in, social gatherings began. Many of the feasts, ceremonies, and other meetings were held in the *kashim* (see "Buildings"), or men's hall. In villages without a separate building, the festivities occurred in a large home. The Alutiiq held a variety of dances, masked performances, special ceremonies, feasts, and other rituals. The celebrations continued, one after the other, as long as the people had enough food to share.

After preparing foods and making gifts for each guest, the hosts of these celebrations dressed up and waited on the beach to greet their guests with songs. They waded into the water and helped the visitors pull their kayaks ashore, and then everyone feasted for days. When the food ran out, the host handed out gifts to everyone before they departed.

Some of the important events included a memorial feast for those who had died, potlatches, an animal-increase ceremony, gatherings to mark the succession of chiefs or to celebrate milestones in children's lives (a boy's successful hunt and a girl's menstruation), and preparation for war.

Festivals included singing and dancing to the beat of a drum. Traditional drums were carved and painted, and drumheads were made from halibut stomach or seal bladder or hide; puffin beaks decorated the rims. Drum handles were carved or painted. Some even had tiny masks attached to them. Rattles and whistles also accompanied the drum as the Alutiiq acted out stories or history, or sang to honor their ancestors.

Gift-giving Gift-giving was a major part of winter celebrations. Chiefs gave out clothing and other goods. The more lavish the gifts, the more they revealed the chief's ability to organize, delegate, and gather necessary resources. To show their wealth, the chiefs sometimes gave each guest a squirrel-skin parka. The practice of gift-giving also extended to the spirit world. Hunters thanked the animals they caught, and women gathering berries or herbs left a present for the plants. The people also left offerings of food for the dead (see "Death and mourning").

Modern holidays Nowadays, friends and relatives still gather to celebrate major holidays, such as national U.S. holidays. Many Alutiiq also observe the traditional Orthodox Christian seasons of Christmas and Easter. Russian New Year is another major religious holiday. The people hold masquerade balls or visit neighbors, who feed them and try to guess the identities of the costumed guests. *Sláwiq* (Starring) happens on January 7 to enact the wise men's journey to find baby Jesus. While carrying a replica of the Star of Bethlehem, people sing hymns in three languages—English, Russian, and Alutiiq. *Maskalatalhít,* or masked dancers, represent King Herod's soldiers who were sent to kill the baby. Accordions, guitars, and whistles provide accompaniment.

CURRENT TRIBAL ISSUES

Many Alutiiq communities are still recovering from the various natural disasters they suffered during the late 1900s (see "History"). Only seven of the thirty animal species have returned to the pre-oil-spill levels after the Valdez incident.

Since 2007, the Kodiak Alutiiq/Sugpiaq Repatriation Commission has been collecting grave goods and ancestral remains from museums around the country. Material items are housed in the Alutiiq Museum. The museum also stores bones temporarily until the villagers give them a proper burial.

Other efforts aimed at revitalizing the culture began in the 1980s. The Kodiak Area Native Association (KANA) took a new approach to dealing with social and health problems that plagued the people. They focused on instilling pride in the Alutiiq culture and helping people develop self-esteem. A major success in combating alcohol abuse occurred in Akhiok village in 1988. The residents began a sobriety movement and were successful in getting all their citizens to stop drinking. The movement spread to other communities. A large part of the healing is tied to participating in traditional subsistence activities with their families. Some of the initiatives that have been developed are arts and crafts classes, oral history program, elders' conferences, and language instruction, which allow older community members to pass along vital skills and culture. These programs continue into the twenty-first century, giving the Alutiiq more pride in their heritage.

Ecotourism and archaeological excavations bring in visitors and stimulate the economy, but they also encourage Alutiiq students to learn more about their heritage. The Alutiiq communities are becoming stronger as their members preserve their traditions and culture.

NOTABLE PEOPLE

Sugpiaq sculptor and painter Alvin Eli Amason (1948–) was born in Kodiak and raised by his grandfather, who was a bear guide. After years of teaching in various areas of the United States, Amason returned to his native Alaska, where he taught at the University of Alaska and the Visual Arts Center of Alaska. He later became director of the Native Art Center of the University of Alaska in Fairbanks and a member of the Alaska Native Arts Foundation board of directors. Amason's work has been shown and purchased internationally. His daughter Lena Amason has followed in his footsteps as a painter who also carves wood panels.

A 2007 MacArthur Fellow, Sven Haakanson (1967–) is known for his work in revitalizing and preserving Alutiiq culture, traditions, and language. After graduating from Harvard University with a Ph.D., Haakanson accepted a position as the executive director of the Alutiiq Museum in Kodiak, Alaska, where he organized traveling exhibits that made the world aware of the rich heritage of his people. He also began leading a study of ancient petroglyphs and stone carvings on the island. Haakanson, who is also a carver and photographer, passed along his knowledge by teaching at the college level and serving as the chair of the Alaska State Council on the Arts. His interests also extend to serving on the Alaska Native Science Commission.

BOOKS

Bielawski, Ellen. *In Search of Ancient Alaska: Solving the Mysteries of the Past.* Anchorage: Alaska Northwest Books, 2007.

Crowell, Aron L. *Living Our Cultures, Sharing Our Heritage: The First Peoples of Alaska.* Washington, DC: Smithsonian Books, 2010.

Haakanson, Sven D., Jr., and Amy F. Steffian, eds. *Giinaquq Like a Face: Suqpiaq Masks of the Kodiak Archipelago.* Fairbanks: University of Alaska Press, 2009.

Luehrmann, Sonja. *Alutiiq Villages under Russian and U.S. Rule.* Fairbanks: University of Alaska Press, 2008.

Miller, Gwenn A. *Kodiak Kreol: Communities of Empire in Early Russian America.* Ithaca, NY: Cornell University Press, 2010.

Mulcahy, Joanne B. *Birth & Rebirth on an Alaskan Island: The Life of an Alutiiq Healer.* Athens: University of Georgia Press, 2001.

Partnow, Patricia H. *Making History: Alutiiq/Sugpiaq Life on the Alaska Peninsula.* Fairbanks: University of Alaska Press, 2001.

Steffian, Amy F., and April G. Laktonen Counceller. *Alutiiq Traditions—An Introduction to the Native Culture of the Kodiak Archipelago.* Kodiak, AK: Alutiiq Museum & Archeological Society, 2009.

Williams, Maria Shaa Tláa. *The Alaska Native Reader: History, Culture, Politics.* Durham, NC: Duke University Press, 2009.

Wilson, Kenneth F., Jr., and Jeff Richardson, eds. *The Aleutian Islands of Alaska: Living on the Edge.* Fairbanks: University of Alaska Press, 2009.

WEB SITES

"Alutiiq." *Afognak Native Corporation.* http://www.alutiiq.com/ (accessed on August 15, 2011).

"Alutiiq Heritage." *Kodiak Island Convention & Visitors Bureau.* http://www.kodiak.org/explore-kodiak/history-a-culture/alutiiq-heritage.html (accessed on August 15, 2011).

Aluttiq Museum. http://alutiiqmuseum.org/ (accessed on August 15, 2011).

"Alutiiq Natives." *Kodiak Island Internet Directory.* http://kodiakisland.net/alutiiq2.html (accessed on August 15, 2011).

"Liicugtukut Alutiiq." *Alaska Humanities Forum.* http://www.alutiiqlanguage.org/ (accessed on August 15, 2011).

National Museum of the American Indian: Indigenous Geography. "The Alutiiq." *Smithsonian Museum.* http://www.indigenousgeography.si.edu/uploads/pdfs/Akhiok_4-8_ENG.pdf (accessed on August 15, 2011).

Old Harbor Native Corporation. http://www.oldharbornativecorp.com/ (accessed on August 15, 2011).

"Unangax & Alutiiq (Sugpiaq)." *Alaska Native Heritage Center.* http://www.alaskanative.net/en/main_nav/education/culture_alaska/unangax/ (accessed on August 15, 2011).

Inuit

Name

Inuit (pronounced *IN-yoo-it*) is the tribe's name for themselves and means "the people." In the past, the Inuit were sometimes called *Eskimo,* which may mean "eaters of raw meat" in the Algonquian language, although some linguists (people who study languages) say the name most likely comes from an Ojibway word meaning "to net snowshoes." Another recent theory is that it came from the Montagnais language and should be translated as "people who speak a different language." The people in Canada and Greenland prefer to be called Inuit. In Alaska, the word *Eskimo* refers to all indigenous peoples of both Yupik and Inuit origin.

Location

The Inuit inhabit the area around the Arctic Circle, including Greenland, northern Canada, Alaska, and the Chukokta region of Russia.

Population

There were approximately 127,000 Inuit in the mid-1990s, including 44,000 in Alaska, 32,000 in Canada, 49,000 in Greenland, and 2,000 in Russia. In 2000, there were 45,919 Inuit in the United States. Canada's 2001 census indicated an Inuit population of 29,005. An estimate in 2005 placed Greenland's Inuit population at 50,100, and Russia's at less than 1,000. The 2010 U.S. Census identified 24,859 Inupait, the term used to identify populations previously identified by the census as Eskimo.

Language family

Eskimoan or Eskimaleut.

Origins and group affiliations

Scientists think the Inuit migrated from Asia on foot and by dogsled up to ten thousand years ago, by crossing a land bridge that once connected Siberia to Alaska across the Bering Sea. From there some groups

Traditional Inuit Communities

Shaded area

☐ Traditional Inuit lands encompassing present-day Alaska, Siberia, Canada, and Greenland

Inuit Territories today

The Inuit occupy a 5,000-mile stretch of territory around the Arctic Circle.

A map of traditional Inuit lands. MAP BY XNR PRODUCTIONS. CENGAGE LEARNING, GALE. REPRODUCED BY PERMISSION OF GALE, A PART OF CENGAGE LEARNING.

continued eastward through northern Canada and into Greenland. In the early twenty-first century, most Inuit inhabit a large territory around the Arctic Circle.

The Inuit are divided into three major groups: the Alaskan Inuit, including those living in Chukotka, Russia; the Central Inuit, which encompasses the groups in northern Canada, including Labrador and Baffin Island; and the Greenland Inuit.

The Inuit are a people of great ingenuity and endurance who, over thousands of years, survived and thrived in the harsh and icy environment of the Arctic. Although they were spread across more than one continent, they nevertheless retained cultural tiesthrough similar customs and languages. To uphold their rights, the Inuit became active in the economics and politics of their countries and have been working to preserve the best of their old ways while adopting the best of the new.

HISTORY

Inuit migration theory

The Inuit were probably among the last of the Native groups to migrate to North America by crossing a land bridge across the Bering Strait between Siberia and Alaska, according to many scientists. Scholars disagree as to when the crossings occurred. The earliest evidence of Inuit civilization remains hidden because much of the land they would have crossed in Alaska and northern Canada now lies underwater. The Aleut, who now occupy the border islands of western Alaska, probably split off from the Inuit first, whereas other bands of Inuit migrated east into Greenland.

Despite being spread over many thousands of miles and throughout different continents, all Inuit speak varieties of the same language, which supports this theory. They also have similar customs, body types, and skin color.

Some anthropologists (people who study the cultures of different civilizations) think the Inuit first lived in eastern Alaska, long before western Alaska and the Canadian Arctic were inhabited. By 4000 BCE, the Inuit reached the coast of Alaska; some even ventured into the interior. By 1200 BCE, the Arctic was inhabited from the west coast of Alaska to the eastern part of northern Canada. Permanent coastal settlements existed in Alaska around 1600 BCE, and by 600 CE, these settlements had grown larger and more stable. From 600 to about 1800, the Inuit lived in coastal and inland villages and developed more sophisticated tools and more complex ways of life. Contact with non-Natives during the 1800s brought tremendous changes to the lives of the Native people.

First European-Inuit encounters

Because of their remote locations, few Inuit had early contact with Europeans. The Inuit of Greenland were the first to encounter Europeans when the Vikings, under Erik the Red (c. 950–c. 1003), traveled there

Important Dates

984: The Vikings under Erik the Red first encounter the Inuit of Greenland.

1576: British explorer Martin Frobisher first comes into contact with the central Inuit of northern Canada.

1741: Russian explorer Vitus Bering is the first European to reach the Inuit of Alaska.

1867: The United States purchases the Alaska Territory from Russia.

1971: Through the Alaska Native Claims Settlement Act (ANCSA), the Inuit and other Alaska Natives receive $962 million and 44 million acres in exchange for giving up claims to another 335 million acres.

1999: The Canadian government transfers control of a newly formed province, Nunavut, to the Inuit. At 818,962 square miles (2,121,101 square kilometers), Nunavut covers one-fifth of the total landmass of Canada.

in the year 984. Six centuries passed before British explorer Martin Frobisher (c. 1535–1594) encountered the Inuit of Greenland and northern Canada during his unsuccessful searches for the Northwest Passage. (The Northwest Passage is a water route through the islands north of Canada that connects the Atlantic and Pacific oceans.)

In 1741, the Russian explorer Vitus Bering (1681–1741), for whom the Bering Strait was named, was the first European to meet the Inuit of Alaska. Russian emperor Peter the Great (1672–1725) had first sent Bering to Alaska in 1724, and Bering later returned to establish settlements. Soon, Russian fur traders arrived in the area.

Samuel Hearne (1745–1792) of the Hudson's Bay Company, a wealthy British trading firm, reached the Inuit of northern Canada by land in the late 1700s. Canadian Inuit did not have major dealings with Europeans until the arrival of nineteenth-century whaling fleets and the later development of the fur trade there.

Inuit lifestyle changes

From the seventeenth to the early nineteenth century, hundreds of Scottish, British, and American whalers came to the Arctic. The Inuit supplied them with oil, blubber, whalebone, and furs. In return, the Inuit received tea, tobacco, flour, crackers, matches, lead, molasses, brandy, rifles, and ammunition. In the early 1800s, some Inuit replaced Native tools with European goods and traded for metal knives, kettles, lamps, guns, cloth, and alcohol.

In the 1800s, whalers from New England sailed to the Arctic and spent the winters living ashore. In the spring, they returned to their ships, and the Inuit took their places in the winter dwellings. The Natives and the New Englanders hunted together, and in time their cultures blended. Many white men took Inuit wives, and their children were raised as Inuit.

Also during the 1800s, Russian fur hunters and traders moved into western Alaska. Soon, the Russian-American Company controlled the fur trade in Alaska and the Aleutian Islands. About that same time, on the peninsula of Labrador in northeastern Canada, German missionaries established missions to convert the Inuit to Christianity. Germans traded for Inuit furs, introduced seal nets to Native hunters, and encouraged them to produce baskets, carvings, and other crafts. The Inuit generally had friendly relations with these traders, for whom they served as guides and interpreters.

New technology and diseases

In the mid-1800s, large-scale trading, fishing, and whaling industries ended on the coast of Alaska. By 1850, seal, salmon, bear, and walrus were scarce, and by 1860, whales were no longer plentiful either. Non-Native hunters moved farther north and west in search of wildlife. The Inuit by then were dependent on the U.S.-produced goods for which they traded their furs.

After the United States purchased the Alaska Territory from Russia in 1867, there was much greater contact between Alaskan Inuit and the Americans, who established fur-trapping, gold-mining, and commercial whaling operations in Inuit territory. Despite the ever-growing number of white explorers and settlers, several Inuit bands managed to avoid all contact with non-Native peoples into the early 1900s.

The newcomers brought diseases for which the Natives had no immunity. Epidemics of smallpox, influenza, measles, and scarlet fever killed great numbers of Native people in the Arctic. Prior to European contact the Inuit population was estimated at approximately sixty thousand. Disease had cut their numbers in half by 1900.

Inuit and non-Native relations in Canada

After the decline of whaling in the late 1800s, three main groups managed the central and northern Arctic: traders, missionaries, and the Canadian police. They looked for new occupations for the Inuit to replace the old ones.

In the 1920, the Canadian government–run Hudson's Bay Company, which controlled all the trading posts in the region, imported reindeer from Norway. They tried to turn the Inuit into herders but failed to train them properly. Moving Inuit to new hunting and trapping grounds did not succeed either because the people were heartsick at being separated from their relatives.

Next Anglican and Roman Catholic missionaries established schools for the Inuit and supervised education and healthcare in the Arctic until 1945, when the Canadian government took over. In the 1900s, the Royal Canadian Mounted Police, or "Mounties," kept peace among the non-Natives and the Inuit in Canada's western provinces. This proved difficult for the Inuit, who were used to policing themselves.

During World War II (1939–45; a war in which Great Britain, France, the United States, and their allies defeated Germany, Italy, and

Japan), airfields, weather stations, and a radar lines were built across Canada's North. Soon, mining exploration and development increased. Later, discoveries of large oil and gas reserves brought thousands of people from the south into the Inuit lands.

In recent decades, the Canadian government has begun to provide education, healthcare, and other social services to the Inuit. As a result, the government presence grew, and the Inuit moved to a smaller number of large, more permanent communities.

Alaskan land claim disputes

For years, Inuit struggled with land-claims issues, but major ones were not settled until the late twentieth century. In 1971, the Alaska Native Claims Settlement Act (ANCSA) gave Alaska Natives $962.5 million and 44 million acres, and they ceded their claims to another 335 million acres. The agreement allowed the government to build the Alaskan Pipeline from north to south through Alaska to transport oil.

From ANCSA, the Inuit and other Native groups received legal ownership of 12 percent of the total lands of Alaska and much-needed money for economic growth. They developed local corporations to manage their land and money and invested in businesses, such as oil fields,

Paul Okalik (right), the new premier of Nunavut, signs the official documents creating the new province of Nunavut, Canada, in April 1999.
© NICK DIDLICK/STRINGER/AFP/ GETTY IMAGES.

mining operations, hotels, and shipping companies. In 1980, ANCSA was amended to restore Native hunting and fishing rights.

Major land claims of Inuit and other Canadian Natives were finally successful in 1982 when legislation passed calling for the formation of a new territory called Nunavut in the Northwest Territories.

The Inuit in modern times

By the end of the twentieth century, the Inuit population had recovered to earlier peak levels. Traditional ways are increasingly being exchanged for those of modern life. Many Inuit have adopted aspects of mainstream American culture, including guns, knives, clothes made of modern fabrics, sewing machines, boats with motors, snowmobiles rather than dog sleds, and wooden houses, which have made their traditional ways seem obsolete. The environmental impact of oildrilling, mining, commercial fishing and whaling, and military activities in the Arctic regions has greatly decreased the numbers of sea mammals and land animals available to Inuit hunters. Anti-sealing, anti-trapping, and anti-whaling movements have lessened the value of these Inuit industries.

In recent years, some Inuit bands have settled in one place to grow crops or herd reindeer and cattle. In Alaska, the Inuit people are moving into urban areas. In 1960, 12 percent of Inuit people lived in cities, but by 1990, the number had grown to 44 percent.

On April 1, 1999, the Canadian government divided the Northwest Territories and turned part of it over to the Natives. This new territory, called Nunavut (meaning "Our Land"), is an area about the size of France. Nunavut citizens live by Canadian laws, but they can govern the territory the way other Canadian provinces do. About 85 percent of Nunavut inhabitants are Inuit, so they are the major political power in legislation (lawmaking). The largest community in Nunavut, Iqaluit, is the capital.

RELIGION

The Inuit believe that all aspects of nature, including animals and weather, had spirits. Among their gods were Sedna, who lived at the bottom of the ocean and controlled the year's supply of sea mammals, and the guardian of the caribou, who controlled caribou numbers during their migration across the Arctic.

Human beings were said to have two types of souls: the "breath of life" disappeared when a person died; the "soul" separated from the

Inuit Words

Many Inuit words have gained wide usage in English, including *kayak, parka, igloo, husky,* and *malamute,* the name of a dog breed. The common Inuit expression *Ajurnamat,* which means "it cannot be helped," demonstrates the calm and stoic approach to life that is typical of the Inuit. Here are some other Inuktitut words:

angun	"man"
arnaq	"woman"
atausiq	"one"
imiq	"water"
malruk	"two"
pingasut	"three"
sisamat	"four"
siqiniq	"sun"
taqqiq	"moon"

body but existed after death. In the afterworld, most souls went into the earth, whereas those of women who died giving birth or people who perished violently or by suicide went to the sky.

The Inuit also believed evil spirits sometimes disrupted people's lives. They tried to eliminate the influence of evil spirits. Individuals who suffered from bad fortune wandered away from the tribe and spent several days alone. They contacted spirits of their dead ancestors to reverse their situation.

Religious rituals were performed to ensure good weather or success in hunting. Sometimes carved decorative objects of wood, bone, or ivory, with attached feathers or fur, were used to summon the attention of the spirits. During ceremonial dances, Inuit men often wore masks on their faces, while women wore tiny masks on their fingers, fashioned to resemble animals or other spirits in nature.

By the late 1900s, many Inuit were Christians, but most retained some of their original beliefs. For example, the Inuit believe that bragging during good times invites bad luck, so they complain about their good fortune.

LANGUAGE

The language of the Inuit is Inuktitut. Despite being scattered over great distances, all Inuit bands speak closely related dialects (varieties) of the Eskimoan or Eskimaleut language family. Only two different linguistic groups are found among the Inuit: the Pacific or Alaskan group, which includes the Yup'ik (see entry); and the Canadian or Northern group, which includes the Inuit of Greenland.

Since 1900, Inuit contact with non-Natives resulted in a mixed language of three hundred to six hundred words, based on Inuktitut as well as English and other languages. This mixed language is sometimes mistaken for the actual Inuit language.

Inuit languages use body signals, such as squinting. They also are extremely rich in specific words. Inuktituit speakers can add many suffixes to a single word to make it more exact. Some words end up expressing as much meaning as a whole sentence. For this reason, people often say that the Inuit have fifty or even hundreds of different words meaning "snow". The truth is that, by increasing the length of their words, the Inuit can make their descriptions of snow, or of any object, much more precise.

GOVERNMENT

The Inuit spent so much time hunting and protecting themselves from the harsh environment that they had little time for social or political organization. They did not have chiefs. Unofficial leaders, usually the strongest hunters, were consulted on matters that involved the whole tribe. Other than that, each person took charge of himself.

The cooperative spirit of the Inuit caused problems when they dealt with Europeans. Dishonest traders often took advantage of them. Additionally, they had for centuries preferred not to have a central government, so other nations had difficulty forming political relationships with them.

In modern times, the Inuit are very involved in political activities at the local, national, and international levels. International organizations allow Inuit of different countries to work together on matters of economic, social, and cultural importance. The Inuit are also taking a greater part in the policymaking of the governments under which they live. Inuit villages in Alaska are governed by various elective systems. In Canada, elected councils oversee most Inuit communities. Inuit members now sit in both houses of Canada's parliament.

ECONOMY

In early times, the Inuit did not use money, and people had few possessions. Families had dogs, a dwelling, and a few handmade items that may have included tools, sleds, weapons, or kayaks, and an occasional piece of craftwork, such as a whalebone carving.

The basic materials needed for survival were freely shared among members of the community, and the land belonged to all. Fishing and

ESQUIMAUX DOGS.

An Inuit family and dog sled team, circa 1800s. © NORTH WIND PICTURE ARCHIVES/ ALAMY.

hunting could be undependable, but no one went without food. Successful hunters regarded it an honor to share the fish they caught with others. Sod homes, abandoned by one group as they moved elsewhere in pursuit of game, were available for others who came along later.

No part of the animals caught by the Inuit went to waste. They made tools from bones and teeth; melted fat into oil to burn for light, heat, and cooking; and fashioned clothing, coverings for boats, and tents from the skin. Because few trees grow in the Arctic, the Inuit relied on stones, driftwood, bones, and antlers to make tools. Sometimes they traveled hundreds of miles to find the right type of stones for making knives. This way of life went on century after century.

In the early twenty-first century, the people's economic base has expanded. Artistic products by the Inuit, such as carvings and paintings, are in demand in the world art market and provide a steady source of income. The growth of Inuit communities has provided the people with jobs in community services, industry, and government.

DAILY LIFE

Adapting to an extreme environment

For thousands of years, the lives of the Inuit were regulated by the seasons. Between October and February, the sun never rises, and the temperature can reach -80 degrees Fahrenheit (-62 degrees Celsius). Average winter temperatures hover around -29 degrees Fahrenheit (-34 degrees

An Inuit village during seal hunting season, circa 1800s.
© NORTH WIND PICTURE ARCHIVES/ALAMY.

Celsius). The short, wide bodies of the Inuit conserve heat. The Inuit also have many more blood vessels in their hands and feet than other people, allowing them to stay warm enough even in very cold weather.

Because the Arctic region has few edible plants, the Inuit learned to live almost entirely by hunting and fishing. To kill enough game to feed and clothe their families, Inuit men spent most of their time hunting.

The hunting cycle

In the winter, about a dozen families lived together in small communities. Each day, hunters crawled over the ice to net or harpoon seals. Sometimes they waited patiently by holes in the ice for hours until seals came up for air. A hunter could easily fall asleep, so he had to concentrate to stay awake.

The Inuit used teams of trained dogs to hunt polar bears, cornering the bears and then killing them with spears. Hunting took place at night and was extremely dangerous because spears had to be thrown from close range.

In the spring, the communities broke up. Some families went off in kayaks (skin-covered one-person boats) to hunt seals. Sometimes Inuit captured seals using rawhide nets. Walrus and sea lion were available in the summertime, but unlike seals they migrated south in winter. Occasionally, the Inuit hunted whales. They used boats to herd them close to shore; they then struck them with harpoons attached to floats. When the whale became exhausted from dragging a float, hunters hauled it ashore with their boats.

The main summer activity was pursuing caribou as the herd made its way back north. Hunters crept up on the caribou or hid in a pit until the animals approached and then killed them using spears or bows and arrows. Sometimes, they drove the caribou into the water to capture them.

Depending on their geographic region, Inuit bands hunted a wide range of other game including musk oxen, mountain sheep, wolves, wolverines, foxes, hares, marmots, squirrels, and birds. They hunted animals from blinds (concealed places), caught them in traps, or entangled them in weighted nets called *bolas*. As colder weather approached, families and communities rejoined each other.

Families

Men hunted and built homes, whereas women prepared food, worked on skins, and made clothing. Women were not permitted to hunt; in fact, it was considered bad luck for a woman to touch a harpoon or a bow.

To survive in the Arctic, the Inuit developed a cooperative culture, and the extended family (parents, children, grandparents, and other relatives) was the most important unit in society. Often two or more related families lived together in one house, working, traveling, and eating together. The oldest man was usually in charge of a household, but he had to display hunting skills and be generous and reasonable.

People depended on their relatives for help with everyday tasks, especially in times of trouble. Those unable to feed themselves were "adopted" by families.

Buildings

Igloos and other early structures The Native term *igloo* refers to any type of dwelling, but it is used here to mean an ice house. Not all Inuit lived in igloos, although they were highly practical in the Arctic environment. Igloos were common among some bands in northern Canada, where

Inuit family gathers inside an igloo. © WAYNE R. BILENDUKE/GETTY IMAGES.

snow was plentiful. The circular, dome-shaped structures were made of blocks of hard-packed snow cut with long knives of bone, metal, or ivory. The inside walls were melted with the heat of a blubber lamp, then quickly refrozen to make a solid, windproof barrier. The outside walls were covered with a layer of soft snow for insulation.

Most igloos had a hole at the top to let smoke and air escape. Some had a clear block of ice for a window, and some had skylights. To enter an igloo, a person crawled through a long, low tunnel. Inside, people slept on a low platform of snow covered with twigs and caribou furs. Sometimes, several igloos were linked together to provide separate living, sleeping, and storage facilities. A simple igloo could be built in about one hour.

The Inuit of Alaska and Greenland more commonly lived in *karmats,* cabins made of stones or logs and covered with sod. These rectangular houses were usually low to the ground and set over shallow pits. As with igloos, a long entrance tunnel kept out cold air. Windows were sometimes fashioned by stretching transparent animal intestines over small openings. Inside the karmat, people burned animal fat in shallow, saucer-shaped soapstone lamps over which fish and meat could be cooked. In warmer weather, when they traveled frequently in pursuit of game, many groups made tents of driftwood or whalebones covered with sealskin or caribou hides.

Modern housing Government officials complained that traditional Inuit sod houses were damp, smelly, and unsanitary, so they supplied prefabricated (already put together) houses; the homes were shipped on barges during warmer months. Most Inuit live in these wood houses set on stilts or gravel pads to insulate them from the permanently frozen earth beneath. Although the houses arrive painted, the paint soon wears away and is seldom reapplied. Most houses have front doors that open out, a problem when winter snow piles up. The freezing and thawing cycles cause the houses to warp, so many have leaky windows and are often drafty.

Inside, one large room is divided into separate eating and sleeping areas. Few communities have indoor plumbing, so a five-gallon bucket often serves as the toilet, and bathtubs are used for storing dirty clothes. Most families use the front porch for freezers or other infrequently used appliances. Despite these problems, many people choose to use the houses because they provide more space than traditional dwellings.

Transportation

The Inuit built kayaks and *umiaks* (large, deep boats rowed with conventional oars). Men built the umiaks of wooden or whalebone frames covered with sealskin, and women rowed them.

The Inuit also built sleds, called *komatiks,* by tying a platform onto wooden or bone runners. They rubbed the surface of the runners with mud, then brushed them with water that froze to a smooth, slippery finish. A team of sturdy northern dogs called huskies usually drew the sleds.

In modern times, the Inuit travel by four-wheel-drive vehicles, airplanes, motor boats, and snowmobiles, although dog sleds and kayaks remain important vehicles.

Clothing and adornment

Basic apparel for men and women consisted of a hooded parka, pants, stockings, boots, and mittens. Mittens were made of waterproof sealskin for the summer or warm, lightweight caribou skin for the winter. The Inuit also made clothing from hides of polar bears, wolves, foxes, dogs, marmots, squirrels, and birds.

Inuit clothing had to allow a person to sleep out in the open in temperatures reaching -60 degrees Fahrenheit (-51 degrees Celsius). In extremely cold weather, people wore two of each garment with the fur side facing the body. Parkas fit snugly around the wrists, neck, and waist to keep cold air out. Women's parkas sometimes featured large, fur-lined hoods for carrying babies.

The Inuit crafted boots, or *mukluks,* from four layers of sealskin; they placed moss and down between the layers for insulation. Women's boots came all the way up the leg, whereas men's boots were usually shorter. Snow goggles with narrow eyeholes cut down the glare of the bright snow.

Special occasions called for clothing decorated with fur borders or embroidered designs. Some Inuit wore earrings, nose rings, or lip plugs made of ivory, shell, sandstone, or wood.

The importance of dry clothing Inuit women made and maintained all the clothing. As young girls, they learned to sew waterproof seams with thread made of tendons. When men returned from hunting, they used bone or wood scrapers, which were kept in the tunnel entrances of their homes, to remove ice crystals from their clothing. The women then chewed the frosty fabric to make it soft again and hung it on a rack over a blubber lamp to dry. This was important because wet clothes froze quickly in the frigid weather. Indoors, it was usually warm enough to go naked.

Some women made waterproof garments to pull over outerwear. Because seal, whale, and sea lion intestines are impervious to water (do not let liquid through), women washed and scraped these guts, then filled them with air and let them dry. Afterward, they sewed the strips together to make *kamleikas.* Some *kamleikas* were decorated with puffin beaks and feathers. The process could take a month, but when the parka was finished, it was water-repellent. People often sewed the bottom edges of their jackets to their kayaks to stay warm and dry on the water.

Food

The major food source for the most northern Inuit were seals and walruses along with a few land animals. Most people also ate salmon, trout, and smelt. In the summer, they built dams to trap salmon that swam upstream from the sea. Men waded waist-deep into the water to spear them with three-pronged harpoons.

The Inuit who lived below the Arctic Circle had wider food choices than their neighbors farther north. They hunted birds, fished in rivers, collected clams, and ate berries and other edible plants. Cranberries, blueberries, and young willow root were especially prized.

The people believed that if they offended the spirits of animals, they could bring on sickness or famine. For this reason they had complicated rules about food preparation. Products of the sea and products of the land were kept separate. They also had strict rules about how meat was distributed. For example, women ate the head, eyes, front legs,

The Inuit Diet

The question is often asked: Can a diet such as the one consumed by the Inuit, 40 to 70 percent based on meat, be healthy? At one time, the Canadian government encouraged the Inuit to consume mostly powdered milk, cereals, and grains, but the food made many of them sick, and they returned to eating frozen meat known as *quaq.* Most raw meat is eaten soon after it is killed, when it tastes best. Quaq is easy to eat because ice crystals in the blood and meat help in the chewing process.

By eating animals raw, the Inuit absorbed vast quantities of vitamins and minerals stored up in the animal tissues, and the vitamins counteracted the onset of heart disease. For example, the skin of the white whale was rich in vitamin C; raw liver, another staple item, had plenty of vitamin A and D. Recent studies indicate that fat from wild animals is easily converted into energy and provides a rush of rapid body heat, important for people in frigid climates.

The Inuit who eat the traditional diet have low rates of diet-linked diseases such as heart disease. In the early twenty-first century, the real threat in the traditional Inuit diet is concentrated pollutants showing up in the meat of certain animals, including whales and seals. Inuit who move to the south often have problems adjusting to common American ways of eating.

and heart, while men got the backbones. The hunter who captured the prey received the ribs, breastbone, and attached meat, and everyone else shared the rest.

Most meat was eaten raw, and only the toughest parts were boiled. The Inuit hunted caribou and polar bear primarily for their fur, rather than for meat, although caribou antler tips made a crunchy snack. In times when food was scarce, the Inuit ate their clothing, sleds, and even their dogs, but during periods of plenty, they enjoyed big feasts.

Education

Inuit children learned the importance of friendliness and cooperation, most often by being treated that way by their parents and extended families. Children received much attention and affection. They learned by example and encouragement from playful parents, rather than by being punished.

At about age eight, boys received their first training as hunters. They learned to build an igloo, track game, and make weapons. A feast was held after a boy captured his first seal or caribou. Girls were taught to trap animals, care for stone lamps, and make and repair clothing. Handling dogs, driving a sled, estimating the thickness of ice, tracking animals, and assessing the environment and weather were skills taught to both sexes.

In the 1940s and 1950s, Christian missionaries started the first Inuit schools to teach reading and mathematics. They tried to teach the Native people to assimilate—live according to the ways of the rest of society. Lessons taught in English forced students to learn the language. At school, Inuit children were forbidden to use their own language or practice their religion or culture. Teaching methods conflicted with the Inuit traditions of learning by doing, and. in many schools throughout the Arctic, students were victims of physical or sexual abuse.

Schools were mainly located in larger communities in Alaska and Canada because there were relatively few missionaries. Parents in remote locations were encouraged to send their children to these faraway boarding schools. Many did, and the separation proved painful for both children, who missed their families, and parents, who worried that their sons and daughters would forget their Native way of life.

In modern times, Inuit children are required to attend elementary school; most must leave their home communities to attend high schools or trade schools. Schools in Canada conduct many classes for elementary-school children in their native language. Adult education centers help older people qualify for jobs in industry and government.

Healing practices

When an Inuit became ill, a healer called a shaman (pronounced *SHAH-mun* or *SHAY-mun*) or an *angakok* might be called in to help. A shaman often put himself into a trance to study the problem and develop a solution. The shaman contacted the spirits by singing, dancing, and beating on drums. When the spirits entered the shaman's body, he rolled around on the floor or spoke a strange language. The patient took comfort in having the shaman intercede with the spirits on his or her behalf.

The Inuit now have access to medical personnel who visit their communities. Those who live in remote places are flown to bigger cities that have hospitals.

ARTS

The ancient Inuit made ivory carvings of people, bears, birds, seals, whales, walruses, and caribou. They also made masks for dancing that depicted various human expressions. Later, they expanded their materials to include antlers, bone, stone, and wood.

Modern Inuit artists continue the tradition by carving animal and human figures of soapstone and ivory. They also create paintings as well as embroidered clothing and tapestries that are sold throughout the world. All of these items are displayed at the annual Great Northern Art Festival in Canada. The event also features music, dance, storytelling, and fashion shows.

Oral literature

Storytelling was a favorite form of entertainment during harsh winters. The Inuit preserved their culture by passing down stories, songs, and poems from one generation to the next. Often, the songs and stories told of nature and the spirit world. They explained how the world worked and taught values. Sometimes, storytellers illustrated tales by drawing pictures in the snow with a knife. Scholars point out that the stories often showed the tension between opposites, such as male/female, land/sea, winter/summer, or dark/light.

The Kivigtok

The *kivigtok* is a person who has completely abandoned Inuit society and gone off alone to live in inland Greenland. The kivigtok is considered particularly wise and gifted because he had the ingenuity necessary to survive, for inland Greenland was nearly an impossible place for humans to live. Stories about the kivigtok like the one presented here are popular among the Inuit.

There was once a man who had several sons; of these, the second son turned *kivigtok* (viz., fled the society of mankind). This happened in the wintertime; but next summer the father, as well as his other sons, went away from home in order to search for the fugitive. In this manner summer went by and winter came round, but still they had not found him. When summer was again approaching, they made all preparations for another search, this time to other places, along another firth. Late in autumn they at length chanced to find out his solitary abode, in an out-of-the-way place, after having traversed the country in every direction for ever so long. His habitation was a cave or hollow in a rock, the inside being covered with reindeer-skin, and the entrance of which had been carefully closed up. At the time of their arrival the kivigtok was still out hunting; but a little later they saw him advance toward the place from the inland, dragging a whole deer along with him. The brothers were lying in ambush for him; and when he came close to them they seized hold of him. He recognised them at once, and gave a loud cry like that of a reindeer, and said, "Do let me off; I

Throat-singing

Regular singing is done by everyone and is usually accompanied by hand drums and dancing, but throat-singing is done by two singers, often women, facing each other. One of the pair starts the rhythm, and the other singer follows. Singers make rhythm sounds in their throats—deep, breathy sounds—while they are singing; in this way, they make two sounds at one time.

Sometimes throat-singing is a contest; the person who runs out of breath first or who cannot keep up with the other's pace loses. These contests can last from one to three minutes each, though some singers can go on for hours by using a circular breathing technique.

shan't flee." The father now asked him to return with them, adding, "This is the second summer in which we have given up our hunt in order to find thee out, and, now we have succeeded, thou really must come home with us;" and he answered, "Yes, that I will." They remained in the cave during the night, enjoying each other's company. Next day they had much to do with the things that had to be taken back with them, the store-room, besides his dwelling-place, being filled with dry meat and skins. They tied up bundles to be taken down one by one to the tent of his relatives, which was pitched at some distance near the firth by which they were to travel home. When they were about to set off with the first loads, they wanted him to follow them; he excused himself, however, saying, "When ye go down the last time I shall follow; but I must stay and take care of these things." They went without him; but on their return the kivigtok had disappeared, and taken the remainder of the provisions with him, and the brothers grew exceedingly vexed with themselves, that they had thus relied on his word, without leaving any one in charge of him. But all too late. Some time afterwards, when they had gone out again to look for him, he terrified them by yelling and howling at them from the summit of a steep and altogether inaccessible rock. How he had got there they could not make out, but finding it impossible to follow him, they were obliged to give him up for lost.

SOURCE: Rink, Henry. *Tales and Traditions of the Eskimo.* 1875. Available online at *Sacred Texts.* http://www.sacred-texts.com/nam/inu/tte/tte2-040.htm (accessed on August 15, 2011).

When the Catholic Church banned throat-singing, it was only practiced in secret. The tradition has been making a comeback over the past few decades, as much with young Inuit as with their elders.

CUSTOMS

Names

The Inuit were superstitious about names. After a person's death, it was bad luck to mention his or her name aloud until a baby received the same name and brought the spirit back to life. The baby inherited all the good qualities of the deceased person. People never said their own names aloud; instead, they announced their presence by saying, "Someone is here."

Feasting customs

Because the Inuit moved often and might not see their relatives for months on end, they took advantage of all opportunities to visit and feast. Most feasts were held in fall, when food was plentiful and winter supplies were already stored. People gathered at a family home or at a big snow house to dance to the music of drums, dine, tell stories, and practice religious rites.

When a successful hunter hosted a feast, he invited his guests to the meat rack outside to help him fetch the main course. All the while he apologized for the sorry quality of his offering, even if he was secretly proud of it. As they helped him haul the meat into the house, visitors complained loudly about how heavy it was, while complimenting their host on his great skills as a hunter. At the end of the feast, the well-fed guests fell asleep. When they woke, it was time to dine once again.

Games and celebrations

The Inuit held two annual ceremonies to thank the natural world that supported them. The Bladder Dance freed spirits of sea mammals killed during the year's hunt. Because they believed animals' spirits resided in their bladders, the Inuit saved them and inflated them with air. After several days of dancing and rituals, they returned the bladders to the sea. Another annual ceremony took place in the spring, when the sun rose again over the Arctic after several months of darkness. The Inuit welcomed the sun with special dances; to symbolize the creation of the world, they dressed in costumes that represented both sexes.

In the early twenty-first century, Arctic villages hold special celebrations at the beginning or end of summer as well as to welcome the new year. They share food and compete in dogsled races, wrestling, a form of baseball, and the "two kick" game, where a player jumps up and kicks an object as far as possible, using both feet at the same time, then lands on the floor on both feet.

The Inuit were fond of games, including one resembling soccer that was played without goals. Two teams kicked a caribou-skin ball around in the snow to see which team could keep possession of the ball longer. Children also enjoyed jumping trampoline-style on stretched-out walrus skins in a game called "skin toss."

In modern times, basketball has become a central part of Inuit culture. High school basketball occupies the young people during the long, dark winters, and team rivalries instill pride in communities. Because villages may be hundreds of miles apart, young basketball players travel to their games by plane and ferryboat.

War and hunting rituals

Before departing in search of game, Inuit hunters performed special ceremonies, spoke prayers, and sang songs to guarantee a successful catch. Through prayers and offerings of fish, the Inuit sought the help of the Sea Mother, who lived in land and sea animals, and the Raven Father, who was associated with storms, thunder, and lightening. Hunters had faith in charms fashioned in the shape of ravens. When a hunter caught a polar bear, he ate a small portion of the meat, not only for survival, but also to show reverence for the beast.

Courtship and marriage

Inuit men married when they could support a family. Women married shortly after their first menstruation. Courtship customs varied. Sometimes children were pledged to one another from birth. Other times, a man asked another for permission to marry his daughter. Occasionally, a man would simply take a woman from her house and ask her to live with him. Successful hunters often had more than one wife, and women sometimes had more than one husband. Wife exchange was common. People were so dependent on one another that no one remained unmarried.

A hunter setting off on a large trip might "borrow" the wife of another, if his wife was unable to go. Partnerships among hunters were sometimes strengthened in this way. Men were expected to be prepared to "lend" their wives, but women were not asked about their feelings in the matter.

In the Inuit culture, newly married couples usually lived with the husband's parents for a while. During that time, the man worked hard to show that he would be a good provider. Among the Inuit, plumpness was a sign of beauty and plenty, and men preferred plump wives.

Death

It was common for an old person who could no longer contribute to the community to stay behind when the family moved, thereby sealing his or her own fate. The souls of the dead were thought to join the world of the spirits, and they could become hostile to their surviving relatives or others.

An Inuit hunter takes aim from a boat. © JOEL SARTORE/CONTRIBUTOR/NATIONAL GEOGRAPHIC/GETTY IMAGES.

CURRENT TRIBAL ISSUES

On April 1, 1999, Nunavut became a new Canadian province, governed by the Inuit. Nunavut, meaning "Our Land," is made up of land from the eastern and northern sections of the Northwest Territories. The Inuit also received a financial settlement of $1.14 billion along with 818,962 square miles (2,121,102 square kilometers) of land, one-fifth the landmass of Canada. In exchange, the Inuit gave up claims to other lands in Canada.

In modern times, the Inuit struggle with economic and health concerns, including high rates of alcohol and substance abuse and suicide. Animal rights activists oppose Inuit hunting and fishing practices; pollutants affect their food sources; and global warming could destroy the Arctic region. Because children who attended church-run schools during the mid-1900s were often subjected to physical and sexual abuse, Inuit communities now have major problems with domestic violence, sexual abuse, alcoholism, depression, and suicide. Former victims tend to become abusers themselves and thus pass along the cycle of violence. Others turn their anger, shame, and grief inward, which often leads to substance abuse and severe depression. Many programs have been started to deal with these problems and to help victims heal.

In conjunction with Carleton University, Inuit elders and hunters have created the "Inuit*siku* (sea ice) Atlas." For thousands of years, the Inuit passed down their knowledge of weather, tides, currents, and sea ice to each new generation. This vital data will be made available via the Internet along with Arctic survival skills and oral history.

NOTABLE PEOPLE

Kenojuak Ashevak (1927–) is one of the best-known Inuit artists in Canada. Her stone-block prints of birds and human beings involve intertwined figures and fantasies. They are strong, colorful, richly composed, and were recognized almost immediately as unique and valuable in the art community. They are sought after by national and international collectors and museums. Kenojuak also carves and sculpts soapstone and other materials. The National Film Board of Canada produced a film about Kenojuak's work in 1962, and her work was featured in a limited edition book published in 1981.

Another notable Inuit is William J. Hensley (1941–; Iggiagruk or "Big Hill"), a former Alaska state senator and cofounder of the Northwest Alaska Native Association and the Alaska Federation of Natives.

BOOKS

Burgan, Michael. *Inuit History and Culture*. New York: Gareth Stevens, 2011.

Doak, Robin S. *Arctic Peoples*. Chicago: Heinemann Library, 2012.

Doherty, Craig A., and Katherine M. Doherty. *Arctic Peoples*. New York: Chelsea House, 2008.

Falconer, Shelley, and Shawna White. *Stones, Bones, and Stitches: Storytelling through Inuit Art*. Toronto, Ontario: Tundra Books, 2007.

Hauser, Michael. *Traditional Inuit Songs from the Thule Area*. Copenhagen: Museum Tusculanum Press, 2010.

Hessel, Ingo. *Inuit Art: An Introduction*. Vancouver, British Columbia: Douglas & McIntyre, 2002.

Houston, James A. *James Houston's Treasury of Inuit Legends*. Orlando, FL: Harcourt, 2006.

King, David C. *The Inuit*. New York: Marshall Cavendish Benchmark, 2008.

Leroux, Odette, and Marion E. Jackson. *Inuit Women Artists: Voices from Cape Dorset.* Vancouver, British Columbia: Douglas & Mcintyre, 2006.

Mcgrath, Melanie. *The Long Exile: A Tale of Inuit Betrayal and Survival in the High Arctic.* New York: Knopf, 2007.

McPherson, Robert. *New Owners in Their Own Land: Minerals and Inuit Land Claims.* Alberta, Canada: University of Calgary Press, 2004.

Stern, Pamela R. *Daily Life of the Inuit.* Santa Barbara, CA: Greenwood, 2010.

Stuckenberger, Nicole. *Thin Ice: Inuit Traditions Within a Changing Environment.* Hanover, NH: Hood Museum of Art, 2007.

Van Deusen, Kira. *Kiviuq: An Inuit Hero and His Siberian Cousins.* Montreal: McGill-Queen's University Press, 2009.

Wallace, Mary. *Make Your Own Inuksuk.* Toronto, Ontario: Maple Tree Press, 2004.

WEB SITES

Arctic Library. "Inuit" *Athropolis.* http://www.athropolis.com/library-cat. htm#inuit (accessed on August 15, 2011).

The Canadian Great Northern Art Festival. http://www.gnaf.org/ (accessed on August 15, 2011).

Deschenes, Bruno. "Inuit Throat-Singing." *Musical Traditions.* http://www. mustrad.org.uk/articles/inuit.htm (accessed on August 15, 2011).

"Inuit." *Indian and Northern Affairs Canada.* http://www.ainc-inac.gc.ca/ap/in/ index-eng.asp (accessed on August 15, 2011).

"The Inuit." *Newfoundland and Labrador Heritage.* http://www.heritage.nf.ca/ aboriginal/inuit.html (accessed on August 15, 2011).

Inuit Tapiriit Kanatami. http://www.itk.ca/ (accessed on August 15, 2011).

"Inuit*siku* (sea ice) Atlas." *Inuit Sea Ice Use and Occupancy Project (ISIUOP).* http://sikuatlas.ca/sea_ice.html (accessed on August 15, 2011).

"Land Claims." *Department of Labrador and Aboriginal Affairs.* http://www.laa. gov.nl.ca/laa/land_claims/index.html (accessed on August 15, 2011).

Ottawa Inuit Children's Centre. http://www.ottawainuitchildrens.com/eng/ (accessed on August 15, 2011).

Redish, Laura, and Orrin Lewis. "Inuktitut (Eskimo/Inuit Language)." *Native Languages of the Americas.* http://www.native-languages.org/inuktitut.htm (accessed on August 15, 2011).

"Throat Singing." *Inuit Cultural Online Resource.* http://icor. ottawainuitchildrens.com/node/30 (accessed on August 15, 2011).

Unangan

Name

The Unangan (pronounced *oo-NUNG-an,* meaning "the people," or "coast people," is the name these Alaskan island dwellers have called themselves since ancient times. *Unangax* is the plural; *Unangam* is the adjective form. Russian fur traders of the eighteenth century gave the people the name Aleut (pronounced *AHL-lee-ay-LOOT, a-LOOT,* or *AL-ee-oot*), a name that is still sometimes used. *Aleut* may have originated from the Chukchi word *aliat,* or "island." It also may have come from *allíthuh,* meaning "community."

Location

The Unangam homeland began at the western tip of the Alaska Peninsula and stretched across the Aleutian Island chain and into Russia. It included the Pribilof and Shumagin Islands. During World War II (1939–45), the Japanese took the Attu islanders to their country. During that same time, the U.S. government put the rest of the Unangam people in refugee camps in southwestern Alaska. Following the war, most people returned to their traditional homelands, with the exception of Attu residents.

Population

Precontact population estimates differ. Getting an accurate count from early writers is difficult, because many only counted the hunters or guessed at the size of the villages. Some sources indicated 16,000 to 20,000 Unangan, but one of the more reliable sources suggested the count should be 12,000 to 15,000. Even when a census was taken, the Russian figures did not match those of the Americans. A Russian census in 1790 counted sixty-six villages on eighteen islands and the mainland, but some communities may have been overlooked. The Unangam population fell by 80 to 90 percent from the mid-1700s to 1800 due to disease, malnutrition, forced labor and punishments, and suicide. The1845 Russian census showed 4,287Unangan, although that may have included some Eskimos (Inuit). In 1890, the number of villages had decreased to twenty-two, and by 1920, the U.S. Census indicated only 2,942 Unangan. Those numbers more than doubled to 6,581 by 1960. However, in the 1990s, the population had decreased to 4,000, and only ten villages remained. The U.S. Census counted 10,787 in 2000.

Traditional Unangan Communities

Shaded area

☐ Traditional lands of the Unangan on the Alaska Peninsula and the Aleutian, Pribilof, and Shumagin Islands

A map of traditional Aleut Unangan (Aleut) communities. MAP BY XNR PRODUCTIONS. CENGAGE LEARNING, GALE. REPRODUCED BY PERMISSION OF GALE, A PART OF CENGAGE LEARNING.

Language family

Eskaleut.

Origins and group affiliations

Some experts believe the Unangan were one of the first groups to cross the ancient land bridge that once connected Asia and North America. Some of these early travelers settled throughout the Americas, whereas the Unangan remained in the northern regions of the continent. Other anthropologists believe the Unangan arrived later by boat with the Eskaleut peoples. The Unangam people may have once shared a language with other Eskaleut speakers, such as the Inupiat and Yup'ik (see entry). The Unangan considered the Kenaitze, Chugach, Yakutats, and Kolosh as relatives. Often the Alutiiq, or Supiag, to the north were sometimes erroneously classified as Aleut. Attacks by the Tlingit (see entry) and enslavement by the Russians decimated the Unangam population during the 1700s and 1800s.

For nearly five thousand years, the Unangan lived on the abundant natural resources of their homeland. That changed after the Russians, and later the Americans, took control of the area. The Russians forced

Unangam hunters to supply pelts and fish that benefited the Russian economy. The once-vibrant Unangam population decreased rapidly from 1745 to the late 1800s, when the United States purchased Alaska. Life under the Americans included the curtailment of rights for more than a century, internment during World War II, and huge losses of land in the mid-1900s. Not until the final decades of the twentieth century did the Unangan regain some of the territory and freedoms they had lost. In spite of outside influences, the Unangam peoples have retained much of the traditional culture and values passed down by their ancestors over thousands of years.

HISTORY

Ancient peoples

Archaeologists have found settlements in the Aleutian area dating back as far as 8,000 or 9,000 years, leading them to speculate that the Unangan may have crossed the land bridge across the Bering Sea that connected Asia and North America thousands of years ago. Other experts believe that the Unangan arrived in the area around 4,000 BCE, traveling by boat from northeastern Asia. In either case, the Unangam culture has had strong roots in the people's traditional homeland for millennia.

The Unupiat and Yup'ik (see entry) may once have shared the Eskaleut language with the Unangan. These groups separated about 1000 BCE. The Unangan settled on the islands, whereas the other two groups made their homes along the Alaskan coast. After they divided, the languages of the three groups changed to reflect the differences in their homelands.

Archaeologists have found goods from many different Native Alaskan groups far distant from their area of origin. The Unangan with their sailing abilities were able to establish trading relationships with other villages. The Unangan also fought among themselves and with other area tribes in the area until the 1700s, when all of the Native peoples of western Alaska united against their common enemy, the Russians.

Important Dates

1720s–30s: Russian fur traders arrive on the Shumagin Islands.

1745: Russians kill fifteen Unangan on Attu Island.

1867: The United States purchases Alaska from Russia.

1939–45: The Japanese take Unangam captives from Attu to Japan. The United States confines Unangan to internment camps.

1958: Alaska becomes a state; 104 million acres of Native land are taken.

1971: The Unangan get large tracts of land under the Alaska Native Claims Settlement Act.

1988: The Aleutian and Pribilof Islands Restitution Act is signed. Two years later, more than five hundred Unangans receive restitution payments.

1994: Amchitka's nuclear testing facility closes.

Arrival of the Russians

Although some Russian fur trappers may have landed on the Shumagin Islands in the 1720s and 1730s, the Unangan had little contact with the Russians until Vitus Bering (1681–1741), a Danish explorer for Russia, sighted the Aleutian Islands in 1741. Bering's discovery prompted more fur traders to set sail for these rich hunting grounds in 1745. The first Russian party to reach the island of Attu slaughtered fifteen Unangan who resisted them. The inlet where the incident occurred is now called Massacre Bay.

This encounter set the tone for Unangan-Russian relations over the next century. The two groups engaged in bloody battles as the Unangan resisted the newcomers determined to take over their lands and resources. In 1764, Umnak and Unalaska Island residents murdered some Russians. Following this rebellion, the Russians retaliated by killing many Unangan, as well as destroying all their boats and tools, until they dominated the Unangan.

Pribilof Islands discovered

In 1786, the Russian explorer Gerasim Pribilof sighted Saint George Island, and the following year, trappers discovered Peter and Paul Island (now Saint Paul Island). These two islands formed part of a group of uninhabited islands called the Pribilof Islands, which had a huge seal population. Eager to take advantage of the bounty, the Russians forced Unangan men to move to the area to harvest pelts. Many Unangan hunters lost their lives in the dangerous seas around the islands.

Aleut people interact with traders at a Russian settlement, circa 1800s. © INTERFOTO/ ALAMY.

While the men were gone, the Russian often stole their wives, slaves, and possessions. In many villages, women and children, who no longer had men to provide food, suffered and even starved to death. At the same time, contact with the Russians passed along diseases. The Unangan had no immunity to these strange new illnesses, and many people died. During the first few decades of Russian control, the Unangam population decreased by about 85 percent due to forced labor, epidemics, and slaughter.

Russian-American Company takeover

To prevent other nations from harvesting pelts in their colony, the Russian government gave the Russian-American Company, a private fur-trading business, the authority to govern and protect the Aleutian Islands in 1799. The company's second charter, signed in 1821, declared that the Unangan were now Russian subjects.

Prior to this, the Unangan had chiefs and councils of elders to govern themselves (see "Government"), but the company set up a new system of government that gave the Russians more political control. Now the Russians could remove and appoint chiefs. They also reduced the chiefs' power to settle disputes and make decisions; the main role of Unangan leaders became to organize company work parties.

Resettlement into *artels*

The Russian-American Company also moved the Unangans from their hundreds of villages into *artels,* or temporary settlements, to make it easier to maintain control. The artels were located close to the fur-trapping areas. Eventually, these temporary homes became permanent. By 1834, the Unangan had only twenty-seven villages left.

The government forced all Unangan slaves to work for the company. Creoles, who were part Unangan and part Russian, had to work for ten to fifteen years. Unangan men between the ages of eighteen and fifty were legally bound for three years of service, but the company often ignored the law and made them continue working after their term was up. Everyone else in the villages, even the children and elderly, were required to do jobs, such as making parkas for the hunters. The people could not leave their villages without permission. The government also set limits on the amount of hunting and fishing the Unangan did for food, and the company forbid the people to trade with any other countries or businesses.

Americans take control

The Unangan may have hoped for a better life when the United States bought Alaska from Russia in 1867, but Pribilof Island residents only exchanged one company's domination for another. The U.S. government hoped to regain the $7.2 million they had paid to purchase the land. They granted to the Alaska Commercial Company a lease to handle the fur trade in the area. Although the lease specified that the company provide for the Unangam people's well-being, the owners, supported by government policy, had differing ideas from the Unangan as to what that meant.

Life on the Pribilof Islands

The Americans, as had the Russians before them, paid the Unangan workers for each pelt. Seal hunters made good wages compared to many laborers in other parts of the United States. Because their homes were company-owned, the Unangan could save a good portion of their pay. For example, in 1874, more than 50 percent of the Pribilof workers had saved as much as $40,000.

Although they were economically prosperous, the people were denied basic rights. They could not own their own homes, and they had access to only a small portion of the money they earned. Workers' wages went into a company account. Seal hunters used credit in the company store, and whatever money they spent was deducted from their accounts. The company limited the amount of cash the Unangam workers could withdraw. In addition, the workers were not allowed to leave the island without permission.

During the off-season, the men had to work for the government. Some received ten cents an hour for maintenance and construction work. Most workers, however, received no pay for their months of labor repairing roads and community buildings or guarding the rookeries. If the men refused to work, government agents put them in irons, fined them, and sometimes even banished them from the island. Other injustices included a ban on liquor and sugar, a government takeover of the chiefs' authority to administer justice, and the company's insistence that men marry to ensure a large future seal-hunting population.

Pribilof under new management

In 1890, the Alaska Commercial Company's twenty-year lease ran out. Under political pressure, the government awarded the next lease to the North American Commercial Company, but overharvesting had decimated the seal population. As seals grew scarce, the government reduced the amount of seals it permitted the Aleut to kill for food. At the same time, the hunters' wages, based on the number of seals they harvested, also declined sharply. The hunters went from earning one of the highest average incomes for U.S. workers to one of the lowest.

Over the next few decades, Pribilof Island residents ended up as recipients of government funds. They had an unusual status: they were not on welfare because they worked, but their wages did not cover their expenses. They had no access to the money they earned; all their funds went into the company account. Thus, the company, with government backing, tightly controlled the islanders' lives and restricted their freedom.

World War II confinements

After World War II (1939–45) began, the Unangan faced even greater hardships. The Japanese took over the island of Attu and sent many Unangan as captives to Hokkaido, Japan. To maintain security in the Aleutian Islands, the U.S. government moved the Unangam people into refugee camps in southwestern Alaska. The living conditions of most of these camps were unfit.

Because of the Aleutians' proximity to Japan, the U.S. military set up bases on many of the islands. The Americans also fought to regain the islands of Attu and Kiska from the Japanese and succeeded, but the damage throughout the archipelago was considerable. After the war, the Unangam people returned from the internment camps to find that the soldiers had damaged their homes and stolen their possessions. On Atka Island, all the homes had been burned to the ground to prevent a Japanese advance.

Rebuilding after the war

The residents of Attu were forbidden to return to their homes, so the government relocated them to Atka. The U.S. Navy rebuilt homes on the island, but the move away from their original homelands and exposure to the outside world had changed many Unangan. Some chose not to return to their homes. Many of those who had died in the camps were elders, so in addition to the personal tragedies the Unangam people endured, they suffered great losses in culture, language, and traditional life ways.

Conditions at the Internment Camps

When the government evacuated the Unangan during World War II, the people moved them from their island homes to abandoned sites on the Alaskan mainland. They had to leave behind most of their possessions, as they were allowed to bring only a single suitcase. The refugees often arrived to find no bedding, food, or other necessities at the camps.

The quarters at Killisnoo, for example, had three outdoor pit toilets, contaminated water, bad electrical wiring, and no heat or bathing facilities. The neighboring Tlingit donated blankets and some food, but when a nearby town offered the Unangan more supplies, the government refused them, saying that the situation was being taken care of—a claim far from the truth. Eighteen percent of the people at Killisnoo died during the war years.

A burned-out cannery site at Burnett Inlet offered a bunkhouse with no heat, electricity, beds, or plumbing. The area was also home to a large wolf population. Although the Unangan begged the government several times to let them leave, they were forced to stay until the war ended.

Thirty-two people died at Funter Bay, where detainees were housed in a cannery barracks with holes in the roofs and rotten floors. Many buildings had no doors or windows. Heat, electricity, and sewage systems were nonexistent.

Most people only ate one meal a day, because food supplies were so scarce.

More than 160 people crowded into Ward Lake, a Civilian Conservation Corps camp built to hold 70 people. The government supplied lumber and expected the people to repair the buildings and construct new ones. People who had made their living from the sea were now supposed to find a way to survive in the rainforest around the camp. Estimates indicate that as many as one-fourth of the residents died during the three years at the camp.

Philemon M. Tutiakoff, who had been moved from Unalaska, explained:

> The overcrowded conditions were an abomination. There were 28 of us forced to live in one designated 15x 20 foot [4.6 by 7.6 meter] house. There existed no church, no school, no medical facility, no store, no community facility, no skiffs or dories, no fishing gear and no hunting rifles. We had to abandon our heirlooms and pets even before the evacuation.

When the detainees returned home, many found they had no homes, or their homes had been ransacked. Churches, too, had been destroyed, looted, or used for target practice. The Unangan who had spent the past three years trying to make their camps livable now had to repeat the process in their homelands.

In the 1950s, the Unangan, along with the Japanese Americans who also had been placed in internment camps during the war, sued the federal government. After more than thirty years, Congress granted the Unangan about $12,000 each in restitution in 1988. The government also paid more than $20 million for property damage, much of which went to the Aleut Native Corporation. This organization, formed after the Alaska Native Claims Settlement Act of 1971 passed, oversees and enhances the resources of the region for the Unangam people.

For several decades, the Aleutian Islands continued to be the site of various U.S. military bases or installations. These were kept intact for surveillance during the Cold War with Russia, a time of tense political relations that began after World War II and lasted until 1991. By the mid- to late 1990s, some of these bases were abandoned. The Aleutian Islands were also used for testing nuclear bombs, in spite of many protests. The final bomb was exploded in 1971, but the testing facility on Amchitka Island did not close until 1994 (see "Current Tribal Issues").

RELIGION

Traditional beliefs

The Unangan believed all objects in nature had spirits, so they respected them and had rituals and taboos for handling them. A person in mourning or a menstruating woman could not touch tools that came in contact with animals or fish, because it would offend the animal spirits. Games and dances were held before and after whaling (see "Festivals") to please the whale's spirit, so more whales would appear. The people cared for their environment, believing it would then respond by providing food and shelter.

As part of their worship of the natural world, they venerated the sun, because life originated from light. The men rose at dawn and came out onto the rooftops. Facing east, they greeted the day and "swallowed light." "East"and "above" both stood for the sacred directions of the creator, *Agugux* or *Agudar.*

According to the Unangan, the world was divided into three parts. Many people lived in the highest world, *Akadan Kougoudakh,* where it was always daylight. Earth represented the middle world, and the lower world, *Sitkoughikh Kouyudakh,* held the afterlife.

Offerings and amulets

In addition to holding public ceremonies, each village maintained a shrine where adult males made offerings of skins and feathers smeared with paint. Children and women were forbidden to go to these sacred places, which were usually secreted high on a cliff or rock, or in a cave. Whalers may have also used these shrines for their secret society rites.

Amulets (good luck charms) were important to the Unangan and connected them to the spirit world. They valued belts that had been knotted from grasses and sinew during incantations. They wore these under their clothes to protect them from death. Men hid a special two-colored stone to draw sea otters to them. Hunters hats (see "Clothing") and *baidarkas,* small boats used for hunting, had carved ornaments on them that may have served as amulets (see "Transportation").

Russian Orthodox Church

The first Russian missionaries arrived in 1796. Soon after, many Unangan accepted the Russian Orthodox faith. A church was built on St. Paul in 1819, and the first permanent missions opened in 1824 on Unalaska and in 1825 on Atka.

The Unangan may have been drawn to the Catholic religion for several reasons. In the early years, church membership exempted people from paying tributes for three years (the Russians demanded a tribute, a certain amount of pelts due to the fur trading company). Also, the priests did not force the Unangan to give up their language or culture. Instead, they studied the language and conducted services in both Russian and Unangan.

The richness of the ceremonies likely appealed to the people, who had many rituals of their own. Churches and masses also emphasized art and music, two traditional Unangam interests. Church services and hymns became rituals of everyday life. The people remained faithful to the Christian religion; as of the 2000s, most Unangan were Russian Orthodox, and the church remained a central part of community life.

LANGUAGE

The Unangam language had two main branches: the Eastern and Western. The Western was further subdivided into two main dialects, Atkan and Attuan. Attuan had become nearly extinct by the late 1900s, but Atkan was still being spoken. The Eastern dialect, Unalaskan, is used on the Alaskan Peninsula and on various islands.

Before the Russians arrived, the Unangan had no written language. By the 1800s, the Russian priest Ivan Veniaminov (1797–1879) had developed a writing system based on Cyrillic script. Although many people learned this system, they later stopped using it because the letters were so unusual. The Unangan also adopted quite a few Russian words into their language.

By the twenty-first century, *Unangam Tunuu,* the Aleut language, was endangered. Fewer than one hundred people could speak it. To preserve and revitalize their language, the Aleutian Pribilof Islands Association (APIA), founded in 1976, began recording speakers and translating written material into two major dialects: *Niiɫuɫ im Tunuu* (Atka dialect) and *Qagaaadan Tunuu* (Eastern dialect). APIA also developed language-learning materials for lessons and classrooms.

Unangan Words

The people call their language *Unangam Tunuu.* Many words in the language have many suffixes, which makes them long. Most sentences have a similar structure to English; the usual order is subject-object-verb.

qas	"fish"
tanĝaaĝim	"bear"
alax̂	"whale"
tiĝlax̂	"eagle"
sabaakax̂	"dog"
uskaanax̂	"rabbit"

GOVERNMENT

Traditional leadership

Most people in a village were related, and a chief and a council of elders were responsible for the group's welfare. The chiefs, called *toyons* (or *toions*), protected their people's hunting boundaries and led their warriors during battle. Before declaring war or passing judgment for a crime, the chief met with all the other toyons on the island. Villages sent representatives to the council meetings. These leaders were chosen for their wisdom, bravery, and hunting abilities.

The position of chief was not hereditary, but a son or nephew often took over when the chief died. To hold the position, though, the new leader had to prove himself worthy. Otherwise, another man, usually a great hunter, was chosen in his place. Although chiefs were honored and respected, they received no special privileges.

Russian and American takeovers

After the Russians arrived, they declared the Unangan to be Russian citizens and set up the Russian-American Company as the main authority. The company managers chose three chiefs rather than one, which diluted the chiefs' power, and the Russians reserved the right to appoint or remove the chiefs from office. Under that system, the company stripped the chiefs of their authority to settle disputes if either party was Russian or Creole. Instead, the Unangan leaders were put in charge of recruiting and organizing company workers. Some chiefs were given extra pay for policing the work force.

This trend continued under the Americans, who bought Alaska from the Russians in 1867. The fur-trading companies who leased the Aleutian Islands from the United States took over the decision-making for the Unangan. They kept them in a dependent position by controlling their finances and freedom.

Present-day authority

Through all the centuries of domination, the Unangan still looked to their main chiefs to make decisions for the community and settle disputes. After the Alaska Native Claims Settlement Act (ANCSA) passed in 1971, the Aleut Corporation became one of the thirteen regional Native corporations set up under its terms. The government gave the Aleut Corporation $19.5 million, 66,000 acres of land, and 1.572 million acres of subsurface property. The corporation oversees thirteen village corporations, which have presidents.

In addition, the Unangan in 1976 established the Aleutian Pribilof Islands Association (APIA), a nonprofit company that secures government and private funding to support social services and strengthen economic development throughout the region. Each of the thirteen Unangan tribal communities appoints a representative to the board of directors.

ECONOMY

For thousands of years, the Unangan supported themselves with the rich natural resources available along their coasts. Marine mammals and fish provided the mainstay of their subsistence lifestyle, along with some gathering. After the Russians arrived, many Unangan were enslaved and forced to fish or hunt for their captors. Families left without a father often had inadequate food. That, coupled with the harsh treatment of the Unangan and the spread of disease, led to a sharp decline in the population. Rather than remaining in their traditional villages, most people were moved close to Russian ports and trading posts.

Russian conservation practices helped maintain thriving seal colonies. By the time the Americans took over, the seal population was estimated to be more than two million. The Americans, however, exploited the natural resources. By the early 1900s, many food supplies had been depleted. Sea otter and codfish almost disappeared. Some Unangan worked on fox or sheep farms; others found work as longshoremen or construction workers. Most, though, still depended on the sea for their livelihoods, and this remained the primary occupations throughout the twentieth century. The major industries in the twenty-first century continue to be fishing and seafood canning. Cod, salmon, and halibut are the mainstays of economy.

DAILY LIFE

Families

In the early days, several clans lived together in a village. Each home usually held a few related families. A man and his wife, or wives, and their children often lived with the eldest son and his family. The man's younger brother and family might also live in the home, and so might a nephew, his sister's son, whom he would train and who might later marry his daughter.

Buildings

Traditional homes Archaeologists have uncovered several ancient building sites. Many ancient Unangan made their homes of whalebones and boulders. Inside, families dug into the floor to create a hearth and storage pits lined with stones or clay. Other Unangam groups constructed houses of driftwood and sod over whalebone frames. Summer camp sites show depressions that may have held tents or other portable structures.

To build their homes, called *barabaras,* the Unangan excavated about 3 to 5 feet (1 to 1.5 meters) into the ground. The pit was often about 50 feet (15 meters) long and 20 feet (6 meters) wide. Some homes reached 240 feet (73 meters) by 40 feet (12 meters), and as many as forty families lived there. The people anchored driftwood or whalebones into the floor to support the roof and walls. Grass mats covered with sod formed the exterior of the home. Two square holes in the roof served as the window and door. To exit, the Unangan climbed a notched log that served as a ladder. These rooftop doors only allowed one person to enter or exit at a time, a fact the Russians took advantage of by luring the Unangan out and killing them one at a time.

Living areas in the interior of the house were separated by hanging woven grass mats. Mats also lined the floor. Some homes had benches and a raised platform for tanning hides. Large storage containers were usually waterproof and often made of animal intestines or of sealskin with the head and flipper holes tied shut. Other utensils included wooden buckets and dune-grass baskets. Some baskets were woven so tightly that they could hold water.

Fires were rare because the people usually ate their meat raw, but stone lamps holding seal or whale oil provided light.

Above-ground houses After the American fur-trading companies took responsibility for the economy of the Aleutian Islands, they provided supplies for frame homes. The Unangan did not want to move from their underground homes into above-ground homes that needed to be heated with coal or wood. To convince the people to do so, the Americans destroyed the barabaras. The Unangan built the wooden homes with company materials, but they did not own their homes, because the company held the titles.

Clothing and adornment

One of the most important items of clothing was the *kamleika,* a long coat made of sea mammal intestines. Some were made from cormorant or other bird skin. Some of these parkas had hoods with drawstrings.

These garments kept men dry when they went to sea, because the material was waterproof. Men often had their parkas stitched to their *baidarkas* (kayak-like boats; see "Transportation") when they went out hunting. The kamleika was decorated with bird feathers, fur, caribou hair embroidery, yarn, and even human hair.

Women wore *suks,* floor-length waterproof parkas made from sea otter intestines or sometimes from whale tongue. These parkas had collars that stood up to block the wind. They also had a special pouch on the back for carrying a baby. To stay warm, women donned coats of woven grass capes or of fur-seal with the fur inside. Mittens and foot coverings tightly woven from grass repelled water.

Boots were constructed from seal hide and had soles made sea lion flippers. The boots were often thigh high and waterproofed at the top with seal esophagus. People often carried their boots so they would not wear out. Most Aleutian Islanders preferred to go barefoot.

Belts had sacred meanings (see "Religion") for the Unangan. People tied them around their waists to protect themselves from attacks by enemies or animals. A belt made by a girl during her first menstruation was thought to cure illness. Dancers' belts might be adorned with fur seal tassels and caribou embroidery.

Men wore special wooden hats or visors for whaling and hunting (see "War and hunting rituals"). Women's hats for ceremonies were round caps that looked like Russian sailors' hats, but they were made from intestine and decorated with embroidery and fringes of painted seal esophagus. These waterproof hats sometimes covered cloth caps worn underneath. Men wore hats of similar shape, but they might be made of leather with fur, yarn, and embroidery.

Clothing was dyed using natural materials, such as flowers, plants, and soil. A sparkling black dye was created from volcanic minerals mixed with octopus bile.

An Aleut couple is depicted wearing traditional costumes in an 1889 engraving.
© MEDIACOLOR'S/ALAMY.

The Unangan tattooed their faces and hands. Before Russian contact, they pierced their babies' lower lips and inserted an ivory labret (a barbell-shaped stud). Their ears were also pierced.

Food

The Unangan took advantage of the rich natural resources of the seas around them. Seals, otters, whales, sea lions, walruses, and porpoises provided food, oil, clothing, and tools. The waters supplied a variety of fish and shellfish. The people ate few land animals, although caribou, reindeer, fox, and sea birds were sometimes added to their diets. Men climbed the cliffs to the rookeries for ducks, geese, and their eggs. These were divided among all the villagers.

Because the Unangan lived in such a damp climate, they had trouble drying food, so meat had to be eaten soon after it was caught. Meat was usually eaten raw. Only when preparing for feasts did the people store food.

Women gathered cranberries and other berries in addition to plants such as anemone greens and roots, lily bulbs, cowslip, wild celery and parsnips, and kelp. They also collected greens found along the beach, and men brought home seaweed. These plant products were an important food source when meat was scarce. Seal oil was used to flavor the food; it also provided important nutrients.

Later, the Americans introduced rice, potatoes, and dried fruit, which the Unangam people added to their meals. With sea mammal hunting restricted, most Unangan came to rely on halibut and salmon, geese and ptarmigan, shellfish, reindeer, and berries and plants.

Transportation

Life along the coastline meant boats were vital to early travelers. The Unangan developed *baidarkas,* small skin boats that were light enough to be carried in one hand. The boats were made of seal or sea lion skins over a driftwood frame. They usually had one round opening, although some had two holes—one for the hunter and one for a paddler. Men often had their *kamleikas* (waterproof parkas; see "Clothing") sewn to the opening to keep themselves dry. Later boats sometimes had three openings. Historians have suggested these boats were made for the Russians, who could not manage the boats well; they may have been designed so that a Russian could sit between two Unangam paddlers. Longer and thinner than kayaks, baidarkas were easy to maneuver, and Unangam sailors could navigate them well even in dense fog.

Women and families traveled in larger open boats made of walrus skins over driftwood frames. These *baidaras,* as the Russians called them, could hold up to forty people.

Most villages are accessible only by sea or air, so modern Unangan travel by plane. All villages have a landing strip or airport.

Education

Russian church schools In 1825, the Russian Orthodox priest Ivan Veniaminov started the first school on Unalaska. Before that, families taught their children all the skills they needed to be successful adults. As they got older, nephews would be trained by their mother's brother and then marry his daughter (see "Marriage").

In addition to giving religious instruction, Veniaminov taught the Unangan the skills they needed to work for the fur-trading companies. He also added art, music, Russian language, and Aleut language lessons to the curriculum. To teach people to read, Veniaminov had to develop an Aleut alphabet (see "Language"). Even the adults learned to read and speak Russian, and Veniaminov noted that the Unangan were quick learners.

American education Later, when the American fur-trading company took over on the Pribilof Islands (see "History"), more schools were opened. Once again the people proved to be good students, and the adults learned English. (Many older Unangan can speak three languages—Russian, English, and Aleut.)

Because the new schools worked to assimilate the Unangam students (make them more like mainstream Americans), encouraging them to forget the Russian language and church teachings, many parents objected. Unangam parents worried that their children would lose an important part of their culture and religion. By 1873, only a few students attended the American schools.

The government began arresting parents who did not send their children to school. The truant students were also punished. One account recorded by Dorothy M. Jones in her report to the government, later published in *A Century of Servitude: Pribilof Aleuts under U.S. Rule,* told of a father who was arrested by a treasury agent:

[The agent] put handcuffs on, and lodged him (the father) in the cellar of the company's house, a very cold, damp place, and kept him four days on bread and water, and during all this time the son had been confined in a dark closet in the company's house and kept on bread and water.

Even confining the parents did not always work, so the company imposed a fine for every school day a child missed. The money was deducted directly from the parents' company account (see "History"). Most parents eventually gave in and sent their children to the American school, but unlike in earlier years, the students did poorly and refused to learn.

Education today After a century of being taught to deny their culture, Unangam students are now learning to respect their heritage. The Aleutian Pribilof Islands Association (APIA) holds a culture camp every year, at which children learn traditional arts, songs, and dances as well as their language. APIA also provides materials for classrooms to help students become fluent in *Unangam Tunuu*.

Healing practices

Because they mummified their dead (see "Death and mourning"), the Unangan had a knowledge of medicine and anatomy. Sometimes, they even performed autopsies. To alleviate pain, they practiced piercing. On Atka Island, they pinched the skin together around an aching joint and sewed through it with thread covered in gunpowder. The Unangan also used bloodletting, making a cut to let out "bad blood." They may have copied this from the Russians in the eighteenth century.

Most families could cure simple physical ailments with various plants. For example, crushed yarrow leaves and anemone root juice stopped bleeding. Cow parsnip leaves heated in water relieved achy muscles. Tea made from the wild iris root worked as a laxative.

More complicated healing, though, was done by shamans (pronounced *SHAH-munz* or *SHAY-munz*). These healers cured illness by dancing, singing, and drum-playing. The Unangan believed their shamans had a connection to the spiritual world that gave them special powers. Shamans not only healed but also foretold the future and provided amulets, or good luck charms, for protection or better hunting. When epidemics introduced by the Russians and Americans killed many people, shamans lost their power and respect in the Unangan community because they could not control the rapid spread of these diseases.

ARTS

Collectors prized Unangam baskets, which were tightly woven and decorated with embroidered designs. Some made of white or light-colored grasses with colored designs looked almost like pottery from a distance because they were shaped like bottles or lidded jars. To create them, women had to keep the dune grass wet and weave the more complicated shapes upside down. Many baskets had such a tight weave that they could hold water. This same weave was also used for mittens and foot coverings to make them waterproof.

Dance masks, carved and decorated with beards and mustaches to look realistic, were worn for *ukamax,* or plays that were presented during feasts and gift-giving. The performers reenacted battles, hunts, and legends to the music of drums and songs (see sidebar, "Song of an Atkan Aleut"). Men and women danced at winter festivals in colorful costumes, swinging rattles made from inflated seal stomachs, to the beat of the drums. After the ceremony, the performers destroyed the masks and drums or put them in caves because they could only be used once.

Unangam hunters made special hats with visors that protected their eyes from the sun's glare. These hats were shaped from wood to curve around the head. Painted bright colors, the hats were adorned with bones and sea lion whiskers (see "War and hunting rituals").

Traditional Unangam Values

A Russian priest who helped record the Unangam language, Father Ivan Veniaminov, spent from 1825 to 1834 with the people. During that time, he recorded details of the Unangam culture. He listed the main principles the Unangan followed before missionaries introduced them to Christianity:

Respecting and caring for parents

Strictly observing family structure

Respecting and caring for all elders

Assisting the poor

Being modest, humble, and merciful to the less fortunate

Extending hospitality to strangers

Listening rather than speaking

Being brave and fearless

Avoiding behavior and actions that hurtothers or the environment

CUSTOMS

Social organization and family life

Villages were divided along kinship lines, but they cooperated with each other to hunt or defend their territory. The Unangam people stressed loyalty to relatives and respect for parents. The traditional code of values also emphasized caring for elders (see sidebar, "Traditional Unangam Values"). Following these family values is still important to the people today, because most villagers continue to have strong kinship ties.

Unangan society had several classes—honorables, commoners, and slaves, or *kalgi*. Chiefs came from the highest level of society, the honorables. This upper class received better space in the longhouses and had more elaborate burials. They also owned slaves, who did the menial labor and protected their masters. Most slaves were captured during warfare or raids. If their fathers were free, the children of slaves would also be free. Those fathered by slaves remained part of the slave class.

Birth and childrearing

Because water gave strength, parents bathed newborns in the sea. The parents chose an elder in their family to be the baby's godparent. The godparent made sure the child was raised properly and received all that he or she needed. This relationship was called *anaaqisagh*. Godparents took it personally whenever someone criticized the child. In later life children helped their godparents.

By age eight, boys learned to make and use tools and weapons. An uncle or male relative on his mother's side taught the boy to hunt, fish, and fight. Girls learned to cook, sew, weave, and gather plants.

Puberty

Girls were secluded during their first menstruation for thirty days. They were then tattooed on their chins. By age thirteen, girls were ready for marriage, even if they had not reached puberty, if they were competent in household chores.

At about age fifteen, boys often had visions of animals or other beings. They needed to submit to these spirits. By age eighteen, if they had become good hunters, young men were ready to marry.

Marriage

A man usually worked for his future wife's parents for a year or two. He often married his uncle's (mother's brother) daughter, called his cross-cousin. Once the couple married, they usually lived with the wife's parents until their first child was born. They then moved to the man's family home unless his wife's parents needed more help than his family did.

Both men and women could have more than one spouse, usually the sisters or brothers of their first spouse. Male transvestites were accepted in the community if they did women's work.

Death and mourning

Ancient burial sites show that some Unangan preserved the bodies of their dead in caves or rock crevasses. Archaeologists have found both male and female mummies buried with their possessions. The Unangan put dishes, baskets, mats, fishing nets, combs, and clothing in the graves. Burials of warriors included slat armor, shields, and kayaks. Slaves were killed to accompany their owners into the afterlife.

Pits were another common burial spot. Bodies were placed in a flexed position. In some areas, the Unangan wrapped corpses with mats and placed them in sarcophagi, or wooden boxes made of driftwood.

Usually, only honorables (see "Social organization and family life") and beloved children were mummified. The Unangan took out the organs, cleaned the body in a cold stream, stuffed it with oiled moss or dried grass, and wrapped it furs or bird skin. After tying matting around it, they hung the mummy in a dry cave.

Mourners fasted, gave away possessions, and sometimes committed suicide. Spouses mourned for sixty days. For a death at sea, mourning lasted thirty days. The Unangan believed the "shadows" or souls of the dead stayed with the living, so people called on them when they were in danger.

War and hunting rituals

Before the Russian arrived, the Unangan fought amongst themselves. They also battled with and raided other groups. War captives were sometimes tortured and killed, but many became slaves, particularly women.

The Unangan worked together to capture sea mammals. First, they surrounded their prey in their *baidarkas* (see "Transportation"). The hunters then used throwing boards to hurl barbed darts at small sea mammals or to harpoon larger animals with spears. The throwing boards steadied their weapons and added distance to their throws. A line attached to the darts or spears allowed the men to pull the animal close to the boat so they could club it to death. The person whose spear landed closest to the head owned the animal.

Festivals

Every spring, the people had ceremonies when they caught the first whale. Most celebrations, though, were held in the winter. People gathered to dance, feast, and play games. The villages also shared stories and songs about their ancestors.

Masks were used for ceremonial dances, but they were destroyed afterward.

CURRENT TRIBAL ISSUES

The Unangam people have faced many environmental difficulties over the years. Overharvesting of sea mammals and fish caused some species to become endangered. In 1983, Congress passed the Fur Seal Act Amendments. The government no longer controlled the Pribilof Islands seal harvests. Instead, the community took over management of the seal population. Within two years, St. Paul stopped all commercial harvests. It is now illegal to own seal pelts, and individuals may only kill seals for subsistence (food necessary to stay alive).

In addition to the large-scale depletion of their traditional food supplies from overharvesting, the Unangan have been affected by other disasters that continue to have an impact on their communities. For example, in the 1960s, the U.S. Atomic Energy Commission set up a nuclear testing facility on Amchitka. Three major nuclear bombs were exploded, including the five-megaton "Cannikan" bomb, which in 1971 created the largest underground nuclear explosion in American history. Although the nuclear facility closed in 1994, the cleanup of the radioactive, chemical, and toxic waste remains ongoing.

In 2011, the Unangan faced several other environmental concerns. One of these was PSP, or paralytic shellfish poisoning, caused by a toxin found in clams, scallops, mussels, cockles, and some crabs. If people eat the poisoned shellfish, their chest and abdominal muscles become paralyzed. Unable to breathe, victims can die in as little as thirty minutes. In 2009, the Environmental Protection Agency (EPA) funded a two-year program to test shellfish on the Alaskan beaches. That support ended in 2011, so the Unangan are at risk if they eat untested seafood. To protect themselves, communities must plan group harvests. Prior to the scheduled event, they have to capture samples of the shellfish and send them to a testing laboratory. If the tests show low levels of PSP, the harvest can proceed. Otherwise, the harvest is cancelled.

Another major concern occurred during a nuclear meltdown in Japan following the 2011 earthquake and tsunami. Because many of the Aleutian Islands are only a short distance from Japan, the atmosphere had to be monitored to be sure excess levels of radioactive material did not reach Alaska.

NOTABLE PEOPLE

Singer, actor, and director Jane Lind (1950–) founded the Native American Theater Ensemble in the 1970s. She has appeared in movies and plays and on television. Other notable Unangan include sculptors John Hoover (1919–2011), Bill Prokopiof (1944–1999), and Alvin Amason (1948–).

BOOKS

The Aleut Relocation and Internment during World War II: A Preliminary Examination. Anchorage, AK: Aleutian/Pribilof Islands Association, 1981.

Black, Lydia. *Aleut Art: Unangam Aguqaadangin.* Anchorage, AK: Aleutian/Pribilof Islands Association, 2003.

Braje, Todd J., and Torben C. Rick. *Human Impacts on Seals, Sea Lions, and Sea Otters: Integrating Archaeology and Ecology in the Northeast Pacific.* Berkeley: University of California Press, 2011.

Crowell, Aron L. *Living Our Cultures, Sharing Our Heritage: The First Peoples of Alaska.* Washington, DC: Smithsonian Books, 2010.

Doherty, Craig A., and Katherine M. Doherty. *Arctic Peoples.* New York: Chelsea House, 2008.

Laut, Agnes C. *Pioneers of the Pacific Coast: A Chronicle of Sea Rovers and Fur Hunters.* Victoria, British Columbia: TouchWood Editions, 1915, rep. 2011.

Lubischer, Joseph. *The Baidarka as a Living Vessel: On the Mysteries of the Aleut Kayak Builders.* Port Moody, British Columbia: Baidarka Historical Society, 1988.

Oleksa, Michael J. *Alaskan Missionary Spirituality.* 2nd ed. Crestwood, NY: St. Vladimir's Seminary Press, 2010.

Reedy-Maschner, Katherine L. *Aleut Identities* Kingston, Ontario: McGill-Queens University Press, 2010.

Williams, Maria ShaaTláa. *The Alaska Native Reader: History, Culture, Politics.* Durham, NC: Duke University Press, 2009.

WEB SITES

Alaska Native Collections. "Unangan."*Smithsonian Institution.* http://alaska.si.edu/culture_unangan.asp (accessed on August 15, 2011).

Aleutian Pribilof Islands Association. http://www.apiai.com/cultural_heritage.asp?page=culturalheritage (accessed on August 15, 2011).

"Alutiiq and Aleut/Unangan History and Culture."*Anchorage Museum.* http://www.anchoragemuseum.org/galleries/alaska_gallery/aleut.aspx (accessed on August 15, 2011).

Anderson, Dana G. "Aleut Images."*State of Alaska and Alaska Pacific University.* http://www.alaskool.org/projects/traditionalife/Aleutian_Chain/Text.htm (accessed on August 15, 2011).

"Culture& History." *Aleut Corporation.* http://www.aleutcorp.com/index. php?option=com_content&view=section&layout=blog&id=6&Itemid=24 (accessed on August 15, 2011).

Veniaminov, Ivan. "Song of an Atkan Aleut." *Notes on the Atkin Aleuts and the Koloshi.* Reprinted in "Cultural Change in the Aleutian Islands: Contact with Another Culture," by Mary Ann Hanak. *University of Alaska Fairbanks.* http://www.ankn.uaf.edu/ancr/aleut/culturalchange/append.a-f.html (accessed on August 15, 2011).

Jones, Dorothy M. "A Century of Servitude: Pribilof Aleuts under U.S. Rule."*University of Connecticut.* http://arcticcircle.uconn.edu/HistoryCulture/ Aleut/Jones/ch2.html (accessed on August 15, 2011).

Lienhard, John H. "Ivan Veniaminov."*Engines of Our Ingenuity.* http://www. uh.edu/engines/epi668.htm (accessed on August 15, 2011).

Museum of the Aleutians. http://www.aleutians.org/index.html(accessed on August 15, 2011).

Martinson, Charles."Unangan/Aleut Culture."*Unimak Area of Alaska.* http:// unimak.us/ethnography.shtml (accessed on August 15, 2011).

National Park Service. "Aleutian World War II: Evacuation and Internment." *U.S. Department of the Interior.* http://www.nps.gov/aleu/historyculture/ unangan-internment.htm (accessed on August 15, 2011).

Redish, Laura, and Orrin Lewis. "Aleut Language (Unangan, Aleutian, Atkan)."*Native Languages of the Americas.* http://www.native-languages.org/ aleut.htm#language (accessed on August 15, 2011).

"Unangax& Alutiiq (Sugpiaq)." *Alaska Native Heritage Center.* http://www. alaskanative.net/en/main_nav/education/culture_alaska/unangax/ (accessed on August 15, 2011).

Yup'ik

Name

Yup'ik (pronounced *YOU-pik*), or Yupiaq, applies not only to the people but also to the language. It comes from two words—*yuk*, meaning "person" or "human being," and *pik*, meaning "real." The plural is *Yupiit*, the "real people." When *Yup'ik* is spelled with the apostrophe, it refers only to the Central Alaskan Yup'ik and shows that the "p" sound is long. The Siberian and Naukanski Yupik do not use the apostrophe. The Central Alaskan Yup'ik who live on Nunivak Island call themselves *Cup'ig* (plural *Cup'it*). Those who live in the village of Chevak call themselves *Cup'ik* (plural *Cup'it*). Their names for themselves also mean "real people."

Location

The Yup'ik live in western, southwestern, and south-central Alaska and the Russian Far East. Although the ancestors of the Yupik in Russia may have once inhabited a large territory along the Bering and Arctic Sea coasts, in the early twenty-first century, they reside mainly in three small areas—Naukan, Chaplino (Central Siberian Yupik), and Sireniki.

Population

Before the Europeans arrived, the estimated population in Nunivak was 500; in Yukon-Kuskokwim, 13,000; and in Bristol Bay, 3,000. According to statistics from the U.S. Bureau of the Census, the population count for Yup'ik in 2000 was 21,937; in 2010, it was 28,927. Prior to European contact, the Sugpiaq numbered around 20,000; afterward, their numbers fell to less than 5,000. The 2000 census showed 2,355 Sugpiaq. About 1,700 Yupik were living in Russia in the early twenty-first century.

Language family

Eskimo-Aleut.

Origins and group affiliations

About six thousand years ago, the Inupiat spread through much of the Arctic and Greenland. The Alutiiq (or Sugpiaq), Aleut (see entries), and Yup'ik descended from the Inupiat. Groups such as the Tlingit, Haida (see entries),

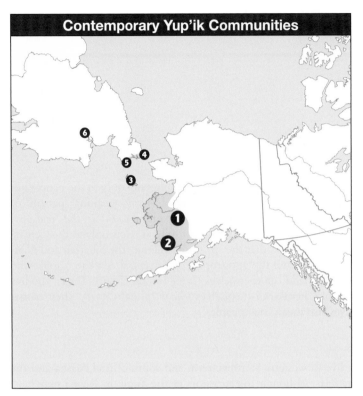

Contemporary Yup'ik Communities

Alaska
1. Alutiiq, or Sugpiaq (25 occupied villages)
2. Central Yup'ik (63 occupied villages)
3. Siberian Yup'ik

Russia
4. Naukan
5. Chaplino
6. Sireniki

Shaded area
☐ Traditional lands of the tribes of the Yup'ik in present-day Alaska and Siberia

A map of contemporary Yup'ik communities. MAP BY XNR PRODUCTIONS. CENGAGE LEARNING, GALE. REPRODUCED BY PERMISSION OF GALE, A PART OF CENGAGE LEARNING.

Athabascan, and Eyak broke off from these earlier groups and became migrating hunters. In Russia, the Chukchi and Korak tribes moving north displaced the Siberian Yupik, and the Yupik engaged in frequent warfare with the Chukchi (Anqallyt). In modern times, the groups that speak related branches of the Eskimo-Aleut language include Sugpiaq, Central Yup'ik, Naukan or Naukanski Yupik, and Siberian Yupik. The Sirenikski of Siberia are sometimes included in that grouping, but their language and culture are now almost extinct.

The Arctic has many diverse habitats, and the people who dwell there are as unique as their landscapes. Spread across great distances, many Yup'ik villages are cut off from their neighbors and cannot be reached by land, except in winter. The nearest town may be hundreds of miles away, so people rely on boats or planes for outside contact. This isolation, however, has helped the Yup'ik maintain their way of life for centuries without interference from outsiders. Throughout the late twentieth and early twenty-first centuries, however, they have adapted to many changes. Small towns have replaced winter communities, and jobs for wages or government funds have replaced the subsistence lifestyle for many. In spite of modernization, however, the Yup'ik have retained much of their traditional culture, religion, and language.

HISTORY

Ancient history

Researchers believe Siberian hunters were the first humans in the Americas. During the Ice Age, Native Americans likely crossed a land bridge across what is now the Bering Sea in pursuit of animals. When the ice melted, the seas rose and covered the strip of land between Alaska and Siberia. The earliest artifacts found in Alaska are about twelve thousand years old.

The Inupait culture developed in western Alaska about six thousand years ago. These peoples spread south and west to the Aleutian Islands and as far east as Greenland. They and their descendants—the Alutiiq, Aleut (see entries), and Yup'ik—hunted sea animals and, occasionally, caribou. Oral traditions and artifacts indicate that there were clashes as well as frequent trade among these groups and with those in the Pacific Northwest. Some Alaskan Athabaskan (see entry) men traveled as far as Siberia to obtain coral jewelry for their brides.

Pre-European contact

For centuries, the Yup'ik lived in groups called *tungelquqellriit* ("those who share ancestors"). People in the group were part of an extended family of several generations living together. Each group had its own dialect (variety of language), social and religious ceremonies, and seasonal routine of hunting, fishing, and gathering. In times of war, neighboring societies became allies.

Russian arrivals

The first Alaskan contact with Europeans occurred in 1741 when the Danish-born explorer Vitus Bering (1681–1741) led a Russian expedition to the area. His mission was to see if Siberia and North America

Important Dates

1741: Vitus Bering leads first expedition to Alaskan territory.

1784: Russians establish a settlement on Kodiak Island.

1867: Alaska is sold to the United States.

1884: Congress passes the Alaska Organic Act, making Alaska a territory of the United States.

1959: Alaska becomes a state.

1971: The Alaska Native Claims Settlement Act (ANCSA) creates for-profit corporations to be owned by Natives, but not tied to any specific entities.

were part of the same continent. Although that was not the case, these explorers brought back sea otter furs.

Russian merchants soon funded fur-trading expeditions. At first, most traders did not establish settlements, and some traveled along the coast as far south as California. They enslaved Aleut hunters and forced them to bring in more furs. In 1784, the first Russian settlement was established on Kodiak Island, and the Russian American Company had the sole right to all fur trade. A fort at Sitka served as the Russian capital in the United States until Alaska was sold to the United States in 1867.

Russian Orthodox missionaries, hoping to convert the Natives, arrived soon after the fur traders. Because of their isolation, the Yup'ik were one of the last groups to come in contact with Europeans. The missionaries worked on Kodiak Island and then in the Yukon-Kuskokwim Delta, where they encountered the Yup'ik in the late 1800s. Although the Yup'ik accepted some Christian teachings, they also retained many elements of their traditional beliefs.

Lifeways change

In 1884, Presbyterian minister Sheldon Jackson (1834–1909) asked American churches to support his efforts to start schools. The Moravians (members of a Protestant church that originated in Moravia, present-day Czech Republic) opened Bethel mission in 1885, and the Catholics built Holy Cross in 1888. The missionaries tried to change Yup'ik life. They banned many traditional religious practices and insisted that families live together in homes of their own rather than living in separate men's and women's quarters.

At first, the Yup'ik did not comply, but after a measles outbreak killed many of their people, some agreed to the missionaries' demands. Because many children had lost their parents, the Catholics and Moravians opened orphanages. Although most parents were reluctant to send their children to mission schools, they had little choice once education became compulsory.

Then gold was discovered just north of Yup'ik territory in 1906. Within a few years, a trail opened from Seward to Nome. Mail and people could now reach the area, even in the winter. The first plane landed in Bethel in 1926, and contact with the outside world increased.

By 1950, the Bureau of Indian Affairs began flying students to distant high schools, where they stayed for nine months of the year. Parents worried that because their children were gone so long, they would not learn traditional skills. One family filed a lawsuit that led to the establishment of local high schools in 1976. In the early twenty-first century, all villages had schooling for kindergarten through twelfth grade.

Looking toward the future

In modern times, the Yup'ik, along with other native groups, are struggling to balance the many innovations of modern society with traditional culture and values. New technology such as snowmobiles, outboard motors, CB radios, and telephones have made life easier, but they have also increased pollution and altered the environment.

Other changes have resulted from the Alaska Native Claims Settlement Act (ANCSA), passed in 1971. Under this act, Alaskan Natives gave up their rights to any future land claims. The people received 44 million acres and $962.5 million. The land, however, was divided among non-profit corporations, and the people were given shares. Although owning land conflicts with Native beliefs, the Yup'ik had to develop skills to run the corporations and follow government rules.

Since then, the people have worked together to improve their community economies. Various Yup'ik village corporations merged to lower their costs. One of the largest groups, Calista Corporation, represented fifty-six villages, many of them Yup'ik, At first, the group lost a great deal of money, but they have since turned the corporation into a profitable venture by combining the original towns into forty-five for-profit ANCSA village corporations.

These many rapid changes in such a short time have resulted in many social problems among Alaskan Natives. Alcoholism, suicide, and domestic violence are problems many Native communities currently face.

RELIGION

Traditional beliefs

The Yup'ik believed that everything had a soul. Souls never died; they instead entered a new body. For this reason, the people returned the seals' innards to the sea at the annual Bladder Festival (see "Festivals") and named new babies after someone who had recently died.

Because they believed dead animals would return, the people never broke the animals' bones, and they only cut the meat apart at the joints. To show their respect for the seals they caught, hunters offered them a drink of fresh water. After a man caught a whale, he treated it as a guest, entertaining it with drumming and music and offering it good foods. If the dead seal or whale was pleased, it would return, ensuring successful future hunts.

The Siberian Yupik considered many animals sacred. The killer whale, which they believed turned into a wolf in winter, protected hunters. At the end of ritual meals, the people threw a piece of meat into the sea to thank the killer whales who helped them by driving the walrus to shore. Before hunting boats departed, the Yupik held special ceremonies to placate the sea animals they were about to hunt. They also threw tobacco into the sea for the whales.

Amulets protected people against harm and insured successful hunts. Some of these small figures, such as walrus or dog heads, were carved from stone and worn by individuals. Hunters attached wooden whale carvings to their belts. Some people hung a carved raven's head in their homes for protection. In addition to Raven, who created the world, other sacred animals included the swallow and the spider.

Christian influence

In the late 1800s, Russian Orthodox missionaries arrived to convert the Yup'ik. Although other denominations, such as the Moravians and Catholics, later set up churches in Yup'ik territory, the Russian Orthodox influence remained strong. This is especially evident in the Yup'ik tradition of celebrating *Selaviq*, Russian Orthodox Christmas. This festival lasts for ten days and nights after January 7. People get together to sing, pray, and feast.

As a result of missionary influence, many people adopted Christianity. Some, such as the Sugpiaq, were forced into baptism to escape slavery. Those who accepted the Russian Orthodox religion and let the priest baptize them became Russian citizens. Russian fur traders could no longer force them to work as slaves. To prevent this, some traders imprisoned the priest so he could not baptize the Natives. Other Yup'ik accepted Christian teachings but combined them with their traditional beliefs.

LANGUAGE

The four main dialects of the language include Alutiiq (Sugpiaq), spoken on the coast of the Gulf of Alaska; Central Yup'ik, used on the Alaskan mainland and some offshore islands; Naukanski, with a few speakers on

Cup'ig Words

Yup'ik words are often more descriptive than English words. For example, an American might say someone is a liar. In Cup'ig (a Yup'ik dialect), different words may be used: *iqlungar-* is "to have a tendency to tell lies," whereas *iqluqu-* means "to lie constantly."

In English, people say they feel sick, but the Cup'ig word explains the circumstances. If a person uses the word *kiinguaqerte*, everyone not only knows that the speaker feels queasy, but that he or she has that "sudden eerie feeling from seeing someone with a large flesh wound." Americans might say someone is humming, but the Cup'ig word, *uyurua-*, means "to hum or sing a wordless tune, especially when going out in the morning to check the weather."

The Yupik can use one word to describe things precisely that take many words in other languages. An example would be in the way seals are identified. Not only does one word give the seal breed, it also pinpoints its gender and activities. Thus *qalzrir* is a "bull [male] bearded seal 'singing' under water" and *qamuqatag2* is a "mother bearded seal swimming with a cub on her back." A few other Cup'ig words and phrases are found below:

aana	"mother"
aang	"yes"
Cangacit?	"How are you?"
cass'ar	"clock"
elissar-	"to teach or study"
ellallug	"rain"
iqallii-	"to fish"
nacar	"hat"
napa	"tree"
quyana	"thank you"
Uss'ur	"Hey, you!"
wigtua-	"to try"
yaani	"over there"

the Siberian side of the Bering Strait; and Siberian Yupik, which is used on both St. Lawrence Island and in Chukotka in Siberia.

Central Yup'ik has the largest group of speakers. The two main dialects of the Central Yup'ik are Cup'iq (or Cup'ik) and Yup'ik. One-third of the children learn it as their first language. In modern times, though, most people in Alaska also speak English, especially the young. In Siberia, the majority of Yupik also speak Chukchi and Russian; some people believe these languages will eventually replace Yupik dialects.

Yup'ik was not written until a missionary, John Hinz, worked with some of the people to translate the Bible and other religious texts. In Siberia, most people learned to write Yupik using the Cyrillic alphabet, which is used to write Russian. In the 1960s, a group of Yup'ik met with scholars

A Yup'ik man holds a traditional seal-hunting harpoon.
© MARILYN ANGEL WYNN/
NATIVESTOCK PICTURES/CORBIS.

at the University of Alaska and updated their alphabet so it could be written on a keyboard.

GOVERNMENT

Most early settlements consisted of extended families or small groups of families. An individual's skills largely determined his social rank in the village. The most successful hunters, *nukalpiit*, usually became group leaders. Some Yupik traders used their wealth to gain positions as village chiefs. Most leadership roles were based on generosity and abilities. Although the Yup'ik did not have formal leadership, a chief might open and close the hunting season, mediate quarrels, and decide when to go on trade journeys. In the early twenty-first century, most villages have elected officials who work as part of tribal or city councils.

ECONOMY

Traditional Yup'ik economy was based on the sea. The people hunted seal, whale, and walrus from boats or from the shore with harpoons, and later guns. They also fished and dried their catch for winter, hunted fur-bearing land animals, and gathered plants and berries.

Coastal villages traded seal oil, herring eggs, and other products from the sea with villages further inland for moose, caribou, and furs. In the late 1800s, the people began trading with the Russians. Some peoples, such as the Sugpiaq, were enslaved and forced to work for the Russians. The Central Yup'ik traveled seasonally, migrating in search of game, fish, and plants.

The Siberian Yupik hunted sea mammals and fished. Some also bred reindeer cooperatively with their neighbors, the Chukchi. Under the Soviet government, new equipment and occupations were introduced to improve the economy. Soviet policies, however, also forced people to leave "unproductive" villages. This meant the Naukanski Yupik were made to leave their homeland and move to the mainland.

In modern times, many people still practice their subsistence lifestyle of hunting and fishing, but they find it harder to make a

Eskimo Branch of Eskimo-Aleut Speakers

Alutiiq, or Sugpiag

The Alutiiq, who speak Sugpiaq, live on Kodiak Island and around Prince William Sound in Alaska. The name Alutiiq came from the Russians, who mistook them for Aleuts, so many prefer to be called Sugpiaq. The majority of the people accepted the Russian Orthodox religion during the 1800s (often to escape slavery), and in the early twenty-first century, quite a few have Russian names.

The two Sugpiaq dialects and cultures, Koniag and Chugash, are quite different from each other. The Koniag live on Kodiak Island and the upper Alaska Peninsula. Before the Russians arrived, they were warlike. In modern times, the Koniag support themselves by fishing. The Chugash, though, were influenced by other groups such as the Tlingit, Aleut (see entries), Athabascan, and Eyak. At one time, they were skilled sea mammal hunters, but today, their five villages have become assimilated (more like mainstream American society).

In the early 2000s, about four hundred of the three thousand Sugpiaq spoke their native language, but the people have been working to restore their heritage.

Central Yup'ik

The largest group of Yup'ik speakers—thirteen thousand out of about eighteen thousand—is found in the southwestern area of Alaska. Some live along the Bering Sea; others live inland along the rivers. Many still fish and gather berries as their ancestors did, but more people have turned to wage labor to support themselves and their families. The Central Yup'ik have retained much of their culture because they were one of the last groups to have contact with the Europeans. In the 2000s, they have the most villages of

any Native group in the United States, although many of their villages are small.

Naukan or Naukanski Yupik

On the Russian side of the Bering Sea, Naukan was a large town dating from two thousand years ago. It was once a busy place with pit homes that housed as many as six hundred people. The homes were about 30 feet (9 meters) in diameter and had driftwood and whalebone roofs.

During Soviet times, the government closed down "unproductive" villages, so the people were relocated to the mainland. Of the remaining 350 people, only 75 spoke the Naukan language in 1990. By the early 2000s, the language was almost extinct.

Siberian Yupik

In Alaska, the Siberian Yupik live in two villages, Savoonga and Gambell, on St. Lawrence Island. Because they are only 50 miles (80 kilometers) from Siberia, they have close ties with the Russian Yupik. For many years, they could not communicate with relatives and friends because of the Cold War (1945–91; an intense political and economic rivalry between the United States and the Soviet Union falling just short of military conflict). In modern times, they continue to fish, hunt sea mammals, and gather berries and plants. They have kept their language vital; almost all children learn it from their parents.

In Siberia, the people are named for their main village, Chaplino, and they and their language were called *Yuit*, a name assigned by the Soviet Union in 1931. The Yuit live along the coast of the Chukchi Peninsula in the northeastern area of Russia.

In Alaska, about 1,050 of the 1,100 Siberian Yupik speak their Native language. In Russia, only 300 of the 1,200 to 1,500 people speak Siberian Yupik.

living. Most villages are hundreds of miles from towns, so people must leave their homes and move to cities to work for wages. Those who stay in their villages sometimes face poverty and must rely on government aid.

DAILY LIFE

Families

Most groups were family-based clans, each with their own seasonal patterns and lifestyles. Society was patrilineal (descent traced through the father). In a life geared toward survival, cooperation played an important role in both community and family life.

Respect for elders was also important. Older people who were feeble and needed to be cared for like babies and those whose minds reverted to childhood were said to be moving to the next stage of life. They were preparing for rebirth. Family members considered it a privilege to chew up food and feed it to an elder who had lost his or her teeth.

Buildings

All males in a Yup'ik village lived together in a *qasgiq*, or men's house. Boys stayed with their mothers until they were about six years old. Then they joined the other men in this communal building. Women carried food to the qasgiq, and the building also served as a dance hall, meeting place, and community center.

Women and children lived in an *ena*, which was smaller than a qasgiq. Light came in through a skylight window made of seal or walrus intestine. One Yup'ik woman said that the windows made a lot of noise when it was windy. Both the qasgiq and the ena had a partially underground passageway that kept snow from blowing into the house. The women used this entrance to the ena for cooking. Food caches were built nearby; they were either on stilts to keep them out of reach of animals or in underground storage areas. Carved stone bowls held seal oil. When these were burning, they served as lamps.

To build sod houses, the Yup'ik dug a round hole about 3 to 4 feet (1 meter) deep and then made a frame from driftwood or whalebone. They cut sod and put it on the frame with the grass inside. More grass was sometimes added for insulation. The seal or walrus gut skylight could be removed as needed to make a smoke hole for the fire.

A Yup'ik sod house stands at the Alaska Native Heritage Center in Anchorage. © MARILYN ANGEL WYNN/NATIVESTOCK PICTURES/CORBIS.

In Russia, the early Yupik lived in dugouts of snow and ice (sometimes called igloos); later, walrus hide and plank tents served as homes. In the summer, the Yupik made rectangular homes of wood and stretched walrus skins over them. The roof sloped toward the rear. The people often piled rocks, large bones, or dirt mounds around the edges of the hides.

By the early twenty-first century, most Yup'ik lived in modern houses with electricity and central heating systems.

Tools and transportation

The tools a Siberian Yupik used for hunting dated back thousands of years. He went out in a *baidara*, a boat made of split walrus hides and used a toggling harpoon tied to a sealskin float. His whalebone clapper made a sound like a killer whale, which frightened walrus and seal onto land, where other hunters killed them with spears and clubs. The Yupik also used ice canes, bows and arrows, and snow goggles. They decorated many of their tools with special symbols for good luck in hunting.

The most important tool a Yup'ik woman used was a fan-shaped slate knife called a *uluaq*. She needed this for skinning animals and scraping hides. She also had sewing implements made from stone, bone, or walrus tusk.

For transportation, the Yup'ik used kayaks (one-person, closed canoes made of skin or leather), bidarkas (open, flat-bottomed boats), and whaleboats. On land, they used dog teams and sleds. Umiaks (boats made from walrus skins) are still used, but now instead of oars or sails, most boats have outboard motors. Land transportation is mainly by all-terrain vehicles and snowmobiles.

Clothing and adornment

Women used the skins of birds, fish, sea mammals, and land animals to make clothing. Hunting clothes had to be warm and waterproof. They usually made boots and mittens from sealskin. Grass insulated socks and served as waterproof thread. Furs such as muskrat made warm winter hats.

Fish skins and seal or walrus intestines were used for waterproof jackets and boots. Because animal intestines do not let liquid through, women washed and scraped the guts, then filled them with air and let them dry. Afterward, they sewed the strips together to make lightweight, see-through parkas. The process took a long time, but when a jacket was finished, it was water-repellent.

Sugpiaq whalers were often shamans (pronounced *SHAH-munz* or *SHAY-munz*) who used secret rituals and poisons. They wore special wooden hats to show their high status. These tall hats were ornately decorated and usually had a brim that shaded the shamans' eyes from the sun so they could spot whales more easily. Other than that, most shamans did not wear any special clothing and could only be distinguished by their pendants, tassels, and fringes.

Food

The Yup'ik diet centered around fish and sea mammals. They kept walrus and whale meat semi-cold so it fermented; then they boiled it. Walrus and seal meat might be dried in strips; seal was sometimes frozen. For a special treat, whale skin with pink blubber on it was eaten raw. Most people fed walrus to their dog teams. They turned the meat into *tuugtaq* (meatballs) and stored it in underground caches

In addition to sea mammals, men caught salmon, cod, halibut, and herring. Shellfish, large game (moose, caribou, and bear), birds, bird eggs, edible greens, and berries were also important. People also ate seaweed. Sometimes, they bartered for reindeer meat from inland people.

In modern times, many Yup'ik still follow the traditional hunting patterns of migrating with the seasons, but most people also supplement their diets with store-bought foods. Villages generally have grocery stores that sell canned and packaged goods. One item that is always well-stocked in stores is soda. The availability of soft drinks and candy has greatly increased the number of children who need to have their teeth filled or capped.

Because many people now eat large amounts of sugared foods, obesity (being very overweight) has become a major problem. The change in lifestyle has also contributed to this problem. People who were once very physically active are now using snowmobiles and planes. Children no longer have to haul water or chop wood, so they do not burn excess calories the way they once did. In the 2000s, many health professionals are encouraging Natives to return to their traditional diets.

Healing practices

Every village had a shaman. Most often, they were men, but women sometimes served in this role. Shamans could be good or evil. Those who were good healed illness, fought off curses, asked the spirits to provide necessities such as food and water, and helped hunters find animals. Evil shamans placed curses on people and could even kill them. Shamans who were suspected of casting evil spells were sometimes murdered.

ARTS

Carving

The Siberian Yupik are known for their ivory and whalebone carvings. Some of them create moving sculptures using pulleys to make scenes, such as walrus hunting or traditional dances, come alive.

Skillful carvers also used wood to create masks for winter dances. Some were very realistic looking, such as a wolf's head with its tongue protruding or other animal masks, including fox, bear, and caribou heads.

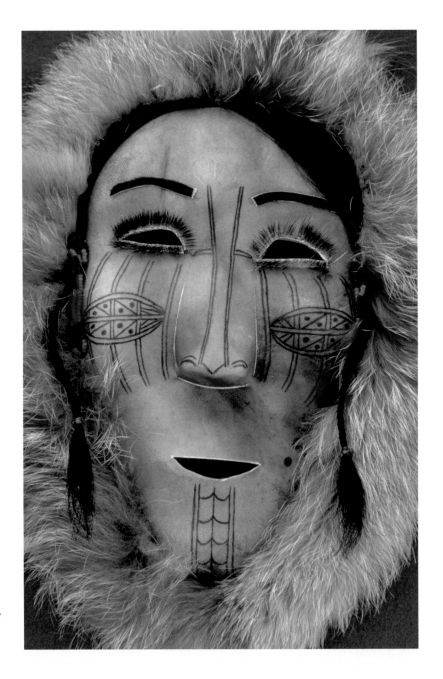

A Siberian Yupik dance mask is made from caribou hide.
© WOLFGANG KAEHLER/CORBIS.

Some masks represented spirits. Raven, the creator of the world in Yup'ik stories, often appears on these ceremonial masks. Although many of the subjects are the same, each mask tells a different story. Only the mask's creator could share the meaning behind the mask he had made.

Colors have special significance as well. Red, which means life or blood, can protect the wearer. Black often represents death or the after-life, and white might symbolize life or winter. Painted spots on the masks can stand for snowflakes, stars, or eyes. Most masks were made in pairs but, although they were similar, they never matched exactly.

Dance

Masked dancing took place during the winter in the *qasgiq* or men's house. To prepare, the Yup'ik carved masks under the direction of the shaman. They also created theatrical devices that they hung from the roof. Women sewed special costumes.

The people danced and sang to the beat of a drum. A musician held the drum in his left hand and beat it with thin wood rods called drum handles. These were usually highly decorated.

After the missionaries arrived in the late 1800s, they banned masked dancing, telling the people it was sinful. Although it is not done in

Yupik dancers perform in Russia wearing traditional dress. © PAT O'HARA/CORBIS.

modern times as often as it was in the past, some villages still get together during the cold months to dance. Most of the time, though, masks are no longer used. In the late 1990s, many of these masks were collected and shown in a traveling exhibition, *Agayuliyararput* ("Our Way of Making Prayer"), which also featured dancing and drumming.

CUSTOMS

Birth and naming

Pregnant women had to get up quickly and leave their homes each morning to guarantee that their labor would be short and that their babies would enter life quickly. Babies received the name of a relative who had recently died. The gender of the person did not matter. At the naming ceremony, a little water was put in the baby's mouth or on its head. The Yup'ik believed that the dead person's soul went into the child's body.

Puberty

Some Yup'ik tattooed the wrists of teens with the motif of a dot within a circle that represented an eye. This design not only helped to catch game, it also symbolized passing from one world into the next and enhanced the ability to see into the spirit world.

When menstruation began, a girl was isolated. To avoid spoiling the hunts, she stayed indoors. If she had to go out to go to the bathroom, she kept her hood up and her head bowed. After her first menses, a girl gave her dolls to a younger relative.

Marriage and divorce

The Yup'ik had arranged marriages, and pre-teen girls were often given in marriage. Because they married so young, many marriages did not last. Serial marriages were common and accepted, especially if the couple did not have any children. When they did have children, they kept strong kinship relationships with their former spouse's family.

Hunting rituals

Men used the smoke of wild celery, Labrador tea, and blackberry bushes before they hunted to give them the smell of the land and to attract animals. They also avoided women, since the female smell was said to repel game. They carried hunting fetishes (objects that represent the spirits of animals or the forces of nature) because these could help hunters sight game even at great distances. Tools often had the traditional design of a dot inside a circle painted on them. This represented an eye to help them see the animals. Men guarded their vision carefully so they would not miss seeing game. They practiced this by keeping their eyes lowered when talking to others and never looking at women.

War etiquette

In Siberia, warfare was common. Men made armor from double layers of toughened sealskin or from whalebone covered with sealskin. Shin guards were made from mammoth tusks. To cover their heads and upper bodies, they used wooden shields covered with dried animal skin.

Death rituals

When someone died, the Yup'ik first placed the corpse in each of the four corners of the house, then they pulled it through the smoke hole. Going through the smoke hole symbolized the passage between life and death. Afterward, they placed the body in a fetal position with knees to chest. They wrapped the arms around the knees and bound them together at the wrists. Because this is the position a baby takes in the womb, it showed that the dead person was ready to be reborn into another body. The Yup'ik then covered the corpse with driftwood or rocks. Sometimes they overturned a canoe or kayak with the body inside.

Festivals

The Yup'ik had five major traditional ceremonies that they celebrated each winter. Festivals began in November after the freeze-up. The first and most important of these was the Bladder Festival.

Bladder Festival The people believe that animals watch to see what happens to their bodies and bones. Game will only reappear to be hunted if the remains have been treated with respect. To show their respect for the animals they have killed, the Yup'ik held the Bladder Festival.

Because the Yup'ik believed bladders held the seals' souls, they hung them on the back wall of the men's house and treated them as honored guests. To start the festival, young boys had their bodies painted and went from house to house, where they were given food. Next, two older men (called "mothers") dressed up in gutskin parkas and led boys (called "dogs") around the village to collect bowls of *akutag* (a type of Alaskan ice cream).

During the five days of the festival, men purified themselves with sweat baths and with smoke from wild celery plants. No one worked; instead they competed in sports, sang songs, and feasted to entertain the seals. On the last night, everyone gathered in the men's house. Parents gave gifts to celebrate their children's achievements. Then a big giveaway was held; fish and seal oil were given out. This ensured that no one would go hungry during the long winter months.

Afterward, pairs of young men took the inflated bladders out the smoke hole to an opening in the ice. There they deflated them and returned them to their underwater home. Everyone hoped the seals would tell their kin how well they had been treated, so that many seals would let themselves be caught the following season.

Other celebrations The Feast for the Dead was a time to invite the spirits of the ancestors back for a feast. Children who had the names of deceased relatives wore clothing of that person's gender.

Before the Gift Festival, men made little replicas of things they wanted—grass socks, fish-skin mittens, bird-skin caps. They hung them from a stick and took them to the women. Women each chose one and made that item. When everyone gathered, the women gave the men their gifts, and the men had presents for the women. Since no one knew who had chosen their replicas, they had fun finding out who they were paired up with for the evening.

Messenger Feasts were a time to invite guests from another village to a dance and giveaway. Villages took turns hosting these and, when they did, they made up songs about each gift. One of the purposes of this festival was to ensure that everyone in the village received an equal share of wealth and food.

The last festival of the year was *Agayuyaraq*. The people sang songs to the animals and performed masked dances led by shaman. Masks with special powers were made for this ceremony and represented the various spirits, including the shaman's helper spirits. By remembering past spiritual encounters, the people hoped to attract them again in the future.

CURRENT TRIBAL ISSUES

The biggest difficulty the Yup'ik face is the erosion of their culture. Although modernization has benefited them, they have also suffered many losses to their traditions. It is sometimes difficult to strike a balance between the old and new. Perhaps Paapi Merlin Koonoka, an elder from St. Lawrence Island who is quoted in James H. Barker's book, *Always Getting Ready*, expressed it best: "And as I see it now, it is important for our children to get a modern education. By doing that they will be in a stronger position to preserve our culture and tradition."

One of the ways the people have been preserving their culture is through a grant from the National Science Foundation. Village elders are sharing their names for the places on maps of western Alaska. These names include historic sites and underwater channels as well as rivers, valleys, lakes, and hills. Along with the names, the Calista Elders Council is recording the stories behind the names so that this information can be passed along to the next generations. The maps can be viewed at http://mapserver.eol.ucar.edu/best.

NOTABLE PEOPLE

Angayuqaq Oscar Kawagley (1934–2011) taught at the University of Alaska. He was a member of the Executive Committee of the Inuit Circumpolar Conference and the writer of many articles on indigenous education. Another educator, Helen Slwooko Carius (1928–1998), overcame many hardships, including a childhood bout with polio, to become an internationally recognized Siberian Yupik doll maker. She wrote and illustrated two books—one on Yupik culture, the other a dictionary of her language. Storyteller Chuna McIntyre (1955–) is an artist and a musician who has performed throughout the world. He shares traditional stories he learned from his grandmother along with different sounds and images from the Yupik culture. He is also the founder and director of *Nunamfca* ("Of Our Land") Yup'ik Eskimo Dancers.

BOOKS

Ayagalria, Moses K. *Yupik Eskimo Fairy Tales and More*. New York: Vantage Press, 2006.

Barker, James H. *Always Getting Ready: Upterrlainarluta: Yup'ik Eskimo Subsistence in Southwest Alaska*. New York: University of Washington Press, 1993.

Barker, James H., and Ann Fienup-Riordan. *Yupiit Yuraryarait = Yup'ik Ways of Dancing*. Fairbanks: University of Alaska Press, 2010.

Charles, Nicholas and Maria. *Messenger Spirits: Yup'ik Masks and Stories*. Anchorage, AK: N & M, 2009.

Fienup-Riordan, Ann. *Wise Words of the Yup'ik People: We Talk to You Because We Love You*. Lincoln: University of Nebraska Press, 2005.

Fienup-Riordan, Ann, ed. *Yup'ik Words of Wisdom: Yupiit Qanruyutait*. Lincoln: University of Nebraska Press, 2005.

Guthridge, George. *The Kids from Nowhere: The Story Behind the Arctic Education Miracle*. Anchorage: Alaska Northwest Books, 2006.

Inupiaq and Yupik People of Alaska. Anchorage: Alaska Geographic Society, 2004.

Jenness, Aylette, and Alice Rivers. *In Two Worlds: A Yu'pik Eskimo Family*. New York: Houghton Mifflin, 1989.

Jolles, Carol Zane. *Faith, Food, and Family in a Yupik Whaling Community*. Seattle: University of Washington Press, 2002.

Kawagley, Angayuqaq Oscar. *A Yupiaq Worldview: A Pathway to Ecology and Spirit*. Long Grove, IL: Waveland Press, 2006.

Kerttula, Anna M. *Antler on the Sea: The Yupik and Chukchi of the Russian Far East*. Ithaca, NY: Cornell University Press, 2000.

Luehrmann, Sonja. *Alutiiq Villages under Russian and U.S. Rule*. Fairbanks: University of Alaska Press, 2008.

WEB SITES

Alaska Native Heritage Center. http://www.alaskanative.net/ (accessed on August 15, 2011).

Alaska Yup'ik Eskimo. http://www.yupik.com (accessed on August 15, 2011).

"Always Getting Ready: Yup'ik Eskimo Subsistence." *University of Tennessee: Frank H. McClung Museum*, 1999. http://mcclungmuseum.utk.edu/archives/eskimo/index.shtml (accessed on August 15, 2011).

"Arctic Circle: History and Culture." *University of Connecticut*. http://arcticcircle.uconn.edu/HistoryCulture/ (accessed on August 15, 2011).

Arctic Studies Center. "Agayuliyararput: Our Way of Making Prayer." *Smithsonian Institution National Museum of Natural History*. http://www.mnh.si.edu/arctic/features/yupik/index.html (accessed on August 15, 2011).

Cook, Franklin A. "Nunapitchuk, Alaska: A Yup'ik Eskimo Village in Western Alaska." *Anna Tobeluk Memorial School, Nunapitchuk, Alaska*. Lincoln: University of Nebraska Press, 2005.

"Peoples of Alaska and Northeast Siberia." *Alaska Native Collections*. http://alaska.si.edu/cultures.asp (accessed on August 15, 2011).

Redish, Laura, and Orrin Lewis. "Yupik (Alutiiq, Sugpiaq, Cup'ik, Chugach Eskimo)." *Native Languages of the Americas*. http://www.native-languages.org/yupik.htm (accessed on August 15, 2011).

"St. Lawrence Island Yupik (Siberian Yupik)." *University of Alaska Fairbanks*. http://www.uaf.edu/anlc/languages/sy/ (accessed on August 15, 2011).

"The Yup'ik and Cup'ik People—Who We Are." *The Alaska Native Heritage Center Museum*. http://www.alaskanative.net/en/main_nav/education/culture_alaska/yupik/ (accessed on August 15, 2011).

"The Yup'ik of Western Alaska." *University of Connecticut*. http://www.ucc.uconn.edu/~epsadm03/yupik.html (accessed on August 15, 2011).

"Yup'ik Tundra Navigation." *Center for Cultural Design*. http://www.ccd.rpi.edu/Eglash/csdt/na/tunturyu/index.html (accessed on August 15, 2011).

"Yuungnaqpiallerput: The Way We Genuinely Live." *Calista Elders Council*. http://www.yupikscience.org/ (accessed on August 15, 2011).

Where to Learn More

Books

Abel, Kerry. *Drum Songs: Glimpses of Dene History.* Montreal, Quebec: McGill–Queen's University Press, 1993.

Adams, Richard C. *A Delaware Indian Legend and the Story of Their Troubles.* Whitefish, MT: Kessinger Publishing, LLC, 2006.

Adamson, Thelma, ed. *Folk-tales of the Coast Salish.* Lincoln: Bison Books, 2009.

Aderkas, Elizabeth, and Christa Hook. *American Indians of the Pacific Northwest.* Oxford: Osprey Publishing, 2005.

Adil, Janeen R. *The Northeast Indians: Daily Life in the 1500s.* Mankato, MN: Capstone Press, 2006.

Agonito, Joseph. *Lakota Portraits: Lives of the Legendary Plains People.* Guilford, CT: TwoDot, 2011.

Agoyo, Herman, and Joe S. Sando, eds. *Po'pay: Leader of the First American Revolution.* Santa Fe, NM: Clear Light Publishing, 2005.

Akers, Donna L. *Culture and Customs of the Choctaw Indians.* Santa Barbara, CA: Greenwood, 2012.

The Aleut Relocation and Internment during World War II: A Preliminary Examination. Anchorage, AK: Aleutian/Pribilof Islands Association, 1981.

Alexander, Annie Lou. *Blood Is Red…So Am I.* New York: Vantage Press, 2007.

Alexie, Sherman. *The Absolutely True Diary of a Part-Time Indian.* Waterville, ME: Thorndike Press, 2008.

Alfred, Agnes. *Paddling to Where I Stand: Agnes Alfred, Kwakwaka'wakw Noblewoman.* Seattle: University of Washington Press, 2005.

Alger, Abby L. *In Indian Tents: Stories Told by Penobscot, Passamaquoddy and Micmac Indians.* Park Forest, IL: University Press of the Pacific, 2006.

Allen, John W. *Legends and Lore of Southern Illinois.* Carbondale: Southern Illinois University Press, 2010.

Andersen, Raoul R., and John K. Crellin. *Miśel Joe: An Aboriginal Chief's Journey.* St. John's, Newfoundland: Flanker Press, 2009.

Anderson, Jeffrey D. *One Hundred Years of Old Man Sage: An Arapaho Life.* Lincoln: University of Nebraska Press, 2003.

Andersson, Rani-Henrik. *The Lakota Ghost Dance of 1890.* Lincoln: University of Nebraska Press, 2008.

Angell, Tony, and John M. Marzluff. *In the Company of Crows and Ravens.* New Haven, CT: Yale University Press, 2007.

Anthony, Alexander E., Jr., David Neil Sr., and J. Brent Ricks. *Kachinas: Spirit Beings of the Hopi.* Albuquerque, NM: Avanyu Publishing, 2006.

Archer, Jane. *The First Fire: Stories of the Cherokee, Kickapoo, Kiowa, and Tigua.* Dallas, TX: Taylor Trade, 2005.

Arnold, Caroline, and Richard R. Hewett. *The Ancient Cliff Dwellers of Mesa Verde.* New York: Clarion Books, 2000.

Aron Crowell, ed. *Living Our Cultures, Sharing Our Heritage: The First Peoples of Alaska.* Washington, DC: Smithsonian Institution, 2010.

Augaitis, Daina, Lucille Bell, and Nika Collison. *Raven Travelling: Two Centuries of Haida Art.* Seattle: University of Washington Press, 2008.

Ayagalria, Moses K. *Yupik Eskimo Fairy Tales and More.* New York: Vantage Press, 2006.

Bahti, Mark. *Pueblo Stories and Storytellers.* 3rd ed. Tucson, AZ: Rio Nuevo Publishers, 2010.

Bahti, Mark, and Eugene Baatsoslanii Joe. *Navajo Sandpaintings.* 3rd ed. Tucson, AZ: Rio Nuevo Publishers, 2009.

Bailey, Garrick, ed. *Traditions of the Osage: Stories Collected and Translated by Francis la Flesche.* Albuquerque: University of New Mexico Press, 2010.

Baker, Wendy Beth. *Healing Power of Horses: Lessons from the Lakota Indians.* Irvine, CA: BowTie Press, 2004.

Ball, Eve, Nora Henn, and Lynda A. Sánchez. *Indeh: An Apache Odyssey.* Reprint. Norman: University of Oklahoma Press, 1988.

Ballantine, Betty, and Ian Ballantine, eds. *The Native Americans: An Illustrated History.* Atlanta: Turner Publishing, 1993.

Bancroft-Hunt, Norman. *People of the Totem: The Indians of the Pacific Northwest.* Photographs by Werner Forman. New York: Putnam, 1979.

Barbeau, Marius. *Huron and Wyandot Mythology.* Ottawa, Ontario: Government Printing Bureau, 1915.

Barbour, Jeannie, Amanda J. Cobb, and Linda Hogan. *Chickasaw: Unconquered and Unconquerable.* Ada, OK: Chickasaw Press, 2006.

Barker, James H., and Ann Fienup-Riordan. *Yupiit Yuraryarait = Yup'ik Ways of Dancing.* Fairbanks: University of Alaska Press, 2010.

Barkwell, Lawrence J. *Women of the Metis Nation.* Winnipeg, Manitoba: Louis Riel Institute, 2009.

Barnett, James F., Jr. *The Natchez Indians: A History to 1735.* Jackson: University Press of Mississippi, 2007.

Barrett, Samuel Alfred. *Ceremonies of the Pomo Indians and Pomo Bear Doctors.* University of California Publications in American Archeology and Ethnology. 1917. Reprint. Whitefish, MT: Kessinger Publishing, 2010.

— — —. *The Washo Indians.* 1917. Reprint. Charleston, SC: Kessinger Publishing, 2010.

Barron, Donna Gentle Spirit. *The Long Island Indians and their New England Ancestors: Narragansett, Mohegan, Pequot and Wampanoag Tribes.* Bloomington, IN: AuthorHouse, 2006.

Bartram, William, and Gregory A. Waselkov. *William Bartram on the Southeastern Indians.* Lincoln: University of Nebraska Press, 2002.

Basel, Roberta. *Sequoyah: Inventor of Written Cherokee.* Minneapolis, MN: Compass Point Books, 2007.

Bastedo, Jamie. *Reaching North: A Celebration of the Subarctic.* Markham, Ontario: Red Deer Press, 2002.

Bauerle, Phenocia, ed. *The Way of the Warrior: Stories of the Crow People.* Lincoln: University of Nebraska Press, 2003.

Bean, Lowell John, ed. "Introduction." In *The Ohlone Past and Present: Native Americans of the San Francisco Bay Region.* Menlo Park, CA: Ballena Press, 1994.

Bean, Lowell John, and Florence C. Shipek. "Luiseño." In *Handbook of North American Indians.* Vol. 8: *California,* edited by Robert F. Heizer. Washington, DC: Smithsonian Institution, 1978.

Bean, Lowell, Frank Porter, and Lisa Bourgeault. *The Cahuilla.* New York: Chelsea House, 1989.

Beasley, Richard A. *How to Carve a Tlingit Mask.* Juneau: Sealaska Heritage Institute, 2009.

Becenti, Karyth. *One Nation, One Year: A Navajo Photographer's 365-Day Journey into a World of Discovery, Life and Hope.* Los Ranchos, NM: Rio Grande Books, 2010.

Beck, Mary G. *Heroes and Heroines: Tlingit-Haida Legend.* Anchorage: Alaska Northwest Books, 2003.

Beckwourth, James. *The Life and Adventures of James P. Beckwourth, Mountaineer, Scout, and Pioneer, and Chief of the Crow Nation of Indians.* Paris, France: Adamant Media Corporation, 2005.

Behnke, Alison. *The Apaches.* Minneapolis, MN: Lerner Publications, 2006.

Behrman, Carol H. *The Indian Wars.* Minneapolis, MN: Lerner Publications, 2005.

Belting, Natalia. *Whirlwind Is a Spirit Dancing: Poems Based on Traditional American Indian Songs and Stories.* New York: Milk and Cookies Press, 2006.

Bergon, Frank. *Shoshone Mike.* New York: Viking Penguin, 1987.

Berleth, Richard. *Bloody Mohawk: The French and Indian War and American Revolution on New York's Frontier.* Hensonville, NY: Black Dome, 2009.

Betty, Gerald. *Comanche Society: Before the Reservation.* College Station: Texas A&M University Press, 2005.

Bial, Raymond. *The Chumash.* New York: Benchmark Books, 2004.

— — —. *The Cree.* New York: Benchmark Books, 2006.

— — —. *The Delaware.* New York: Benchmark Books, 2006.

— — —. *The Menominee.* New York: Marshall Cavendish Benchmark, 2006.

— — —. *The Tlingit.* New York: Benchmark Books, 2003.

Bibby, Brian. *Deeper than Gold: A Guide to Indian Life in the Sierra Foothills.* Berkeley: Heyday Books, 2004.

Bielawski, Ellen. *In Search of Ancient Alaska: Solving the Mysteries of the Past.* Anchorage: Alaska Northwest Books, 2007.

Birchfield, D.L., and Helen Dwyer. *Apache History and Culture.* New York: Gareth Stevens, 2012.

Biskup, Agnieszka. *Thunder Rolling Down the Mountain: The Story of Chief Joseph and the Nez Percé.* Mankato, MN: Capstone Press, 2011.

Bjorklund, Ruth. *The Cree.* Tarrytown, NY: Marshall Cavendish, 2009.

— — —. *The Hopi.* Tarrytown, NY: Marshall Cavendish Benchmark, c. 2009.

Blackbird, Andrew J. *History of the Ottawa and Chippewa Indians of Michigan.* Charleston, SC: Nabu Press, 2010.

Bodine, John. "Taos Pueblo." *Handbook of North American Indians,* Vol. 9: *Southwest.* Ed. Alfonso Ortiz. Washington DC: Smithsonian Institution, 1979.

— — —. *Taos Pueblo: A Walk Through Time.* Tucson, AZ: Rio Nuevo, 2006.

Bodinger de Uriarte, John J. *Casino and Museum: Representing Mashantucket Pequot Identity.* Tucson: University of Arizona Press, 2007.

Bogan, Phebe M. *Yaqui Indian Dances of Tucson Arizona: An Account of the Ceremonial Dances of the Yaqui Indians at Pascua.* Whitefish, MT: Kessinger Publishing, 2011.

Bonvillain, Nancy, and Ada Deer. *The Hopi.* Minneapolis, MN: Chelsea House Publications, 2005.

— — —. *The Nez Percé.* New York: Chelsea House, 2011.

— — —. *The Zuñi.* New York: Chelsea House Publishers, 2011.

Boule, Mary Null. *Mohave Tribe.* Vashon, WV: Merryant Publishers Inc., 2000.

Bourque, Bruce J., and Laureen A. LaBar. *Uncommon Threads: Wabanaki Textiles, Clothing, and Costume.* Augusta: Maine State Museum in association with University of Washington Press, 2009.

Bowes, John P. *The Choctaw.* New York: Chelsea House, 2010.

Bradley, Donna. *Native Americans of San Diego County, CA.* Mt. Pleasant, SC: Arcadia, 2009.

Bragdon, Kathleen J. *The Columbia Guide to American Indians of the Northeast.* New York: Columbia University Press, 2005.

Braje, Todd J., and Torben C. Rick, eds. *Human Impacts on Seals, Sea Lions, and Sea Otters: Integrating Archaeology and Ecology in the Northeast Pacific.* Berkeley: University of California Press, 2011.

Bray, Kingsley M. *Crazy Horse: A Lakota Life.* Norman: University of Oklahoma Press, 2006.

Breen, Betty, and Earl Mills, Sr. *Cape Cod Wampanoag Cookbook: Wampanoag Indian Recipes, Images & Lore.* Santa Fe, NM: Clear Light Books, 2001.

Brehm, Victoria. *Star Songs and Water Spirits: A Great Lakes Native Reader.* Tustin, MI: Ladyslipper Press, 2010.

Brimner, Larry Dane. *Pocahontas: Bridging Two Worlds.* New York: Marshall Cavendish Benchmark, 2009.

Bringhurst, Robert. *A Story as Sharp as a Knife: The Classical Haida Mythtellers and Their World.* 2nd ed. Vancouver, BC: Douglas & McIntyre, 2011.

Bringing the Story of the Cheyenne People to the Children of Today. Northern Cheyenne Curriculum Committee. Helena, MT: Office of Public Instruction, 2009.

Broker, Ignatia, *Night Flying Woman: An Ojibway Narrative.* St. Paul: Minnesota Historical Society Press, 1983.

Brown, Dee. *Bury My Heart at Wounded Knee: An Indian History of the American West.* New York: Holt, Rinehart, and Winston, 1970.

Brown, James W., and Rita T. Kohn, ed. *Long Journey Home: Oral Histories of Contemporary Delaware Indians.* Bloomington: Indiana University Press, 2008.

Brown, John A., and Robert H. Ruby. *The Chinook Indians: Traders of the Lower Columbia River.* Norman: University of Oklahoma Press, 1988.

Brown, Joseph. *The Spiritual Legacy of the American Indian: Commemorative Edition with Letters while Living with Black Elk.* Bloomington, IN: World Wisdom, 2007.

Brown, Tricia, and Roy Corral. *Children of the Midnight Sun: Young Native Voices of Alaska.* Anchorage: Alaska Northwest Books, 2006.

———. *Silent Storytellers of Totem Bight State Historical Park.* Anchorage: Alaska Geographic Association, 2009.

Brown, Virginia Pounds, Laurella Owens and Nathan Glick. *The World of the Southern Indians: Tribes, Leaders, and Customs from Prehistoric Times to the Present.* Montgomery, AL: NewSouth Books, 2011.

Browner, Tara, ed. *Music of the First Nations: Tradition and Innovation in Native North America.* Urbana: University of Illinois Press, 2009.

Bruchac, Joseph. *Flying with the Eagle, Racing the Great Bear: Tales from Native North America*. Golden, CO: Fulcrum, 2011.

Bruemmer, Fred. *Arctic Visions: Pictures from a Vanished World*. Toronto, Ontario: Key Porter Books, 2008.

Brugge, Doug, Timothy Benally, and Esther Yazzie-Lewis. *The Navajo People and Uranium Mining*. Albuquerque: University of New Mexico Press, 2006.

Bullchild, Percy. *The Sun Came Down: The History of the World as My Blackfeet Elders Told It*. Lincoln: University of Nebraska Press, 2005.

Burgan, Michael. *The Arapaho*. Tarrytown, NY: Marshall Cavendish Benchmark, 2009.

— — —. *Inuit History and Culture*. New York: Gareth Stevens, 2011.

Burke, Heather, et al, eds. *Kennewick Man: Perspectives on the Ancient One*. Walnut Creek, CA: Left Coast Press, 2008.

Burns, Louis F. *A History of the Osage People*. Tuscaloosa: University of Alabama Press, 2004.

— — —. *Osage Indian Customs and Myths*. Tuscaloosa: University of Alabama Press, 2005.

Button, Bertha P. *Friendly People: The Zuñi Indians*. Santa Fe, NM: Museum of New Mexico Press, 1963.

Calloway, Colin G. *The Shawnees and the War for America*. New York: Viking, 2007.

Carbone, Elisa. *Blood on the River: James Town 1607*. New York: Viking, 2006.

Carlos, Ann M. *Commerce by a Frozen Sea: Native Americans and the European Fur Trade*. Philadelphia: University of Pennsylvania Press, 2010.

Carlson, Paul H., and Tom Crum. *Myth, Memory, and Massacre: The Pease River Capture of Cynthia Ann Parker*. Lubbock: Texas Tech University Press, 2010.

Carlson, Richard G., ed. *Rooted Like the Ash Trees: New England Indians and the Land*. Naugatuck, CT: Eagle Wing Press, 1987.

Carpenter, Cecelia Svinth, Maria Victoria Pascualy, and Trisha Hunter. *Nisqually Indian Tribe*. Charleston, SC: Arcadia, 2008.

Carter, John G. *The Northern Arapaho Flat Pipe and the Ceremony of Covering the Pipe*. Whitefish, MT: Kessinger Publishing, 2007.

Cashin, Edward J. *Guardians of the Valley: Chickasaws in Colonial South Carolina and Georgia*. Columbia, SC: University of South Carolina Press, 2009.

Cassidy, James J., Jr., ed. *Through Indian Eyes: The Untold Story of Native American Peoples*. Pleasantville, NY: Reader's Digest Association, 1995.

Cassinelli, Dennis. *Preserving Traces of the Great Basin Indians*. Reno, NV: Jack Bacon & Company, 2006.

Castillo, Edward D. *The Pomo*. Austin: RaintreeSteck-Vaughn, 1999.

Chalcraft, Edwin L. *Assimilation's Agent: My Life as a Superintendent in the Indian Boarding School System.* Lincoln: University of Nebraska Press, 2007.

Champagne, Duane, ed. *The Native North American Almanac.* Detroit: Gale, 1994.

Charles, Nicholas and Maria. *Messenger Spirits: Yup'ik Masks and Stories.* Anchorage, AK: N & M, 2009.

Chatters, James C. *Ancient Encounters: Kennewick Man and the First Americans.* New York: Simon and Schuster, 2001.

Chaussonnet, Valerie, ed. *Crossroads Alaska: Native Cultures of Alaska and Siberia.* Washington, DC: Arctic Studies Center, National Museum of Natural History, Smithsonian Institution, 1995.

Chehak, Gail, and Jan Halliday. *Native Peoples of the Northwest: A Traveler's Guide to Land, Art, and Culture.* Seattle: Sasquatch Books, 2002.

Chenoweth, Avery, and Robert Llewellyn. *Empires in the Forest: Jamestown and the Making of America.* Earlysville, VA: Rivanna Foundation, 2010.

Childs, Craig. *House of Rain: Tracking a Vanished Civilization across the American Southwest.* 2nd ed. New York: Back Bay Books, 2008.

Clark, Cora, and Texa Bowen Williams. *Pomo Indians: Myths and Some of Their Sacred Meanings.* Reprint. Charleston, SC: Literary Licensing, 2011.

Clark, Ella E. *Indian Legends of the Pacific Northwest.* Berkeley: University of California Press, 2003.

Clark, Jerry E. *The Shawnee.* Lexington: University Press of Kentucky, 2007.

Clow, Richmond L., ed. *The Sioux in South Dakota History: A Twentieth-Century Reader.* Pierre, SD: South Dakota State Historical Society Press, 2007.

Cobb, Amanda J. *Listening to Our Grandmothers' Stories: The Bloomfield Academy for Chickasaw Females, 1852–1949.* Lincoln: University of Nebraska Press, 2007.

— — —. *Massacre at Camp Grant: Forgetting and Remembering Apache History.* Tucson: University of Arizona Press, 2007.

Cone, Marla. *Silent Snow: The Slow Poisoning of the Arctic.* New York: Grove Press, 2005.

Confederated Salish and Kootenai Tribes. *Bull Trout's Gift: A Salish Story about the Value of Reciprocity.* Lincoln: University of Nebraska Press, 2011.

Cook, Franklin A. "Nunapitchuk, Alaska: A Yup'ik Eskimo Village in Western Alaska." *Anna Tobeluk Memorial School, Nunapitchuk, Alaska.* Lincoln: University of Nebraska Press, 2005.

Cook, R. Michael, Eli Gifford, and Warren Jefferson, eds. *How Can One Sell the Air?: Chief Seattle's Vision.* Summertown, TN: Native Voices, 2005.

Corwin, Judith Hoffman. *Native American Crafts of the Northwest Coast, the Arctic, and the Subarctic.* New York: Franklin Watts, 2002.

Costa, David J. *Narratives and Winter Stories.* Oxford, OH: Myaamia Publications, 2010.

Coté, Charlotte. *Spirits of Our Whaling Ancestors: Revitalizing Makah, and Nuu-chah-nulth Traditions.* Seattle: University of Washington Press, 2010.

Coyote, Bertha Little, and Virginia Giglio. *Leaving Everything Behind: The Songs and Memories of a Cheyenne Woman.* Norman: University of Oklahoma Press, 1997.

Cozzens, Peter. *The Army and the Indian.* Mechanicsburg, PA: Stackpole Books, 2005.

Crediford, Gene J. *Those Who Remain.* Tuscaloosa: University of Alabama Press, 2009.

Crompton, Samuel Willard. *The Mohawk.* Edited by Paul C. Rosier. New York: Chelsea House Publishers, 2010.

Medicine Crow, Joseph. *Counting Coup: Becoming a Crow Chief on the Reservation and Beyond.* Washingon, DC: National Geographic, 2006.

— —. *From the Heart of the Crow Country: The Crow Indians' Own Stories.* Lincoln: University of Nebraska Press, 2000.

Crowell, Aron L. *Living Our Cultures, Sharing Our Heritage: The First Peoples of Alaska.* Washington, DC: Smithsonian Books, 2010.

Croy, Anita. *Ancient Pueblo: Archaeology Unlocks the Secrets of America's Past.* Washington, DC: National Geographic, 2007.

Cunningham, Kevin, and Peter Benoit. *The Wampanoag.* New York: Children's Press, 2011.

Curtin, Jeremiah. *Myths of the Modocs.* Whitefish, MT: Kessinger Publishing, 2006.

— —. "The Yanas." In *Creation Myths of Primitive America.* Boston, MA: Little, Brown, and Company, 1903.

Curtain, Jeremiah, and Roland B. Dixon, eds. *Achomawi and Atsugewi Myths and Tales.* Reprint.Sandhurst, UK: Abela Publishing, 2009.

— —. *The Plains Indian Photographs of Edward S. Curtis.* Lincoln: University of Nebraska Press, 2001.

— —. "Salishan Tribes." In *The North American Indian.* Vol. 7. Edited by Frederick Webb Hodge. Norwood, MA: The Plimpton Press, 1911. Available online from http://curtis.library.northwestern.edu/curtis/viewPage. cgi?showp=1&size=2&id=nai.07.book.00000075&volume=7 (accessed on August 11, 2011).

— — "Taos." In *The North American Indian (1907–1930).* Vol. 26. Reprint. New York: Johnson Reprint Corporation, 1970.

— —. "Umatilla." In *The North American Indian,* edited by Fredrick Webb Hodge. Vol. 8. 1911. Available online from http://curtis.library. northwestern.edu/curtis/viewPage.cgi?showp=1&size=2&id=nai.08. book.00000129.p&volume=8#nav (accessed on August 11, 2011).

———. "The Washoe." In *The North American Indian.* Vol. 15. Edited by Frederick Webb Hodge. Norwood, MA: The Plimpton Press, 1926: 89–98. Available online from Northwestern University. http://curtis. library.northwestern.edu/curtis/viewPage.cgi?showp=1&size=2&id=nai.15. book.00000141&volume=15 (accessed on August 15, 2011).

Cushing, Frank H. *Zuñi Folk Tales.* Charleston, SC: Kessinger Publishing, 2011)

Cwiklik, Robert. *King Philip and the War with the Colonists.* Englewood Cliffs, NJ: Silver Burdette Press, 1989.

Dahlin, Curtis A., and Alan R. Woolworth. *The Dakota Uprising: A Pictorial History.* Edina, MN: Beaver's Pond Press, 2009.

Damas, David, ed. *Handbook of North American Indians,* Vol. 5: *Arctic.* Washington, DC: Smithsonian Institution, 1984.

Dangberg, Grace, translator. *Washo Tales.* Reprint. Carson City: Nevada State Museum, 1968.

De Angulo, Jaime. *Indian Tales.* Santa Clara, CA: Heyday Books, 2003.

De Capua, Sarah. *The Shawnee.* New York: Marshall Cavendish Benchmark, 2008.

De Laguna, Fredericæ. "Tlingit." In *Handbook of North American Indians: Northwest Coast.* Vol. 7, edited by Wayne Suttles. Washington, DC: Smithsonian Institution, 1990, pp. 203–28.

Decker, Carol Paradise. *Pecos Pueblo People through the Ages: "—AndWe're Still Here": Stories of Time and Place.* Santa Fe, NM: Sunstone Press, 2011.

Decker, Peter R. *"The Utes Must Go!": American Expansion and the Removal of a People.* Golden, CO: Fulcrum Publishing, 2004.

DeJong, David H. *Forced to Abandon Our Fields: The 1914 Clay Southworth Gila River Pima Interviews.* Salt Lake City: University of Utah Press, 2011.

Deloria, Vine, Jr. *Red Earth, White Lies: Native Americans and the Myth of Scientific Fact.* New York: Scribner, 1995.

Dempsey, L. James. *Blackfoot War Art: Pictographs of the Reservation Period, 1880–2000.* Norman: University of Oklahoma Press, 2007.

Denetdale, Jennifer. *The Long Walk: The Forced Navajo Exile.* New York: Chelsea House, 2008.

———. *The Navajo.* New York: Chelsea House, 2011.

Densmore, Frances. *American Indians and Their Music.* Kila, MN: Kessinger Publishing, 2010.

DeRose, Cat. *Little Raven: Chief of the Southern Arapaho.* Palmer Lake, CO: Filter Press, 2010.

Dial, Adolph L., and David K. Eliades. *The Only Land I Know: A History of the Lumbee Indians.* Syracuse: Syracuse University Press, 1996.

Dickey, Michael E. *The People of the River's Mouth: In Search of the Missouria Indians.* Columbia: University of Missouri, 2011.

Ditchfield, Christin. *Northeast Indians.* Chicago: Heinemann Library, 2012.

— — —. *Plateau Indians.* Chicago: Heinemann Library, 2012.

Doak, Robin S. *Arctic Peoples.* Chicago: Heinemann Library, 2012.

— — —. *Subarctic Peoples.* Mankato, MN: Heinemann-Raintree, 2011.

Doherty, Craig A. *California Indians.* New York: Chelsea House Publications, 2007.

— — —. *Northeast Indians.* Broomall, PA: Chelsea House Publications, March 2008.

— — —. *Southeast Indians.* Minneapolis, MN: Chelsea House, 2007.

Doherty, Craig A., and Katherine M. Doherty. *Arctic Peoples.* New York: Chelsea House, 2008.

— — —. *Great Basin Indians.* Minneapolis, MN: Chelsea House, 2010.

— — —. *Plains Indians.* New York: Chelsea House, 2008.

— — —. *Plateau Indians.* New York: Chelsea House, 2008.

— — —. *Southwest Indians.* Minneapolis, MN: Chelsea House, 2007.

Dolan, Edward F. *The American Indian Wars.* Brookfield, CT: Millbrook Press, 2003.

Donlan, Leni. *Cherokee Rose: The Trail of Tears.* Chicago, IL: Raintree, 2007.

Downum, Christian E. *Hisatsinom: Ancient Peoples in a Land without Water.* Santa Fe: School for Advanced Research Press, 2011.

Dresser, Thomas. *The Wampanoag Tribe of Martha's Vineyard: Colonization to Recognition.* Charleston, SC: History Press, 2011.

Driver, Harold E., and Walter R. Goldschmidt. *The Hupa White Deerskin Dance.* Whitefish, MT: Kessinger Publishing, 2007.

Drury, Clifford M., ed. *Nine Years with the Spokane Indians: The Diary, 1838–1848, of Elkanah Walker.* Glendale, CA: Arthur H. Clark Company, 1976.

DuBois, Cora. *The 1870 Ghost Dance.* Reprint. Lincoln: University of Nebraska, 2007.

Duncan, Kate C. *Northern Athapaskan Art: A Beadwork Tradition.* Seattle: University of Washington Press, 1989.

Dunn, Jacob Piatt. *Massacres of the Mountains: A History of the Indian Wars of the Far West 1815–1875.* Whitefish, MT: Kessinger Publishing, 2006.

Dutton, Bertha P. *Indians of the American Southwest.* Englewood Cliffs, NJ: Prentice-Hall, 1975.

Duval, Kathleen. *The Native Ground: Indians and Colonists in the Heart of the Continent.* Philadelphia: University of Pennsylvania Press, 2006.

Dwyer, Helen, ed. *Peoples of the Southwest, West, and North.* Redding, CT: Brown Bear Books, 2009.

Dwyer, Helen, and D. L. Birchfield. *Cheyenne History and Culture.* New York: Gareth Stevens, 2012.

Dwyer, Helen, and Mary A. Stout. *Nez Percé History and Culture.* New York: Gareth Stevens, 2012.

Eastman, Charles A. *The Essential Charles Eastman (Ohiyesa), Revised and Updated Edition: Light on the Indian World.* Michael Oren Fitzgerald, ed. Bloomington, IN: World Wisdom, 2007.

— — —. *From the Deep Woods to Civilization.* Whitefish, MT: Kessinger Publishing, 2006.

— — —. *The Soul of the Indian.* New York: Dodo Press, 2007.

Eaton, William M. *Odyssey of the Pueblo Indians: An Introduction to Pueblo Indian Petroglyphs, Pictographs and Kiva Art Murals in the Southwest.* Paducah, KY: Turner Publishing Company, 2001.

Ember, Melvin, and Peter N. Peregrine, eds. *Encyclopedia of Prehistory,* Vol. 2: *Arctic and Subarctic.* New York: Kluwer Academic/Plenum Publishers, 2001.

Englar, Mary. *The Iroquois: The Six Nations Confederacy.* Mankato, MN: Capstone Press, 2006.

Erb, Gene, and Ann DeWolf Erb. *Voices in Our Souls: The DeWolfs, Dakota Sioux and the Little Bighorn.* Santa Fe: Sunstone Press, 2010.

Erdoes, Richard. *The Sun Dance People: The Plains Indians, Their Past and Present.* New York: Random House, 1972.

Erickson, Kirstin C. *Yaqui Homeland and Homeplace.* Tucson: University of Arizona Press, 2008.

Erickson, Winston P. *Sharing the Desert: The Tohono O'Odham in History.* Tucson: University of Arizona Press, 2003.

Erikson, Patricia Pierce. *Voices of a Thousand People: The Makah Cultural and Research Center.* Lincoln: University of Nebraska Press, 2005.

Ezell, Paul H. "History of the Pima." In *Handbook of North American Indians,* Volume 10: *Southwest,* edited by Alfonso Ortiz. Washington, DC: Smithsonian Institution Press, 1983.

Falconer, Shelley, and Shawna White. *Stones, Bones, and Stitches: Storytelling through Inuit Art.* Toronto, Ontario: Tundra Books, 2007.

Fariello, Anna. *Cherokee Basketry: From the Hands of Our Elders.* Charleston, SC: History Press, 2009.

Field, Ron. *The Seminole Wars, 1818–58.* New York: Osprey, 2009.

Fitzgerald, Judith, and Michael Oren Fitzgerald, eds. *The Spirit of Indian Women.* Bloomington, IN: World Wisdom, 2005.

Forczyk, Robert. *Nez Percé 1877: The Last Fight.* Long Island City, NY: Osprey, 2011.

Foreman, Grant. *Indian Removal.* Norman: University of Oklahoma Press, 1972.

Foster, Martha Harroun. *We Know Who We Are: Métis Identity in a Montana Community.* Norman: University of Oklahoma Press, 2006.

Foster, Sharon Ewell. *Abraham's Well: A Novel.* Minneapolis, MN: Bethany House, 2006.

Fowler, Loretta. *The Columbia Guide to American Indians of the Great Plains.* New York: Columbia University Press, 2005.

Fradin, Dennis B. *The Pawnee.* Chicago: Childrens Press, 1988.

Frank, Andrew. *The Seminole.* New York: Chelsea House, 2011.

Freedman, Russell. *The Life and Death of Crazy Horse.* New York: Holiday House, 1996.

Gagnon, Gregory O. *Culture and Customs of the Sioux Indians.* Westport, CT: Greenwood, 2011.

Garfinkel, Alan P., and Harold Williams. *Handbook of the Kawaiisu.* Kern Valley, CA: Wa-hi Sina'avi, 2011.

Geake, Robert A. *A History of the Narragansett Tribe of Rhode Island: Keepers of the Bay.* Charleston, SC: History Press, 2011.

Geronimo. *The Autobiography of Geronimo.* St. Petersburg, FL: Red and Black Publishers, 2011.

Giago, Tim A. *Children Left Behind: Dark Legacy of Indian Mission Boarding Schools.* Santa Fe, NM: Clear Light Publishing, 2006.

Gibson, Karen Bush. *The Chumash: Seafarers of the Pacific Coast.* Mankato, MN: Bridgestone Books, 2004.

— — —. *The Great Basin Indians: Daily Life in the 1700s.* Mankato, MN: Capstone Press, 2006.

— — —. *New Netherland: The Dutch Settle the Hudson Valley.* Elkton, IN: Mitchell Lane Publishers, 2006.

Giddings, Ruth Warner. *Yaqui Myths and Legends.* Charleston, SC: BiblioBazaar, 2009.

Gipson, Lawrence Henry. *The Moravian Indian Mission on White River: Diaries and Letters, May 5, 1799, to November 12, 1806.* Indianapolis: Indiana Historical Bureau, 1938.

Girdner, Alwin J. *Diné Tah: My Reservation Days 1923–1938.* Tucson: Rio Nuevo Publishers, c2011.

Glancy, Diane. *Pushing the Bear: After the Trail of Tears.* Norman: University of Oklahoma Press, 2009.

Goddard, Pliny Earle. *Hupa Texts.* Reprint. Charleston, SC: BiblioBazaar, 2009.

— — —. *Life and Culture of the Hupa.* Reprint. Charleston, SC: Nabu Press, 2011.

— — —. *Myths and Tales from the San Carlos Apache.* Whitefish, MT: Kessinger Publishing, 2006.

— — —. *Myths and Tales of the White Mountain Apache*. Whitefish, MT: Kessinger Publishing, 2011.

Goodman, Linda J. *Singing the Songs of My Ancestors: The Life and Music of Helma Swan, Makah Elder*. Norman: University of Oklahoma Press, 2003.

Goodwin, Grenville. *Myths and Tales of the White Mountain Apache*. Whitefish, MT: Kessinger Publishing, 2011.

Gordon, Irene Ternier. *A People on the Move: The Métis of the Western Plains*. Surry, British Columbia: Heritage House, 2009.

Grafe, Steven L. ed. *Lanterns on the Prairie: The Blackfeet Photographs of Walter McClintock*. Norman: University of Oklahoma Press, 2009.

Grant, Blanche Chloe. *Taos Indians*. 1925 ed. Santa Fe: Sunstone Press, 2007.

Grant, Campbell. *Rock Paintings of the Chumash: A Study of a California Indian Culture*. Reprint. Santa Barbara, CA: Santa Barbara Museum of Natural History/EZ Nature Books, 1993.

Gray-Kanatiiosh, Barbara A. *Cahuilla*. Edina, MN: ABDO, 2007.

— — —. *Modoc*. Edina, MN: ABDO, 2007.

— — —. *Paiute*. Edina, MN: ABDO Publishing, 2007.

— — —. *Yurok*. Edina, MN: ABDO, 2007.

Graymont, Barbara. *The Iroquois*. New York: Chelsea House, 1988.

Green, Michael D., and Theda Perdue. *The Cherokee Nation and the Trail of Tears*. New York: Viking, 2007.

— — —. *The Columbia Guide to American Indians of the Southeast*. New York: Columbia University Press, 2001.

Grinnell, George Bird. *Blackfeet Indians Stories*. Whitefish, MT: Kessinger Publishing, 2006.

— — —. *The Cheyenne Indians: Their History and Lifeways*. Bloomington, IN: World Wisdom, 2008.

Guigon, Catherine, Francis Latreille, and Fredric Malenfer. *The Arctic*. New York: Abrams Books for Young Readers, 2007.

Gunther, Vanessa. *Chief Joseph*. Greenwood, 2010.

Guthridge, George. *The Kids from Nowhere: The Story behind the Arctic Education Miracle*. Anchorage: Alaska Northwest Books, 2006.

Hagan, William T. *The Sac and Fox Indians*. Norman: University of Oklahoma Press, 2008.

Hahn, Elizabeth. *The Pawnee*. Vero Beach, FL: Rourke Publications, Inc., 1992.

Haig-Brown, Roderick. *The Whale People*. Madeira Park, BC: Harbour Publishing, 2003.

Hancock, David A. *Tlingit: Their Art and Culture*. Blaine, WA: Hancock House Publishers, 2003.

Handbook of North American Indians, Vol. 6: *Subarctic.* Ed. June Helm. Washington, DC: Smithsonian Institution, 1981.

Harpster, Jack, and Ken Stalter. *Captive!: The Story of David Ogden and the Iroquois.* Santa Barbara, CA: Praeger, 2010.

Harrington, Mark Raymond. *Certain Caddo Sites in Arkansas.* Charleston, SC: Johnson Press, 2011.

Hayes, Allan, and Carol Hayes. *The Desert Southwest: Four Thousand Years of Life And Art.* Berkeley, CA: Ten Speed Press, 2006.

Hearth, Amy Hill. *"Strong Medicine Speaks": A Native American Elder Has Her Say: An Oral History.* New York: Atria Books, 2008.

Hebner, William Logan. *Southern Paiute: A Portrait.* Logan: Utah State University Press, 2010.

Heinämäki, Leena. *The Right to Be a Part of Nature: Indigenous Peoples and the Environment.* Rovaniemi, Finland: Lapland University Press, 2010.

Heizer, R. F., ed. *Handbook of North American Indians.* Vol. 8: *California.* Washington, DC: Smithsonian Institution, 1978.

Hessel, Ingo. *Inuit Art: An Introduction.* Vancouver, British Columbia: Douglas & McIntyre, 2002.

Hicks, Terry Allan. *The Chumash.* New York: Marshall Cavendish Benchmark, 2008.

— — —. *The Zuñi.* New York: Marshall Cavendish Benchmark, 2010.

Hill, George, Robert H. Ruby, and John A. Brown. *The Spokane Indians: Children of the Sun.* Norman: University of Oklahoma Press, 2006.

Himsl, Sharon M. *The Shoshone.* San Diego, CA: Lucent Books, 2005.

Hirst, Stephen. *I Am the Grand Canyon: The Story of the Havasupai People.* Grand Canyon, AZ: Grand Canyon Association, 2006.

Hobson, Geary. *Plain of Jars and Other Stories.* East Lansing: Michigan State University Press, 2011.

Hodge, Frederick Webb. "Dwamish." *Handbook of American Indians North of Mexico.* New York: Pageant Books, 1959.

Hogeland, Kim, and L. Frank Hogeland. *First Families: Photographic History of California Indians.* Berkeley: Heyday Books, 2007.

Holm, Bill. *Spirit and Ancestor: A Century of Northwest Coast Indian Art in the Burke Museum.* Seattle: Burke Museum; University of Washington Press, 1987.

Hooper, Lucile. *The Cahuilla Indians.* Kila, MN: Kessinger Publishing, 2011.

Hoover, Alan L. *Nuu-chah-nulth Voices, Histories, Objects, and Journeys.* Victoria: Royal British Columbia Museum, 2000.

Hopping, Lorraine Jean. *Chief Joseph: The Voice for Peace.* New York: Sterling, 2010.

Houston, James A. *James Houston's Treasury of Inuit Legends.* Orlando, FL: Harcourt, 2006.

Hungrywolf, Adolf. *Tribal Childhood: Growing Up in Traditional Native America.* Summertown, TN:Native Voices, 2008.

Hyde, Dayton O. *The Last Free Man: The True Story behind the Massacre of Shoshone Mike and His Band of Indians in 1911.* New York: Dial Press, 1973.

Hyde, George E. *Indians of the Woodlands: From Prehistoric Times to 1725.* Norman: University of Oklahoma Press, 1962.

Indians of the Northwest Coast and Plateau. Chicago: World Book, 2009.

Indians of the Southwest. Chicago: World Book, 2009.

Inupiaq and Yupik People of Alaska. Anchorage: Alaska Geographic Society, 2004.

Jacknis, Ira. *The Storage Box of Tradition: Kwakiutl Art, Anthropologists, and Museums, 1881–1981.* Washington, DC: Smithsonian Institution Press, 2002.

Jackson, Helen Hunt. *The Indian Reform Letters of Helen Hunt Jackson, 1879–1885.*Edited by Valerie ShererMathes. Norman: University of Oklahoma Press, 1998.

— — —. *Ramona.* New York: Signet, 1988.

James, Cheewa. *Modoc: The Tribe That Wouldn't Die.* Happy Camp, CA: Naturegraph, 2008.

Jastrzembski, Joseph C. *The Apache.* Minneapolis: Chelsea House, 2011.

— — —. *The Apache Wars: The Final Resistance.* Minneapolis: Chelsea House, 2007.

Jenness, Aylette, and Alice Rivers. *In Two Worlds: A Yu'pik Eskimo Family.* New York: Houghton Mifflin, 1989.

Jennys, Susan. *19th Century Plains Indian Dresses.* Pottsboro, TX: Crazy Crow, 2004.

Jensen, Richard E., ed. *The Pawnee Mission Letters, 1834-1851.* Lincoln: University of Nebraska Press, 2010.

Jeter, Marvin D. *Edward Palmer's Arkansaw Mounds.* Tuscaloosa: University of Alabama Press, 2010.

Johansen, Bruce E. *The Iroquois.* New York, NY: Chelsea House, 2010.

Johnsgard, Paul A. *Wind through the Buffalo Grass: A Lakota Story Cycle.* Lincoln, NE: Plains Chronicles Press, 2008.

Johnson, Jerald Jay. "Yana." In *Handbook of North American Indians.* Vol. 10: *Southwest,* edited by Alfonso Ortiz. Washington, DC: Smithsonian Institution, 1983.

Johnson, Michael. *American Indians of the Southeast.* Oxford: Osprey Publishing, 1995.

———. "Duwamish." *The Native Tribes of North America.* New York: Macmillan, 1992.

———. *Native Tribes of the Northeast.* Milwaukee, WI: World Almanac Library, 2004.

Johnson, Michael, and Jonathan Smith. *Indian Tribes of the New England Frontier.* Oxford: Osprey Publishing, 2006.

Johnson, Thomas H., and Helen S. Johnson. *Also Called Sacajawea: Chief Woman's Stolen Identity.* Long Grove, IL: Waveland Press, 2008.

———. *Two Toms: Lessons from a Shoshone Doctor.* Salt Lake City: University of Utah Press, 2010.

Jonaitis, Aldona. *Art of the Northwest Coast.* Seattle: University of Washington Press, 2006.

Joseph, Frank. *Advanced Civilizations of Prehistoric America: The Lost Kingdoms of the Adena, Hopewell, Mississippians, and Anasazi.* Rochester, VT: Bear & Company, December 21, 2009.

Josephson, Judith Pinkerton. *Why Did Cherokees Move West? And Other Questions about the Trail of Tears.* Minneapolis: Lerner Publications, 2011.

Josephy, Alvin M., Jr. *500 Nations: An Illustrated History of North American Indians.* New York: Knopf, 1994.

———. *Nez Percé Country.* Lincoln: University of Nebraska Press, 2007.

Kallen, Stuart A. *The Pawnee.* San Diego: Lucent Books, 2001.

Kaneuketat. *I Dreamed the Animals: Kaneuketat: the Life of an Innu Hunter.* New York: Berghahn Books, 2008.

Kavasch, E. Barrie. *Enduring Harvests: Native American Foods and Festivals for Every Season.* Old Saybrook, CT: The Globe Pequot Press, 1995.

Keegan, Marcia. *Pueblo People: Ancient Tradition, Modern Lives.* Santa Fe, NM: Clear Light Publishers, 1999.

———. *Taos Pueblo and Its Sacred Blue Lake.* Santa Fe: Clear Light Publishers, 2010.

Keegan, Marcia, and Regis Pecos. *Pueblo People: Ancient Traditions, Modern Lives.* Santa Fe, NM: Clear Light Publishers, 1999.

Kegg, Maude. *Portage Lake: Memories of an Ojibwe Childhood.* Edmonton: University of Alberta Press, 1991.

Kennedy, J. Gerald. *Life of Black Hawk, or Ma-ka-tai-me-she-kia-kiak. Dictated by Himself.* New York: Penguin Books, 2008.

King, David C. *The Blackfeet.* New York: Marshall Cavendish Benchmark, 2010.

———. *First People.* New York: DK Children, 2008.

———. *The Inuit.* New York: Marshall Cavendish Benchmark, 2008.

———. *The Nez Percé.* New York: Benchmark Books, 2008.

———. *Seminole.* New York: Benchmark Books, 2007.

Kiowa and Pueblo Art: Watercolor Paintings by Native American Artists. Mineola, NY: Dover Publications, 2009.

Kirkpatrick, Katherine. *Mysterious Bones: The Story of Kennewick Man.* New York: Holiday House, 2011.

Kissock,Heather, and Jordan McGill. *Apache: American Indian Art and Culture.* New York: Weigl Publishers, 2011.

Kissock, Heather, and Rachel Small. *Caddo: American Indian Art and Culture.* New York: Weigl Publishers, 2011.

Koyiyumptewa, Stewart B., Carolyn O'Bagy Davis, and the Hopi Cultural Preservation Office. *The Hopi People.* Charleston, SC: Arcadia Publishing, 2009.

Kristofic, Jim. *Navajos Wear Nikes: A Reservation Life.* Albuquerque: University of New Mexico Press, 2011.

Kroeber, Theodora. *Ishi in Two Worlds: A Biography of the Last Wild Indian in North America.* Berkeley: University of California Press, 2004.

Krupnik, Igor, and Dyanna Jolly, eds. *The Earth Is Faster Now: Indigenous Observations of Arctic Environmental Change.* Fairbanks, Alaska: Arctic Research Consortium of the United States, 2002.

Kuiper, Kathleen, ed. *American Indians of California, the Great Basin, and the Southwest.* New York: Rosen Educational Services, 2012.

— — —. *American Indians of the Northeast and Southeast.* New York: Rosen Educational Services, 2012.

— — —. *American Indians of the Plateau and Plains.* New York: Rosen Educational Services, 2012.

— — —. *Indigenous Peoples of the Arctic, Subarctic, and Northwest Coast.* New York: Rosen Educational Services, 2012.

Lacey, T. Jensen. *The Blackfeet.* New York: Chelsea House, 2011.

— — —. *The Comanche.* New York: Chelsea House, 2011.

Lankford, George E., ed. *Native American Legends of the Southeast: Tales from the Natchez, Caddo, Biloxi, Chickasaw, and Other Nations.* 5th ed. Tuscaloosa: University of Alabama Press, 2011.

Lanmon, Dwight P. and Francis H. Harlow. *The Pottery of Zuñi Pueblo.* Santa Fe: Museum of New Mexico Press, 2008.

Larsen, Mike, Martha Larsen, and Jeannie Barbour. *Proud to Be Chickasaw.* Ada, OK: Chickasaw Press, 2010.

Lenik, Edward J. *Making Pictures in Stone: American Indian Rock Art of the Northeast.* Tuscaloosa: University of Alabama Press, 2009.

Levine, Michelle. *The Delaware.* Minneapolis, MN: Lerner Publications, 2006.

— — —. *The Ojibway.* Minneapolis, MN: Lerner Publications, 2006.

Levy, Janey. *The Wampanoag of Massachusetts and Rhode Island.* New York: PowerKids Press, 2005.

Liebert, Robert. *Osage Life and Legends: Earth People/Sky People.* Happy Camp, California: Naturegraph Publishers, 1987.

Life Stories of Our Native People: Shoshone, Paiute, Washo. Reno, NV: Inter-tribal Council of Nevada, 1974.

Liptak, Karen. *North American Indian Ceremonies.* New York: Franklin Watts, 1992.

Little, Kimberley Griffiths. *The Last Snake Runner.* New York: Alfred A. Knopf, 2002.

Lloyd, J. William. *Aw-aw-tam Indian Nights: The Myths and Legends of the Pimas.* Westfield, NJ: The Lloyd Group, 1911. Available online from http://www.sacred-texts.com/nam/sw/ain/index.htm (accessed on July 20, 2011).

Lobo, Susan, Steve Talbot, and Traci L. Morris, compilers. *Native American Voices: A Reader.* 3rd ed. Upper Saddle River, NJ: Prentice Hall, 2010.

Lourie, Peter. *The Lost World of the Anasazi: Exploring the Mysteries of Chaco Canyon.* Honesdale, PA: Boyds Mills Press, 2007.

Macdougall, Brenda. *One of the Family: Metis Culture in Nineteenth-Century Northwestern Saskatchewan.* Vancouver, British Columbia: UBC Press, 2010.

Mann, John W.W. *Sacajawea's People: The Lemhi Shoshones and the Salmon River Country.* Lincoln, NE: Bison Books, 2011.

Margolin, Malcolm. *The Ohlone Way.* Berkeley, CA: Heyday Books, 1981.

———. *The Way We Lived: California Indian Stories, Songs, and Reminiscences.* Reprint. Heyday Books, Berkeley, California, 2001.

Marriott, Alice, and Carol K. Rachlin. *Plains Indian Mythology.* New York, NY: Thomas Y. Crowell, 1975.

Marshall, Ann, ed. *Home: Native People in the Southwest.* Phoenix, AZ: Heard Museum, 2005.

Marshall, Bonnie. *Far North Tales: Stories from the Peoples of the Arctic Circle.* Edited by Kira Van Deusen. Santa Barbara, CA: Libraries Unlimited, 2011.

Marsi, Katie. *The Trail of Tears: The Tragedy of the American Indians.* New York: Marshall Cavendish Benchmark, 2010.

McDaniel, Melissa. *Great Basin Indians.* Des Plaines, IL: Heinemann, 2011.

———. *The Sac and Fox Indians.* New York: Chelsea Juniors, 1995.

———. *Southwest Indians.* Chicago: Heinemann Library, 2012.

Mcmullen, John William. *Ge Wisnemen! (Let's Eat!): A Potawatomi Family Dinner Manual.* Charleston, SC: CreateSpace, 2011.

Melody, Michael E., and Paul Rosier. *The Apache.* Minneapolis: Chelsea House, 2005.

Merriam, C. Hart. *The Dawn of the World: Myths and Tales of the Miwok Indians of California.* Kila, MN: Kessinger Publishing, 2010.

Michael, Hauser. *Traditional Inuit Songs from the Thule Area.* Copenhagen: Museum Tusculanum Press, 2010.

Miles, Ray. "Wichita." *Native America in the Twentieth Century, An Encyclopedia.* Ed. Mary B. Davis. New York: Garland Publishing, 1994.

Miller, Debbie S., and Jon Van Dyle. *Arctic Lights, Arctic Nights.* New York: Walker Books for Young Readers, 2007.

Miller, Frederic P., Agnes F. Vandome, and John McBrewster, eds. *Nuu-chah-nulth People.* Beau Bassin, Mauritius: Alphascript Publishing, 2011.

Miller, Raymond H. *North American Indians: The Apache.* San Diego: KidHaven Press, 2005.

Milner, George R. *The Moundbuilders: Ancient Peoples of Eastern North America.* New York: Thames & Hudson, 2005.

Mooney, James. *Calendar History of the Kiowa Indians.* Whitefish, MT: Kessinger Publishing, 2006.

— — —. *Myths of the Cherokee.* New York: Dover Publications, 1996.

Mosqueda, Frank, and Vickie Leigh Krudwig. *The Hinono'ei Way of Life: An Introduction to the Arapaho People.* Edited by Susan Scott Hill. Concho, OK: Cheyenne and Arapaho Tribes of Oklahoma, 2008.

— — —. *The Prairie Thunder People: A Brief History of the Arapaho People.* Edited by Susan Scott Hill. Concho, OK: Cheyenne and Arapaho Tribes of Oklahoma, 2008.

Mossiker, Frances. *Pocahontas: The Life and the Legend.* New York: Alfred A. Knopf, 1976.

Mundell, Kathleen. *North by Northeast: Wabanaki, Akwesasne Mohawk, and Tuscarora Traditional Arts.* Gardiner, ME: Tilbury House, Publishers, 2008.

Myers, Albert Cook, ed. *William Penn's Own Account of the Lenni Lenape or Delaware Indians.* Somerset, NJ: Middle Atlantic Press, 1970.

Myers, Arthur. *The Pawnee.* New York: Franklin Watts, 1993.

Myers, James E. "Cahto." In *Handbook of North American Indians.* Vol. 8: *California,* edited by R. F. Heizer. Washington, D.C.: Smithsonian Institution, 1978: 244–48.

Neeley, Bill. *The Last Comanche Chief: The Life and Times of Quanah Parker.* New York: Wiley, 1996.

Nelson, Sharlene, and Ted W. Nelson. *The Makah.* New York: Franklin Watts, 2003.

Nez, Chester, and Judith Schiess Avila. *Code Talker.* New York: Berkley Caliber, 2011.

Nichols, Richard. *A Story to Tell: Traditions of a Tlingit Community.* Minneapolis: Lerner Publications Company, 1998.

Nowell, Charles James. *Smoke from their Fires: The Life of a Kwakiutl Chief.* Hamdon, CT: Archon Books, 1968.

O'Neale, Lila M. *Yurok-Karok Basket Weavers.* Berkeley, CA: Phoebe A. Hearst Museum of Anthropology, 2007.

Opler, Morris Edward. *Myths and Tales of the Chiricahua Apache Indians.* Charleston, SC: Kessinger Publishing, 2011.

Ortega, Simon, ed. *Handbook of North American Indians.* Vol. 12: *The Plateau.* Washington, DC: Smithsonian Institution, 1978.

Ortiz, Alfonso, ed. *Handbook of American Indians.* Vols. 9–10. *The Southwest.* Washington, DC: Smithsonian Institution, 1978–83.

Owings, Alison. *Indian Voices: Listening to Native Americans.* New Brunswick, N.J.: Rutgers University Press, 2011.

Page, Jake, and Susanne Page. *Indian Arts of the Southwest.* Tucson, AZ: Rio Nuevo Publishers, 2008.

Page, Susanne and Jake. *Navajo.* Tucson, AZ: Rio Nuevo Publishers, 2010.

Paige, Amanda L., Fuller L. Bumpers, and Daniel F. Littlefield, Jr. *Chickasaw Removal.* Ada, OK: Chickasaw Press, 2010.

Palazzo-Craig, Janet. *The Ojibwe of Michigan, Wisconsin, Minnesota, and North Dakota.* New York: PowerKids Press, 2005.

Peltier, Leonard. *Prison Writings: My Life Is My Sun Dance.* New York: St. Martin's, 2000.

Penny, Josie. *So Few on Earth: A Labrador Métis Woman Remembers.* Toronto, Ontario: Dundurn Press, 2010.

Peoples of the Arctic and Subarctic. Chicago: World Book, 2009.

Perritano, John. *Spanish Missions.* New York: Children's Press, 2010.

Philip, Neil, ed. *A Braid of Lives: Native American Childhood.* New York: Clarion Books, 2000.

Pierson, George. *The Kansa, or Kaw Indians, and Their History, and the Story of Padilla.* Charleston, SC: Nabu Press, 2010.

Pijoan, Teresa. *Pueblo Indian Wisdom: Native American Legends and Mythology.* Santa Fe: Sunstone Press, 2000.

Pritzker, Barry, and Paul C. Rosier. *The Hopi.* New York: Chelsea House, c. 2011.

Riddell, Francis A. "Maidu and Concow." *Handbook of North American Indians.* Vol. 8: *California.* Edited by Robert F. Heizer. Washington DC: Smithsonian Institution, 1978.

Rielly, Edward J. *Legends of American Indian Resistance.* Westport, CT: Greenwood, 2011.

Riordan, Robert. *Medicine for Wildcat: A Story of the Friendship between a Menominee Indian and Frontier Priest Samuel Mazzuchelli.* Revised by

Marilyn Bowers Gorun and the Sinsinawa Dominican Sisters. Sinsinawa, WI: Sinsinawa Dominican Sisters, 2006.

Rollings, Willard H. *The Comanche.* New York: Chelsea House Publications, 2004.

Rosoff, Nancy B., and Susan Kennedy Zeller. *Tipi: Heritage of the Great Plains.* Seattle: Brooklyn Museum in association with University of Washington Press, 2011.

Ruby, Robert H., John A. Brown, and Cary C. Collins. *A Guide to the Indian Tribes of the Pacific Northwest.* Norman: University of Oklahoma Press, 2010.

Russell, Frank. *The Pima Indians.* Whitefish, MT: Kessinger Publishing, 2010.

Ryan, Marla Felkins, and Linda Schmittroth. *Tribes of Native America: Zuñi Pueblo.* San Diego: Blackbirch Press, 2002.

— — —. *Ute.* San Diego: Blackbirch Press, 2003.

Rzeczkowski, Frank. *The Lakota Sioux.* New York: Chelsea House, 2011.

Seton, Ernest Thompson. *Sign Talk of the Cheyenne Indians.* Mineola, NY: Dover Publications, 2000.

Sherrow, Victoria. *The Iroquois Indians.* New York: Chelsea House, 1992.

Shipek, Florence Connolly. "Luiseño." In *Native America in the Twentieth Century: An Encyclopedia,* edited by Mary B. Davis. New York: Garland Publishing, 1994.

Shipley, William. *The Maidu Indian Myths and Stories of Hanc'Ibyjim.* Berkeley: Heyday Books, 1991.

Shull, Jodie A. *Voice of the Paiutes: A Story About Sarah Winnemucca.* Minneapolis, MN: Millbrook Press, 2007.

Simermeyer, Genevieve. *Meet Christopher: An Osage Indian Boy from Oklahoma.* Tulsa, OK: National Museum of the American Indian, Smithsonian Institution, in association with Council Oak Books, 2008.

Simmons, Marc. *Friday, the Arapaho Boy: A Story from History.* Albuquerque: University of New Mexico Press, 2004.

Sita, Lisa. *Indians of the Northeast: Traditions, History, Legends, and Life.* Milwaukee, WI: Gareth Stevens, 2000.

— — —. *Pocahontas: The Powhatan Culture and the Jamestown Colony.* New York: PowerPlus Books, 2005.

Slater, Eva. *Panamint Shoeshone Basketry: An American Art Form.* Berkeley: Heyday Books, 2004.

Smith, White Mountain. *Indian Tribes of the Southwest.* Kila, MN: Kessinger Publishing, 2005.

Snell, Alma Hogan. *A Taste of Heritage: Crow Indian Recipes & Herbal Medicines.* Lincoln: University of Nebraska Press, 2006.

Sneve, Virginia Driving Hawk. *The Cherokee*. New York: Holiday House, 1996.

— — —. *The Cheyenne*. New York: Holiday House, 1996.

— — —. *The Iroquois*. New York: Holiday House, 1995.

— — —. *The Nez Percé*. New York: Holiday House, 1994.

— — —. *The Seminoles*. New York: Holiday House, 1994.

Snyder, Clifford Gene. *Ghost Trails: Mythology and Folklore of the Chickasaw, Choctaw, Creeks and Other Muskoghean Indian Tribes*. North Hollywood, CA: JES, 2009.

— — —. *The Muskogee Chronicles: Accounts of the Early Muskogee/Creek Indians*. N. Hollywood, CA: JES, 2008.

Solomon, Madeline. *Koyukon Athabaskan Songs*. Homer, AK: Wizard Works, 2003.

Sonneborn, Liz. *The Choctaws*. Minneapolis, MN: Lerner Publications, 2007.

— — —. *The Creek*. Minneapolis: Lerner Publications, 2007.

— — —. *The Chumash*. Minneapolis, MN: Lerner Publications, 2007.

— — —. *The Navajos*. Minneapolis, MN: Lerner Publications, 2007.

— — —. *Northwest Coast Indians*. Chicago: Heinemann Library, 2012.

— — —. *The Shoshones*. Minneapolis, MN: Lerner Publications, 2006.

— — —. *Wilma Mankiller*. New York: Marshall Cavendish Benchmark, 2010.

Spalding, Andrea. *Secret of the Dance*. Orca, WA: Orca Book Publishers, 2006.

Spence, Lewis. *Myths and Legends of the North American Indians*. Whitefish, MT: Kessinger Publishing, 1997.

Spragg-Braude, Stacia. *To Walk in Beauty: A Navajo Family's Journey Home*. Santa Fe: Museum of New Mexico Press, 2009.

Sprague, DonovinArleigh. *American Indian Stories*. West Stockbridge, CT: Hard Press, 2006.

— — —. *Choctaw Nation of Oklahoma*. Chicago, IL: Arcadia, 2007.

— — —. *Old Indian Legends: Retold by Zitkala--Sa*. Paris: Adamant Media Corporation, 2006.

— — —. *Standing Rock Sioux*. Charleston, SC: Arcadia, 2004.

St. Lawrence, Genevieve. *The Pueblo And Their History*. Minneapolis, MN: Compass Point Books, 2006.

Stanley, George E. *Sitting Bull: Great Sioux Hero*. New York: Sterling, 2010.

Stern, Pamela R. *Daily Life of the Inuit*. Santa Barbara, CA: Greenwood, 2010.

Sterngass, Jon. *Geronimo*. New York: Chelsea House, 2010.

Stevenson, Matilda Coxe. *The Zuñi Indians and Their Uses of Plants.* Charleston, SC: Kessinger Publishing, 2011.

Stevenson, Tilly E. *The Religious Life of the Zuñi Child.* Charleston, SC: Kessinger Publishing, 2011.

Stewart, Philip. *Osage.* Philadelphia, PA: Mason Crest Publishers, 2004.

Stirling, M.W. *Snake Bites and the Hopi Snake Dance.* Whitefish, MT: Kessinger Publishing, 2011.

Stone, Amy M. *Creek History and Culture.* Milwaukee: Gareth Stevens Publishing, 2011.

Stout, Mary. *Blackfoot History and Culture.* New York: Gareth Stevens, 2012.

— — —. *Hopi History and Culture.* New York: Gareth Stevens, 2011.

— — —. *Shoshone History and Culture.* New York: Gareth Stevens, 2011.

Strack, Andrew J. *How the Miami People Live.* Edited by Mary Tippman, Meghan Dorey and Daryl Baldwin. Oxford, OH: Myaamia Publications, 2010.

Straub, Patrick. *It Happened in South Dakota: Remarkable Events That Shaped History.* New York: Globe Pequot, 2009.

Sullivan, Cathie, and Gordon Sullivan. *Roadside Guide to Indian Ruins & Rock Art of the Southwest.* Englewood, CO: Westcliffe Publishers, 2006.

Sullivan, George. *Geronimo: Apache Renegade.* New York: Sterling, 2010.

Suttles, Wayne, and Barbara Lane. "Southern Coast Salish." *Handbook of North American Indians.* Vol. 7: *Northwest Coast.* Edited by Wayne Suttles. Washington, DC: Smithsonian Institution, 1990.

Swanton, John R., and Franz Boas. *Haida Songs; Tsimshian Texts (1912).* Vol. 3. Whitefish, MT: Kessinger Publishing, 2010.

Sweet, Jill Drayson, and Nancy Hunter Warren. *Pueblo Dancing.* Atglen, PA: Schiffer Publishing, 2011.

Tenenbaum, Joan M., and Mary Jane McGary, eds. *Denaina Sukdua: Traditional Stories of the Tanaina Athabaskans.* Fairbanks: Alaska Native Language Center, 2006.

Tiller, Veronica E. Velarde. *Culture and Customs of the Apache Indians.* Santa Barbara, CA: ABC-CLIO, 2011.

Underhill, Ruth. *The Papago Indians of Arizona and their Relatives the Pima.* Whitefish, MT: Kessinger Publishing, 2010.

Van Deusen, Kira. *Kiviuq: An Inuit Hero and His Siberian Cousins.* Montreal: McGill-Queen's University Press, 2009.

Vanderwerth, W. C. *Indian Oratory: Famous Speeches by Noted Indian Chieftains.* Norman: University of Oklahoma Press, 1979.

Vaudrin, Bill. *Tanaina Tales from Alaska.* Norman: University of Oklahoma Press, 1969.

Viola, Herman J. *Trail to Wounded Knee: The Last Stand of the Plains Indians 1860–1890.* Washington, DC: National Geographic, 2004.

Von Ahnen, Katherine. *Charlie Young Bear.* Minot, CO: Roberts Rinehart Publishers, 1994.

Wade, Mary Dodson. *Amazing Cherokee Writer Sequoyah.* Berkeley Heights, NJ: Enslow, 2009.

Wagner, Frederic C. III. *Participants in the Battle of the Little Big Horn: A Biographical Dictionary of Sioux, Cheyenne and United States Military Personnel.* Jefferson, NC: McFarland, 2011.

Waldman, Carl. "Colville Reservation." In *Encyclopedia of Native American Tribes.* New York: Facts on File, 2006.

— — —. *Encyclopedia of Native American Tribes.* New York: Facts on File, 2006.

Wallace, Mary. *The Inuksuk Book.* Toronto, Ontario: Maple Tree Press, 2004.

— — —. *Make Your Own Inuksuk.* Toronto, Ontario: Maple Tree Press, 2004.

Wallace, Susan E. *The Land of the Pueblos.* Santa Fe, NM: Sunstone Press, 2006.

Ward, Jill. *The Cherokees.* Hamilton, GA: State Standards, 2010.

— — —. *Creeks and Cherokees Today.* Hamilton, GA: State Standards, 2010.

Warm Day, Jonathan. *Taos Pueblo: Painted Stories.* Santa Fe, NM: Clear Light Publishing, 2004.

Waters, Frank. *Book of the Hopi.* New York: Viking Press, 1963.

White, Bruce. *We Are at Home: Pictures of the Ojibwe People.* St. Paul, MN: Minnesota Historical Society Press, 2007.

White, Tekla N. *San Francisco Bay Area Missions.* Minneapolis, MN: Lerner, 2007.

Whitehead, Ruth Holmes. *The Micmac: How Their Ancestors Lived Five Hundred Years Ago.* Halifax, Nova Scotia: Nimbus, 1983.

Whiteman, Funston, Michael Bell, and Vickie Leigh Krudwig. *The Cheyenne Journey: An Introduction to the Cheyenne People.* Edited by Susan Scott-Hill. Concho, OK: Cheyenne and Arapaho Tribes of Oklahoma, 2008.

— — —. *The Tsististas: People of the Plains.* Edited by Susan Scott-Hill. Concho, OK: Cheyenne and Arapaho Tribes of Oklahoma, 2008.

Wiggins, Linda E., ed. *Dena—The People: The Way of Life of the Alaskan Athabaskans Described in Nonfiction Stories, Biographies, and Impressions from All Over the Interior of Alaska.* Fairbanks: Theata Magazine, University of Alaska, 1978.

Wilcox, Charlotte. *The Iroquois.* Minneapolis, MN: Lerner Publishing Company, 2007.

— — —. *The Seminoles.* Minneapolis: Lerner Publications, 2007.

Wilds, Mary C. *The Creek.* San Diego, CA: Lucent Books, 2005.

Wiles, Sara. *Arapaho Journeys: Photographs and Stories from the Wind River Reservation.* Norman: University of Oklahoma Press, 2011.

Williams, Jack S. *The Luiseno of California.* New York: PowerKids Press, 2003.

— — —. *The Modoc of California and Oregon.* New York: PowerKids Press, 2004.

— — —. *The Mojave of California and Arizona.* New York: PowerKids Press, 2004.

Wilson, Darryl J. *The Morning the Sun Went Down.* Berkeley, CA: Heyday, 1998.

Wilson, Elijah Nicholas. *The White Indian Boy: The Story of Uncle Nick among the Shoshones.* Kila, MN: Kessinger Publishing, 2004.

Wilson, Frazer Ells. *The Peace of Mad Anthony: An Account of the Subjugation of the Northwestern Indian Tribes and the Treaty of Greeneville.* Kila, MN: Kessinger Publishing, 2005.

Wilson, Norman L., and Arlean H. Towne. "Nisenan." In *Handbook of North American Indians.* Vol. 8: *California.* Edited by Robert F. Heizer. Washington DC: Smithsonian Institution, 1978.

Winnemucca, Sarah. *Life among the Paiutes: Their Wrongs and Claims.* Privately printed, 1883. Reprint. Reno: University of Nevada Press, 1994.

Wolcott, Harry F. *A Kwakiutl Village and School.* Walnut Creek, CA: AltaMira Press, 2003.

Wolfson, Evelyn. *The Iroquois: People of the Northeast.* Brookfield, CT: The Millbrook Press, 1992.

Woolworth, Alan R. *Santee Dakota Indian Tales.* Saint Paul, MN: Prairie Smoke Press, 2003.

Worl, Rosita. *Celebration: Tlingit, Haida, Tsimshian Dancing on the Land.* Edited by Kathy Dye. Seattle: University of Washington Press, 2008.

Wright, Muriel H. *A Guide to the Indian Tribes of Oklahoma.* Norman: University of Oklahoma Press, 1951.

Wyborny, Sheila. *North American Indians: Native Americans of the Southwest.* San Diego: KidHaven Press, 2004.

Wynecoop, David C. *Children of the Sun: A History of the Spokane Indians.* Wellpinit, WA, 1969. Available online from http://www.wellpinit.wednet.edu/shorthistory (accessed on August 11, 2011).

Wyss, Thelma Hatch. *Bear Dancer: The Story of a Ute Girl.* Chicago: Margaret K. McElderry Books, 2010.

Zepeda, Ofelia. *Where Clouds Are Formed: Poems.* Tucson: University of Arizona Press, 2008.

Zigmond, Maurice L. *Kawaiisu Mythology: An Oral Tradition of South-Central California.* Banning, CA: Malki-Ballena Press, 1980.

— — —. "Kawaiisu." In *Handbook of North American Indians, Great Basin.* Vol. 11. Edited by Warren L. D'Azavedo. Washington, DC: Smithsonian Institution, 1981, pp. 398–411.

Zimmerman, Dwight Jon. *Tecumseh: Shooting Star of the Shawnee.* New York: Sterling, 2010.

Zitkala-Sa, Cathy N. Davidson, and Ada Norris. *American Indian Stories, Legends, and Other Writings.* New York: Penguin, 2003.

Periodicals

Barrett, Samuel Alfred, and Edward Winslow Gifford. "Miwok Material Culture: Indian Life of the Yosemite Region" *Bulletin of Milwaukee Public Museum* 2, no. 4 (March 1933).

Barringer, Felicity. "Indians Join Fight for an Oklahoma Lake's Flow." *New York Times.* April 12, 2011, A1. Available online from http://www.nytimes.com/2011/04/12/science/earth/12water.html (accessed on June 18, 2011).

Beck, Melinda. "The Lost Worlds of Ancient America." *Newsweek* 118 (Fall–Winter 1991): 24.

Bourke, John Gregory. "General Crook in the Indian Country." *The Century Magazine,* March 1891. Available online from http://www.discoverseaz.com/History/General_Crook.html (accessed on July 20, 2011).

Bruchac, Joseph. "Otstango: A Mohawk Village in 1491," *National Geographic* 180, no. 4 (October 1991): 68–83.

Carroll, Susan. "Tribe Fights Kitt Peak Project." *The Arizona Republic.* March 24, 2005. Available online at http://www.nathpo.org/News/Sacred_Sites/News-Sacred_Sites109.htm (accessed on July 20, 2011).

Chief Joseph. "An Indian's View of Indian Affairs." *North American Review* 128, no. 269 (April 1879): 412–33.

Collins, Cary C., ed. "Henry Sicade's History of Puyallup Indian School, 1860 to 1920." *Columbia* 14, no. 4 (Winter 2001–02).

Dalsbø, E.T., "'We Were Told We Were Going to Live in Houses': Relocation and Housing of the Mushuau Innu of Natuashish from 1948 to 2003." *University of Tromsø,* May 28, 2010. Available from http://www.ub.uit.no/munin/bitstream/handle/10037/2739/thesis.pdf?sequence=3 (accessed on May 26, 2011).

Dixon, Roland B. "Achomawi and Atsugewi Tales." *Journal of American Folklore* 21. (1908): 159–77.

Dold, Catherine. "American Cannibal." *Discover* 19, no. 2 (February 1998): 64.

Duara, Nigel. "Descendants Make Amends to Chinook for Lewis and Clark Canoe Theft." *Missourian.* (September 23, 2011). Available online from http://www.columbiamissourian.com/stories/2011/09/23/descendants-make-amends-chinook-lewis-clark-canoe-theft/ (accessed on November 2, 2011).

Elliott, Jack. "Dawn, Nov. 28, 1729: Gunfire Heralds Natchez Massacre." *Concordia Sentinel*. November 5, 2009. Available from http://www.concordiasentinel.com/news.php?id=4321 (accessed on June 27, 2011).

Eskin, Leah. "Teens Take Charge. (Suicide Epidemic at Wind River Reservation)." *Scholastic Update,* May 26, 1989: 26.

Et-twaii-lish, Marjorie Waheneka. "Indian Perspectives on Food and Culture." *Oregon Historical Quarterly,* Fall 2005.

Griswold, Eliza. "A Teen's Third-World America." *Newsweek.* December 26, 2010. Available online from http://www.thedailybeast.com/articles/2010/12/26/a-boys-third-world-america.html (accessed on July 20, 2011).

ICTMN Staff. "Washoe Tribe's Cave Rock a No-go for Bike Path" *Indian Country Today Media Network,* February 10, 2011. Available online at http://indiancountrytodaymedianetwork.com/2011/02/washoe-tribes-cave-rock-a-no-go-for-bike-path/ (accessed on August 15, 2011).

Johnston, Moira. "Canada's Queen Charlotte Islands: Homeland of the Haida." *National Geographic,* July 1987: 102–27.

Jones, Malcolm Jr., with Ray Sawhill. "Just Too Good to Be True: Another Reason to Beware False Eco-Prophets." *Newsweek.* (May 4, 1992). Available online at http://www.synaptic.bc.ca/ejournal/newsweek.htm (accessed on November 2, 2011).

June-Friesen, Katy. "An Ancestry of African-Native Americans." *Smithsonian.* February 17, 2010. Available online from http://www.smithsonianmag.com/history-archaeology/An-Ancestry-of-African-Native-Americans.html#ixzz1RN1pyiD1 (accessed on June 21, 2011).

Kowinski, William Severini. "Giving New Life to Haida Art and the Culture It Expresses." *Smithsonian,* January 1995: 38.

Kroeber, A. L. "Two Myths of the Mission Indians." *Journal of the American Folk-Lore Society* 19, no. 75 (1906): 309–21. Available online at http://www.sacred-texts.com/nam/ca/tmmi/index.htm (accessed on August 11, 2011).

Lake, Robert, Jr."The Chilula Indians of California." *Indian Historian* 12, no. 3 (1979): 14–26. Available online fromhttp://www.eric.ed.gov/ERICWebPortal/search/detailmini.jsp?_nfpb=true&_&ERICExtSearch_SearchValue_0=EJ214907&ERICExtSearch_SearchType_0=no&accno=EJ214907

Parks, Ron. "Selecting a Suitable Country for the Kanza." *The Kansas Free Press.* June 1, 2011. Available online from http://www.kansasfreepress.com/2011/06/selecting-a-suitable-country-for-the-kanza.html (accessed on June 17, 2011).

Rezendes, Michael. "Few Tribes Share Casino Windfall." *Globe.* December 11, 2000. Available online from http://indianfiles.serveftp.com/TribalIssues/Few%20tribes%20share%20casino%20windfall.pdf(accessed on July 4, 2011).

Roy, Prodipto, and Della M. Walker. "Assimilation of the Spokane Indians." *Washington Agricultural Experiment Station Bulletin.* No. 628.

Pullman: Washington State University, Institute of Agricultural Science, 1961.

Shaffrey, Mary M. "Lumbee Get a Win, But Not without Stipulation." *Winston-Salem Journal* (April 26, 2007).

Shapley, Thomas. "Historical Revision Rights a Wrong." *Seattle Post-Intelligencer.* (December 18, 2004). Available online from http://www.seattlepi.com/local/opinion/article/Historical-revision-rights-a-wrong-1162234.php#ixzz1WBFxoNiw (accessed on August 15, 2011).

"Q: Should Scientists Be Allowed to 'Study' the Skeletons of Ancient American Indians?" (Symposium: U.S. Representative Doc Hastings; Confederated Tribes of the Umatilla Indian Reservation Spokesman Donald Sampson). *Insight on the News* 13, no. 47 (December 22, 1997): 24.

Siegel, Lee. "Mummies Might Have Been Made by Anasazi." *Salt Lake Tribune,* April 2, 1998.

Stewart, Kenneth M. "Mohave Warfare." *Southwestern Journal of Anthropology* 3, no. 3 (Autumn 1947): 257–78.

Trivedi, Bijal P. "Ancient Timbers Reveal Secrets of Anasazi Builders." *National Geographic Today,* September 28, 2001. Available online at http://news.nationalgeographic.com/news/2001/09/0928_TVchaco.html (accessed on June 29, 2007).

Trumbauer, Sophie. "Northwest Tribes Canoe to Lummi Island." *The Daily.* (August 1, 2007). Available online at http://thedaily.washington.edu/article/2007/8/1/northwestTribesCanoeToLumm (accessed on November 2, 2011).

Van Meter, David. "Energy Efficient." *University of Texas at Arlington,* Fall 2006.

Wagner, Dennis. "Stolen Artifacts Shatter Ancient Culture." *The Arizona Republic,* November 12, 2006.

Warshall, Peter. "The Heart of Genuine Sadness: Astronomers, Politicians, and Federal Employees Desecrate the Holiest Mountain of the San Carlos Apache." *Whole Earth* 91 (Winter 1997): 30.

Win, WambliSina. "The Ultimate Expression of Faith, the Lakota Sun Dance." *Native American Times.* July 4, 2011. Available online from http://www.nativetimes.com/index.php?option=com_content&view=article&id=5657:the-ultimate-expression-of-faith-the-lakota-sun-dance&catid=46&Itemid=22 (accessed on July 4, 2011).

Web Sites

"Aboriginal Fisheries Strategy." *Fisheries and Oceans Canada.* http://www.dfo-mpo.gc.ca/fm-gp/aboriginal-autochtones/afs-srapa-eng.htm (accessed on August 15, 2011).

"Aboriginal Peoples: The Métis." *Newfoundland and Labrador Heritage.* http://www.heritage.nf.ca/aboriginal/metis.html (accessed on August 4, 2011).

"About the Hopi." Restoration. http://hopi.org/about-the-hopi/ (accessed on July 20, 2011).

"Acoma Pueblo." *ClayHound Web.* http://www.clayhound.us/sites/acoma.htm (accessed on July 20, 2011).

"Acoma Pueblo." *New Mexico Magazine.*http://www.nmmagazine.com/native_american/acoma.php (accessed on July 20, 2011).

"Acoma'Sky City'" *National Trust for Historic Preservation.*http://www.acomaskycity.org/ (accessed on July 20, 2011).

"Address of Tarhe, Grand Sachem of the Wyandot Nation, to the Assemblage at the Treaty of Greeneville, July 22, 1795." *Wyandotte Nation of Oklahoma.* http://www.wyandotte-nation.org/history/tarhe_greenville_address.html (accessed May 12, 2011).

"The Adena Mounds." *Grave Creek Mound State Park.* http://www.adena.com/adena/ad/ad01.htm (accessed June 7, 2011).

Adley-SantaMaria, Bernadette. "White Mountain Apache Language Issues." *Northern Arizona University.* http://www2.nau.edu/jar/TIL_12.html (accessed on July 20, 2011).

Akimoff, Tim. "Snowshoe Builders Display Their Craft at the Anchorage Museum." *KTUU.* May 5, 2011. http://www.ktuu.com/news/ktuu-snowshoe-builders-display-their-craft-at-the-anchorage-museum-20110505,0,7760220.story (accessed on June 6, 2011).

Alamo Chapter. http://alamo.nndes.org/ (accessed on July 20, 2011).

Alaska Native Collections. *Smithsonian Institution.* http://alaska.si.edu/cultures.asp (accessed on August 15, 2011).

— — —. "Unangan."*Smithsonian Institution.* http://alaska.si.edu/culture_unangan.asp(accessed on August 15, 2011).

"Alaska Native Language Center." *University of Alaska Fairbanks.* http://www.uaf.edu/anlc//anlc/languages/ (accessed on June 4, 2011).

Alaska Yup'ik Eskimo. http://www.yupik.com (accessed on August 15, 2011).

All Indian Pueblo Council. http://www.20pueblos.org/ (accessed on July 20, 2011).

Allen, Cain. "The Oregon History Project: Toby Winema Riddle."*Oregon Historical Society.* http://www.ohs.org/education/oregonhistory/historical_records/dspDocument.cfm?doc_ID=000A9FE3-B226-1EE8-827980B05272FE9F (accessed on August 11, 2011).

"Alutiiq and Aleut/Unangan History and Culture."*Anchorage Museum.* http://www.anchoragemuseum.org/galleries/alaska_gallery/aleut.aspx (accessed on August 15, 2011).

Aluttiq Museum. http://alutiiqmuseum.org/ (accessed on August 15, 2011).

"Anasazi: The Ancient Ones." *Manitou Cliff Dwellings Museum.* http://www.cliffdwellingsmuseum.com/anasazi.htm (accessed on July 20, 2011).

"Anasazi Heritage Center: Ancestral Pueblos." *Bureau of Land Management Colorado.* http://www.co.blm.gov/ahc/anasazi.htm (accessed on July 13, 2011).

"The Anasazi or 'Ancient Pueblo.'" *Northern Arizona University.* http://www.cpluhna.nau.edu/People/anasazi.htm (accessed on July 20, 2011).

"Ancient Architects of the Mississippi." *National Park Service, Department of the Interior.* http://www.cr.nps.gov/archeology/feature/feature.htm (accessed on July 10, 2007).

"Ancient DNA from the Ohio Hopewell." *Ohio Archaeology Blog,* June 22, 2006. http://ohio-archaeology.blogspot.com/2006/06/ancient-dna-from-ohio-hopewell.html (accessed on July 10, 2007).

"Ancient Moundbuilders of Arkansas." *University of Arkansas.* http://cast.uark.edu/home/research/archaeology-and-historic-preservation/archaeological-interpretation/ancient-moundbuilders-of-arkansas.html (accessed on June 10, 2011).

"Ancient One: Kennewick Man." *Confederated Tribes of the Umatilla Reservation.* http://www.umatilla.nsn.us/ancient.html (accessed on August 11, 2011).

Anderson, Jeff. "Arapaho Online Research Resources." *Colby College.* http://www.colby.edu/personal/j/jdanders/arapahoresearch.htm (accessed on July 2, 2011).

"Anishinaabe Chi-Naaknigewin/Anishinabek Nation Constitution." *Anishinabek Nation.* http://www.anishinabek.ca/uploads/ANConstitution.pdf (accessed on May 16, 2011).

"Antelope Valley Indian Peoples: The Late Prehistoric Period: Kawaiisu." *Antelope Valley Indian Museum.* http://www.avim.parks.ca.gov/people/ph_kawaiisu.shtml (accessed on August 15, 2011).

"Apache Indian History." *Access Genealogy.* http://www.accessgenealogy.com/native/tribes/apache/apachehist.htm (accessed on July 15, 2011).

"Apache Indians." *AAA Native Arts.* http://www.aaanativearts.com/apache (accessed on July 15, 2011).

"Apache Nation: Nde Nation." *San Carlos Apache Nation.* http://www.sancarlosapache.com/home.htm (accessed on July 15, 2011).

"Apache Tribal Nation." *Dreams of the Great Earth Changes.* http://www.greatdreams.com/apache/apache-tribe.htm (accessed on July 15, 2011).

"The Apsáalooke (Crow Indians) of Montana Tribal Histories." *Little Big Horn College.* http://lib.lbhc.edu/history/ (accessed on July 5, 2011).

Aquino, Pauline. "Ohkay Owingeh: Village of the Strong People" (video). *New Mexico State Record Center and Archives.* http://www.newmexicohistory.org/filedetails.php?fileID=22530 (accessed on July 20, 2011).

"The Arapaho Tribe." *Omaha Public Library.* http://www.omahapubliclibrary.org/transmiss/congress/arapaho.html (accessed on July 2, 2011).

Arctic Circle. http://arcticcircle.uconn.edu/Museum/ (accessed on June 10, 2011).

"Arctic Circle." *University of Connecticut.* http://arcticcircle.uconn.edu/VirtualClassroom/ (accessed on August 15, 2011).

"The Arctic Is…." *Stefansson Arctic Institute.* http://www.thearctic.is/ (accessed on August 15, 2011).

Arctic Library. "Inuit" *Athropolis.* http://www.athropolis.com/library-cat.htm#inuit (accessed on August 15, 2011).

"Arikira Indians." *PBS.* http://www.pbs.org/lewisandclark/native/ari.html (accessed on June 19, 2011).

"Arkansas Indians: Arkansas Archeological Survey." *University of Arkansas.* http://www.uark.edu/campus-resources/archinfo/ArkansasIndianTribes.pdf (accessed on June 12, 2011).

Arlee, Johnny. *Over a Century of Moving to the Drum: Salish Indian Celebrations on the Flathead Reservation.* Helena: Montana Historical Society Press, 1998. Available online from http://www.archive.org/stream/historicalsketch00ronarich/historicalsketch00ronarich_djvu.txt (accessed on August 11, 2011).

Armstrong, Kerry M. "Chickasaw Historical Research Page." *Chickasaw History.* http://www.chickasawhistory.com/ (accessed on June 16, 2011.

"Art on the Prairies: Otoe-Missouria." *The Bata Shoe Museum.* http://www.allaboutshoes.ca/en/paths_across/art_on_prairies/index_7.php (accessed on June 20, 2011).

"Assiniboin Indian History." *Access Genealogy.* http://www.accessgenealogy.com/native/tribes/assiniboin/assiniboinhist.htm (accessed on June 7, 2011).

"Assinboin Indians." *PBS.* http://www.pbs.org/lewisandclark/native/idx_ass.html (accessed on June 7, 2011).

"Assiniboine History." *Fort Belknap Indian Community.* http://www.ftbelknap-nsn.gov/assiniboineHistory.php (accessed on June 6, 2011).

"Athabascan." Alaska Native Heritage Center Museum. http://www.alaskanative.net/en/main_nav/education/culture_alaska/athabascan/ (accessed on June 6, 2011).

Banyacya, Thomas. "Message to the World." *Hopi Traditional Elder.* http://banyacya.indigenousnative.org/ (accessed on July 20, 2011).

Barnett, Jim. "The Natchez Indians." *History Now.* http://mshistory.k12.ms.us/index.php?id=4 (accessed on June 27, 2011).

Barry, Paul C. "Native America Nations and Languages: Haudenosaunee." *The Canku Ota—A Newsletter Celebrating Native America.* http://www.turtletrack.org/Links/NANations/CO_NANationLinks_HJ.htm (accessed on June 5, 2011).

"Before the White Man Came to Nisqually Country." *Washington History Online.* January 12, 2006. http://washingtonhistoryonline.org/treatytrail/teaching/before-white-man.pdf (accessed on August 15, 2011).

Big Valley Band of Pomo Indians. http://www.big-valley.net/index.htm (accessed on August 11, 2011).

Bishop Paiute Tribe. http://www.bishoppaiutetribe.com/ (accessed on August 15, 2011).

"Black Kettle." *PBS.* http://www.pbs.org/weta/thewest/people/a_c/blackkettle. htm (accessed on July 4, 2011).

"Blackfeet." *Wisdom of the Elders.* http://www.wisdomoftheelders.org/ program208.html (accessed on July 2, 2011).

"Blackfoot History." *Head-Smashed-In Buffalo Jump Interpretive Centre.* http:// www.head-smashed-in.com/black.html (accessed on July 2, 2011).

Blackfeet Nation. http://www.blackfeetnation.com/ (accessed on July 2, 2011).

Boyer, Ruth McDonald, and Narcissus Duffy Gayton. "Apache Mothers and Daughters: Four Generations of a Family. Remembrances of an Apache Elder Woman." *Southwest Crossroads.* http://southwestcrossroads.org/ record.php?num=825&hl=Apache (accessed on July 20, 2011).

British Columbia Archives. "First Nations Research Guide." *Royal BC Museum Corporation.* http://www.royalbcmuseum.bc.ca/BC_Research_Guide/ BC_First_Nations.aspx (accessed on August 15, 2011).

Bruchac, Joe. "Storytelling." *Abenaki Nation.* http://www.abenakination.org/ stories.html (accessed on June 5, 2011).

Brush, Rebecca. "The Wichita Indians." *Texas Indians.* http://www.texasindi- ans.com/wichita.htm (accessed on June 9, 2011).

"Caddo Indian History." *Access Genealogy.* http://www.accessgenealogy.com/ native/tribes/caddo/caddohist.htm (accessed on June 12, 2011).

"Cahto (Kato)." *Four Directions Institute.* http://www.fourdir.com/cahto.htm (accessed on August 11, 2011).

"Cahto Tribe Information Network." *Cahto Tribe.* http://www.cahto.org/ (accessed on August 11, 2011).

"Cahuilla." *Four Directions Institute.* http://www.fourdir.com/cahuilla.htm (accessed on August 11, 2011).

Cahuilla Band of Mission Indians. http://cahuillabandofindians.com/ (accessed on August 11, 2011).

"California Indians." *Visalia Unified School District.* http://visalia.k12.ca.us/ teachers/tlieberman/indians/ (accessed on August 15, 2011).

California Valley Miwok Tribe, California. http://www.californiavalleymiwoktribe- nsn.gov/ (accessed on August 11, 2011).

Cambra, Rosemary, et al. "The Muwekma Ohlone Tribe of the San Fran- cisco Bay Area." http://www.islaiscreek.org/ohlonehistcultfedrecog.html (accessed on August 11, 2011).

"Camp Grant Massacre—April 30, 1871." *Council of Indian Nations.* http:// www.nrcprograms.org/site/PageServer?pagename=cin_hist_campgrantmas- sacre (accessed on July 20, 2011).

Campbell, Grant. "The Rock Paintings of the Chumash." *Association for Humanistic Psychology.* http://www.ahpweb.org/articles/chumash.html (accessed on August 11, 2011).

Canadian Heritage Information Network. "Communities& Institutions: Talented Youth." *Tipatshimuna.* http://www.tipatshimuna.ca/1420_e.php (accessed on May 19, 2011).

Carleton, Kenneth H. "A Brief History of the Mississippi Band of Choctaw Indians." *Mississippi Band of Choctaw.* http://mdah.state.ms.us/hpres/A%20Brief%20History%20of%20the%20Choctaw.pdf (accessed on June 12, 2011).

Central Council: Tlingit and Haida Indian Tribes of Alaska. http://www.ccthita.org/ (accessed on November 2, 2011).

Cherokee Nation. http://www.cherokee.org/ (accessed on June 12, 2011).

"Cheyenne Indian." *American Indian Tribes.* http://www.cheyenneindian.com/cheyenne_links.htm (accessed on July 4, 2011).

"Cheyenne Indian History." *Access Genealogy.* http://www.accessgenealogy.com/native/tribes/cheyenne/cheyennehist.htm (accessed on July 4, 2011).

"Chickasaw Indian History." *Access Genealogy.* http://www.accessgenealogy.com/native/tribes/chickasaw/chickasawhist.htm (accessed on June 16, 2011).

The Chickasaw Nation. http://www.chickasaw.net (accessed on June 12, 2011).

"Chief Joseph." *PBS.* http://www.pbs.org/weta/thewest/people/a_c/chiefjoseph.htm (accessed on August 11, 2011).

"Chief Joseph Surrenders." *The History Place.* http://www.historyplace.com/speeches/joseph.htm (accessed on August 11,2011).

Chief Leschi School. http://www.leschischools.org/ (accessed on November 2, 2011).

"Chief Seattle Speech." *Washington State Library.* http://www.synaptic.bc.ca/ejournal/wslibrry.htm (accessed on November 2, 2011).

"The Children of Changing Woman." *Peabody Museum of Archaeology and Ethnology.* http://www.peabody.harvard.edu/maria/Cwoman.html (accessed on July 15, 2011).

"The Chilula." *The Indians of the Redwoods.* http://www.cr.nps.gov/history/online_books/redw/history1c.htm (accessed on August 11, 2011).

Chinook Indian Tribe/Chinook Nation. http://www.chinooknation.org/ (accessed on November 2, 2011).

"Chinookan Family History." *Access Genealogy.* http://www.accessgenealogy.com/native/tribes/chinook/chinookanfamilyhist.htm (accessed on November 2, 2011).

"Chippewa Cree Tribe (Neiyahwahk)." *Montana Office of Indian Affairs.* http://www.tribalnations.mt.gov/chippewacree.asp (accessed on June 3, 2011).

"Chiricahua Indian History." *Access Genealogy.* http://www.accessgenealogy. com/native/tribes/apache/chiricahua.htm (accessed on July 20, 2011).

Chisolm, D. "Mi'kmaq Resource Centre," *Cape Breton University.* http://mrc. uccb.ns.ca/mikmaq.html (accessed on May 15, 2011).

"Choctaw Indian History." *Access Genealogy.* http://www.accessgenealogy.com/ native/tribes/choctaw/chostawhist.htm (accessed on June 21, 2011).

"Choctaw Indian Tribe." *Native American Nations.* http://www.nanations.com/ choctaw/index.htm (accessed on June 21, 2011).

Choctaw Nation of Oklahoma. http://www.choctawnation.com (accessed on June 12, 2011).

"Chumash." *Four Directions Institute.* http://www.fourdir.com/chumash.htm (accessed on December 1, 2011).

The Chumash Indians. http://www.chumashindian.com/ (accessed on August 11, 2011).

Clark, William. "Lewis and Clark: Expedition Journals." *National Geographic.* http://www.nationalgeographic.com/lewisandclark/record_tribes_020_5_1. html (accessed on June 19, 2011).

— — —. "Lewis and Clark: Missouri Indians." *National Geographic.* http:// www.nationalgeographic.com/lewisandclark/record_tribes_012_1_9.html (accessed on June 20, 2011).

"Coast Miwok at Point Reyes." *U.S. National Park Service.* http://www.nps. gov/pore/historyculture/people_coastmiwok.htm (accessed on August 11, 2011).

"Coastal Miwok Indians." *Reed Union School District.* http://rusd.marin. k12.ca.us/belaire/ba_3rd_miwoks/coastalmiwoks/webpages/home. html(accessed on August 11, 2011).

"Comanche." *Edward S. Curtis's The North American Indian.* http://curtis. library.northwestern.edu/curtis/toc.cgi (accessed on July 4, 2011).

"Comanche Indian History." *Access Genealogy.* http://www.accessgenealogy. com/native/tribes/comanche/comanchehist.htm (accessed on July 4, 2011).

"Comanche Language." *Omniglot.* http://www.omniglot.com/writing/coman-che.htm (accessed on July 4, 2011).

Comanche Nation of Oklahoma http://www.comanchenation.com/ (accessed on July 4, 2011).

"Community News." *Mississippi Band of Choctaw Indians.* http://www.choctaw. org/ (accessed on June 12, 2011).

Compton, W. J. "The Story of Ishi, the Yana Indian." *Ye Slyvan Archer.* July 1936. http://tmuss.tripod.com/shotfrompast/chief.htm (accessed on August 11, 2011).

The Confederated Salish and Kootenai Tribes. http://www.cskt.org/ (accessed on August 11, 2011).

Confederated Tribes and Bands of the Yakama Nation. http://www.yakamana-tion-nsn.gov/ (accessed on August 11, 2011).

Confederated Tribes of the Colville Reservation. http://www.colvilletribes.com/ (accessed on August 11, 2011).

Confederated Tribes of Siletz. http://ctsi.nsn.us/ (accessed on November 2, 2011).

Confederated Tribes of the Umatilla Indian Reservation. http://www.umatilla.nsn.us/ (accessed on August 11, 2011).

"Confederated Tribes of the Umatilla Indians." *Wisdom of the Elders.* http://www.wisdomoftheelders.org/program305.html (accessed on August 11, 2011).

"Confederated Tribes of the Yakama Nation." *Wisdom of the Elders.* http://www.wisdomoftheelders.org/program304.html (accessed on August 11, 2011).

"Connecting the World with Seattle's First People."*Duwamish Tribe.* http://www.duwamishtribe.org/ (accessed on November 2, 2011).

Conrad, Jim. "The Natchez Indians." *The Loess Hills of the Lower Mississipi Valley.* http://www.backyardnature.net/loess/ind_natz.htm (accessed on June 27, 2011).

Cordell, Linda. "Anasazi." *Scholastic.* http://www2.scholastic.com/browse/article.jsp?id=5042 (accessed on July 20, 2011).

"Costanoan Indian Tribe." *Access Genealogy.* http://www.accessgenealogy.com/native/tribes/costanoan/costanoanindiantribe.htm (accessed on August 11, 2011).

Costanoan Rumsen Carmel Tribe. http://costanoanrumsen.org/ (accessed on August 11, 2011).

"Costanoan Rumsen Carmel Tribe: History." *Native Web.* http://crc.nativeweb.org/history.html (accessed on August 11, 2011).

Cotton, Lee. "Powhatan Indian Lifeways." *National Park Service.* http://www.nps.gov/jame/historyculture/powhatan-indian-lifeways.htm (accessed on June 1, 2011).

Council of the Haida Nation (CHN). http://www.haidanation.ca/ (accessed on November 2, 2011).

"A Coyote's Tales—Tohono O'odham." *First People: American Indian Legends.* http://www.firstpeople.us/FP-Html-Legends/A_Coyotes_Tales-TohonoOodham.html (accessed on July 20, 2011).

"Creek Indian." *American Indian Tribe.* http://www.creekindian.com/ (accessed on June 12, 2011).

"Creek Indians." *GeorgiaInfo.* http://georgiainfo.galileo.usg.edu/creek.htm (accessed on June 12, 2011).

"Crow/Cheyenne." *Wisdom of the Elders.* http://www.wisdomoftheelders.org/program206.html (accessed on July 5, 2011).

"Crow Indian Tribe." *Access Genealogy.* http://www.accessgenealogy.com/native/tribes/crow/crowhist.htm (accessed on July 5, 2011).

Crow Tribe, Apsáalooke Nation Official Website. http://www.crowtribe.com/ (accessed on July 5, 2011).

"Culture and History."*Innu Nation.*http://www.innu.ca/index.php?option=com_content&view=article&id=8&Itemid=3&lang=en (accessed on May 19, 2011).

"Culture& History." *Aleut Corporation.* http://www.aleutcorp.com/index.php?option=com_content&view=section&layout=blog&id=6&Itemid=24 (accessed on August 15, 2011).

"Culture and History of the Skokomish Tribe." *Skokomish Tribal Nation.* http://www.skokomish.org/historyculture.htm (accessed on November 2, 2011).

Curtis, Edward S. *The North American Indian.*Vol.13. 1924. Reprint. New York: Johnson Reprint Corporation, 1970. Available online from *Northwestern University Digital Library Collections.* http://curtis.library.northwestern.edu/curtis/viewPage.cgi?showp=1&size=2&id=nai.13.book.00000192&volume=13#nav-Edward (accessed on August 11, 2011).

"Dakota Indian Tribe History." *Access Genealogy.* http://www.accessgenealogy.com/native/tribes/siouan/dakotahist.htm (accessed on July 5, 2011).

"Dakota Spirituality." *Blue Cloud Abbey.* http://www.bluecloud.org/dakotaspirituality.html (accessed on July 5, 2011).

"Dams of the Columbia Basin and Their Effects on the Native Fishery." *Center for Columbia River History.* http://www.ccrh.org/comm/river/dams6.htm (accessed on August 11, 2011).

Deans, James. "Tales from the Totems of the Hidery." *Early Canadiana Online.* http://www.canadiana.org/ECO/PageView/06053/0003?id=986858ca5fbdc633 (accessed on November 2, 2011).

Deer Lake First Nation. http://www.deerlake.firstnation.ca/ (accessed on June 5, 2011).

"Delaware Indian Chiefs." *Access Genealogy.* http://www.accessgenealogy.com/native/tribes/delaware/delawarechiefs.htm (accessed on June 8, 2011).

"Delaware Indian/Lenni Lenape." *Delaware Indians of Pennsylvania.* http://www.delawareindians.com/ (accessed on June 8, 2011).

"Delaware Indians." *Ohio Historical Society.* http://www.ohiohistorycentral.org/entry.php?rec=584 (accessed on June 2, 2011).

The Delaware Nation. http://www.delawarenation.com/ (accessed on June 2, 2011).

Delaware Tribe of Indians. http://www.delawaretribeofindians.nsn.us/ (accessed on June 2, 2011).

DelawareIndian.com. http://www.delawareindian.com/ (accessed on June 2, 2011).

Dene Cultural Institute. http://www.deneculture.org/ (accessed on June 10, 2011).

Deschenes, Bruno. "Inuit Throat-Singing." *Musical Traditions.* http://www. mustrad.org.uk/articles/inuit.htm (accessed on August 15, 2011).

"Desert Native Americans: Mohave Indians." *Mojave Desert.* http:// mojavedesert.net/mojave-indians/ (accessed on July 20, 2011).

Dodds, Lissa Guimarães. "'The Washoe People': Past and Present." *Washoe Tribe of Nevada and California.* http://www.Washoetribe.us/images/ Washoe_tribe_history_v2.pdf (accessed on August 15, 2011).

"Duwamish Indian Tribe History." *Access Genealogy.* http://www.accessgeneal-ogy.com/native/tribes/salish/duwamishhist.htm (accessed on November 2, 2011).

"The Early History and Names of the Arapaho." *Native American Nations.* http://www.nanations.com/early_arapaho.htm (accessed on July 2, 2011).

Eastern Shawnee Tribe of Oklahoma. http://estoo-nsn.gov/ (accessed on June 12, 2011).

Eck, Pam. "Hopi Indians." *Indiana University.* http://inkido.indiana.edu/ w310work/romac/hopi.htm (accessed on July 20, 2011).

Edward S. Curtis's The North American Indian. http://curtis.library.northwest-ern.edu/curtis/toc.cgi (accessed on August 11, 2011).

Elam, Earl H. "Wichita Indians." *Texas State Historical Association.* http://www. tshaonline.org/handbook/online/articles/bmw03 (accessed on June 9, 2011).

Ely Shoshone Tribe. http://elyshoshonetribe-nsn.gov/departments.html (accessed on August 15, 2011).

Etienne-Gray, Tracé. "Black Seminole Indians." *Texas State Historical Associa-tion.* http://www.tshaonline.org/handbook/online/articles/bmb18 (accessed on June 12, 2011).

Everett, Diana. "Apache Tribe of Oklahoma." *Oklahoma Historical Soci-ety.* http://digital.library.okstate.edu/encyclopedia/entries/A/AP002. html(accessed on July 15, 2011).

"Eyak, Tlingit, Haida, and Tsimshian." *Alaska Native Heritage Center Museum.* http://www.alaskanative.net/en/main_nav/education/culture_alaska/eyak/ (accessed on August 15, 2011).

Fausz, J. Frederick. "The Louisiana Expansion: The Arikara." *University of Missouri–St. Louis.* http://www.umsl.edu/continuinged/louisiana/Am_ Indians/8-Arikara/8-arikara.html (accessed on June 19, 2011).

———. "The Louisiana Expansion: The Kansa/Kaw." *University of Missouri-St. Louis.* http://www.umsl.edu/continuinged/louisiana/Am_Indians/3-Kansa_Kaw/3-kansa_kaw.html (accessed on June 17, 2011).

———. "The Louisiana Expansion: The Missouri/Missouria." *University of Missouri–St. Louis.* http://www.umsl.edu/continuinged/louisiana/Am_ Indians/2-Missouria/2-missouria.html (accessed on June 20, 2011).

— — —. "The Louisiana Expansion: The Oto(e)." *University of Missouri-St. Louis.* http://www.umsl.edu/continuinged/louisiana/Am_Indians/4-Oto/4-oto.html (accessed on June 20, 2011).

Feller, Walter. "California Indian History." *Digital Desert.* http://mojavedesert.net/california-indian-history/ (accessed on August 11, 2011).

— — —. "Mojave Desert Indians: Cahuilla Indians." *Digital-Desert.* http://mojavedesert.net/cahuilla-indians/ (accessed on August 11, 2011).

"First Nations: People of the Interior." *British Columbia Archives.* http://www.bcarchives.gov.bc.ca/exhibits/timemach/galler07/frames/int_peop.htm (accessed on August 11, 2011).

"First Peoples of Canada: Communal Hunters." *Canadian Museum of Civilization.* http://www.civilization.ca/cmc/home (accessed on June 10, 2011).

"Flathead Indians (Salish)." *National Geographic.* http://www.nationalgeographic.com/lewisandclark/record_tribes_022_12_16.html (accessed on August 11, 2011).

"Flathead Reservation." http://www.montanatribes.org/links_&_resources/tribes/Flathead_Reservation.pdf (accessed on August 11, 2011).

Flora, Stephenie. "Northwest Indians: 'The First People.'" *Oregon Pioneers.* http://www.oregonpioneers.com/indian.htm (accessed on August 15, 2011).

Forest County Potawatomi. http://www.fcpotawatomi.com/ (accessed on June 5, 2011).

Fort McDowell Yavapai Nation. http://www.ftmcdowell.org/ (accessed on July 20, 2011).

"Fort Mojave Indian Tribe." *Inter Tribal Council of Arizona, Inc.* http://www.itcaonline.com/tribes_mojave.html (accessed on July 20, 2011).

Fort Peck Tribes. http://www.fortpecktribes.org/ (accessed on June 4, 2011).

Fort Sill Apache Tribe. http://www.fortsillapache.com (accessed on July 20, 2011).

"Fort Yuma-Quechan Tribe." *Inter-Tribal Council of Arizona, Inc.* http://www.itcaonline.com/tribes_quechan.html (accessed on July 20, 2011).

Gangnier, Gary. "The History of the Innu Nation." *Central Quebec School Board.* http://www.cqsb.qc.ca/svs/434/fninnu.htm (accessed on May 24, 2011).

Gerke, Sarah Bohl. "White Mountain Apache." *Arizona State University.* http://grandcanyonhistory.clas.asu.edu/history_nativecultures_whitemountainapache.html (accessed on July 20, 2011).

"Geronimo, His Own Story: A Prisoner of War." *From Revolution to Reconstruction.* http://www.let.rug.nl/usa/B/geronimo/geroni17.htm (accessed on July 20, 2011).

"Gifting and Feasting in the Northwest Coast Potlatch." *Peabody Museum of Archaeology and Ethnology.* http://www.peabody.harvard.edu/potlatch/ (accessed on November 2, 2011).

Glenn Black Laboratory of Archaeology. "Burial Mounds." *Indiana University.* http://www.gbl.indiana.edu/abstracts/adena/mounds.html (accessed June 7, 2011).

— — —. "The Ohio Valley-Great Lakes Ethnohistory Archives: The Miami Collection." *Indiana University.* http://gbl.indiana.edu/ethnohistory/ archives/menu.html (accessed on June 7, 2011).

Glover, William B. "A History of the Caddo Indians." Formatted for the World Wide Web by Jay Salsburg. Reprinted from *The Louisiana Historical Quarterly*, 18, no. 4 (October 1935). http://ops.tamu.edu/x075bb/caddo/ Indians.html (accessed on June 12, 2011).

GoodTracks, Jimm. "These Native Ways." *Turtle Island Storytellers Network.* http://www.turtleislandstorytellers.net/tis_kansas/transcript01_jg_tracks. htm (accessed on June 20, 2011).

"Grand Village of the Natchez Indians." *Mississippi Department of Archives and History.* http://mdah.state.ms.us/hprop/gvni.html (accessed on June 27, 2011).

Great Basin Indian Archives. http://www.gbcnv.edu/gbia/index.htm (accessed on August 15, 2011).

Great Basin National Park. "Historic Tribes of the Great Basin." *National Park Service: U.S. Department of the Interior.* http://www.nps.gov/grba/histo-ryculture/historic-tribes-of-the-great-basin.htm (accessed on August 15, 2011).

Greene, Candace S. "Kiowa Drawings." *National Anthropological Archives, National Museum of Natural History.* http://www.nmnh.si.edu/naa/kiowa/ kiowa.htm (accessed on July 4, 2011).

"Haida." *The Kids' Site of Canadian Settlement, Library and Archives Canada.* http://www.collectionscanada.ca/settlement/kids/021013-2061-e.html (accessed on November 2, 2011).

"Haida Heritage Center at Qay'llnagaay." *Haida Heritage Centre.* http://www. haidaheritagecentre.com/ (accessed on November 2, 2011).

"Haida Language Program." *Sealaska Heritage Institute.* http://www.sealaska-heritage.org/programs/haida_language_program.htm (accessed on November 2, 2011).

"Haida Spirits of the Sea." *Virtual Museum of Canada.* http://www.virtualmuseum. ca/Exhibitions/Haida/nojava/english/home/index.html (accessed on November 2, 2011).

Handbook of American Indians. "Arikara Indian Tribe History." *Access Geneal-ogy.* http://www.accessgenealogy.com/native/tribes/nations/arikara.htm (accessed on June 19, 2011).

Handbook of American Indians.. "Quapaw Indian Tribe History." *Access Gene-alogy.* http://www.accessgenealogy.com/native/tribes/quapaw/quapawhist. htm (accessed on June 20, 2011).

"History—Incident at Wounded Knee." *U.S. Marshals Service.* http://www.usmarshals.gov/history/wounded-knee/index.html (accessed on July 4, 2011).

"History: We Are the Anishnaabek." *The Grand Traverse Band of Ottawa and Chippewa.* http://www.gtbindians.org/history.html (accessed May 13, 2011).

"History and Culture." *Cherokee North Carolina.* http://www.cherokee-nc.com/history_intro.php (accessed on June 12, 2011).

"A History of American Indians in California." *National Park Service.* http://www.nps.gov/history/history/online_books/5views/5views1.htm (accessed on August 15, 2011).

"History of Northern Ute Indian, Utah." *Online Utah.* http://www.onlineutah.com/utehistorynorthern.shtml (accessed on August 15, 2011).

"History of the Confederated Tribes of the Siletz Indians." *HeeHeeIllahee RV Resort.* http://www.heeheeillahee.com/html/about_tribe_history.htm (accessed on November 2, 2011).

Hollabaugh, Mark. "Brief History of the Lakota People." *Normandale Community College.* http://faculty.normandale.edu/-physics/Hollabaugh/Lakota/BriefHistory.htm (accessed on July 4, 2011).

Holt, Ronald L. "Paiute Indians." *State of Utah.* http://historytogo.utah.gov/utah_chapters/american_indians/paiuteindians.html (accessed on August 15, 2011).

Holzman, Allan. "Beyond the Mesas [video]." *University of Illinois.* http://www.vimeo.com/16872541 (accessed on July 20, 2011).

———. "The Indian Boarding School Experience [video]." *University of Illinois.* http://www.vimeo.com/17410552 (accessed on July 20, 2011).

Hoopa Tribal Museum and San Francisco State University. http://bss.sfsu.edu/calstudies/hupa/Hoopa.HTM (accessed on August 11, 2011).

Hoopa Valley Tribe. http://www.hoopa-nsn.gov/ (accessed on August 11, 2011).

"Hopi." *Four Directions Institute.* http://www.fourdir.com/hopi.htm (accessed on July 20, 2011).

"Hopi." *Southwest Crossroads.* http://southwestcrossroads.org/search.php?query=hopi&tab=document&doc_view=10 (accessed on July 20, 2011).

"Hopi Indian Tribal History." *Access Genealogy.* www.accessgenealogy.com/native/tribes/hopi/hopeindianhist.htm (accessed on July 20, 2011).

"Hopi Tribe." *Inter Tribal Council of Arizona, Inc.* http://www.itcaonline.com/tribes_hopi.html (accessed on July 20, 2011).

"Hupa." *Four Directions Institute.* http://www.fourdir.com/hupa.htm (accessed on August 11, 2011).

"Hupa Indian Tribe." *Access Genealogy.* http://www.accessgenealogy.com/ native/tribes/athapascan/hupaindiantribe.htm (accessed on August 11, 2011).

Huron-Wendat Nation. http://www.wendake.com/ (accessed May 12, 2011).

Hurst, Winston. "Anasazi." *Utah History to Go: State of Utah.* http://historytogo. utah.gov/utah_chapters/american_indians/anasazi.html (accessed on July 20, 2011).

Indian Country Diaries. "Trail of Tears." *PBS.* http://www.pbs.org/indiancountry/ history/trail.html (accessed on June 12, 2011).

"Indian Peoples of the Northern Great Plains." *MSU Libraries.* http://www.lib. montana.edu/epubs/nadb/ (accessed on July 1, 2011).

Indian Pueblo Cultural Center. http://www.indianpueblo.org/ (accessed on July 20, 2011).

"Indian Tribes of California." *Access Genealogy.* http://www.accessgenealogy. com/native/california/ (accessed on August 11, 2011).

"Indians of the Northwest—Plateau and Coastal." *St. Joseph School Library.* http://library.stjosephsea.org/plateau.htm (accessed on August 11, 2011).

"Innu Youth Film Project."*Kamestastin.* http://www.kamestastin.com/ (accessed on May 24, 2011).

"The Inuit." *Newfoundland and Labrador Heritage.* http://www.heritage.nf.ca/ aboriginal/inuit.html (accessed on August 15, 2011).

"Jemez Pueblos." *Four Directions Institute.* http://www.fourdir.com/jemez.htm (accessed on July 20, 2011).

"Jemez Pueblo." *New Mexico Magazine.*http://www.nmmagazine.com/native_ american/jemez.php (accessed on July 20, 2011).

Jicarilla Apache Nation. http://www.jicarillaonline.com/ (accessed on July 15, 2011).

Johnson, Russ. "The Mississippian Period (900 AD to 1550 AD)" *Memphis History.* http://www.memphishistory.org/Beginnings/PreMemphis/ MississippianCulture/tabid/64/Default.aspx (accessed June 7, 2011).

"The Journals of the Lewis and Clark Expedition: Nez Percé." *University of Nebraska.* http://www.nationalgeographic.com/lewisandclark/record_ tribes_013_12_17.html (accessed on August 11, 2011).

Jozhe, Benedict. "A Brief History of the Fort Sill Apache Tribe." *Oklahoma Historical Society.* http://digital.library.okstate.edu/Chronicles/v039/v039p427. pdf (accessed on July 20, 2011).

"Kansa (Kaw)." *Four Directions Institute.* http://www.fourdir.com/kaw.htm (accessed on June 17, 2011).

"Kanza Cultural History." *The Kaw Nation.* http://kawnation.com/?page_id=216 (accessed on June 17, 2011).

"Kansa Indian Tribe History." *Access Geneology.* http://www.accessgenealogy.com/native/tribes/siouan/kansahist.htm (accessed on June 17, 2011).

Kavanagh, Thomas W. "Comanche." *Oklahoma Historical Society.* http://digital.library.okstate.edu/encyclopedia/entries/C/CO033.html (accessed on July 4, 2011).

— — —. "Reading Historic Photographs: Photographers of the Pawnee." *Indiana University.* http://php.indiana.edu/-tkavanag/phothana.html (accessed on July 6, 2011).

"Kawaiisu." *Four Directions Institute.* http://www.fourdir.com/Kawaiisu.htm (accessed on August 15, 2011).

"The Kawaiisu Culture." *Digital Desert: Mojave Desert.* http://mojavedesert.net/kawaiisu-indians/related-pages.html (accessed on August 15, 2011).

Kawaiisu Language and Cultural Center. http://www.kawaiisu.org/KLCC_home.html (accessed on August 15, 2011).

Kawno, Kenji. "Warriors: Navajo Code Talkers." *Southwest Crossroads.* http://southwestcrossroads.org/record.php?num=387 (accessed on July 20, 2011).

Kidwell, Clara Sue. "Choctaw." *Oklahoma Historical Society.* http://digital.library.okstate.edu/encyclopedia/entries/C/CH047.html (accessed on June 21, 2011).

"Kiowa Indian Tribe History." *Access Genealogy.* http://www.accessgenealogy.com/native/tribes/kiowa/kiowahist.htm (accessed on July 4, 2011).

"Kiowa Indian Tribe." *Kansas Genealogy.* http://www.kansasgenealogy.com/indians/kiowa_indian_tribe.htm(accessed on July 4, 2011).

*Kiowa Tribe.*http://www.kiowatribe.org/(accessed on July 4, 2011).

Kitt Peak National Observatory. "Tohono O'odham." *Association of Universities for Research in Astronomy.* http://www.noao.edu/outreach/kptour/kpno_tohono.html (accessed on July 20, 2011).

"Kwakiutl." *Four Directions Institute.* http://www.fourdir.com/kwakiutl.htm (accessed on November 2, 2011).

Kwakiutl Indian Band. http://www.kwakiutl.bc.ca/ (accessed on November 2, 2011).

"Lakota, Dakota, Nakota—The Great Sioux Nation." *Legends of America.* http://www.legendsofamerica.com/na-sioux.html (accessed on July 4, 2011).

"Lakota Page: The Great Sioux Nation." *Ancestry.com.* http://freepages.genealogy.rootsweb.ancestry.com/-nativeamericangen/page6.html (accessed on July 4, 2011).

"Lakota-Teton Sioux." *Wisdom of the Elders.* http://www.wisdomoftheelders.org/program203.html (accessed on July 4, 2011).

Larry, Mitchell. *The Native Blog.* http://nativeblog.typepad.com/the_potawatomitracks_blog/potawatomi_news/index.html (accessed on June 5, 2011).

"Leschi: Last Chief of the Nisquallies." *WashingtonHistoryOnline.* http://washingtonhistoryonline.org/leschi/leschi.htm (accessed on August 15, 2011).

"Lewis & Clark: Chinook Indians." *National Geographic.* http://www.nationalgeographic.com/lewisandclark/record_tribes_083_14_3.html (accessed on November 2, 2011).

"Lewis and Clark: Crow Indians (Absaroka)." *National Geographic Society.* http://www.nationalgeographic.com/lewisandclark/record_tribes_002_19_21.html (accessed on July 5, 2011).

"Lewis and Clark: Native Americans: Chinook Indians." *PBS.* http://www.pbs.org/lewisandclark/native/chi.html (accessed on November 2, 2011).

"Lewis & Clark: Tribes: Siletz Indians." *National Geographic.* http://www.nationalgeographic.com/lewisandclark/record_tribes_090_14_8.html (accessed on November 2, 2011).

"Lewis & Clark: Yankton Sioux Indians (Nakota)." *National Geographic.* http://www.nationalgeographic.com/lewisandclark/record_tribes_019_2_8.html (accessed on June 12, 2011).

Lewis, J.D. "The Natchez Indians." *Carolina—The Native Americans.* http://www.carolana.com/Carolina/Native_Americans/native_americans_natchez.html (accessed on June 27, 2011).

Lipscomb, Carol A. "Handbook of Texas Online: Comanche Indians." *Texas State Historical Association.* http://www.tshaonline.org/handbook/online/articles/bmc72 (accessed on July 4, 2011).

"The Long Walk." *Council of Indian Nations.* http://www.nrcprograms.org/site/PageServer?pagename=cin_hist_thelongwalk (accessed on July 20, 2011).

"Luiseño." *Four Directions Institute.* http://www.fourdir.com/luiseno.htm (accessed on August 11, 2011).

"Luiseno/Cahuilla Group." *San Francisco State University.* http://bss.sfsu.edu/calstudies/nativewebpages/luiseno.html (accessed on August 11, 2011).

"Lumbee History & Culture." *Lumbee Tribe of North Carolina.* http://www.lumbeetribe.com/History_Culture/History_Culture%20Index.html (accessed on June 4, 2011).

"Métis: History & Culture." *Turtle Island Productions.* http://www.turtle-island.com/native/the-ojibway-story/metis.html (accessed on June 4, 2011).

Métis Nation of Ontario. http://www.metisnation.org/ (accessed on June 4, 2011).

MacDonald, George F. "The Haida: Children of Eagle and Raven." *Canadian Museum of Civilization.* http://www.civilization.ca/cmc/exhibitions/aborig/haida/haindexe.shtml (accessed on November 2, 2011).

"Maidu." *Four Directions Institute.* http://www.fourdir.com/maidu.htm (accessed on August 11, 2011).

"The Maidu." *The First Americans.* http://thefirstamericans.homestead.com/Maidu.html (accessed on August 11, 2011).

"Maidu People." *City of Roseville.* http://www.roseville.ca.us/parks/parks_n_facilities/facilities/maidu_indian_museum/maidu_people.asp (accessed on August 11, 2011).

Makah Cultural and Research Center. http://www.makah.com/mcrchome.html (accessed on November 2, 2011).

The Makah Nation on Washington's Olympic Peninsula. http://www.northolympic.com/makah/ (accessed on November 2, 2011).

Manning, June. "Wampanoag Living." *Martha's Vineyard Magazine.* May–June 2010. http://www.mvmagazine.com/article.php?25216 (accessed on June 9, 2011).

Mashantucket Museum and Research Center. http://www.pequotmuseum.org/ (accessed on June 1, 2011).

Mashpee Wampanoag Tribe. http://mashpeewampanoagtribe.com/ (accessed on June 1, 2011).

"Massacre at Wounded Knee, 1890." *EyeWitness to History.* http://www.eyewitnesstohistory.com/knee.htm (accessed on July 4, 2011).

"Massai, Chiricahua Apache." *Discover Southeast Arizona.* http://www.discoverseaz.com/History/Massai.html (accessed on July 20, 2011).

May, John D. "Otoe-Missouria." *Oklahoma Historical Society.* http://digital.library.okstate.edu/encyclopedia/entries/O/OT001.html (accessed on June 20, 2011).

McCollum, Timothy James. "Quapaw." *Oklahoma Historical Society.* http://digital.library.okstate.edu/encyclopedia/entries/Q/QU003.html (accessed on June 20, 2011).

— — —. "Sac and Fox." *Oklahoma Historical Society.* http://digital.library.okstate.edu/encyclopedia/entries/S/SA001.html (accessed on June 5, 2011).

McCoy, Ron. "Neosho Valley: Osage Nation." *KTWU/Channel 11.* http://ktwu.washburn.edu/journeys/scripts/1111a.html (accessed on June 12, 2011).

McManamon, F. P. "Kennewick Man." *Archaeology Program, National Park Service, U.S. Department of the Interior.* http://www.nps.gov/archeology/kennewick/index.htm (accessed on August 11, 2011).

Media Action. "Excerpt from Youth-led Interview with Phillip Esai." *Vimeo.* http://vimeo.com/15465119 (accessed on June 6, 2011).

— — —. "A Portrait of Nikolai." *Vimeo.* 2010. http://vimeo.com/14854233 (accessed on June 6, 2011).

"Menominee Culture." *Menominee Indian Tribe of Wisconsin.* http://www.mpm.edu/wirp/ICW-54.html (accessed on June 7, 2011).

"Menominee Indian Tribe of Wisconsin." *Great Lakes Inter-Tribal Council.* http://www.glitc.org/programs/pages/mtw.html (accessed on June 7, 2011).

Menominee Indian Tribe of Wisconsin. http://www.menominee-nsn.gov/ (accessed June 8, 2011).

"Menominee Oral Tradition." *Indian Country.* http://www.mpm.edu/wirp/ICW-138.html (accessed on June 7, 2011).

Mescalero Apache Reservation. www.mescaleroapache.com/ (accessed on July 15, 2011).

"Metis Communities." *Labrador Métis Nation.* http://www.labradormetis.ca/home/10 (accessed on June 4, 2011).

"Miami Indian Tribe." *Native American Nations.* http://www.nanations.com/miami/index.htm (accessed on June 7, 2011).

"Miami Indians." *Ohio History Central.* http://www.ohiohistorycentral.org/entry.php?rec=606 (accessed on June 7, 2011).

Miami Nation of Oklahoma. http://www.miamination.com/ (accessed on June 7, 2011).

Miccosukee Seminole Nation. http://www.miccosukeeseminolenation.com/ (accessed on June 12, 2011).

"Mi'kmaq Resources" *Halifax Public Libraries.* http://www.halifaxpublicli-braries.ca/research/topics/mikmaqresources.html (accessed on June 1, 2011).

Mississippi Valley Archaeology Center at the University of Wisconsin–La Crosse, "Early Cultures: Pre-European Peoples of Wisconsin: Mississippian and Oneota Traditions." *Educational Web Adventures.* http://www.uwlax.edu/mvac/preeuropeanpeople/earlycultures/mississippi_tradition.html (accessed on June 20, 2011).

"Missouri Indian Tribe History." *Access Genealogy.* http://www.accessgenealogy.com/native/tribes/siouan/missourihist.htm (accessed on June 20, 2011).

"Missouri Indians." *PBS.* http://www.pbs.org/lewisandclark/native/mis.html (accessed on June 20, 2011).

"Miwok." *Four Directions Institute.* http://www.fourdir.com/miwok.htm (accessed on August 11, 2011).

Miwok Archeological Preserve of Marin. "The Miwok People." *California State Parks.* http://www.parks.ca.gov/default.asp?page_id=22538 (accessed on August 11, 2011).

"Miwok Indian Tribe History." *Access Genealogy.* http://www.accessgenealogy.com/native/california/miwokindianhist.htm (accessed on August 11, 2011).

"Modoc." *College of the Siskiyous.* http://www.siskiyous.edu/shasta/nat/mod.htm (accessed on August 11, 2011).

"Modoc." *Four Directions Institute.* http://www.fourdir.com/modoc.htm (accessed on August 11, 2011).

"Modoc Indian Chiefs and Leaders." *Access Genealogy.* (accessed on August 11, 2011). http://www.accessgenealogy.com/native/tribes/modoc/modocindianchiefs.htm

Modoc Tribe of Oklahoma. http://www.modoctribe.net/ (accessed on August 11, 2011).

"Mohave Indian Tribe History." *Access Genealogy.* http://www.accessgenealogy.com/native/tribes/mohave/mohaveindianhist.htm (accessed on July 20, 2011).

"Mohave National Preserve: Mohave Tribe: Culture." *National Park Service.* http://www.nps.gov/moja/historyculture/mojave-culture.htm (accessed on July 20, 2011).

"The Mohawk Tribe." *Mohawk Nation.* http://www.mohawktribe.com/ (accessed on June 7, 2011).

Montana Arts Council. "From the Heart and Hand: Salish Songs and Dances: Johnny Arlee, Arlee/John T., Big Crane, Pablo."*Montana Official State Website.* http://art.mt.gov/folklife/hearthand/songs.asp (accessed on August 11, 2011).

Morris, Allen. "Seminole History." *Florida Division of Historical Resources.* http://www.flheritage.com/facts/history/seminole/ (accessed on June 12, 2011).

Muscogee (Creek) Nation of Oklahoma. http://www.muscogeenation-nsn.gov/ (accessed on June 12, 2011).

Museum of the Aleutians.. http://www.aleutians.org/index.html (accessed on August 15, 2011).

Mussulman, Joseph. "Osage Indians." *The Lewis and Clark Fort Mandan Foundation.* http://lewis-clark.org/content/content-article.asp?ArticleID=2535 (accessed on June 12, 2011).

Muwekma Ohlone Tribe. http://www.muwekma.org/ (accessed on August 11, 2011).

The Myaamia Project at Miami University. http://www.myaamiaproject.com/ (accessed on June 7, 2011).

Myers, Tom. "Navajo Reservation" (video). *University of Illinois.* http://www.vimeo.com/8828354 (accessed on July 20, 2011).

Nametau Innu. "Your First Steps in the Innu Culture." *Musée Régional de la Côte-Nord.* http://www.nametauinnu.ca/en/tour (accessed on May 26, 2011).

Narragansett Indian Tribe. http://www.narragansett-tribe.org/ (accessed on June 1, 2011).

"Natchez Indian Tribe History." *Access Genealogy.* http://www.accessgenealogy.com/native/tribes/natchez/natchezhist.htm (accessed on June 27, 2011).

Natchez Nation. http://www.natchez-nation.com/ (accessed on June 27, 2011).

"Natchez Stories." *Sacred Texts.* http://www.sacred-texts.com/nam/se/mtsi/#section_004 (accessed on June 27, 2011).

National Library for the Environment. "Native Americans and the Environment: Great Basin." *National Council for Science and the Environment.* http://www.cnie.org/nae/basin.html (accessed on August 15, 2011).

National Museum of American History—Smithsonian Institution. "Pueblo Resistance: We Are Here." *Mexico State Record Center and Archives.* http://www.newmexicohistory.org/filedetails.php?fileID=23042 (accessed on July 20, 2011).

National Museum of the American Indian. "Central Plains." *Smithsonian.* http://americanindian.si.edu/searchcollections/results.aspx?regid=58 (accessed on July 4, 2011).

— — —. "Prairie." *Smithsonian.* http://americanindian.si.edu/searchcollections/results.aspx?regid=60 (accessed on June 12, 2011).

— — —. "Southern Plains." *Smithsonian.* http://americanindian.si.edu/searchcollections/results.aspx?regid=61 (accessed on June 20, 2011).

"Native Americans: Osage Tribe." *University of Missouri.* http://ethemes.missouri.edu/themes/1608?locale=en (accessed on June 12, 2011).

"Navajo (Diné)." *Northern Arizona University.* http://www.cpluhna.nau.edu/People/navajo.htm (accessed on July 20, 2011).

Navajo Indian Tribes History. *Access Genealogy.* http://www.accessgenealogy.com/native/tribes/navajo/navahoindianhist.htm (accessed on July 20, 2011).

The Navajo Nation. http://www.navajo-nsn.gov/history.htm (accessed on July 31, 2007).

"Nde Nation." *Chiricahua: Apache Nation.* http://www.chiricahuaapache.org/ (accessed on July 20, 2011).

"New Hampshire's Native American Heritage." *New Hampshire State Council on the Arts.* http://www.nh.gov/folklife/learning/traditions_native_americans.htm (accessed on June 5, 2011).

"Nez Percé." *Countries and Their Culture.* http://www.everyculture.com/multi/Le-Pa/Nez-Perc.html (accessed on August 11, 2011).

"Nez Percé (Nimiipuu) Tribe." *Wisdom of the Elders.* http://www.wisdomoftheelders.org/program303.html (accessed on August 11, 2011).

"Nez Percé National Historical Park." *National Park Service.* http://www.nps.gov/nepe/ (accessed on August 11, 2011).

Nez Percé Tribe. http://www.nezperce.org/ (accessed on August 11, 2011).

"Nisqually Indian Tribe, Washington." *United States History.* http://www.u-s-history.com/pages/h1561.html (accessed on August 15, 2011).

Nisqually Land Trust. http://www.nisquallylandtrust.org (accessed on August 15, 2011).

"NOAA Arctic Theme Page." *National Oceanic and Atmospheric Administration.* http://www.arctic.noaa.gov/ (accessed on August 15, 2011).

"Nohwike Bagowa: House of Our Footprints" *White Mountain Apache Tribe Culture Center and Museum.* http://www.wmat.us/wmaculture.shtml (accessed on July 20, 2011).

"Nootka Indian Music of the Pacific North West Coast." *Smithsonian Folkways.* http://www.folkways.si.edu/albumdetails.aspx?itemid=912 (accessed on August 15, 2011).

Northern Arapaho Tribe. http://www.northernarapaho.com/ (accessed on July 2, 2011).

Northern Cheyenne Nation. www.cheyennenation.com/ (accessed on July 4, 2011).

"Northwest Coastal People." *Canada's First Peoples.* http://firstpeoplesofcanada.com/fp_groups/fp_nwc5.html (accessed on August 15, 2011).

"Nuu-chah-nulth." *Royal British Columbia Museum.* http://www.royalbcmuseum.bc.ca/Content_Files/Files/SchoolsAndKids/nuu2.pdf (accessed on August 15, 2011).

"Nuu-chah-nulth (Barkley) Community Portal." *FirstVoices.* http://www.firstvoices.ca/en/Nuu-chah-nulth (accessed on August 15, 2011).

Nuu-chah-nulth Tribal Council. http://www.nuuchahnulth.org/tribal-council/welcome.html(accessed on August 15, 2011).

"Official Site of the Miami Nation of Indians of the State of Indiana." *Miami Nation of Indians.* http://www.miamiindians.org/ (accessed on June 7, 2011).

Official Site of the Wichita and Affiliated Tribes. http://www.wichitatribe.com/ (accessed on June 9, 2011).

Official Website of the Caddo Nation. http://www.caddonation-nsn.gov/ (accessed on June 12, 2011).

Ohio History Central. "Adena Mound." *Ohio Historical Society.* http://www.ohiohistorycentral.org/entry.php?rec=2411 (accessed June 7, 2011).

"Ohkay Owingeh." *Indian Pueblo Cultural Center.* http://www.indianpueblo.org/19pueblos/ohkayowingeh.html (accessed on July 20, 2011).

*Ohlone/Costanoan Esselen Nation.*http://www.ohlonecostanoanesselennation.org/(accessed on August 11, 2011).

Oklahoma Humanities Council. "Otoe-Missouria Tribe." *Cherokee Strip Museum.* http://www.cherokee-strip-museum.org/Otoe/OM_Who.htm (accessed on June 20, 2011).

Oklahoma Indian Affairs Commission. "2011 Oklahoma Indian Nations." *Pocket Pictorial Directory.* Oklahoma City: Oklahoma Indian Affairs Commission, 2011. Available from http://www.ok.gov/oiac/documents/2011.FINAL.WEB.pdf (accessed on June 12, 2011).

The Oregon History Project. "Modoc." *Oregon Historical Society.* http://www.ohs.org/education/oregonhistory/search/dspResults.cfm?keyword=Modoc&type=&theme=&timePeriod=&region= (accessed on August 11, 2011).

"The Osage." *Fort Scott National Historic Site, National Park Service.*http://www.nps.gov/fosc/historyculture/osage.htm (accessed on June 12, 2011).

Osage Nation. http://www.osagetribe.com/ (accessed on June 12, 2011).

"Osage Indian Tribe History." *Access Genealogy.* http://www.accessgenealogy.com/native/tribes/osage/osagehist.htm (accessed on June 12, 2011).

The Otoe-Missouria Tribe. http://www.omtribe.org/ (accessed on June 20, 2011).

Ottawa Inuit Children's Centre. http://www.ottawainuitchildrens.com/eng/ (accessed on August 15, 2011).

Ottawa Tribe of Oklahoma. http://www.ottawatribe.org/history.htm (accessed May 13, 2011).

"Our History." *Makah Cultural and Research Center.* http://www.makah.com/history.html (accessed on November 2, 2011).

"Pacific Northwest Native Americans." *Social Studies School Service.* http://nativeamericans.mrdonn.org/northwest.html (accessed on August 15, 2011).

Paiute Indian Tribe of Utah. http://www.utahpaiutes.org/ (accessed on August 15, 2011).

The Pascua Yaqui Tribe. http://www.pascuayaqui-nsn.gov/ (accessed on July 20, 2011).

"The Pasqu Yaqui Connection." *Through Our Parents' Eyes: History and Culture of Southern Arizona.* http://parentseyes.arizona.edu/pascuayaquiaz/ (accessed on July 20, 2011).

"Past and Future Meet in San Juan Pueblo Solar Project." *Solar Cookers International.* http://solarcooking.org/sanjuan1.htm (accessed on July 20, 2011).

Pastore, Ralph T. "Aboriginal Peoples: Newfoundland and Labrador Heritage." *Memorial University of Newfoundland.* http://www.heritage.nf.ca/aboriginal/ (accessed on August 15, 2011).

Paul, Daniel N. "We Were Not the Savages."*First Nation History.* http://www.danielnpaul.com/index.html (accessed on June 1, 2011).

"Pawnee." *Four Directions Institute.* http://www.fourdir.com/pawnee.htm (accessed on July 6, 2011).

"Pawnee Indian Museum." *Kansas State Historical Society.* http://www.kshs.org/places/pawneeindian/history.htm (accessed on July 6, 2011).

"Pawnee Indian Tribe History." *Access Genealogy.* http://www.accessgenealogy.com/native/tribes/pawnee/pawneehist.htm (accessed on July 6, 2011).

Pawnee Nation of Oklahoma. http://www.pawneenation.org/ (accessed on July 6, 2011).

"Pecos Indian Tribe History." *Access Genealogy.* http://www.accessgenealogy.com/native/tribes/pecos/pecoshist.htm(accessed on July 20, 2011).

"Pecos National Historical Park." *Desert USA.* http://www.desertusa.com/pecos/pnpark.html (accessed on July 20, 2011).

"Pecos Pueblos." *Four Directions Institute.* http://www.fourdir.com/pecos.htm (accessed on July 20, 2011).

"People of Pecos." *National Park Service.* http://www.nps.gov/peco/historyculture/peple-of-pecos.htm (accessed on July 20, 2011).

"People of the Colorado Plateau: The Hopi." *Northern Arizona University.* http://www.cpluhna.nau.edu/People/hopi.htm (accessed on July 20, 2011).

"People of the Colorado Plateau: The Ute Indian." *Northern Arizona University.* http://cpluhna.nau.edu/People/ute_indians.htm(accessed on August 15, 2011).

"The People of the Flathead Nation."*Lake County Directory.* http://www.lakecodirect.com/archives/The_Flathead_Nation.html (accessed on August 11, 2011).

"Peoples of Alaska and Northeast Siberia." *Alaska Native Collections.* http://alaska.si.edu/cultures.asp (accessed on August 15, 2011).

"Pequot Lives: Almost Vanished." *Pequot Museum and Research Center.* http://www.pequotmuseum.org/Home/MashantucketGallery/AlmostVanished.htm (accessed June 8, 2011).

Peterson, Keith C. "Dams of the Columbia Basin and Their Effects of the Native Fishery." *Center for Columbia River History.* http://www.ccrh.org/comm/river/dams7.htm (accessed on August 11, 2011).

Peterson, Leighton C. "Tuning in to Navajo: The Role of Radio in Native Language Maintenance." *Northern Arizona University.* http://jan.ucc.nau.edu/-jar/TIL_17.html (accessed on July 20, 2011).

"Pima (AkimelO'odham)." *Four Directions Institute.* http://www.fourdir.com/pima.htm (accessed on July 20, 2011).

"Pima Indian Tribe History." *Access Genealogy.* www.accessgenealogy.com/native/tribes/pima/pimaindianhist.htm (accessed on July 20, 2011).

Pit River Indian Tribe. http://www.pitrivertribe.org/home.php (accessed on August 11, 2011).

"Pomo People: Brief History." *Native American Art.* http://www.kstrom.net/isk/art/basket/pomohist.html (accessed on August 11, 2011).

Porter, Tom. "Mohawk (Haudenosaunee) Teaching." *FourDirectionsTeachings.com.* http://www.fourdirectionsteachings.com/transcripts/mohawk.html (accessed June 7, 2011).

"Powhatan Indian Village." *Acton Public Schools: Acton-Boxborough Regional School District.* http://ab.mec.edu/jamestown/powhatan (accessed on June 1, 2011).

"Powhatan Language and the Powhatan Indian Tribe (Powatan, Powhatten, Powhattan)." *Native Languages of the Americas: Preserving and Promoting Indigenous American Indian Languages.* http://www.native-languages.org/powhatan.htm (accessed on on June 1, 2011).

"Preserving Sacred Wisdom." *Native Spirit and the Sun Dance Way.* http://www. nativespiritinfo.com/ (accessed on July 5, 2011).

"Pueblo Indian History and Resources." *Pueblo Indian.* http://www.puebloindian.com/ (accessed on July 20, 2011).

Pueblo of Acoma. http://www.puebloofacoma.org/ (accessed on July 20, 2011).

Pueblo of Jemez. http://www.jemezpueblo.org/ (accessed on July 20, 2011).

Pueblo of Zuñi. http://www.ashiwi.org/(accessed on July 20, 2011).

Puyallup Tribe of Indians. http://www.puyallup-tribe.com/ (accessed on November 2, 2011).

Quapaw Tribe of Oklahoma. http://www.quapawtribe.com/ (accessed on June 20, 2011).

"The Quapaw Tribe of Oklahoma and the Tar Creek Project." *Environmental Protection Agency.* http://www.epa.gov/oar/tribal/tribetotribe/tarcreek.html (accessed on June 20, 2011).

"Questions and Answers about the Plateau Indians." *Wellpinit School District 49 (WA).* http://www.wellpinit.wednet.edu/sal-qa/qa.php (accessed on August 11, 2011).

"Questions and Answers about the Spokane Indians." *Wellpinit School District.* http://wellpinit.org/q%2526a (accessed on August 11, 2011).

Redish, Laura, and Orrin Lewis. *Native Languages of the Americas.*http://www. native-languages.org (accessed on August 11, 2011).

"Research Starters: Anasazi and Pueblo Indians." *Scholastic.com.* http://teacher. scholastic.com/researchtools/researchstarters/native_am/ (accessed on July 20, 2011).

"The Rez We Live On"(videos). *The Confederated Salish and Kootenai Tribes.* http://therezweliveon.com/13/video.html (accessed on August 11, 2011).

The Rooms, Provincial Museum Division. "Innu Objects."*Virtual Museum Canada.* 2008. http://www.museevirtuel-virtualmuseum.ca/edu/ViewLoit Collection.do;jsessionid=3083D5EEB47F3ECDE9DA040AD0D4C956? method=preview⟨=EN&id=3210 (accessed on May 24, 2011).

Sac and Fox Nation. http://www.sacandfoxnation-nsn.gov/ (accessed on June 5, 2011).

"Sac and Fox Tribe." *Meskwaki Nation.* http://www.meskwaki.org/ (accessed on June 5, 2011).

San Carlos Apache Cultural Center. http://www.sancarlosapache.com/home.htm (accessed on July 20, 2011).

"San Carlos Apache Sunrise Dance." *World News Network.* http://wn.com/ San_Carlos_Apache_Sunrise_Dance (accessed on July 20, 2011).

"San Juan Pueblo." *New Mexico Magazine.* http://www.nmmagazine.com/ native_american/san_juan.php (accessed on July 20, 2011).

"San Juan Pueblo O'Kang." *Indian Pueblo Cultural Center.* http://www.indianpueblo. org/19pueblos/ohkayowingeh.html (accessed on July 20, 2011).

"The Sand Creek Massacre." *Last of the Independents.* http://www.lastoftheinde-pendents.com/sandcreek.htm (accessed on July 2, 2011).

"Seminole Indian Tribe History." *Access Genealogy.* http://www.accessgenealogy. com/native/tribes/seminole/seminolehist.htm (accessed on June 12, 2011).

Seminole Nation of Oklahoma. http://www.seminolenation.com/ (accessed on June 12, 2011).

Seminole Tribe of Florida. http://www.seminoletribe.com/ (accessed on June 12, 2011).

"Sharp Nose." *Native American Nations.* http://www.nanations.com/arrap/ page4.htm (accessed on July 2, 2011).

"The Shawnee in History." *The Shawnee Tribe.* http://www.shawnee-tribe.com/ history.htm (accessed on June 12, 2011).

"Shawnee Indian Tribe History." *Access Genealogy.* http://www.accessgenealogy. com/native/tennessee/shawneeindianhist.htm (accessed on June 12, 2011).

"Shawnee Indians." *Ohio Historical Society.* http://www.ohiohistorycentral.org/ entry.php?rec=631&nm=Shawnee-Indians (accessed on June 12, 2011).

Shawnee Nation, United Remnant Band. http://www.zaneshawneecaverns.net/ shawnee.shtml (accessed on June 12, 2011).

"A Short History of the Spokane Indians." *Wellpinit School District.* http://www.wellpinit.wednet.edu/shorthistory (accessed on August 11, 2011).

"Short Overview of California Indian History." *California Native American Heritage Commission.* http://www.nahc.ca.gov/califindian.html (accessed on August 15, 2011).

Sicade, Henry. "Education." *Puyallup Tribe of Indians.* http://www.puyallup-tribe. com/history/education/ (accessed on November 2, 2011).

"Simon Ortiz: Native American Poet." *The University of Texas at Arlington.* http://www.uta.edu/english/tim/poetry/so/ortizmain.htm (accessed on July 20, 2011).

Simpson, Linda. "The Kansas/Kanza/Kaw Nation." *Oklahoma Territory.* http:// www.okgenweb.org/-itkaw/Kanza2.html (accessed on June 17, 2011).

The Skokomish Tribal Nation. http://www.skokomish.org/ (accessed on November 2, 2011).

Skopec, Eric. "What Mystery?" *Anasazi Adventure.* http://www.anasaziadventure. com/what_mystery.pdf (accessed on July 20, 2011).

Smithsonian Folkways. "Rain Dance (Zuñi)." *Smithsonian Institution.* http:// www.folkways.si.edu/TrackDetails.aspx?itemid=16680 (music track) and http://media.smithsonianfolkways.org/liner_notes/folkways/FW06510.pdf (instructions for dance). (accessed on July 20, 2011).

Snook, Debbie. "Ohio's Trail of Tears." *Wyandotte Nation of Oklahoma*, 2003. http://www.wyandotte-nation.org/culture/history/published/trail-of-tears/ (accessed May 11, 2011).

The Southern Arapaho. http://southernarapaho.org/ (accessed on July 2, 2011).

Southern Ute Indian Tribe. http://www.southern-ute.nsn.us/ (accessed on August 15, 2011).

Splawn, A. J. *Ka-mi-akin, the Last Hero of the Yakimas.* Portland, OR: Kilham Stationary and Printing, 1917. Reproduced by Washington Secretary of State. http://www.secstate.wa.gov/history/publications_detail.aspx?p=24 (accessed on August 11, 2011).

"Spokane Indian Tribe." *Access Genealogy.* http://www.accessgenealogy.com/ native/tribes/salish/spokanhist.htm (accessed on August 11, 2011).

"Spokane Indian Tribe." *United States History.* http://www.u-s-history.com/ pages/h1570.html (accessed on August 11, 2011).

Spokane Tribe of Indians. http://www.spokanetribe.com/ (accessed on August 11, 2011).

Sreenivasan, Hari. "'Apache 8' Follows All-Women Firefighters On and Off the Reservation." *PBS NewsHour.* http://video.pbs.org/video/2006599346/ (accessed on July 20, 2011).

Stands In Timber, John. "Cheyenne Memories." *Northern Cheyenne Nation.* http://www.cheyennenation.com/memories.html (accessed on July 4, 2011).

Stewart, Kenneth. "Kivas." *Scholastic.* http://www2.scholastic.com/browse/ article.jsp?id=5052 (accessed on July 20, 2011).

"The Story of the Ute Tribe: Past, Present, and Future." *Ute Mountain Ute Tribe.* http://www.utemountainute.com/story.htm (accessed on August 15, 2011).

Sultzman, Lee. *First Nations.* http://www.tolatsga.org/sf.html (accessed on June 5, 2011).

Swan, Daniel C. "Native American Church." *Oklahoma Historical Society.* http://digital.library.okstate.edu/encyclopedia/entries/N/NA015.html (accessed on August 11, 2011).

"Taos Pueblo." *Bluffton University.* http://www.bluffton.edu/-sullivanm/taos/ taos.html (accessed on July 20, 2011).

"Taos Pueblo." *New Mexico Magazine.* http://www.nmmagazine.com/native_ american/taos.php (accessed on July 20, 2011).

Taos Pueblo. http://www.taospueblo.com/ (accessed on July 20, 2011).

"Taos Pueblo: A Thousand Years of Tradition." *Taos Pueblo.* http://taospueblo. com/ (accessed on July 20, 2011).

"Territorial Kansas: Kansa Indians." *University of Kansas.* http://www. territorialkansasonline.org/-imlskto/cgi-bin/index.php?SCREEN=

keyword&selected_keyword=Kansa%20Indians (accessed on June 17, 2011).

"Throat Singing." *Inuit Cultural Online Resource.* http://icor.ottawainuitchildrens. com/node/30 (accessed on August 15, 2011).

"Tlingit Tribes, Clans, and Clan Houses: Traditional Tlingit Country." *Alaska Native Knowledge Network.* http://www.ankn.uaf.edu/ANCR/Southeast/ TlingitMap/ (accessed on November 2, 2011).

"Tohono O'odham (Papago)." *Four Directions Institute.* http://www.fourdir. com/tohono_o'odham.htm (accessed on July 20, 2011).

"Totem Pole Websites." *Cathedral Grove.* http://www.cathedralgrove.eu/ text/07-Totem-Websites-3.htm (accessed on November 2, 2011).

"Trading Posts in the American Southwest." *Southwest Crossroads.* http:// southwestcrossroads.org/record.php?num=742&hl=chiricahua:: apache (accessed on July 20, 2011).

"Traditional Mi'kmaq Beliefs."*Indian Brook First Nation.* http://home.rushcomm. ca/-hsack/spirit.html (accessed on June1,2011).

"Tsmshian Songs We Love to Sing!" *Dum Baaldum.* http://www.dumbaaldum. org/html/songs.htm (accessed on August 15, 2011).

"Umatilla Indian Agency and Reservation, Oregon." *Access Genealogy.* http:// www.accessgenealogy.com/native/census/condition/umatilla_indian_ agency_reservation_oregon.htm (accessed on August 11, 2011).

"Umatilla, Walla Walla, and Cayuse." *TrailTribes.org: Traditional and Con-temporary Native Culture.* http://www.trailtribes.org/umatilla/home.htm (accessed on August 11, 2011).

"Unangax & Alutiiq (Sugpiaq)." *Alaska Native Heritage Center.* http://www. alaskanative.net/en/main_nav/education/culture_alaska/unangax/ (accessed on August 15, 2011).

Unrau, William E. "Kaw (Kansa)." *Oklahoma Historical Society.* http://digital. library.okstate.edu/encyclopedia/entries/K/KA001.html (accessed on June 17, 2011).

Urban Indian Experience. "The Duwamish: Seattle's Landless Tribe." *KUOW: PRX.* http://www.prx.org/pieces/1145-urban-indian-experience-episode-1-the-duwamish(accessed on November 2, 2011).

The Ute Indian Tribe. http://www.utetribe.com/ (accessed on August 15, 2011).

"Ute Nation." *Utah Travel Industry.* http://www.utah.com/tribes/ute_main.htm (accessed on August 15, 2011).

Virtual Archaeologist. "The Like-a-Fishhook Story." *NDSU Archaeology Tech-nologies Laboratory.* http://fishhook.ndsu.edu/home/lfstory.php (accessed on June 19, 2011).

"A Virtual Tour of California Missions." *MissionTour.* http://missiontour.org/ index.htm (accessed on August 11, 2011).

"Visiting a Maidu Bark House." *You Tube.* http://www.youtube.com/watch?v=fw5i83519mQ (accessed on August 11, 2011).

"The Wampanoag." *Boston Children's Museum.* http://www.bostonkids.org/educators/wampanoag/html/what.htm (accessed on June 1, 2011).

"Washoe." *Four Directions Institute.* http://www.fourdir.com/washoe.htm (accessed on August 15, 2011).

"Washoe Hot Springs." *National Cultural Preservation Council.* http://www.ncpc.info/projects_washoe.html (accessed on August 15, 2011).

"Washoe Indian Tribe History." *Access Genealogy.* http://www.accessgenealogy.com/native/tribes/washo/washohist.htm (accessed on August 15, 2011).

"We Shall Remain." *PBS.* http://www.pbs.org/wgbh/amex/weshallremain/ (accessed on July 20, 2011).

Weiser, Kathy. *Legends of America.* http://www.legendsofamerica.com (accessed on July 20, 2011).

"White Mountain Apache Indian Reservation." *Arizona Handbook.* http://www.arizonahandbook.com/white_mtn_apache.htm (accessed on July 20, 2011).

"White Mountain Apache Tribe." *InterTribal Council of Arizona.* http://www.itcaonline.com/tribes_whitemtn.html (accessed on July 20, 2011).

"White Mountain Apache Tribe: Restoring Wolves, Owls, Trout and Ecosystems" *Cooperative Conservation America.* http://www.cooperativeconservation.org/viewproject.asp?pid=136 (accessed on July 20, 2011).

"Who Were the Lipan and the Kiowa-Apaches?" *Southwest Crossroads.* http://southwestcrossroads.org/record.php?num=522&hl=chiricahua:: apache (accessed on July 20, 2011).

"Wichita." *Four Directions Institute.* http://www.fourdir.com/wichita.htm (accessed on June 9, 2011).

Wind River Indian Reservation. http://www.wind-river.org/info/communities/reservation.php (accessed on July 2, 2011).

Wind River Indian Reservation: Eastern Shoshone Tribe. http://www.easternshoshone.net/ (accessed on August 15, 2011).

WMAT: White Mountain Apache Tribe. http://wmat.us/ (accessed on July 20, 2011).

"Wounded Knee." *Last of the Independent.* http://www.lastoftheindependents.com/wounded.htm (accessed on July 4, 2011).

The Wounded Knee Museum. http://www.woundedkneemuseum.org/ (accessed on July 4, 2011).

Wyandot Nation of Anderdon. http://www.wyandotofanderdon.com/ (accessed May 13, 2011).

Wyandot Nation of Kansas. http://www.wyandot.org/ (accessed May 13, 2011).

Wyandotte Nation of Oklahoma. http://www.wyandotte-nation.org/ (accessed May 13, 2011).

"Yakima Indian Tribe History." *Access Genealogy.* http://www.accessgenealogy. com/native/tribes/yakimaindianhist.htm (accessed on August 11, 2011).

Yakama Nation Cultural Heritage Center. http://www.yakamamuseum.com/ (accessed on August 11, 2011).

"Yaqui." *Four Directions Institute.* http://www.fourdir.com/yaqui.htm (accessed on July 20, 2011).

"Yaqui and Mayo Indian Easter Ceremonies." *RimJournal.* http://www.rimjournal. com/arizyson/easter.htm (accessed on July 20, 2011).

"Yaqui Sacred Traditions." *Wisdom Traditions Institute.* http://www.wisdomtraditions. com/yaqui2.html (accessed on July 20, 2011).

"Yuma (Quechan)." *Four Directions Institute.* http://www.fourdir.com/yuma. htm (accessed on July 20, 2011).

Yuman Indian Tribe History." *Access Genealogy.* http://www.accessgenealogy. com/native/tribes/yuman/yumanfamilyhist.htm (accessed on July 20, 2011).

"The Yup'ik and Cup'ik People—Who We Are." *The Alaska Native Heritage Center Museum.* http://www.alaskanative.net/en/main_nav/education/ culture_alaska/yupik/ (accessed on August 15, 2011).

"Yup'ik Tundra Navigation." *Center for Cultural Design.* http://www.ccd.rpi. edu/Eglash/csdt/na/tunturyu/index.html (accessed on August 15, 2011).

"The Yurok." *California History Online.* http://www.californiahistoricalsociety. org/timeline/chapter2/002d.html# (accessed on August 11, 2011).

"Yurok." *Four Directions Institute.* http://www.fourdir.com/yurok.htm (accessed on August 11, 2011).

The Yurok Tribe. http://www.yuroktribe.org/ (accessed on August 11, 2011).

Zeig, Sande. *Apache 8* (film). http://www.apache8.com/ (accessed on July 20, 2011).

"Zuñi." *Northern Arizona University.* http://www.cpluhna.nau.edu/People/zuni. htm (accessed on July 20, 2011).

"Zuñi." *Southwest Crossroads.* http://southwestcrossroads.org/record. php?num=2&hl=zuni (accessed on July 20, 2011).

"Zuñi Pueblo." *New Mexico Magazine.* http://www.nmmagazine.com/native_ american/zuni.php (accessed on July 20, 2011).

"Zuñi Pueblos (Ashiwi)." *Four Directions Institute.* http://www.fourdir.com/ zuni.htm (accessed on July 20, 2011).

Index

Italics indicates volume numbers; **boldface** indicates entries and their page numbers. Chart indicates a chart; ill. indicates an illustration, and map indicates a map.

O

P

T

U

V

W

X

Y

U•X•L Encyclopedia of Native American Tribes, 3rd Edition